NM4HPP

True to the Democratic Party ... ory ... r defea...

D0271438

...R 18, 1903. TWELVE PAGES. ... COPY.

...TEETH ...N OF HIGH WIN... OVER
...T KITTY HAWK ON CAROLINA COAST

...EN THE

"WANTS CANAL BUILT ... PICION OF ... DISHONOR"

... Fiery Debate on ... ate

...RAPH COMPANY.

...VICE TO ALL THE WORLD.

...which have been assented to by the sender of the following message. ...rison, and the Company will not hold itself liable for errors or delays ...any case where the claim is not presented in writing within sixty days

...conditions named above.

...General Manager.

170

all against twenty one mile
...wer alone average speed
...57 seconds inform Press 525P
Orevelle Wright

... about to attack another, is ...fore the blow is struck, in ... the assailed party, and ...r the assault has been ...policeman is justified in ...pocketbook which has been ...e victim by the assailant ...ed over to him (the po... ground that he was the ...

...ook the floor as soon as ...oncluded, and there was ...vident interest in what ...e began with reference ...eech and compliment... highly on his attitude ...e democratic attitude ...stion. On the latter ... democratic senators ...avorable to tre con...nal as are republi... said the facts were ..., and he proceeded ...sion of the execu... that thsi influence ...rom time to time ...d become practi... executive." ...na, he declared, ...t act of trans... taken place in ...y, and it should ...rd to party."

... Mr. Loomis for ...nama situation ... before injunc... moved by the ... Mr. Loomis ... situation at ...s many were ... given infor...ad not had ... from any ...orman con... the facts, ...rtion that ...reat man, ...d the pa...rines and seize a ...territory of the repblic of ...olombia, which we were under contract to guarantee to that country. This is," he added, "in the light of the facts before us, nothing less than usurpation."

Mr. Gorman then discussed the president as a "second Napoleon," which title had, he said, "been assigned to him by some." "A second Napoleon, indeed," he exclaimed. Had it come to this that the United States must have a Napoleon to shape its destinies and to distort the presidential office from its proper functions?

Here Mr. Aldrich interrupted Mr. Gorman with a question as to whether it

(Continued on Page 9.)

... correspondence ... revolution, and asked: ...his great anxiety before any disturbance had occurred?" It was, he said, clear that if the correspondence so far printed included all the information possible to give on the subject, that from twenty-four to forty-eight hours before the revolution broke out this government had instructed a man-of-war to prevent Colombia from doing anything to prevent it. "I want to know, and the American people want to know and have a right to know, whether this mighty policeman on the isthmus, see...

... advan... clamored for by ...tic ports, ... the time of that ... would take the ...next congress con...eavor to secure in ...arbor bill a provi...g, straightening ...channel.

SHORTS

THIRTY MILLION

NO BALLOO... ATTACHED TO AID IT

Three Years of Hard, S... Work by Two Ohio Broth... Crowned With Succes...

ACCOMPLISHED WHAT ... LANGLEY FAILE...

With Man as Passenger ... Machine Flew Like B... Under Perfect Control

BOX KITE PRINCIPLE WITH TWO PROPEL...

The problem of aerial navi... without the use of a balloon ha... solved at last.

Over the sand hills of the Nort...olina coast yesterday, near Kitty ... two Ohio men proved that they ... soar through the air in a flying m... of their own construction, wi... power to steer it and speed it a...

This, too, in the face of a wind... ing at the registered velocity of t... one miles an hour.

Like a monster bird the in... hovered above the breakers and ... over the rolling sand hills at th... mand of its navigator and, afte... ing for three miles, it gracefu... scended to earth again and reste... ly upon the spot selected by th... in the car as a suitable landing...

While the United States gove... has been spending thousands of ... in an effort to make practica... ideas of Professor Langley, ... Smithsonian Institute, Wilber a... ville Wright, two brothers, nat... Dayton, O., have, quietly, even se... perfected their invention, and p... a successful test.

They are not yet ready that the... should know the methods they ... adopted in conquering the air, ...

The Wright Brothers

By the same author:

CRUSADER FOX KING

RESCUE BELOW ZERO

PACIFIC ORDEAL (with Captain Kenneth Ainslie)

INTO THE SILK

LONG NIGHT'S JOURNEY

TOM ROLT AND THE CRESSY YEARS

JEAN BATTEN: THE GARBO OF THE SKIES

SMITHY: THE LIFE OF SIR CHARLES KINGSFORD SMITH

The Wright Brothers

The Remarkable Story of the Aviation Pioneers Who Changed the World

IAN MACKERSEY

LITTLE, BROWN

A *Little, Brown* Book

First published in Great Britain in 2003 by Little, Brown

Endpapers: Telegram courtesy of Special Collections, Wright State University; Newspaper courtesy of Library of Congress.

A CIP catalogue record for this book is available
from the British Library.

ISBN 0 316 86144 8

Typeset in Berling by M Rules
Printed and bound in Great Britain by
Clays Ltd, St Ives plc

Little, Brown
An imprint of
Time Warner Books UK
Brettenham House
Lancaster Place
London WC2E 7EN

www.TimeWarnerBooks.co.uk

Contents

The Wright Brothers

Preface

Isn't it astonishing that all these secrets have been preserved for so many years just so that we could discover them!!

Orville Wright, 7 June 1903

Few inventors can have been commemorated as frequently, and as passionately, as the creators of the aeroplane. In their Midwest home town of Dayton, Ohio, the imagery of the Wright Brothers greets the visitor on every side. It's as if their deeds were the very purpose of the city's existence. The airport carpet on to which you step from the plane is woven with a pattern of the famous first flying machine. Signs welcome you to the home of flight. The car number plates proclaim 'Birthplace of Aviation'. It is possible to spend whole days touring more than twenty sacred places where Wilbur and Orville lived and laboured, built bicycles, studied soaring birds, designed and flew their aeroplanes.

On the remote Outer Banks of the Atlantic coast of North Carolina there is more consecrated ground. At a place called Kill Devil Hills, grey- and green-uniformed park rangers guard the holy site among huge, golden sandhills where the historic first flights were made on a December morning in 1903. At a museum in Dearborn in Michigan there are on display the transplanted Wright family house and cycle shop in which the brothers argued their way towards aeronautical truths. And on the Indiana plains, east of Indianapolis, near the small township of Millville, stands yet another shrine – a reconstruction of the lonely farmhouse in which Wilbur was born in 1867. A hundred years after the birth of the modern aeroplane, people continue to come great distances to see the simple dwelling in which one of its architects spent the early months of his life.

Nor do the memorials end with the human sites. Almost every year a fresh replica of one of the Wrights' aeroplanes is created, assiduously matching the original in every minuscule detail. Modern aerodynamicists, marvelling at the scientific brilliance of the untutored brothers, continue to subject these re-creations to the rigorous analysis of twenty-first-century testing in wind tunnels, one of them provided, in 2003, by NASA itself. Aerospace engineers are astonished at the sheer efficiency of the brothers' machine and the way its design so wonderfully overcame the centuries-old barriers to mechanical flight.

More than any other invention in modern history the Wright Brothers' achievement has sustained a uniquely unceasing flow of books. A search of the Internet declares the existence of more than a hundred separate titles. Nor does this include an ever-growing library of subsidiary works affectionately devoted to such specifics as: their bicycle business; their earlier career in the printing trade; the life of their mechanic; the stormy United Brethren Church career of their father; the recipes of the meals they enjoyed. Three published volumes contain their hundreds of private and business letters. A definitive chronology of their lives logs their thousands of gliding and powered flights. A thesis was devoted to the single subject of how news of the first flight reached the world. There is even an informative publication about the Wright family funerals.

This extensive literature owes much to the rich documentation the Wrights so conscientiously created. They – especially Wilbur – were prolific record-keepers and correspondents. They left behind boxes of letters in which they wrote about their aviation experiments in extensive detail. They timed every flight to a fifth of a second. They measured distances flown to the nearest foot and clocked the precise wind strength. They photographed everything. Week after week historically valuable aeronautical data poured into their notebooks. To family and a few trusted friends they confided, in often witty and humorous letters, their failures and privations, frustrations and triumphs.

This wealth of material, today preserved in the Library of Congress in Washington and in the Paul Laurence Dunbar Library of their home-town Wright State University, enabled a succession of biographers to do what the brothers never got around to doing: chronicling for posterity with technical precision how man learnt to become a bird.

Sitting today in the great manuscript reading room of the Library of Congress on Capitol Hill, sifting through the boxes of the brittle original documents in the brothers' beautifully clear handwriting arouses many emotions, chiefly amazement at the sophistication and technical grasp of these small-town bicycle makers as, with sublime confidence, they ventured into uncharted aeronautical seas of daunting peril and complexity, taking in their stride abstruse scientific concepts that were defined by formidable chains of algebra and trigonometry far above the heads of most people. But, day after day, as I pored over these historic papers, I found my interest and curiosity seized by something else as well. It was apparent that the full story of flight was much more than just that of two remarkable men. It was a saga of the entire Wright family. Swept up in the maelstrom of triumphs and tragedies that surrounded the invention, some of them had been thrust into the limelight as prominently as the brothers themselves.

They were a singular clan, as interesting as the aeroplane. There was the towering, demanding figure of their litigious, Puritan father, Bishop Milton Wright, who created the uncompromisingly rigid moral climate in which the machine was conceived; his meek and submissive wife, Susan, who did not live to see even the conception of the flying machine; the brothers' warm-tempered and forthright sister, Katharine, a woman ahead of her time, who was sucked so deeply into it all she was sometimes actually credited with part of the aerodynamic achievement; the shadowy figures of two elder brothers whose lives were eclipsed in the penumbra of monumental fame.

The Wrights were no ordinary family. They functioned as a highly efficient, self-contained unit, fiercely loyal to one another, passionate about each other's causes, piercingly critical of the outside world and most other mortals. They trusted only one another and communicated with obsessive frequency; their need when separated for copious streams of personal news was never satisfied. Happily, much of this lively intercourse, brimming with advice, criticism and affection, has survived to add poignant and deeply human strands to the record of the aeroplane's birth.

Forty years after Orville's death in 1948, aviation historians had assumed that all Wright family records had long ago surfaced. Yet this was not so. I learnt that, in the 1990s, some sensational new material had emerged. It threw important fresh light on Orville's opposition to Katharine's marriage in the autumn of her life which had, incredibly, led Orville never to speak to her again. A discreet veil had apparently been drawn over this traumatic event; biographers, unable to substantiate it, appeared to have brushed it under the carpet. At the time his anger had shaken and divided the Wright family, yet, to protect and preserve Orville's image, no more than a hint of these distressing events had previously been made public. The new documents were hundreds of revealing love letters from the, by then, middle-aged spinster Katharine Wright, written secretly in the mid-1920s from the home she shared with Orville to the man she had decided to marry. They foreshadowed her brother's hostility to the marriage and the shock of unhappiness it was to deal him. But why Orville, so often portrayed as a patient, gentle and fair-minded man, should have reacted so badly was not explained for another twelve years.

Earlier Wright biographers had got wind of the existence of some reputedly anguished letters written after her marriage by Katharine and her husband, Henry Haskell, to an old friend in England. Copies of these letters were believed to have been deposited before his death in 1981 by the prominent British aviation historian Charles Gibbs-Smith with his papers at the National Museum of Science and Industry in London. Several searches of his archive, however, failed to throw up any trace of the Haskell letters. But, early in 2003, as this book was in the final stages of editing, a fresh search made at the Science Museum on my behalf unearthed them at long last. Having lain fallow for more than seventy years, they contained the only explanation that Orville was ever to give for his extraordinary actions, over which history had drawn a kindly veil.

In my four-year quest for understanding of the family of flight I was helped by many people. As biographical subjects the Wright Brothers have tended to be the preserve of American writers. Yet as a foreigner intruding into this heroic, much trodden territory I was welcomed on all sides into the community of the Wright historical and commemoration industry with great warmth and unfailing helpfulness.

At first I was regularly pointed to one reputedly omniscient centre of expertise. 'Have you talked to Tom Crouch?' people would say. A senior curator at the National Air and Space Museum in Washington, DC and author of a major biography of the brothers, Tom Crouch proved to have a quite encyclopedic knowledge of the Wrights. Himself a Daytonian, he had enjoyed the special confidence of one of the brothers' nieces, Ivonette Wright Miller, who, born in 1896, had vivid memories of Wilbur, Orville, Katharine and her grandfather Bishop Wright. I am deeply grateful to Tom for his readiness to share with me so generously his fathomless store of information on the Wright phenomenon.

Equal gratitude is due to Dr Adrian Kinnane, a Washington psychologist and historian who, fascinated by the personal style of the brothers, had devoted several years of his life, for no reward, to writing a penetrating study of the unusual pair. His diligently researched, unpublished book, *The Crucible of Flight*, a psychological biography, critically examined the roots of their characters, their extraordinary family nest and the exceptional forces that bound them as brothers. Dr Kinnane's professional insights into the phenomenon of the Wright family have been an invaluable help towards my understanding of them all.

Since Orville Wright's death in 1948, successive descendent relatives have assumed the responsibility of family spokesperson. 'There will always be one,' a Dayton historian told me. 'As one dies another is soon appointed. It's a bit like the papal succession.' By 2002 the role had descended to a great-niece, Marianne Miller Hudec. To Marianne and her late husband Bob I am grateful for warm hospitality at their home in Boston and for much valuable family information. I must especially thank Marianne for her personal and very affectionate memories of great-uncle 'Orv' and for the prodigies of fresh research she so willingly undertook for me into the sad events that clouded Katharine Wright's marriage in 1926.

My further thanks – and admiration – go to former USAF colonel Bill Sloan, the 81-year-old ex-World War II pilot who in Dayton took me for a memorable flight on a replica of a Wright Model B aircraft, even bravely allowing me to fly it for a few frightening seconds. Although the machine, at first sight, looked like a Wright *Flyer*, its creators had been required to add some un-Wrightlike refinements. It had a more powerful engine. It had a seat harness. It had ailerons, flight instruments and radio. Its occupants were obliged to wear helmets. Nonetheless, sitting there, unshielded from the buffeting airflow, struggling unsuccessfully with the alarmingly erratic controls, was to sample the primitive and perilous way in which it had all begun.

Unexpected as a source of Wright folklore was my octogenarian pilot's doctor, who regularly endorsed his enviable fitness to fly. Professor Stanley Mohler, in his seventies himself still an active pilot, was Director of Aerospace Medicine at Dayton's Wright State University. As well as having a profound technical knowledge of the Wrights' aeroplanes, he had, intriguingly, made a brain comparison study of the brothers' respective personalities, and another of some 1908 X-rays which explained why Orville had spent forty years of his life in pain. I am grateful to him for much helpful emailed advice in all his areas of expertise.

I also owe sincere thanks to Dawne Dewey, Head of Special Collections and Archives, Wright State University Libraries, in Dayton, Ohio, for the hospitable way in which she opened the Wright Brothers Collection to my time-consuming study; to Darrell Collins, the National Park Service historian at the Wright Brothers National Memorial at Kill Devil Hills for allowing me to walk the ground beneath the flight path of Wilbur's and Orville's first four flights; to Harry Fraser-Mitchell for his aerodynamics expertise and for so willingly checking my manuscript for technical errors; to Len

Bruno, Science Manuscript Historian, Library of Congress, for consistent kindness in responding to a continuous bombardment of requests for the retrieval of obscure material from an author 9000 miles away; to retired airline captain Ken Hyde for driving me across Virginia to show me the Wright *Flyers* and gliders he and his team were re-creating with fanatical authenticity to be flown at Kill Devil Hills in celebration of the centennial; to Peter Jakab, author of the most accessible book ever written to explain the technical brilliance of the Wrights' achievement, for much helpfulness; to Harry Haskell, grandson of Katharine Wright's husband, Henry J. Haskell, for much information about his grandfather and for permission to quote from Katharine's private letters to Henry; to Lois Walker, a USAF historian at Tyndall AFB, Florida, who is writing a major biography of Katharine Wright, for her many shared insights into Katharine's life; to William Hunt, Windsor Herald at the College of Arms in London, for his methodical search of the pedigrees of the Wrights' forebears which clarified the brothers' previously misunderstood English ancestry; to retired French Air Force General Pierre Lissarrague, historian at the aviation museum at Le Bourget airport, Paris, for the endless trouble he took to research for me elusive threads in the record of the Wrights' unhappy attempts to sell their machine to the French government, and for the evidence he produced of Octave Chanute's 1903 disclosure of the Wrights' secrets to the French Aéro-Club; to Randy Neuman, archivist at the United Brethren Historical Center, Huntington, Indiana, for the light he threw on the perpetual strife that swirled around Bishop Milton Wright; to Ann Honious, historian, Lawrence Blake, superintendent, and Bob Petersen, park ranger, at the Wright Brothers Station, Dayton Aviation Heritage National Historical Park, for enlightening tours of the legendary places; to Madeline Iseli, executive director of Inventing Flight, for introducing me to the bewildering array of city, state and federal committees, societies, commissions and boards that, during my research, seemed to spring up around the country almost every week to organise centennial celebrations; to Mary Oliver, archivist and curator of the Montgomery County Historical Society, for the privilege of a private tour of the Wrights' stately home, Hawthorn Hill, allowing me to visit its mysterious 'blue room' and the bedroom from which Katharine poured out her letters to Henry Haskell; to Jim Bebbington, city hall and county politics reporter, *Dayton Daily News*, for his explanations of the decay of the once attractive city of Dayton. To Peter Davison, assistant curator, aeronautics at London's National Museum of Science and Industry for his persistence in helping my four-year-long search for the Haskell papers held by Charles Gibbs-Smith; to Brian Riddle, librarian, Royal Aeronautical Society, for his constant prompt helpfulness in steering my research into fruitful areas; to Margaret Edwards-Brown in California for telling me about her grandfather, Reuchlin, eldest and least known of the Wright Brothers; to Bernd Lukasch, curator at the Otto Lilienthal Museum in Anklam, Germany, for increasing my slender knowledge of the life and work of the world's first successful glider pilot; to Martin Zink for solving all my computer problems; to my daughter Paula for many unpaid research chores in London; and finally, for their encouragement and huge enthusiasm for the project, I owe very great thanks indeed to my publisher, Alan Samson, and my editors, Stacey McNutt, Juliet Van Oss and Viv Redman.

While this book was being written in Auckland, New Zealand, international aviation was preparing to celebrate the 2003 centennial; but here at the bottom of the world the biggest commemorative event was staged, not on 17 December, but on 31 March. That was the day in 1903 when, according to persistent local belief, a South Canterbury farmer called Richard Pearse had become the world's true father of flight by flying a powered aeroplane nine months before the Wrights. 'I hope you're going to acknowledge Richard Pearse,' I was repeatedly warned. Well, Pearse was clearly a remarkable individual whose experimental aeroplanes deserve to be taken seriously by aviation history, but did he make a controlled, sustained powered flight, landing undamaged, before Wilbur and Orville? Alas he did not.

In the early years of the twentieth century, when the American brothers were consistently putting a practical flying machine into the air, Pearse, at his remote farmhouse in the Waitohi district, built – out of bamboo and metal tubes – a monoplane with elevator, ailerons and tricycle undercarriage. Looking surprisingly like a modern microlight, it was powered by a two-cylinder petrol engine ingeniously built from lengths of steel farm irrigation pipes. Arguments over whether he ever managed to make it fly have never ceased. Unfortunately it wasn't until fifty years after his turn-of-the-century experiments – in 1954 – that researchers became aware of his ingenious work.

Unlike the Wrights, Pearse, who had died in 1953, left behind little record of the two aeroplanes he designed and built. All witnesses to a flight he was alleged to have made in March 1903 were very young at the time. According to the memories of many, the aeroplane finished up in a gorse bush. Significantly, Richard Pearse himself never claimed to have properly flown, let alone beaten the Wrights to it. In a 1928 letter to a newspaper he admitted: 'It would start to rise off the ground when a speed of twenty miles an hour was attained. This speed was not sufficient to work the rudders so, on account of its huge size and low speed, it was uncontrollable and would spin round broadside on directly it left the ground. So I never flew with my first experimental plane . . . I had successful aerial navigation within my grasp . . . But I decided to give up the struggle as it was useless to try and compete with men who had factories at their backs.'*

Predictably, the centennial year revived other counterclaims that had refused to die, but no one researching the carefully documented and authenticated work of the Wrights can be left in the least doubt: it was the bicycle-makers from Dayton who conquered the air.

Ian Mackersey,
Auckland,
New Zealand,
August 2003

*The *Star*, Christchurch, New Zealand, 15 September 1928.

Prologue

When, as a young newspaper reporter, I indulged ten shillings a week of my £6 salary on the extravagance of flying lessons, my instructor, a veteran World War II pilot, used to delight in bewildering people by answering the phone as 'Wilbur Wright'. It was a game, I discovered, that he'd begun with another instructor at an airfield fifty miles away. They had nicknamed one another Wilbur and Orville.

I think this must have been the first I'd ever heard of the legendary brothers to whose combined genius I owed the existence of the little open-cockpit biplane on which I was learning to fly at this small town in the centre of New Zealand's North Island. After five hours and fifty minutes of instruction at the grass aerodrome, there came the memorable day when Vic climbed out of the front cockpit and uttered the magic words: 'She's all yours. Do just one circuit.'

As, in that moment of heady excitement, I slipped the bonds of gravity alone for the first time and the wood and fabric wings gently bore me into the air, I had only the barest understanding of the physical forces that, on that joyous day, made me a bird. The elementary facts of powered flight I'd taken for granted – that the spinning airscrew, pouring cold slipstream into my face, was driving the machine forward, overpowering the resistance of its bulky structure and magically creating above the cambered wings the invisible suction that supported the entire weight of the aircraft and its occupant. Likewise I had accepted the traditional functions of the simple controls, well known to every schoolboy: the stick that, through the elevators, raised and lowered the nose and, when tilted sideways, nudged the ailerons to bank left or right; the foot pedals which moved the rudder to turn.

Flying instruction in those days rarely bothered to explain the arcane aerodynamic theory of all this. The simple process was much more concerned to demonstrate what the controls did, not why they did it. Pupils were only too grateful to be spared the science and difficult mathematics of it all. It was, however, the ability to control a flying machine safely in the three dimensions of the air that had presented its inventors with their biggest challenge.

The phenomenon of human flight, one of the supreme achievements of the second millennium, had been discovered and perfected less than fifty years before my own triumphant first solo. On 17 December 1903, among the sand dunes of the bleak and gale-swept Atlantic coast of North Carolina, two American bicycle mechanics, Wilbur and Orville Wright, lying prone on the lower wing and dressed in suits and ties, made the world's first piloted sustained and controlled powered flights in a heavier-than-air machine. They flew twice each. The longest flight, by Wilbur, lasted nearly a full, conclusive minute. These sons of a devout Brethren bishop in the Midwestern city of Dayton, Ohio, had that day fulfilled man's great dream to emulate the birds that had defeated inventive minds since the Middle Ages. With their primitive wood and fabric machine looking like a large box kite, its propellers driven by clanking bicycle chains, they had launched the age of aviation. Amazingly, most of the world would not know about it for nearly five years.

1

The Bishop's Sons

The yearning to rise into the air, to cruise above the earth, had given birth to man-lifting kites, had prompted desperate leaps from high places by brave individuals with flapping wings, and brought, in the eighteenth century, the exciting breakthrough of balloon flight that had led to powered airships. But winged flight that truly copied the birds, safely cruising the three dimensions of the sky with a workable means of propulsion and control, remained tantalisingly out of reach.

Brilliant men had struggled to understand the physical theory and complex mechanics of bird flight without success. Some had tried to replicate the process by designing contraptions in which, with only the power of their arms and legs, they hopelessly flapped bird-shaped wings of wood and fabric; they never left the ground – unless they jumped off a tower, inevitably to maim or kill themselves. The reason was terribly simple. The musculature of man, compared with that of a bird, was too pathetically inadequate to keep him in the air. What the would-be aviators were yet to discover was that the wing-operating breast muscles of birds represent as much as a huge one-third of their body weight. To match that a man would need a six-foot chest to hold the muscle mass necessary for flight.

Nor did the experimenters know that birds' hearts are relatively much larger and stronger than those of mammals – that man's heart comprises a bare half of one per cent of his total weight compared with the 8 per cent of some eagles and the colossal 22 per cent of the tiny hummingbird. Birds are powered by much higher revving engines than humans', which turn over at a dawdling 70 beats a minute. Compare this with the pumping capacity of the chaffinch, helped by a supercharged pulse rate of 700. Nor can man ever hope to compete with the efficiency of a bird's lungs, which are uniquely connected to a series of air sacs distributed through their bodies, potently charging their flight muscles with high-octane oxygen fuel. And their wing bones are weight-savingly hollow.

Human flight, it came to be realised, would have to be aided mechanically. It required something else, too, that few experimenters had ever succeeded in getting their heads around – an understanding of the immutable and unforgiving laws of aerodynamics, a science still at the dawn of its creation.

So who were these brothers, a couple of unknown bicycle-makers with no scientific training, neither of whom had formally graduated from high school, who with systematic determination succeeded in cracking the technological secrets of manned flight and changing the face of the world?

Nothing about Wilbur and Orville Wright suggested a shred of the greatness that would become theirs that historic day in 1903 near remote and inaccessible Kitty Hawk, where they took their revolutionary machine in search of reliable winds and to escape the prying eyes of newsmen. The astonishing thing about their conquest of the air was the speed with which such an untutored pair accomplished it. Only five years earlier, aviation had not seriously entered their lives. They scarcely knew the difference between lift and drag. Their world was entirely involved with the simple mechanics of the humble pedalled bicycle. Equally astounding was the fact that their four historic flights that day, a feat of sheer inventive genius, created, internationally, scarcely a ripple of interest. The meagre reports of this significant event for humankind that did appear were characterised by inaccuracies beyond belief. And not only was the way it was communicated to the world a public relations disaster, but the brothers' marketing efforts to find anyone to buy the fabulous machine were met with lack of interest and sceptical disbelief. Astonishingly their own government was so uninterested that its army, which could have seized it and led the world into the revolutionary era of military aviation, declined even to see it demonstrated.

The advent of modern aviation was delayed for years while the Wrights, in possession of this hot property, cloaked its ingenious mechanism in secrecy as they tried unsuccessfully to persuade nations to buy it. Their uphill struggle was to see their lives turned upside down, their health affected, their word doubted, the invention misunderstood by their contemporaries, hopelessly misdescribed by the press, their trust shattered by con men and corrupt officials. The journey to eventual modest riches and fame was to take a huge toll.

The small Dayton West Third Street cycle shop in which the aeroplane was conceived and built was one of fourteen in this industrial city of 80,000. In the last years of the nineteenth century, Wilbur and Orville would arrive there promptly at 6 o'clock every morning and conscientiously toil at their work benches until 10 o'clock at night. The brothers eked out a modest living from the bicycles they built and repaired in the unpretentious brick building they shared with an undertaker. Both, despite the grimy nature of their trade, were always smartly dressed in the middle-class attire of the era – suits, fresh daily stiff white collars and bowler hats. Wilbur was thirty-two, Orville approaching twenty-eight. Neither had ever married – or had any intention of doing so. Neither had ever touched alcohol, smoked, or used the Lord's name in vain. Model citizens of puritanical outlook, they were courteous, good-humoured, intelligent, widely read and subscribed to a tireless work ethic. They were, it seems, near-perfect beings.

Of the two, who bore little immediate resemblance to each other, Wilbur was instantly the more striking personality. Taller, leaner, more angular than his brother, he very rarely smiled and gave the impression to those who didn't know him of cold aloofness. He was a rather strange, unflappable, very reserved man of startling intellect. He could, with his rapidly balding head, have passed quite easily for a preoccupied academic: a most unlikely sort of person to be working as a mechanic.

A more conventional, stockier individual, Orville was a warmer, more gregarious personality. His curly dark brown hair was also rapidly thinning, but his approaching baldness was offset by a thick bushy moustache. Friends described him as a bit of a dandy, deeply concerned about his appearance, always immaculately scrubbed and groomed. He was also a creatively practical man. A natural-born engineer who revelled in the face of mechanical challenge, he complemented the intensely cerebral Wilbur.

The two were inseparable. People said an almost unnatural harmony existed between them – described by some as almost a kind of marriage. 'From the time we were little children,' Wilbur wrote, 'my brother Orville and myself lived together, worked together and, in fact, thought together. We usually owned all our toys in common, talked over our thoughts and aspirations so that nearly everything that was done in our lives has been the result of conversations, suggestions and discussions between us.'[1]

The immutable union was forged in the crucible of a uniquely close-knit family shaped by a caring but autocratic father. Milton Wright was a bishop in the highly pietistic Church of the United Brethren in Christ, an evangelical sect that had taken root in rural America. With his white beard and stern countenance, Bishop Wright comes across today in photographs as an austere, rather forbidding character. In 1899, at the time the brothers began to address the challenge of flight, both were still living under his roof and in the thrall of his moral influence and emotional spell.

The family home at 7 Hawthorn Street, in Dayton's westside suburbs west of the Miami River, was just a few minutes' walk from the cycle shop. It was a narrow two-storey wooden frame dwelling separated by barely two feet from the house next door. Bishop Wright had bought it for $1800 in 1870 and he lived here with Wilbur and Orville and his unmarried daughter Katharine, who was in her early twenties. His wife, Susan, had died ten years earlier, twins – Otis and Ida – had perished in infancy, and his two eldest sons, Reuchlin and Lorin, had left home. The bishop and his three grown-up children had become a domestic unit of extraordinary self-sufficiency.

The Wrights believed they could track their ancestry back to

Saxon England. Milton Wright, an enthusiastic amateur genealogist, claimed to have traced his own direct forebears to the late 1400s and an English country squire, John Wrighte, who, in 1538, built a baronial three-storey mansion at Kelvedon Hatch between Brentwood and Chipping Ongar, today on the north-eastern edge of London.

'His grandson's grandson, Samuel Wright,' Milton wrote, 'came to America probably in the year 1630 and in the year 1636 was a first settler at Springfield, Massachusetts. At that place he was deacon of the first church of the Puritans and soon after, in the continued absence of the pastor, was chosen to dispense the word of God for the present. He removed years later to Northampton (Mass) where he died in 1665, sleeping in his chair.'[2]

However, if Deacon Samuel Wright was indeed the first of the clan to arrive in America – and it appears that he was – it is by no means certain that he was descended from the landed gentry of Essex. A staggering amount of dedicated research into the Wright Brothers' ancestry was conducted by one of Milton's distant cousins, Curtis Wright, a Carthage, Missouri stone quarry owner, who published a 320-page book of breathtaking sweep on the subject, still on sale today.[3] The book claims a long line of distinguished ancestors – a duke, no less, plus a string of baronets, knights, a Lord Mayor of London, a privy counsellor, a British ambassador, one of Cromwell's physicians and numerous eminent academics. Deacon Samuel Wright, according to Curtis, could trace his pedigree directly back to the noble Kelvedon line through his father, a wealthy London merchant, Nathaniel Wright, one of the founders of the Massachusetts Bay Company. However, in London, at the College of Arms – a branch of the Royal Household and the ultimate authority on the pedigrees of the English gentry – the records reveal a quite different story.

Attempting to check Deacon Samuel's lineage for this biography in 2001, Windsor Herald of Arms William Hunt quickly discovered that merchant Nathaniel Wright's son, Samuel, had not in fact ever gone to America. He had become the minister of Stockton church in Wiltshire, dying there, an untravelled man, in 1663. His four children had all been daughters. Mr Hunt also investigated the ranks of three of the Kelvedon line, claimed by Curtis Wright to have been knighted or ennobled. 'None,' he declared, 'was entitled to call himself "Sir" or "Lord".'[4] Indeed a peerage wasn't given to a Wright, he established, until 1932.

So who exactly were the true forebears of the first of the aeronautical Wrights to arrive in America? To trace them safely would have involved a costly search of close to a hundred pedigrees the College of Arms hold for Wright, of whom a small swarm joined the seventeenth-century emigration wave. But whoever he was and from wherever he may have come to America in the early 1630s, the Puritan Samuel Wright appears to have been accurately tracked through six generations of perilous frontier life down to Milton Wright. Certainly the bishop was to inherit some of his steely and righteous character.

The Wrights' forebears lived mainly by farming or as clerics. From Massachusetts they migrated west and south in their wagons, carving farms and log cabins out of the forests. They made their own clothes and ground their own flour. Life was a harsh, endless round of hard labour, struggling to keep hunger and disease at bay. They sprinkled the progeny that survived with Old Testament and Puritan names like Ebenezer, Seth, Hannah, Rebecca, Helped and Thankful. They intermarried with other settlers of Dutch and German blood. They fought battles with Indians and were caught up in the 1770s in the bloody War of Independence in which Milton's grandfather served in the Patriot Army fighting the British at Bemis Heights and Saratoga. Milton's father, Dan Wright, and his mother, Catharine Reeder, of German and Dutch descent, settled in Indiana. There, in green woodland in what today is Rush County, east of Indianapolis, they felled trees, built a simple cabin, cleared ten acres, and planted a crop of corn. They later moved to a larger farm nearby where Milton was born in 1828.

Milton left a vivid description of the austere Indiana frontier life into which he arrived. His parents 'were poor and so were their neighbours; and they saw hardships as also did their neighbours all; but the soil was as rich as they were poor'. His father, Dan, whom a photograph portrays as a dogged-looking man of severe gaze, was phlegmatic and slow speaking, yet 'his intellect', Milton recorded, 'was a busy and incessant workshop'. His strength of character and rigidly high moral resolve was to be acquired in turn by his son and later by Wilbur and Orville. In that hard-drinking frontier society, Dan would rather accept a smaller price for his corn than sell it to the local distilleries. 'In 1833 he banished liquor from his house, and raised us all without it. 'There was', wrote Milton with pride, 'not a drinking man among his children.'[5]

His mother, Catharine, Milton effusively describes as another paragon of virtue. 'Industry, affection and conscientiousness were three of her chief characteristics. Home was her sphere and her children her jewels. She was tenderly and constantly pious.'[6] Unlike her husband, who refused to join any of the established churches because of their failure to oppose slavery, Catharine became an ardent member of a local Methodist church. Four of her sons obliged her daily prayers and became ministers.

In 1840, when Milton was twelve, the family bought a farm in Orange Township in neighbouring Fayette County where, at the local school, Milton recalled proudly, he 'devoured books with remarkable rapidity . . . and with a memory which at that time was a marvel to the family.'[7] He set out on a disciplined path of self-improvement. 'I patiently trained my mind to think. I did it daily, purposely and sometimes laboriously as systematically as I knew how.'[8] The mind-training regime led him to join a debating society. And it took him out into the fields and woods where he would stand alone and deliver heartfelt speeches 'which often attracted the ears of the family and sometimes of the neighbours'.[9] It was out here, at the age of fourteen, that, at the urging of his mother, he found religion for himself. 'I was converted in my father's field in 1843 . . . while labouring in the growing corn of June.' He suddenly 'felt called to labour in some public way for the cause of God and humanity. It was not by voices or visions or signs but by an impression that spoke to the soul powerfully and abidingly.'

To practise his goodness Milton joined the Church of the United Brethren in Christ. Older than its better-known namesake, the Plymouth Brethren, to which it was not related, it had been formed by a group of evangelical preachers in Maryland in 1800. Fanatically pious in its teachings, it owed some of its theology to the Methodist, Mennonite and Dutch and German Reformed traditions.

The new church grew rapidly. It created its own ministers and bishops, the latter, in the spirit of frontier egalitarianism, elected for four-year terms by delegates to quadrennial conferences. There was little ritual. Congregations democratically chose their own forms of communion and baptism. Good Brethren were exhorted to forswear alcohol, and encouraged to support the anti-slavery cause. Membership in the Masonic order, or any other secret society, was specifically forbidden on pain of expulsion.

Milton not only joined the United Brethren – being baptised by immersion – he decided to dedicate his life to this church, and to his wider idealistic goal of helping create a universally practising Christian America. He became a minister and was admitted to the White River Conference, the governing body of the local church district in central Indiana. By the mid-1850s he'd become a travelling circuit preacher, spreading God's word through the countryside on horseback, steadily enrolling converts whose totals he proudly logged in his diary each evening. But by now he had more than just the Lord on his mind. At Hartsville College, the church's training establishment, he had met a fellow student, a 'smart young lady' of German descent called Susan Catherine Koerner.

Susan, who was studying literature, was also a committed Christian. She had joined the Brethren at fourteen as the result, apparently, of a 'significant religious experience'.[10] Her father, John Koerner, was a wagon and carriage-maker who, in 1818, to avoid conscription, had come from Saxony in Germany to America, where he had married Catherine Fry, the daughter of an American-born farmer of Swiss extraction. By the time Milton and Susan met, the Koerners had a farm in Union County, Indiana. Here, as well as farming, John Koerner continued to practise his basic trade from a carriage workshop in which Susan as a child spent much of her time, acquiring in the process an unusual degree, for a young girl, of mechanical aptitude.

The courtship became a protracted affair, conducted chastely, largely by letter. 'Both wanted to be absolutely certain that the other had the character and strength of purpose required to face the difficulties of a Christian life.'[11] Much less is known about Susan and her family than about the hugely documented Wrights. She didn't keep a diary and few of her letters have survived. Milton's tenacious genealogical researches appear not to have uncovered much material about the Koerners. His own diaries contain minimal references to her.

What is known is that she was bright, but painfully shy. 'Like myself, in school, she excelled,' Milton once wrote immodestly.[12] In the few photographs that exist of her, Susan appears as a serene, rather plain woman, her short hair bobbed in a central parting that gives her a decidedly severe look. The few of her letters that exist – written to Milton during the marriage – are brief and stiffly formal, strictly factual and devoid of much emotion.

The slowly developing understanding between them was cautiously drawn out over six years, during which Milton, having bought his own Indiana property, was mixing farming with teaching and pastoral duties. In 1857 the United Brethren offered him a three-year assignment as a missionary to the West Coast – to join one of its operations in Oregon. The Pacific coast, before the transcontinental railway had linked it to the east, was virtually a foreign country, an independent frontier society, a lengthy sea voyage distant. Milton, afraid he would lose Susan, whom he was now satisfied met all his demanding specifications for a minister's wife, arranged what appears to have been one of their rare premarital meetings. 'Had my first private talk with Susan Koerner,' his diary records. 'I asked her to go to Oregon with me.'[13] She refused, but agreed to wait and marry him on his return.

In Oregon Milton preached at remote farmhouses, travelling his district by horseback and canoe. He taught at a Brethren school, Sublimity College, where he acquired a reputation as a strict disciplinarian, expelling a boy for attending a ball. Dancing was prohibited by the Brethren. The town, it was said, 'became noted during Wright's tenure for its peacefulness and purity of morals'.[14] He was a fiery preacher. Some of his sermons would roll on for a continuous hour and a half. His persuasive force was dramatic. People found 'the joys of conversion' so overwhelming they would break into shouting. Some of them wept. His evangelical spell was hypnotic. People would fall helpless to the ground in religious trances. Intoxicated by his own outpourings, Milton himself once keeled over in front of the congregation.

The young preacher fell in love with the wilderness world of Oregon. He wanted to return to Indiana, marry Susan and bring her back to make their life together there. At the end of 1859 he made the long voyage home and, within days of arrival, they were married. He was thirty-one, she twenty-eight. However, the raw pioneer life of the West Coast held little appeal for Susan. They were never to go.

Instead, in the bitter, icy Indiana winter of 1859, they moved into their first home, a three-roomed house on a farm in Rush County, south-east of Indianapolis. It proved a good marriage. Susan, despite chronic ill health from then widespread malaria, rheumatism and a host of other recurring ailments, fulfilled impeccably Milton's ideal of the perfect wife. She was, he was later to tell Wilbur, 'so humble, cheerful, meek and true'[15] – the model companion for a farmer-preacher in the austere rural Midwest of the 1860s. According to Wright legend she was, behind her acute shyness, level-headed, patient, practical, self-reliant and self-sacrificing. Within the harmony of the marriage Susan was to remain her own person, a quietly dominant emotional force, her crippling shyness masking a will as strong as her husband's. And with his constant, lengthy absences from home on the preaching circuit it was certainly she who ran the house.

There were to be many houses. In thirty years of married life they would move twelve times, and the process began almost immediately. Two moves took them, in 1860, to Grant County, to a farm Milton had earlier purchased there. Here, in a hewed log cabin, they remained for four years while he preached throughout the district and farmed his land, which produced a tiny income from its crops and timber. Their first child, Reuchlin, was born here in 1861. Milton wanted distinctive names for his brood. Reuchlin's was that of an obscure fifteenth-century German theologian.

Their second child, another boy, arrived the following year. Named Lorin, after a town randomly chosen from a map, he was born in Milton's parents' home where his father Dan, 'in full hope of heaven', had recently died. Milton's mother helped to deliver her latest grandson.

To the east and south the Civil War was now raging. But Brethren were pacifists, and although they opposed slavery and supported the Union cause as serving God's will, Milton did not fight. While whole companies of men were being formed up around him to join the Yankee army, he wrote, 'I am but little stirred about the war.' Reading his diaries during the five years of the conflict, in which nearly three million served and more than 600,000 died in battle on American soil, one could almost believe the country was still at peace. His diary remains a determined chronology of the minutiae of country pastoring, attending to the world of sin that flourished on the home front.

The untamed Midwest, into which settlers were pouring, was, in the Brethren view, breeding a raw society rife with moral corruption. Hard drinking, gambling, dancing and fornication were the target of its itinerant preachers. Milton was in his element. By horseback and wagon and winter sleigh he pursued his dedicated routines, baptising, marrying, burying, comforting, converting, moving his family through a succession of rented houses throughout Indiana.

In 1865, when the war was over, the Wrights settled on a second property which Milton – possibly with wedding present money – had bought near Millville on the fertile farmland east of New Castle, between Indianapolis and the Ohio border. On its five acres they lived self-sufficiently, keeping cows, pigs and chickens, growing wheat, maize and flax. Susan milked, wove the flax and did most of the farm work to free Milton to pursue his calling.

It was a frugal and bleak existence in a climate that veered from the extremes of Siberian cold to scorching summer heat. The tiny farmhouse, with its ham-curing smokehouse, outside toilet and wooden-bucket well, had just three rooms. Here, on 16 April 1867, Susan gave birth to her third child, another boy.

As the infant emerged into the world there was something arrestingly different about him. This was no ordinary baby. He had, Milton wrote, 'a head of extraordinary height – two stories high'. After a clergyman much admired by Milton, they named this unique progeny Wilbur.

2

A House of Piety (1868–1886)

Wilbur was still a baby when the peripatetic family moved on from Millville. They went, in 1868, back to Hartsville, to the United Brethren college where Milton, despite his lack of academic qualifications, had been appointed its first professor of theology. His singular qualities had begun to be recognised by the church establishment. However, Hartsville was to be but a brief interlude: more challenging work was awaiting him.

It involved the contentious issue of male secret societies whose members the Brethren barred. Since the Civil War, Freemasons had become a significant power in America. Large numbers of prominent businessmen, politicians and clergymen had flocked to join. The church's ban had begun to affect its own recruitment and a growing number of younger Liberal ministers were pushing for a relaxation of the inflexible rule. But they had not reckoned with the messianic determination of the Brethren's elders to bar what they viewed as the agents of the Devil. The philosophical disagreement was threatening to split the normally placid church asunder. The conservative right wing, the Radicals, preparing to fight the issue to the death, saw Milton Wright as a doughty champion of their cause.

Milton regarded the secret societies with special dread and loathing. They may have been dedicated to the worthy ideals of fraternity, charity and high moral standards, welcoming men of every religion, but he took issue with their secrecy, the covert way in which they helped colleagues, and their esoteric rituals which emphasised man's relationship to God while ignoring Christ's name. He believed that the Masons were a force for evil. They ranked in his mind alongside Catholic immigrants whose papal plan, he was convinced, was to destroy Protestantism, Asians who threatened to 'heathenise' America, Sunday newspapers, Sunday mail and train services. He believed the suffering of the Civil War and railroad accidents on the sabbath were God's judgement. He campaigned for the total prohibition of alcohol. He believed absolutely in the innate depravity of man – that all were born inherently evil.

The secret society controversy dominated the Brethren's quadrennial conference of 1869 at Lebanon, Pennsylvania, where the Radicals loudly opposed the smallest relaxation of the anti-Masonic doctrine. Their most powerful weapon was the hectoring Puritan oratory of the uncompromising Milton. He leapt into the fray with guns blazing. There were no grey zones in his view of right and wrong. The secret societies, he thundered, were the 'dark-visaged sister of the now defunct institution of slavery'.[1] He saw Masons covertly infiltrating the Brethren as enemy agents. The lines were drawn for a protracted doctrinal battle that would pit Brethren against Brethren. The Radicals wanting stiffer propaganda from the church's influential weekly, the *Religious Telescope*, fired the too moderate editor and replaced him with the aggressive Milton Wright. The move brought the family to Dayton, Ohio.

The United Brethren Publishing House had its own large brick building in the centre of town. Milton, now forty, arrived there in June 1869 to take up his crusading pen. It was one of the most prestigious roles in the church, in which he was entrusted with its chief instrument of power. He had soon convinced himself that God had chosen him for the task – helping to Christianise America ahead of the Second Coming, due at the 1900 millennium.

Milton, Susan and the three boys, eight-year-old Reuchlin, Lorin, six, and two-year-old Wilbur, lived initially in rented houses in Dayton in one of which the short-lived twins, Ida and Otis, were born. Then, in April 1871, they moved into the house they had bought at 7 Hawthorn Street on the west side of the city. With two breaks, it would be Milton's home for the next forty-three years. Here, on 19 August 1871, their sixth child, another boy, was born. Milton called him – after another minister he admired – Orville. In contrast to his reaction when the startlingly big-headed Wilbur had arrived four years earlier, Milton left no first impression of his latest son. All he wrote in his diary that evening was 'Orville was born this morning'.

The Dayton into which Orville had arrived was a typical Midwest city of the era. With a population of around 37,000, it sat astride the Miami River, an unremarkable place that had sprung up on the rolling plains of south-west Ohio, with low, rectangular brick buildings, wide main streets and a profusion of churches and factories. People travelled about in wagons, buggies and horse-drawn streetcars.

The shingle-roofed, clapboarded Hawthorn Street house was around a mile from downtown Dayton, a horse-tram ride away along West Third Street. A thriving new working-class neighbourhood, the detached houses were close-packed. Number 7 had been built on a lot just thirty-seven feet wide. On one side you had to turn sideways to pass between it and its neighbour. The seven rooms comprised a downstairs parlour, dining room and kitchen, with four modest bedrooms upstairs. A small cellar extended beneath the parlour and at the rear of the lot stood a wooden carriage shed beside the tiny outdoor lavatory. The house had no plumbing, no bath. They would sluice themselves in relays once a week, sitting in a tub on the kitchen floor with the curtains drawn. Water came from an open well with a wooden pump at the back door, and lighting from oil and, later, gas lamps. Susan cooked on a wood-burning kitchen range. A coal stove heated the house in winter. 'When I saw this house,' wrote the Wright Brothers' first biographer, John McMahon, in 1930, 'I felt its pre-eminence in a street of meagre homes. It was large . . . it had style.'[2]

Every morning Milton Wright, in sombre clerical garb, took the streetcar to the *Telescope* office at the corner of Main and Fourth Streets. Here he energetically immersed himself in his new job, pouring out three or four pungent editorials a week, often completing them in one swift draft. He outspokenly addressed almost every major issue of the day, from global and ecclesiastical politics, farming and theology to the corruption of youth. Every week he identified fresh moral perils for his Brethren; and he unceasingly attacked the burgeoning secret societies.

While Milton savoured his newfound power, Susan managed the Hawthorn Street home. She did all the cooking, mending, washing, cleaning. She even cut the boys' hair and made not only many of her own clothes but sometimes clerical suits for her husband. As Reuchlin and Lorin grew out of theirs, the cast-offs were remodelled for Wilbur and Orville. From her father, John Koerner, she had learnt an unfeminine range of mechanical skills which she put to use doing carpentry round the home. Once, famously, she built a sled for the older boys. When Milton came back in the evening she would serve him dinner, after which he would insist on reading aloud, for her opinion, the editorials he'd written during the day.

Unfortunately his bigoted propaganda soon so upset the Liberals that they launched a rival newspaper. Its appearance shocked Milton Wright. He saw it as little short of rebellion – as the thinly disguised voice of Freemasonry. The battle within the church became bitter and now deeply personal. Wright was singled out by the Liberals for special ridicule. 'The only pity is that he was not born in time to enjoy all the glories of the old Spanish Inquisition,' cried the rival *Tribune*.[3]

Stubbornly, despite the winds of change billowing around him, he demanded even more draconian sanctions against Masons. In response, the Liberals succeeded in having him dumped as editor. To get him out of the way the Brethren made him a bishop, whisking him to its far-off district of West Mississippi, a vast, lightly populated frontier territory lying between the great river and the Rockies. At first he tried to preside over this far-flung domain from Dayton, but the travelling proved too exhausting. So, in June 1878, the family rented out Hawthorn Street and moved west to Cedar Rapids, Iowa. The four sons had been joined by a daughter, Katharine, born three years to the day after Orville, on 19 August 1874.

The five children, now spanning thirteen years – from four-year-old 'Katie' to seventeen-year-old Reuchlin – were not to see much of their father as he plunged into his new role as a travelling bishop, riding the Union Pacific week after week into a Wild West in which General Custer and his men had not long before made their fatal last stand against the Sioux of Chief Sitting Bull. Milton's diary records the exhausting journeys that took him as far west as Denver, as roving administrator of the fifteen church districts of his huge diocese, once more visiting congregations on horseback, delivering streams of sermons, staying in rough hotels, stranded in winter snowdrifts, trying to sleep on uncomfortable trains on which his companions would offend him with their smoking and swearing.

His flow of letters to Susan and the children persistently demanded more frequent news from home. If it didn't come regularly he was quick to rebuke. His need for family contact was impossible to satisfy. Milton would return to Cedar Rapids with gifts and educational toys for the children. One in particular, some time in 1878, was a primitive rubber-driven helicopter made of cork, bamboo and paper which Wilbur and Orville would identify years later as the tiny seed of their interest in flight. When it finally wore out they tried to create much larger replicas, but the bigger versions refused to fly. The larger they made them the less successful they were. One day they would discover the immutable law of aerodynamics that explained this – that doubling the size in fact required a great deal more power. Trying to overcome the difficulty, Orville was admonished by his teacher for playing with one of the replicas at his desk in the classroom. He is said to have pleaded that he was working on a flying machine which might enable him, in a still larger version 'to fly with his brother'.[4]

Little distinguished the childhoods of the Wrights from thousands of others in the 1870s Midwest. They went swimming and fishing in the rivers, had pet chickens and kittens, made bows and arrows and painted themselves as Indians. Orville, at five, skilfully played truant from school for a month, carefully timing his return home each day to deceive his mother.

In winter they went tobogganing and played ice hockey on frozen ponds. They lit bonfires, experimented with cigars rolled from grape leaves, played at pirates, and Orville, who appears to have been the most enterprising, formed an army of school friends, appointing himself general. He and Katharine were paid $5 a year each to do the family dishes, which Orville supplemented by selling scrap iron and bones. He also, according to a much repeated anecdote, once made and sold sugared pine tar as chewing gum to other children. The Wright boys made their own stilts, floated home-made rafts across ponds and baked potatoes over fires in the woods. Wilbur and Orville made and flew kites which they would sell to friends – but the pastime didn't apparently arouse any scientific curiosity about the lifting forces that might hoist objects or people into the air.

The older children teased the younger. Reuchlin and Lorin would abandon Wilbur when escorting him away from home. Wilbur delighted in making Katharine cry, something he learnt to do simply by crooking his finger. Most of them acquired nicknames which they were privately to endure all their lives. Reuchlin was 'Reuch', pronounced 'Roosh', Lorin 'Fiz', Orville 'Orv' or 'Bubbo' or 'Bubs' (Wilbur's infant pronunciation). Wilbur was Will, but in letters they liked to refer to him as 'Ullam' (short for Jullam – German for William), Katharine was Kate, but in correspondence became 'Swes' or 'Sterchens', diminutives for the German *Schwesterchen* – 'little sister'.

Whippings – administered with a cane – were sparing, perhaps because the chief dispenser was so frequently away. They were usually for disobedience or dangerous conduct. Milton once beat Wilbur and Orville for throwing stones at a passing carriage, a punishment Orville tried unsuccessfully to avoid by hiding in the cellar. 'I governed them,' Milton, at eighty-seven, recalled for a biographer. 'They were pretty good boys, but mischievous. I had little trouble with them.'[5] Wilbur was last caned at the age of twelve.

None of the children, although diligent, especially excelled in their early years at school, but the home was filled with books and Milton and Susan, encouraging reading from an early age, developed in them a lively general knowledge. Their early education was a mix of formal schooling and home tuition. Of the five, it was Wilbur – whose emerging analytical abilities quite early had him beating his older brothers at draughts – who began to show the greatest intellectual potential. His ability to concentrate and absorb great amounts of information was phenomenal. From an early age it was clear that here was someone special.

He was described as a dreamer, frequently uncommunicative to the point of withdrawal. His remote self-confidence his teachers found unnerving. Once, at eleven, he was harshly reprimanded in front of the class for a wrong answer to an arithmetical problem chalked on the blackboard. Ordered to stay in after school, he was then humiliated to have a younger pupil, a girl, instructed to help him arrive at the correct answer. The two went into a huddle – in which Wilbur proved that his answer had actually been correct. They went back to the teacher, who had to concede Wilbur was right.

A voracious reader, Wilbur began to devour *Ivanhoe, Robinson Crusoe*, encyclopedias and the Greek biographer Plutarch's *Parallel Lives* in Milton's library. His mind, said Milton, 'was a storehouse of dates, figures, names, things trifling and important with every item instantly available for inspection'.[6] So lost would Wilbur become in the pages of a book, he would fail to hear people calling him. In the trundle bed he at one time shared with Orville, he would delight in terrifying his younger brother in the dark with the bloodthirsty tales he'd devoured during the day.

The Wright family life was driven by religious devotions. Unfailingly after breakfast there would be a quarter-hour of family prayer around the table to launch the day. At bedtime they would all regather for another prayer session led by Milton or Susan. Grace was said before all meals. Sunday school was compulsory and they were usually expected to attend a full church service as well, in addition to 'religious experience meetings' at which they would be further inculcated with piousness. Wilbur was thirteen when Milton's diary recorded his son's 'conversion' to Christianity. It happened in Cedar Rapids at a revival meeting at which his father was preaching. Following the sermon, Wilbur 'rose for prayers', professing a new birth in Christ as his saviour. There is no record of Orville's conversion. But from formal religion there was no escape. It was such an integral part of their existence that it didn't seem either excessive or oppressive. Nor did the absence of a tree at Christmas – banned by the bishop as pagan. Presents arrived instead on the table with Christmas dinner.

Their lives in Cedar Rapids were regularly interrupted by serious illness. The horrors of typhoid, diphtheria and tuberculosis were never far away. While Milton himself enjoyed huge stamina and a robust constitution, he nonetheless recorded regular bouts of debilitating sickness on his incessant travels. At home, Susan and the children were periodically struck down. The bishop's diary, in November 1878, recorded a typical spate of family ill health: 'Orville continues very sick . . . Orville has sinking spells and appears to be nearly gone . . . Orville nearly died . . . Orville some better, but feeble . . . Orville much improved . . . Lorin gets up with fever – has diphtheria . . . Reuchlin took sick with diphtheria.' All this within six days, during which Orville clearly came close to death. How much unrecorded illness laid them low when Milton was away – which was most of the time – is anybody's guess.

The four years of Milton's reign as bishop of West Mississippi were a watershed in his troubled career. As he roamed his prairie parishes far from the centre of United Brethren power, he began steadily to lose political ground within the church. When, in 1881, at Lisbon, Iowa, the quadrennial conference loomed up again, his enemies dealt him two depressing blows. He was neither re-elected as a bishop nor reappointed to the editorship of the *Telescope*. He was thrust into the wilderness – paying, for his uncompromising and abrasive style, a heavy price. He had offended too many colleagues. Indeed by now he had alienated not only the Liberal bloc within the Brethren but a growing number of his right-wing Radical colleagues as well. Stripped of bishop's power and authority, Milton returned merely as a presiding senior clergyman to the church's White River district. He was back almost to where he had begun over twenty years earlier, travelling the Indiana plains as a nomadic preacher on a sadly reduced salary.

Once again he uprooted the family, moving them back to Indiana – to a farm in Henry County, near Richmond. They chose Richmond because Susan's sister and their widowed mother lived there. Susan's health had become a major worry, with one illness following another. Now showing the ominous early symptoms of tuberculosis, she wanted to be near relatives during Milton's long absences.

Although he was back on the preaching circuit it did not prevent him re-energising, from his new headquarters, his war against secret societies and the rising menace of the Liberal movement, which had now set out to overhaul the entire pantheon of the church's outmoded policies. Despite attempts by the church to suppress it, he launched his own mouthpiece, a monthly newspaper, *The Richmond Star*.

The four Wright sons were now deeply caught up in their father's religious crusades. Wilbur, fifteen, and Orville, now eleven, had been pressed into service at his newspaper, folding and addressing copies. Reuchlin was hovering on the brink of a career in the church. He had gone from high school to a Brethren clergy training school. Later, he and Lorin had enrolled at the tiny fifty-student – and rather second-rate – Brethren university at Hartsville where they roomed together. However, neither ever graduated or entered the church. Instead, chronically short of money and in debt, they left home and went back to Dayton to find work, Reuchlin as a timber-yard clerk, Lorin as an assistant bookkeeper in a carpet shop.

Reuchlin had begun to rebel against his father's domination. Of all the children, he would be the only one successfully to cut loose from its pervasive power. A handsome and serious-looking young man, he appears, in the few photographs, perennially despondent and much older than his years. As one of the Wrights' biographers was to put it, 'an air of resignation hung over him – an indication that dutiful adulthood had been purchased at the price of self defeat and touchiness'.[7] In his mid-twenties Reuchlin married the daughter of a United Brethren missionary. Susan habitually complained about her daughter-in-law, claiming that her relatives were 'sponging' off Reuchlin. It was the beginning of his more or less permanent disengagement from his own family.

Lorin was also to marry. Unlike Reuchlin, he would remain happily on the fringes of the family and, like his siblings, was to be drawn in to his father's doomed religious causes. Kind and easy-going, he lacked the drive that was to distinguish his younger brothers. Yet Lorin and Reuchlin, at a time when only 7 per cent of American children ever got to high school, were launched into the world with the most schooling of the four sons. 'Reuch and Lorin were talented men with more formal education than most of their contemporaries, yet both gave the impression of being constantly overwhelmed by responsibility and circumstance. They suffered from chronic poor health and seemed to be perpetually on the brink of failure.'[8]

Of all the bishop's children, Wilbur continued to show the greatest academic promise. Starting his senior year at Richmond High School, he was confidently taking in his academic stride Greek, Latin, geometry, philosophy and geology, effortlessly gaining consistent 95 per cent results. Milton and Susan had begun to discuss sending him to Yale.

At Richmond High the descriptions are of a quiet, almost introvertedly grave young man, contemplative, excessively private, and inclined towards gloominess. Although he mixed easily with others of his own sex, from all the evidence he suffered an acute aversion to female company. A suggestion by some biographers that he once had a crush on a young woman classmate seems to have had no basis in fact.

Despite his academic brilliance there, Wilbur did not graduate from Richmond High School.* In June 1884, just a few months before he was due to, Milton abruptly moved the family back to Dayton to be nearer the centre of church power. Because they couldn't reclaim their own leased-out home in Hawthorn Street for sixteen months, they had to rent another. It was a most uncomfortable place. Susan, torn away from her mother and sister and with tuberculosis spreading through her lungs, described it bluntly as 'miserable'.

Back in Dayton, Milton wanted to marshal support for the next round of the power struggle, but the tide had turned against him. The reforming Liberals were now in a majority determined to make the church more liberal and democratic. To remove its stormy petrel, the Brethren re-elected Milton as a bishop and banished him

*Although he had met the requirements for high school graduation, Wilbur failed to apply for his diploma. It was presented 110 years later to Wright family members at a banquet in 1994.

again – this time to the smallest of all its kingdoms on the Pacific West Coast. Worried about Susan's ailing health he negotiated a deal allowing him to limit his time in this latest isolation to six months in the year.

The bishop didn't go to his outpost quietly. Before departing he boldly tried to create, complete with its own newspaper, a new rival church – the Constitutional Association – within the shrinking ranks of the conservatives. In an unwise act of nepotism, he appointed Reuchlin as secretary and left the family in Dayton.

In the winter of what was probably 1885–86 – the precise date is uncertain – during one of his stints on the West Coast, some bad news reached Milton from Hawthorn Street. Wilbur, he learnt, had been badly injured while playing ice hockey. The physical and psychological trauma was to alter the course of his son's life.

3

Trials of the Righteous (1886–1889)

The accident happened on a frozen artificial lake in Dayton. In a game between the high school, where Wilbur was taking some esoteric subjects in philosophy to prepare himself for Yale, and the sons of Civil War veterans, one of the players lost his grip on his stick. It flew out of his hand, striking Wilbur in the face and knocking him down. 'It smote him on the mouth with such force as to knock out all his front upper teeth. It was a cruel and terrible injury. An army surgeon bandaged the gory face.'[1]

There are several versions of the accident – and of its severity. This one came from the Wright Brothers' first biographer, John McMahon, who got it from Orville about thirty years after the event. Milton Wright left a less alarming account in which, many years later, he recalled that the bat had knocked Wilbur down, 'but not injuring him much'.[2]

According to Milton, a few weeks later he 'began to be affected with nervous palpitations of the heart' which precluded his going to Yale. It is also recorded that he developed 'digestive complications'. How much the physical symptoms were merely psychosomatic – a subtle interaction triggering organic dysfunction after the emotional shock of painful injury – we shall never know, but it caused a devastating interruption to the academic career of the hugely promising eighteen-year-old.

He had, at the central high school, just been awarded astonishingly high marks in the two abstract subjects of Cicero, the Roman orator, and 'rhetoric' – the latter's special subject. Wilbur, once active and athletic, withdrew from all school activities. A deeply introspective personality at the best of times, he became convinced that the accident had permanently weakened his heart and nervous system. He retreated into inactivity and despondency.

Suddenly the family was very vulnerable. The two elder boys had left home, but Orville, at fifteen, and twelve-year-old Katharine were still in need of care. Milton was constantly away for months at a time and Susan, dying of tuberculosis, had become a helpless invalid confined to bed. Seeing no immediately active future for himself, and anxious that his father shouldn't have to resign his duties as a bishop, Wilbur stepped into the breach to devote the greater part of his life and energy to the care of his dying mother and younger siblings. 'Such devotion of a son has rarely been equalled,' Milton said, 'and the mother and son were fully able to appreciate each other. Her life was probably lengthened, at least two years, by his skill and assiduity.'[3]

Wilbur became, in short, housekeeper and nurse. The intellectually stimulating years he might have enjoyed at Yale were abandoned. Every morning, through the last two years of her life, he would help the bedridden Susan hobble painfully down the stairs to the parlour, where during the day he would attend to her every need. In the evening he would gently pick her up and carry her back upstairs. And all the while he also acted as substitute father to Orville and Katharine.

Wilbur's withdrawal began to cause concern within the family, some of whom, as year followed year, wondered if his protracted recuperation was perhaps more attitudinal than physical. When, towards the end of 1888, his disengagement from the world had stretched into three years, Lorin, making a precarious living in a frontier town in Kansas, wrote to ask fourteen-year-old Katharine: 'What does Will do? He ought to do something. Is he still cook and chambermaid?'[4]

No amount of research has ever successfully established a credible medical explanation for Wilbur's extraordinarily protracted convalescence as he moved from nineteen into his early twenties. On the surface of it, the facial injury, which Milton dismissed so lightly, could only have laid him up for a few weeks at the most while the wound healed. But no medical or dental records of the accident have survived to tell us what really happened. It's not even known if Wilbur subsequently had to wear a partial denture.

During his protracted convalescence, he was nonetheless putting the time to productive use. Day after day he assiduously educated himself in ancient and modern history, literature, ethics and science from the books in Milton's library. He reread Plutarch's twenty-three biographies of Greek and Roman statesmen and soldiers, Gibbon's *Decline and Fall of the Roman Empire*, Boswell's *Life of Samuel Johnson*. He devoured histories of England and France, the *Encyclopaedia Britannica*, the works of Sir Walter Scott, and even the books of a celebrated agnostic which Milton had, perhaps surprisingly, acquired. By the time Lorin had made his unsympathetic enquiry, Wilbur, now twenty-one, was probably as well read as any university graduate at that time. He was also, by late 1888, beginning at last to rise out of his brooding blues. He had begun some part-time work in a grocery store. Ready to face the world again, and in need of intellectual challenge, he decided to launch himself into the United Brethren affray – to go into battle in support of his father amid the mounting strife still corroding the church.

When a Brethren commission announced modernising proposals, it was now Wilbur who set out with relish to condemn every one of them. Some of the Liberal elders were stung by the bluntness of his tracts and articles, by the impudence of one so young. But Wilbur was unrepentant. To one deeply offended elderly minister he replied:

> You seem to infer that I am too young to tell the truth. Is there any precise age at which men become able to speak the truth? I know children not five years old who tell the truth. It has not been the custom, therefore, to grade the truth of statements by the age of the person giving voice to them . . . it is unworthy of a

man in your position in the church to take advantage of my youth to discredit statements which you would not venture to discredit otherwise.[5]

Susan, despite ebbing strength, wrote detailed letters to Milton in California, keeping him abreast of the Liberals' machinations. She devoured the *Religious Telescope*, noting that its new editor had called the outspoken Wilbur 'a fool' and had begun to turn against Bishop Wright. 'I have it in mind,' she told Milton, 'to write him a note thanking him for the interest he takes in your welfare and that of your district and suggest that Judas also took quite an interest in his Lord.'[6]

Only a few of Susan's letters to Milton have survived. Written on lined paper, briefly to the point and ending always 'Love to you, S. C. Wright', they report regularly on the debt-ridden, jobless Reuchlin's unhappy marriage to Lulu Billheimer, whose family were 'still sponging' off him, forcing him to borrow from Susan. 'It is not worth while to try to help him till he shakes the Billheimers off,' she told Milton in exasperation. Her letters supplied a running commentary on the totals of one of Wilbur's tracts, 'going fast' as it was poured out to the Brethren faithful across the country.

The propaganda pamphlet was in fact being printed by Wilbur and Orville in their first joint business enterprise as the 'Wright Brothers'.[7] Orville, now seventeen, was at high school in Dayton. Unlike his brother he was an unmotivated scholar, said to have been more interested in gadgets than books. He regularly received only 'medium' ratings for 'application'. Not greatly interested in his school work, he had acquired a reputation for persistent minor mischief which led teachers to keep him under surveillance, often seated in the front of the class, where his mind was usually on his interests outside the classroom. He and a fellow pupil, a Hawthorn Street neighbour, Edwin Sines, between whose houses they'd rigged a telegraph line, had acquired a small, rudimentary printing press with which they produced a newspaper for the eighth grade, *The Midget*. The paper claimed confidently, 'We have secured as contributors some of the finest literary talent of our city.' But *The Midget* was short-lived. Milton Wright, home from the West Coast and seizing a copy hot off the press, was dismayed to see that page three of the four pages was virtually blank. It merely carried the name 'Sines & Wright' printed twice across it diagonally. The publishers had found the task of filling the paper, typeset painfully character by character, more than they'd bargained for. Accusing them of dishonesty and laziness, the bishop promptly banned its distribution. *The Midget* never appeared again.

Printing, however, had now entered Orville's blood so deeply that he wanted to make it his career. He went on from job printing work, setting up the type for the Radical Brethren tracts on the Wrights' dining room table, to spend two summer vacations learning the craft doing sixty-hour weeks in a Dayton printing works. And as, in the spring of 1888, Wilbur began to emerge from the years of his withdrawal he, too, became involved. He helped Orville build his own press in the barn at the back of the Hawthorn Street garden. They made it together from lengths of firewood, bits of junk iron and hinged steel bars scavenged from the folding canopy of the old family buggy. The completed press was big enough to print a newspaper. It could thump out a thousand sheets an hour.

As she sat in the Hawthorn Street parlour penning her cryptic communiqués to Milton that summer of 1888, Susan was sinking. Her tuberculosis, which today antibiotics would have cured, was slowly consuming the tissue of her lungs. No clinical accounts of her final months exist, but she would have been suffering increasing pain and probably coughing up blood. She was also beginning to feel neglected by Milton, who was far away, busily evangelising on the West Coast. 'I thought I would surely get a letter this morning,' went a peeved note to him in June, 'but you don't seem to be much given to writing this trip.'[8] Wilbur, too, was growing anxious. By August he was so worried about Susan's health that he wrote tactfully to his father: 'Mother thinks that while it is not absolutely necessary on account of her health that you should return before your time is up, yet she would feel more comfortable if you were here.'[9]

The bishop seemed to feel that Susan's health was much more immediately in the hands of her children. To Katharine and Orville he sent a moralising lecture, urging them, in a joint letter, to be 'real good and agreeable to one another, so Mother will enjoy the times and live longer.'[10] He was not prepared, it seems, to be deflected from the Lord's work. In September, now feeling very ill, Susan decided to make her own direct plea:

> Dear Milton, I received your letter of Sep 19th this morning. I felt a good deal disappointed for I thought may be you [would] come home this week. I have been a good deal under the weather for a couple of weeks. When I wrote you before I was taking a cold but as it has been coming on for several days and still was not bad I thought it would not amount to much but it kept getting worse until [sic] it was most as bad as last spring . . . The cold was not so bad but I had not as much strength to start on and I am very weak . . . Come home when you think best. I guess I will get along all right. Love to you, S. C. Wright.[11]

This sad, rambling letter did the trick. The week in late September that he received it in California, Milton decided at last to return to Dayton. Strangely, his diary makes not a single reference to the failing health of his wife that brought him rushing home. It gives instead praise to the Lord for the success of the four years of his West Coast mission. 'Providence has very greatly favoured me those years. Praise his name.'[12]

Although he had returned at last to Susan's bedside, back in Dayton there were soon other things to disturb his peace of mind. In November a crucial church-wide referendum to decide the future character of the Brethren delivered him a shattering blow. A raft of liberalising proposals – including relaxation of the secret societies ban – was carried by an overwhelming majority of the voting church membership. Although it was now clear that the reforming winds would sweep the proposals into law at the church's 1889 quadrennial conference, Milton refused to accept the democratic will. He was prepared to split the church: to cleanse it of secretism would be 'pleasing to God', he railed.[13]

In the early months of 1889, as his wife lay dying in Hawthorn Street and members of the diehard Radicals were one by one beginning to waver, Milton rallied his shrinking forces for the final battle. Wilbur and Orville joined the war of words. Orville's home-made press was now publishing a profitable weekly newspaper, *The*

West Side News. Wilbur had become editor and Orville printer and publisher. Although most of the content was casually lifted from other newspapers and magazines, its editorials spoke with Wilbur's caustic independent voice. His columns fiercely promoting the Radical cause in the church row now became a mouthpiece for Milton as they issued dire warnings to Liberal parishioners that they were law-breakers.

The issue came to its dramatic head at the May 1889 convention. The theatrical setting for the final act of this divine tragedy was the opera house in the town of York, Pennsylvania. A photograph taken at the start of the meeting shows the delegates as a group of severe-looking elderly men in dark grey clerical uniform, most hugely bearded, some clutching top hats. Milton, now sixty, his trim beard snow white, a flinty and implacable figure, sat with the six bishops in an atmosphere crackling with high tension.

The result was a foregone conclusion. The changes were overwhelmingly swept into law. Yet still the mesmerising, fanatical star of the conference refused to capitulate. To the acrimonious end, Wright repeatedly leapt to his feet to denounce the reforms as illegal. 'I vote "no!"' he rumbled with great emotion, predicting disaster for the entire movement. 'Bishop Wright stood like a hero,'[14] wrote one of his colleagues. 'He stood faithful among the faithless.'

Events now took a dramatic turn. Bishop Wright and a small rump of fourteen Radical followers walked out. They rented another opera house and convened their own rival caucus. The Brethren that day divided into two irreconcilably opposed factions. They became known respectively as the churches of the United Brethren in Christ (New Constitution) and the Church of the United Brethren in Christ (Old Constitution).

Though elected one of the tiny breakaway church's new bishops, he was about to move into the saddest, most testing years of his life. The war of the rival Christian camps was far from over. A fresh battle for the church's extensive worldly assets, spread across America, was about to begin. Milton arrived back in Dayton in the third week of May 1889, mentally and physically drained, to find his wife of thirty years close to death.

4

The Bird-watching Bicycle-makers

(1890–1899)

Susan Wright lingered on for another six weeks. Milton was torn between the religious tumult in which he was engulfed and the demands of nursing her. On Wednesday 3 July he was due to go to north Dayton to meet a lawyer to launch lawsuits against the Liberals. He asked Susan if she would prefer that he cancel. She insisted that he go. When he got back she was much worse.

At 4 o'clock next morning, Independence Day, 'I found Susan sinking,' he wrote, 'and about five awakened the family. She revived about 7:00 somewhat, but afterward continued to sink till 12:20 afternoon, when she expired, and thus went out the light of my home.'[1]

That afternoon Milton went to Woodland cemetery where he chose 'a beautiful lot' on a wooded hillside for the burial two days later. For years thereafter he would visit the grave on the anniversary of her death to lay flowers at precisely 4 o'clock, the time of the interment. He was to feel her loss acutely; on top of the havoc he had generated within the church, two of the sustaining pillars of his existence had collapsed within weeks. 'In intellect, in sensibilities, and in disposition, she was all that heart could desire,' he grieved. 'At home her shining was gentle and pure as the glory of a pearl, and she had no ambition to shine anywhere else.'[2] In an obituary in the

West Side News one of the family wrote: 'her children have lost their best, their truest friend on earth.'[3]

In the nest there remained only Wilbur, Orville and Katharine. Lorin was still trying to make a living out west. Reuchlin and Lulu, now with a two-year-old daughter and a second child on the way, had moved to Kansas City where he had found office work with a railroad company.

In Hawthorn Street the crises of 1889 had brought the family to a major crossroads. Milton, in the midst of the Brethren tempest, was beset by grief. Wilbur, released from his nursing role and recovered at last from the trauma of his accident, suddenly found himself free to seek a new life direction. Orville, too, felt unleashed: free finally to quit school and become a full-time printer, though continuing to take part-time Latin lessons in case he decided on university; like Wilbur, he had eventually left before the term's end without a high school diploma.

Katharine, now fifteen and still at school, was talkative, witty, outspoken to a fault and had a ready sense of humour. Quick to anger and argue, she was gregarious and mature beyond her years. Photographs show a petite, dark-haired young woman with warm, expressive, slightly tomboyish features, more handsome than pretty. A pince-nez, from childhood onwards permanently clipped to her nose to correct a serious vision problem, gave her a distinctly academic, slightly bossy appearance. Milton expected her to step into her mother's shoes. He had begun to prepare her two years earlier when she was barely thirteen; from the preaching circuit he'd written to his adolescent daughter urging her: 'Be good. Learn all you can about housework. Do not worry Mother. Be my nice pet daughter.'[4] Half a year later he'd begun to reinforce the message:

> You must take care of Mother while I am gone. Take especially good care of yourself. You have a good mind and good heart, and being my only daughter, you are most of my hope of love and care, if I live to be old.[5]

Concerned that his daughter appeared to display little of the meekness he had admired in her mother, Milton had added:

> I am especially anxious that you cultivate modest feminine manners and control your temper, for temper is a hard master.[6]

Barely a month after the funeral, when Katharine had gone to visit family friends in another town, Milton, extending his needs to the imperial 'we', put her under fresh pressure:

> Dear Daughter: I hope this will find you well and enjoying life finely. We very much miss you, but we are satisfied if you are well and enjoying life and being real good as we suppose you are. Home however seems lonesome without you. But for you we should feel like we had no home. Yet we are so busy, we do not stop much to think whether we have any home or not.
>
> I often think of something or see or hear of something that Mother would know and care something about, but she is not here, and there is no-one knows or cares anything about it.[7]

The letter ended: 'Come home when you get your visit out,' adding ominously, 'if we do not send for you before.' Fifteen-year-old Katharine was left in little doubt that her life and conduct were now being directed by her father. She was expected to run the house – to where Lorin, having failed to make a life in Kansas, had, homesick and unhappy, returned dejectedly soon after the shock of his mother's death. As Katharine moved into her late teens and, in the early 1890s, began to prepare for university, she was forced to accept her new lot as Milton's secretary and housekeeper. It was a role in which she was soon showered with constant, meticulously detailed letters.

There were regular church statistics – 'lay these away carefully in the left-hand pigeonholes in my desk'. There was money. It would arrive with precise directives for its use – down to pots of paint with which Wilbur and Orville were expected to redecorate the house. There were frequent complaints. 'I want you to raise a racket if the boys do not send me the Conservator as soon as it's in print – two copies – and not wait for me to get it by the mailers. I have not seen last week's paper yet! A week after it is in print!'[8]

'I want you and the boys to be real good while I am away.'

(Wilbur was twenty-five and Orville twenty-one.) 'Make business first; pleasure afterward, and that guarded.'[9] The same letter commanded Katharine to be diligent about a financial task: 'Do not neglect nor be careless about it,' he instructed. His need for mail was obsessive – 'I want you to raise a racket if I do not get letters from home every week. I have not heard from home since I left nearly two weeks ago! There is no use in such work.'[10] A later letter to Wilbur made the point more bluntly: 'After this one of you boys must reach me by letter each week promptly.'[11]

Wilbur and Orville wrote when they chose. They were busy making a living. The printing business was proving more successful than their newspapers – a succession of three failed within months of launching. Now trading as Wright & Wright, Job Printers, they had replaced the *West Side News* with a daily, the *Evening Item*. It was an ambitious venture, appearing six days a week, mixing local news with national news supplied by a wire service. Trying to compete with twelve other Dayton newspapers, it promised readers they would get 'the clearest and most accurate possible understanding of what is happening in the world from day-to-day'. In the circulation battle it didn't shrink from sensational stories with headlines like ROASTED IN RED, ROARING AND TERRIBLE FLAMES, DIED FOR LOVE – TRAGIC SUICIDE IN AN OHIO HOTEL. Wilbur's trenchant editorials supported women's suffrage, opposed the expansion of American power, and promoted honesty and personal morality in politics. But the brave enterprise couldn't compete with Dayton's weighty, illustrated dailies now being poured off high-speed presses. The *Item* lasted less than four months.

A third and final publishing adventure also quickly foundered. The *Dayton Tattler* was printed by the Wrights for one of Orville's school friends, Paul Laurence Dunbar. Dunbar was a conspicuous member of the class as its lone black student in a heavily segregated society. An exceptionally gifted writer, he had become editor of the school newspaper and president of the debating society. But most famously, this son of freed slaves shone as a poet. His ability to express lyrically the dialects, misery and inferiority of slavery in his verse, fiction and songs was to bring him national fame long before America was to hear of the Wright Brothers, but in 1890, when

Orville, who claimed him in this racist city as a close friend, was turning out the *Tattler*, this solemn, sad-faced black youth whose writing would one day bring him prosperity could only get work as a lift operator in Dayton. Much quoted is a snatch of affectionate doggerel Dunbar is said to have scribbled on the printing shop wall one day while working there with Orville:

Orville Wright is out of sight
In the printing business
No other mind is half so bright
As his'n is[12]

The *Tattler*, which carried advertisements for $3 trousers and $15 suits, was to die from lack of income after only three issues.* Its demise ended Wilbur's and Orville's tenuous publishing career. They decided to stick to more profitable job printing. Some of their work began, helpfully, to come from Milton, who had been appointed the Radicals' publishing agent. Split off in his mid-sixties from Brethren friends and close colleagues of forty years, he was the renegade dynamo at the centre of a frenzy of activity among the tiny breakaway 'Old Constitution' group to build a whole new church almost from nothing. Most of the machinery of the original church – the funds, the colleges, the Sunday schools, the publishing house, indeed the very church buildings themselves, with their pastors – had remained with the Liberal main body. Milton found himself presiding over a tiny splinter movement in chaos. The legal squabbles for the assets raged in the courts of seven states for eight years. In state after state supreme courts and courts of appeal found in favour of the Liberal majority. Milton was convinced that the depressing pattern of defeat, stripping the Radicals of almost every vestige of their property, was the work of crooked judges. The elected judiciary, he believed, was now corrupted by Freemasons.

---

*Dunbar, too, was to enjoy in his celebrity a depressingly brief life. His marriage to another talented black writer failed when he turned to drink to ease the pain of the tuberculosis that killed him at thirty-three.

In Dayton the Wright family had belonged to the United Brethren church in Summit Street, but most of the congregation was staunchly Liberal; the local Radicals were forced to disband, and Wilbur, Orville and Katharine suddenly found themselves without a church. They later joined another of Radical persuasion, but Wilbur and Orville, appalled by the vilification of their father which, following the split, arose from all sides of the once united church, became permanently alienated from formal religion. 'They continued,' said Bishop Wright's biographer, Dr Daryl Elliott, 'to support their father in his church battles and respect him as a man of God. Nevertheless they chose to practice their Christianity in a private manner. Milton never challenged them on their choice even though he must have been disappointed.' However, 'there is no evidence to suggest that Wilbur and Orville ever became agnostics or rejected their faith.'[13]

In 1890 Dayton, Milton's own faith was being severely tested. Despite his formidable constitution, the strain and disappointment of the church's internal warfare began to take its toll. As he watched the steady desertion to the Liberals of more and more clergy, he was nearly brought to his knees. Not only was he, as senior bishop, effectively the head of the disabled new church, he was also still a travelling preacher, spending sleepless nights on trains jolting through Ohio, Pennsylvania, Virginia and up into Canada. And he was constantly haranguing judges, sometimes spending whole days standing in the witness box being grilled by Liberal counsel. 'I am over taxed with work,' he wrote. 'Somewhat worn down & Nervous.' To help preserve his health he had begun a spartan fitness regime – it included daily bathing, even in the sub-zero Dayton winter, in ice-cold water – 'and have found,' he wrote, 'much comfort and health in it.'[14]

When the overburdened Milton was at home, the family would rally to lighten his load. Lorin became his scribe, slowly penning an incessant stream of briefs to attorneys as his father dictated them in measured sentences. And Wilbur would give hours of his time to reading his father's interminable legal persuasions as one expensive suit followed another. On at least one occasion, Wilbur himself took the stand to give evidence for the Radicals. He never doubted the absolute rightness of Milton's beliefs and the revolutionary measures he took to pursue them. He had become one of his most passionate and articulate disciples: there was not the least uncertainty that Milton, because he was their father, knew best and must always be right. It was a view shared unequivocally by Orville and Katharine. They, too, came to believe in the innate wickedness of mankind – that the world out there was filled with people not to be trusted.

The church strife brought the Wrights even closer together. Though Milton's character seems to have seethed with contradictions, his children's loyalty to his religious purposes was total and unquestioned. As exacting and demanding as he may have been, it is also clear that, beneath his forbidding exterior, he cared very much for his children's welfare; his love for them was undeniable.

Once Lorin had married a Dayton schoolteacher, Ivonette ('Netta') Stokes, and created a home of his own not far away in West Dayton, and Katharine had been sent off by Milton to university at Oberlin College in northern Ohio, there was often only Wilbur and Orville in residence at Hawthorn Street. They shared not only their fraternity but, in their vice-free lives, the strict moral values implanted by their parents, their work habits and a capacity for piercingly critical judgements of their fellow men. The special affinity that drew them together, the complementarity of the relationship, was a force that fed common interests and a powerful joint energy. Their bachelor existence was, as Wilbur wrote to Katharine, characterised by blissful, if austere, harmony:

> Orville cooks one week and I cook the next. Orville's week we have bread and butter and meat and gravy, and coffee three times a day. My week I give him more variety. You see that by the end of his week there is a big lot of cold meat stored up, so the first half of my week we have bread and butter and 'hash' and coffee and the last half we have bread and butter and eggs and sweet potatoes and coffee. We don't fuss a bit about whose week it is to cook. Perhaps the reason is evident. If Mrs Jack Spratt had undertaken to cook all fat, I guess Jack wouldn't have kicked on cooking every other week either.[15]

Cooking wasn't the only shared interest outside the printing shop. They had both bought one of the new 'safety' bicycles – machines with wheels the same size that had begun to replace the 'penny-farthing' which, with its perilously high saddle and huge front wheel, needed acrobatic skills to master. As millions of new chain-drive easy-to-handle bikes had poured on to the market, a cycling craze had begun to sweep America. Orville had taken up racing, winning medals. Wilbur, who had been an outstanding ice skater, athlete and footballer before his hockey incident, avoided racing for fear of another painful accident. Instead he acted as Orville's 'starter', launching him with a shove. The two, always in suits and ties, had begun to go for long rides together far out into the country.

Suddenly, both seemed to have time on their hands – enough to build the veranda, seen in most photographs of the Hawthorn Street home, along the front and side of the house. In truth they'd become bored with printing. Wilbur now had no newspaper for his literary talents; Orville was also losing interest since Sines had begun to cope with most of the small stream of work.

Looking around for a fresh business in which to immerse themselves, they decided to capitalise on the bicycle boom. In West Third Street they rented the first of a succession of premises and set up as the Wright Cycle Exchange to sell and repair bicycles. Despite intense competition, the venture, which offered bikes from $50 upwards, flourished. Soon it was their main source of income, and within a few months they had to move to bigger premises down the street, where they renamed the business the Wright Cycle Company.

They appear to have brought equal engineering skill to the business. In photographs both can be seen at work in hats, ties and waistcoats, bent over their lathes. They carefully harboured the profits in their joint bank account; it was said they never ever queried each other's drawings. And not a cent, it seems, was ever squandered on the smallest pleasure:

> The brothers were abstemious in their habits . . . They used no liquor, beer or tobacco . . . They were sparing of tea and coffee . . .

> Parties and dissipations were unknown to them. They went home nights, read, talked and so to bed.[16]

They worked in great harmony. They whistled, sang snatches of *Swanee River*, *Annie Laurie* and *Oh Susanna*, and hummed themes from Schubert and Schumann. At home the pair would engage in endless conversation. 'Their voices were so much alike that a person in the next room couldn't always distinguish between them. If the quiet, even staccato became extra fast and choppy, like a bit of rapids in a sober low-murmuring brook, it was probably Wilbur.' But they could also argue forcefully, a process they relished while alarming others. 'I love to scrap with Orv,' Wilbur once said, 'he's such a good scrapper.'[17] Yet the heated arguments never became personal squabbles – they were invariably disagreements on a higher plane: about scientific ideas, technical matters and theories. Their congeniality seems to have been complete. Orville summed it up years later: 'I can remember when Wilbur and I could hardly wait for morning to come to get at something that interested us. *That's* happiness!'[18]

Both, outside their brotherly arguments, were even-tempered. The mildest curse never escaped their lips, and customers had to mind their language. The differences in their temperaments seemed only to cement their unity. Never was it threatened by Wilbur's greater maturity, the intimidating force of his intellect, or by Orville's inability to grow up, the adolescent pranks that were essential to his being. According to his first biographer he would perform a regular goodnight trick. It involved 'going upstairs on all fours, slapping each step with his hands . . . at twenty-eight he was not quite grown up . . .'[19]

Although profitable, the bicycle business had its ups and downs. It was acutely seasonal, regularly dying in the autumn and winter. In 1896 they merged the printing and cycle businesses under one roof at 22 South William Street, just around the corner from 7 Hawthorn Street. Here they decided to manufacture their own machines – each bike a beautifully handmade original – building them over the winter when trade was slack.

Just as the cycle business was getting off the ground, Wilbur came close to death with acute appendicitis. Surgery then involved such a dangerously high infection risk that he was treated with bedrest and a bland diet. He was off work for over two and a half months. As he lay in bed he began to ponder his future. He had drifted into the printing and cycle businesses but saw neither as his destiny. Back at work amid the mentally unstimulating routines of the machine shop, he found himself hankering again for university. 'I have thought about it more or less for a number of years,' he wrote to Milton on his travels,

> but my health has been such that I was afraid that it might be time and money wasted to do so, but I have felt so much better for a year or so that I have thought more seriously of it and have decided to see what you think of it and would advise.
>
> I do not think I am specially fitted for success in any commercial pursuit . . . Intellectual effort is a pleasure to me and I think I would be better fitted for reasonable success in some of the professions than in business.
>
> I have always thought I would like to be a teacher. Although there is no hope of attaining such financial success as might be attained in some of the other professions or in commercial pursuits, yet it is an honourable pursuit, the pay is sufficient to enable one to live comfortably and happily and is less subject to uncertainties than almost any other occupation. It would be congenial to my tastes, and I think with proper training I could be reasonably successful.
>
> Of course I could not attempt a college course unless you are able and willing to help me some . . . I think with six or eight hundred dollars I could complete the course which would probably take about four years. I would be glad to have you think the matter over and give me your advice on it.[20]

Wilbur added that by continuing to work in the cycle shop he himself could fund 'the greater part of the expense'.

'I received your letter,' Milton replied a few days later. 'Yes, I will help you what I can in a collegiate course. I do not think a commercial life will suit you well.'

Wilbur didn't go to university. His life, and Orville's, continued to revolve around bicycles. They began to build their own hand-crafted models for sale. They raced them – at least Orville did – and experimented with novel designs. They created a minor sensation by building from the high wheels of two penny-farthings a freak tandem – which only they ever had the skill to ride.

With the exception of an 1893 visit to the World's Columbian Exposition in Chicago at which they had admired the latest bicycle designs, they had never travelled more than a few miles from their home town. Their lives centred wholly on Dayton, where hunting and fishing trips on nearby rivers regularly figured in their well-ordered lives. Their limited social activity seemed to centre on musical evenings at which both, according to the custom of the day, would sing heartily around the piano. Wilbur was said to have had a fine bass voice. Both were members of an informal local singing group.

On Sunday mornings when, to please Milton, they avoided work of any description, they would sometimes cycle the three miles out to some sandstone pinnacles on the bank of the Miami River in the Moraine neighbourhood, south-west of the city. Here, where the breeze swept up the side of these long-since-disappeared sharp-pointed rocks sculptured like little Matterhorns, they would lie on their backs in the sun for hours watching the hawks and buzzards soaring on the updraught.

As they lazed by the spiky rocks on the outskirts of town, the brothers talked idly, as so many before them had done, about how man might emulate the birds that glided overhead. What particularly fascinated them was the ability of the buzzards to hang stationary in the breeze without an apparent flick of a feather. 'We could not understand,' Orville wrote, 'that there was anything about a bird that would enable it to fly that could not be built on a larger scale and used by man. If the bird's wings would sustain it in the air without the use of any muscular effort we did not see why man could not be sustained by the same means.'[21]

Their working lives, however, continued to be devoted to bicycles and printing – an existence that almost certainly brought more contentment to the less ambitious Orville than to Wilbur who, as he entered his thirties, felt no real affinity for either occupation. He had continued to drift, registering little more than passing shock and interest in the event he was later to quote as igniting the first embers of his fascination with the riddle of heavier-than-air flight: the death in August 1896 of a German aeronautical experimenter called Otto Lilienthal.

News of Lilienthal's fatal glider crash in the Rhinow Hills appeared as a small paragraph in the Dayton newspapers in the middle of a Wright family crisis. Orville had gone down with typhoid, the killer that lurked in almost every Midwest water supply. He'd been lying for weeks in a feverish delirium, drifting in and out of consciousness, hovering yet again between life and death. Milton was away fighting his grim church battles, so Katharine had postponed her return to college to nurse her brother. She and Wilbur took turns to keep vigil by his bed. There was still no cure for typhoid; they were advised merely to feed him a diet of milk and beef soup, regularly sponge him down – and hope for the best.

Although Wilbur was to cite the German's death as arousing only 'a passive interest which had existed from my childhood' in what he called 'aeronautical problems', the event has nevertheless acquired in Wright legend the status almost of an epiphany. Orville would have learnt of Lilienthal's fate much later when, for the first time in six weeks, he was able to sit up in bed. When he was well enough to join Wilbur back at the cycle shop in the autumn of 1896, their curiosity about flight seems to have continued, but only in a detached sort of way. The newspapers had been carrying reports of other attempts to fly much nearer home. Near Chicago some American enthusiasts were also successfully gliding off small hills. And in Washington, DC the head of the Smithsonian Institution, Professor Samuel Langley, had managed to fly two steam-powered model aeroplanes: they had remained in the air over the Potomac River for an historic 90 seconds.

Yet it wasn't for another three years – until the spring of the last year of the century – that the brothers' aeronautical curiosity appears to have taken serious root. They came across a book on ornithology[22] which galvanised them for the first time into a burst of positive aerial activity. 'My brother and I became seriously interested in the problem of human flight in 1899,' Wilbur was to recall many years later:

> We knew that men had by common consent adopted human flight as the standard of impossibility. When a man said, 'It can't be done; a man might as well try to fly,' he was understood as expressing the final limit of impossibility. Our own growing belief that man might nevertheless learn to fly was based on the idea that while thousands of the most dissimilar body structures, such as insects, fish, reptiles, birds and mammals, were flying every day at pleasure, it was reasonable to suppose that man might also fly.[23]

The conviction led Wilbur, in May 1899, to write to the Smithsonian one of the most historically important letters the great research institution would ever receive:

> Dear Sirs, I have been interested in the problem of mechanical and human flight ever since as a boy I constructed a number of bats of various size after the style of Cayley's and Pénaud's machines,

the letter began, in terms that must have been all too familiar to an organisation regularly showered by letters from eccentrics and enthusiastic amateurs with schemes for flying machines.

> My observations since have only convinced me more firmly that human flight is possible and practicable . . . I am about to begin a systematic study of the subject in preparation for practical work to which I expect to devote what time I can spare from my regular business. I wish to obtain such papers as the Smithsonian Institution has published on the subject and, if possible, a list of other works in print in the English language.[24]

5

Some Aeronautical Theories (1899)

> I am an enthusiast, but not a crank in the sense that I have some pet theories as to the proper construction of a flying machine. I wish to avail myself of all that is already known and then, if possible, add my mite to help on the future worker who will attain final success . . .[1]

Wilbur's letter to the Smithsonian was opened by Professor Langley's assistant, Richard Rathbun. Langley had the previous year been granted by the US Army the then very large sum of $50,000 to develop his successful steam-powered model aeroplanes into full-size man-carrying machines. The announcement had sharply escalated the flood of mail from would-be inventors, but Rathbun replied to them all courteously. To Wilbur he promptly posted a helpful consignment of material. It included reprints of four articles which had appeared in the institution's annual reports. The authors were Otto Lilienthal, a lone French artist and glider experimenter called Louis-Pierre Mouillard, Samuel Langley, and one of Langley's aeronautical assistants, Edward Huffaker.[2]

Adding suggestions for further reading, Rathbun recommended a book, *Progress in Flying Machines*, by Octave Chanute. It had been Chanute's gliders that had been making news in Chicago. Also on the list was Langley's own scientific work on flight, *Experiments in Aerodynamics*, and a publication called the *Aeronautical Annual*. The latter was an influential journal edited by a wealthy Boston shoe manufacturer, James Means, who had retired from the footwear business to devote his life to the cause of flight. In his 1896 annual, in an article entitled 'Wheeling and Flying',[3] Means had, by happy coincidence, linked the two forms of locomotion, urging those who struggled to fly to master first, in gliders, the balance and control that was the basis of cycling: 'To learn to wheel one must learn to balance. To learn to fly one must learn to balance,'[4] he declared. He was right – but still no one knew how to do it.

One of the first to address the mysteries of flight scientifically, the Wrights learnt, was the awesomely talented Italian artist, philosopher, architect, engineer and scientist, Leonardo da Vinci. Flight was said to have been 'the most obsessing, most tyrannical of his dreams'. He would buy caged birds in the market in Florence for the sheer pleasure of releasing them to fly to freedom. While painting the *Mona Lisa* and *The Last Supper*, his mind was grappling with the theory of aerodynamics and the forces that created lift and drag. He designed a test rig to measure these things. Most of his aeronautical work, in the late fifteenth century, was preoccupied with flapping flight. He sketched wonderfully clear drawings of flying machines with windmill-like wings, manually cranked by a complex system of windlasses, pulleys and levers.

Human engines would never have lifted Leonardo's ornithopters off the ground. Moreover, he had designed his wings to 'row downwards and backwards'. But to defy gravity, birds' wings (we now know from high-speed photography) do not actually beat backwards. The action of flapping up and down provides simultaneously both lift and propulsion. On the downstroke the outer primary feathers of most birds twist into miniature high-speed propellers, moving forward and down in a kind of figure-of-eight action. This pulls the bird forward to create an airflow over the entire length of the wings to supply the lift.*

---

*Despite the biological reality, human ingenuity eventually did achieve the apparently impossible. A human-powered propeller-driven aeroplane, *Gossamer*

Da Vinci's work in the late fifteenth century was not immediately to inspire others. His precious aeronautical notebooks lay in obscurity in private hands for over three hundred and fifty years. Not until 1874 did the world begin to learn the extent of his scientific work. By then aeronauts were making long-distance flights of hundreds of miles, sitting in the baskets of balloons drifting in always uncertain directions at the whim of the wind.

Balloons had been the inspiration of a French paper-maker, Joseph Montgolfier. 'Ruminating in front of his fireplace' in Avignon one evening, he had been intrigued by the rising flow of smoke and sparks. Could the force driving them be harnessed to lift something bigger? he wondered. He made a bag of fine silk and lit a fire beneath it. The bag promptly swelled and rose to the ceiling. With the help of his brother Etienne, Joseph made a much bigger bag which they tested outside. It ascended over 70 feet into the air before cooling and deflating. In the marketplace at Annonay, near Lyon, in 1783, they demonstrated their 'aerostatic machine' in public. They later sent aloft a sheep, a rooster and a duck. Before the year was out their balloons were carrying people on long journeys across France.

When the gasbags evolved into airships, they were made controllable – at first propeller-driven by smoke-belching steam engines into which the pilots shovelled coal. Even when the internal combustion engine arrived in the 1880s, the ponderous creeping blimps were to remain mistress of the air for the rest of the nineteenth century. But through this era of leisurely lighter-than-air flight there had persisted the view that bird flight still held the secret to man's great dream.

'We were much impressed,' Orville wrote, 'with the great number of people who had given thought to it – among these some of the greatest minds the world has produced.' He named an English experimenter, Sir George Cayley, Sir Hiram Maxim (inventor of the machine gun who had ventured into aeronautics), Alexander Graham

Albatross, built of ultra-light materials, was, in 1979, flown by an athletic pilot, Bryan Allen, across the English Channel in 2 hours, 50 minutes. Nine years later Allen's achievement was eclipsed when another pilot successfully emulated Daedalus by pedalling an astonishing 74 miles across the sea from Crete to the island of Santorini.

Bell (who had invented the telephone and was also now trying to solve the problem of flight), Otto Lilienthal and Samuel Langley.

Wilbur had read of Cayley's work in James Means' *Aeronautical Annual* which, in 1895, had reprinted some intriguing articles from an obscure journal with a tiny circulation in which, in 1809 and 1810, Cayley had described his research.[5] In these learned aeronautical papers he had set out with astounding accuracy what today are recognised as the scientific truths lying at the root of the aerodynamics that would create the 747 and Concorde. Before the locomotive had been invented, and while the world was still struggling to drive and steer gasbags round the sky, Cayley had put his important discoveries into practice, building fixed-wing aeroplanes that actually flew with men on board. The Wrights may not have known a lot about these dramatic events, for the full extent of the Yorkshire baronet's aeronautical genius did not emerge for more than a hundred years. Even to this day his name is scarcely known outside aviation circles.

Born in 1773 into the comfortable and privileged world of the land-owning upper classes, Cayley was a self-taught scientist and philosopher. His inventions were numerous – from railway safety devices and artificial limbs to theatre safety curtains and caterpillar tractors. But his most significant work was in aeronautics and the construction of successful man-carrying flying machines. This shy, chubby country squire set out to understand the forces that kept birds so effortlessly in the air. He was convinced they could be translated into mechanical flight – into his bold vision of mass air travel across the 'uninterrupted navigable ocean that comes to the threshold of every man's door'.

Working alone in a stone workshop on his baronial estate, Brompton Hall, near Scarborough, he had divined by 1799 the physical basis of flight, correctly identifying at long last the baffling fundamental force of lift. He saw that the wings of the herons and rooks he studied achieved their lift because they were cambered – curved convexly from front to rear. He discovered that a cambered wing's lifting power was produced by the passage of the air flowing over it. Although he didn't manage to identify the true principal reason – the creation of a region of low pressure 'suction' on the upper surface caused by the increased speed of the air rushing over the curved wing top – he was the first since da Vinci to conduct a scientific examination of lift. He even established where the centre of this elusive force was, and the equally crucial importance of the centre of the opposing force of gravity. He copied into aircraft design the feature called dihedral – having noticed how gliding birds held their wings up in a shallow V to correct lateral rolling. When the birds rolled one way, he observed that their lower wings generated more lift than the upper ones, swinging them back on to an even keel. He observed, too, that birds' wings were slightly tilted above the horizontal.

To simulate flight, Cayley built a whirling arm machine to measure the variations in the force of the lift generated by airflow passing over a wing with its leading edge raised to face the flow, as the birds' did, at different angles – what today is known as the angle of attack of an aircraft wing. He mounted his spinning arm on a tripod, setting it up at the top of the sweep of the grand baronial stairs at Brompton. It was rotated by a cord pulled by a weight which he dangled above the entrance hall. On one side of the arm he attached a flat wing surface exactly one foot square, balancing it on the other with small ounce weights from the kitchen scales. As the arm rotated he raised the angle of the wing in 3-degree stages. As it rose it produced – as he had observed with the crows' wings – more lift and supported progressively heavier weights. But the lift, he discovered, only increased up to an angle of so many degrees. When the wing was raised too far, its lifting power quite suddenly diminished. Cayley had discovered the classic aerodynamic process, crucially demonstrated to every student pilot to this day, by which an aircraft wing, if raised on modern aeroplanes beyond around 12 degrees, causes the airflow over the top surface to break up and the wing rapidly to lose its supportive lift and stall.

Cayley's discoveries marked a turning point in the understanding of flight. Where, throughout history, people had persisted futilely in trying to provide both lift and propulsion from their own puny arm and leg power, Cayley concluded that these basic forces had to be divorced – that the power must be found from some other source. In a major intellectual leap, he began to design an aeroplane which, for the first time, would have separate systems for lift, propulsion and control. In the process he gave the world the cambered aeroplane wing. And, in an historic textbook phrase, he analysed the basis of mechanical flight: *to make a surface support a given weight by the application of power to the resistance of air*.

Having identified these physical forces he began, around 1809, to build gliders, launching them across a shallow valley on his estate. Later he built and flew two man-carrying machines. Their flights firmly sealed his place as a giant of aeronautical invention, though, sadly, not at the time. The world's first full-sized aeroplanes, they had cambered wings beneath which the pilot sat in an open-boat fuselage with three wheels. An adjustable tail unit could be trimmed on the ground and a separate rudder and elevator were pilot-operated. The only vital control the gliders lacked was any form of ailerons – reliable devices to correct rolling movements were not to arrive for another half-century. In the first of Cayley's machines, which had hand-pumped flappers protruding from the sides like dragonfly wings, a ten-year-old boy was flown in 1849. In another, around 1853, Cayley's petrified coachman flew several hundred yards across the valley, climbing out to shout the much quoted: 'Please, Sir George, I wish to give notice. I was hired to drive, not to fly.'[6]

To what degree the coachman controlled the historic glide is nowhere recorded. Nor are any subsequent manned flights.* Cayley never used propellers and never succeeded in producing a lightweight engine to connect to the bird-type flappers he favoured for propulsion. But his aerodynamic work had taken the development of mechanical flight further than it had travelled in the whole course of human history. When he died, aged eighty-four, in 1857, his obituary in *The Times*[7] made not a single reference to his aeronautical achievements. No newspaper reported the events in the Yorkshire valley for which he would one day be recognised as

*In the early 1970s Cayley's glider was re-created for an Anglia Television programme. For safety it was made of stronger and heavier material – but it flew. Taken to the very Yorkshire valley of the original flight, it did so with its modern pilot with surprising efficiency. So did another replica in July 2003, piloted by British billionaire Sir Richard Branson.

the inventor of the aeroplane. This honour was not to come until his private papers were made public for the first time in 1927, and his historically significant notebooks in 1961. The Wrights knew nothing of his epoch-making manned flights.

They did know about the flights of the publicly acclaimed glider pioneer Otto Lilienthal. They had seen magazine photographs of the German's machines spectacularly scything through the air. He appeared to have mastered manned flight – yet, sadly, not quite.

A mechanical engineer born in 1848, Otto Lilienthal was the son of a cloth merchant whose failing business had led him into alcoholism and premature death. In common with the Wrights, there had grown between Otto and his younger brother, Gustav, an uncommonly deep and trusting bond. As children in the north-east German town of Anklam they'd become fascinated by the storks that nested on the local roofs and barns and had tried to copy the big ungainly birds that they noticed always made their take-offs into wind. They made a set of beechwood and cloth wings, unsuccessfully experimenting at night to avoid the jibes of their schoolmates. Later, at technical academies in Berlin, Otto and Gustav began to address the aerodynamic challenges of human flight with Teutonic thoroughness.

Convinced that the birds alone held the secrets of ascent, the Lilienthal brothers analysed their mechanics and aerodynamics to a degree never before attempted by anyone. They became the first since Cayley had discovered the principles to explain that birds achieved their propulsion by the 'propellering' airscrew action of the outer primary feathers. Then they built all manner of testing devices: treadle-operated wings working like see-saws whose lift they measured with counterweights, and whirling arms like Cayley's. They flew bird-shaped kites in stiff breezes to observe the lift over their curved wings. They produced reams of tables, logging figures for the forces of lift and drag from air flowing over surfaces set at different angles. They calculated the size of the wing needed to support the weight of a machine and its pilot.

'It took much time and study to arrive at the conclusion that the slight curvature of the wing was the real secret of flying,' Otto wrote. So was the ratio of its greatest depth of curvature to its fore and aft breadth. They settled for a relationship of 1:15 to 1:18. But because they decided not to reveal the historic findings publicly for fear of ridicule, this fundamental aerodynamic data lay effectively dormant in their notebooks for over a decade.

It was not until 1889, by which time he was drawing a modest income from his own Berlin company that was making steam boilers, that Otto at last found the courage to publish, at his own expense, the details of their significant research. The book, *Birdflight as the Basis of Aviation*,[8] attracted only a tiny readership. By the time the book had made its unobtrusive appearance, Otto Lilienthal had entered the uncharted domain of the air to learn its moods at first hand. From 1891 to his death in 1896 he built eighteen gliders, most with a fixed rear tailplane and fin. All his cambered wings were closely modelled on soaring birds. In mid-air he was said to have looked like a flying squirrel. They were in effect hang-gliders – on which he made more than 2000 flights. Although Gustav was still involved, the enterprise had now largely become his brother's. Gustav never flew.

The world has been left both movie footage and a rich collection of photographs of Otto's flights. They show him in hat and knickerbockers, torso and legs swung forward, high above the German countryside, hanging by his armpits within the wings as he flew exultantly over villages and farms. Lilienthal grew adept at these gravity-shifting body swings. They were his sole means of steering his gliders – or preventing them from pitching up, running out of lift and diving earthward in the fatal stalls he so dreaded. The world's media, dubbing him 'the winged Prussian', hailed him as a genius. American newspapers began to send reporters to Europe to observe the phenomenon. Yet, successful as his aircraft were, he never managed to produce a powered machine. On a gloriously sunny, calm Sunday morning in August 1896, he was caught, gliding off a hilltop, by an unexpected thermal eddy. The machine stalled, nosed down and plunged to the ground. He died without regaining consciousness. One of his favourite sayings was *Opfer müssen gebracht werden* – 'sacrifices must be made'. He was forty-eight.

By the autumn of 1899 the Wright Brothers were already

immersed in the history of flight. Aeronautics, they decided, had been brought into disrepute by men of inadequate ability 'who had hoped to solve the problem through devices of their own invention which had all of them failed, until finally the public was led to believe that flying was as impossible as perpetual motion'.[9] Their minds focused by the literature, the Wrights decided for the first time that they wanted to try to fly themselves. 'After reading the pamphlets . . . we became highly enthusiastic with the idea of gliding as a sport,' Orville said over twenty years later:

> We found that Lilienthal had been killed through his inability to properly balance his machine in the air. Pilcher, an English experimenter, had met with a like fate.
>
> We found that both . . . had attempted to maintain balance merely by the shifting of the weight of their bodies . . . We at once set to work to devise a more efficient means of maintaining the equilibrium . . .[10]

Although in these recollections two decades later Orville referred to 'we', it was Wilbur's initiative alone that launched them into aviation. Wilbur was now patently the more restless of the two, the most inwardly dissatisfied with his lot, the one in search of something more fulfilling than assembling and repairing bicycles in a slumping market now saturated with machines. It was his need for a personal challenge rather than any long-standing ambition to find the aeronautical grail that led him, rather than the more contented Orville, to launch into serious research. And now, surrounded by a heap of state-of-the-art writing on the subject, it was Wilbur who was seized with the deep desire to do more. For three months, through the summer of 1899, he methodically analysed the history of failure:

> Men of the very highest standing in the profession of science and invention had attempted to solve the problem . . . But one by one, they had been compelled to confess themselves beaten, and had discontinued their efforts . . . there was no flying art in the proper sense of the word, but only a flying problem. Thousands of men

> had thought about flying machines and a few had even built machines . . . but these were guilty of everything except flying. Thousands of pages had been written on the so-called science of flying but for the most part the ideas set forth, like the designs for machines, were mere speculations and probably ninety per cent was false.[11]

Wilbur brought some penetrating thought processes to aeronautics. His ability to reduce problems to essentials led him, with extraordinary speed, to the heart of the matter. More brilliantly than anyone for nearly a century, he identified the three fundamentals of manned powered flight. Today they seem almost too obvious to be stated, but at the end of the nineteenth century they were far from so – Wilbur spelt them out. A successful flying machine, he said, would require wings to sustain it in the air, a power plant to drive it forward, and a means of balancing and steering it in flight. All these things had of course been identified by Sir George Cayley nearly a hundred years earlier, but the Yorkshireman had never brought these fundamentals together into a fruitful trinity.* Thus it was not Cayley's but Lilienthal's footsteps that Wilbur set out to follow.

Wings of sorts already existed. So did power plants. But no one had yet brought them together in an aeroplane that a pilot could safely manoeuvre at will about the sky. It was 'the problem of equilibrium,' Wilbur decided, 'that constituted the problem of flight itself.'[12] Something more precise and a lot safer than the crude and dangerous process of body-swinging that had killed Lilienthal was needed.

As the German had done, Wilbur and Orville decided to turn again to the birds for inspiration. They had been impressed by

---

*Although Wilbur was aware from Cayley's 1809–10 articles of his aerodynamic discoveries, he knew nothing of the sophisticated flying machines the baronet had, in his scientific isolation, remarkably created. The man-carrying gliders had been described, with clear sketches, by Cayley in a popular technical magazine in London in 1852. The report had gone unnoticed by the aviation community. It was not to be rediscovered until 1960 when the British air historian Charles Gibbs-Smith stumbled upon it. 'Here,' said Gibbs-Smith, 'was the modern aeroplane – except for its engine and for its ailerons: and nobody took any notice!'

the writing of a French experimenter, Louis-Pierre Mouillard. Mouillard had dabbled with gliders while farming in North Africa. His studies of the mechanics of the flight of hawks, vultures and albatrosses had culminated in a remarkably detailed book of ornithology, *The Empire of the Air*, which had made him pre-eminent in this field.* The 1881 book had inspired many a would-be birdman, though none of the Frenchman's own attempts to build a flying machine was successful. Mouillard claimed that birds maintained fore and aft balance and pitched up and down by folding their wings forwards and backwards. This, he said, brought the centre of lifting pressure of the wings to the front or rear of the centre of gravity, thereby tilting the bird up or down.

Cycling once more out to the pinnacle rocks, Wilbur and Orville studied with fresh insight the manoeuvres of the soaring clusters of birds. They were diving and climbing using exactly the backwards and forwards wing movements Mouillard had described. However, when they came to roll, the brothers saw that they did it rather differently than the Frenchman had suggested. He had claimed that birds banked in flight by 'drawing inward' one wing to reduce its area, and therefore its lifting power, to less than that of the opposite wing, thus causing the temporarily larger wing with the greater lift to rise into the start of a roll towards the reduced wing. The Wrights saw that it was more complicated than that. Watching a pigeon they noticed that, in banking, it was making rapid adjustments to its wingtips – 'so as to present one tip at a positive angle and the other at a negative angle, thus, for the moment, turning itself into an animated windmill'.[13] The birds' balance was controlled 'by utilising dynamic reactions of the air instead of shifting weight'.

If a pilot could manipulate his aircraft's wings in similar fashion, the Wrights reasoned, he could surely maintain equilibrium in the rolling plane, as well as bank himself into controlled turns. It was, after all, a familiar concept: the banking action of leaning into a turn

---

**The Empire of the Air* is today one of flying's rarest books. The precious few surviving copies change hands on the Internet for up to $1000 each.

on a bicycle. They resolved to find a way of mechanically replicating the animated windmilling.

What they didn't know was that a wing-twisting suggestion for lateral control – soon to become known as wing 'warping' – was not entirely new. Two little-known English patents for it had been granted some years before but never developed. Much more recently, an American, a physics instructor at Yale, Edson Gallaudet, who wanted to build a flying machine, had also alighted on the idea. In 1898, only six months before Wilbur had written to the Smithsonian, he had used it in a box kite to which he had added a horizontal tail attached to the wings by a boom. The wings were made to twist in opposite directions to each other by gears operated from the ground by cords. Gallaudet had secretly test-flown this promising device off floats on Long Island Sound only the previous November. It had risen into the air, bobbed about, then fallen into the water. Gallaudet had planned to resume testing in the spring of 1899, but, unfortunately, his university masters had got wind of the experiment. They decided that, if publicised, the lunatic venture would make Yale a laughing stock. He was instructed to cease work on it or resign. Reluctantly he had abandoned the trial.

The brothers' first banking system was a design of Orville's. It was to pivot the outer sections of the wings on metal shafts, geared to rise and fall like giant ailerons in opposite directions when the pilot moved a lever. It would probably have worked, but the mechanism would have been too heavy. They were forced to think of another, lighter method. An idea came to Wilbur in the late summer of 1899.

Katharine, who had the previous year graduated from Oberlin in Greek and Latin, invited a college friend, Harriet Silliman, to stay at Hawthorn Street. Orville, as the marginally less girl-shy of the brothers, had been assigned as their escort on an evening visit into Dayton. When he got home late that night he found an excited Wilbur clutching a small cardboard box, bursting to show him something. Wilbur had been minding the cycle shop on his own when a customer had come in to buy an inner tube. After he'd handed it over, Wilbur had stood chatting to the man, idly toying with the empty box. As he did so he noticed that, in twisting it between his fingers, he had absent-mindedly given it a spiral distortion. With Archimedian triumph, the story goes, Wilbur realised in a flash that he had stumbled on a solution to flight control – helical twisting of the wings. Within days he and Orville, at the bike shop, had begun to make a small bamboo, paper and string model to check out the twisting feasibility. So encouraging did it look that they immediately went on to build a larger version – a pair of biplane wings they intended to test as a kite.

The exact date of this famed 1899 flight in a West Dayton field, now part of Sunrise Park, is not known. The double-wing box kite, measuring only 5 feet by 13 inches, had a horizontal stabiliser on a boom at the back. Wilbur carried it through the streets collecting, like the Pied Piper, a bunch of excited boys that began to grow as they went. He created quite a stir, this balding man in a business suit striding along with a kite clutched in his arms. On the open common near the Miami River, Wilbur laid his pair of fabric-covered pine wood wings on the ground and began, encircled by chattering boys, to arrange it for flight.

This primitive contraption, now recognised as a direct ancestor of the modern aeroplane, was constructed principally to demonstrate a banking capability under ground control. After barely two months in the aviation business, its designers had introduced some ingenious features. The vertical wooden struts that linked the wings were hinged to allow the top surface to be shifted backwards and forwards. The purpose of this was to move the centre of lift in relation to the centre of gravity so that the wings, as well as banking when twisted, could also be made to pitch up or down. All these actions were controlled by four cords that ran from the outer front corners of the two wings to a pair of sticks which Wilbur held. By juggling the sticks he could make the tethered biplane pitch up or down and roll to the left or right. Its response was positive and dramatic. The kite obediently banked as commanded and pitched up and down, almost overobligingly, when directed. Indeed 'the model made such a rapid dive to the ground that the small boys present fell on their faces to avoid being hit, not having time to run.'[14] The tethered prototype was apparently flown only that once, but it was enough to demonstrate the uncanny ability of the Wrights to convert an abstract concept with impressive speed into practical working technology.

The five-foot kite, with its shellac-coated fabric wings and its highly original control features, had lived the brief existence of a butterfly. It had served its purpose. The simple contraption went back to the cycle shop where it was hung on the wall of the upstairs workshop, eventually – in 1905 – to be destroyed because it was in the way.

6

To Ride a Flying Machine

(1899)

The brothers now had the bit between their teeth. Excited by their rapid initial success they decided to build a much bigger machine – a man-carrier. They would fly it at first as a kite so as to perfect a control system without risk of maiming themselves if things went wrong. Not only had the gifted Lilienthal met a tragic end, but now the unforgiving sky had claimed another victim – a Scottish marine engineer called Percy Pilcher.

Inspired by the German's success, Pilcher had in England built his own glider. Before testing it he had travelled to Berlin to look at Lilienthal's machines and pick his brains. Otto had generously taken him out to one of his flying hills, and even allowed him to make several glides. Pilcher was so impressed he bought one of the monoplanes on the spot, using it for reference in the design of his own four hang-gliders. The most successful of these, on which he fitted a wheeled undercarriage, he named the *Hawk*. It looked like a crude ellipsoid umbrella.

Unlike Lilienthal, Pilcher often dispensed with hill launching. He had himself hoisted into the air, on his 250-yard flights, at the end of a long fishing line frantically towed by his assistants. If nothing else, his experiments made him Britain's first true aviator.

On the last day of September 1899 he went up to Leicestershire to demonstrate the *Hawk* to Lord Braye at his estate near Market Harborough. Towed off by two cantering horses, he rose high into the air, but within seconds something went badly wrong. A bamboo rod in the tail unit snapped. The glider dived into the ground, breaking both Pilcher's legs. He was alive when pulled from the wreckage, but died the next day.

Though shocked by news of the latest tragedy, the Wrights knew there was no completely safe way to discover the techniques of bird flight – trial and error had to happen in the air itself. 'There are two ways of learning how to ride a fractious horse,' Wilbur said:

> One is to get on him and learn by actual practice how each motion and trick may be best met; the other is to sit on a fence and watch the beast awhile, and then retire to the house and at leisure figure out the best way of overcoming his jumps and kicks. The latter system is the safest; but the former, on the whole, turns out the larger proportion of good riders. It is very much the same in learning to ride a flying machine; if you are looking for perfect safety you will do well to sit on a fence and watch the birds; but if you really wish to learn you must mount a machine and become acquainted with its tricks by actual trial.[1]

Until now experimenters had assumed that because the turbulence of air currents was sudden and unpredictable, a machine had to be given inherent stability to enable it, when bumped about, to bounce back automatically to equilibrium independently of the pilot's actions. Some pioneers had used dihedrally upwardly angled wings. Others had incorporated spring-loaded flexible wings or tails intended to provide momentary responses to wind gusts. But neither they nor Lilienthal had considered it necessary to develop means by which the pilots could control their gliders in the three-dimensions of pitch, yaw and roll. Wilbur questioned the need for automatic stability – the notion that a plane had to remain as rigidly level in the air as a train on its tracks. He believed that the unstable birds had got it right – that the operator, like a cyclist, had to be given the means to climb, descend, turn or bank at will. This, he insisted, was much more vital than building in inherent stability. In fact successful flight, it is now known, is possible with either a stable or an unstable aircraft; it is the control system that is the most critical – and the essence of stability.

Although in 1899 the early research initiatives were indisputably Wilbur's, Orville was soon involved. He became quickly sensitive to the balance of power in the partnership, resenting any suggestion of being treated as Wilbur's kid brother, as the junior partner. And he was especially touchy about Wilbur's use of 'I' when Orville believed he should have said 'we'. Flying began to dominate their conversation. 'We had taken up aeronautics merely as a sport,' they wrote in a joint article. 'We reluctantly entered upon the scientific side of it. But we soon found the work so fascinating that we were drawn into it deeper and deeper.'[2]

They had gone in with equal enthusiasm – but it was some time before the man-lifting kite would take shape. For nearly a year they were forced to return their physical energies to the bicycle business. The profits from the small shop – they had now sold the printery – were their only source of funds for their next flying experiment. In the workshop at 1127 West Third Street they toiled sixteen hours a day at their benches, turning out from their cycle boutique, in competition with a flood of mass-produced models, a trickle of handsome handcrafted machines with elegant names like St Clair and Van Cleve, but the talk between them through the autumn and winter of the turn of the century was increasingly now of aeronautics.

They began to take a sharp interest in the work of the American experimenters, among whom one was pre-eminent: Octave Chanute, a French-born American civil engineer. He had conducted the gliding trials near Chicago and in 1894 had written the classic *Progress in Flying Machines* which they had read from cover to cover. Chanute's comprehensive and definitive record of man's attempts to fly in this devotedly researched book stretched exhaustively back to the 1500s. It analysed with a scientist's rigour all the attempts through history, sifting the techniques into dead ends doomed to failure and those realistically worth pursuing. *Progress in Flying Machines*, which remains eminently readable to this day, had become an essential textbook for every serious experimenter.

A distinguished railroad and bridge builder now in his prosperous late fifties and approaching comfortable retirement, he seemed an unlikely candidate to be drawn to the eccentric domain of human flight. But Chanute was no ordinary man. In his life's autumn he had begun a remarkable second career in aviation that was destined to make him one of its great pioneers. He saw the flying machine as an engineering and intellectual challenge of irresistible fascination. He had hurled himself into it with such energy and enthusiasm that he'd soon created for himself the role of international aeronautical coordinator.

In a world sprinkled with pockets of uncoordinated aviation research and experimental activity, awash with failed aeroplanes and ideas, this elegant, balding, white-bearded engineer of great ability and personal charm had arrived like Moses to lead the growing army of experimenters to the promised land of mechanical flight. Not only was he endowed with the financial resources, he brought the mental discipline of a scientist and the skills of an engineer to the quest for the technological solution.

Octave Chanute had been brought to America in 1838 at the age of six by his father. Rigidly protected from the world, Octave grew up a prudish young man who didn't smoke, drink, dance or swear, ignorant of even the most common American slang. At seventeen he had left home and gone to work in a survey gang on the new Hudson River Railroad. At twenty-one he was a fully fledged engineer, laying track for the Chicago and Mississippi Railroad; by the time of the great railway boom he'd become one of the country's foremost construction engineers, creating new lines through the American west and flinging a great bridge across the Missouri River in Kansas City. He had also built canals and had chaired the technical committee that planned New York's elevated city rail system. Chanute had become an eminence, prominent on numerous professional bodies, with a town in Kansas even named in his honour.[3]

His interest in aviation had begun as a hobby he'd been too busy to pursue – and often too embarrassed to admit to. At a Kansas City dinner party, asked how he spent his spare time, he is said to have replied: 'Wait until your children are not present, for they would laugh at me.' But aeronautics had become a drug he was unable to abandon. When, in the mid-1870s, on the verge of collapse from the stress of the New York mass transit assignment, he had taken his family on a holiday to France, his eyes had been opened by aviation developments in Europe. However, it was not until his retirement in 1885 that he'd found himself with the leisure and, from a timber preservation business in Chicago the money, to indulge his passion.

Chanute didn't do things by halves. He threw himself into the floundering aviation scene like an aeronautical messiah, energising and stirring it internationally. In the study of his comfortable Chicago home he created a remarkable information centre that soon contained more data on man's attempts to fly than had ever before existed in one place. He subscribed to cuttings agencies and scoured bookshops and libraries, collecting every scrap of aerial information in print. He organised aviation conferences, and in his neat copperplate fired off thousands of letters on long sea-mail journeys to every faltering flying-machine builder whose experiments, however ill conceived, had made even the smallest news anywhere in the world.

By the 1890s Chanute was in touch with virtually everyone who had seriously dabbled in pursuit of the fantasy. He corresponded with the colourful American-born Sir Hiram Maxim in England who, believing that all a successful aeroplane required was masses of lift from a huge array of wing surfaces and enormous thrust from powerful engines, had built such a mammoth – only to find it uncontrollable.* Chanute became friendly with Langley, and leapt into keen dialogue with Mouillard in Egypt, to whom he sent money to help with his latest glider, a bird-like contraption with cartwheels which was never to fly. He began an active correspondence with a well-shod English émigré in Australia, Lawrence Hargrave, a man of independent means who, in the

---

*A self-described 'chronic inventor' whose brainchildren ranged from mousetraps to light bulbs, Hiram Maxim had been knighted by the British for his invention of the world's first fully automatic machine gun. His huge aeroplane with a 104-foot wingspan and 18-foot steam-driven propellers weighed four tons and carried a crew of three. Photographs of it are among the most publicised in the story of flying. Never intended to become properly airborne, it was tested on launching railway tracks at Dartford in Kent in 1894. With engines convulsing and blades threshing, it rose a few inches into the air before crashing. With just two primitive elevators it would have been uncontrollable in the air.

scientific isolation of the Antipodes, had quite remarkably designed a small fleet of gliders, powered aeroplanes, streams of aircraft engines and, most famously, the inherently stable, powerfully lifting box kite that was to inspire the biplane. In France, which was beginning to lead the world with nationalistic zest to produce the first manned, powered aeroplane, Chanute tracked down the locally acclaimed experimenter Clément Ader. And although he was never to meet him, he engaged, until the glider pilot's death, in brisk technical dialogue with Otto Lilienthal in Germany.

Chanute constantly risked his professional reputation, facing ridicule in a world convinced that human flight was impossible. At an 1886 meeting in Buffalo, New York, of the American Association for the Advancement of Science, of which he was vice-president, he had risked the derision of his engineering colleagues by introducing an aeronautical item to the agenda. He invited along to speak an ornithologist, Israel Lancaster, who had been experimenting with model birds as a prelude to human flight. To Chanute's embarrassment the address was greeted with guffaws of laughter. The audience, said the *Buffalo Courier*, was 'in a quandry [*sic*] as to whether Mr Lancaster is a crank or a sharp practical joker who has been giving the great association of America savants guff'.[4]

But not all the learned scientists were laughing. Sitting in the audience had been Samuel Langley, then better known as a physics professor at Pittsburgh University, of whose Allegheny Observatory he was director, more concerned at that time with the study of solar energy than aeronautics. Langley had been riveted by Lancaster's assertion, derided by his audience, that a man-made wing, like the soaring birds', could be made to move in the air against the wind by the very power of the opposing wind itself. He had left the conference fired by the scientific vision of mechanical flight. Convinced that no one had yet unravelled the physical principles, he'd gone back to his observatory impatient to begin his own aerodynamic research. He had built an enormous outdoor, steam-driven whirling arm, 60 feet in diameter, rigging it with all manner of sophisticated electromechanical devices in an attempt to uncover the basic physical laws affecting wing surfaces rushing through the air at up to 70 miles an hour.

The work began to dominate Langley's professional life – even after his appointment, in 1887, to head the giant edifice of the Smithsonian. Acquiring there a prodigious range of scientific responsibilities, he did not allow them to interfere with his aviation sideline; it would eventually take possession of him.

Langley used the institution's resources to build the scores of model flying machines that would lead eventually to his triumphs over the Potomac. Uninterested in gliders and three-dimensional control, he concentrated from the outset on powered flight, producing a famous research document that set out to prove its feasibility and that suitable power already existed in the shape of lightweight steam engines. He claimed to have discovered the surprising phenomenon 'that the faster the speed the less the force required'. This declaration of the seemingly advantageous relationship between power and speed came to be known as the 'Langley Law'. Unhappily it was to prove quite misleadingly sweeping.

Although Langley's research was marked by great technical thoroughness and catapulted him to international prominence as a leading aerodynamic scientist, the whirling arm was a crude research tool. Its measurements were clouded in error – some of which, to Langley's distress, were quickly identified by sceptical scientific colleagues in Britain.

Yet Langley was to remain one of pioneer aviation's most memorable figures. An elegant, enormously self-confident upper-middle-class Bostonian, a lifelong bachelor, who liked to dress in a frock coat and silk top hat, he directed the institution's affairs with an iron fist. He compensated for shyness and loneliness with a tyrannical management style, creating ripples of fear as he strode about the corridors in morning coat and striped trousers, intimidating his subordinates who were required to walk several paces behind him. Despite the aura of aeronautical omniscience this royal figure radiated, it was five heartbreaking years before his experimental aircraft factory managed to give birth to the models that were eventually successfully to fly. To help with the dispiriting task that saw close on a hundred designs fail, Langley, who dreamed of large passenger aeroplanes cruising the world, brought into this awesome place some bright young men whose lives were soon to cross those of the Wright Brothers.

One was a gifted mathematics and physics graduate, Edward Huffaker. Fluent in Latin, Greek and French, with a masters degree in civil engineering, he came from Tennessee where he had worked as a railroad construction engineer. Excited by the possibility of powered flight he had, like Israel Lancaster, built some models shaped from his observations of soaring birds. He'd offered his inventions to Chanute, who was so impressed with Huffaker's unusual grasp of the principles of flight that he wrote to Langley urging that he snap him up. Langley had done so in December 1894, giving him the task of designing some efficient wings.

At first Huffaker had been thrilled to work alongside the famous professor. He had demonstrated one of his own gliders, launching it into an impressive 600-foot flight from one of the Smithsonian's parapets. The amazed Langley had asked him, he claimed, to introduce a similar cambered-wing design on one of the steam models. But Langley wasn't, at heart, convinced of the lifting advantage of camber. He was wedded to flat surfaces.

The young engineer's pleasure at working with the celebrated scientist was short-lived. Huffaker's impressive academic credentials had not, unfortunately, endowed him with all the social graces Langley expected of his staff. Walking past Huffaker's office one morning on an inspection tour, the elegantly morning-coated Langley was aghast to see his new employee sitting not only coatless and tieless, but with his feet propped up on his desk. With even greater horror he spotted, crudely nailed to the wall, a tin-can spittoon which had all too obviously been put to full use by its tobacco-chewing owner. Although the professor was forced to suffer this uncouthness as the price for the scientific ideas his struggling programme so badly needed, it didn't stop him now making Huffaker's life intolerable.

Observing the unpleasant process was another engineer, Augustus Herring, a young experimental glider builder from New York whom Langley had recruited. The son of a wealthy Georgian cotton broker, thirty-year-old Herring was a tall, good-looking man with a pleasing Southern accent. Said to 'move easily among the upper crust',[5] he had been at school in Switzerland and Germany and spoke French and German. He had failed to graduate at the New York technology institute where he'd studied mechanical engineering, having devoted too much of his time to the less respectable field of aeronautics. Degreeless, he had been reduced to working as a chain-man on railroad construction. However, in 1894, inspired by Lilienthal's success, he had returned to aviation, building and flying two gliders modelled on the German's bird-wing designs. When he learnt of this, Langley had signed him up as his chief aeronautical assistant.

Within days of his arrival Herring was deeply regretting the move. Almost immediately he had clashed with the autocratic Secretary, amazed to find him still wedded to inefficient flat wing surfaces. He had also been shocked to see how Huffaker's health was being visibly affected by Langley's treatment of him. Describing how the professor constantly interfered with his own design work, regularly ordering details changed behind his back, Herring said, 'it is more than any respectable engineer ought to be willing to submit to'.[6] Herring contributed more significant designs to Langley's powered aeroplanes than anyone else, but he found the Secretary impossible to work with. Within a few months he resigned to join Octave Chanute in Chicago.

By the mid-1890s Chanute had become so quietly obsessed with the challenge of manned flight and so encyclopedically knowledgeable about history's trail of failed attempts that he had decided to build some aeroplanes of his own. Like Lilienthal he believed that man had to learn to soar before risking powered flight, but unlike the German, who directed his gliders by throwing his body about, he wanted a system of automatic equilibrium which would eliminate the need for these mid-air gyrations.

In Chicago Chanute had created a small collective of plane-makers. Too old to fly himself, he had drawn together a group of young experimenters whose various glider constructions he agreed to fund alongside the building and testing of his own machines. He hired a carpenter, William Avery, whose workshop had, by early 1896, become a small aircraft factory. Here were assembled both the creatures of Chanute's aeronautical imagination and one of the Lilienthal bird-wing machines which Augustus Herring had shipped across from New York. An immigrant Russian seaman, Paul Butusov, who had studied the soaring flight of albatrosses at sea, and who dubiously claimed to have flown his own glider secretly for several miles in Kentucky, had been invited to join the team to build, at Chanute's expense, a large new machine.

In Avery's workshop, an assortment of strange-looking hang-gliders had begun to take shape. The first of Chanute's creations, aiming for a potent concentration of lifting surfaces, had six pairs of wings – four in a stack at the front with two more sitting behind. Because of its resemblance to the American bush cricket they dubbed it the *Katydid*. In the summer of 1896 they took this insectile brainchild of Chanute's, together with Herring's Lilienthal glider, to a remote place in the Indiana sand dunes on the southern shore of Lake Michigan. Chanute had chosen the remote location thirty miles east of Chicago for its reliable windflow off the lake and for the soft landings from the great dunes. He also hoped that, in this bleak wilderness, the secret trials would escape the notice of reporters.

They launched their gliders, leaping off a wooden plank on top of a hundred-foot-high dune. Herring's Lilienthal machine didn't perform well. When it flipped over and was broken beyond repair, they turned to Chanute's multiplane, testing it as a kite and glider. Almost every day they rearranged the permutations of the wing stacks, all able flexibly to swivel backwards and forwards under sudden gusts, in the hope of making the glider automatically stable. They finished up with five stacks in the front and one behind. The *Katydid* performed reliably enough, but could never be made to go very far.

The fact that it was flying at all, however, was sufficient to make news across America. Word of the activities of 'the crazy old man of the dunes' had reached the Chicago newspapers. When reporters converged on the site, Chanute promptly abandoned the trials. Back in Chicago they assembled a brand new glider, a triplane, the joint creation of Chanute and Herring. It owed to the older man's railroad engineering background its rigid box-frame construction with crossed diagonal piano-wire bracing – a system called the Pratt truss. Widely used in bridge construction, it was to become an integral feature of multiplane design for decades to come. The new plane's stabilising cruciform tail unit, mounted on a spring to bounce with gusts, was Herring's major contribution to the joint venture – though the basic cruciform arrangement could hardly be considered a startlingly new conception, having been used by both Cayley and Lilienthal.

When the experimenters, now encumbered by Butusov's monster glider, returned to the lakeside dunes, they chose an even more remote site, travelling there secretly from Chicago by ship. The triplane produced too much lift when Herring first flew it. When they cut it down to a biplane it performed much better. The simple, classic, rectangular-winged biplane they had arrived at is now regarded as one of the landmarks in the evolution of the aeroplane. Herring and Avery flew it over distances of more than 100 yards, remaining airborne on glides of up to 14 seconds that were soon, despite their retreat deeper into the wilderness, being witnessed by a fresh stream of Chicago newsmen who arrived, with cameras, by buggy, bicycle and boat.

Once again, to his embarrassment, the elderly Chanute found himself hailed across America as a celebrity. But much more distressing was the public disclosure of major tensions within the team. At the centre of the conflict was Augustus Herring.

Now one of aviation's most knowledgeable technocrats, and its most experienced living glider pilot, Herring had already contributed much to the development of the aeroplane in America. He desperately wanted to be the first man to fly a powered machine, something he believed could be accomplished sooner than Chanute was prepared to try. Irritated by the elderly engineer's caution, Herring considered Chanute less talented than himself, his judgements clouded by age, his pursuit of 'automatic stability' unnecessary. He thought his support of the Russian seaman absurd and Butusov's giant contrivance outright dangerous. Ridiculously, the Russian planned to control its rise and fall in the air by striding backwards and forwards along a running board. Although the Russian's machine did prove incapable of flight, Herring's arrogance and independence had upset the others. What might have merely festered below the surface was brought to a head when Herring shared his personal grievances with the newspapers. Suddenly the dissension in the camp had become a public spectacle. Herring, proclaiming the jointly created glider as substantially his own invention, walked out, vowing to build a powered machine of his own.

He had found a new sponsor, a young banker, a Yale man, Matthias Arnot, of Elmira in New York State. The latest machine, the Herring–Arnot biplane, looked almost identical to its Chanute–Herring parent. In September 1897 they took it to the Indiana dunes to try it out, inviting all the Chicago newspapers to come and watch. The machine made superb glides of up to 200 yards, and reporters who were allowed to fly it wrote ecstatically of the experience.

The newspapers hailed Herring as a hero with powered flight within his grasp – and he set out to prove they were right. Again funded by Arnot, he built a two-propeller biplane driven by a compressed-air motor. In October 1898 he attempted to fly it at St Joseph, on the eastern shore of Lake Michigan, where he had gone to live. Hoisting the glider on to his shoulders, he started the engine and the propellers pulled him into the air. With his knees tucked up, he managed to skim for 50 feet before settling back on to the sand. It wasn't a sustained flight, but the machine had left the ground under its own power.

A photograph, taken just too late by Arnot, shows Herring at the moment of landing. He had achieved what aviation historians would describe kindly as an 'airborne condition'. But Herring was so pumped he dashed off a telegram to Chanute in Chicago summoning him to witness a repeat of the historic event next day. He had repaired his friendship with the older man, who obligingly took the night boat to St Joseph. But next day there was no wind. The machine was unable to fly. Chanute refused to wait. He sailed back to Chicago in disgust, convinced that powered flight was still a long way off.

As the turn of the century approached, still no experimenter had addressed the problem of powered piloted flight in its entirety. They had learnt to glide short distances. They had powered models in exciting brief excursions. They had made pointless uncontrolled hops to prove they could fleetingly defy gravity. But no one had yet successfully brought together the three crucial elements that an English county squire had so simply identified a hundred years earlier. Nobody had yet united George Cayley's seemingly obvious ingredients of sustaining wings, propulsion and control in a safe and practical vehicle.

In Dayton, Ohio, however, well out of the public eye, a flying machine designed to do all these things for the first time was quietly taking shape in its creators' minds.

7

Complexities of the Invisible Forces

(1900)

By late 1899, the Wright brothers' pilot-controlled biplane was not only in a state of advanced planning, they were looking for somewhere to fly it.

There was a world of difference, they knew, between raising a 5-foot model into the breeze on the end of four cords and launching, into what would have to be a stiff wind, a heavy machine with wings big enough to support the weight of a man. They doubted the Dayton breezes would be adequate. And although they were confident their warping device had cracked the problem of lateral stability, they weren't convinced they yet had the answer to the equally critical matter of pitch control – a lack of which could kill them just as quickly. The fore and aft sliding hinged-top wing method they had used on the kite to shunt the centre of lift backwards and forwards with strings would not be practical in a full-sized machine.

Instead, they conceived of a smarter idea – an elevator: the hinged surface used for pitch control on almost all aeroplanes to this day. But rather than fitting the horizontal device – which, confusingly, they insisted on calling a 'forward rudder' – in its now familiar position behind the wing at the tail, they decided to locate it on a boom out in front and connected it to a pilot-controlled lever. The arrangement was known as a *canard* for its resemblance to the head and neck of a flying duck. The pilot, they decided, instead of dangling below the machine would lie prone, facing forward along the middle of the lower wing, thus reducing a lot of the drag that had made other gliders so inefficient. The wings were to be cambered for maximum lift.

Wilbur and Orville were convinced that full flight control had eluded so many inventors for so long because no one had been able to stay in the air for long enough to practise the art and diagnose the difficulties. 'We figured that Lilienthal, in five years, had spent only about five hours in actual gliding through the air,' Wilbur said. 'The wonder was not that he had done so little, but that he had accomplished so much . . . We thought that if some method could be found by which it would be possible to practice by the hour instead of by the second there would be hope of advancing the solution . . .'[1]

To do this, they calculated, the piloted machine would need a substantial wing area which, to be sustained, tethered, in the air would have to be flown in a steady breeze of 18 miles an hour. As no constant wind of this force could be found on the Ohio plains anywhere near Dayton, they tried to find a breezier locality. Chicago had a reputation as one of the country's windiest cities; Chanute and Herring had flown in Lake Michigan's steady breezes in the dunes nearby. So, in November 1899, Wilbur wrote to the US Weather Bureau seeking details.

'We have been doing some experimenting with kites, with a view to constructing one capable of sustaining a man,' he explained. 'We expect to carry the experiments further next year.' He asked the bureau for records of wind consistencies and strengths around Chicago in the months from August to November. The information he was sent confirmed the windy city's reputation. The bureau, for good measure, also enclosed statistics for 120 other weather stations across America; one of these caught Wilbur's eye. It was a place in North Carolina he'd never heard of, a remote station on the Atlantic coast called Kitty Hawk. It boasted the country's sixth highest average wind strength. The brothers put it on their shortlist, from which they decided, on reflection, to delete Chicago for fear that flying experiments close to a big city would attract something they utterly dreaded – the attention of newspapers.

Beyond this enquiry about winds, the Wrights' flying project went no further for some time. Through the winter of early 1900 they were too busy again building bicycles for the spring market. They may have sketched the control concept of a piloted glider, but nothing actually got built. There was, after all, no incentive to expedite the aeroplane. They saw themselves in competition with no one, saw no imminent success, nor prospect of great reward. It was still little more than a hobby, a scientific challenge they could discuss as they worked their lathes or sat by the fire after dinner back at Hawthorn Street – where domestic life had become much cosier.

In contrast to their once spartan bachelor existence they were now being fussed over by two women. Katharine, who had become a Latin and English teacher at Steele High School, the city's biggest, was back home running a briskly efficient house, producing three hot square meals a day. Early in the New Year she had acquired a permanent domestic help. Milton had engaged a fourteen-year-old girl, Carrie Kayler. Carrie was so petite she had, at first, to stand on a chair to reach the kitchen gas light. Orville, who was, psychologically, to remain all his life a boy with an abiding need to tease, had found a new victim. He would taunt the tiny maid mercilessly, intending it for fun but never quite knowing when to stop. Carrie's diminutive height became a fixation. He would regularly make her stand up to be measured against a set of marks on the kitchen door frame.

'Most of Mr Orville's teasing was fun,' Carrie, who was to stay with the Wrights for nearly fifty years, recalled a long time later. 'But at times he would keep it up until he would almost have a person in tears. Then you could count on a word from Mr Will. When he saw things were getting close to the breaking point, he'd say, "I guess that's about enough Orv". And Mr Orville would stop instantly. Mr Orville always listened to Mr Will, but *never* to anyone else.'[2]

Wilbur's self-absorption and powers of concentration Carrie found awesome. He could become oblivious of his surroundings and of the presence of others, slowly pacing the floor, hands clasped behind him, quietly humming popular songs. The words would sometimes disconcertingly die on his lips as his mind wrestled with some abstract thought. On one occasion Lorin's children heard him softly singing 'The flowers that bloom in the . . .' After a minute or so one of his nieces yelled: 'Uncle Wilbur, aren't you *ever* going to say *spring*?'

He was also, Carrie noticed, a creature of almost obsessive quirky habit:

> When he came home from the bicycle shop at noon, and for supper, he would *always* do these things and in this order: come through the back door into the kitchen and drop his hat on the nearest chair; reach to the top of the cupboard where he kept a comb and carefully smooth down his fringe of hair; and then cross to the sink to wash his hands. After that he would go directly to a cracker box on the dining room sideboard, pick out one cracker and nibble it as he went to the front of the house. That was a signal to set food on the table.
>
> Promptly, when the noon hour was over, Mr Will would come through the kitchen, looking straight ahead and saying nothing. He'd go out the back door and down the alley. But in a minute he'd come back, with a queer little one-sided smile, for his hat.

Wilbur, Carrie thought, lived on a different plane from other people – certainly from the down-to-earth Orville who 'never once forgot his hat. And, no matter how absorbed he was in what he was doing or thinking, he always knew what was going on around him.'[3]

Mr Orville, Carrie learnt, was extraordinarily finicky about the way his food was cooked, in particular his gravy, for which he had an excessive weakness. 'He showed,' she remembered, 'a violent prejudice against what he called white lump gravy.' Miss Katharine had warned her on the first day about this singular aversion of Orville's. But Carrie had been slow to acquire gravy expertise. Wilbur came into the kitchen one day and 'peered into the pan as she anxiously stirred her mixture. He reached over and gently took the pan from her. "Now then, Carrie," he said cheerfully, "let's just pour this out and start over." He rolled back his sleeves and went to work. While Carrie looked on, fascinated, he made the smoothest, savoriest [*sic*] gravy without a lump.'[4]

Carrie frequently witnessed the ritual of the brothers' fierce after-dinner arguments over the riddles of aeronautics. From the next room she would be aware of long silences between them 'as each was just thinking over what the other had said'. And whenever she went into the living room she would see them seated on opposite sides of the fireplace. 'Mr Orville would be sitting straight in his chair with arms folded; but Mr Will was more likely to be sitting on the small of his back with legs stretched out, his hands clasped behind his head and elbows spread wide. After a while one of them would say, "Tisn't either," and the other would say, "Tis too." After keeping that up for a while they'd swing back into full-size argument.'[5]

Carrie Kayler had little idea what they were talking about. She was just conscious of the heat and passion behind the endless debates – and how synchronously they always seemed to think. 'Their minds seemed to act as one,' said Orville's friend, the author Fred Kelly:

> One night after they had been working late at their shop, Orville returned home ahead of Wilbur. He was in bed when Wilbur came in. A surprising thing was that Wilbur, contrary to his invariable habit, forgot to bolt the front door. Orville, nearly asleep, reminded him of his oversight. Then, when Wilbur went back to put on the lock, Orville thought to himself, 'I'll bet he does something else peculiar. He'll blow out the gas in his room.' Why he thought Wilbur would blow out the gas instead of turning it off he could never explain. Fearing he would drop off to sleep, he sat up in bed until the light in Wilbur's room was off. Then he went to investigate and found the gas was still turned on. Wilbur had blown out the flame. Except for Orville's presentiment, both could have been asphyxiated.[6]

For Bishop Wright, 1900 brought, at last, a merciful ceasefire in the destructive decade-long war between the Brethren factions. Milton's bitterness had begun to fade; he was now too weary of the rancorous conflict for further fight. Now seventy-two, he had the previous year mellowed sufficiently to attend a rival Liberal church service and had later actually been persuaded to preach to an enemy congregation. By early 1900 the warring bishops, worn down by the years of resentment and litigation, had met to discuss a truce. They agreed on a peace formula that would abandon any further lawsuits and accept as binding all previous court decisions. Any property still in dispute would be divided.

Milton now had some more commercial things on his mind – he had developed some business interests which were competing with his spiritual duties. He had sliced off part of the farm in Grant County, Indiana purchased as an investment more than forty years earlier, where Reuchlin had been born, to create a township that was to become the present Fowlerton. In this brand new community between Indianapolis and Fort Wayne the bishop had enterprisingly created a tiny island of industry – a sawmill, cannery, grain elevator and bottle factory. The small boom had been sparked by a local gas and oil discovery on which he had also capitalised by installing five pumping wells on his farm.[7] The venture was never to bring him any great wealth.

In the spring of 1900, as Wilbur and Orville grappled with the myriad unknowns of mechanical flight, they were so confounded by a succession of stumbling blocks that they were finally compelled to seek out some expertise. Wilbur sat down to write a long letter to the grand old man of aeronautics, Octave Chanute, upon whose biplane glider they intended more or less to model their own structure.

Chanute was still a revered figure in international aviation circles. Although he had ceased to experiment with his own aeroplanes, he remained the most up-to-date source of information on global efforts to crack the conundrum. To someone of such renown, Wilbur's letter was suitably deferential. 'For some years,' he began, 'I have been afflicted with the belief that flight is possible to man. My disease has increased in severity and I feel that it will cost me an increased amount of money if not my life. I have been trying to arrange my affairs in such a way that I can devote my entire time for a few months to experiment in this field.' He went on:

> My general ideas of the subject are similar to those held by most practical experimenters, to wit: that what is chiefly needed is skill rather than machinery. The flight of the buzzard and similar sailers is a convincing demonstration of the value of skill, and the partial needlessness of motors. It is possible to fly without motors, but not without knowledge and skill. This I conceive to be fortunate, for man, by reason of his greater intellect, can more reasonably hope to equal birds in knowledge than to equal nature in the perfection of her machinery.[8]

Wilbur repeated to Chanute his belief that Lilienthal had failed because he hadn't created a safe and positive mechanical means of regaining equilibrium while his glider was being tossed about in flight. Nor had he been able to spend enough time airborne to discover the inadequacy of his crude flight control system. 'Even the simplest intellectual or acrobatic feats could never be learned with so short practice, and even Methuselah could never have become an expert stenographer with one hour per year for practice.'[9]

Making no mention of Orville, Wilbur described the wing-twisting banking device he proposed experimenting with. 'I make no secret of my plans for the reason that I believe no financial profit will accrue to the inventor of the first flying machine, and that only those who are willing to give as well as to receive suggestions can hope to link their names with the honour of its discovery. The problem is too great for one man alone and unaided to solve in secret.'[10]

He planned, he said, to go aloft on his biplane flown as a kite, tethered by a counterweighted rope attached to a wooden tower. He asked for any 'suggestions as your great knowledge and experience might enable you to give me' and added a request for advice on a suitable winter locality 'where I could depend on winds of about fifteen miles per hour without rain or too inclement weather. I am certain that such localities are rare.' In the absence of any motive power, a steady windflow over the wings was essential to provide lift for both kiting and gliding if they decided to cut loose.

The letter was to be the first of nearly four hundred the two would exchange over the next ten years. It was to open one of the most endearing, and ultimately deeply unhappy, friendships in the history of aviation.

Now sixty-eight and living in prosperous comfort on the income from his Chicago timber preservation business, Octave Chanute was impressed by the thoughtful letter from Dayton written on the pale blue paper of an obscure cycle company. It reflected a surprising understanding of the core of the problem of manned flight. Here was someone clearly deserving of his encouragement. Promptly and affably he replied, sending Wilbur some helpful literature on manned kites, but cautioned against tethering the machine to a tower which, he warned, risked collision with the structure. For reliable winter sea breezes he suggested San Diego, California, and St James City, Pine Island, Florida. These, however, he added, were deficient in sandhills for soft landings. 'Perhaps even better locations can be found on the Atlantic coasts of South Carolina or Georgia.' Chanute concluded warmly: 'If you have occasion at any time to be in this city, I shall be glad to have you call on me, and can perhaps better answer the questions that have occurred to you.'[11]

Writing to thank Chanute, Wilbur still made no mention of his co-experimenter.

> I shall consider your suggestions carefully in making my plans. For the present I have but little time for aeronautical investigations, in fact I try to keep my mind off this subject during the bicycle season as I find that business is neglected otherwise . . . Just now I am content with trying to settle upon a general plan of operations, and for a suitable location.[12]

Promising that he wouldn't inflict on Chanute 'a voluminous correspondence about mere theories and untried experiments', he said he would 'be pleased to have the benefit of your advice when my plans are more fully matured.'

> What one man can do himself directly is but little. If however he can stir up ten others to take up the task he has accomplished much. I know of no man in America so well fitted as yourself to do this missionary work.[13]

A cordial relationship was firmly established. Wilbur was impatient for the cycle shop's summer trade spate to end and for him and Orville to build their man-lifting box kite and get it into the air. But where to fly it? Chanute's suggestion of the Atlantic led them to look again at the Weather Bureau list which had identified one such place. Kitty Hawk, in North Carolina, met their sea breeze needs. But did it have sand, and was it free of obstructing vegetation? Early in August Wilbur wrote directly to the weather station there to find out. The reply, which came from the sole observer, Joseph Dosher, was brief, but reassuring:

> . . . I will say the beach here is about one mile wide, clear of trees or high hills and extends for nearly sixty miles same condition. The wind blows mostly from the north and north-east September and October . . . I am sorry to say you could not rent a house here, so you will have to bring tents. You could obtain board.[14]

Dosher showed Wilbur's letter to William Tate, one of the most prominent and best educated of the locals in this tiny isolated community. Tate was a notary public, the postmaster and a county commissioner. He followed up Dosher's letter with a cordial invitation of his own:

> I would say that you would find here nearly any type of ground you could wish; you could, for instance, get a stretch of sandy land one mile by five with a bare hill in centre 80 feet high, not a tree or bush anywhere to break the evenness of the wind current. This in my opinion would be a fine place; our winds are always steady, generally from 10 to 20 miles velocity per hour . . . We have Telegraph communication & daily mails. Climate healthy . . .

He urged Wilbur to come before the weather pitched into November's storms. Tate concluded: 'If you decide to try your machine here & come I will take pleasure in doing all I can for your convenience & success & pleasure, & I assure you you will find a hospitable people when you come among us.'[15]

The combination of reporter-free remoteness, sand, wind and

generosity was irresistible. Wilbur and Orville settled there and then for Kitty Hawk. Almost immediately they began to build their man-lifter. Into its design they methodically factored more sophisticated aerodynamic features than any experimenter before them. They had done their homework with clinical care. Sifting through every available technical record of their failed predecessors, they arrived at their own judgements to produce the most advanced heavier-than-air flying machine ever created up to that time.

Two fundamentals had concerned them – the needs for efficient lifting surfaces and effective flying controls. On the latter they were confident that their experimental kite had proved the success of their wing-twisting banking system, and that an elevator out front would provide a safe and reliable form of pitch control. On the actual shape of the wing they faced a bewildering array of mathematical data documented by their predecessors.

The ideal wing seemed to require the seemingly unachievable marriage of a multitude of conflicting criteria. These included the velocity of the wing through the air (whether powered or gliding under the influence of gravity), the speed of the wind into which it was flying, the total area of lifting surfaces, the all-up weight the wings had to support, the resistance – drag – created by the bulk of the machine and its occupant and, critically, the wing geometry: its shape, size, depth of camber and the angle at which it attacked the airflow.

A lot of conflicting mathematical formulae had been published in the course of a hundred and fifty years of research into all this. One of the most crucial, which was to give them more problems than most, was the elusive figure to feed into their calculations for the quantity of the lifting force they could expect from wings raised to meet the airflow at various angles. For these air pressure figures they settled for those arrived at a century and a half earlier by an English engineer, John Smeaton, who had studied the aerodynamics of windmill sails. Both Lilienthal and Chanute had used them.

All this aerodynamic science is far too arcane and complicated for most people readily to comprehend. That the high-school-educated brothers, neither with even the beginnings of a mathematics or engineering degree, managed to grasp and wrestle with the still evolving algebraic laws and concepts which daily confronted them as they floundered through these uncharted seas is staggering. They were later to try to illustrate the sheer complexity, citing the variables in the lift generated by different wing shapes thus:

> The pressures on squares are different from those on rectangles, circles, triangles or ellipses, arched surfaces are different from planes, and vary among themselves according to the depth of curvature; true arcs differ from parabolas, and the latter differ among themselves; thick surfaces differ from thin, and surfaces thicker in one place than another vary in pressure when the positions of maximum thickness are different; some surfaces are most efficient at one angle, others at other angles. The shape of the edge also makes a difference, so that thousands of combinations are possible in so simple a thing as a wing.[16]

Through this tangled web of theoretical confusion they appear to have had a quite uncanny ability to identify the most promising quantum in each case.

In August 1900, between cycle shop and Hawthorn Street parlour, bouncing ideas in closed-circuit dialogue, they arrived at a shape for the machine they would take to Kitty Hawk. Its design detail flowed from the simple requirement to lift the 140 or so pounds weight of either brother and support him in a lift-generating wind of around 15 miles an hour. This, they calculated, required a total surface area of something like 180 square feet shared between the two wings. Each wing would therefore be 18 feet by 5 feet.

To the precise camber of both they had given much thought. Lilienthal and Chanute had built theirs in the shape of a circular arc with its greatest depth of curvature halfway between the front and back; the deepest part was one-twelfth of the front-to-rear distance – a camber ratio of 1:12. The Wrights weren't happy with this proportion – they had their own ideas about it. They broke with tradition and positioned the high point of the curve close to the leading edge, arguing that a centrally humped camber exposed too much of its top surface to the oncoming airflow, creating downward pitching pressure and making it unstable. They settled, too, for a much less curved wing, giving theirs almost half the camber at 1:23. Both these changes they thought would create a safer, more powerful lifting surface than the deeper camber with its potential for disastrous sudden downward flicks.

The wings were to be rigged one above the other, 5 feet apart, linked by upright posts and trussed laterally across the span with criss-crossing wires. But they deliberately avoided the rigidity of bracing wires from front to back to allow the outer edges of the wings freedom to twist for banking. This 'warping' action, as Chanute was to dub it, was activated by cables connected to a swivelling crossbar in the middle of the rear of the lower wing. The pilot, stretched out prone, would operate the bar with his feet. This would leave his hands free to move a lever connected by cable to the front elevator on the *canard* which, as on their earlier kite, would again sit out on a boom in front of the pilot's nose. They had thus provided for control of roll and pitch, but not for the third dimension of yaw. The machine had no rudder; they were assuming – wrongly, as it turned out – that when they began to bank it would happily turn as well.

Why the brothers adopted the *canard* arrangement – which to modern eyes creates the illusion that the aircraft is flying backwards – was never documented at the time. But much later Orville was to explain: 'We retained the elevator in front for many years because it absolutely prevented a nose-dive such as that in which Lilienthal and many others have since met their deaths.'[17]

The German pilot's crash had resulted – it is now known – from a stall. But in 1900, the phenomenon of the stall – today demonstrated to every pupil pilot early in their training – was not understood. Experimenters were unaware of what it was, what precipitated it. They had not discovered that when an aircraft slowed down or went into an extreme nose-up attitude, and the speed of the lift-making airflow over the wings dropped, the flow began to break up into destructive turbulence causing the wings to drop, often into a dive. Although they didn't at the time know why, aerodynamically, the forward stabiliser prevented the more violent consequence of a stall, the intuitive fact for the Wrights was that it acted like a parachute, helping the aircraft to drop gently rather than whipping into the frightening nosedive they so dreaded.

In August 1900 Wilbur began to assemble the machine. He appears to have built it on his own. He chose ash for the wing ribs, steaming them into cambered shape, covering them with sateen. He wanted to use spruce for the 18-foot spars but couldn't find any in Dayton, so he decided to get some up in Norfolk, Virginia, on his way to Kitty Hawk.

Milton, who knew of his sons' burgeoning interest in aeronautics, appears not yet to have been aware of their flight test plans; he was away at a church conference in Indiana. Wilbur broke the news in a letter which reflected the challenge flight now represented for him:

> I am intending to start in a few days for a trip to the coast of North Carolina . . . for the purpose of making some experiments with a flying machine. It is my belief that flight is possible and, while I am taking up the investigation for pleasure rather than profit, I think there is a slight possibility of achieving fame and fortune from it. It is almost the only great problem which has not been pursued by a multitude of investigators, and therefore carried to a point where further progress is very difficult. I am certain I can reach a point much in advance of any previous workers in this field even if complete success is not attained just at present.[18]

The letter, which made no reference to Orville, concluded nonchalantly: 'At any rate, I shall have an outing of several weeks and see a part of the world I have never before visited.'

There is no record of Milton's reaction to what must have been mildly alarming news. He made no mention in his diary. A myth was later to develop that Bishop Wright opposed his sons' flying experiments. On the contrary, there is ample testimony that, despite his deeply held fundamentalist beliefs, he took an alert interest in the scientific revolutions unfolding around him, believed in their power for good and even saw in the aeroplane its eventual value as a vehicle that could expedite the spread of Christianity.

Whatever – if any – misgivings he may have felt on receipt of Wilbur's letter, Milton would have been perhaps a little comforted to hear two days later from Katharine:

> We are in an uproar getting Will off. The trip will do him good. I don't think he will be reckless. If they can arrange it, Orv will go down as soon as Will gets the machine ready.[19]

This is the first record of the fact that Orville was part of the glider test team. But it was Wilbur who would pioneer the adventurous route to the bleak and extraordinarily inaccessible Kitty Hawk. On the evening of 6 September, with boxes of disassembled aeroplane wings, he boarded a train at Dayton's Union Station on the first stage of the longest journey he had ever made.

8

A Place Called Kitty Hawk (1900)

Wilbur hadn't bargained for the sheer difficulty of getting to Kitty Hawk. The 750-mile journey which he'd reckoned at a couple of days took a week. The place could only be reached by boat. It lay offshore on one of a long chain of narrow sand islands called the Outer Banks. They stretched for 175 miles in a great arc, in places thirty miles offshore, southward from the Virginia border, providing a protective barrier against the pounding Atlantic for half the length of the swampy North Carolina coast. A desolate place with a harsh climate, the banks were inhabited by small communities of fishermen and men who manned the lighthouses and the ever-busy lifesaving stations. It was a landscape dominated by sand – long, flat stretches of it, great hundred-foot-high dunes and rolling hummocks on which here and there grew trees misshapen by the wind.

To reach the hamlet of Kitty Hawk, Bill Tate told Wilbur, he had to get a boat from the North Carolina port of Elizabeth City to Roanoke Island, the site of Sir Walter Raleigh's disastrous late sixteenth-century 'lost colony' whose 120 settlers, the first in North America, had famously disappeared off the face of the earth. From the town of Manteo on this renowned island a thrice-weekly mail boat ran across the sound to Kitty Hawk. But Wilbur never made it to Roanoke.

When on the evening of the second day he disembarked, travel weary, from the overnight train at Old Point Comfort on Chesapeake Bay, he took a steamer across Hampton Roads to Norfolk, Virginia, where he booked into a hotel. The next day he scoured the city's lumber yards in vain for the 18-foot lengths of spruce he needed for his spars. There weren't any to be had, nor anything in 18-foot lengths. Reluctantly he was forced to settle for 16-foot sections of pine. He bought them, history records, from a timber merchant glorying in the name of Cumpston Goffigon. It meant that the wings would now have to be scaled down and the sateen coverings resewn in Kitty Hawk. The pine spars cost $2.70, bringing the total outlay for the glider to around $15 – around $300 today.

That afternoon he loaded his boxes on to a second train and travelled down to Elizabeth City, on the Pasquotank River, where he spent another night in a hotel. Kitty Hawk was now only thirty-five miles away across Albemarle Sound, but he had missed the weekly boat to Manteo by one day. Rather than hang around he decided to charter one direct to Kitty Hawk, but at the river port he discovered that not only was there a dearth of hire boats but no one even seemed to have heard of Kitty Hawk. Stuck in Elizabeth City for three days, despairing of ever reaching the Outer Banks, Wilbur began to feel pangs of guilt that he had shared so little of his hazardous flying plans with his father, especially as Milton had, from the sale of some Iowa prairie land he'd bought over twenty years earlier with an inheritance from his father, recently made to each of his four sons a generous present of $3000 each.[1] This tidy sum – worth over $60,000 today – Wilbur had not drawn upon for the Kitty Hawk venture, but he clearly felt he owed it to his father to minimize his anxiety. From his hotel he wrote, 'I have no intention of risking injury to any great extent, and have no expectation of being hurt. I will be careful, and will not attempt new experiments in dangerous situations.' Possibly with his hockey accident in mind he added optimistically: 'I think the danger much less than in most athletic games.'[2]

After three days' searching, Wilbur found a boatman who knew Kitty Hawk. His name was Israel Perry and he quoted a modest $3 for the passage. Perry, a native of Kitty Hawk described as a 'loquacious' fisherman, owned and lived on a flat-bottomed schooner, the *Curlicue*, anchored in deeper water three miles downriver. Leaving most of his crates to follow on the weekly cargo boat, Wilbur loaded the wing spars, his trunk and suitcase on to a small, leaking, unseaworthy skiff, and nervously set off down the Pasquotank with Perry and his young deckhand.

As they clambered on to the *Curlicue* Wilbur's heart sank. He was appalled by her stench and state of decay. 'The sails were rotten, the ropes badly worn and the rudder post half rotted off, and the cabin so dirty and vermin infested that I kept out of it from first to last.'[3] The boat was cockroach-infested, stank of fish and the fastidious Wilbur suspected that Perry rarely washed. It was to be an uncomfortable and terrifying voyage.

When at nightfall they crept out of the river into Albemarle Sound they were hit by a storm. The flat-bottomed boat, with its large cabin superstructure, had difficulty making way into a south-east headwind that soon rose to a full gale. The strain of rolling and pitching in the heavy sea proved too much for the decrepit schooner. To Wilbur's alarm it sprang a leak and, with waves crashing in over the bow, they began to take on water. He was convinced they were going to founder.

As they bailed for their lives, Wilbur, his city suit soaked, saw that they were gradually being driven ashore. Since to turn risked a fatal capsize, the skipper was forced to hold her grimly into the gale, but the wind finally got the better of the helpless vessel: first the foresail then the mainsail were torn loose. They had been caught in the tail of a full-blown hurricane. Their only chance now was to make a straight run over the bar of a nearby estuary, driven only by the jib. While Wilbur held his breath, Perry went about. It was a risky manoeuvre, but they managed it without capsizing. The gale was now behind them and ferocious waves began to crash over the stern. Somehow they survived to anchor further up the estuary for the night. Refusing to go into the stinking cabin, Wilbur curled up and tried to sleep on deck. For most of the next day, as the high winds subsided, they remained there making repairs. Wilbur was by now famished. Nauseated by the very sight of the cooked food Perry had offered him, he made polite excuses and retrieved a pot of jam that Katharine had tucked into his suitcase as he was leaving. It was all he was to eat for forty-eight hours.

The rest of the voyage was mercifully uneventful. Under patched-up sails, the *Curlicue* delivered Wilbur to the wharf at Kitty Hawk around 9 o'clock on their second night at sea. The village was in darkness, everyone asleep, so Wilbur spent another uncomfortable night afloat, sleeping again on the hard deck, eaten by mosquitoes. At daybreak, stiff, damp, sleepless, with a painfully sore back and very hungry, he went ashore.

A handful of basic, unpainted, cedar-shingle-roofed houses built on the sand among scattered trees appeared to be all there was of Kitty Hawk. The only sign of life was a fourteen-year-old boy, Elijah Baum, standing on the wharf. He offered to guide Wilbur to the Tates' house, a quarter of a mile away. Wilbur hadn't actually replied to Tates' letter of welcome. Bill and Addie Tate were therefore taken aback that morning to find Elijah standing there with 'a strange gentleman' in a business suit and cap.

'He took off his cap,' Tate said, 'and introduced himself as Wilbur Wright of Dayton, Ohio, "to whom you wrote concerning this section."'[4] Tate immediately invited Wilbur in and introduced him to his wife. When the couple learnt that he'd not eaten for forty-eight hours, Addie hurried into the kitchen and whipped him up a great platter of ham and eggs. 'Mr Wright done a he-man's part by that humble breakfast,'[5] Tate recalled.

Wilbur asked if he could possibly board with the Tates until Orville arrived in a couple of weeks with their tent and bedding. Tate and Addie hesitated. They excused themselves and retreated to another room to confer. Through the open door Wilbur overheard what was bothering them. Addie was concerned that their primitive home and plain fare would not be good enough for the well-dressed stranger from the city. Wilbur quickly joined them to offer reassurance. 'Mrs Tate,' he interrupted. 'We shall be guests in your house; your fare will be our fare.'[6] The Tates were impressed – convinced that their boarder was 'a gentleman of breeding'. They weren't surprised to learn that he was the son of a bishop and must therefore have 'been brought up in the Christian way of life'.[7]

There were only two bedrooms. To provide one for Wilbur, Tate and Addie and their two young daughters crowded into the other. The interior of the two-storey house of rough-sawn boards matched the bleakness of its surroundings. The unplastered walls were unpainted, there were no carpets, not a single picture or book, and very little furniture. But what it lacked in comfort was more than made up for by the sheer warmth of the hospitality. When Wilbur's baggage had been fetched from the wharf in a horse cart and he'd been shown to his upstairs room, he asked to see where their drinking water came from. It was a shallow open well; it looked like a classic source of typhoid – the last thing he could afford to contract in this outlandish place. He requested that they bring him each morning a gallon pitcher of boiled water.

In the days following his arrival Wilbur was taken by Tate on a tour of Kitty Hawk. The origin of the name no one seemed to know for sure. One version claimed it was a corruption of 'skeeter' hawk, a local mosquito-eating dragonfly; another that it had come from 'Killy Honk', an Indian expression for killing the island's wild geese.

In 1900 the place boasted two churches and a one-teacher school. Because wind-blown sand was constantly migrating inland from the ocean beach, sometimes burying entire houses and big trees in its path, most of the habitation was on the western, leeward side of the Banks. With his city attire and educated turn of speech, Wilbur was immediately an object of curiosity in this frugal, reserved community unaccustomed to visits by outsiders. In the infertile sandscape, the islanders raised cattle and pigs and meagre crops of corn and vegetables. Everybody seemed to own a boat. Everybody fished and gathered oysters from the sounds. Most of the houses were even more rudimentary than the Tates'. Liable to be blown down in hurricanes, some had removable floorboards to relieve the pressure of the flood waters the storms brought in. Life was austere in the extreme.

The island was around a mile wide at Kitty Hawk. It rose, Sahara-like, four miles to the south into huge barren dunes known as the Kill Devil Hills, and further south still was a summer resort called Nags Head to which North Carolina families came in paddle steamers to stay in holiday cottages. But the fishing community of

Kitty Hawk was separated from this contact with the outside world by a long stretch of uninhabited sand dotted here and there with woods in which there were squirrels and bears.

On Kitty Hawk's ocean beach Wilbur was introduced to the men of the US Life Saving Service. Later to become the Coast Guard, its station provided storm season employment for fishermen who regularly risked their lives rowing to rescues through the dangerous surf. A 1900 photograph shows a group of tough, sullen, almost identical-looking men who, with their brass-buttoned jackets and caps and enormous drooping moustaches, look as if they could have stepped out of a Coen Brothers movie. The station, with its lookout tower and boat ramp, was one of seven dotted along the Outer Banks. Still visible skeletons of ships bore testimony to the long history of wrecks on the treacherous shoals that girded the coast. The ocean beach had for centuries regularly received bodies from the sea and harvests of wreckage and flotsam. Legend had it that the seventeenth-century pirate Blackbeard had caroused here and that Bankers had once maintained the flow of ill-fated cargo by plundering ships they would murderously lure to destruction with lamps waved from the beach.

Installed at the Tates', Wilbur lost no time in unpacking his boxes and assembling the glider beneath a canvas awning he rigged up in the backyard. Borrowing Addie's sewing machine, he worked on the porch to cut down the larger panels to fit the smaller spars he'd been forced to settle for. Addie, who helped with some of the work, was much impressed by his stitching skills. A warm friendship blossomed between Wilbur and Bill Tate. While Tate, who had had four years' schooling, was fascinated by the flying experiment and insisted on lending practical help at every turn, most of the Bankers, who had much less education, privately regarded Wilbur as a crank. As Tate said of this insular community, 'We were set in our ways. We believed in a good God, a bad Devil and a hot Hell, and more than anything else we believed that the same good God did not intend man should ever fly.'[8]

As the machine began to take shape, Wilbur wrote again to Milton. 'I have my machine nearly finished. It is not to have a motor and is not expected to fly in any true sense of the word,' he said.

> My idea is merely to experiment and practice with a view to solving the problems of equilibrium . . . When once a machine is under proper control under all conditions, the motor problem will be quickly solved. A failure of motor will then simply mean a slow descent and safe landing instead of a disastrous fall. In my experiments I do not expect to rise many feet from the ground and in case I am upset there is nothing but soft sand to strike on. I do not intend to take dangerous chances, both because I have no wish to get hurt and because a fall would stop my experimenting, which I would not like at all . . .
>
> I am constructing my machine to sustain about five times my weight and am testing every piece. I think there is no possible chance of its breaking while in the air . . . My machine will be trussed like a bridge and will be much stronger than that of Lilienthal . . .
>
> I have not taken up the problem with the expectation of financial profit. Neither do I have any strong expectations of achieving the solution at the present time or possibly any time. My trip would be no great disappointment if I accomplished practically nothing. I look upon it as a pleasure . . .[9]

Attempting to set his father's mind further at ease, Wilbur concluded: 'I am watching my health very closely and expect to return home heavier and stronger than I left. I am taking every precaution about my drinking water.' Again his letter made no reference to his brother.

However, Orville was about to become fully involved. He had hired two men to run the cycle shop – on which both Katharine and Lorin had agreed to keep a close eye – and was preparing to join Wilbur. When, on 24 September, he boarded the train at Dayton, he was loaded with camping equipment, blankets, acetylene lamps, his mandolin and a supply of coffee, tea and sugar unobtainable in Kitty Hawk's few sparsely stocked stores, most run as sidelines out of private houses.

'I was glad to get Orv off,' Katharine wrote to Milton. 'He had worked so hard and was so run down. They never have had a trip anywhere since the World's Fair.' Orville made it to Kitty Hawk without mishap in four days – two of which were spent becalmed in Albemarle Sound – arriving on 28 September. He stayed for a while with the Tates, then he and Wilbur moved into their large rectangular 22-foot-long tent, which they erected on the edge of the dunes about a quarter of a mile away. The site looked out over Kitty Hawk bay. To prevent it blowing away they roped one end to a scraggy wind-bent oak that had somehow managed to survive the relentlessly rolling mountains of sand, and installed their folding cots, a small workbench and a gasoline stove. They drew their water from the Tates' well, boiling it and carrying it every day across the sand. Some nearby bushes became their lavatory.

Quickly they settled into a harmonious labour-sharing routine. Orville volunteered to cook and Wilbur washed the dishes; to save water he scoured the pots and plates with sand. They dined on bacon, canned vegetables, rice, tomatoes, eggs, corn bread and Orville's milkless biscuits – which were said to have been delicious.

The biplane glider was soon ready to fly. With wooden bows added to the ends, it now had a wingspan of 17½ feet by 5 feet across. The total surface area of around 177 square feet included 12 square feet of the forward horizontal stabiliser which incorporated the moveable elevator. It had no tail fin or rudder. In its centre section an 18-inch wide gap had been cut out of the lower wing. In this space the pilot was to lie stretched out full length, his hand operating the elevator lever for pitch control, his feet resting upon the swivelling bar which warped the wings to bank. The wing again criss-cross wire braced laterally, but not fore and aft – was free to twist.

Later the Wrights kept meticulously detailed records of their flying experiments, but in early October 1900, on that first visit to Kitty Hawk, their logging of events was scanty, to say the least. Although they had acquired an expensive Korona-V camera – at $85 it had cost six times more than all the glider's materials put together – they took only three pictures of the historic machine and left few written records of the flight tests. It is believed that they first hoisted the aircraft into the air on Wednesday 3 October. Although they had planned to try it out thoroughly as a kite before attempting to board it, and Wilbur had solemnly promised Milton he would take no risks, it appears that on that very first flying day, after just a few kitings, he threw caution to the winds.

Bill Tate had come out to help. On the side of the dune he and Orville, both holding about twenty feet of coiled rope attached to the machine, gripped a wingtip each while Wilbur stood inside the open lower wing space, grasping the two interior ribs. 'At his signal, all three men trotted forward into the wind until the craft began to lift, at which point Wilbur pulled himself aboard, stretching his feet out to the T-bar at the rear and placing his hands on the elevator control.'[10]

As the glider began to rise in the stiff breeze, Orville and Tate gently paid out the lines until it was bobbing about in the air. But almost immediately Wilbur, alarmed by the violent pitching which he found he couldn't control, began to panic. 'Lemme down! Lemme down!' he is said to have shouted. When he'd been hauled back to earth, Orville apparently expressed his surprise that he had given up so easily – to which, it is recorded, Wilbur responded: 'I promised Pop I'd take care of myself.'

According to the Wrights' first biographer, John McMahon – who got most of his material from long interviews with Orville fifteen years later – Orville also had a go at flying aboard the kite that day: 'Orville did have a wild ride,' wrote McMahon. 'It ended with a mild smash from which he rose unscathed.'

However, for most of the limited flying that the wind made possible, the machine was operated as an unmanned kite. The biggest problem was the wind itself. The records that had lured them to this wild place had actually referred to monthly average velocities of 15 and 20 miles an hour. The reality was frustratingly very different. Some days there was dead, unflyable calm; on others, 60 mile-an-hour gales would sweep across the Outer Banks, blinding them with showers of stinging sand and threatening to tear the tent from its tree anchor. But when it was possible to send the kite up it became clear that, despite its control innovations, the machine was still a long way from being safe and efficient. Disappointingly, they were not going to get the hours of airborne time as pilots they so badly wanted in order to try and master the problem of flight control that had eluded all their predecessors.

Operating the warping and pitch with cords from the safety of the ground, they had such difficulty coordinating them that they tied off the warp to concentrate on pitch operation alone. Sometimes they got local boys who hung around the camp to fly the plane while they operated the control cords. To simulate its behaviour with the weight of a man they loaded it with a ballast of heavy chains borrowed from Tate. They measured the wind speed with a hand-held anemometer lent by the weather station man, Joe Dosher, and tried to assess the drag, the total air resistance, of the glider's structure by hooking into the tethering line a standard spring scale borrowed from a fisherman.

They also on several occasions sent aloft a boy who had taken to visiting their camp, proudly showing them huge fish he was catching in the sound. Tom Tate was the son of Bill Tate's half-brother, Dan. Although only eleven years old and weighing forty pounds less than the brothers, Tom nonetheless presented roughly the same drag as an adult when in the air. And because he was so much lighter, it was possible to send him up in much lighter winds than their own weight required. Tom appears to have flown on a number of occasions and become a local celebrity – as well as, subsequently, the subject of at least one book.

But they needed an aeroplane that would fly a man, not a boy. Again and again they reworked the mathematics they had based on Lilienthal's figures. They had calculated that their glider, lifting a 140-pound man plus its own weight of 52 pounds – an all-up 192 pounds – would fly with its wings attacking the horizontal windflow of between 15 and 20 miles per hour at an angle of around 3 degrees. This was an ideal angle for gliding and for the effectiveness of the controls. The reality was proving dispiritingly different. The thing needed to rear up into a dramatic, unglidable 20-degree angle just to support the weight of an adult. It was an angle that created a disastrous amount of drag. To get it down to around a flyable 3 degrees would need, they realised, a mild gale of 35 to 40 miles an hour.

As they began to suspect the validity of the sacred German formulae, their frustration deepened. Wilbur became withdrawn and morose. For relief he went off birdwatching. 'Will was so mixed up,'

Orville wrote to Katharine, 'he couldn't even theorise. It has been with considerable effort that I have succeeded in keeping him in the flying business at all. He likes to chase buzzards, thinking they are eagles and chicken hawks . . .'[11]

On these escapes from the depressing experiments, Wilbur, wandering the dunes alone, began to fill his notebook with pertinent observations: 'No bird soars in a calm'; 'the object of the tail is to increase the spread of surface in the rear when the wings are moved in light winds and thus preserve the centre of pressure at about the same spot. It seems to be used as a rudder very little.' But bird flight, which was to continue to fascinate and baffle Wilbur, was, despite its parallels, never to provide more than aerodynamic insights into mechanical flight control. The birds of Kitty Hawk that October did little more than soothe Wilbur's disheartened state of mind. He knew that only through dogged experimentation with man-made contraptions would the solution be found – if, indeed, ever.

Meanwhile their antics were creating a mighty stir in the tiny backwoods community. The Wrights dressed, at all times in all weathers, like businessmen bound for the office, in suits and ties with starched white collars that they changed daily. They were friendly and unfailingly courteous, but most people didn't quite know what to make of this oddball pair who had come all this way, camping uncomfortably in their midst, just to fool around with a big kite. After a storm one night 'the Kitty Hawkers were out early,' Orville wrote, 'peering around the edge of the woods and out of their upstairs windows to see whether our camp was still in existence.'[12]

People addressed them respectfully as 'Mr Wright', but Bill Tate felt able to advance familiarity with 'Mr Wilbur' and 'Mr Orville'. Those who went out to watch them at work were fascinated by their powers of concentration. 'I never saw two men so wrapped up in their work in my life,' said one of the lifesavers. 'When they were working we could come around and stand right over them and they wouldn't pay any more attention to us than if we weren't there at all. After their day's work was over they were different; then they were the nicest fellows you ever saw and treated us fine.'[13] They demonstrated amazing fixity of purpose and self-discipline, and were impressively efficient in the way they worked. 'A nail dropped is not worth the time it takes to pick it up,' Wilbur is said to have told a frugal local carpenter.

Despite their punctilious politeness and pleasantness, the brothers tended to keep themselves to themselves. 'They didn't have much to do with people,' said the wife of one of the lifesavers. 'They just stayed in their camp . . . and would only go down to the station to collect their mail. I never saw them go inside. They would just go to the door and someone would take their mail out to them. It wasn't that they didn't like people, they were just very secretive about what they were doing.'[14]

For their part, the Wrights were reporting on the Kitty Hawkers. They wrote to the family on Sundays when, continuing to please Milton, they didn't work – though they didn't go to church. Telling Katharine about the spartan existence of the islanders, Orville observed: 'They never had anything good in their lives and consequently are satisfied with what they have . . . satisfied in keeping soul and body together.' Orville complained: 'No-one down here has any regular milk. The poor cows have such a hard time scraping up a living that they don't have any time for making milk. You never saw such poor pitiful looking creatures as the horses, hogs and cows are down here. The only things that thrive and grow fat are the bedbugs, mosquitoes and wood ticks.'[15]

The night storms whipping in off the Atlantic hurled rain and sheets of hissing sand at the tent, flapping its sides in thunderous claps. They would lie in bed with their clothes on, shivering in the freezing cold, waiting for the tent to fly away, ready to rush outside to hold it down. When they left the glider pegged down outside at night it would often be buried by morning under several feet of sand.

On a nearby dune they erected a wooden tower. Over a pulley on the top they ran a rope from the machine to some dangling counterbalancing weights which rose and fell as the glider twitched about in the pulsing wind. It was intended to give them hours of practice, but the glider didn't fly very happily from the structure: it soared too high and kept plunging to earth. Soon disaster struck. While they were tinkering with the kite on the ground, it was whipped out of their grasp and blown twenty feet away – and wrecked. Disconsolately they dragged the mangled heap back to their camp. They seriously talked of packing in the whole experiment and going home, but in the morning they changed their minds. The whole point of coming to Kitty Hawk had been to fly the plane. They'd only managed it for a few seconds at a time. Admitting defeat seemed unthinkable. They had the skills to repair it and they did so. It took three days.

When the glider was finally rebuilt they decided the time had come to test it properly in piloted flight. They were especially anxious to master the temperamental pitch control while soaring free as a bird. To do so they needed a better launching site. There was nowhere high enough around Kitty Hawk, so they took the now rather battered set of wings four miles south to the nest of huge dunes that were the Kill Devil Hills – named after the bad quality rum once consumed there. Bill Tate helped them carry it down in a cart drawn by his horse Quixote. However, when they arrived at Kill Devil the wind, perversely, had died. To get enough lift to support their weight when the machine was tethered had needed a wind of around 25 miles an hour. Flying free, the aircraft's forward speed, adding to the lifting pressure of the wind, required a breeze of only half that velocity – but when they staggered up to the top of the tallest sand mountain, over a hundred feet high, there wasn't even this much breath of air.

In desperation they resorted to tossing the empty machine off the brow of the dune to see what it would do on its own. To their delight it performed surprisingly well, happily gliding out over the slope before stalling and plummeting into the sand. Apart from minor fractures, it survived the crashes intact. Filled with renewed confidence, they went back to Kitty Hawk determined to resume the trials in the morning.

Next day the weather smiled. It brought, their anemometer showed, an ideal gliding wind of around 12 miles an hour. They hurried back to the top of the biggest Kill Devil sand mountain. Here, gingerly, with adrenalin pumping, Wilbur took up his position standing inside the lower wing while Orville and Bill Tate gripped a wingtip each. To simplify the flying they had again tied off the warping controls, leaving only the forward elevator free to vary the pitch.

They began gently, walking down the slope, then trotting, then running, holding the wings level until the glider, lift sucking it into the air, outran them. Wilbur, now prone, was airborne, hissing along in free flight for the first time. Without the complication of the banking control, he had only his pitch lever to worry about. He was amazed at how well, how positively, it worked. Gliding down the 10-degree slope he was able to hold the glider just a few feet off the sand. To avoid injury he had intended pulling himself up into a sitting position for landing, but it was unnecessary. He found he could bring the machine down, even touching at 30 miles an hour, with such smooth precision there was no risk of being hurt. As the thing ploughed gently in, the sole discomfort was a face-full of sand.

Wilbur made around a dozen descents that historic day, 19 October 1900, each time going a little further until comfortably making glides of 300 to 400 feet and remaining triumphantly airborne for as long as 15 to 20 seconds. Nearly fifty years earlier George Cayley's coachman had flown in a glider with the ability to control it, but no one knows whether he ever overcame his terror of doing so. Now, for the first time in the development of the aeroplane, one had most certainly been controlled in flight with a more sophisticated means than body swinging.

Although most of the Wrights' numerous biographers have accepted that the glides that day were made exclusively by Wilbur, the brothers' subsequent writing on the subject was to go out of its way to create the impression that both men had done so. There is no log to identify which of them was riding the wings from day to day. The only biography ever written with the blessing of either man was published long after Wilbur's death.[16] Reluctantly approved by Orville after much quibbling, it carefully avoided naming pilots and with references such as 'the brothers repeatedly made landings' leaves the clear impression that the flying was shared. The same inference is to be drawn from a subsequent letter about the flights that Wilbur wrote to Chanute, confusingly referring to 'the operators' and 'the man on the machine' rather than himself. One could be forgiven for believing that in that cold, wind-battered tent at Kitty Hawk they had entered into a solemn pact to take no individual credit for any of the perilous flights that year – whether or not they had been made by only one of them. Certainly their corporate entity had now been firmly launched.

The mystery of the 1900 pilotage may now never be solved, for no photographs were taken of those brief gliding moments. Regardless of their respective contributions, it is clear that Wilbur was the dominant force at Kitty Hawk. 'He was the leading spirit of the team,' Bill Tate's daughter, Pauline, was to recall. 'He led and Orville followed.'[17]

But whether one or both made those faltering first free-flying excursions, the Wrights were still far from solving the secrets of flight. Their pitch and banking control systems had worked well, but their wings, designed using Lilienthal's air pressure data, did not provide anything like enough lift. Even allowing for the smaller wings they had been forced to use, the result was disappointing. The glider when loaded – both tethered and flying free – had needed much stronger winds than they had calculated from the Lilienthal figures. It led them to believe that two things might need to be changed: the total wing area enlarged and a greater camber introduced to boost the lift. Their camber, at a 1:23 thickness ratio, had been a good deal flatter than the 1:12 used both by the German and in Chanute's gliders. What's more, their already modest curvature had grown even flatter as the steam-bent ribs had begun to straighten out. They were correct in both these suspicions, but it was not a total explanation. There were other factors – beyond their understanding at that time – that were also contributing to the wing's poor performance.

However, at Kitty Hawk that October their experiments had gone as far as they could go. They had flown the repeatedly crashed glider almost to destruction, and there was a problem back in Dayton at the cycle shop now demanding their return. A telegram had come from Katharine telling them that she and Lorin had dismissed, as unsatisfactory, one of the two men they had engaged at the shop.

Before they folded their tent on 23 October they decided to give the glider one final symbolic flight. They took it to the top of a dune and hurled it into the air. The tired machine skimmed a few yards before collapsing on to the ground where, to prevent it blowing away, they shovelled sand over it. They told Bill Tate he was welcome to salvage the bits if he wished.

Israel Perry's leaking schooner took them back to Elizabeth City. They had flown in free controlled flight – whether both or Wilbur alone – for a total of barely two airborne minutes. But, said Wilbur, 'we were very much pleased with the general results . . . we considered it quite a point to be able to return without having our pet theories completely knocked on the head . . . and our own brains dashed out into the bargain.'[18]

Back at Kitty Hawk Addie Tate walked out to the dune and dug the tattered glider out of the sand. With a pair of scissors she trimmed the green sateen off the wings. The fabric was of a fine, silky quality unknown on the Outer Banks. She washed it, cut it up and made a dress with a pretty bow at the back for each of her two daughters.

9

The Maestro's Disciples (1901)

Back home in late October 1900, Wilbur and Orville were quickly reimmersed in the cycle business. But their minds were really on flight – on the glider which, apart from its control system, had proved so aerodynamically disappointing. They had begun to redesign it and were already discussing a return to Kitty Hawk for further experiments. The challenge was beginning to take over their lives.

Wilbur wrote to Chanute to report on their experiments. Chanute had no idea they had so quickly developed such an advanced aeroplane, and for the first time he learnt that the young bicycle-maker was not alone in the project. 'In October my brother and myself spent a vacation of several weeks at Kitty Hawk, North Carolina, experimenting with a soaring machine,'[1] Wilbur had begun his downbeat letter, sending details and sketches of the glider. He described the success of their elevator and warping controls, and how the machine had been flown with the pilot lying prone.

Chanute, notwithstanding his purported expertise as aviation's global coordinator, appears to have acquired only a limited understanding of the complicated forces involved. He was still wedded to the body-swinging method of control, and his distinguished engineering career, building railways and bridges, somehow hadn't equipped him to understand the physical facts of the three dimensions of the sky. He didn't appreciate that, in the space of just a few months, the Wrights had advanced the technique of aircraft control further than anyone in the history of flight. Chanute merely congratulated Wilbur on the reduction of drag he had achieved by use of the prone piloting position. 'This is a magnificent showing,' he had applauded, 'provided that you do not plough the ground with your noses.'[2] Wilbur's letters to Chanute leave no record of who the pilots actually were. He needlessly continued to obfuscate it with the anonymous 'we', 'the man on the machine', 'the operators', 'the aeronaut'.

In spite of his failure to grasp the full stunning significance of the Wrights' flight control innovations – he seemed capable of understanding flight only in two dimensions and saw warping as merely an aid to turning – Chanute was impressed that these new arrivals, coming from nowhere, had made such startling progress. They were clearly candidates for the exclusive club of the young experimenters he encouraged and funded and used to put his own ideas into the air. What Chanute didn't know was that the Wrights were already philosophically and technically a long way ahead of him.

Christmas was now approaching and in Dayton the Wright clans were gathering. The extended family had been growing. Reuchlin, still working as a book-keeper in Kansas City, and his wife Lulu now had three children. They all descended on 7 Hawthorn Street for the event. On Christmas Day they were joined by Lorin and Netta with their three children; another was on the way. Wilbur and Orville had become uncles to a small tribe of nieces and nephews whom they would entertain with shadow puppets created in their workshop. Milton's favourite, frequently mentioned with pride in his diary, was Lorin's eight-year-old son, Milton.

It was a crowded house, a happy gathering, one of the few that would see all the generations together. Presiding over the festivities there emerges, too, a different image than the stern crusading figure of Milton who had sent so many shock waves through the hearts of his ecclesiastical brethren. In the bosom of his family, as he descended into old age, Milton became a warm and generous, much loved authoritarian figure, his rigidity tolerated. On New Year's Eve he wrote, 'Having been spared for 72-100ths of the old century, I am permitted to enter upon the new. Praise the Lord for his merciful kindness.'

But the new year brought more anguish for Bishop Wright. Just as the Brethren wounds had begun to heal, he was engulfed, incredibly, in yet another church crisis, this time within the ranks of his own denomination. The new ructions had erupted around a fellow cleric, the Reverend Millard Keiter, who had succeeded Milton as the Radicals' publishing agent. Milton had wanted the job to go to Wilbur, but the church had been unwilling to offer this powerfully influential post to another Wright.

Keiter became the villain who would cast the blackest of all shadows over Milton's stormy career. With his dark beard and bald features sharpened by a coxcomb, he was an unappealing character and a formidable and ambitious Brethren politician. More worryingly, Keiter had begun to embezzle church money. Milton had discovered that he had written, in the printing establishment's name, a $1000 promissory note to a woman in Maryland to cover a personal debt to her. Confronted by the publishing board, Keiter had agreed to cancel the note but became convinced that Bishop Wright had embarked on a crusade to persecute him.

Not satisfied that Keiter could any longer be trusted, Milton asked Wilbur to audit the publishing house books. Wilbur reported, 'there is something rotten somewhere.' Keiter, he declared, was, 'either a liar, a thief, or an incompetent bookkeeper, or all three.'[3] Though not a trained accountant, Wilbur had, through the cycle business, acquired some bookkeeping know-how. He discovered that Keiter had been regularly diverting church money into his own pocket, even using it to buy clothes and building materials for his house.

When Milton had taken the damning evidence to his colleagues on the publishing board, he was astounded by their reaction. Anxious to avoid scandal, all they wanted was for the matter to be quietly covered up. Once again Bishop Wright, identifying a fresh moral evil in their midst, had found himself virtually a lone voice. Now, in 1901, more funds had started mysteriously slipping through the errant cleric's hands. This time, when Milton demanded his prosecution the Indiana court merely referred the case back to the church. It removed Keiter from the publishing post and formed a special investigation committee. Its own audit would take nearly six months.

At the 1901 quadrennial conference, Milton was re-elected bishop for another four-year term. He had planned to retire but, still in good health, and, one suspects, anxious to stay firmly where he could expedite Keiter's nemesis, he was easily persuaded to soldier on.

When Milton got home from the conference in the third week of May, Wilbur and Orville were preparing to return to Kitty Hawk. They had redesigned the 1900 glider to give it much more lift and had become so consumed by the aerial quest that they had decided not to wait until the bicycle season slackened in the autumn but to go in mid-summer when living conditions on the Outer Banks would be more agreeable. They were looking for a mechanic to run the shop in their absence.

The new wings were now bigger, each spanning 22 feet by 7 feet, and they had considerably increased the curvature from the previous year's camber of 1:23 (an inch in depth for every 23 inches across) to the 1:12 used by Lilienthal which formed the basis of his critical lift pressure figures, which had dictated the Wrights' wing shape. Their total wing area, at 290 square feet, had been nearly doubled – on top of which the forward elevator once more added further lifting power. It was the biggest glider ever built – far too large to be controlled by a leg-swinging pilot. Chanute, who still didn't understand the Wrights' revolutionary flight controls, doubted whether it would ever get off the ground.

To protect it from the elements on the Outer Banks they planned to build a wooden hangar. They'd also decided to move their base south from Kitty Hawk to the vicinity of the Kill Devil hills. Wilbur, who conducted virtually all the correspondence with Chanute, invited him to visit them and watch the trials. Chanute, meanwhile, was eager to publicise their limited success to the international aeronautical community. He wanted to refer to their experiments in an article he was writing for *Cassier's Magazine*.

The Wrights didn't welcome the prospect of publicity. Chanute's request put them on their guard. 'It is not our intention,' Wilbur wrote, 'to make a close secret of our machine, but at the same time, inasmuch as we have not yet had an opportunity to test the full possibilities of our methods, we wish to be the first to give them such test. We will gladly give you for your own information anything you may wish to know, but for the present would not wish any publication in detail of the methods of operation or construction of the machine.'[4] Chanute respected their wish. He said he would refer to them as 'Wright Brothers' or 'W. Wright and Bro' – 'as you may prefer'. To which Wilbur replied, 'The form of designation is immaterial but in so far as we have any preference it is for "Messrs Wilbur and Orville Wright".'[5]

Wilbur preferred writing his own carefully guarded articles. He sent a highly technical one on the angle of attack to the Aeronautical Society in London for its journal, and another about the prone piloting position – which carefully ignored the details of their control system – to a German aviation magazine. With these two articles drip-feeding their innovations to the world, plus Chanute's in *Cassier's Magazine*, the Wright Brothers' name now publicly joined the ranks of the serious experimenters. They were beginning to be talked about.

Chanute was eager to meet the Wrights and involve them in his magic circle. An opportunity came in the summer of 1901. He had arranged to go from Chicago down to Chuckey City in Tennessee to meet Edward Huffaker, whose life had recently been beset by sadness and tragedy. After the triumphant launch of Samuel Langley's steam-powered models over the Potomac he had begun to work for a time at the Smithsonian on the professor's full-size piloted successor, the *Great Aerodrome*, being built for the War Department. But his already strained relationship with Langley had grown worse; at the end of 1898 Huffaker had resigned and gone home to his wife and children in Tennessee. Devastatingly, the following year, she had died of typhoid. The bereft Huffaker had been rescued by Chanute, who'd hired him to build a full-size glider – the machine that Chanute was now on his way to inspect.

Breaking his journey at Dayton on 26 June, Chanute was invited to dinner at 7 Hawthorn Street. The event has gone down as one of the defining encounters in the chronicles of aviation. Chanute, now in his seventieth year, was revealed to the family as a prosperous, immaculately dressed figure of enormous gentle charm and courtesy. Elegantly bald, his side-hair snow-white, he looked, with his moustache and small tuft of goatee beard, every bit the elder statesman of flight.

At the dinner – joined by the bishop – Katharine was an apprehensive hostess. She went to inordinate trouble, fussing over Carrie Kayler's preparation of the desert melon. Miss Katharine, Carrie was to recall, gave instructions that if one melon, on cutting, proved to be better than the other, she was to ensure that 'Mr Chanute got a piece of the better one'. However, Carrie, noticing that one of the two melons was not fully ripe, decided democratically to cut the other into small pieces to give everyone a portion. Katharine severely rebuked the nervous young maid. 'For a while it seems, there was some doubt in Carrie's mind that she would ever be forgiven.'[6]

Lost in aeronautical discussion, it is unlikely that anyone actually registered what they were eating. They apparently talked into the small hours of the morning and met again before Chanute, having visited the cycle shop to see the new glider under construction, left for Tennessee that afternoon. Before he went, he put to the brothers a request which they disliked but felt unable to refuse. He asked them if they would allow, in addition to himself, two of his protégés to visit their Outer Banks camp during the forthcoming trials. One was Edward Huffaker, whose paper on soaring flight the Smithsonian had sent them; the other man they had never heard of. His name was George Spratt.

Spratt was a 31-year-old Pennsylvanian with medical training. He was sometimes described as Dr Spratt, though doubts exist as to whether he had ever fully qualified.[7] Whatever his true qualifications, he had, while still in his twenties, quit medicine for health reasons and retreated to his family's farm at Coatesville, west of Philadelphia. Depressed by his forced abandonment of medicine, Spratt had confronted a large void in his life. However 'there seemed to be,' he wrote, 'a voice within that quietly bid me hope that there was a mission for me to fulfil.'[8] That mission, he had eventually decided, was to join the growing ranks of experimenters and crack the secret of manned flight. 'It will,' he wrote, 'come out on top of all methods of transportation in time.' Flying, Spratt declared, had been 'the dream of my life. I never scared a bird up or saw it cross a valley but what I longed to go with it and envied it.'[9]

Spratt had begun experiments on the farm in the late 1890s to try and measure the forces of lift, and built a small model glider to test his theories. He had written to Chanute for advice and the two had entered into a warm correspondence; the older man had sent him money. Soon he had joined the privileged ranks of Chanute's would-be aviators and the latter had offered to fund a full-sized man-carrying glider.

Early in 1900 Spratt had made a perceptive aerodynamic discovery about the lifting performance of a cambered wing. He identified a characteristic of the centre of pressure to creep forward when the angle of attack was decreased, then suddenly, bewilderingly, to reverse as the wing approached the horizontal. At this moment the point where all the lifting force was concentrated began to travel back, away from the wing's leading edge. The reversal did not occur with flat uncambered surfaces. Chanute believed it was an original discovery. At the time Spratt, though pleased with his achievement, had considered it merely of academic interest. He was soon, on the Outer Banks, to realise that it was much more than that. The aerodynamic quirk he had stumbled upon was actually something quite critical to survival in the air.

At the Dayton meeting of aviation's eminence and the bishop's experimenting boys, Chanute's priority was Huffaker, whom he wanted to have test, in the stiff breezes at Kill Devil, the glider he was paying him to build. But, with the risk of injury they ran, Spratt's medical knowledge and aviation passion was also worth, he suggested, adding to the team.

The independent-minded Wrights wanted neither of these two strangers foisted upon them. They preferred to work on their own, not as part of a group of enthusiasts crowding their primitive camp in the wilderness, but they were still in awe of the doyen of world aviation and too polite to refuse outright. Besides, they were already in Chanute's debt. He had brought to Dayton an anemometer which he lent them; down at Kill Devil, away from the weather station, they would need their own means of measuring the wind strength.

Two days later Chanute wrote to Wilbur from Chuckey City where Huffaker had unveiled his glider. He had unwisely built all its frames, for lightness, out of paper tubes. 'I fear,' wrote the disenchanted Chanute, 'they will not stand long enough to test the efficiency of the ideas in its design.'[10] Notwithstanding this failure, Chanute still wanted to send Huffaker and his unpromising contraption to the Outer Banks so the Wrights could help him test it. Chanute would pay all his expenses.

Wilbur's heart must have sunk as he read this now formal proposition; and also that George Spratt, likewise at Chanute's expense, was now definitely to be tacked on to the expedition – 'to serve under your orders'. Chanute, who had earlier described Huffaker as 'a trained experimenter' who 'lacks mechanical instinct', and Spratt as 'an amateur', asked for Wilbur's reaction to his suggestions. Although it seemed as if the greater benefits of the arrangement would be for Chanute's nominees, the Wrights now felt trapped. Reluctant to offend Chanute, Wilbur responded that they would 'welcome the arrival of Messrs Huffaker and Spratt' at their new camp. 'We would be very glad to have the assistance of both these men but do not feel that we have a right to ask you to bear the expense entailed, unless you feel that you yourself are getting your money's worth.'[11]

Sensing that the Wrights were worried about the confidentiality of their invention when exposed to the eyes of two more rival experimenters, Chanute wrote of Spratt, 'I think he is discreet concerning other people's ideas. Huffaker I consider quite reliable. I mention this as you told me you have no patents.'[12]

Wilbur replied:

> We have felt no uneasiness on this point, as we do not think the class of people who are interested in aeronautics would naturally be of a character to act unfairly. The labours of others have been of great benefit to us in obtaining an understanding of the subject

> and have been suggestive and stimulating. We would be pleased if our labours should be of similar benefit to others.
>
> We of course would not wish our ideas and methods appropriated bodily, but if our work suggests ideas to others which they can work out on a different line and reach better results than we do, we will try hard not to feel jealous or that we have been robbed in any way.[13]

Wilbur would be compelled before long to modify these charitable sentiments. Meanwhile it was agreed that Chanute, Huffaker and Spratt would all make their way independently to the Outer Banks. Wilbur and Orville, who had now engaged a permanent mechanic, Charlie Taylor, to run the shop under Katharine's strict eye, left Dayton for Kitty Hawk on 7 July. They were heavily burdened with the big new glider, disassembled for the journey, their large tent and camping paraphernalia. A heap of timber for the hangar had been railed ahead to Elizabeth City.

They arrived in Kitty Hawk in the middle of a fearful storm. It was raining so hard they put up for the first night with Bill and Addie Tate. They got little sleep, having to share a bed which sagged like a hammock. Orville described it in a letter to Katharine in which he drew a funny sketch of them both lying on the U-shaped mattress:

> That's Will down in the centre and that little fellow hanging onto the side with both hands is me. When I played out and couldn't stand it any longer, I rolled down into the bottom and made Will crawl up the side. The fellow in the bottom could get along pretty comfortably, for when he was attacked by any foe (which roams at large over most of the beds in these southern places) he had the opportunity of slapping back, but the poor fellow on the side was in a pretty fix, having both hands occupied, and had to endure the attacks the best he could.[14]

In driving rain Bill Tate drove them the four miles south to their new headquarters near the base of the three Kill Devil hills. It was a remote and lonely site. Their only neighbours here would be the men at the Kill Devil lifesaving station three-quarters of a mile away. In a pelting downpour they pitched the big tent and began to erect the shed in which to assemble the glider, but the rain was so drenching they finally retreated into the sodden tent, soaked to the skin and acutely thirsty. Apart from the rain pouring from the low-scudding black clouds, there was no fresh water at Kill Devil. They set up the portable drilling equipment they'd brought and tried to sink a well. In the middle of the operation the drill bit broke off; they were reduced to collecting rainwater off the tent walls. It tasted soapily of waterproofing oil and Orville was violently sick all night.

It was two days before the rain let up. They emerged from the tent to find the surrounding sand flats dotted as far as they could see with great lakes of water in which mosquitoes were breeding in hordes unmatched in local memory.

It took three days to erect the hangar. It was 25 feet long, 16 feet wide and nearly 7 feet high; it had big doors at each end, hinged at the top so they could be propped up as awnings. They were in the middle of assembling the glider when the first of their guests arrived, bringing his five-winged paper tube glider.

The brothers took an instant dislike to Edward Huffaker. Between him and Wilbur there seems to have been a major personality clash from the moment the good-looking young engineer walked into their camp. Partly a collision of culture, it was also professional. Huffaker, as a result of his own work with gliders and public lectures on soaring, his brilliant academic record with high university honours in mathematics and philosophy, his fluency in Latin, Greek and French, his experience as a civil engineer, and his hands-on involvement with Professor Langley's powered flying machines at the Smithsonian, together with his association with the famous Chanute, had become a figure of considerably more significance at that moment than the unknown brothers. Huffaker saw the Wrights as a team devoid of academic credentials, floundering, out of their depth in the uncharted universe of aerodynamic endeavour, gifted only with the mechanical skills he sadly lacked. He was to describe them disparagingly as mere 'bicycle mechanics'.

Huffaker found the Wrights far too fussy and formal for life under canvas in a barren, insect-infested desert. They were, he later contemptuously told people back in Tennessee, a couple of 'sissies'. His own nature, shaped by life in the hills of Appalachia, was easy-going – laid-back to a degree that offended his meticulous hosts. He couldn't understand why Wilbur and Orville washed and shaved every day, regularly changed their clothes, and had brought to this primitive camp a stock of celluloid collars to wear fresh daily. He couldn't comprehend why they insisted that the pots and dishes be washed after every meal and that each item had to be returned to an exact spot on the storage shelves. On the other hand, Huffaker, who may have possessed a formidable intellect, appeared to the Wrights as lazy and dirty. He refused to help with the dishes. He didn't bother to wash. He wore the same white shirt for four weeks until it was offensively grubby. He helped himself to their tools without so much as a by-your-leave. He was careless with equipment, leaving instruments lying in the sand, and he began to use their precious camera as a stool. The antipathy was mutual.

To make matters worse, Huffaker was fond of sermonising. Like Wilbur and Orville, he was the son of a clergyman; unlike the brothers he delivered regular moral lectures on subjects which had the Wrights quietly fuming. But they bit their tongues and were coldly polite. In Victorian style they addressed one another formally as Mr Huffaker and Mr Wright. The rising tension between the brothers and this unwanted guest was not helped by the discomforts of life under canvas. Worst, without question, were the mosquitoes. They had arrived, Orville wrote dramatically to Katharine, 'in a mighty cloud, almost darkening the sun'. It was, he said, the beginning of the most miserable experience of his life.

> The agonies of typhoid fever . . . are as nothing in comparison. But there was no escape. The sand and grass and trees and hills and everything was fairly covered with them. They chewed us clear through our underwear and socks. Lumps began swelling up all over my body like hen's eggs. We attempted to escape by going to bed which we did a little after five o'clock. We put our cots out under the awnings and wrapped up in our blankets with only our noses protruding from the folds . . . Alas! Here nature's complicity

in the conspiracy against us became evident. The wind, which until now had been blowing over twenty miles an hour, dropped off entirely. Our blankets then became unbearable. The perspiration would roll off us in torrents . . . Misery! Misery![15]

They rigged nets, but the mosquitoes penetrated them. 'The tops of the canopies were covered with mosquitoes till there was hardly standing room for another one; the buzzing was like the buzzing of a mighty buzz saw.' They moved their cots away from camp, out on the sand. They lit fires but the smoke was more distressing than the insect hordes. 'In desperation we fled from them, rushing all about the sand for several hundred feet around, trying to find some place of safety. But it was of no use.'

After a week of wretchedness they had – despite having now successfully sunk a well with a pipe driven twelve feet into the sand – begun seriously to talk of abandoning the site. As well as mosquitoes the place was alive with aggressive sand fleas. Orville was to tell his biographer, Fred Kelly, that there were some nights so miserable that he decided that if he could survive until morning he would happily pack up and go home. But eventually a blessed wind sprang up. Magically the mosquitoes disappeared.

Meanwhile, the second of Chanute's apostles had pitched up. George Spratt was a very different character from Huffaker. The brothers liked him immediately. He was affable and unassuming with a lively sense of humour, had an impressive knowledge of aerodynamics, was inordinately willing to turn his hand to any chore in the camp, and his standards of personal hygiene matched their own. He was also brimming with biological know-how – he was a veritable textbook of information on the flora and bird life of the Outer Banks. And he constantly entertained them with endless stories and anecdotes.

Spratt and Wilbur clicked immediately. The bond that blossomed between them owed something to their shared histories of ill health, filial sacrifice and career frustration. Spratt had been following his father into medicine, but a rheumatic fever-damaged heart had forced him to give it up and commit his life to running the paternal farm. Both men had come to aeronautics from disappointment, lack of direction and lack of fulfilment – in both cases after spells of depression and acute self-doubt. The commonality of their backgrounds slowly led them to bare their souls to each other. Not only was Spratt a delightful companion, he turned out to be a hard-working, endlessly willing assistant, helping again and again in oppressive heat to lug the glider laboriously up the sandhill and launch it down the slope.

The flight trials began on 27 July. They were probably once more flown by Wilbur alone. On that first day, off the highest, at 100 foot, of the three great dunes, he made seventeen flights. The results were bitterly disappointing. On two of the glides the machine performed so dangerously that his colleagues on the ground thought he was going to go the way of Lilienthal.

The problem appeared to lie with the forward elevator. Wilbur, in cap, white shirt, tie and braces, stretched out prone on the lower wing, was launched into the air by his ground crew, which now sometimes included the faithful Bill Tate and his half-brother, Dan Tate. As they watched him float out over the long sand slope into the sea breeze they saw he was having difficulty controlling the pitch – the machine was making big undulating swoops which he couldn't fully correct. Although on some of the flights the glider was airborne for up to 20 seconds, the new wings weren't performing nearly as well as the smaller predecessors. The plane was exhibiting some frightening, unexplained tendencies.

The control problems had come with the very first attempt – the thing seemed determined to dive into the sand. It would lurch forward reluctantly for only a few feet before flopping back to earth. To counter this, Wilbur began inching his body rearwards to try and move the centre of gravity back to keep the nose up. He had to move so far he had difficulty reaching the elevator control lever. Furthermore, the elevator needed a huge amount of movement to respond at all – in fact, he estimated, four times that of the previous glider.

But on the ninth glide, after they had all laboured in the July heat to manhandle the machine through the soft sand back up the slope, there came what seemed for the onlookers like a triumphant moment. When they trotted Wilbur into the air, the glider, cruising just a few feet above the sand, flew for the first time on and on. It went over 300 feet before landing in a shower of sand. The cheering launch team bounded down the slope to congratulate Wilbur, but to their surprise he greeted them glumly, shaking his head in disappointment. He had had, he said, to apply full deflection to the elevator throughout the glide just to stay above the ground. The first machine had required only tiny movements. Something was radically wrong.

Someone suggested that they wrap it up for the day and go back to camp to discuss the problem, but Wilbur said no. There was only one way to learn how to make an aeroplane fly – in the air. He insisted on trying again immediately.

Once more they lugged the awkward contraption back up the hill. Once more they flung it into the air. Carefully hugging the slope, he proceeded to glide a promising 100 feet. But then something terrifying happened. The machine began to run amok: of its own volition it started to climb. As Wilbur's heart froze, he applied full down pressure on the elevator, desperately trying to level off and stay near the ground, but the glider was out of control. Amid shouts of alarm from below, he found that he couldn't arrest the ascent. Even with the elevator at the limit of its travel, the machine continued to rise until it was over 20 feet in the air. At the same time it rapidly began to lose forward speed.

As the glider approached the stall, Wilbur heard Spratt shouting to him to depress the elevator to bring the nose down, but he was already desperately doing that. It was having no effect. In a final effort to pitch the nose down he pulled his body as far forward as he could go, but the aircraft was now totally stalled. It had run out of lift. A modern aeroplane, with its elevator in the rear, could have dropped a wing and begun a spin into the ground. The Wrights' large front elevator prevented it from doing this. In this critical situation the device paid off. It allowed the glider to mush down safely in a flat descent, pancaking into the sand undamaged, Wilbur's protruding knees thankfully protected by the skids fitted beneath wing and forward elevator.

As he climbed out the others gathered around. None of them had any idea what was wrong. They still didn't know what a stall was.

They just knew that they had reached a new potentially dangerous aerodynamic frontier. 'This,' Orville wrote sombrely to Katharine, 'is precisely the fix Lilienthal got into when he was killed. His machine dropped head first to the ground and his neck was broken.'[16]

Despite the bad fright, Wilbur insisted on trying again – at least he knew he would not plunge to earth as the German had done. But on the next launch the same thing happened: the nose came up, the glider again climbed, ran out of speed and, blown back by the wind, began a tail slide which Wilbur was only just able to arrest, and dropped on to the sand.

In the tent that night they sat on their cots in the hurricane lamplight and discussed the impasse. The Wrights were temporarily out of their depth. Why was the machine rearing up and dangerously losing lift? None of them knew for sure – but Huffaker and Spratt offered a suggestion. They both believed that the sudden uncontrollable pitching was being caused by the phenomenon of the reversal of the lift pressure centre. As the glider gathered speed down the hill to around 20 miles an hour, its angle of attack to the windflow became progressively lower, bringing the centre of lift forward – thereby pitching the wing up. But, as Spratt had discovered from the experiments he had reported to Chanute, there came a point at the efficient flying angle of around 3 or 4 degrees, when the centre of the sustaining lift travelled back to the rear of the centre of gravity, thus pivoting the wing down into a nosedive. Huffaker agreed with Spratt that this was probably the explanation.

Next day the Wrights decided to test the theory. They removed the top wing and flew it in winds of different strength as a kite. What they observed seemed to confirm the theory. In light winds the front of the wing rose up, indicating that the centre of lifting pressure was ahead of the centre of gravity. In stronger winds the wing flew at a much lower angle to the breeze: it nosed down, demonstrating that the pressure centre had moved behind the centre of gravity, sucking the rear of the wing up. The 1900 machine – built with thinner-cambered 1:23 ratio wings – had not behaved like this, but it hadn't produced very much lift either. On the other hand, Lilienthal's fatal stall had resulted from the thicker

1:12 camber they had copied into the new machine. They decided immediately to reshape both wings to restore the thinner camber. It was fairly simply done because they had astutely designed the wings to enable quick camber changes on location. The slimmer remodelled wings finished up with a camber of around 1:19. And to reduce the drag, which they had found was greater than the previous model's, they reshaped the wings' leading edges, making them rounder and smoother.

The invisible aerodynamic influences that kept a wing in stable flight were proving more complex – and potentially dangerous – than the Wrights had imagined. It was clear that the opposing forces of lift and gravity were permanently at war with one another. There seemed, Wilbur declared, 'to be an almost boundless incompatibility of temper which prevents their remaining peaceably together for a single instant, so that the operator who . . . acts as peacemaker, often suffers injury to himself while attempting to bring them together.'[17]

While they were busy at their hangar workbench, reshaping the wing in search of a permanent truce between these warring forces, Huffaker had been preparing his own machine for a test glide. It was destined, regrettably, never to take to the air. As there wasn't space for it in the shed it had to sit outside exposed to the weather. A heavy rainstorm now dealt an ignominious end to its ill-conceived life. The sodden paper tubes collapsed; the machine crumpled into a pathetic heap of wreckage. In later years the resentful Huffaker was to complain that the Wrights had falsely promised him hangar space. It was not so. The brothers' 1901 glider filled almost the entire interior of the hut. Nonetheless, the demise of the Chanute-designed paper glider, which the Wrights privately ridiculed, did not help the already strained relationship.

Chanute arrived in the sticky heat of early August by horse and cart from the ferry wharf at Nags Head. He was dismayed to be confronted by the bedraggled remains of the glider that had been the sole purpose of Huffaker's presence at Kill Devil. Despite having invested $1000 in the disastrous project, aviation's mastermind seems to have accepted its fate with equanimity. As he unpacked his unsuitable city clothing and set up his cot in the now crowded tent, he cannot have failed to sense the cool atmosphere that lay between

Wilbur and his protégé. The antagonisms were only subdued by the conventional civilities and innate politenesses that the bishop had inculcated in his sons. A famous photograph shows Chanute, with his distinguishing small, white, pointed beard, winged collar, bow tie and Homburg, sitting with Orville and Huffaker on a camp stretcher under the awning of the shed. Wilbur stands in front of them. Of all the images that captured the human face of the aeroplane's development, this one recorded some of its most colourful folk heroes at what was to become flying's most famous of all locations.

Chanute was impatient to see the Wrights' aeroplane in action, so up the big hill they humped it and Wilbur climbed aboard again. To his immense relief the thinner cambered wings appeared to have solved the pitch problem. The machine now responded sensitively to the elevator control, enabling him to hiss along, safely close to the sand slope, and fly, again, impressive distances of over 300 feet. Spratt was especially cheered by the remedy. He believed that the alarming pressure centre reversal he had suggested was an original discovery of his. The Wrights were certainly grateful for the diagnosis.

Filled with the new hope of safe control in the air, they were now emboldened to risk some turns. Until now, Wilbur had flown with the banking warp system tied off. They now reconnected it. But, to make it easier to coordinate the pitch and bank controls simultaneously, they replaced the foot-operated bar with a laterally sliding cradle in which the pilot lay. He operated it simply by moving his hips to left or right in the direction he wanted to turn. Proud of this ingenious improvement, Wilbur set out to test it. The machine was borne up the long hill on the shoulders of five men: Wilbur, Orville, Huffaker, Spratt and Bill Tate. The lonely, portly figure of the puffing Chanute followed some distance behind. For the latter the event held promise of being aeronautically historic – the first ever piloted turn made without body-swinging.

Launched down the slope, Wilbur began with a gentle turn to the left, cautiously shifting his hips in that direction. The turn began promisingly. The warping cables twisted the right wing's trailing edge down and the left one up. With the increased lift on that side the right wing rose and the glider began to bank to the left, pivoting about the lower left wing. But suddenly something happened. Quite abruptly the machine reversed direction: it began to turn to the *right*.

Wilbur was flabbergasted. Once again the glider had become uncontrollable. Startled by a 'peculiar feeling of instability', he hurriedly landed. When he tried again the same thing happened. Their masterly invention, wing warping (forerunner of the modern aileron), was suddenly failing to do what up to now it had done so well. The brothers were bewildered and shattered – all their dreams were collapsing around them. Chanute was mystified. So were Huffaker and Spratt. And when Wilbur insisted on pressing on, trying out more gliding turns, he finally became so confused by the puzzling responses of the controls that he allowed the left wingtip to drop as he skimmed close to the ground. It hit the sand and the machine slewed, skidding and bouncing to a stop. Not being strapped to the wing, he was thrown forward into the elevator, collecting a black eye, bruised nose and cut face. He had become the first casualty of their experiments. Undaunted, he insisted on making more flights, but he now flew nervously, warily attempting very cautious turns for fear of skidding out of control in the wrong direction.

Chanute conscientiously logged all the distances and flight times in his diary with fantastic precision – '4.3 sec . . . 110 ft; 5.1 sec . . . 93 ft; 12.5 sec . . . 366 ft' and so on. The flights were watched with amazement by the lifesavers at the nearby Kill Devil station. Not all of them understood why grown men in suits and waistcoats were engaged in this repetitive, apparently pointless activity. Adam Etheridge's wife, Lillie, commented: 'They looked just like little children playing, they did.'[18] On days when they didn't fly, the brothers would amaze the lifeboat men as they wandered the Atlantic Ocean beach, studying the soaring manoeuvres of marine birds. 'They seemed,' said John Daniels, 'to be interested in gannets . . . they would imitate their movements with their arms and hands. They could imitate every movement of the wings of those gannets; we thought they were crazy.'[19]

Despite their scepticism, the Bankers were helpfulness itself to these strange visitors. They came in their spare time to watch and help with glider humping and launching, constantly astonished at the patience and politeness they received. Always they were welcomed, sometimes invited to stay for a meal. Orville, who continued to do all the cooking, kept eggs in quantities that staggered them. Years later Bankers still spoke of Orville's especially flavoursome scrambled eggs.

By the middle of August, when more bad weather arrived, it was apparent that the perplexing turning problem wasn't going to be solved that summer. They were flying a potentially lethal machine which, despite its remoulded wings, was still delivering a dismal amount of lift and, according to their grocers' scales, attached during kiting, far too much inhibiting drag. As the rain came pelting back to further dampen their spirits, they decided it was time to pack it in and return to Dayton. One by one their guests departed – first Chanute, then Spratt and finally, to their great relief, the irritating Huffaker. After he had gone, Wilbur was mortified to discover that the Tennessean had helped himself to one of his blankets.

Leaving the glider in its lonely shed in the Kill Devil sand wastes, Wilbur and Orville packed up the big tent and started for home on 20 August. They were convinced that the unexpected complexities of controlled flight had beaten them. 'We doubted that we would ever resume our experiments,' Wilbur later wrote:

> Although we had broken the record for distance in gliding, and although Mr Chanute assured us that our results were better than had ever before been attained, yet when we looked at the time and money which we had expended and considered the progress made and the distance yet to go, we considered our experiments a failure. At that time I made the prediction that men would sometime fly, but that it would not be within our lifetime.[20]

On the long train journey across the Virginias back to Dayton, they were so dejected they hardly spoke. They were nagged by the suspicion that something, inconceivable as it seemed, was radically wrong with Lilienthal's sacred wing lift performance figures, around which they were designing their machines. How to set about proving this was something they didn't for the moment want to think about. Ill with an appalling cold he had caught at Kill Devil, a dispirited Wilbur is said to have uttered to Orville that, 'Not within a thousand years would man ever fly.'[21]

10

A Wing of Perfect Shape

(1901)

So depressed were the brothers by the Kill Devil trials they'd forgotten to telegraph Katharine that they were on their way home. 'The boys walked in unexpectedly on Thursday morning,' she reported to Milton, who was in Indiana at a church conference. She added: they 'haven't had much to say about flying. They can only talk about how disagreeable Huffaker was . . . Will is sick too and with a cold or he would have written to you before this.'[1]

Katharine had been on her own in Dayton, teaching at Steele High School, coordinating family affairs, looking after the empty house and keeping a vigilant eye on the cycle shop. She had taken a rapid dislike to the new mechanic, Charlie Taylor. Taylor had long been a good friend of the brothers, who had sometimes subcontracted cycle repair work to him. He had left school at the age of twelve and his considerable skills were self-taught. Now married with children, he was someone whom Wilbur and Orville were happy, for $18 a week, to trust with the business in their absence. To Katharine, he belonged on the wrong side of the class divide. An uncomplicated, rough and ready working man of forthright and sometimes crude opinion, he was not prepared to defer to the bosses' sister, who resented his familiarity. She was offended, too, that Taylor filled the workshop with the reek of the cigars he perpetually smoked. Before long Katharine had begun to avoid the shop. On the rare occasions she forced herself to go, the two scarcely spoke. 'I simply can't stand Charles Taylor,' she was to tell Wilbur and Orville. But the brothers were fond of the unpolished mechanic. There was no way he would be sacrificed on the whim of their sister.

In the darkroom they had created in the Hawthorn Street garden shed they processed the Kill Devil photographs. As the images began to take shape on the wet glass negatives, their spirits revived. They had a superb collection of historic pictures – the first ever to show a piloted machine in free flight, flown with its own on-board controls. Wilbur sent some to Chanute with a lengthy technical report. It brimmed, incomprehensibly to the layman, with the mathematics of the flight tests: 'The drift of a plane at this angle is about 1/7 of the lift, making the drift 240÷7 = 34 lbs, which added to the head resistance 10.4 lbs makes a total of 44.4 lbs against an observed total of 240÷6 = 40 lbs, or counting drifts alone, 34 lbs against 29.6 lbs which is the measure of the superiority in economy of power in the curve used over a flat surface under the conditions named.'[2] And so it went on for pages in the abstruse language of the new technology in which they began earnestly to correspond.

Cracking the secret codes of flight was now critically reduced to terms such as these: to the bewildering relationship between the wing area, the resistance of the structure and its occupant, the all-up weight, the velocity (headwind plus machine's forward speed), the wing's angle of attack, the geometry of its camber – and even the position of the thickest part of the camber. Nor was this all. The chain of variables was bound together by some other vital formulae. There was the one they had innocently taken from Lilienthal's published tables purporting to show the amount of lift obtained by a wing of a given size presented to the airflow at various angles and air speeds. But to complicate things further, built into the German's figures was yet another crucial value – one that had not been questioned for around 150 years. It was a multiplier – a number that determined the relationship between velocity and lift pressure in the specific medium of the air, as distinct from water or other fluids of different densities. It was the one given to the scientific world by

John Smeaton back in the 1750s and Lilienthal, Chanute and the Wrights had trustingly accepted it as immutable fact.

Now, in correspondence with Chanute, Wilbur began to question the time-honoured, interlocked figures that underpinned the technology of flight – as understood at that time. Chanute was so impressed by Wilbur's formidable intellect, his swift grasp of aerodynamics and his astonishingly scientific approach that he tried to persuade him to share his newfound knowledge with a wider audience. He invited him to come to Chicago and lecture a distinguished group of his professional engineering colleagues.

Wilbur was at first appalled at the suggestion. He felt he was too newly arrived on the scene; their research still faced too many unsolved problems. Katharine persuaded him to change his mind. 'Will was about to refuse,' she wrote to tell Milton, 'but I nagged him into going. He will get acquainted with some scientific men and it may do him a lot of good. We don't hear anything but flying machine and engine from morning till night. I'll be glad when school begins so I can escape.'[3]

Wilbur's audience for the mid-September speech were to be members of the Western Society of Engineers. Chanute asked him to send photographs and diagrams to be prepared as lantern slides and asked if he had any objections to members' wives being present. Wilbur, who had imagined an informal talk to a small audience, grew nervous. 'I must caution you,' he anxiously wrote to Chanute, 'not to make my address a prominent feature of the programme as you will understand that I make no pretence of being a public speaker . . . As to the presence of ladies, it is not my province to dictate, moreover I will already be as badly scared as it is possible for man to be, so that the presence of ladies will make little difference to me, provided I am not expected to appear in full dress &c.'[4]

Although it was not to be a white tie affair, getting himself kitted out even in a business suit was to present some difficulty. While Orville made a fetish of dressing immaculately, Katharine had frequently to remind Wilbur that his trousers had become baggy at the knees – whereupon he would sheepishly heat up the flat iron and press them. But for the Chicago speech his wardrobe had nothing of adequate elegance to satisfy his sister. He finished up borrowing heavily from Orville. 'We had a picnic getting Will off to Chicago,' Katharine told Milton. 'Orv offered all his clothes so off went "Ullam" arrayed in Orv's shirt, collars, cuffs, cuff-links and overcoat. We discovered that to some extent "clothes do maketh the man" for you never saw Will look so swell.'[5] Of the imminent speech Katharine told Milton: 'We asked him whether it was to be witty or scientific and he said he thought it would be pathetic before he got through with it.'[6]

The address was a resounding success. The text was published internationally, thrusting the unknown Wilbur into the front ranks of aviation science. In Chicago he was entertained by Chanute at his home on the city's fashionable new north side. His host took him up into his study. The holy of holies, to Wilbur's surprise, was a disorganised sea of papers with, hanging from its ceiling, a small forest of model flying machines 'so thick that you can't see any ceiling at all'.

Wilbur's address – prosaically entitled 'Some Aeronautical Experiments' – which rolled forth such statements as 'the drift proper would have been to the lift (108 lbs) as the sine of 13 degrees is to the cosine of 13 degrees', may have passed over the heads of some of the civil engineers better versed in terrestrial matters, but in bringing the world up to date, technically, with the state of the flying art the Wrights had developed, it was masterful. It took the science far beyond the published work of Chanute, Lilienthal and Langley. Chanute, in introducing him, had misguidedly declared that 'the great obstacle in the way of manned flight remained a light enough motor'. But Wilbur had dared to disagree with the revered engineer. He told his learned audience that a suitable power plant would quickly arrive when aviation was ready for it. It was the least of the unsolved problems. Of much more concern were the sacred figures that lay at the heart of the great Lilienthal's tables. Boldly for one so new to aeronautics, Wilbur decided to tread where no experimenter had hitherto dared to go. He publicly questioned the validity of the sacrosanct data. It was like challenging the equation of Einstein's $E=mc^2$ relativity theory.

Although Chanute was staunchly to defend the German's figures to the last, Wilbur, his confidence boosted by the acclaim his speech had brought, told him in Chicago that he and Orville intended to test them scientifically. They planned a complete recheck of the long accepted assumptions they suspected of falsely supporting the mathematics of lift – the time-honoured Smeaton's as well as Lilienthal's, which compounded the problem by embodying the former's. They believed that all the figures might be flawed.

Back in Dayton the brothers determined to find out. They built a simple test device from a bicycle wheel, which they mounted on a rig so that it could revolve like a horizontal windmill. Set apart on the wheel's rim they attached vertically two small rectangles of metal – one flat-on to the wind, the other cambered in the shape of a wing. According to Lilienthal's tables, if the mini-wing was set at an angle of 5 degrees to an airstream flowing simultaneously over both plates, they would exactly balance each other – the wheel would remain stationary when exposed to a strong wind. But in the light winds of Dayton, the device had refused to work properly. So they mounted the horizontal rim on the front of a bicycle. Pedalling furiously up and down the street they got it to work. The result immediately confirmed their suspicions. Far from balancing the flat vane at 5 degrees the cambered surface had to be angled up to nearly 18 degrees – more than three times the value in the Lilienthal tables.

Sticklers for accuracy, the Wrights wanted to be sure that this shattering finding was correct. To double-check it Orville built a crude wind tunnel. He used an old starch box which he fitted with a glass observation window on top. Air was driven through it by a fan powered by a single-cylinder internal combustion engine fuelled by the shop's natural gas lighting supply. Once more they used a miniature cambered wing section set at an angle to the airstream. Now on a rod, it was again balanced against an opposing flat plate – mounted on opposite sides of a sort of weathervane. The deflections were measured on scraps of wallpaper laid on the bottom of the box. Again the result did not show anything like the amount of lift promised by the Lilienthal tables.

They began to wonder how it was that the German himself had managed to glide so apparently successfully. No one would now ever know if his spectacular swoopings off the German hillsides actually correlated with the performance predicted by his design data. They suspected that the whirling arm device with which they at first believed he had measured the lift on wing surfaces had produced results distorted by the centrifugal force and swirling air. They didn't know if the inaccuracy lay with the German aviator's calculations, or with the standard figure for air pressure he had mathematically locked into his formula from the long trusted Smeaton value. The brothers decided to do more sophisticated tests.

In October 1901 they built a bigger wind tunnel. It was a rectangular wooden box, 6 feet long and 16 inches square, again with a glass window on top. Inside they set up a device that is today regarded as one of their greatest strokes of inventive brilliance. It was a deceptively crude and spindly-looking balance made from bicycle spokes and old hacksaw blades. Suspended on this flimsy structure they once more hung a flat plate – now split into four fingers – and opposing it, via delicate metal links, a small cambered wing section. When the fan began pumping a 30-mile-an-hour airflow through the box, it played equally on the flat vanes and the small wing section. Their respective deflections were cleverly measured by pointers. The pressure on the flat plates served as a datum against which the different lifting capacities of various wing shapes could be evaluated.

Additionally they built a separate balance to measure the drag that impeded the force of lift. The pointer of this second inventive gadget showed a wing's all important ratio of drag-to-lift. This latter yardstick of a lifting surface's effectiveness George Spratt had first suggested to them at Kill Devil. He had attempted to do it himself, he said, back in Pennsylvania, but had failed. The brothers were more successful, and it was another of the valuable technical contributions they would receive from Spratt.

With these inventive, deceptively crude instruments the Wrights suddenly had the means to check the efficiency of wings of every description. With the help of Orville's facility with geometry and trigonometry, in the space of just a few weeks in the autumn and early winter of late 1901 they began skilfully to do something that no one had ever managed to achieve – to define mathematically an efficient man-made wing that would mimic the birds and support a flying machine.

Wilbur faithfully kept Milton in touch with what they were doing. 'We have been experimenting somewhat with an apparatus for measuring the pressure of air on variously curved surfaces at different angles, and have decided to prepare a table which we are certain will be much more accurate than that of Lilienthal.'[7]

It wasn't long before they discovered that the celebrated Lilienthal data that had been shaping their sluggish gliders' wings did indeed appear to be inaccurate. So, too, was the even holier lift figure of Smeaton's that had been misleading experimenters since the mid-eighteenth century. They dumped, forthwith, the erroneous data of both. Starting with a clean slate they began to create their own brand new tables of lift and drag.

But were Lilienthal's celebrated figures really that far out? The Wrights had been reluctant to rubbish the data of one so eminent, specially when they learnt that the German's tables had not, after all, been derived from a distorting whirling arm but had been obtained with wing sections exposed, as their own had been, to a stream of air. Modern aerodynamicists have actually established that the Wrights' and Lilienthal's data were in fact surprisingly similar. Quite simply, what explained the problem was the wrong assumption the Wrights initially made that the German's figures applied universally to cambered wings of all shapes and sizes. The truth was they worked only for the circular arc Lilienthal had used – not for the thinner one, cambered near the leading edge, that had so disappointed Wilbur and Orville. Nor did his figures apply to wings of every aspect ratio – the ratio of length to breadth, which could vary from long and narrow to short and stubby or somewhere in between.

As the gas combustion engine blasting air through the tunnel in the back room of the cycle shop thundered hour after hour, it shook the dead at Fetters and Shank, the undertakers' next door. It was also helping to beget something that, since the days of Leonardo da Vinci, had eluded researchers – the subtle anatomy of the ideal aeroplane wing that the world now takes for granted. Effectively, its modern shape was born in that noisy back room at 1127 West Third Street.

Wilbur and Orville tested more than two hundred different wing surfaces. They wanted one that generated the smallest drag for the most lift – still the ideal of designers to this day. Methodically noting the figures in dusty notebooks, they tried little square-shaped wings, rectangular ones, ellipses, semi-circular, and some with tips that varied from square to pointed. They cut them out of thin sheet metal with tinsnips and moulded their curvatures with hammer and file, adding beads of solder and mounds of wax. They tested them inclined at angles of attack from zero to 45 degrees. They experimented with pairs of wings mounted in tandem, with biplanes and triplanes with the surfaces set at different distances apart. They checked out aspect ratios. They tried wings of varying camber with the deepest point at different positions. They tested sharp and blunt leading edges. Suspecting that their fabric wing coverings might be too porous and have been sucking away the precious lift they needed, they conducted further experiments. They tried more tightly woven muslin and varnished the surface. But these refinements, they found, made no difference to the lift.

The results of their wind tunnel tests – added to the data they had obtained with their full-size gliders at Kill Devil – were carefully recorded; their observation methods were meticulous; nothing short of perfection would satisfy them. Their faithfully drawn sketches of the profiles of the dozens of wing shapes they methodically worked through, today preserved in their historic notebooks in the Library of Congress in Washington, bring modern aerodynamicists to marvel at the sheer prescience of it all. The angle to the airstream at which the first flicker of lift could be detected they established within one quarter of a single degree.

By December 1901 they had systematically amassed the largest body of information anyone had ever collected on the aerodynamic properties of almost every conceivable permutation of wing form. It was a monumental breakthrough. They had effectively rewritten the textbook of flight. They had freed themselves at last from the flawed data that had bedevilled the efforts of their predecessors.

In the 1980s, aviation scientists at the National Air and Space Museum in Washington accurately re-created the Wright Brothers' wind tunnel and its imaginative balancing devices and reran some of the experiments. More than eighty years later the historic apparatus was still yielding surprisingly accurate data. Indeed the lift value the Wrights eventually substituted for the much maligned Smeaton figure has been confirmed by modern aerodynamicists to be accurate within a few per cent. One of the museum's curators and biographer of the brothers' aeronautical achievements, Peter Jakab, said: 'The lift balance is among the most brilliant examples of how the Wrights merged their many talents to produce a useful resolution to a problem. Their ability to think through a problem clearly, their technical skill, their engineering sense, and their consistent focus on what specifically was required to proceed with the overall project came together in a particularly impressive and effective way. Over and over again these attributes enabled the Wrights to find solutions to daunting challenges.'[8]

One of the Wrights' unique qualities, said Peter Jakab, was their ability to think visually. The forces they were trying to measure were invisible, but by the use of graphic imagery they were able, with rare skill, to visualise the direction and interplay of those unseen forces.

As the aerodynamic truths – or what they hoped were now truths – poured into their notebooks, Wilbur shared the revelations in a stream of letters to Chanute. 'It is perfectly marvellous to me how quickly you get results with your testing machine,' Chanute wrote. 'You are evidently better equipped to test the endless variety of curved surfaces than anybody has ever been.'[9] The long letters, stuffed with tables and diagrams, provide historians with a unique record of the process of perfecting the flying machine. The letters became increasingly technical as aerodynamic niceties flew back and forth between Dayton and Chicago. The doyen of aviation's experimenters was staggered by the speed and brilliance of the research of these self-taught men. He was generous with his praise. 'If your method and machine are reliable you have done a great work, and have advanced knowledge greatly. Your charts carry conviction to my mind and your descriptions and comments are clear.'[10]

So enthusiastic was Chanute that he offered to tackle some of the weeks of mathematical drudgery – that a computer would have done in a trice today – to produce the stack of reference tables for the scores of wing shapes their wind tunnel data had analysed. When Wilbur gratefully accepted, the dedicated Chanute took sheaves of the work with him on a beach holiday to California where he had taken his ailing wife for the winter.

Freed now from the Lilienthal formula, the brothers began to design what they hoped might at last be an aerodynamically perfect aeroplane. Not quite ready to experiment with the complications of a powered machine, they cautiously decided to build just one more glider.

Scientifically promising as their project was, it was not producing a cent of income. Their livelihood, and funding of the experiments, still depended on the cycle business, but for months now, ever since their return from the Outer Banks, they had scarcely touched a bicycle; they had left it all to Charlie Taylor. Now, as Christmas 1901 approached, they knew that if they didn't interrupt their aeronautical dabbling and get back to assembling the next season's cycles, they would soon run out of money.

When Chanute learnt that their seminal aerodynamic research had ceased he was shocked. 'I very much regret in the interest of science that you have reached a stopping place. If however some rich man should give you $10,000 a year to go on, to connect his name with progress, would you do so? I happen to know Carnegie. Would you like for me to write to him?'[11]

The legendary Andrew Carnegie, an immensely wealthy Scottish-born American industrialist, was well known for his generous philanthropy. He believed a rich man should distribute his wealth for the benefit of society. He wouldn't have needed much persuading to attach his beneficence to the birth of the aeroplane, but the Wrights didn't want anyone else's money – or the strings that would accompany it. As a matter of principle they insisted on remaining financially independent. They had no debts, each had several thousand dollars in the bank, a steady income from a business. They saw no reason to encumber the intellectual assets they were creating.

Wilbur wrote quickly to decline. 'Nothing,' he said, 'would give me greater pleasure than to devote my entire time to scientific investigations; and a salary of ten or twenty thousand a year would be no insuperable objection, but I think it possible that Andrew is too hardheaded a Scotchman to become interested in such a visionary pursuit as flying.'[12]

The Wrights knew that, despite their late arrival in aviation, their dogged perfectionist methods had already taken them into the forefront of discovery. No one before them had come anywhere near understanding the factors that made for a flight-efficient wing – or indeed a control system. As Orville was later to write: 'I believe we possessed more data on cambered surfaces, a hundred times over, than all of our predecessors put together.'[13] From initial modest hopes – born of little more than simple curiosity – of making perhaps a small contribution, they were for the first time daring to see themselves, just possibly, as the architects of mechanical flight.

They were also getting to be known in the international aviation community. Chanute had seen to that: he'd distributed the text of Wilbur's Chicago address far and wide. In England, France and Germany the work of the Dayton bicycle-makers was being talked about. Rival experimenters were starting to write to them, pleading for information. They were having to consider protecting their discoveries – something that was becoming increasingly urgent as the enthusiastic Chanute seemed determined that the priceless knowledge pouring out of the cycle shop should be shared with the world.

Chanute had a fresh proposition: that the brothers enter an aeronautical exhibition being planned in St Louis for 1903. It was likely to be dominated by balloons, but large prizes were to be offered for the best demonstrations of 'aerial apparatus'. Chanute had in mind a Wright powered aeroplane. The brothers were not immediately interested, doubting one could be produced in time. Nor did the cool-headed and thrifty Wilbur see it as a profitable investment. 'I have little of the gambling instinct . . .' he told Chanute. 'Mathematically it would be foolish to spend two or three thousand dollars competing for a hundred thousand dollar prize if the chance of winning be only <u>one</u> in a hundred.'[14]

Chanute didn't give up. He tried to pressure Wilbur into writing an article publicly sharing the technical fruits of the wind tunnel tests.

Yet again Wilbur hesitated. He feared their data would be seized by a competitor to build a machine that triumphed in the competition. 'It would,' he said, 'be hardly advisable to make public information which might assist others to carry off the prize from us.'[15]

Increasingly the brothers were aware that in the masses of tables, utterly incomprehensible to most people, they were now guarding formulae of incomparable commercial value. Chanute had several times urged them to patent the crucial principles; but proving the figures in the air was for the moment their higher priority.

Christmas 1901 was a subdued occasion at Hawthorn Street. Milton had only just returned from his incessant travels and wasn't very well. Katharine, Wilbur and Orville spent the day with their father. Lorin and Netta held their own festivities and Reuchlin and Lulu, still living far away, were in the throes of a major change in their lives.

Reuchlin, who had suffered much ill health, had left his clerical job in Kansas City. They had bought a dairy farm at Tonganoxie, about twenty miles away, in the hope that the outdoor life would benefit him. 'Reuch' still remained isolated on the edge of the family circle and seemed to prefer to remain there. Eternally criticised by Lulu for his lack of drive and success in life, he appears by now to have developed a permanent sense of inferiority. A few months earlier he had handled for Milton the sale of his Iowa land. When the deal had been completed he had begun to agonise that he had overpaid the agent's commission by $100 – thereby reducing the sum divided among the four brothers. Guiltily he had written to Milton offering to pay the others the difference from his own share. 'I don't want them to feel that their interests have been injured by anything I did.'[16]

Wilbur replied:

> Some matters connected with the sale seem to have worried you and led you to fear that we felt disposed to blame you for something. We have certainly had no such feeling. We saw . . . that if foresight had been equal to hindsight we might have realised a little more from the sale, perhaps, but as we felt that any of us would have made the same errors, we had no disposition to blame you.[17]

On New Year's day 1902 Milton entered in his diary his customary gratitude to God for sparing him yet another year: 'Seventy-three years of Divine blessings to me.' But his peace of mind was about to be threatened again. The Keiter affair was beginning to boil.

In November the final audit of the church's publishing house accounts had confirmed that at least $1400 was missing. And now, within a few weeks of the New Year, Milton learnt of a second financial irregularity involving the same woman in Maryland. This time she had been persuaded by Keiter to lend the church $1000 for a spurious purpose – but the money had never been deposited in the church's accounts. And with a further bequest, from a woman in Indiana, the value of her cheque had been mysteriously raised from $1000 to $3000, Keiter apparently pocketing the difference. Despite the abundant evidence, the church's publishing board, fearing the devastating effect on fund-raising, shrank from prosecuting. Bishop Wright was so disgusted he set out to collect his own cast-iron evidence. Once more he called upon Wilbur.

Wilbur needed little urging to join this latest moral crusade. He didn't hesitate to give it a higher priority than the cycle business or the pursuit of the dream of flight. He took the train to Brethren headquarters, now in Huntington, Indiana. Once more he spent days sifting through the publishing house books for his father. Again he found evidence of flagrant embezzlement.

'The question of whether officials shall rob the church, and trustees deceive the church for fear of injuring collections, must be settled now for all time,' he declared trenchantly in a letter to Milton:

> To cheat the people by lying reports is more dishonest than Keiter's stealing . . . The quicker the matter can be brought to a focus the better it will be . . . My chief regret is that the strain and worry which you have borne for fifteen years past shows no sign of being removed. I had hoped that you could spend your remaining years in peace. It would seem however that the fight only increases in intensity.[18]

And now Milton learnt of a fresh enormity committed by his clerical colleagues. To avoid further scandal, Bishop Barnaby had quietly repaid the Maryland woman from church funds. Convinced that a Brethren mafia was at work, Milton began to pour out embittered tracts which Wilbur helped him write and post by the thousand. The pamphlets vehemently attacked Barnaby and his pro-Keiter colleagues with accusations that threw concern for libel to the winds. Within the highest ranks of the church the bishop and his son saw the creeping spectre of Freemasonry at large again.

Nonetheless, Keiter did find himself back in the dock – facing a jury in the Huntington court in April 1902, charged with forging the bequest note. He emerged as a Machiavellian figure prepared to go to extraordinary lengths to cover his tracks. Yet, despite the overwhelming evidence, he was acquitted on abstruse legal technicalities after a four-day hearing. Keiter now turned on his accuser with a vengeance. Incensed by the stream of damaging tracts pouring from Milton and Wilbur into Radical Brethren homes, he launched, under the provisions of the church's law, formal disciplinary charges against its stormy petrel and most senior bishop. Wright was charged with libel, insubordination and violation of the Brethren precept that forbade going to law against a fellow Christian.

The formal trial, to be held at the Brethren college in Huntington, was set for 7 August. The prosecutor, to Milton's astonishment, was to be Millard Keiter himself.

The defendant's comforter, adviser and unofficial attorney, his pamphleteer and often his spokesman, would be Wilbur Wright.

11

Tumult in the Church (1902)

Milton's trial at the hands of his fellow churchmen deeply affected the entire Wright family. The rank injustice of it all hung like a black cloud over Hawthorn Street through the spring and summer of 1902 and began to jeopardise the test flights of the new machine Wilbur and Orville were planning. At the cycle shop they had magically converted the wind tunnel figures into scientifically the most accurately devised shape the world had yet seen. But the project was constantly interrupted.

Four times Wilbur dropped work on the new glider and hurried across country to Huntington to help Milton prepare for his martyrdom. He bolstered his father's bruised morale and polished his case against the cluster of allegations now flung at him. In May he confided to Chanute that 'attending to some matters for my father' had 'occupied much of my time and attention recently'.[1] Wilbur had been ghosting a string of bluntly worded tracts – some of them typed by Orville – for the Brethren faithful throughout the Midwest. Milton increasingly relied upon Wilbur. More than any of the Wright children his rigidly moral character had come to reflect Milton's own. When it came to good versus evil, Milton's battles were automatically Wilbur's battles. He had seen the evidence of Keiter's misappropriations with his own eyes in the church's books.

He knew where his duty lay. Even to the point of postponing the new Kill Devil trials, he was prepared to pour his intellectual and emotional energies into challenging the scandalous cover-up perpetrated by frightened men within the church. If ever Wilbur had needed evidence of his father's insistent thesis that men were innately savage creatures never to be trusted, it was being revealed in all its disillusioning truth. The sordid events in the church were to shape his attitude toward his fellow beings for ever.

Katharine, at the centre of the family, worried about the effect of it all on her father's health. As Milton continued to journey from parish to parish, railing against his accusers, she sent him a stream of affectionately supportive letters, entreating him not to yield to his colleagues' attempts to silence him. 'Don't let them bluff you out with their rascality,' she urged. 'It will give them too much satisfaction to see you giving up. The boys will be so disappointed too.'[2] She pleaded with him: 'Be sure to be careful of yourself, in every way. Are you getting the right kind of things to eat?' She begged him to get plenty of sleep, 'not to spend your strength on unnecessary travel'. And to replace his worn clothes – 'Really, Pop, you ought to have a better looking overcoat.'

She also kept up a flow of news from Dayton; about the students she was teaching at Steele High – 'The pupils who sit in my room are not so nice as they were last year, I think. I had five or six notoriously bad boys assigned to my room. I was ready for them and nipped their smartness in the bud.'[3] And she kept him in constant touch with the aeronautical developments that pervaded the home. 'The boys have finished their tables – of the action of the wind on various surfaces.'[4] And as the new glider began to grow she described the cottage industry it had brought to Hawthorn Street, apparently infiltrating every room. 'The flying machine is in process of making now. Will spins the sewing machine around by the hour while Orv squats around marking the places to sew. There is no place in the house to live . . .'[5]

Wilbur's spinning was interrupted by Milton's formal trial. The ordeal began in the first week of August at the Radical Brethren's central college in Huntington. Wilbur travelled ahead to marshal the damning evidence against Keiter he was convinced would exonerate his father.

The hearing was conducted by bearded men in dark grey suits amid solemn ritual as if it were a court of law. From the outset the odds were stacked heavily against the accused bishop, whose defence was not helped by a sleepless night from a bout of cholera. Milton's colleague, Bishop Barnaby, the principal instigator of the cover-up, was unfortunately presiding. Keiter himself was, quite incredibly, allowed to appear as the chief prosecutor, charging Bishop Wright, quaintly, with 'agitating controversy'. Of this Milton was openly and defiantly guilty. Milton, for his part, with two fellow ministers had circulated a report demanding that the elders covering up Keiter's 'crookedness' confess their wrongdoing or cease to be paid by the church. In this polarised atmosphere of great personal bitterness the trial proceedings rapidly descended into uproar and had to be abandoned. But Keiter had not finished with Milton. He knew that the bishop's and Wilbur's aggressive pamphleteering, questioning the integrity of some of the church's most respected senior figures, had upset many. Wright was now a vulnerable and isolated figure. Keiter took the case to another church forum – this time in the heart of Milton's own kingdom – to the White River district where he was the presiding bishop. The second trial was scheduled for 28 August.

Milton's troubles were now clashing head-on with Wilbur and Orville's summer flight plans at Kill Devil. Wilbur was increasingly torn. A week before the White River inquisition was due to start in Huntington, Katharine wrote to tell Milton how it was affecting her brothers – and offering her father a refuge on the Outer Banks:

> They are talking of going next Monday – though sometimes Will thinks he would like to stay and see what happens at Huntington next week. They really ought to get away for a while. Will is thin and nervous and so is Orv. They will be all right when they get down in the sand where the salt breezes blow etc. They insist that, if you aren't well enough to stay out on your trip you must come down with them. They think that life at Kitty Hawk cures all ills, you know.[6]

In the event, Kitty Hawk claimed them. When Milton declared the latest trial unlawful and decided to boycott it, there was no longer a need for Wilbur to stand by his father in the Brethren dock. On 25 August, leaving Charlie Taylor to run the shop, the brothers shipped the new glider to Elizabeth City and boarded the train.

The latest glider was a major advance on the 1901 machine. It sprang from the host of tiny winglets whose complex subtleties they had measured in the wind tunnel. Based on the characteristics of three that had demonstrated the best ratios of lift over drag, the biplane's wings were the biggest and most powerfully lifting yet. They had increased the span by 10 feet to 32 feet and had made them, at only 5 feet across, a lot slimmer and more graceful with a much higher aspect ratio – now 6:1 compared with the previous 3:1. They had also chosen a thinner camber whose thickness could be cleverly varied by adjusting its rigging from 1:24 to as slender as 1:30 (which would prove the best). And, guided again by the wind tunnel results, they had moved the high point of the wing's curvature to a position around a third of the way back from the leading edge. Once more, for pitch control, there was a forward elevator, now smaller – and wing-shaped, which helped give the machine a bit more lift as well. And in the rear, attached to tail booms, they had fitted their first rudder – two fixed vertical vanes.

Not controllable in flight, the double rudder was an attempt to cure the frightening problem Wilbur had encountered the previous year when, warping the wings to bank left or right, the machine had unnervingly swung in the opposite direction. They had eventually identified the trouble as a serious flaw in their wing warping system. What was happening, they finally established, was that when the pilot moved the hip cradle to turn, say, to the left, the right wing – effectively its starboard aileron – would twist down, creating more lift on that side and causing the right wing to rise and begin a bank to the left. However, in warping down, the outer right wing was also creating a significant amount of drag against the airflow. This drag was actually causing the wing to pinwheel back to the right. The fixed rear rudder was intended to counteract that. At Kill Devil they would discover if it did.

Back at Kitty Hawk they learnt that Bill Tate was too busy – working at a sawmill further north – to help them this time. His half-brother, Dan, took them down the inside coast in his sailing boat to a fishing wharf near Kill Devil. They went inland to the big sandhills by horse cart which, bogged down in deep sand, they had to push much of the way. The wooden shed, with the 1901 glider still sitting inside, had suffered badly in the winter gales. The sand had been scoured away beneath it, collapsing the ends. The roof, Wilbur said, looked like 'a dromedary's back'.

It took them eleven days to repair the building and to wind- and sand-proof it with tar paper and battens nailed over the cracks. This time they were determined to live in comfort. They added an extension in which they created a combined kitchen, dining room and sleeping quarters. The bunks, of heavy sacking stretched between frames, they put up in the rafters with a ladder for access. They drilled a new sixteen-foot well for their old pump, striking, below sea level, pure fresh water. They covered their dining table with oilcloth and upholstered the chairs with sacking and wood shavings. A photograph of the kitchen shows how fastidiously everything was arranged: cups and pans hang in rows with military orderliness; food cans, boxes and jars are lined up with immaculate precision. It was said that the five eggs seen in the picture – laid by a hen they kept in a coop – had been neatly pencil-numbered in sequence.

What toilet arrangements they made is nowhere recorded. Wide-angle photographs of the camp from the nearby dunes show the lonely building sitting exposed in a vast expanse of sand; there is not a sign of a privy for hundreds of yards around. Perhaps they trudged to the seclusion of distant woods out of the camera's view. But, as one of their biographers wrote, 'Sanitary arrangements, in those days, were not something to write home about.'[7]

They had decided this time to speed up communication with Kitty Hawk, four miles to the north. They had brought a bicycle with balloon tyres which they had specially built with a very low gear for pedalling in soft sand. It was a great success, reducing the former three-hour walk to collect mail to one hour.

They discovered that the camp, for the moment mercifully mosquito free, had become, in their absence, overrun by wildlife. Outside they had to drive away wild pigs, and inside the hut was infested with mice which, despite being hunted with sticks and gun, continued to plague their living quarters. In his diary Orville became preoccupied with the extermination of one in particular:

> At 11 o'clock last night I was awakened by the mouse crawling over my face. Will had advised me that I had better get something to cover my head, or I would have it 'chawed' off like Guillaume Mona had by the bear. I found on getting up that the little fellow had only come to tell me to put another piece of corn bread in the trap. He had disposed of the first piece. I have sworn 'vengeance' on the little fellow for this impudence and insult.[8]

Once again they were to be hosts to a number of guests. The charming and amiable Chanute was due to come: his wife had died in California and he had been knocked sideways with grief. He was still 'endeavouring to regain my mental poise', he told Wilbur. Nonetheless, he was impatient to see the latest glider perform.

To the brothers' dismay he was also trying yet again to wish other people's experiments upon them. In California, Chanute met a man-lifting kite enthusiast, a jeweller called Charles Lamson who had earlier built and flown the first Lilienthal glider in America. Lamson had recently patented a kite with an oscillating wing that rocked fore and aft in response to the quirks of the erratic centre of lift. Notwithstanding the wildly impractical notion of the invention, Chanute, who still at heart believed automatic stability was the answer to fixed-wing flight, commissioned him to build a glider using the rock-and-roll wing. He then wrote to ask Wilbur if they would be prepared to flight-test the improbable device on the Outer Banks.

That wasn't all. Chanute also wanted them to build a new version of one of the now hopelessly redundant body-swinging gliders he and his disciples had tested on the Indiana dunes six years earlier. The brothers, with their efficient wind tunnel-designed wings and pilot-operated controls, had progressed light years ahead of these outmoded concepts with which the old man was still dabbling. Chanute suggested that, by testing their own glider up against a clutch of his own sponsored designs, 'you will get some good out of it'.

Wilbur and Orville saw the potential for not a shred of good. They saw only, despite Chanute's insistence that he would pay for everything, a great deal of unwanted work that would merely shunt aeronautics into a retrogressive backwater. The truth, which aviation's ardent mover and shaker had not yet divined, was that the Dayton mechanics were rapidly running aerodynamic rings around him – in both the theory of flight and its practice. They were acutely conscious that they were still newcomers to the scene alongside the internationally respected Chicago engineer, yet, unfortunately, by 1902 he had little to offer the Wrights. 'More often than not,' said Peter Jakab, 'he ruminated over antiquated or wrong-headed theories and designs that the brothers had long since discarded. By now, the Wrights' sharing of information with him was far more an act of courtesy toward a respected, well-liked friend than a forum for substantive intellectual exchange.'[9]

Chanute appears to have been quite naively unaware of the extensive inconvenience he was inflicting on the Wrights. Time subtracted from their own work would be devoted to building contraptions they knew to be inherent failures. How did he think they would provide the hangar space for the rival machine at Kill Devil – not to mention the accommodation and catering for Chanute and the pilot he would need to bring?

Out of respect for Chanute's many kindnesses and his great encouragement of their own early experiments, they reluctantly agreed to have the Lamson machine fly at Kill Devil and the new hang-gliders built in Dayton. Wilbur had, however, made it clear that all he and Orville would have time for would be to oversee the construction. The work would have to be subcontracted to a carpenter. Nor could it begin, he said, until after the summer cycle season. What's more, it was to be clearly understood that the gliders would be entirely Chanute's babies, not their own. There was no way they wanted to turn the clock back and start body-swinging off the Kill Devil hills.

Chanute reluctantly accepted the arrangement. But something then happened to change his plans. Augustus Herring, the ambitious and quarrelsome young aeronautical experimenter who had rowed with Samuel Langley at the Smithsonian and later created ructions among Chanute's Indiana dunes gliding team, had suddenly re-entered his life.

Herring, still an immensely proud and self-confident man, had fallen on hard times. After he had abandoned Chanute for his new patron, Matthias Arnot, in 1897 to build his own powered hang-glider, on which he'd made a couple of inconclusive hops, he had been struck down by personal disasters. His workshop, complete with new aircraft and aerial steam engines he was building, had been destroyed by fire. Soon afterwards his financier, Arnot, had died. Herring's health had collapsed and he had suffered a nervous breakdown. Trying to rebuild his life, he had heard of the glittering prizes being offered in the St Louis flying machine competition and had written to Chanute with a proposal. He'd read Wilbur's acclaimed account of the brothers' aerodynamic work and been fired with the desire to race them to successful powered flight. If Chanute would fund him, he confidently offered, he could actually 'beat Mr Wright'.

Chanute didn't immediately jump at the offer. He hadn't forgotten the bad terms on which he and Herring had parted back in 1896, nor the unhappiness the latter's defiance and disloyalty had created among the dunes gliding team, nor the resentment Herring had subsequently levelled at him for not adequately crediting him publicly for his inventive contribution to their joint glider. Herring might then have been one of the world's most determined and experienced pilots, but he was rebellious, obstinate and quick to sulk. However, Chanute took pity on him. He offered to involve him in his new flying programme, suggesting that he, rather than the busy Wrights, tackle the glider-building work.

Wilbur and Orville couldn't have been more relieved. 'To tell the truth,' Wilbur told Chanute, 'the building of machines for other men to risk their necks on is not a task that I particularly relish.'[10] It had been left, therefore, that Chanute would come to Kitty Hawk with his own pilot to fly the Lamson and the glider Herring would re-create for him. But who would be that pilot who would have to join them at the Kill Devil camp and share their cramped and spartan existence? Since their bad experience with Huffaker they were on their guard. 'It was our experience last year,' Wilbur reminded Chanute, 'that my brother and myself, while alone, or nearly so, could do more work in one week than in two weeks after Mr Huffaker's arrival.'

On a visit to Dayton early in July, Chanute had raised the matter again. The Wrights told him that whoever his pilot turned out to be, he would be expected to help them launch their own new glider. They appear to have got wind of Herring's disruptive reputation and saw him as another potential irritant to life at Kill Devil. More than that there was the fear that he sounded like someone fully capable of pirating their aircraft's sacred features to claim as his own. Despite Chanute's constant urging, they had not yet protected their design work with a patent. Although they had never met him, the more they worried about Herring's character the more nervous they grew for the security of their priceless wind tunnel breakthrough.

None of these worries appeared to surround the alternative candidate, William Avery, Chanute's plodding Chicago carpenter who had also piloted gliders on the Indiana dunes. Following Chanute's Dayton visit, Wilbur had written to reinforce their view that 'for reasons not necessary to mention' they hoped he would bring Avery. Alas, Avery was too busy to come. Chanute brought Herring.

In the hope of adding to their complement someone they at least knew to be agreeable and helpful, Wilbur had written to George Spratt to try to persuade him to join them again. The warm bond that had sprung up between them the previous year had grown through lively subsequent correspondence. Wilbur's letters had even been dispensing psychological counselling for a depression into which the young Pennsylvanian had sunk, beset by a sense of worthlessness at the failure of his own experiments with wing shapes:

> I see from your remark about the 'blues' that you still retain the habit of letting the opinions or doings of others influence you too much. We thought we had partly cured you of this at Kitty Hawk. It is well for a man to be able to see the merits of others and the weaknesses of himself, but if carried too far it is as bad, or even worse, than seeing only his <u>own merits</u> and <u>others</u>' weaknesses. In the present case there was no occasion for your 'blueness' except in your own imagination. Such is usually the case.[11]

Having endeavoured to soften Spratt's melancholy, Wilbur had generously proceeded to try to help him with his aerodynamic research. Not only had he enclosed a detailed working diagram of their own precious wind tunnel with full directions for its use, he had sent Spratt four of the actual miniature wing surfaces they had created for their own lift/drag tests.

While waiting at Kill Devil that September for Spratt's response to the invitation to join them, there came shattering news from Dayton. Milton had been found guilty in absentia by his Brethren colleagues at his Huntington trial. Led by Bishop Floyd, an investigation committee of Wright's own White River district elders had voted to condemn him on the three substantive counts of libelling fellow churchmen, insubordination, and taking legal action against a fellow Christian. Bishop Wright had been ordered 'to confess his error to the church and the offended parties within 60 days' – or be indefinitely suspended from the Brethren. He was also ordered 'to cease his efforts to arouse the church'. Among the allegedly injured parties was the bent but resilient Keiter, still, for the sake of the church's image, curiously uncondemned by the majority. The church had chosen to sacrifice Bishop Wright.

When news of his conviction and sentence finally reached Milton, he condemned the trial as an unprecedentedly wicked device to conceal the sins of a criminal embezzler. How dare they, he seethed, try 'to close the mouth and silence the tongue of a bishop in this church'.[12] He had no intention of confessing, apologising or ceasing his campaign against the cover-up. His suspension did not remain a dark secret within the church community. It made newspaper headlines throughout the Midwest, was splashed on the Chicago front pages. To defend their action, the Brethren rushed to distribute 5000 pamphlets explaining why Milton had been punished. Throughout the Wright family it caused shock waves of hurt and resentment.

Katharine and Lorin, trying to counter the damning publicity in Dayton, sent an indignant letter to a local newspaper defending their victimised father. To Milton Katharine wrote: 'Isn't that a noble idea of theirs to give you sixty days to confess . . . Not one of that crowd knows what common honour, honesty or gratitude means.'[13]

Sending to Kill Devil a bunch of newspaper clippings featuring the sensational story of crime and punishment within the now ludicrously dissension-ridden Brethren, Katharine wrote:

> Dear boys,
>
> I haven't heard one word from you yet . . . you didn't tell me how I could reach you. We ought to have some arrangement . . . It's a wonder I have any mind left. I'm worried . . . about both you and Daddy . . .
>
> Pop seems all right but I'm afraid he is worrying a good deal. You ought to see the sympathy he gets from all the decent folks in town. The bank people think that it is an outrage.

Katharine also relayed Milton's rising anxieties about their gliding ventures:

> Dad seems worried over your flying business this year. The habit of worry is strong in him. I am not much alarmed, having learned how 'Ullam' considers his father and sister (ha! ha!) but don't run any risks. We've been worried enough for one year.[14]

Over his ostracism within the church, Katharine showered her father with letters of reassurance and comfort. Wilbur, she told him, would help deal with his spineless Brethren colleagues on his return:

> We'll never stop fighting now Pop until we've shown those rascals up – not if it takes some money for it. We are not going to let this thing go – not by a long chalk. Just wait till the boys are back again, with Will feeling strong again![15]

She urged Milton 'to telegraph Will' should church officials attempt to rein him in by legal suit – Wilbur had effectively become his father's de facto lawyer. When the details of the Brethren's latest iniquity had first reached Kill Devil it had blown the brothers' minds right off aeronautics and set them heatedly discussing how Milton's oppressors should be dealt with. From their lonely wooden shack, by the light of a paraffin lamp, Wilbur sat down and wrote to his father: 'This action was an infamous outrage and when I get back home I will see that the members of the committee who made this finding sign a written retraction.'[16]

The letter is one of many that illustrate the depth of Wilbur's emotional involvement in Milton's Brethren battles. The injustices his father was suffering were now increasingly competing with aeronautics for his singular wisdom. Reading the letters in the Library of Congress today, one cannot fail to be struck by the power and influence he had by now assumed in his role as his father's adviser. Many of the letters read more like the instructives one would expect to be issuing from a father to a troubled son. Distinguished by their reasoning and logic, they bristle with brisk imperatives telling Milton precisely what he should do: 'You should make it clear . . . that the convention was not a body having authority over you'; 'your reply should be that you will overlook their insubordination . . .'; 'the resolutions should be published and widely circulated . . . someone should attend to it.'[17] In letter after letter, many written from the wilderness of Kill Devil, the incisive flow of dos and don'ts poured forth. They reflect an astonishingly intimate knowledge of Brethren affairs and of its warring factions – and a perennial concern for Milton's welfare. 'Be very careful of your health – you can not afford to be sick just now . . . do not worry about church affairs – things are moving nicely and the Keiterites rising to their fall.'

Millard Keiter was not to be vanquished that easily. For Bishop Wright justice was slow to arrive. The process of his redemption would drag on acrimoniously for years, continuing to divert Wilbur from his aeronautical destiny.

12

An Unscrupulous Guest at Kill Devil Hills

(1902)

By the second week of September 1902, Wilbur and Orville had the Kill Devil camp shipshape again and had begun to assemble the new glider. They cannibalised the old machine, using its inter-wing struts, and, helped by their assistant, Dan Tate, now on their payroll, tested the biplane as an unmanned kite.

Kiting was still the most prudent way to observe design changes in the air before risking human ascent. From their wind tunnel performance records they were confident they could now pretty much predict how any wing of a precise aspect ratio and cambered shape, at different angles of attack, would fly in what strength of wind down what angle of glideslope carrying what weight. The latest glider was the product, they hoped, of all this technical certainty.

And as it ascended into the air above the dun-coloured sand, their hearts rose with it as they observed all the indications of flight more seemingly perfect than they had ever witnessed before. The slender new wings met all the expectations raised by the weeks of work in the thundering wind tunnel. The flying cords swung up almost vertically as the empty machine soared effortlessly on the breeze in a clear blue sky. They could see immediately that their aerodynamically sophisticated wing was generating much more lift than ever before. It was postponing to very low and efficient angles of attack the reversal of the crucial lift pressure centre that had earlier had such alarming earth-plummeting consequences for the pilot.

Any wing, bird or mechanical, has to be angled above the horizontal to maintain flight. The smaller that angle the more efficient the wing. The Wrights had created one that was now rivalling the soaring birds'. With its longer span and brand new tail it had also begun to look like a modern aeroplane. It performed brilliantly.

Again it was Wilbur who flew. Once more he had a hip cradle for warp control, but, to complicate things, they had decided to reverse the action of the hand lever that operated the forward elevator. It meant learning to coordinate the controls all over again. Launched by Orville and Dan Tate, he sailed down the slope of the biggest sand dune with great precision. When he gingerly banked into a turn, the fixed double rudder appeared to have completely solved the previous year's sudden terrifying lurches back in the opposite direction. The new machine serenely glided at a much shallower angle and the elevator delicately controlled the pitch.

Wilbur made numerous flights of up to 200 feet. They provided surging moments of exhilaration, coursing on the wind, harnessing the forces of nature. But much of it was sheer drudgery. There were only three of them to repeat, dozens of times in just one afternoon, the exhausting task of carrying a hundred awkward pounds of glider through loose sand back up the long slope, sometimes tripping and stumbling. It stretched everyone's physical fitness.

To gusts striking it side-on, the new glider was more sensitive than its predecessors. It would disconcertingly tremble and twist as if bent on wresting control from the pilot. It would sometimes refuse to maintain a straight heading, instead wildly yawing from side to side. To try to solve the problem – to reduce the impact of crosswinds tipping the underside of the wings – Orville made some modifications. He retrussed the wings to droop the tips several inches lower than the centre; but although this cured the crosswind instability, it was still not the end of their control troubles. Almost immediately they faced a fresh aerodynamic hiccup. The piloting dramas it created were to be shared for the first time by Orville. The time had come for him to earn his wings – and share the dangers. On 23 September he made his first documented flight from the big hill.

In what must have been one of the world's earliest flying lessons, Orville nervously stepped into the gap between the wings. No instructor could go with him; all the tuition would be shouted into the wind from the ground. There would be no confident hand to seize the controls in the highly possible event that he did something dangerous; he was going to have to learn to be a bird on his own. To diminish the bewilderment of it all they tied off the hip cradle, limiting his control to the elevators. He could rise and fall, but not turn and bank.

As Wilbur and Dan Tate seized the wingtips, Orville gripped one of the forward elevator struts with his right hand and took the pitch lever in his left. After a short trot down the slope into the breeze, his legs were pedalling in space and he was airborne, followed down the slope by Tate and Wilbur, the latter's instructing shouts now blown away by the wind in his ears. The glider went about 50 yards – Orville had flown without mishap, skidding into the ground in a shower of sand as Wilbur rushed up. There is no record of brotherly congratulations, only a matter-of-fact technical note in Orville's diary:

> After dinner [always in the middle of the day] we took the machine out again (having housed it on account of threatening rain) and began gliding on the N.N.W slope of the big Kill Devil Hill, where the slope at its greatest was 9½°. I here took my first free flight, and after about a half dozen attempts made a glide of 160 feet, with a total angle of descent of 6°57′.[1]

How, in 1902, they measured a descent angle to within a minuscule one-sixtieth of a degree is anybody's guess. But nothing short of perfection would ever satisfy them.

Later the same day Orville tried a flight with all the controls operative. This one was to end in disaster. 'I noticed that one wing was getting a little too high and that the machine was slowly sliding off in the opposite direction,' he wrote. So busy was he concentrating on moving the cradle with his body towards the high wing to lower it that he forgot his elevator control. Within seconds the nose had pitched up to nearly 45 degrees as anxious warning shouts came from the ground. They were too late. 'I found suddenly that I was making a descent backwards toward the low wing, from a height of 25 or thirty feet . . .' All too swiftly the stalled glider had smashed into the sand in 'a heap of flying machine, cloth, and sticks in a heap, with me in the centre without a bruise or a scratch.'[2]

The others were amazed to find Orville unharmed. Bishop Wright would have had a seizure had he accepted their invitation to escape from his ecclesiastical woes to come to Kill Devil and witness his sons dicing with death like this. Yet it's unlikely he would have seen either of them killed, so robustly and flexibly built was the glider's structure. Not only had they used light resilient woods, but the frames were not rigidly attached to one another. They floated within the fabric covering which itself had been cleverly laid, angled on the bias for greater strength. The whole thing was thus marvellously forgiving in a crash – like a rubber box it bounced back into shape with incredible persistence. Orville's scratch-free escape was testimony to its ability to survive potentially fatal impacts. Certainly the dramatic accident appears in no way to have dampened their spirits. 'In spite of this sad catastrophe we are tonight in a hilarious mood,'[3] Orville cheerfully wrote in his diary that evening. But why so happy?

It is probable that they ascribed the crash merely to Orville's inexperienced control fumbling and that they were celebrating – non-alcoholically, as always – the huge advance of the new glider and its demonstrably improved performance over the earlier machines. In just three flying days they had notched up around 125 glides – more than the grand total for the whole of 1900 and 1901. Apart from some remaining control problems, the aeroplane was performing beyond their wildest dreams.

The new worries with the banking system, however, could not be ignored. The cause of the alarming intermittent tailslides, in which the glider had literally fallen out of Orville's hands into the ground, was still a mystery. Disquietingly, the mysterious plunges soon happened again. It was clearly more than inexperienced control handling, and it began to cloud their conversation. They even created a name for the phenomenon: after the small crater the crashing wingtip gouged out of the sand, they called it 'well digging'.

In the three days it took to rebuild the wrecked machine – one of the lifeboatmen's wives sewed up the torn wing fabric on her machine – they searched their minds for an explanation, without success. With some nervousness they resumed flying, the cause of the latest warping aberration still a mystery. It was still unsolved when, several days and a few more glides later, about to set off for Big Hill, they spotted in the distance two heavily burdened figures approaching across the sand from Kitty Hawk. One was the ferry skipper, helping carry someone's baggage towards their camp. Hoping it was George Spratt, who had written to say he was coming, they parked the glider and hurried out to meet them.

To their surprise the visitor was Lorin. They had known he might be coming, but weren't expecting him so soon. He had been ill and was in need of a holiday from his bookkeeping job with a Dayton builder. Short of money, he hoped that a few days at the fabled flying camp by the sea would provide a cheap convalescence. 'Make it as easy and inexpensive as you can for him,' Katharine had urged them in a letter. In a later note to 'Dear Bubbos' she added: 'Do see to it that he has a roaring good time and send him back fattened up a little.'[4] Lorin was to stay a fortnight. Another bunk was nailed up in the rafters and he began to make himself useful, running errands to Kitty Hawk, helping hump and launch the glider and taking many of the photographs of it in the air that have made the 1902 flight trials so well documented pictorially.

Despite the sluggish shutter speeds and emulsions of the day, Lorin captured on glass plate negative some remarkably vivid action on the Kill Devil hills. Day after day he recorded the gliding activity with the flair of a news photographer. He got dramatic pictures of both Wilbur and Orville in the air in their caps, ties and braces, stretched out on the lower wing, at every stage of a glide from the moment of launch to the instant of ploughing back on to the sand. Even by the standards of the twenty-first century there are some superb action shots of people frozen with thrusting arms upright at the second of hurling the machine into the air. Others have caught members of the team, legs and arms swinging, as they scamper down the slope trying to keep pace with the glider above. More than the dry scientific records of their notebooks and diaries, the photographs re-create a moving sense of the heady success and deadly seriousness of it all.

George Spratt arrived the day after Lorin, and an under-roof bunk was created for him too. The brothers welcomed Spratt as an old friend. The likeable amateur experimenter had had a discouraging year since Wilbur's counselling letters had tried to deal with his chronic blues. He badly wanted an achievement of his own, but success continued to elude him. He hadn't managed to use the detailed wind tunnel design and sample winglet information Wilbur had sent him to replicate it all for himself. Instead he had tried unsuccessfully to gather wing lift data with a swinging arm facing the natural wind. Equally unrewarding had been his attempts to create his own breeze with a pedal-driven fan. He hadn't even succeeded in copying the Wrights' miniature metal test wings; he'd finished up trying to carve the shapes unsatisfactorily out of wood.

Spratt saw himself sinking into the aviation community's second league, yet he was affectionately and hospitably welcomed as an equal at Kill Devil – and now quickly proceeded to strike up a warm friendship with Lorin as well. The pair soon teamed up and began to go off on fishing expeditions together.

It was a buoyant foursome who, that first week in October 1902, sat in the lamplight after supper each night, drinking coffee and talking flying. The subject now never far away was the latest unhappy 'well-digging' occurrence. It represented the last obstacle to safe controlled flight and they stayed up late, as the Atlantic wind rocked the frail shack, wrestling with the problem. It is said that the discussion at times became characteristically heated between Wilbur and Orville, that they fell to 'shouting and arguing', scribbling their theories diagramatically on scraps of paper and thrusting them at each other. All they could agree, it seems, was that the trouble lay with the new tail. The fixed rudder had cured the dangerous banking reversal habit merely to replace it with another equally frightening response.

It was Orville who finally solved it. On Thursday 2 October they had all sat up debating the problem far beyond their normal half past seven bedtime. Orville had drunk one cup of coffee too many – when he climbed up into his cot he couldn't get to sleep. For hours he tossed and turned, listening to the moaning of the wind and the creaking of the timbers, the tail problem circling in his mind.

In the small hours there had come the shaft of insight – so obvious that he wondered that it hadn't occurred to them sooner. What was happening, he became convinced, was that when the glider was banked into a turn, say to the left, the wing on that side dipped and, unless swiftly checked, began to side-slip. As the machine slid towards the ground, the left-side-pressure on the rigid rudders began to pivot the tail to the right, thus winding the plane into an even more uncontrollable side-slip, and a corkscrewing left-hand spin to earth. The remedy was obvious: allow the rudder to be moved in flight to ease the pressure build-up that was triggering the alarming plunge.

Pleased by his diagnosis, Orville lay there agonising about how to put it to his older brother. It would need to be presented carefully, for Wilbur, he felt, tended still to regard him as the kid brother – a junior partner to whose suggestions he often responded negatively on principle. It apparently took Orville some time at breakfast to find the courage to raise the matter at all. Finally, signalling with a wink to Lorin that he was about to utter something possibly provocative, he came out with his theory. To his surprise Wilbur didn't rubbish it. Not only did he take it seriously, but after a few moments' deep thought he added a further astute suggestion of his own. Making the rudder moveable would require a third control for the pilot to have to bother with. He already had enough to think about just coordinating the elevator and warp systems. As the rudder, in turning, would need to be operated in a delicate sympathy with the bank control, why not, he said, link the two? Couple a swinging rudder to the warp cradle? Orville had to agree it made a lot of sense. The problem had been solved, as so often in their partnership, by joint ingenuity. But would it work in the air?

That very day they began to modify the glider. They removed the fixed twin vertical tail fins, replacing them with a single hinged rudder. This they wired up to the warp system. Sliding the hip cradle from side to side now turned the rudder synchronously. But before they could test this hook-up in the air, Chanute and Herring walked into camp.

The two men arrived in the middle of a violent rainstorm on 5 October drenched to the skin. Fortuitously it was a Sunday, when the Wrights were carefully doing nothing that could be construed as work. Two more cots were squeezed up into the rafters as they set about organising routines in this now overcrowded environment. The Wrights were punctiliously considerate hosts, rapidly sending to Elizabeth City for more canned food to boost their supplies.

What gems of historical aviation dialogue would a recording of their ceaseless aerodynamic discourse have provided on this the eve of man's true conquest of the air? There was the generous-hearted worrier and workaholic Octave Chanute, rather too old, as he approached his seventy-first year, to relish the rigours of camp life; aviation's delightful wise old owl who must, at least in his heart, have conceded that these unique brothers had already left him technically for dead in the race for mechanical flight. There was the frustrated, opinionated, 35-year-old short-fused Gus Herring, convinced that, on the Lake Michigan beach four years earlier, he had already achieved powered flight in the brief hop he'd made in his body-swinging biplane and that, given the money he now lacked, he could quickly overtake the Wrights. There was the equally frustrated but much sadder figure of George Spratt, whose shafts of aeronautical perception were not enough to lift him from the role of one of life's congenial but chronic losers, a description that could also have attached to Lorin, who must have found himself out of his depth as recondite aerodynamic talk rippled around him in this very special place. From time to time in the evening they would apparently relax in bursts of song, when 'the sound of Orville's mandolin accompanying a chorus of voices could be heard far into the night'.[5]

Soon there were more gliders in the air at Kill Devil. The triplane built at Chanute's expense by the Californian jeweller, Lamson, had arrived in Elizabeth City and was waiting to be shipped across. The separate biplane glider Herring had built for Chanute had come with its builder. Quickly assembled and test-flown, it was not a great success. On his second glide, Herring, legs dangling, flew only 20 feet in a few pathetic hops and jumps before crashing on to a wing and breaking it. It just wasn't robust enough: its wings buckled and twisted in flight. Chanute was furious – it had to be abandoned. He blamed Herring, telling Samuel Langley in a subsequent letter, 'I fear that he is a bungler.' But, in fairness to Herring, Chanute had inspected the hang-glider during construction and approved it.

Herring and his patron turned their hopes towards the Lamson device with the oscillating wings which presently arrived in a cart from Kitty Hawk. It proved equally disappointing. Sent aloft as a kite, it performed moderately well. But when Herring climbed aboard it refused to glide more than 50 feet.

The successive failures of Chanute's latest flawed machines, neither embodying pilot control systems, sent Herring into a highly nervous state. Before one flight he fainted and had to be revived by Spratt, whom everybody at Kill Devil generously addressed as 'Doctor'. The incident followed what had been for Herring a night sleepless with worry and foreboding, in the middle of which his shouts had suddenly startled them all. Orville wrote:

> We were all awakened about 2 o'clock in the morning by an announcement by Mr Herring that the chicken had been stolen by a fox. As he had not always proved a true prophet in his previous predictions that it would be stolen in the night, we took little stock in the announcement. Daylight revealed the chicken safe and sound.[6]

As one of the Wrights' biographers wrote: 'A man capable of waking his sleeping camp fellows in the middle of the night to report the non-theft of a chicken by a possibly non-existent fox was quite capable of feigning illness the next morning – or actually fainting – to avoid any more glides in a rickety glider with oscillating wings, slack trussing and weak joints . . .'[7]

How true any of this was we will never know, but if Herring was actually reduced to this demoralised state it would in the circumstances have been scarcely surprising, for while Chanute and

Herring were witnessing the failure of their pitiful contraptions, Wilbur and Orville had been making aviation history. Before their dispirited guests' eyes, from the same sandhills, they had been testing their own new amazing, now modified, glider. The inter-coupled rudder and warp controls had completely eliminated the dangerous side-slipping. The machine was now performing flawlessly – the first in flying history to be totally controllable by the pilot in all the planes of movement. Humiliatingly for aviation's most eminent and knowledgeable figure, Chanute was observing the total eclipse of his bankrupt philosophy of flight. The aeroplane was not to be an automatically stable vehicle with dancing, springy wings guided about the sky by a man's threshing legs. It would be made effortlessly to pitch, bank and turn with three pilot-controlled systems that would still be serving world aviation a century hence. The Wrights had quietly accomplished something that not the genius of Leonardo da Vinci, the scientific imagination of George Cayley, the brilliance of Lilienthal, nor the huge resources of Langley had ever achieved.

Chanute and Herring watched Wilbur and Orville making magnificent flights which almost daily stretched ever further across the coastal sands. As their confidence and mastery of the machine grew, so did the daring of their manoeuvres and the wind strengths in which they were brave enough to fly. Confidently they began to launch in velocities of 30 miles an hour. They made glides of more than 600 feet in flights lasting up to 26 seconds. Wilbur became so competent that he began to hold the glider stationary in the air, comfortably cushioned on the sustaining breeze flowing up the big hill. They took aerial turns in their stride – now without even the flicker of an aberrant control spasm. They banked from left to right and flew boldly across the wind when they chose. Always the machine obeyed the pilot. Always, now, it was under precise control.

From the top of the big hill Lorin snapped a dramatic high-angle picture of Wilbur negotiating a right-hand turn. One can see the port wing warped downward and rudder angled to balance the banking manoeuvre, and his hips pressing the cradle to the right. Their launch assistant, Dan Tate, was in awe of their prowess. 'All she needs,' he commented, 'is a coat of feathers to make her light and she'll stay in the air indefinitely'.[8] The flights were now the talk of the Kill Devil lifeboat station. A steamer cruising by in Albemarle Sound slowed down while the passengers rushed to the rail to watch – unknowingly – the nativity of the modern aeroplane.

In all the Wrights between them made more than 700 flights. They were intoxicated with success. 'Our machine is a very great improvement over anything we had built before and over anything anyone has built,' Wilbur wrote triumphantly to Milton. 'We have far beaten all records for flatness of glides as we in some cases have descended only 5⅓ degrees from the horizontal while other machines descended from 7½° to 11°. This means that in soaring we can descend much slower and in a power machine can fly with much less power . . . We are being very careful and will avoid accidents of serious nature if possible . . . We now believe that the flying problem is really nearing its solution.'[9] And Orville wrote with equal pride to Katharine:

> We now hold all the records! The largest machine that we handled in any kind [of weather] made the longest distance glide (American), the longest time in the air, the smallest angle of descent, and the highest wind!!! Well, I'll leave the rest of the 'blow' till we get home.[10]

Plaintively Katherine had earlier written: 'I am deserted by my family.' Unhappy to remain in the house alone, she had gone to stay with friends. After what appear to have been emotionally draining days teaching Latin to difficult pupils, she would call in at the cycle shop to check on Charlie Taylor, then, at 7 Hawthorn Street, would collect the mail. The latter invariably contained garrulous notes from Milton complaining that his children weren't getting – as he demanded – letters to all his ports of call on the preaching circuit. Katharine would spend her evenings writing apologetic letters to placate him – and notes to keep Wilbur and Orville informed about affairs at the shop.

According to Taylor, 'the business,' she wrote, 'is about to go up the spout . . .' :

> Say, he makes me too weary for words. He is your judge, it seems. Everything that happens he remarks that it struck him that you left too much for the last minute. Today I got wrathy and told him that I was tired of hearing him discuss your business . . . I wish you would send me a check for $25 – I don't enjoy going to the store after money. Mr Taylor knows too much to suit me. I ought to learn something about the store business. I despise to be at the mercy of the 'hired man'.[11]

But the brothers were in too euphoric a state to be much concerned by the cash-flow problems of their shop. More to the point, perhaps they were soon going to need Charlie Taylor's expertise for a challenging new venture: to help them create their ultimate flying machine – to give the glider an engine and propellers. At Kill Devil they had already begun to plan it.

By the third week of October all their guests had left. To their relief they had the place to themselves once more. The chill of autumn – they needed five blankets each at night and sometimes kept their clothes on – had descended on the Outer Banks and gales arrived to set the shed swaying. Every evening now they would sit by their driftwood-burning stove until late, working with the symbiotic harmony that so immutably bound them, drawing up the first specifications for the motorised glider.

The era of dependence on gravity to power their leisurely one-way descents off hillsides was coming to an end. The new machine would be launched from a stationary start on flat ground into sustained level flight. The mathematics of the propulsion system they carefully worked through from their now proven wind tunnel data. The powered vehicle would have to carry a lot more weight than the gliders. With engine, propellers, extra supporting structure and the pilot, they reckoned it would be lifting all of 625 pounds into the air. This, they calculated, would need an increase in their present 300 or so square feet of wing area to more than 500 square feet. They were looking at a significantly bigger machine with something like a 40-foot wingspan. And to produce the thrust to overcome all that drag and sustain level flight at an airspeed of 23 miles an hour against a moderate headwind, their meticulous equations told them the engine would have to generate around 8 horsepower. The aeroplane would be designed with more engineering exactitude than any of its predecessors and competitors.

Chief among their rivals at that moment, as far as they knew, was Samuel Langley's piloted *Great Aerodrome*, impatiently awaited for its great military potential by its customer, the US War Department. The army had been persuaded to invest in its development following the Spanish–American War of 1898 in which the country's navy and land forces found themselves in action in Cuba and the Philippines. The professor had lobbied President McKinley, convincing him that he could create this powerful new weapon of war for $50,000. He told McKinley he was confident he could build a bigger version of his successful steam models, powering it with a lightweight petrol engine. The Smithsonian had promptly been awarded the lucrative contract. Edward Huffaker had briefly worked on the venture before fleeing from Langley's tyranny. The new project manager was an electrical and mechanical engineer, Charles Manley. Unlike the coarse-mannered Tennessean, Manley more than fully measured up to Langley's demanding criteria. The two were to enjoy what, for the Smithsonian's Secretary, was to become one of his rare warm and happy relationships.

But the philologically confusing *Great Aerodrome* had been less successful. Langley was convinced that by simply scaling up the models and again launching over the Potomac his would be the triumph of manned flight. But now, four years later, after the expenditure of huge sums of government money, the *Great Aerodrome*, shrouded in a tight veil of secrecy, was still far from ready to fly. Technologically, except for its lightweight engine, it was in every way inferior to the Wrights' machines. Langley continued to exude an air of great confidence, though reports of the Wrights' startling successes on the North Carolina coast had begun to make him anxious to know more about their work.

From the Outer Banks, Chanute and Herring had travelled together to Washington to meet the Smithsonian's director. Chanute wanted to bring his friend up to date with the Wrights' staggering progress. The less scrupulous Herring, correctly divining that he would be getting no more work from Chanute, had a less worthy purpose: he wanted to trade the brothers' precious control secrets for a job back at the institution. Certainly he could have presented Langley with priceless information to help him catch up with the Dayton mechanics.

Langley received Chanute, from whom he now learnt with what must have been rising misgiving of the remarkable breakthrough the Wrights had achieved, but he hadn't forgotten his earlier experience with Herring and refused to meet him. Nor did he respond with any enthusiasm to a letter soon after from Herring hinting at the revolutionary secrets he would barter for fresh employment. Chanute had urged Langley to hurry to Kitty Hawk and witness, before it was too late, the astonishing flights for himself. More than eager to do so, Langley had dashed off a telegram to Wilbur at Kill Devil: 'MR CHANUTE HAS INTERESTED ME IN YOUR EXPERIMENTS. IS THERE TIME TO SEE THEM? KINDLY WRITE ME.'

But the Wrights now saw Langley as a serious rival – one with large resources at his command with which to help himself to their still unpatented ideas. For the first time they had begun to believe that they themselves might be on the brink of inventing the powered aeroplane. Why invite a competitor into their camp to share the years of heartbreak and hard-earned discovery – all funded by no one but themselves?

Wilbur replied to Langley that there wasn't time. It was now late October and they were preparing to pack up and return to Dayton. Langley persisted, writing to Chanute to try to get him to persuade the brothers to reveal to him the details of their aeroplane. 'I should be glad,' he said, 'to hear more of what the Wright Brothers have done, and especially of their means of control . . . I should be very glad to have either of them visit Washington at my expense, to get some of their ideas on the subject, if they are willing to communicate them.'[12] Chanute, passing the letter on to Wilbur, frankly described the approach from the great man as 'cheeky'.

The brothers declined to go to Washington. 'It is not at all probable that either Orville or myself will find opportunity to visit Prof. Langley,' Wilbur wrote back firmly to Chanute.

In fact had they been happy to show Langley their machine there would have been plenty of time to do so. For in that last week of

October, free of visitors, they indulged, with Dan Tate's help, in a veritable orgy of masterful flying that would undoubtedly have both staggered and depressed the professor. 'We crowded more glides than in all the weeks preceding,' Wilbur reported to Chanute. 'In two days we made about two hundred and fifty . . . This practice enabled us to very greatly increase our skill in the management of the machine. We increased our record for distance to 622½ ft.'[13]

Occasionally Bill Tate came down from the sawmill to visit them. Amazed at the length of the flights they were now making, he is said to have told them: 'What in the hell is the matter with you boys; you know that it will fly, why in hell don't you put an engine on it and *fly*?'[14] Tate noticed how competitive things had become between the two. They egged each other along and constantly tried to outdistance the other or make smoother landings. They were gliding, he thought, 'almost better than the gannets'.

They would have liked to stay longer at Kill Devil, but Dan Tate, their only remaining launch assistant, had to leave to join a fishing crew. On 28 October, having made nearly 1000 flights, they stored the glider and its two hapless rivals in the shed, gathered up a collection of shells and starfish for Lorin's children, and walked in cold drizzling rain the four miles to Kitty Hawk to take the schooner back to Elizabeth City. In contrast to the previous year they were returning in a mood of buoyant elation.

Milton was waiting to greet them off the train in Dayton. The bishop was in grim war mode. He'd been rallying his forces for a frontal attack on 'the Keiterites'. Within hours of his return to Hawthorn Street Wilbur found himself drawn back into the fray, resolved to avenge the 'infamous outrage' that had been perpetrated upon his father.

Milton had decided to challenge Keiter's defenders en masse; he had called a revolutionary conference of Brethren opposed to his impeachment and demanding Keiter's prosecution. It was scheduled for 25 November in Huntington. For the next three weeks Wilbur poured his lawyerly and filial energies into preparations for the rebel gathering. Letters from Chanute and Langley with urgent aeronautical questions went unanswered.

Father and son sat together at the tense conference. Sixty-two ministers and lay Brethren, all loyal to Milton and willing to split the church yet again, attended. Wilbur, who, but for the absence of a beard, would not, with his measured words and stern unsmiling countenance, have seemed out of place amidst this band of religious zealots, delivered a speech fiercely defending Milton 'whose degradation is being sought because he took a stand for righteousness and honest administration of sacred funds'. It is unlikely that any of the delegates would have had a clue that the bishop's son was in the process of creating an invention that would change the world; yet he was clearly a force in his own right. He was even elected to a committee set up to pursue recovery of the embezzled funds, and his damning audit of Keiter's accounts was circulated to shock and rally people to the bishop's defence.

Resolutions praised Milton's fifty-two stainless years of service to the Brethren church, but the militant gathering merely drove a deeper wedge into the heart of the battle-weary Radical Brethren. The Keiterites responded aggressively. Even before Milton and Wilbur had left Huntington, the still flourishing Millard Keiter had filed an $11,000 lawsuit for libel against Bishop Wright and eight of his rebel colleagues. Wilbur was named as one of the defendants. It heralded a new phase of ferocity in the seemingly insoluble conflict.

It wasn't until the end of November that Wilbur was able to return to aeronautics. 'Affairs at Huntington have required much of my time and thought recently, so I have not found opportunity to verify the calculations,' he apologised to Chanute, who was badgering him for technical data on the Kill Devil flights – and again pressing the brothers urgently to patent their invention.

They hadn't yet invented the powered aeroplane, but, with their three-dimensional control system and sophisticated wing design, had come a lot nearer than anyone else. As a result of the persistent publicity Chanute had given their experiments, the risk of appropriation was growing by the week. He couldn't have more vigorously disseminated the details of their success to the aeronautical world. As a result it was not only Langley who was beginning to sniff around. In Europe, where fixed-wing aviation since the deaths of Lilienthal and Pilcher was virtually at a standstill, the Wrights' work was suddenly attracting attention.

In England, the Aeronautical Society of Great Britain, whose membership still consisted mainly of professional engineers and gentlemen amateurs, was in decline. Its president, a brother of the founder of the Boy Scouts, had in 1902 decided to ginger things up. Himself an indefatigable but not very successful aeronautical experimenter, the complicatedly named Major Baden Fletcher Smyth Baden-Powell was a British Army officer, a 'sturdy, upright and honest Victorian soldier', who had served with camels on the Upper Nile, at the relief of Mafeking in the South African War, and had tried to interest the War Office in man-lifting observation kites. What he lacked in aeronautical understanding was more than compensated for by an energetic enthusiasm for the subject. He'd got wind of the Wrights' activities and had written to Chanute demanding information about 'the interesting Mr Wright'.

When Chanute had sent him a glowing account of the brothers' inventions, Baden-Powell had promptly shared it all in an address to the society which had electrified some of the members. One of them, Patrick Young Alexander, a young man of independent means, had been so intrigued he'd promptly booked a passage to America determined to meet the brothers. On arrival in December 1902 he had gone straight to Chicago to call on Chanute for a letter of introduction to Wilbur and Orville.

Chanute had been impressed by Alexander, a tall Englishman with an engaging charm. His father, the manager of the well-known Cammells steelworks in Sheffield, had been one of the founders of Britain's Aeronautical Society. Patrick had served a brief apprenticeship in the dark rolling mills before becoming a deckhand on a sailing ship from whose rigging, in the Indian Ocean, he had fallen and become permanently crippled with an unset broken leg. He had subsequently, with the help of a £60,000 fortune inherited from his father (worth several million pounds today), joined the host of amateurs seeking a role for themselves in the exciting field of aviation.

It was Alexander's serious ambition to be the first man in Britain to pilot a powered aeroplane. A zestful dilettante who owned his own balloons from which he made parachute jumps, he was extensively well connected and knowledgeable in aviation circles.

Generously shovelling money into projects, he travelled the world in first-class comfort to meet experimenters and scoop up information. He'd been to see Pilcher, Hiram Maxim, Lilienthal and Count Zeppelin, the German airship pioneer – even to meet aviators in Russia and China. He had set up his own balloon and motor research workshop, and eccentrically cherished a dream of human flight powered by electrical energy drawn from the air. But this aeronautical gadfly lacked Chanute's professional engineering background and had become involved in some unpromising inventions, patenting in the 1890s a balloon steered by oars. Without his infinite leisure and wealth it is unlikely that he would ever have become as prominent as he did. Certainly in December 1902 the Wright Brothers had never heard of him.

Completely unannounced, Alexander knocked on the door of 7 Hawthorn Street on Christmas Eve, clutching his introduction from Chanute, who had described him kindly as a leading 'aeronautical investigator'. When the hospitable Wrights invited him in out of the snow, he found the family in the midst of wrapping gifts and the bishop busy mailing out a stack of Keiter campaign pamphlets.

Wilbur and Orville took to this limping, pushy stranger. 'We were much pleased with him,' Wilbur later told Chanute. But they had still been cautious with revelation. Their rapid success had led them to revise their earlier proclaimed intentions to share their inventive fruits for the general good. And they were right to be careful with this prying member of the British aeronautical establishment so anxious to develop friendships with successful inventors. Pat Alexander, with his worldly English charm, was the brothers' first encounter with the subtleties of British diplomacy. They weren't quite sure whose interests he represented, but for the moment they welcomed him as an honourable man, a likeable fellow enthusiast. Surprisingly, given how little they knew about him, they didn't reject a suggestion that he might be permitted to come to the Outer Banks to watch their next aeroplane fly.

Chanute's efforts to spread details of their unprotected invention did not end with Alexander. Within months they learnt that a French Army artillery officer, a Captain Ferdinand Ferber, encouraged by Chanute, had audaciously built a rough copy of their

1901 glider. Ferber, said to have been an unenthusiastic, rather overweight, chronically short-sighted soldier, had been unsuccessfully experimenting with gliders since 1899. After Chanute had sent him a copy of Wilbur's Chicago address, he had commissioned a carpenter to build him a flimsy imitation of the machine – but without a warp control for banking, which he had for some reason decided was useless. Ferber had made a few brief uncontrolled flights in it when, in March 1903, Chanute, on a visit to Europe, had gone to meet him in Nice and been shown his crude version of the Wrights' glider. By now the pertinacious Frenchman, in the hope of achieving powered flight ahead of the American brothers, had attached to it a petrol engine and propeller. Afraid to risk his neck in free flight, he was testing the device by hanging it from a big whirling arm around which it slowly drove itself. Unhappy with it, Ferber pleaded with Chanute to persuade Wilbur and Orville to sell him their state-of-the-art 1902 glider and teach him to fly it at Kill Devil. But the Wrights had already moved beyond gliding flight. They planned to fly their first powered machine at Kill Devil in the late summer.

While the brothers were grappling with a multitude of perplexing new problems that surrounded propeller propulsion, Chanute had travelled up to Paris where he was fêted by the aeronautical community as a celebrity. Here, at a dinner in his honour in the first week of April 1903, he spilt most of their technological beans before an audience of many of the wealthiest, most influential members of the country's aviation establishment. In an historic, well-illustrated lecture to the Aéro-Club de France – which the ubiquitous Patrick Alexander had rushed from England to attend – he had described, for all to hear, the three-dimensional control system of the 1902 glider. He had even revealed, to his spellbound audience's fascination, the crucial and exclusive secret of its successful rudder linkage to the warp control.

The lecture has taken its place in flying history as the moment when Europe was suddenly awakened to the sobering truth that fixed-wing flight technology had all but arrived in the New World. The full text of Chanute's address, delivered in his native French, has not survived, but the essence of what he disclosed – reported in careful detail by members of his audience – has been minutely analysed by aviation historians ever since. He had begun by describing his own hang-glider experiments on the Indiana dunes six years earlier. When he moved on to discuss the Wrights' revolutionary 1902 machine, he left his audience with the impression that it was he who had actually inspired its design. He said that the brothers' gliders had been developed directly from his own machines, details of which he had gladly supplied them.

That the fundamental secrets of the Wrights' three-dimensional control system were not handed carte blanche to the French that night was not for the want of Chanute's indiscretion. All that prevented it was the seemingly astonishing fact that he didn't fully understand the system he was describing. His technical descriptions were just vague enough not to have been of immediate practical help to a competitor.

From published reports of his speech in the French aeronautical press (which ran pictures of the Wrights' latest glider captioned as 'the Chanute machine') it is clear that he – whose own machines had never had either controllable elevator or rudder – did not really know how the two vital controls had been connected by the Wrights in one of their greatest of all triumphs, and more to the point *why* they were physically linked in the first place. This despite his having, at Kill Devil, been a close witness to the system in action.

In what was far from one of his finest hours, the ageing engineer led his audience to believe that the brothers were not original workers. He described them as 'young, intelligent and daring pupils' merely working under his inventive guidance. They had seized on his own designs and proceeded to perfect them. 'With all due charity,' wrote the British aviation historian Charles Gibbs-Smith, 'one can only conclude that this fine old man, finding himself in 1903 in the romantic country of his birth, and surrounded by the warmth, respect and indeed adulation of his audience, succumbed to the temptation of acting the part of inspirer, teacher and mentor of the Wrights. Chanute's greatest contribution to the development of aviation was as encourager, critic and propagandist-in-chief; not as technical innovator or adviser.'[15]

In one evening in Paris Chanute had given life to a myth that was to take the Wrights years to extinguish. Chanute, people said, was not a petty self-seeking man. He genuinely had, as one historian put it, 'a bee buzzing around in his bonnet that told him the Wright Brothers would never have achieved what they had without his advice and assistance.'[16]

The elderly inspirer was not to be content to limit these extraordinary claims to the mainland of Europe.

13

'Our Turn to Throw'

(1903)

By the time he crossed to England later in April 1903, it seems that Chanute had really convinced himself that the Wrights had been working under his tutelage and actually flying his gliders. He'd gone to meet a clergyman whose hobby was ballooning, the Reverend J. M. Bacon. His daughter, Gertrude, herself a keen balloonist, recalled how she listened to 'the courteous, keen-eyed, white-haired old American gentleman, sitting at our table and telling us in modest, matter-of-fact tones, of a gliding machine of his own design on which two young men were even then accomplishing most successful flights . . . He said they were brothers of the names of Orville and Wilbur Wright.'[1]

It is unlikely that the Wrights were ever to read Chanute's claims recorded much later by the vicar's daughter. Nor is it probable that they knew how he had hijacked in Paris the aeronautical inventions they had pioneered almost entirely on their own. They had never been very interested in Chanute's body-steering hang-gliders from which their own giant leap had drawn little inspiration. Yet the damage had been done.

The truth was that a major philosophical gulf was steadily developing between the Wrights and their mentor. Chanute still couldn't escape from the belief that the brothers' research and ingenious designs should, for the benefit of humankind, be revealed to the world. The Wrights knew they were in possession of a precious and exclusive property that was now attracting growing international curiosity. More than ever they were determined to guard the secrets and at long last extract some reward for their years of self-funded work. Unfortunately, Chanute, with his international prestige and connections into every crevice of aviation endeavour, was becoming a major threat to these commercial hopes.

When Chanute arrived back in Chicago in May 1903 his brisk correspondence with Wilbur resumed happily for a time. Lengthy letters bursting with technical minutiae flowed again at the rate of several a week, but it wasn't long before the sensitive matter of publicity was once more to raise its head. Chanute had agreed, as a follow-up to his Aéro-Club address, to write an article on the progress of aviation in America for a French science journal. In it he attempted to describe the latest Wright glider and its interconnected control system, but preparing the text he rapidly floundered out of his depth and was forced to shower a string of queries upon Hawthorn Street. 'Should the warping of the wings be mentioned?' he asked. 'Somebody may be hurt if it is not.'[2] To which Wilbur responded firmly: 'It is not our wish that any description of this feature of our machine be given at present.'[3]

When Chanute sent the draft to Wilbur for approval, the brothers were shocked by some of its inaccuracies. Not only had he got some key dimensions wrong, he had claimed that the rudder was operated 'by twines leading to the hand of the aviator'. Wilbur had written back a little testily: 'Really, this is news to me!', requesting that he drop the curious reference – whereupon Chanute was forced to admit his blinding ignorance of the controls. 'How,' despite having seen it at Kill Devil, he asked, 'is the vertical tail operated?' He had to substitute something, he pleaded – in effect seeking to disclose the critical information that lay at the very heart of the invention. If published, Wilbur replied, it could seriously jeopardise their ability to protect the machine in France and Germany where prior published disclosure invalidated patent applications. 'I only see three methods of dealing with this matter:

(1) Tell the truth. (2) Tell nothing specific. (3) Tell something not true. I really cannot advise either the first or the third course.'[4]

Reluctantly, Wilbur had sketchily described how the rudder and warp systems were locked together by wires, but added firmly, 'This statement is not for publication, but merely to correct the misapprehension in your mind.' At last, it appears, the confused aviation patriarch got the message, but the terseness of some of Wilbur's gently exasperated letters had upset him. 'I was puzzled,' Chanute wrote woundedly, 'by the way you put things . . . you were sarcastic and I did not catch the idea that you feared that the description might forestall a patent.'

Chanute said he would 'suppress' the contentious passage, but, to the brothers' bewilderment, added peevishly that the information – the design feature that had cracked one of the central problems of human flight – 'would have proved quite harmless as the construction is ancient and well known'.[5] Wilbur and Orville were flabbergasted. How could someone of Chanute's great international eminence, the author of one of the finest technical histories of the great quest, be so unfathomably ignorant? Patiently Wilbur wrote to chide him for accusing them of 'ancient methods which we do not use'.

Yet the Wrights were genuinely anxious to keep the relationship alive. The correspondence continued, but with Wilbur increasingly cagey about the things he disclosed. Reading the formally polite – 'Dear Mr Chanute', 'Dear Mr Wright' – letters that passed between them in that summer of 1903 one can feel the technical divide growing and Wilbur's rising, always polite, impatience with the other man's preoccupation with analyses of their most recent flights. The engineer in Chanute was obsessed with the mathematics of it all. He bombarded Dayton with requests for figures from their notebooks, which Wilbur considered now all somewhat academic. To yet another demand – for detailed aerodynamic information of eight glides made on one specific day – he replied a trifle offhandedly: 'I am really a little rusty at figuring per cents of error in such a case, but, at a guess, say we put it at 100,000 per cent – at any rate it is more than 50 per cent.'[6]

In spite of these aggravations he continued to humour Chanute, obligingly sending him sheaves of performance tables. The Wrights' minds, however, were already focused on new priorities: the development of the engine and propellers.

The work had begun soon after their return from the Outer Banks in the autumn of 1902. While Wilbur was being distracted by the tumult in the church, Orville had built a new larger wind tunnel with which they made final checks on the lift and drag figures for the big new wings that would have to support a motor. Hoping to buy a ready-made petrol engine from a motor manufacturer, Wilbur wrote to ten companies seeking a specially light one of 8 to 9 horsepower weighing no more than 180 pounds (82 kg). None of the makers was in the least interested in this one-off job. The brothers decided to build their own.

In 1902 the motor car internal combustion engine was a primitive machine. Theirs would have to run extra smoothly and vibration-free to avoid damaging the transmission chains with which they planned to link it to two propellers. They gave the job to Charlie Taylor. 'They had never done much machine work,' Taylor recalled in 1948, 'and anyway they were busy on the airframe. It was up to me. My only experience with a gasoline engine was an attempt to repair one in an automobile in 1901.'[7]

Taylor did a remarkable job, working only from rough sketches drawn by Wilbur and Orville and stuck on a spike on his bench in the cycle workshop. The crankcase was cast in aluminium alloy by a local foundry, and Taylor bored into it the holes for the cylinders and moulded the cast-iron pistons with his lathe. He made the crankshaft from a slab of steel, shaving and sculpturing it into shape. When finished 'she balanced up perfectly', he proudly remembered.

The engine had four water-cooled in-line cylinders, but no fuel pump or carburettor. Petrol – to be gravity-fed from a small tank attached to a wing strut – was injected directly into the horizontal cylinders and vaporised in a heated steel chamber on the manifold through which air passed on its way to the engine. Nor were there plugs – the sparks were created by arcs leaping between contact points inside each cylinder. Dry-cell batteries and a coil started the engine after the cylinders were primed with a few drops of petrol.

Once it was ticking over, the ignition came from a flywheel-driven magneto. There was no throttle: it ran at one speed.

When, early in February 1903, this small, very crude, home-made engine was ready for testing, the result was disappointing. The cooling system didn't work properly because the water wasn't circulated; it was merely replenished, as it evaporated, from a tank which was to be strapped to a strut between the wings. The valve box became red-hot within minutes and the engine had to be rapidly shut down. Next day, when they tried again, the bearings seized, shattering the crankcase. 'The boys broke their little gas motor in the afternoon,' Milton recorded quaintly in one of his rare references to his sons' aviation ventures.

It wasn't until April that a fresh casting arrived and testing resumed. This time, with valves popping noisily and a cloud of blue exhaust smoke filling the workshop, the engine ran successfully. To measure its power they connected it to a large resistance fan whose revolutions per minute they simply counted. To their delight this showed that it was delivering much more than the 8 horsepower they needed – it was giving a healthy 12 horsepower. So as not to waste the extra 150 pounds of weight this allowed them they used it to strengthen the machine with additional structure. It had all been achieved in six weeks with constant interruptions to attend to the shop whose customers were still their only source of income.

According to Charlie Taylor the new aeroplane was not born in an atmosphere of continuous harmony. Bent over his lathe he would sometimes be startled to hear from the room upstairs, where Wilbur and Orville were building the airframe, violent arguments breaking out. Forty-five years later Taylor could still remember the shouting matches:

> Both the boys had tempers . . . but I never heard them use a profane word . . . They were working out a lot of theory in those days and occasionally they would get into terrific arguments. They'd shout at each other something terrible. I don't think they really got mad, but they sure got awfully hot.
>
> One morning following the worst argument I ever heard, Orv came in and said he guessed he'd been wrong and they ought to

> do it Will's way. A few minutes later Will came in and said he'd been thinking it over and perhaps Orv was right. First thing I knew they were arguing the thing all over again, only this time they had switched ideas. When they were through though they knew where they were and could go ahead with the job.[8]

The new biplane with its 40-foot wingspan was too big to assemble in the shop. The centre section alone occupied so much space when it was brought downstairs and so blocked the way that, when a customer arrived, one of them would have to go out of a side door and re-enter by the front.

The propellers, they had assumed, would present the least of all their design problems. How wrong they were. The propeller was to confront them with a challenge almost as great as the quest for efficient wings and safe controls. Somehow they had imagined they would simply draw on the technology of marine propellers which, after all, had been in use for around a hundred years.

The brothers went to the Dayton public library in search of scientific information on the theory of ship propulsion and propeller design. Theoretical data appeared to be non-existent. Marine propellers, it seemed, were designed purely empirically. Their size and pitch (the distance travelled forward in one revolution) were merely arranged to suit the needs of each vessel. No helpful tables had apparently ever been compiled on which they could simply substitute air for water pressures. They were also surprised to discover that marine propellers operated at barely 50 per cent efficiency in their thrust compared with the power of the engine driving them. Although the crude flat-bladed propellers used by powered-flight experimenters like Maxim and Langley had operated at even lower levels of effectiveness, this wasn't good enough for the Wrights. Their new aeroplane's propellers would, they had already calculated, require, with their 12 horsepower motor, to be at least 66 per cent efficient. As they had neither the time nor the money to plod through an array of trial and error shapes, they were back in the business of invention:

> What at first seemed a simple problem became more complex the longer we studied it. With the machine moving forward, the

Sir George Cayley, the little-known English baronet who was the true inventor of the modern aeroplane. His glider flew a man across a Yorkshire valley in 1853. *Royal Aeronautical Society*

The 'Winged Prussian', Otto Lilienthal. His widely publicised glider flights in the early 1890s helped to inspire the Wright Brothers. *Otto Lilienthal Museum*

Lilienthal gliding off a German hill. His leg-swinging control technique led him to stall and plunge to his death in 1896. *Otto Lilienthal Museum*

Bishop Milton Wright, whose church wars competed with aeronautics to dominate family life. *Special Collections and Archives, Wright State University*

Susan Wright, the brothers' mother, who did not live to see the aeroplane conceived under her roof. *Special Collections and Archives, Wright State University*

The house at 7 Hawthorn Street, West Dayton, that witnessed much of the agony and ecstasy of the birth of flight. *Special Collections and Archives, Wright State University*

A composite picture of the Wright family. From left: Wilbur, Katharine, Susan, Lorin, Milton, Reuchlin, Orville. *Special Collections and Archives, Wright State University*

Downtown Dayton, Ohio, in the early 1900s, with the electric inter-urban railcars on which the brothers travelled to their flying field at Simms station, Huffman Prairie. *Dayton & Montgomery County Public Library*

The Wright Brothers' cycle shop at 1127 West Third Street, Dayton, in which the world's first successful powered aeroplane was built. *Special Collections and Archives, Wright State University*

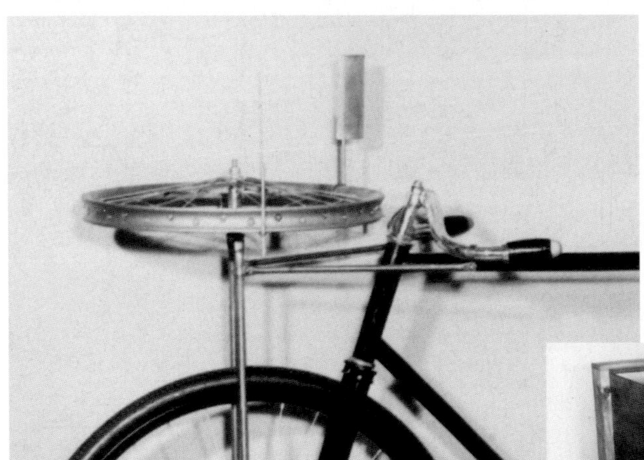

The miniature wing sections, which the Wrights used to test with this rig mounted on a bicycle. *Special Collections and Archives, Wright State University*

A replica of the wind tunnel in which more than 100 wing shapes were tested. *Special Collections and Archives, Wright State University*

Wilbur soars above the Kill Devil sandscape in the 1902 glider. Their camp is visible in the distance. *Special Collections and Archives, Wright State University*

Above: The Kill Devil shed in August 1901. Seated, from left: Octave Chanute, Orville, Edward Huffaker. Wilbur is standing on the right. *Special Collections and Archives, Wright State University*

Left: Camp kitchen, 1902. The food cans and utensils were kept arranged with obsessive military tidiness. *Special Collections and Archives, Wright State University*

14 December 1903. Four lifesavers, two boys (and a dog) wait expectantly by the *Flyer* mounted on its rail for the first powered take-off attempt. Wilbur stalled: the machine went only sixty feet. *Special Collections and Archives, Wright State University*

Kill Devil Hills, North Carolina, 10.35 a.m., 17 December 1903. In one of the world's most reproduced pictures, lifesaver John Daniels got this photograph at the moment Orville lifted off the rail on his historic first flight. Wilbur, running alongside, has just released his steadying hand from the wingtip. *Special Collections and Archives, Wright State University*

Samuel P. Langley, Secretary of the Smithsonian Institution, whose rival aeroplanes disastrously failed to fly. *Special Collections and Archives, Wright State University*

Octave Chanute, the French born aviation pioneer with whom the Wrights shared some of their most precious aeronautical secrets before the friendship ended in bitter acrimony. *Library of Congress*

Langley's ill-fated aeroplane, the *Great Aerodrome*, at the moment of launching from the top of a houseboat in October 1903. The machine and its pilot dived straight into the Potomac. *NASM, Smithsonian Institution (SI 89-12604)*

Airborne at Huffman Prairie, Dayton, in November 1904, the *Flyer* can now stay up for five minutes. *Special Collections and Archives, Wright State University*

The *Flyer* on its launch rail at Fort Myer, Washington, DC, 1908. The launching weights were raised and dropped in the tower behind. *Special Collections and Archives, Wright State University*

Below: At Pau in France, in 1909, a farmer looks up from his hay wagon as Wilbur flies overhead. *Special Collections and Archives, Wright State University*

> air flying backward, the propellers turning sidewise, and nothing standing still, it seemed impossible to find a starting point from which to trace the various simultaneous reactions. Contemplation of it was confusing. After long arguments we often found ourselves in the ludicrous position of each having been converted to the other's side, with no more agreement than when the discussion began.[9]

The upshot of this latest round of arguments in the spring of 1903 was agreement that an aeroplane's propeller could not be treated like a ship's, which pushed the vessel forward by displacing the water through which it was passing. It functioned quite differently. It was actually, they discovered in a brilliant shaft of perception, a rotating wing 'travelling in a spiral course'. Instead of being driven passively against the air to produce lift it was itself spun to generate thrust aerodynamically.

To design one of efficient thrusting size and shape they went back to their wind tunnel wing data. From the scores of miniature metal sections they had tested in their search for the ideal wing they looked for one that would best suit the rotary purposes of a propeller. The process by which they eventually found one was never, in the view of some modern aerodynamicists, given the recognition it deserved. 'Their propeller theory revealed,' according to aerospace engineering professor John Anderson at the University of Maryland, 'a degree of technical sophistication in applied aerodynamics never seen before. Their application of the theory in designing a real propeller was masterful.'[10] It was such a significant contribution to aviation, Professor Anderson said, that in its own right it would today have certainly merited a major international scientific award.

Five of the brothers' notebooks are devoted entirely to the intricate technical data they amassed in their propeller research. They show the formulae – far more complex than for their wing design – they wrote to help them arrive at blades of the right length, width, subtle curvature, angle and the most efficient speed of rotation. In the workshop they made a small test fan which they ran to check their figures. Their final design produced two very large propellers – each around 8½ feet long. They were made of three laminations of spruce which they shaped with hatchet and knife. How efficient they were they wouldn't know for sure until they put them in the air at Kill Devil – but they were confident they'd got it right.

In a euphoric letter to George Spratt, Orville proudly described their propeller triumph:

> We had been unable to find anything of value in any of the works to which we had access, so that we worked out a theory of our own on the subject, and soon discovered, as we usually do that all the propellers built heretofore are all wrong, and then built a pair of propellers 8⅛ ft in diameter, based on our theory, which are all right! (Till we have a chance to test them down at Kitty Hawk and find out differently). Isn't it astonishing that all these secrets have been preserved for so many years just so that we could discover them!![11]

Orville's letter ended with a postscript asking Spratt to keep their latest plans secret: 'Please do not mention the fact of our building a power machine to anybody. The newspapers would take great delight in following us in order to record our troubles'.

George Spratt was one of the few people with whom they were still confidently prepared to entrust their secrets. Wilbur at this moment was happily conducting, with endless forbearance, a protracted debate over a new abstruse theory of Spratt's he was claiming as a 'momentous' breakthrough – a circular-section wing that would 'guarantee absolute stability'. When Wilbur had challenged the soundness of the theory, Spratt's fragile self-esteem had collapsed and he had sunk back into depression. Accustomed to the stimulation of passionate argument with Orville, Wilbur told Spratt: 'I see that you are back at your old trick of giving up before you are half beaten in an argument. I . . . was anticipating the pleasure of a good scrap before the matter was settled. Discussion brings out new ways of looking at things and helps to round off the corners.'

When Spratt expressed envy of his intellect, Wilbur responded with some psychological insight into the Wright family:

> You make a great mistake in envying me any of my qualities. Very often what you take for some special quality of mind is merely facility arising from constant practice, and you could do as well or better with little practice.
>
> It is a characteristic of all our family to be able to see the weak points of anything, but this is not always a desirable quality and it makes us too conservative for successful business men, and limits our friendships to a very limited circle. You envy me, but I envy you the possession of some qualities that I would give a great deal to possess in equal degree . . . You should by all means avoid lying awake at nights studying out problems, as you did sometimes at Kitty Hawk . . .[12]

Wilbur now found himself drawn into a lengthy discussion with Spratt on his belief in the value of argument:

> No truth is without some mixture of error, and no error so false but that it possesses some elements of truth. If a man is in too big a hurry to give up an error he is liable to give up some truth with it, and in accepting the arguments of the other man he is sure to get some error with it. Honest argument is merely a process of mutually picking the beams and motes out of each other's eyes so both can see clearly. Men become wise just as they become rich, more by what they save than by what they receive. After I get hold of a truth I hate to lose it again, and I like to sift all the truth out before I give up an error.[13]

In June Chanute visited them again in Dayton. He announced he was ceasing automatic stability experiments – he was beginning to falter in his belief that, as Wilbur put it, 'human intelligence would be inadequate to cope with the difficulties encountered in the tumultuous aerial seas'. Watching the Wrights' glider performing so perfectly at Kill Devil he had decided that a machine under human control, far from foundering in the aerial tumult, would now almost certainly be the first to achieve powered flight. Chanute persuaded Wilbur to appear again before the Society of Western Engineers. In his address he described their 1902 Kill Devil experiments, prudently avoiding the detail of the new control system and giving not the merest hint that they were on the verge of a powered flight attempt.

The brothers were now doubly cautious since a setback in March to their first patent application registering an unpowered flying machine controlled by their three-dimensional system. The US Patent Office, inundated for decades now with flying vehicle applications, had quickly rejected the submission: the drawings were inadequate and their descriptions too vague. To make the principles clearer Wilbur had sent the patent officials one of the cardboard cycle tube boxes that had inspired the wing warping. It was also swiftly dismissed as 'of no assistance'. He was advised to seek the help of a patent lawyer. Bewildered and even more fearful for the security of their intellectual property, the Wrights decided to postpone the application until they had a powered machine to demonstrate.

While during that June of 1903 they were bringing together the motor, propellers and airframe of what they were now calling the *Flyer*, their father was embroiled in renewed guerrilla warfare within the church. For months now, Milton had defied his suspension, continuing to stomp the Brethren circuits through the Midwest, determined to clear his name and put Keiter behind bars. His powerful pro-Keiter fellow bishops, Barnaby and Floyd, decided the time had come for drastic action. They banned Milton from the August conference of his own White River district at Messick, Indiana. Milton defied them and turned up with the formidable Wilbur in tow. To the delegates' amazement the bristling figure of Bishop Wright demanded to take the chair. He strode forward and seized the strategic seat. When he refused to vacate it the conference exploded into uproar. For a moment it looked as if Milton and Bishop Floyd might come to blows. In the ensuing bedlam their angry voices could be heard trying to shout each other down, both beating gavels simultaneously in their battle for control. When neither could restore order, the conference adjourned in disarray. Floyd now decided on forceful measures. Hastily he arranged for an injunction forbidding his opponent from presiding. To the Wrights' dismay a local sheriff arrived and served the order upon Milton.

Next morning the conference resumed to decide Wright's fate. Milton had gone back to Dayton to await the verdict; Wilbur remained to hear the inevitable outcome. He heard his father's activities roundly condemned as anarchist. A committee of elders voted overwhelmingly that he be forthwith expelled from the church.

When Wilbur returned to Hawthorn Street with the news, Milton was philosophical. He said he would ignore the expulsion as illegal and sue the White River elders. He did so seeking $10,000. The Radical Brethren, its dirty linen now hung out publicly amid damaging newspaper headlines, was slowly splitting apart. Ministers were leaving in disgust, no longer trusting the church's ability to safeguard its funds.

Keiter was not summarily kicked out of the church. There was no machinery within the Brethren to resolve the destructive squabble until the next sitting of its quadrennial conference – not due for two more years – in 1905. Shielded from further prosecution by powerful colleagues, Keiter remained within the church as large as life. The two factions continued to denounce each other with flurries of tracts, some written by Wilbur and issued under his own name. By the autumn of 1903, 7 Hawthorn Street had become a propaganda factory, diverting Wilbur's and Orville's minds from aeronautics and employing Lorin and Katharine as well.

At the cycle shop, despite this huge distraction, the world's first powered aeroplane was being crated for shipment to Kill Devil. It hadn't yet been fully assembled – airframe, engine and propellers would finally be bolted together at the flying camp. Wilbur and Orville had planned to leave in August. The Brethren dramas delayed them until late September.

Their fourth journey to the Outer Banks was their least complicated. Steam ships and motor launches had at last begun to replace the unreliable sailing boats and delivered them to Kill Devil on 25 September. Again the winter storms had created havoc at the camp. A 90-mile-an-hour gale driving torrential rain, which had left lakes of water in the sand, had lifted the shed bodily off its foundations and dumped it two feet to the east. But inside, the 1902 glider was intact. They rehired Dan Tate and set to work repairing the building, erecting beside it a new larger shed to house the *Flyer*. They also began to make some impressive glides with the old machine, launching it off the sandhills to polish their piloting skills for powered flying. The new aeroplane was still on its way from Dayton, and while awaiting its arrival they made, between them, over 200 glides, achieving new records in duration and height. For the first time they began to stay in the air for more than a minute.

Interest among the Bankers in their activities was now intense: they soon had a stream of visitors. People still didn't know quite what to make of them, but, crazy as they may have seemed, no one disagreed that they were exceedingly nice people. 'There was nothing high-hat about the Wrights,' said lifeboatman John Daniels, who on an earlier visit had been perplexed to see them leaping about imitating soaring birds. 'They were good company, good mixers with attractive personalities . . . one was instinctively drawn to them.' Both men 'courteously opened doors and gates for companions, told good stories and Orville in particular was a fine cook'.[14]

Curiosity among the locals surged when, on 8 October, a sailing ship brought to Kitty Hawk the crates containing the *Flyer.* Next morning they were taken down to Kill Devil by horse cart. No sooner had the boxes been stored inside the new hangar than a fearful rainstorm burst. The tempest raged for four days with gusts reaching 75 miles an hour and ripping the tar paper off the top of the hangar. In their living quarters next door they lay sleepless in their under-roof bunks as the shrieking wind rose to cyclonic force and the timbers twitched. With every gust they expected to hear the crashing destruction of the frail new shelter and its precious contents. In the middle of the worst night, hearing water sluicing about below, Orville climbed down to find the floor under a sloshing lake of water.

When at last the cyclone moved away their camp had become an island in a landscape of lagoons. Five ships, they learnt, had been driven ashore along the Outer Banks. The body of one of the captains had been washed up on the Kitty Hawk ocean beach.

On 14 October the sun reappeared and Dan Tate returned with a packet of mail. Among the letters was one from a neighbour in Hawthorn Street sending them a newspaper cutting. It was a report of Samuel Langley's long-awaited first flight attempt with his piloted *Great Aerodrome*.

After nearly five years in development, and badly overrunning its original $50,000 budget, the aeroplane the US government had commissioned to revolutionise warfare had finally been test-flown by its project manager, Charles Manly. Huge expectations surrounded it and, despite the secrecy Langley had tried to maintain, a posse of newspaper reporters and photographers had been continuously camped for three months on the malarial mosquito-infested banks of the Potomac at Widewater, thirty-five miles downriver from Washington, waiting to witness the birth of powered flight.

The strange-looking machine, with its tandem wings, had scarcely evolved beyond its small steam-powered predecessors. It was, however, massively powered. Though Manly had developed for it a radial petrol engine of 52 horsepower – more than four times that of the *Flyer* – in most other respects the great machine was technically inferior. The 48-foot by 11-foot dimensions of each of its wings gave it an enormous 1000 square feet of lifting surface, double its rival's, but had Langley, as the Wrights had done, wind-tunnel tested the wings' aspect ratio and curvature he would have discovered how aerodynamically inefficient they were. As was the tandem – one wing behind the other – arrangement.

Critically, it lacked the essential of three-dimensional control. Langley, like Chanute, was a stubborn believer in automatic stability. The only controls the pilot had in his cloth-walled space between the wings were two wheels – one to move the cruciform tail for pitch, the other to operate a frail fabric rudder that lay ineffectually beneath the fuselage. There was no lateral control of any description – no means of raising a dropped wing in flight.

Langley had insisted the machine be launched, like its smaller ancestors, by catapult from the top of a houseboat on the Potomac. Manly, not relishing being flung into space from sixty feet above the river, had protested and suggested a lower-level launch. But Langley had refused.

Wearing sand shoes, a cork life jacket and goggles, Manly had nervously climbed aboard:

> The engine was started and the twin propellers began their whirring song. At 12.30 pm, with power full on and after a quick look around at the impatient vibrating machine, Manly nodded to Smithsonian workmen . . . Two signal rockets were fired. Whistle blasts were the tugs' response. With an axe someone cut the line restraining the catapult launch car. The 850 lb *aerodrome* shot forward toward the edge of the platform.[15]

The flight lasted only seconds. Hurled by the huge launching spring, the *Great Aerodrome* sailed off the houseboat and dived straight into the river. Part of the aeroplane had snagged on the launch mechanism. As one of the watching reporters described it, it dropped 'like a handful of mortar'. Briefly trapped underwater, Manly had struggled up through the tangled mess of guy wires to the surface, grateful to be alive. Langley was in no way discouraged. There was nothing wrong with the machine itself, he told the dismayed War Department. The *Great Aerodrome* would be quickly repaired and ready to take to the air in full flight in a few weeks.

The disaster was gleefully splashed across America by newspapers deeply sceptical of the possibility of human flight. The *New York Times* said it might just happen in 'the next one to ten million years'. Overnight Langley and his ill-starred aeroplane became the nationwide butt of jokes in the press and by comedians on the vaudeville stage.

From the Outer Banks Wilbur wrote to Chanute: 'I see that Langley has had his fling and failed. It seems to be our turn to throw now, and I wonder what our luck will be.'[16]

14

Twelve Famous Seconds (1903)

The Wrights now saw themselves head-to-head in a race for powered flight with the great Samuel Langley. No one else in the world at that moment was anywhere near achieving it. And between the Americans the realistic odds were on the brothers – of whom only a handful of people had ever heard. Unlike Langley who, to his frustration, had never set eyes on the Wrights' machines, they, unknown to him, had been privy to some of the critical aerodynamic data that had shaped his own aeroplanes.

Two years earlier Langley had sent Chanute, in confidence, technical details of the curvature of wings he was testing and the lift they would hopefully produce. Chanute, naughtily, had immediately sent all this private information to Wilbur inviting his opinion. Curious, Wilbur had quickly made a model of the Langley wing and tested it in their wind tunnel. It didn't take him long to discover that, in lifting capability, it wasn't a brilliant performer. 'This surface,' Wilbur had reported, 'is by no means an efficient one for flying.'[1] It was inferior to most of their own experimental wings they had tested, he said. Convinced that the hapless *Great Aerodrome* had inherited these poor flying qualities, the brothers didn't see Langley, even if he solved his launching problems, as a serious threat.

Now they had the satisfaction of learning that they were right.

'He started from a point 60 feet in the air and landed 300 feet away which is a drop of 1 foot for every 5 forward,' Orville wrote to Katharine. 'We are able, from this height, to make from 400 to 600 feet without any motor at all, so that I think his surfaces must be very inefficient.'[2]

In the late October days following the storm they resumed assembling the *Flyer*. Inside the hangar, in which they'd built a workbench, the wing timbers were covered in unvarnished, tightly woven muslin, giving their top and underside surfaces a smoothness that delighted them. 'It is the prettiest we have ever made and of a much better shape,' Orville wrote proudly to tell Milton. The graceful wings had been given a deeper camber of 1:20 compared with the 1:30 of the 1902 glider. They felt the greater curvature would help provide the extra lift the much heavier machine would need.

The engine was mounted on the centre section of the lower wing immediately to the right of the pilot's cradle which, once again, controlled the interlocked wing warping and a revived double rudder. Out in front of the 'whopper flying machine', as Wilbur (quoting one of Lorin's children) described it to Katharine, there was a double elevator which looked like a miniature biplane. Intended to carry a helpful bit of the flight load, it was operated, as on the gliders, by a lever gripped by the pilot's left hand.

The big eight-foot pusher propellers were mounted immediately behind the once again drooped wings on long shafts which ran forward to sprocket wheels connected to the engine by chains. This crude bicycle technology was crucial to the machine's ability to power itself through the air. The brothers' had revealed the seemingly curious fact that the slower their propellers were turning the greater – within certain limits – the thrust they gave. Two large slowly revolving blades would, they discovered, actually push a greater mass of air than a single faster spinning one. To slow the propellers down they geared the sprockets so that 23 revolutions of the engine would produce just 8 turns of the propellers. They also made them counterrotate to neutralise the gyroscopic effect that would have rotated the aeroplane away from the direction of spin. Instead of both blades turning in the same direction, they spun towards each other. They achieved this by the simple expedient of crossing into a figure of eight one of the hollow guide tubes through which the driving trains travelled – thus reversing the direction in which the sprocket turned.

They had hoped the *Flyer* would be ready for its maiden flight by 1 November, but mechanical problems, bad weather and a soon-to-arrive labour crisis were to make the date far too optimistic. When George Spratt arrived in camp in the fourth week of October, they hadn't even begun to test the engine. Spratt was never to see it fly – but he witnessed some remarkable glides which they continued to make with the 1902 machine. One of Orville's, finely timed at 1 minute 11.8 seconds, was a world record that was to stand for eight years, until he himself broke it.

Spratt brought to Kill Devil some bitter weather. Every night the temperature fell a few more degrees and it began to pour with rain again until the sand hollows around the camp were filled once more with great ponds of water. The cold pierced their bones. They hung carpets on the walls to stem the draughts and lit a fire in an empty carbide can. It filled the hut with smoke so choking they were forced to sit on the floor, squatting around the can 'with tears streaming down our cheeks enjoying its kindly rays of heat. Everything about the building was sooted up so thoroughly that for several days we couldn't sit down to eat without a whole lot of black soot dropping down in our plates.'[3] To solve the problem they converted the can into a stove with a stack. 'We are now living in luxurious ease,' Orville reported to Hawthorn Street.

Keeping warm was not their only problem. Their hired labour suddenly deserted them. Dan Tate arrived one morning to announce that the price Bankers were getting for their fish had gone up. To keep him from his main occupation they had to increase his wages, despite the fact that 'whenever we set him at any work about the building he would do so much damage with his awkwardness that we found it more profitable to let him sit around'. But they did need him for launching assistance. 'Of course he was soon spoiled and even went so far as to complain when any work was wanted on the hill.' Tate had begun to resent being treated by the Wrights, he told people, like a housemaid, having to wash their dishes and do other menial domestic tasks. Things came to a head with the cold weather. When Wilbur asked Tate to go over to the ocean beach to collect driftwood for the stove, he refused, saying it was an unreasonable request when they could buy a cord of firewood in Kitty Hawk for just $3. When Wilbur insisted he get the driftwood Tate 'took his hat and left for home.' He never returned.

The willing Spratt quickly filled his shoes, starting by helping them build the 60-foot-long metal-capped wooden rail from which the *Flyer* would hopefully launch itself off level ground into the air. They named it 'the Grand Junction Railroad'. The new aeroplane, with its wingspan of more than 40 feet and all-up weight of around a third of a ton, was too big and heavy to be launched by hand. In any case, to prove that it could lift off unassisted by sloping ground or human energy it was important that its take-off run be made entirely with the thrust of its own engine. The machine was to roll forward along the rail, with its skids sitting on small wooden trolleys on rollers made from bicycle hubs.

But the *Flyer* was still far from ready to test this ingenious railroad. When, on 5 November, they started up the engine for the first time, things went badly. The engine misfired explosively, sending alarming vibrations to the tubular propeller shafts. The sprocket wheels soon worked loose, causing the propellers to turn in jerking fits and starts. In no time the shafts twisted and ripped from their mountings. It was a major setback. They had no means of repairing the damaged shafts at Kill Devil – they would have to go back to Dayton for Charlie Taylor to make replacements. It would all take at least two weeks. Their hopes of getting the *Flyer* into the air that year began to fade.

Spratt offered to cut his stay short and take the shafts to the rail depot at Norfolk, Virginia. Fortuitously a launch was due to leave Kill Devil for Manteo on Roanoke Island at 4 o'clock that afternoon. In Manteo that evening, waiting for the steamer to Elizabeth City, he bumped into Chanute en route to Kill Devil, and told him pessimistically that he was convinced the powered machine would never get off the ground. Chanute had been expecting to bring Patrick Alexander down to see the attempt, the Wrights having agreed that the tenacious Englishman could visit the camp.

Travelling in his customary luxury, Alexander had arrived in America in the last week in October. Chanute appears at last to have accepted that no one, himself included, had an automatic right to observe the Wrights' experiments or expect to share their shrewd, hard-won technical knowledge. With uncharacteristic diffidence he had written to Wilbur at Kill Devil: 'Do not hesitate to say so if you would rather not have me come, and give me also your views as to a visit from Mr Alexander . . . I have not advised him that you are at Kitty Hawk, nor hinted at your plans, so he will not be aggrieved if he is not invited.'[4]

Wilbur replied welcoming both Chanute and Alexander. But, unfortunately for the latter, despite Chanute's letter sending him the good news and arranging to meet him at a hotel in Washington to travel to the Outer Banks together, Alexander failed to wait for him. He actually arrived at Chanute's hotel but, puzzlingly, left him a note to say that he was rushing off to Boston to meet Major Baden-Powell. The bewildered Chanute left for Kill Devil on his own. Alexander missed the aviation experience of his life.

When Chanute reached Kill Devil on 6 November, the weather had become even more bitterly cold and bleak. His elderly bones felt it acutely as sweeping rain drove them all inside to huddle round the makeshift stove. The conversation was as depressing as the conditions outside. Chanute had convinced himself that the *Flyer* wouldn't be able to lift off. His calculations, he argued, showed that the power of the 12 horsepower motor almost exactly matched that required to fly. They hadn't, he said, taken sufficient account of the loss caused by the friction of the chain transmission system. He reckoned it would be as high as 20 per cent. They had allowed for only 5 per cent. With the propeller shafts gone they couldn't test the old man's pessimism. He cast a gloom upon an already cheerless scene.

Nor were their spirits raised by some extraordinary proposals Chanute now put to them. He revealed, to their amazement, that he was trying to buy the remains of an uncontrollable, steam-powered, bat-winged machine, the *Avion III*, which the French experimenter Clément Ader had failed to make fly back in 1897. The weirdly designed aeroplane, looking as if it had leapt from the pages of Jules Verne, had been long ago consigned to a Paris museum. Chanute said he wanted Wilbur and Orville to rebuild it, 'perfect' it, and fly it for him. They couldn't believe he was serious. The Ader machine, which had a crazy pilot-operated hand-cranked swing wing for pitch control, had proved unflyable. It was a bizarre and dangerous exhibit from the past. No way could it ever be made to fly. 'He thinks we could do it!' Orville later told Milton. 'He doesn't seem to think our machines are so much superior as the manner in which we handle them. We are of just the reverse opinion.'[5]

Astoundingly, the doomed Ader machine wasn't the only one Chanute tried to persuade them to fly. He wanted them also to test Augustus Herring's failed oscillating wing glider, now stored at Kill Devil. The brothers firmly declined both proposals. Despite his enormous civil engineering expertise, he was quite unable to get his head around the masterful concepts that had rendered the *Avion* and Herring's body-swinging machine patently redundant.

Chanute spent six miserable days at Kill Devil. Despite the rags they had stuffed into the wall cracks there was no escape from the relentless cold and they were running out of food. They tried to entertain him by demonstrating their piloting skills, gliding the 1902 machine again off the hills, but the wind was so erratic and the cold so severe they had to give up after a few attempts. Back in the smoky fug of the hut they studied photographs Chanute had brought of the *Great Aerodrome* diving into the Potomac. They were staggered by the complexity of Langley's giant launching machinery. 'Our track,' Wilbur wrote home, 'for starting the machine (total cost about $4) amused Mr Chanute considerably, as Langley is said to have spent nearly $50,000 [around $1 million today] on his starting device which failed in the end . . .'[6]

On 12 November Chanute left in a small sailing boat to go back to Manteo where, in a gesture that touched them both, he bought them a pair of gloves each which he sent across to their camp. The gloves were welcome, for the weather had edged even deeper into winter. The ponds around the camp had begun to freeze hard at night, as did the water in the basins inside the hut. To keep warm in their bunks under the roof they had to resort to desperate measures.

'In addition to the classifications of last year, to wit, 1,2,3 and 4 blanket nights, we now have 5 blanket nights & 5 blankets & 2 quilts. Next come 5 blankets, 2 quilts & fire; then 5, 2 & hot-water jug. This is as far as we have got so far. Next comes the addition of sleeping without undressing, then shoes & hats, and finally overcoats. We intend to be comfortable while we are here.'[7]

While waiting for the ship bringing the new propeller shafts and a fresh supply of groceries – they were down to dining on condensed milk and crackers – they found themselves with time on their hands. It was no longer safe to glide the old machine: stored in the back of their living hut its wooden framework, dried out by the warmth from the stove, has become 'rickety' – too risky for serious soaring. They decided, however, that it was safe enough to test the launching rail. They took the 'railroad' in sections up the side of the big hill and placed the glider on the cycle hub trolleys. While one lay prone on the lower wing, the other ran alongside to balance the moving machine. It worked well and in no time the glider was regularly sailing off on brief flights down the hill.

Now, undistracted by visitors, they used the long dark evenings to study languages by lantern light. They were keen to read foreign aviation articles which Chanute had been sending them. Orville, who seems to have been the more enthusiastic, took up both French and German, attacking them diligently. Equally assiduously they both maintained a dutiful flow of correspondence with the family. Long letters went regularly from Kill Devil to Milton, Katharine and Lorin – all of whom were sending their own news.

That autumn of 1903, Milton continued to defy his expulsion, energetically preaching his way from Ohio to Kansas and back. His 'Dear Sons' letters kept Wilbur and Orville informed of the ceaseless machinations of the Keiterites and the rising tide of support he claimed to be generating. Katharine relayed to father and brothers every morsel of information that arrived from the Outer Banks, and every aviation item that appeared in the press. 'Did you see in the papers the Langley machine smashed to pieces?' she asked Milton. 'I wonder if you saw an account of the hurricane that swept the Atlantic coast last week. I'll enclose Orv's letter. I felt worried about them.'[8]

The gregarious Katharine couldn't bear to be on her own. She had sent Carrie off on holiday and 'the house is so lonesome that I hate to stay in it – but I can't rest as well anywhere else.'[9] Women friends would come to stay the night with her; Lorin would call regularly at Hawthorn Street to see if there was anything he could do. Lorin was still struggling to keep his own family afloat. He had set up a part-time business of his own, acquiring horses which he used for haulage work and for pulling a water tank to sprinkle dusty streets for the municipality. It was proving good for his health. 'Lorin,' Katharine noted, 'weighs fifteen pounds more than he did in the spring and looks like a different fellow.'[10]

On the desolate sandbanks, the late November winds that howled in from the Atlantic had begun to bring snow. It didn't bode well for the test flight. Ever since Chanute had left the Wrights had been pondering his conviction that they might not have enough lift-off power. They had estimated that the *Flyer*'s weight with pilot would not exceed 625 pounds, but the true weight had risen well above this. As they worried about the slender power/weight margin between success and failure, Orville had begun to reflect their shrinking confidence in a flow of metaphoric stock market allusions in letters to Charlie Taylor:

> Flying machine market has been very unsteady the past two days. Opened yesterday morning at about 208 (100% means even chance of success) but by noon had dropped to 110. These fluctuations have produced a panic, I think, in Wall Street, but in this quiet place it only put us to thinking and figuring a little. It gradually improved during rest of yesterday and today is almost back to its old mark.[11]

Day after day they brooded on the growing possibility that all their efforts were, like all those before them, headed for failure. 'The more we thought the harder our machine got to running and the less the power of the engine became, until stock got down to a very low figure.'[12]

On 20 November the sailing ship *Lou Willis* brought to Kitty Hawk a large stock of groceries from Elizabeth City. It also brought the replacement shafts which Taylor had made from heavier gauge tubular steel. Haunted by Chanute's belief that they were hopelessly underpowered, and impatient to test the propellers' thrust, they installed the shafts that very day. But when they started the motor their hopes sank again. It ran so erratically that both sprocket wheels worked loose within seconds. They tried tightening the nuts that locked the wheels on to the shafts, but still the sprockets wobbled loose. They were near despair.

> We used a chain and six-foot 2 × 4 to tighten them and the nuts, but ten seconds more run and they were loose again. We kept that up all Friday afternoon and by evening stock had gone still lower, in fact just about as low as it could get, about 100 per cent below par.[13]

'But,' Orville added, 'the darkest hour comes just before dawn. The next morning, thanks to Arnstein's hard cement, which will fix anything from a stop watch to a thrashing machine, we stuck those sprockets so tight I doubt whether they will ever come loose again.'[14]

For the moment the adhesive they used to hold bicycle tyres on their rims had cured the transmission problem. Now at last they could establish the thrust they were going to get. They did so in very basic fashion. Placing rollers under the *Flyer*'s skids they attached to the aeroplane a rope which they ran over a pulley to a dangling box of sand – to which they connected their spring-balance scales. They ran up the engine until the force of the throbbing propellers began to inch the machine forward, raising the sand box and recording the additional pull on the scales.

When the total weight of the *Flyer* had grown to 700 pounds, they calculated that their propellers – originally designed to give 90 pounds of thrust and an airspeed of 24 miles an hour – would now have to achieve nearer 100 pounds. This was necessary to overcome the aircraft's total resistance, which they reckoned to be about 95 pounds. It was a very slender margin, but they were confident it would be enough. Switching off the engine and seizing their notebooks, they hurriedly made the critical calculations. To their great joy the figures brought marvellous news: 'The engine speeded the propellers up to 351 rev. per min. with a thrust of 132 pounds. Stock went up like a skyrocket and is now at the highest figure in its history.'[15] Wonderfully, it appeared that they had after all engineered a healthy margin far beyond their dreams.

'Unless something breaks in the meantime we feel confident of success,'[16] Orville told Charlie Taylor. They were so confident they began to discuss how it should be reported to the world. 'If we should succeed in making a flight and telegraph, we will expect Lorin as our press agent (!) to notify the papers and the Associated Press,' Orville had written to Milton and Katharine. 'Chanute was much surprised that none of the reporters had learned of our experiments. Langley told him that they nearly worried him to death.'[17]

The publicity arrangements were to prove premature. In the last week of November, appalling weather returned. A ferocious gale howled about the sheds, driving the woodsmoke from their chimney across the dismal landscape in a horizontal plume. With the wind came sheets of driving, drizzling rain. The temperature took another dive, the drizzle turned to sleet then snow and the water in their washbasins froze to solid blocks of ice. Inside the hangar they went on tinkering with the *Flyer*, running and rerunning the engine, scribbling the performance figures in their notebooks. To check for vibration and structural strength they suspended it by the wingtips with one of them on board and the motor running. There was no vibration.

On to the machine they attached some instruments: an anemometer with which to calculate distance flown through the air, a stopwatch and, on the engine, a revolution counter to record the number of turns of motor and propellers. All three instruments were cleverly connected by levers and string to be started and stopped synchronously. A small lever on the lower wing simultaneously tripped them all when the fuel valve was shut off.

On 28 November, while running up the engine to test this creative flight data recording system, further catastrophe struck. The new propeller shafts had begun almost immediately to shimmy again. When they shut down the back-firing motor they saw to their consternation that one of the shafts had cracked in the middle. It was a dispiriting moment. With winter daily tightening its grip on the Outer Banks, the chances of an attempt before Christmas now seemed remote. They were already weeks behind their original schedule. By the time Taylor could produce yet more shafts and get them back to Kill Devil it would be mid-December. They retreated to the feeble warmth of their living quarters to talk it over.

There is no record of their discussion that morning. It may have touched on the risk that if they didn't pursue the attempt the stubborn Langley might have another go. It would have revolved around one imperative: their promise to be home by Christmas. What finer gift could they bring the family than the achievement of the world's first powered flight? They decided to have one more try. It was agreed that Orville would go back to Dayton to supervise the manufacture of the new shafts and rush them back to Kill Devil, and that they would abandon the use of vulnerable tubular shafts for high-grade solid steel ones. With luck, the 1500-mile round trip might just be managed in a long week.

It was two days before Orville could get a boat to set off with the failed shafts. He didn't reach Dayton until 3 December. Ironically, the moment he left Kill Devil the weather brightened. It became warmer with clear skies and, perversely, just the right wind strength they needed. With time to kill Wilbur busied himself chopping firewood and writing letters.

Unknown to the brothers, in that first week of December Langley was preparing the repaired *Great Aerodrome* for another brave attempt from his Potomac launching barge. Its wings had been rebuilt, its water-soaked engine dried out and restored. With the grey pall of winter descending upon Washington and ice floes already bobbing on the rapidly freezing river, Langley was in a race against time. He and the still willing Manly would have much preferred to delay the new attempt until spring, but they were under far greater pressure than the publicly invisible Wrights. Langley's hugely expensive project was drawing further criticism in Congress and the growing unease of its customer, the US War Department. With the government's funds now exhausted, Langley's career, and the reputation of the great national institution, was on the line. Regardless of weather and floating ice, he knew the crunch flight now had to be made before Christmas. Furthermore, it would be made this time not at a lonely site thirty-five miles downriver but much more publicly at the confluence of the Potomac and Anacostia Rivers – on Washington's very doorstep. Of a rival pre-Christmas attempt hundreds of miles away in North Carolina the harassed professor was quite oblivious. As indeed were the newspapers.

Orville left Dayton with the new shafts on 9 December. Somewhere on the long journey to Norfolk as the train rocked its way through the wintry vista of the Virginias he bought a newspaper. It carried a story that was both tragic and cheering. Langley's *Great Aerodrome* had the previous day been launched again over the Potomac. Once more it had plunged straight into the river. Manly, a virtually helpless passenger, had been trapped in the wreckage under an ice floe; he was lucky not to have drowned in the freezing water. The aeroplane upon which more time and money had been lavished than any before in aviation history had finally shown itself for what it was – a disastrous technological failure. Despite the persistent faith of its inventor, it was structurally and aerodynamically unsound – at the moment of launch, the rear wing, unable to bear the flight load, had collapsed. One of the earliest photographs to record an aircraft in its death throes dramatically captured the crumpling wing in mid-air as the machine reared up and fell over on its back.

The latest fiasco had been watched by a large contingent of Washington newsmen sitting with cameras in rowing boats. For years they had resented Langley's personal remoteness and the impenetrable cloak of secrecy with which he surrounded his aeroplanes. Their stories next day were merciless. As it crashed, Langley's machine, wrote one, 'pointed straight towards the roofs and towers of the Government Hospital for the Insane'. Perhaps, said another, 'if Professor Langley had only thought to launch his airship bottom-side up, it would have gone into the air instead of down into the water.'

The cartoons were cruel. The *Washington Post*'s depicted a waterlogged buzzard receiving artificial respiration while Langley, in silk top hat, sat dejectedly on the carcase with his head in his hands. 'The time is ripe,' said the *Post*, 'for a really serious appraisement of the so-called aeroplane and for a withdrawal by the government from all further participation in its financial and scientific calamities.'[18] In Congress there were withering criticisms of the public money that had funded Langley's shattered dream. 'If it is to cost us $73,000 to construct a mud duck that will not fly 50 feet,' asked one congressman, 'how much is it going to cost to construct a real flying machine?'[19]*

The mortifying failure of the *Great Aerodrome* left Langley, now approaching seventy, a broken man – exhausted and disheartened. Never in all his distinguished career had he tasted defeat and disappointment so bitter. As public ridicule was heaped upon him he began visibly to age. The secret of powered flight had comprehensively eluded him. For the remaining three years of his life he turned his back on aeronautics, returning to the astrophysics he understood so much better.

The Wrights knew all too well how fine the margins were that, in aviation, separated failure from success. 'I think his treatment by the newspapers and many of his professional friends most shameful,' Wilbur later commented to Chanute. 'His work deserves neither abuse nor apology . . . His fellow scientists will yet be proud of his work in this field.'[20] Langley's belief in powered flight and his spectacular success in flying his steam-powered models had, he said, actually encouraged him and Orville to begin their own studies.

As soon as the shafts were installed, on Saturday 12 December, they rolled the machine out of the shed, lifting it on to the starting track, impatient to try a take-off. Alas, at that moment there wasn't enough wind. All they were able to do was drive it up and down the rail to check the groundspeed – in the process of which the tail

---

*On his return from Dayton, Orville, fascinated to read of the enormous cost to the American taxpayer of the *Great Aerodrome*, had sat down and done a comparison of their own expenditure in creating the *Flyer*. Although he may not have allowed for their labour he meticulously included his boat and train fares to change the shafts. The total cost of the machine's manufacture he arrived at came to less than $1000 – $20,000 in today's money.

frame snagged on the track, damaging the rudders. The *Flyer* had to be returned to the shed for repairs.

Next day, 13 December, dawned with the most ideal weather they could ever have wished for: a perfect take-off breeze sighed across the sands. But it was Sunday. The machine did not leave the shed. Though they knew that this balmy day might be their only chance to get into the air in the precious few days before Christmas, there was no way either was prepared to break his sabbath pledge to Milton. They spent most of the day relaxing, reading, walking along the beach and talking to curious visitors who had begun to trek across the dunes for a glimpse of the motor-driven flying machine that was now the talk of the Outer Banks.

It was not, however, the only centre of interest at that moment. Another quite unexpected event had thrust this obscure corner of America into the country's headline's: one of two US Navy submarines under tow had broken adrift and come ashore on the coast north of Kitty Hawk. Deeply embedded in the sand, the *Moccasin* had for days been resisting all attempts to refloat her while a local telegraphist, camped on the beach, had enterprisingly connected his Morse key to the line to Norfolk and was, rewardingly, sending a stream of progress reports to newspapers. Of the preparations for what promised to be a much more significant event thirty miles to the south, not the merest whisper had reached the media. It seems that, apart from the bemused locals, Chanute, Spratt and the Wright family back in Dayton, no one was aware of the impending attempt at powered flight.

At Hawthorn Street there was already an air of excitement as they waited for news. They had been cheered early in December by one small unrelated triumph. Word had come that Keiter's libel suit against Milton and Wilbur had been dismissed by the court. At the hearing, the attorneys for the nine churchmen Keiter was impudently suing had put some probing questions to the cleric about his honesty and truthfulness. Keiter had refused to answer even when the judge had insisted he must. When he had continued to remain silent the case had been thrown out. But the bishop's mind was now on other things. 'I spend the day,' he told his diary on Monday 14 December, 'largely in getting typewriter copies of the description of the Wright flyer, and copies of a sketch of the inventors.' He didn't know that the first attempts had already been made that very day.

The wind at Kill Devil on the fourteenth had not been strong enough for a take-off from level ground, so they had decided to attempt it with a downhill start off one of the dunes. As they couldn't carry the *Flyer* there unaided, they had arranged with the Kill Devil lifesaving station that they would hang a red flag on the aircraft shed when they were ready to fly and needed manpower. The lifesavers, who were keeping watch on the camp through glasses, were prompt to respond when, at half past one, the flag was displayed for the first time. Five men, two boys and a dog presently arrived.

It took them all forty minutes to lug the heavy machine and its starting rail the quarter-mile on to the lower slopes of the big hill. They rolled it along the rail, moving each of its 15-foot sections from rear to front as they went. On a gentle slope of about 9 degrees they laid out the full 60-foot length of the monorail, facing the gentle, barely adequate 5-mile-an-hour breeze. They tossed a coin to decide who would fly. Wilbur won. He and Orville seized a propeller blade each and swung them in unison. As the motor burst into life, the boys and the dog scampered away in terror to watch from a distance as Wilbur climbed on to the lower wing.

There being no throttle, the propellers were already spinning at take-off power – all Wilbur had to do was flip open a clip that held a restraining rope. But when he tried, the clip, under pressure from the weight of the surging machine on the downward slope, refused to release. Orville and the lifesavers had to heave the *Flyer* back a few inches to slacken the rope. Almost immediately Wilbur unhooked and the *Flyer* began to roll forward with Orville, stopwatch in hand, trying to steady it at the right wingtip. Forty feet down the rail he could no longer keep up. As he let go of the strut, the machine rose into the air. It was a satisfying moment – but a very brief one. Unfamiliar with the sensitivity of the new forward double elevators, Wilbur pitched up into a climb before he had enough flying speed. The *Flyer* stalled and sank into the sand. It had travelled only 60 feet.

Mildly shocked, Wilbur lay there for some time with the propellers turning, too bemused to shut off the engine. When finally he did and they checked for damage, they found it was limited to a few broken parts of the front elevator structure – all quickly repairable. Although the flight, according to Orville's stopwatch, had lasted only 3½ seconds from the end of the launch rail, it was enough to tell them that the machine could probably do all they wanted of it. It could safely power itself off the sloping rail. Now it must do so from flat ground – and sustain level flight.

But for the excessively reactive elevators, which see-sawed about their central pivots, they knew Wilbur would have flown very much further. They were convinced that success was now within their grasp. Bursting to tell the family, Orville next day walked the four miles to Kitty Hawk to send a bullish telegram but instructing them to keep it a secret: 'MISJUDGMENT AT START REDUCED FLIGHT . . . POWER AND CONTROL AMPLE. RUDDER ONLY INJURED. SUCCESS ASSURED. KEEP QUIET.'

At Hawthorn Street, where half an inch of snow had fallen, Milton, with a sense of history, had carefully entered in his diary the text of Orville's wire. With winter and Christmas racing towards them, he must by now have abandoned hope that the boys' dream would be fulfilled that year.

However, at Kill Devil, where bitter cold was creeping back and ice had returned to the ponds, they had not quite given up. Promising as it was, they didn't regard the *Flyer*'s short hop as true powered flight: the machine had left the ground at a higher point than it had landed; the flight had not been sustained; it had landed neither under control nor undamaged.

It took them a day and a half to repair the broken parts. They considered desensitising the front elevators – hingeing them to trail from the front, not oscillate about their middle – but the job would take too long. They would just have to operate them with a specially light touch and hope for the best.

When the *Flyer* was ready to test again on the afternoon of Wednesday 16 December, they carried it out to the launch track which they had now laid about thirty yards from the hangar. During the morning the wind had blown with hopeful strength, but when they were ready to launch and hoist the summoning flag it dropped to a placid rustle. As they stood there waiting for the feeble breeze to stir itself, a stranger arrived:

> After looking at the machine for a few seconds he enquired what it was. When we told him it was a flying machine he asked whether we intended to fly it. We said we did, as soon as we had a suitable wind. He looked at it several minutes longer and then, wishing to be courteous, remarked that it 'looked as if it would fly' if it had a 'suitable wind.' We were much amused for, no doubt, he had in mind the recent 75 mile gale . . .[21]

Not a gale but a strong wind answered their prayers that night. They lay in their bunks, unable to escape the penetrating cold that reached through mountains of blankets and quilts, listening to the magic buffeting on the timbers as they tried to sleep. But dawn on what was now Thursday 17 December did not herald a day of great promise. They needed wind – but not this much. From the distant ocean they could hear the subdued roar of the pounding surf. It was now gusting to levels they considered unsafe for flight.

Around the camp the ponds were again sheathed in ice. Kill Devil that sunless overcast morning was as bleak and inhospitable as they had ever experienced. They steeled themselves to climb down from their bunks and begin their daily washing, shaving and dressing ritual, each selecting from the box a fresh stiff white collar and knotting their ties in the mirror.

After breakfast they ventured outside to check the wind with the hand held anemometer. It was gusting between 22 and 27 mph. 'We thought it would die down before long,' Orville said, 'and so remained indoors the early part of the morning.'

It was beginning to look as if they weren't going to get into the air before they had to retreat for Christmas. If it came to this, they had decided on an alternative plan: to take the *Flyer* home and fly it off a frozen lake they had identified as suitable near the town of St Mary's, around fifty miles north of Dayton. But the plan was not to be needed, for:

> when ten o'clock arrived, and the wind was as brisk as ever, we decided that we had better get the machine out and attempt a flight. We hung out the signal for the men at the Life Saving Station. We thought that by facing the flyer into a strong wind there ought to be no trouble in launching it from level ground about camp. We realised the difficulties of flying in so high a wind, but estimated that the added dangers in flight would be partly compensated for by the slower speed in landing.[22]

As before, the Kill Devil lifesavers responded willingly. While waiting for them the brothers set about laying out the four sections of the junction railroad, aligning them into the punching northerly wind. It was so cold they had to keep stopping to return to the hut to warm their numbed hands over the stove.

Around 10 o'clock five men strolled into camp, hands in pockets, jacket collars turned up against the sub-zero wind chill. The five, whose names have been enshrined in the annals of flight, were three sturdy walrus-moustached men from the rescue station – John Daniels, Will Dough and Adam Etheridge – and two other men who just happened to be at Kill Devil that morning – William Brinkley, a timber buyer from Manteo who had come to salvage lumber from the recent shipwrecks, and Johnny Moore, a seventeen-year-old youth, described as a muskrat trapper and crabber, who had wandered up from Nags Head on a hunting excursion. The brothers had invited Bill Tate to witness the attempt. He and his family now lived nearly twenty miles up the coast; looking at the appalling weather that morning Tate had decided it wasn't worth the long horseback journey south as there couldn't possibly be a flight attempt.

With the help of the volunteer labour force Wilbur and Orville gently carried the *Flyer* from its shed across to the nearby rail. It was Orville's turn. He, as did Wilbur, had a total flying experience at that moment of less than two hours. By half past ten the machine was sitting on its wheels, its delicate structure twitching in the blustering wind. At this point, Daniels was to recall many years later, the brothers 'walked off from us and stood close together . . . talking low to each other for some time. After a while they shook hands and we couldn't help noticing how they held each other's hand like they hated to let up, like two folks parting who weren't sure they'd ever see each other again.'[23]

Drops of petrol were pumped into each of the cylinders and a box with the starting battery lifted on to the wing and connected up. Wilbur and Orville together swung the propellers, coughing the motor into crackling life. While it was warming up Wilbur walked over to the lifesavers and, according to Daniels, 'told us not to look sad, but to laugh and hollo and clap our hands and try to cheer Orville up when he started'.[24]

Before climbing on to the wing, goggleless but wearing a soft cap (one biographer fancifully said he had first removed his bowler hat), Orville, who in photographs appears today an incongruous pilot figure in his smart suit and bow tie, had set up their big bellows camera on its tripod. He had carefully pointed it at the end of the rail and briefed Daniels to squeeze the shutter bulb as the aircraft lifted off.

At ten thirty-five Orville was ready to go. Stretched out in the hip cradle, gripping the dreaded, ultra-sensitive elevator lever, he at last gave a shout. Wilbur whipped away the small wooden stool that had been supporting the right wingtip as Orville snapped open the release rope and started the flight instruments.

Against what was now probably around 24 miles an hour of headwind the *Flyer* was painfully slow to move forward. Steadying the wing, Wilbur was able to keep pace for 40 of the rail's 60 feet. Then effortlessly she lifted into the air and the onlookers obligingly gave a desultory cheer. Daniels squeezed the shutter, taking one of the world's most celebrated photographs of all time.

It was a short flight. Again the clumsy elevator defied smooth control. For 12 exceedingly famous seconds Orville swoopingly rose and fell, once lifting to ten feet, before the flight (which in the face of the headwind had managed less than 8 miles an hour over the ground) ended with a sudden downward dart and an abrupt skid back on to the sand. He had flown only 120 feet: less than the wingspan of a Boeing 747. But, as Orville wrote with careful precision, 'it was nevertheless the first in the history of the world in which a machine carrying a man had raised itself by its own power into the air in full flight, had sailed forward without reduction of speed, and had finally landed at a point as high as that from which it started'.

15

'Damn'd if They Ain't Flew' – An Unnewsworthy Event

(1903)

The six men who had helped launch the *Flyer* into its 12-second hop had rushed over to congratulate Orville. Nobody recorded what he and Wilbur said to each other. When, years later, Orville was asked to recall his emotions on landing that morning, all he could say was: 'I was so interested in whether the thing would work or not that I didn't have time to think about it.'[1] In another interview he said, 'Neither of us felt any great elation over what we did that day. You see we had faith in our calculations and had felt so sure we were going to fly that when we succeeded we weren't surprised.'[2]

'I didn't think it amounted to much,' John Daniels recalled. 'We were used to seeing the glider go up so we weren't much impressed.'[3] But presently he was to be.

The Wrights repaired an elevator skid that had cracked on landing. By twenty past eleven the *Flyer* was back on the rail, ready to go again. It was Wilbur's turn. With the wind still blowing at a stiff 24 miles an hour against the *Flyer*'s modest airspeed of around 30 miles an hour, the second flight would cross the ground, as the first had done, a good deal slower than a man could run.

Struggling to master the unruly elevator, Wilbur did little better than Orville. He switchbacked his way across the sand in a precarious flight also clocked at 12 seconds, but travelling a little further, to 175 feet. Twenty minutes later it was Orville's turn again. He stretched his time to 15 seconds and the distance to a little over 200 feet. At twelve noon, with the motor crackling happily and transmission chains clanking in their metal tubes, Wilbur surged confidently down the rail on his second attempt, determined to conquer the infuriatingly tricky elevators and fly much further.

'The machine,' Orville wrote, 'started off with its ups and downs as it had before, but by the time he had gone over three or four hundred feet he had it under much better control and was travelling on a fairly even course. It proceeded in this manner till it reached a small hummock out about 800 feet . . . when it began its pitching again and suddenly darted to the ground.'[4] Wilbur had flown 852 feet – nearly the length of three football fields. At around 10 miles an hour he had sustained powered flight for 59 seconds. It was, as one biographer put it, as if he had flown through 'some invisible wall in the sky'.

If there had been any suggestion that the first three attempts had been but long undulating hops, there was not a shred of doubt that, with this one, man had really flown. Quite decisively the aeroplane was born. It would be four years before any rival inventor would succeed in making a longer flight.

But for the turbulence over the sand hummock, Wilbur knew he could have flown much further. The elevator supports had been damaged on landing but could be soon repaired. Brimming with confidence, they decided Orville would immediately make another attempt. The small fuel tank held enough to fly around eight miles in still air. In the teeth of the brisk northerly still sweeping the Outer Banks they reckoned it might just get them the four miles across the largely unobstructed sand to Kitty Hawk village.

The damaged *Flyer* was lugged back to camp and temporarily parked outside the hangar, but there disaster struck. A violent gust of wind caught a wingtip, pitching it high into the air. Too late they all rushed to try and grab the toppling aeroplane. Wilbur managed to get a grip on one of the struts, but the wind threatened to lift him bodily into the air and he had to drop off. Orville and John Daniels seized other struts, but Orville, too, had to let go. Daniels' considerable bulk couldn't hold the runaway machine – he screamed as it began to roll over and disintegrate on top of him. Caught up with the engine and driving chains he was helplessly carried across the sand amid a tangle of snapping wires and splintering struts, as the *Flyer* pitched over and over in the wind. When it finally came to a stop the terrified Daniels rolled out on to the ground scratched and bruised.

In the space of a few seconds the *Flyer* had been reduced to a heap of twisted wreckage. The engine had broken loose, the chain guards bent, struts and wing ribs snapped. The world's first aircraft was never to fly again.

The lifesavers helped the Wrights drag the assorted bits into the hangar. Their job done they then wandered off back to the Kill Devil station. The young muskrat trapper, Johnny Moore, immediately sped north with the momentous news. One of the first he is said to have met on the beach was Bill Tate – Tate had changed his mind and ridden south after all. Moore shouted to him: 'They done it! They done it! Damn'd if they ain't flew!'[5]

Word was already beginning to spread through the coastal community. From the Kill Devil lookout tower another surfman, Bob Westcott, had watched some of the flights through his telescope. And much further away, a colleague, Captain S. Joseph Payne, up at the Kitty Hawk station, had, through binoculars, seen at least one of the flights.

On their own again, Wilbur and Orville sorted out the wreckage and then adjourned to their living quarters where they stoked up the fire, cooked their midday meal and sat down quietly to enjoy it. We don't know what they talked about, but it may have touched on thoughts that Orville was, ten years later, to express publicly:

> I would hardly think today of making my first flight on a strange machine in a twenty-seven mile wind, even if I knew that the machine had already been flown and was safe. After these years of experience I look with amazement upon our audacity in attempting flights with a new and untried machine under such circumstances.[6]

After their unhurried meal Wilbur and Orville washed the dishes before setting off on the hour-long walk up to Kitty Hawk to send a telegram to the bishop from the weather bureau. Orville wrote it out for Joe Dosher, the man who had answered their original queries about the Outer Banks: 'SUCCESS FOUR FLIGHTS THURSDAY MORNING ALL AGAINST TWENTY-ONE MILE WIND. STARTED FROM LEVEL WITH ENGINE POWER ALONE. AVERAGE SPEED THROUGH AIR THIRTY ONE MILES. LONGEST 59 SECONDS. INFORM PRESS. HOME CHRISTMAS. ORVILLE WRIGHT.'

The windspeed Orville had quoted was for some reason the minimum they had recorded. In fact the flights had been flown against velocities gusting in the mid twenties; not that it mattered a lot to the family. Dosher had immediately tapped out the message on his Morse key. Along the single wire connecting Kitty Hawk with the outside world it had gone to the weather station at Norfolk for relay to Western Union. Almost as swiftly as it had gone there came a request from the Norfolk operator. Could he please give the news 'to a reporter friend'. The brothers, about to leave the shack, were outraged. 'Absolutely no,' they said. The announcement would be formally issued by the family in Dayton and by no one else.

Despite the Wrights' embargo the news reached a North Carolina newspaper with amazing speed soon after they'd left Dosher's weather shack. The Norfolk telegraph operator, Charles Grant, had decided it was far too big to suppress. In any case had Orville's telegram not said, 'inform press'? Ignoring the ban he had passed the hot news later that afternoon to his friend Edward Dean, a reporter on the *Virginian-Pilot*, when he had called routinely at the weather bureau. Dean, sensing a scoop, but knowing little about the Wrights and less about aviation, had rushed back to his office to tell his bright young city editor, Keville Glennan.

Glennan had heard of the Wrights from lifesavers the previous year while covering a shipwreck on the nearby coast. He seized the story as a major coup for his paper. Only nine days earlier the great Langley machine, with a huge amount of tax-payers' money behind it, had disastrously crashed. 'Now, right in our own private backyard we had an actual flight by two fellows nobody ever heard of except the lifesavers and the seagulls.'[7] He had become friendly with a local lifesaver, Edgar Chadwick, who had kept abreast of the brothers' activities by listening to gossip flowing out of the Kill Devil station along the telephone line that linked the small coastguard bases. Glennan immediately phoned Chadwick demanding full details of the flights. Chadwick promised to ask his Kill Devil colleagues and call back.

The telegram was delivered to 7 Hawthorn Street early that evening. Carrie Kayler took it upstairs to the bishop, who was at work in his room. Presently, Carrie was to recall, he came downstairs. 'He was always calm and showed no excitement, but he looked pleased. All he said was, "Well, they've made a flight."'[8] A short while later the prim, pince-nez'd schoolteacher figure of Katharine arrived home. As soon as she read the telegram (it had suffered in transmission: the flight time had been reduced from 59 to 57 seconds and Orville's name misspelt 'OREVELLE') she told Carrie to delay supper. She put her coat back on and took the wire, the technical notes Wilbur had left Milton about the *Flyer*, and copies of sparsely drawn pen and ink portraits of the brothers which someone had created from photographs. She walked the four blocks to Lorin's house where the family had just sat down to eat. Lorin, unwilling to postpone his meal, said he would take the story to the Dayton newspapers later that evening. On the way home Katharine stopped to send a telegram to Octave Chanute in Chicago. Soon after she returned to Hawthorn Street a reply arrived from the punctilious Chanute. 'It fills me with pleasure,' he wired. 'I am sorely tempted to make the achievement public, but will defer doing so in order that they may be the first to announce their success. I earnestly hope that they will do still better.'

Carrie remembered Katharine and the bishop being in high spirits that night as they sat down to their supper. Their happiness, she noticed, had rather less to do with the aeronautical event than the news that the boys would be home for Christmas. Wilbur had a traditionally important ritual to perform that day. It was he who always stuffed and carved the family turkey, fussily preparing the ingredients and making an elaborate ceremony of it for the benefit of the grandchildren.

After supper Lorin pulled on overcoat, scarf and gloves and set off purposefully on his mission into the winter night. Arriving at the editorial offices of Dayton's morning newspaper, the *Journal,* he was directed to the city editor, Frank Tunison. Tunison, importantly for the wider dissemination of the story, was the Dayton representative of the big national news agency, Associated Press. A hard-bitten 'old timer', he was also, after the Langley fiascos, deeply sceptical. He probably had only the vaguest understanding of the distinction between 'lighter' and heavier-than-air flight and would have been aware that powered airships were no longer a novelty. They could fly and steer for miles, piloted most famously over the rooftops of Paris by the wealthy Brazilian dandy Alberto Santos-Dumont, and in Germany by Count von Zeppelin. Tunison had never heard of the local bicycle-makers whose experiments had been deliberately conducted away from the prying eyes of reporters. Lorin was unable to convince him of the truly epochal significance of the Kill Devil flights. On reading the famed telegram the city editor said disinterestedly: 'Fifty-seven seconds, huh? If it'd been fifty-seven minutes it might have been a news item.' In a decision that was to haunt him all his days, he refused to run even a paragraph in the following morning's *Journal.* He sent out not a line on the AP wire. As far as the city editor was concerned, the only event worth reporting on the Outer Banks at that time was the stranded submarine *Moccasin.*

Meanwhile, Glennan and Dean were trying to draft the story with precious little reliable information. They'd just begun when one of the newspaper's clerks, Harry Moore, walked into the newsroom. He astonished them both by claiming he already had full details of the flights. Although Moore worked at humble duties in the circulation and advertising departments, he had ambitions to be a reporter; he regularly filed Norfolk stories as a stringer for newspapers in other cities. He, too, claimed that his information about 'the two looney Yankees down at Kill Devil' came from lifesavers, one of whom had months earlier promised, 'I will tell you if these birds happen to get up in the air or get killed.'[9] The lifesaver, probably at Kill Devil, had evidently – although Moore refused at the time to name his source – kept his promise; he could only have done so by phone.

When Chadwick failed to phone back, Glennan was forced to turn to Moore for the substance of the story. He was not to know that the latter's facts were a glorious blend of truth, fantasy and inaccuracy. Why Glennan and Dean made no attempt to pass questions to the Kill Devil men through the Norfolk lifesaving station has never been explained.

Before beginning to shape the piece with Moore, Glennan took steps to protect its local exclusivity. To keep it from Norfolk's morning rival, the *Landmark*, he sent Dean back to the weather bureau with instructions to guard the place and prevent Grant from sharing the news with anyone else before he closed at half past eight that evening.

Glennan also decided – for a very different reason than Tunison – to keep the story off the Associated Press wire. He was expected to feed AP with any news item centred within thirty miles of Norfolk; Kill Devil was well outside the contractual radius. But that wasn't the reason he decided to keep one of history's greatest news events from America and the world. Rather it was his determination not to share it with his morning rival. Had the report gone out on AP he knew he would be handing it straight down the wire service to the *Landmark*.

However, Moore, whose enterprise had produced most of the bizarre ingredients, was still anxious to make some money from his initiative. He pleaded to be allowed to offer the story to some of the out-of-town newspapers for whom he acted. Glennan was reluctant. Some of the papers, he feared, might wire back to the *Landmark* for more details. But under pressure from Moore he drew up for him a list of low-risk customers in cities far away from Norfolk.

The front-page lead that greeted the *Virginian-Pilot*'s readers next morning, 18 December 1903, reflected in its embellishments the desperation of its authors. Glennan, who finished up writing most of it, had determined not to let the sparsity of facts stand in the way of a sensational story: FLYING MACHINE SOARS 3 MILES IN TEETH OF HIGH WIND OVER SAND HILLS AND WAVES AT KITTY HAWK ON CAROLINA COAST, declared the imaginative banner headline. 'No balloon attached to aid it,' added a sub-heading – 'Accomplished what Langley failed at.'

'The problem of aerial navigation without the use of a balloon has been solved at last,' began the story. It described just one long flight, launched downhill off a slope and rising to 60 feet, piloted by Wilbur, 'the chief inventor' who sat in the 'operator's car'. The conspicuously bald Wilbur was called 'raven haired and swarthy. He had piercing deep blue eyes and an extremely long sharp nose.'

In his description of the machine as a 'big box', Glennan allowed his creativity to run riot. One propeller pushed it forward while another – an 'underwheel' – exerted an upward force to keep it in the air. During his three-mile flight over sand and sea Wilbur had put the machine 'through all sorts of manoeuvres' before selecting a suitable place to land and 'gracefully circling, drew his invention slowly to earth'. Anxious to give his story a strong quote from the inventor, Glennan took the liberty of providing him with one: '"Eureka," he cried, as did the alchemist of old.'[10]

While the story was on the way to the press, Harry Moore had prepared a shorter version for his own clients. Of the twenty-one newspapers to whom he offered it, only five agreed to buy. Just a few weeks earlier most had carried the pronouncement of the eminent American astronomer Professor Simon Newcomb, who claimed to have produced irrefutable scientific evidence that a practical flying machine was an impossibility. One editor replied offhandedly that he wasn't interested in 'cock and bull yarns'. The editors of three of the purchasing papers had second thoughts: only the Cincinnati *Enquirer* and the New York *American* actually ran it – the latter discreetly burying it on an inside page. Thus the morning after, an event that would come to rank with the moon landings as one of history's greatest milestones was reported by just three newspapers.

Back at Kill Devil, on Friday 18 December Wilbur and Orville were blissfully unaware that their simple plan to have the news announced in a neat brief statement from Dayton had gone so badly awry. They had yet to see Keville Glennan's fertile rendering of their achievement. Milton read the version of it that appeared that morning in the Cincinnati *Enquirer* and was shocked by its 'flaming headlines'and wildly inaccurate content. As the brothers dismantled and crated the crumpled *Flyer* for shipping home, there began to arrive, trudging across the dunes in the hands of lifesavers, a small flood of telegrams. New York newspapers and magazines were asking their price for exclusive rights to the story. Others were demanding immediate 600-word accounts and photographs. Among the messages was one from Chanute: 'Pleased at your success. When ready to make public please advise me.' He didn't know that the Wrights themselves wanted tightly to control every word printed. Yet within hours they had already lost control.

Their 'three-mile' flight supported in the air by a helicopter-type six-bladed rotor revolving beneath the wings was a story reluctant to die. Frank Tunison at the Dayton *Journal*, who had spurned the scoop of the century, was dismayed to see it carried not only by his nearby Cincinnati morning rival but by his city's afternoon papers the same day. DAYTON BOYS EMULATE GREAT SANTOS-DUMONT the *Daily News* headlined its report; it was unaware of the difference between heavier- and lighter-than-air flight, as was the *Herald*, which proclaimed: DAYTON BOYS FLY AIRSHIP.

Associated Press picked it up on the eighteenth from the Norfolk *Virginian-Pilot* and sent it not only nationwide but around the world – complete with all its gross errors and fictions. Across America news editors accustomed to receiving claims that the problem of 'aerial navigation' had been solved by one would-be inventor after another had little idea of the true scientific significance of the achievement. In New York, Chicago and San Francisco the story earned such irrelevant headlines as AIRSHIP FLIES THREE MILES IN A GALE and AIRSHIP FLIES AGAINST WIND.

At Hawthorn Street the bishop was besieged by reporters. In his interviews he did his brave best to correct the travesties of the Norfolk reports, solemnly handing out the text of Orville's telegram and the correct technical specifications of the *Flyer*. Other enquiries came by mail. Milton proudly described his sons to the New York correspondent of a German aeronautical magazine:

> Wilbur is 36, Orville 32, and they are as inseparable as twins. For several years they have read up on aeronautics as a physician would read his books, and they have studied, discussed, and experimented together. Natural workmen, they have invented,

> constructed and operated their gliders and finally their 'Wright Flyer' jointly, all at their own personal expense. About equal credit is due each.[11]

By the time Wilbur and Orville were ready to leave Kitty Hawk with the crated *Flyer* on 21 December they had learnt of the grotesque misreporting that had surrounded their triumph and knew that a contingent of reporters had descended on Norfolk to seize them. The *Virginian-Pilot*, anxious to sustain the drama it had created, reported that they had gone to extraordinary lengths to avoid the media, bypassing Elizabeth City and purportedly making a perilous voyage in an open sailboat through a violent gale to another Albemarle Sound port at Edenton. WILL BRAVE STORM TO ELUDE THE REPORTERS, said the paper's headline. 'Both the men,' confided another report, 'carried disguises with them to be used when Edenton is reached.' Finally arrived in Norfolk, they were said to have recruited decoys to throw newsmen off their trail.

On the train journey back to Dayton, Orville sent a telegram to Hawthorn Street: 'Have survived perilous trip reported in papers. Home tonight.' It was 23 December. At the station to meet them were Milton, Katharine and Lorin plus a handful of reporters. Milton protectively shooed the newspapermen away. Back at the house Carrie had prepared an elaborate homecoming meal. All that is recorded of that reunion dinner is Orville's unquenchable thirst for fresh milk, following months without at Kill Devil.

The family spent a subdued and happy Christmas Day at Lorin's. Wilbur carved the turkey with the expected aplomb, concluding the ritual (according to a painstakingly researched full length book written about the Wright family's recipes) with the solemn proclamation. 'Ah 'tis a fine beast.'[12]

Basking in the reflected glow of his sons' accomplishment, and confident that the Almighty approved of the stand he had taken against iniquity in the church, Milton looked back on a satisfying and financially rewarding year. The bishop had sunk some more oil wells at his Fowlerton property in Indiana and they'd begun to yield a nice return:

> The past year was full of stirring events. I was serene and happy through it all, though grieved at the folly of many, and the wickedness of not a few. I believed that God would at last vindicate the right.[13]

For Wilbur and Orville some small gifts had come at Christmas from Chanute, but early in the New Year the old man sent a mildly piqued letter wondering why Wilbur hadn't written to tell him about the flights so wildly misreported that had him bewildered between fact and fiction. 'I have had no letter from you since I left your camp, but your sister kindly wired me the results of your test of Dec 17. Did you write?' he asked plaintively. Chanute urged Wilbur to give 'the first scientific account of your performances' to the American Association for the Advancement of Science which was about to meet in St Louis, but the Wrights were unwilling to entrust Chanute with much more information. Wilbur responded tersely by telegram: 'WE ARE GIVING NO PICTURES NOR DESCRIPTIONS OF MACHINE OR METHODS AT PRESENT.' Not wishing to hurt Chanute, he wrote him a long letter the same day describing all the flights they had managed to make in the face of a gale – so dangerous that on one of them the aircraft had swooped down and gouged the sand. 'One of the most gratifying features of the trials,' he said, 'was the fact that all our calculations were shown to have worked out with absolute exactness.'[14]

As their accomplishment continued to be described by newspapers in garbled form, and Chicago and New York papers began to send reporters to Dayton to interview them, they decided the time had come for an authoritative statement. Wilbur wrote in a pained preamble:

> It had not been our intention to make any detailed public statement concerning the private trials of our power 'Flyer' on the 17th of December last; but since the contents of a private telegram, announcing to our folks at home the success of our trials, was dishonestly communicated to the newspapermen at the Norfolk office, and led to the imposition upon the public, by persons who never saw the 'Flyer' or its flights, of a fictitious story

> incorrect in almost every detail; and since this story together with several pretended interviews or statements, which were fakes pure and simple, have been very widely disseminated, we feel impelled to make some corrections.[15]

There followed an account of the flights ('two by Orville Wright and two by Wilbur Wright') that should not, they said, have been attempted in a gale, but they had been determined, before returning home, to discover three things: whether the machine had enough power to fly, was strong enough to withstand the shock of landing, and was controllable in 'boisterous winds'. 'When these points had been definitely established, we at once packed our goods and returned home, knowing that the age of the flying machine had come at last.' The statement concluded: 'As all the experiments have been conducted at our own expense without assistance from any individual or institution, we do not feel ready at present to give out any pictures or detailed description of the machine.'

Although the text was distributed to newspapers across America, editors had difficulty reconciling its facts with those of Keville Glennan's earlier fiction. One paper converted the 852-foot distance of Wilbur's flight into the height at which he had flown it. The *New York Herald*, sticking to the Glennan story, even ran detailed sketches and diagrams helpfully showing the pusher propeller at the rear and the vertical lifting one prominently whirling away beneath the lower wing.[16]

The claim the Wrights' statement made that their experiments had been conducted without assistance from anyone deeply upset Chanute when he read it in the Chicago newspapers. Convinced that he had played a significant role, he felt unjustly ignored. 'Please write me just what you had in your mind concerning myself when you framed that sentence in that way,' he wrote woundedly.[17]

The Wrights most definitely had Chanute in mind, for they had eventually read English translations of the French reports of his notorious Aéro-Club address in which they had been made to appear as his young and daring pupils. Chanute had made no attempt to redress this unfortunate impression; the brothers feared that left uncorrected it could undermine their plans to patent their invention in both America and Europe. Yet they still genuinely valued Chanute's friendship, conscious of a quite different debt they owed him – for his unstinting encouragement and the stimulation his seasoned mind had continued to provide.

The purpose of the statement, Wilbur replied, had been to make it clear that they 'stood on quite different ground' from Professor Langley, who received lavish public funds. They felt no obligation to 'make our discoveries public property at this time. We had paid the freight, and had a right to do as we pleased.' Wilbur added they were concerned to read both foreign and American published reports that their experiments had been funded by others – by which he meant Chanute: 'we thought it might save embarrassment to correct this promptly'.[18]

Chanute couldn't understand why they had become so reluctant to earn the international applause wide publicity of their feat would justly bring them. 'They have become very secretive,'[19] he told Patrick Alexander. The two were still in correspondence but relations between them were becoming strained. It seems that despite Chanute's impeccable instructions arranging the Washington hotel rendezvous for their visit to Kill Devil together, Alexander blamed Chanute for his failure to get to the flying camp on the eve of the magnificent events. For some reason he took out his irrational resentment on Chanute, deeply upsetting the older man. Alexander's once warm and forthcoming letters became cool and uncommunicative, to the point where Chanute begged for forgiveness – 'I cannot bear to have a cloud between us' – for whatever the rich Englishman blamed him. Alexander's letters began to wither to brief notes in which he so constantly sought information on the progress of the reticent brothers that it became obvious to Chanute that he was collecting it not for his own idle interest but for the British government. Wilbur and Orville soon arrived at the same conclusion. For the first time they had to address not just how to protect the singular invention, but how to profit from it.

In the middle of January 1904 Wilbur took the train to the nearby town of Springfield. Here he spent hours with a lawyer, Henry Toulmin, an experienced patent attorney. Wilbur discussed with this professional, whom he immediately liked and trusted, a cast-iron patent that would survive piracy and the test of court challenges. To avoid the possibility of having to make a powered flight demonstration of the *Flyer* before sceptical examiners, Toulmin persuaded Wilbur that what they should patent as their exclusive invention was the three-axis control system rather than the totality of the powered aeroplane. Even this would take months to prepare, he warned. Meanwhile, Toulmin urged, they should guard the machine's unique features closely.

In fact the battered *Flyer*, destined to become a national treasure, could scarcely be demonstrated to anyone any longer. It had been unceremoniously dumped in its crates in a shed behind the cycle shop. It would stay there, neglected and regarded by the Wrights as of little further importance, for ten years. It was about to be superseded by a new machine – bigger and more powerful. As rumours of its existence began to circulate in aviation circles – mainly through Chanute – and pressing requests to see their invention in action began to mount, they knew they had involved a patent attorney not a day too soon. The protection would not finally arrive until the middle of 1906; the vital need for it was soon to be demonstrated.

A letter came from a man on Long Island, New York, congratulating them on their successful flights. The writer went on to warn them that he had independently invented and patented the aeroplane ahead of them – he had already overcome the problem of heavier-than-air flight. He had, he claimed, been offered substantial sums to challenge the priority of any patent they might attempt to register. To settle the matter amicably he was prepared to enter into a partnership in which he would acquire a one-third interest in the invention. Failing this he threatened to bring down upon them litigation which, he warned, would be tedious, lengthy and expensive.

The writer was none other than Augustus Herring.

16

Shattering the Five-Minute Barrier

(1904)

Wilbur and Orville read and reread Herring's letter. Although they knew of his open determination 'to beat Mr Wright' and of his cool attempt to barter the secrets of their aeroplane for a job with Langley at the Smithsonian, they couldn't believe his audacity. Wilbur immediately sent a copy of the letter to Chanute. They suspected, he said, that Herring 'was making a frenzied attempt to mount a motor on a copy of our 1902 glider and thus anticipate us . . . But that he would have the effrontery to write us such a letter, after his other schemes of rascality had failed, was really a little more than we expected. We shall make no answer to it at all.'[1]

Chanute took Herring's threat more seriously. He felt guilty at having imposed this talented rogue, with his infinite capacity for mischief, upon the Wrights. 'I am amazed at the impudence of Mr Herring in asking for ⅓ of <u>your</u> invention,' he replied, adding that he wished they had applied for patents when he had long ago urged them. But he thought the fact that Herring had visited Kill Devil and seen the 1902 machine flying would go heavily against him in any suit he was foolish enough to bring.

Chanute was now deeply involved in the organisation of the aeronautical exhibition at the forthcoming St Louis worlds' fair. The exposition had been postponed to September 1904 and a $100,000 prize – worth all of $2 million today – was being offered for the fastest time by a powered flying machine cruising three times round a six-mile circuit. The contest was open equally to airships and fixed-wing machines and the celebrated Santos-Dumont had been persuaded by Chanute to enter. Chanute was hoping the Wrights would pitch their new aeroplane against the Frenchman's airship, but *Flyer II* had yet to make its maiden flight and prove it had the endurance the race would demand.

Meanwhile Herring, in his Walter Mitty world, had written to Chanute seeking his support for a powered machine that would, he claimed, easily take the prize. It would be capable, he wildly asserted, of sustaining flight for ten hours – or up to forty hours for oceanic journeys. The truth was that Herring's own designs had not advanced beyond his 1898 body-swinging glider powered by the compressed air motor he had used to make the inconclusive hop on the Michigan beach that year, and which he was still steadfastly claiming as the world's first powered flight – just as he was insisting in a German aviation magazine[2] that, simultaneously with Lilienthal, he had independently discovered manned gliding flight. In fact he held valid patents for nothing at all. His long-range machine existed only in his imagination. Chanute decided the time had come to sever all contact with Herring.

Herring wasn't their only aggravation. A weekly magazine, the *Independent*, which a few months earlier had published Professor Newcomb's claimed scientific 'proof' that a practical flying machine was an impossibility, had taken the liberty of concocting an article, 'The Experiences of a Flying Man', and shamelessly running it under Wilbur's authorship. A clumsy pastiche, it was woven from Wilbur's two addresses to the Western Society of Engineers, but spiced with some of the more outrageous inaccuracies of the early newspaper stories dreamed up by Keville Glennan. To make matters worse Wilbur recognised the photograph of the 1902 glider that appeared with the article as one taken by Chanute. The latter had innocently supplied the perpetrator of the forgery, a Baltimore journalist called D.A. Willey, who specialised in this sort of fabrication, with both the picture and the text of the lectures. Chanute was horrified when he heard. He wanted Willey to face a criminal prosecution for forgery.

'I am willing to spend some money punishing him,' he told Wilbur. 'I suggest that you consult a lawyer and advise me of what can be done.'[3]

Wilbur had already fired off a vitriolic letter to the magazine's editor, describing the garbled article as 'unmitigated impudence'. The *Independent* duly published a meek apology, buried deep within its pages. It claimed that the article had been submitted by a literary agent. Willey lied that he had a letter of authorisation from Wilbur.

Far from satisfied, Wilbur turned his wrath on the architect of the hoax. 'Please do not think,' he warned Willey in scathing terms he normally reserved for the Keiterites, 'that because your colossal impudence was the means of getting you into trouble it will also be the means of getting you out again.'

> If I were in a position where an exposé would almost ruin me, and was dependent on the forbearance of persons whom I had injured for the suppression of my name in public statements regarding the matter, I think I would try to move them by a show of real penitence rather than by a show of brazen effrontery . . . I never in my life wrote you a letter.[4]

Wilbur declined Chanute's offer to fund a damages case against Willey – if they got judgement he doubted the journalist could pay – and so the matter was pursued no further. If ever the Wrights had doubted the integrity of the press, they were now convinced that no writer could be trusted to report their invention accurately.

They were at a crossroads. They had invented and flown the powered aeroplane – yet it was still far from perfect. It had four times floated into the air and precariously flown a straight course low over a flat stretch of sand. To present it to the world, sell it to the US government and reap financial reward the prototype would have to become a practical flying machine – able to operate anywhere, make turns at will, fly reliably fifty miles or more across country, remain airborne for hours rather than minutes, land without crashing. Its controls needed refinement. The oversensitive forward elevator that had abruptly terminated all their Kill Devil flights, pitching them back to earth in response to the smallest movement, would have to be improved before it could possibly be marketed to anyone.

To do all this, aviation could no longer remain their hobby; it would have to become their principal business. So, in the spring of 1904, they handed over much of the day-to-day running of the cycle business to Charlie Taylor and threw all their energies, in the workroom behind the shop, into building the new aeroplane.

Flyer II was a virtual replica of the 1903 machine, but heavier and with a new, more powerful 16 horsepower engine. Again it was wheelless, sitting on skids. To make it fly faster – they wanted an airspeed this time of around 40 miles an hour – they flattened the curvature of the wings, reducing the camber from 1:20 to 1:25. And in an attempt to dampen the sensitivity of the elevators they mounted them further forward. Later they added weights out front to push out the centre of gravity.

At the cycle shop the new machine grew slowly. There were many interruptions. In February they took time off to go to St Louis to inspect the ground over which the air race would be flown. An aeronautical amphitheatre was already being built. The small fourteen-acre aerodome appeared to have been designed for airships by people who did not understand the needs of fixed-wing aeroplanes. Contestants, they were told, would be required to take off within this absurdly restricted area and to land within fifty yards of the starting point. If they entered, they'd be competing for the grand prize principally with the already distance-proven Santos-Dumont airship. In this tortoise and hare race it would be all or nothing. The only subsidiary prizes were for other airships, gliders, balloons and kites. Given that they hadn't yet flown more than a sixth of a mile, their chances of taking a prize against ships that could stay aloft for hours seemed remote. Surely, Wilbur said of the *Flyer* to the race committee, 'a flight of even one mile by such a machine would be an event of great importance in aeronautical history – yet your rules would give it no recognition even to the extent of a brass medal.'[5] The committee was not in the least moved, and the Wrights, who had also seen the rough country over which the course was to be flown, decided to postpone a decision on entering until the new aeroplane had proved itself.

Back at their workbench there was now another familiar distraction. The warring bishops of the Brethren church were still at each others' throats over the festering Keiter affair and Milton's expulsion. The controversy had become deeply personal. Bishop Floyd sarcastically denounced Milton in the church newspaper, savagely attacking what he called his 'immaculate' ego,

> without spot or blemish, stainless without taint of evil or sin, pure and perfect.
>
> Then it will resolve itself into a court and enter the judgement seat to condemn every one who refuses to worship at its shrine . . . It recognises no power above it. It is infallible. It poses as an example of perfection and measures human character by its own yardstick of selfishness and revenge. Its motives, as adjudged by itself, are of the purest character and of the highest order.[6]

Many in the church shared Floyd's view of the holier-than-thou Bishop Wright, yet a groundswell of sympathy was developing for him and the bitterness between the snarling factions was more than ever threatening the Radical church with self-destruction. Disenchanted parishioners were going off to other churches; donations were drying up. Talks about a 'peace plan' had got nowhere. The Keiterites had proposed that both sides drop their lawsuits, and Wright agree to 'cease all agitation' in return for which he would be reinstated as head of his White River district. Milton wouldn't hear of it. No way would Keiter be allowed to profit from his crimes. To simply stop 'agitation' would mean overlooking a notorious sin against the church.

Instead, Milton aggressively renewed his campaign, reviving his investigations into the publishing house accounts Keiter had falsified. Inevitably Wilbur was drawn back into the fight. In the middle of March he dropped all work on the aeroplane for ten days to help Milton produce a fresh fusillade of indictments spelling out yet again, for all who would read them, Keiter's fiscal iniquities in such detail that no one could possibly misunderstand. Once more Wilbur boarded the train for Indiana. Once more, at the church's Huntington headquarters, he spent days poring over the publishing books, his radar detecting every minute blip of dishonesty.

Back in Dayton he sat down to draft for Milton a counter-proposal to the church's peacemakers. It suggested that an independent panel of three accountants examine the books covering the four years of the alleged stealing. If the panel found no irregularities, the Wright camp would cease to press for Keiter's prosecution. The proposal was rejected. The internecine struggle went on and Wilbur went back to the aeroplane, telling Chanute, 'that church trouble has delayed our work on the machine somewhat'.[7]

By April 1904 *Flyer II* was ready for assembly. To avoid the cost and delay of another expedition to the Outer Banks, they planned to fly it locally. On Huffman Prairie, eight miles north-east of Dayton, they'd found a site. A former swamp, now a cow paddock, it was part of a dairy farm owned by Torrence Huffman, president of one of the city's banks. He had agreed they could use it rent-free on condition that they shoo the cows out of the way before flying. The spread of grassy hummocks was irregularly shaped, a quarter-mile wide by half a mile long. There were trees on two sides, but the field was big enough to fly the oval circuits they now wanted to attempt.

There was only one problem: the place lacked the privacy which more and more obsessed them. Two roads ran past – the busy wagon pike to the neighbouring town of Springfield and a line along which electric trains ran on the Dayton–Springfield inter-urban route. But wherever they flew in the countryside within reach of Dayton, news of it, they accepted, could hardly escape the notice of newspapers for long; and few sites could provide such convenient access from the city – there was a train stop, Simms Station, on the very edge of the field. In April 1904 they borrowed scythes, cut the long grass, built a wooden hangar on one side of the paddock and began to assemble the machine.

As it took shape they discussed how best to handle their public relations. As scores of commuters and local farmers would see the big white bird every time it flew, they decided to take the bull by the horns and tell the world what they were up to. Hoping it might become just a nine-day wonder, Wilbur sent a letter to every daily newspaper in Dayton and Cincinnati announcing they would begin flying at Huffman Prairie on Monday 23 May. With what today seems incredible naivety, he made two requests of the papers: that reports 'not be sensational', and that no photographs be taken.

Around forty people turned up for the Monday morning demonstration. They included Milton and Lorin, who brought his entire excited family along, and a dozen rather cynical reporters. They were all to be disappointed. Heavy rain and high winds delayed the launching off the monorail – now extended to 100 feet to allow for the lighter, less steady winds of the Ohio plains. For most of the day the impatient spectators hung about. The journalists, who had obligingly not brought cameras, grew restless, some complaining that their time was being wasted. When, at last, late in the afternoon, the weather cleared and the high wind subsided, the Wrights decided that, as some had travelled a long way to see them fly, they would at least make an attempt. The machine was rolled out of the hangar and lifted on to the rail. Orville climbed on to the wing. The new *Flyer* accelerated sluggishly, its motor firing badly. There was now very little breeze. The aeroplane struggled down the rail in a succession of explosive fits and starts and flopped off the end, crunching awkwardly on to the ground. Grumbling bitterly, most of the reporters left, never to return. They may have thought that the Wrights meant well and were possibly on to something – but were obviously still far from possessing anything to startle the world.

It was three days before the motor and the weather permitted another try. This time only two or three newspapers bothered to turn up and Lorin and his family decided to give it a miss. Only the bishop came, arriving at Simms Station by train. Around 2 o'clock Orville again mounted the wing. The motor was still playing up, now running on only three cylinders, but a rainstorm was approaching, so he decided – unwisely – to press on quickly. The machine rose about six feet into the air then, as the wind died, with propellers thrashing, fell back to the ground so violently that Orville was hurled off the wing, the top main spar cracked and the upper wing collapsed on top of him. He was lucky not to have been seriously hurt. *Flyer II*, on its maiden flight, had travelled less than ten yards.

The handful of reporters had difficulty making news of the non-event. TEST OF FLYING MACHINE IS DECLARED A SUCCESS, the Chicago *Tribune*'s kindly headline said. FALL WRECKS AIRSHIP declared the *New York Times* more truthfully, blaming the crash on a 'derangement' of the motor. Had Orville flown several hundred yards, the story would have made news around the world. As it was, the reporters who'd bothered to come a second time left that day convinced that the Wrights, whatever they may have achieved at Kitty Hawk, were still a long way from conquering the air. It would be nearly a year and a half before another newsman would set foot on Huffman Prairie.

The brothers couldn't have been more relieved. 'The newspapers are friendly and not disposed to arouse prying curiosity in the community,' Wilbur told Chanute.[8] But had they really tried to impress the world with an impressive flight? There is a belief that they may have set out deliberately to deceive the press to guarantee they were left alone. The theory is given some credibility by a remark of Wilbur's in a letter he wrote a couple of years later to a French colleague with whom he was trying to arrange a secret demonstration flight: 'No doubt an attempt will be made to spy upon us while we are making the trial flights . . . but we have already thought out a plan which we are certain will baffle such efforts as neatly as we fooled the newspapers during the two seasons we were experimenting at Simms.'[9] Would the Wrights have persisted in attempting take-offs twice in succession with a faulty motor had they not had a media audience they were anxious to underwhelm?

It wasn't only the faltering motor that had produced such disappointing performances. Unlike the Outer Banks, where they'd been flying at sea level in stiff, freezing winds, Huffman Prairie sat at an elevation of 815 feet. That in itself was not a great altitude, but on the sultry late-spring day of their first demonstration to the press there was high humidity with a temperature of over 27°C. These three factors – altitude, humidity and heat – all conspired drastically to reduce the density of the air and its ability to support the aeroplane and give bite to its pistons as efficiently as in the cold at sea level. Modern pilots – whose big jets need extra long runways from high-altitude, especially tropical, airports – have calculated that, on 23 May 1904, the difference in the support qualities of the sustaining air – the 'density altitude' – as between Kill Devil and Dayton amounted to a staggering 4700 feet. But in 1904 it is doubtful if the Wrights were fully aware of these penalties in their new physical environment. They blamed poor performance at Huffman Prairie on the lack of reliable wind; they tried to overcome the problem by lengthening the launch rail to 240 feet.

Constantly moving the awkward, heavy timber in its 20-foot sections to face the ever-changing wind began to exhaust and dispirit them. Nor were they helped by the difficulty in finding hummock-free ground on which to connect the whole thing up. And often, having laboriously laid it all out on one heading, the wind would veer to another, forcing them to start all over again. Sometimes they sat around all day waiting for a puff of wind. When they saw a breeze approaching, stirring the distant grass, they would rush to the machine and frantically swing the motor to life to seize the moment, but often the wind would then die within seconds of lifting off and the *Flyer* would drop back to the ground after a few yards. Temporarily unable to obtain spruce for the spars, they had been using pinewood, which easily broke on impact; the aeroplane was sometimes grounded for weeks for major repairs and they were getting precious little flying practice. Their total time at the controls since 1900 still amounted to less than four hours between the two of them, and their powered-flight time was still barely a few minutes. To compete at St Louis in the autumn in the same class as Santos-Dumont's comparatively long-distance airship was out of the question; they postponed entering indefinitely.

Month after month through the summer of 1904 the best they could manage at Huffman Prairie were short hops of less than 200 feet – most ending in a crash with smashed wings, struts and propellers. On every take-off they risked serious injury. Charlie Taylor, who watched some of the attempts, said: 'Every time I saw one of them start on a flight I felt I was seeing him alive for the last time.' A local farmer's wife, who used to watch them from her kitchen window, had begun to rush out with a bottle of arnica every time she witnessed a bad landing; miraculously neither suffered more than bad bruises and cuts.

'I sort of felt sorry for them,' said Luther Beard, managing editor of the Dayton *Journal* which had spurned the world scoop of the first flight. Beard used sometimes to travel out to Simms Station on the train with the Wrights. 'They seemed like well meaning, decent enough young men. Yet there they were, neglecting their business to waste their time day after day on that ridiculous flying machine. I had an idea that it must worry their father.'[10] Beard saw nothing of interest to his paper in the pathetic performance of the constantly crashing machine.

The brothers in their suits and bow ties became a familiar sight to the commuters with whom they travelled to and from the tiny rural halt. Often, now, as they began to run the bicycle business down, they were accompanied by Charlie Taylor, who went out to work on the engine, help with launching and clock the flight times. Taylor, himself a family man, had become an intrigued observer of the pair's almost total lack of interest in one half of the human race, and he used to wonder why, unlike their elder brothers, they appeared to be sexually neutral and had never married. 'I remember,' the mechanic recalled, 'that Orv used to say it was up to Will to marry first because he was the older of the two. And Will kept saying he didn't have time for a wife. But I think he was just woman-shy – young women at least. He would get awfully nervous when young women were around.' Taylor used to observe this on the train. 'If an older woman sat down beside him, before you knew it they would be talking and if she got off at our stop he'd carry her packages and you'd think he'd known her all his life. But if a young woman sat next to him he would begin to fidget and pretty soon he would get up and go stand on the platform until it was time to leave the car.'[11]

As summer melted into autumn and they had still not bettered Wilbur's 59-second Kill Devil flight, the brothers decided that, if they were to continue flying near Dayton, they would have to find a more vigorous means of springing the *Flyer* into the air. Early in September they erected at the starting end of the rail a simple launching device – a 20-foot-high wooden pyramidal structure. The front of the aeroplane was connected, through three pulleys, to a three-quarter-ton weight, which was hoisted up to the top of the tower. When the pilot released a second, holding, rope the weight dropped and its force, boosting the thrust of the propellers, accelerated the machine so powerfully it could now reach flying speed before the end of the rail. It was so efficient it could catapult the *Flyer* into the air off a 60-foot rail even in a light breeze.

Wilbur made the first ten launches. They were hugely successful. Suddenly they were both effortlessly flying the entire length of the field. Soon, cruising cautiously at about ten feet above the ground, they were completing flights of up to half a mile and making their first full half-circle turns in the air. Almost every day now they succeeded in going a bit further. Katharine had begun to bring her women friends out to watch, and Lorin would sometimes help clock the times.

Despite their attempts to time flights between the train schedules they had become the talk of the commuting passengers – but they were still regarded by most as screwballs with an eccentric hobby. Nobody knew they were being privileged to witness the birth of aviation.

Wilbur's diary logged the distance, height, windspeed, manoeuvres and flight times down to a fifth of a second. On 20 September their performance took another leap when he stayed up for 1 minute 35 seconds, successfully flying a complete circle travelling nearly four-fifths of a mile. The flight was watched by a beekeeper, Amos Root, to whom the world is indebted for a full account of the event. Root, hearing of the Wrights' experiments, had, in a remarkable feat for 1904, driven the 175 miles in his primitive motor car from his apiary at Medina in northern Ohio in the hope of seeing the *Flyer* in the air. So keen was he that he had taken lodgings for a few days at a farmhouse nearby. On the day of Wilbur's circumnavigation of the field he'd driven out to their hangar and introduced himself. An earnest and devout Christian, who in his spare time published an obscure trade magazine, *Gleanings in Bee Culture*, he had been welcomed by the brothers who had happily answered all his questions for an article he planned to run. So grateful was Root he had offered the Wrights $100 for all the information they had so willingly given him – but they had refused.

The quaintly told story, when it appeared in the January 1905 issue of the bee journal under the heading 'What God Hath Wrought', was to acquire fame as the first published eyewitness account of a Wright powered aeroplane in sustained flight. 'Dear Friends,' it began, 'I have a wonderful story to tell you – a story that, in some respects, out-rivals the Arabian Nights fables – a story, too, with a moral that I think many of the younger ones need, and perhaps some of the older ones, too, if they will heed it.'

> . . . it was one of the grandest sights of, if not the grandest sight, of my life. Imagine a locomotive that has left its track and is climbing up in the air . . . imagine this white locomotive with wings that spread 20 feet each way, coming right toward you with a tremendous flap of its propellers, and you will have something like what I saw . . . These two brothers have probably not even a faint glimpse of what their discovery is going to bring to the children of men.[12]

Root sent a copy of his article to *Scientific American*. The editors of the popular weekly weren't interested. They thought the Wright machine had no commercial future.

The pair were now regularly making flights of more than a minute. In the middle of October, Orville managed 1 minute 38 seconds, flying nearly a mile. Farmers ploughing and harvesting in adjoining fields had begun to take for granted the sight of the strange noisy contraption with a man sprawled across its bottom wing as a weird fact of life. Often now they didn't even bother to look up. Up there, above the cornfields, the Wrights were still having trouble with the unruly front elevator which continued to send them switchbacking round the circuit, making every airborne moment still perilous. Again and again they tinkered with the structure, trying to solve the frustrating problem. They moved the centre of gravity about, repositioned the engine, suspended weights beneath the elevator – but still the *Flyer* remained only partly controllable. It certainly hadn't reached a state in which to be shown off at St Louis.

They need not have worried. The much vaunted international air race was never to take place. The exposition had run into grave financial difficulties; the organisers were forced to withdraw the glittering $100,000 prize. The great air fair had shrunk to rides in the basket of a tethered balloon (which had eventually burst, plunging its terrified occupants back to earth), and gliding demonstrations of Chanute's resurrected, outmoded, body-swinging 1896 glider. The flying machine that would have stolen the show was never entered.

Although the enormous prize money had always been tempting, the Wrights had remained nervous that exhibiting the *Flyer* risked revealing its secrets to the world before they had safely sold it to the US government. Increasingly the fear haunted them that others were bent on stealing their ideas. 'Intelligence of what we are doing is gradually spreading through the neighbourhood and we are fearful that we will soon have to discontinue experiments,' Wilbur told Chanute, urging him to visit quickly if he wished to see what *Flyer II* could do before they were forced to lock it away from prying eyes. 'We are becoming uneasy about continuing them much longer at our present location. In fact it is a question whether we are not ready to begin considering what we will do with our baby now that we have it.'[13]

Chanute hurried to Dayton and they took him out on the train to Simms Station. It was not to be their day. Orville, anxious to impress their old admirer with a complete circuit of the field, was catapulted off the ramp but immediately hit trouble. Banking into his first turn he found he couldn't come out of it: the machine slewed into the ground. It hit so hard that the skids, engine and both propellers were broken. Orville was shaken and painfully injured his hand. Chanute went back to Chicago still not having seen the Wrights power a machine into steady flight.

It was ten days before they flew again. The turning problem was traced to pilot disorientation. It was easy to bank too steeply or allow the nose to rise so high that the aircraft stalled. A bit of simple Wright ingenuity helped solve the difficulty: they tied a long string to the elevator crossbar. In straight and level flight the string blew back directly toward the pilot. When banking or raising and lowering the nose, this streaming rudimentary flight instrument was a constant reminder of the machine's changing attitude.

In the last week of October 1904, while the *Flyer* was still back in the shed under repair, the Wrights had an important visitor. A dapper British Army officer, Lieutenant Colonel John Capper, accompanied by his attractive and personable wife, breezed into Dayton. Capper had been sent to America by the War Office to discover what the country was up to in aviation. He was especially keen to see the Wrights' aeroplane with a view, if it could be militarily useful, to acquisition by the British government. It was the first hint of a major interest in their baby.

Within days of the garbled newspaper reports of the Kill Devil flights ten months earlier, two brothers, Samuel and Godfrey Lowell Cabot, wealthy businessmen and influential members of a distinguished Boston family, had both – neither, extraordinarily, knowing the other had done so – sent telegrams of congratulation. Godfrey, who believed that if the reports were true something of great significance had happened, followed up his wire with a letter asking if their machine could carry a payload of 100-pound items of freight sixteen miles from his mine in West Virginia over winter-impassable terrain to a railhead. When Wilbur had told him what the *Flyer* could do he had been so impressed that he'd immediately got in touch with a relative, the powerful Republican senator Henry Cabot Lodge, a close friend of President Theodore Roosevelt. 'This may fairly be said to mark the beginning of successful flight through the air by men unaided by balloons,' Godfrey told Lodge. 'It has occurred to me that it would be eminently desirable for the United States Government to interest itself in this invention.[14]

Senator Lodge had passed the letter to the US War Department. The military bureaucrats, with condemnation still ringing in their ears for their squandering of public funds on Langley's failed aeroplanes, were now convinced that heavier-than-air flight was simply not possible. They had no intention of burning their fingers again. Cabot's letter was ignored.

Would the British be more interested? Lieutenant Colonel Capper was an officer in the Royal Engineers who had been recalled from the South African War, hand-picked to help develop the army's use of 'aerial vehicles'. The current vehicles were strings of huge man-lifting kites, gliders, dirigible airships and balloons, operated at Aldershot in Hampshire by an archaically named research and development unit, the Balloon Factory, later to become the famous Royal Aircraft Establishment. The practical military use of the vehicles had become Capper's responsibility; he had been appointed commandant of an associate unit, the 'Balloon Sections', which trained soldiers in the use of observation balloons. His outfit was one of the tiny seeds that would grow into the Royal Air Force.

The lieutenant colonel was a product of his military generation – an ultra-strict disciplinarian, a brave, capable soldier, willing to expose himself to physical danger with his troops in the field and aloft in balloon operations. Though gifted with a sharp mind, he was no scientist and had little understanding of the true complexities of flight. This, nonetheless, hadn't prevented him from recognising the huge potential of military air power: he was determined to see it quickly embraced by the British Army.

Capper's colleague, Colonel James Lethbridge Brooke Templer, who commanded the Balloon Factory, was another martinet – with snuff box in one hand and a long coloured handkerchief in the other, he was fond of making surprise visits to the balloon sheds to check that his instructions were being carried out to the letter. His consuming ambition, like Capper's, was to shake the British Army out of its terrestrial mindset. The army's total budget for air operations stood at what was even then a parsimonious £15,000 (just under a million pounds today). Both Templer and Capper were convinced that their island nation could no longer be defended by its navy: its biggest threat from mainland Europe would soon come from the air. When news of the St Louis air show and the aerial machines it had promised to exhibit from around the world had come to his notice, Templer had persuaded his masters at the War Office to send Capper along.

Preparing for his mission, the lieutenant colonel had gone to see Patrick Alexander whom he described to his superiors as 'a gentleman who is probably better acquainted personally with all interested in aeronautics in Europe and America than any other living individual'. Alexander had given him introductions to Chanute, the recently disgraced Langley, Alexander Graham Bell (still struggling unsuccessfully to add mechanical flight to his invention of the telephone) and to 'Messrs W & O Wright, Dayton'. Capper was to meet them all. Chanute he found 'a truly fine character' who 'had no use for secrecy or personal ambition and was always willing to tell anyone interested all that he knew'.[15] The Wrights, to whom he was clearly devoted, had genuinely mastered powered flight, Chanute said. What's more they were entirely trustworthy.

Capper found the St Louis fair disappointing: not a powered winged machine to be seen. And from what Langley told him of his ill-starred *aerodromes*, it was obvious the professor had nothing practical with which to inspire the British. The British officer came to the conclusion that Americans were 'all so damned certain they know everything and so absolutely ignorant of the theory of aeronautics'.[16] But in Dayton he was forced to revise this conclusion. The two largely unknown bicycle-makers were clearly leading the world in a quite dramatic fashion.

Despite his frustration at the Wrights' seemingly inordinate secrecy, Capper had been instantly taken with them both. They invited him and his wife, Edith, to a meal at Hawthorn Street. The bishop was away but Katharine entertained them hospitably, captivating the rather reserved English visitors with her lively charm. She and Edith, herself a keen balloonist, began a friendship that would last for years. Although the brothers sensed they could trust the British officer, they felt a demonstration flight for him would attract too much attention from the press. Capper wasn't even to be given a glimpse of the machine in its locked shed. It was a huge disappointment, but he accepted it graciously.

Capper was fascinated by these unique brothers: by their obvious decency and integrity; their openness about their work; their quite formidable mastery of the whole science of powered flight. Their invention was clearly an achievement of obvious military value. They took him along to the cycle shop where they let him see the *Flyer*'s motor under repair and, tantalisingly, showed him photographs of the machine, in confident flight, whirring above

Huffman field. But he wasn't allowed to take away any of the pictures; everything they had revealed to him, he was told firmly, was in the strictest confidence.

Although excited by all he'd learnt, Capper had no authority to commit the War Office to anything. He urged the Wrights, when they were ready, to give Britain first option. They said they were not ready, but were left with a feeling of distinct unease when Capper told them that Augustus Herring had already written to the War Office offering a powered machine. Where, they wondered, would his deceitful ploys end?

Back in England, Capper wrote a report for his Whitehall masters warning them that Britain was rapidly falling behind in its development of air power. 'America is leading the way whilst in England practically nothing is being done.' He reported on the startling ascendancy that 'Messrs O. & W. Wright' were giving America:

> The work they are doing is of very great importance as it means that, if carried to a successful issue, we may shortly have as accessories of warfare scouting machines which will go at a great pace and be independent of obstacles of ground, whilst offering from their elevated position unrivalled opportunities of ascertaining what is occurring in the heart of an enemy's country.[17]

The Wrights, whom Capper described as 'most courteous', were 'keeping quiet till perfect'. He added, 'we must have a proper experimental school in England or we shall be left behind.' 'Both these gentlemen,' he said, 'impressed me most favourably; they have worked up step by step; they are in themselves well educated men and capable mechanics, and do not think are likely to claim more than they can perform.'

Capper would have been surprised if he'd known that just two days after he'd left Dayton the Wrights had unlocked the shed and sprung the *Flyer* into the air again. And almost immediately their luck had changed. Wilbur, in one great psychological surge, shot their success to a new level. In nearly four complete rounds of the field he was airborne for over five minutes. A train was stopped while two of the railway company's officials, spellbound by the spectacle, got out to watch. On the first day of December, nearly a year after his 12-second hop at Kill Devil, Orville, too, made a five-minute flight. Proudly watched by his father, now a regular visitor to the field and one of their most passionate observers, he flew nearly three miles. It was the hundredth flight of the season.

The astonishing thing about these two remarkable flights was that, although witnessed by dozens of people, neither was reported by the Ohio newspapers. The Dayton *Journal*'s managing editor, who regularly chatted with the Wrights on the inter-urban train, had asked Orville one day: 'If you ever do something *unusual* be sure and let us know.' Beard's city editor, Frank Tunison, had developed a still deeper aversion to the mere breath of an experimental flying story. 'Why do we print such stuff?' he would declare angrily when occasionally a brief paragraph crept on to an inside page. But Beard felt differently. From time to time he would use the newly installed telephone at Hawthorn Street to ask the brothers if they'd done anything newsworthy. When he'd called on the first of December Orville had proudly reported his five-minute flight.

'Where did you go?' Beard asked.

'Around the field.'

'Oh! Just around the field. I see. Well, we'll keep in touch with you.'[18]

17

Unwanted Baby for Sale (1905)

With two five-minute flights now under their belts, the Wrights, confident they would soon crack the *Flyer*'s remaining control problems, decided the time had come to find a buyer. The obvious customers were military. Ingenuously they cherished the belief that the aeroplane would be a singular power for good in the world: it would enable warring armies to observe each other's every move making it impossible for either to gain an advantage. Not for a moment did they contemplate its use as a terrible new means of delivering destruction. Their immediate patriotic thoughts were to sell it to the US Army. 'We would be ashamed of ourselves if we offered our machine to a foreign government without giving our own country a chance at it . . .' Wilbur told Chanute.[1]

In the first week of January 1905, Wilbur sought the advice of their local congressman, Robert Nevin, at his Dayton home. Nevin said the best way to expedite a sale to the War Department was for them to address a proposal to him: he would personally deliver it to the Secretary of War, William Howard Taft.

The Wrights decided to hedge their bets on a broad front. Wilbur wrote two letters – one to Lieutenant Colonel Capper at Aldershot, the other to Congressman Nevin. Jointly signed by both brothers, they were written on Wright Cycle Company notepaper, the bicycle logos bringing a somewhat incongruous charm to letters from a company apparently in the aeroplane business.

To Nevin they wrote that, after five years of experimentation, they had at last produced a practical flying machine that had made flights of up to three miles:

> The numerous flights in straight lines, in circles, and over S-shaped courses, in calms and in winds, have made it quite certain that flying has been brought to a point where it can be made of great practical use in various ways, one of which is that of scouting and carrrying messages in time of war. If the latter features are of interest to our government, we shall be pleased to take up the matter either on a basis of providing machines of agreed specification, at a contract price, or of furnishing all the scientific and practical information we have accumulated . . . together with a licence to use our patents; thus putting the government in a position to operate on its own account.
>
> If you can find it convenient to ascertain whether this is a subject of interest to our own government, it would oblige us greatly, as early information on this point will aid us in making our plans for the future.[2]

Unfortunately, when the letter arrived in Nevin's Washington office he was away ill. A clerk launched this remarkable offer routinely into the system. It was forwarded without the congressman's endorsement to the War Department's Board of Ordnance and Fortification. Sadly for the Wrights' hopes, the board was the same agency that had poured $50,000 into the Langley projects that had so recently died in shame in the Potomac. As a result of this savagely publicised financial disaster, the board had become the target for bitter congressional censure. In the House of Representatives congressman after congressman had stood up to harangue and ridicule both the War Department and Langley. The only thing the professor ever made fly was government money, shouted one. Still licking its wounds, the board had acquired a decided aversion to offers of flying machines secretly built in small town bicycle shops. And since the Langley scandal, showered with requests for funds from other experimenters and hosts of cranks, it had composed a stock reply. One quickly went back to Nevin:

> I have the honour to inform you that, as many requests have been made for financial assistance in the development and designs for flying machines, the Board has found it necessary to decline to make allotments for the experimental development of devices for mechanical flight and has determined that, before suggestions with that object in view will be considered, the device must have been brought to the stage of practical operation without expense to the United States.

Bewilderingly, as if the author had not properly read the brothers' letter, the reply added:

> It appears from the letter of Messrs Wilbur and Orville Wright that their machine has not yet been brought to the stage of practical operation, but as soon as it shall have been perfected, this Board would be pleased to receive further representations from them in regard to it.[3]

The letter was signed by the board's president, Major-General Gillespie. Wilbur and Orville were astounded that someone of his rank could have so grotesquely misunderstood their abundantly clear offer that, far from seeking development funds, had actually described a machine that was already able to fly several miles. Today a swift email or phone call to the general's secretary would have quickly put the matter right, but the Wrights did nothing to persist. Rather they took the letter as a personal insult to their integrity. When Wilbur reported the 'flat turndown' to Chanute he was shocked. As an American, Chanute wrote, he was appalled that his government was apparently prepared to allow foreign powers to seize the invention. He begged Wilbur to allow him to intervene at the War Department by 'putting a flea in its ear', but the Wrights demurred, hurt and angry at the way they'd been brushed off by their own government. 'It is no pleasant thought to us,' Wilbur told him, 'that any foreign country should take from America any share of the glory of having conquered the flying problem, but we feel that we have done our full share toward making this an American invention and if it is sent abroad for further development the responsibility does not rest upon us. We have taken pains to see that "opportunity" gave a good clear knock on the War Department door.'[4]

But did they knock hard enough? For more than half a century historians have apportioned blame for the seemingly mindless form of the rejection equally to the Wrights and the military bureaucracy – to the Wrights for their naivety in believing that their Christian word that a working aeroplane was now actually flying and theirs for the asking should have been good enough for the army. Why hadn't they sent the powerful proof that was so tellingly available – the photographs of it patently in flight; the signed statements they could have obtained from dozens of witnesses of repute? As for the War Department, why, sceptical as he may have been, had not the general whose job it was to evaluate new military technology at least followed it up with an invitation to demonstrate this allegedly practical machine? Indeed, why had the Wrights not immediately offered to do so? And why, when the letter had so obviously been misunderstood, had they not made a single effort to clarify it? One explanation says they didn't actually trust the military authorities and were afraid to show them too much, believing the army might confiscate both the plane and the entire corpus of their priceless aerodynamic research data.

'Hard though it is a hundred years later for us to understand,' said Adrian Kinnane, 'Wilbur and Orville felt positively offended that anyone should demand further demonstration of what they claimed.' Dr Kinnane, an American psychologist and historian, made an extensive and scholarly study in the early 1980s of the close-knit Wright clan, examining the role the family's internal dynamics played in the birth of the aeroplane. 'Faith in their personal integrity was automatically expected of everyone. It was an attitude of righteousness, bred in the bruising church conflicts in which they reduced everything to the single question: "Who is in the right?" They always were. How dare anyone doubt it.'[5]

Stung with disbelief at their own government's response – one historian was to describe it as 'near the border-line of official insanity'[6] – the Wrights were now forced to pin their hopes of reward on the British with whom, through their friendship with the balloon colonel, they already had a foot firmly in the door. Yet here, though the response was more rational, they were to fare little better. Their stiffly formal 'Dear Sir' letter to Capper, also written on cycle company paper, had attempted to test the British waters. It brought the lieutenant colonel up to date with the exciting five-minute flying achievements of the *Flyer* since he'd visited them a few months earlier and suggested that:

> There is no question but that the government in possession of such a machine as we can now furnish, and the scientific and practical knowledge and instruction we are in a position to impart, could secure a lead of several years over governments which waited to buy perfected machines before making a start in this line.

If the British government were interested, they said, they could, during the coming year, produce an aeroplane that would fly at a minimum of 35 miles an hour and carry two men. It could make possible the creation of 'a corps of aviators for military scouting purposes'.

'If you think it probable that an offer of such character would receive consideration from your government at this time, we will be glad to give further consideration to matters of details, etc.' The letter concluded on a personal note 'with pleasant recollections of the visit from you and Mrs Capper last October, we remain, Respectfully yours, Wilbur and Orville Wright'.[7]

When the letter arrived at the Aldershot office of his balloon unit, Capper read it with quiet elation. He would have been even more pleased had he known that the US Army had that very week rejected this sensational new means of transport and weapon of war that was, amazingly, being offered on a plate to a foreign power. It was a personal coup for the colonel – the trust the Wrights had placed in him. But he knew he would need permission from his superiors to reply.

'I forward herewith letter received by me this day from Messrs Wright Brothers of Dayton, Ohio, USA, with a request that I be informed what sort of an answer I may give to the letter,' Capper wrote correctly to his boss, the General Officer Commanding, Royal Engineers, Aldershot Command. Knowing that, at command headquarters, there would be little comprehension among senior officers more familiar with balloons and kites of the military significance of the Wrights' invention, Capper felt it helpful to explain that 'the machine has no gas bag'. Enthusiastically he went on: 'As it has gone for three miles, it is merely a question of skill, nerve and endurance of the operator for it to go 50 or 100 miles or any required distance.' Urging that the Wrights be given 'every encouragement from us in the interest of progress in our war appliances', the colonel asked that 'I be permitted to answer the letter stating that I think it probable that their offer would receive consideration from His Majesty's Government'.[8]

Aldershot Command, a great deal more comprehending than their American counterparts, decided that this was an important matter for higher authority. Capper's request and the letter from the Wrights was passed to the venerable institution of the War Office in London. It dropped on the Director of Artillery. This senior officer quickly decided that aeroplanes were not within his purview. He sent off a brief polite note of acknowledgement to the Wright Cycle Company and passed the file sideways to his colleague Brigadier-General Richard Ruck, the Director of Fortifications and Works. Ruck, later to be knighted, was a progressive, flexible-minded officer eager to investigate new ideas and with a special interest in aviation that was later to lead him to prominence in the Aeronautical Society. No one could have been more favourably disposed to take the invention seriously. Ruck lost no time in getting in touch with the brothers to confirm genuine British Army interest and to seek more information and a detailed proposal of what precisely they could supply – and at what price.

The Wrights' reply early in March 1905, long regarded as one of the defining documents in the drawn-out birth pangs of flight, was a lengthy typewritten letter with all the hallmarks and legalistic convolutions that Wilbur had perfected in the Brethren wars. After much soulful discussion, he and Orville had decided to divide their offer into two parts: a practical flyable aeroplane; and, quite separately, the intellectual body of their accumulated aeronautical research. The latter, Wilbur said, would equip the British with the technical knowledge to design machines to their own special requirements. However this knowledge package would be so difficult to price – it involved the sale of patents yet to be granted – that he suggested they begin by limiting the deal to one machine with only the data necessary for its operation. The aeroplane would be capable of carrying two men of average weight and flying 50 miles without refuelling at a speed of not less than 30 miles an hour. It would be strong enough 'to make landings without being broken when operated with a reasonable degree of skill'.

The letter proposed that the price be pegged to the distance successfully flown in a trial flight before British Army observers. They were asking £500 for each mile covered, but if none managed to reach ten miles the contract would be void. There was no mention of the number of qualifying flights they would be permitted to attempt which, in theory, suggested the price could be raised to an astronomically open-ended sum merely by flying more and more miles. Brigadier-General Ruck assumed they were talking of a 50-mile ceiling – £25,000. But this was not all. The cycle company was also asking £200 per month as a fee for the flying training one of the brothers would have to give the British student pilots. Though keen to take negotiations further, Ruck had nothing like this sort of money – today around what seems like a modest one and a half-million pounds – in his directorate's budget. However, so convinced was he of the strategic importance of this military opportunity that he decided, at the point where many of his contemporaries would have killed it stone dead, to pass the proposal upwards. It went to a powerful, scientifically minded body called the Royal Engineer Committee concerned with the technical evaluation of new military devices. In April its president recommended that the military attaché at the British embassy in Washington, Colonel Hubert Foster, go to Dayton and witness some flight trials.

Yet nothing happened. For nearly half a year the War Office fell silent. Unfortunately, when its order reached Foster's office at the British embassy in Washington in May 1905 the colonel was away on a protracted visit to Mexico to whose government he was also accredited. Whether or not the instruction was sent to the itinerant attaché in Mexico, the Wrights, who were offering to make Britain the world's first air power, were to be ignored for most of the rest of 1905.

Somehow this does not seem to have bothered them unduly, for they had other immediate problems on their mind. One was the now urgent need to build another aeroplane, hopefully eliminating all the dangerous handling foibles of the 1904 machine. The other preoccupation came from the Brethren. All peace plans had collapsed and the final showdown between the church's squabbling factions was looming at the quadrennial conference at Grand Rapids, Michigan, in the middle of May.

Inevitably Wilbur had hastened to serve as his father's advocate and tract writer. At issue was the running sore of the continued cover-up of Keiter's embezzlement and Bishop Wright's expulsion. Quite bizarrely the crooked minister was still flourishing within the church, while Milton had remained *persona non grata*. He had nonetheless been immensely busy, rallying to his side growing numbers of sympathetic delegates incensed at his treatment by the kangaroo court.

Once again Wilbur thrust aviation aside and boarded the train. He produced an eloquently compelling tract reminding Brethren in damning, clinical detail of Keiter's catalogue of criminality within their midst, while making an emotional case against the unjust treatment of his father. The document was widely distributed with powerful effect at the conference, which Milton, in one of the most thunderingly righteous hours of his career, according to one Keiterite, 'dominated with an iron hand equal to that of any political despot of today'.[9]

By a two-thirds majority the White River district's edict of three years earlier expelling Bishop Wright was declared null and void; he was totally vindicated. His foes, Bishops Barnaby and Floyd, defeated and rebuked, were retired under a cloud, going off, according to the bishop's diary 'to sulk'. Fuelled by Wilbur's latest denouncement of Keiter, the conference also voted overwhelmingly that the publishing house's books should be reinvestigated by independent accountants.

It was a heart-warming victory for Milton Wright. Good had finally vanquished evil – though not entirely, it seems. The moral ambivalence that had for so long sustained Keiter's charmed existence continued to flourish within the top ranks of the Brethren. When the outside accountants duly produced their report, which confirmed his extensive pilfering, the embarrassing document was merely filed and 'the case considered closed'.[10] Astonishingly, Keiter was allowed to remain active in the senior ranks of the church, not only as chairman of its publishing board for another two years but also inspiring a major breakaway movement of his supporters that was, in classic Brethren style, to split the White River district into two churches. Milton, who was never to see him imprisoned, was now seventy-six. It was time, he decided, to retire. He ceased to be a bishop, but was to remain active within the Brethren as a senior churchman – and his path was to cross Keiter's yet again.

Back in Dayton the Wright family rejoiced. 'We won a complete victory,' Wilbur proudly told Chanute, 'turned every one of the rascals out of office and put friends of my father in their places. It will be a relief to have the matter off my mind hereafter.'[11]

'The painful Keiter saga deeply affected the family,' said Adrian Kinnane. 'It had worked powerfully to bring them even closer together. And the stressful events, which Milton's own rigid righteousness had helped create, had greatly reinforced their conservative, mistrustful attitudes towards mankind and wicked people like Keiter and Herring who seemed to be everywhere. It certainly served to heighten Wilbur and Orville's wariness in their dealings with every single potential buyer of their flying machine.'[12]

Freed from the distraction of the church battles, Wilbur rejoined Orville late in May at the cycle workroom where *Flyer III* was under construction. The 1904 machine had been broken up; only its engine was salvaged to power the new aeroplane. The third *Flyer* looked very much like its predecessors except that, to improve longitudinal control, the elevators were pushed further out in front and the twin rudders positioned further out the back. The camber of its 40½-foot wings was increased to 1:20, the propellers, which had begun to twist in flight, were cleverly redesigned to eliminate the distortion, the pilot still lay prone on the lower wing, and it still had no wheels – it sat on long bowed runners looking like a winged sledge. In a major change to the control system they disconnected the rudder from the wing warping to allow the pilot now, as in all modern aeroplanes, to use it independently. They hoped that with the ability to apply more rudder when necessary it would cure the tendency to side-slip into the ground while turning. The disconnection meant, however, that the pilot had three separate controls to coordinate. It was initially to have disastrous results.

When *Flyer III* was assembled at Huffman Prairie and test-flown in the last week of June, they had to learn how to fly all over again. Orville, who went first, failed hopelessly to harmonise the three controls and smacked into the ground. Wilbur next day did the same, breaking a wing spar as he fumbled his way back to earth. For twelve weeks, through the summer of 1905, when they were often grounded by bad weather, neither could manage a flight of more than 20 seconds; every one ended depressingly in accident and damage. They still wore no safety harness or proper head protection, yet always seemed to escape with only cuts and bruises.

Meanwhile, at Hawthorn Street, they were being temporarily looked after by a young visiting relative called Emma – Milton, Katharine and Carrie were all away, but some of Lorin's children had come to stay. However, Katharine, visiting a girlfriend in northern Ohio, was unhappy about Emma's ability to maintain the domestic routines to her high standards. She continued to exercise her housekeeping dominion over Hawthorn Street in an almost daily flow of minute instructions to her brothers:

> I wish you would telephone to Joe Boyd to cut the grass about the middle of this week. It gets so coarse when allowed to grow too long. And please put up one string for that honey suckle vine on the south porch. And see that the flowers get some water . . . Get up early Sunday morning and see that the children get washed and off to Sunday school! . . . You could tell our Emma to get some chickens and make sandwiches and devilled eggs if you

> wanted to have them out in the country for dinner... Tell Emma to have my room cleaned . . . Please forward any letters that come. Emma could go to the post office for the mail or order it delivered . . . I hope Emma won't break the family purse by her grocery bills . . .[13]

As the days passed, Katharine's anxiety that Emma, despite her suspected inadequacies, might have usurped her domestic management role, grew. On the eve of her return she wrote:

> I hope Emma will have something decent to eat. She won't boss that ranch after I strike the place, I can promise her that. I hope things haven't been too uncomfortable.

But Wilbur and Orville had scarcely noticed Katharine's absence. They had been too busy out at Huffman Prairie trying to crack what seemed to be the last remaining problem – the dispiriting bugbear of the hypersensitive pitch controls. They now pushed the elevator unit out still further and significantly increased its surface area by 50 per cent. With this modification Wilbur at last, in the final days of August, managed to fly again for one minute. In the first week of September Orville did nearly five minutes. As the switchbacking ceased and they began to master the new feel of the controls, their flying, suddenly, marvellously, appeared to have become accident-free.

But once more they were congratulating themselves too soon. During the tight banked turns necessary to stay within the boundary of the field they found themselves uncontrollably sinking to earth. Only after Orville had been quite unable to turn away from a tall tree that stood at the far end of the paddock did they diagnose the problem and learn how to prevent it. At the last moment he had desperately pushed the elevator fully down for an emergency landing. The *Flyer*, now descending, picked up speed. And as it did so, to his great surprise, the warp control suddenly came back to life. It allowed him to bank away – though not before collecting a branch which stabbed itself into the wing.

They had discovered a phenomenon that to this day continues to kill inexperienced pilots in low-powered machines in tight steep turns – the increased loading of the centrifugal force was raising the *Flyer*'s stalling speed to a level that their tiny power could not overcome. Orville had stumbled on the solution. By increasing the airspeed in a dive, he'd produced the extra lift to nip a stall in the bud and sustain the aircraft in the air. From now on they used the technique, always 'tilting the machine forward a little', in circling. It was to be the last in the endless succession of handling perils that had bedevilled their journey into the unknown.

Now that they knew how to turn without killing themselves, their flight distances surged in thrilling leaps. In late September, as chill, denser, autumn air arrived to help the launching process, Wilbur stayed up, exultantly, for over 18 minutes. Watched by the amazed white-whiskered figure of his father, he circled the field sixteen times, only being forced to land when he ran out of fuel. He'd travelled over 11 miles.

It was just the beginning. They fitted a bigger fuel tank and three days later Orville flew 12 miles – then 15. In the first week of October he did close to 21. Wilbur then capped it by staying up for a stupendous 39½ minutes during which he made thirty rounds of the field, travelling over 24 miles. The flight was only ended when the tank ran dry. No longer was there even a tiny doubt: they had created a practical flying machine that could be confidently offered to the world. It was the true dawn of modern aviation. And astonishingly still only a handful of people knew about it.

The bishop's boys may have conquered the air, fulfilling man's centuries-old dream with one of the greatest triumphs in the annals of technology, but the Ohio newspapers seemed incapable of recognising that one of history's truly tremendous events had for months been occurring in full public view under their very noses. Week after week through the early autumn of 1905, as word of the remarkable machine spread through the district, their audience grew – some now coming out from Dayton by motor car. The city's newspapers had started getting calls from people puzzled by the absence of any explanation of this unique motorised gadget daily clattering through the sky. For some curious reason the editors simply didn't believe the reports. 'I guess,' said one later, 'that we were just plain dumb.'

But though the local press was silent, word had begun to spread in aviation circles. One day the brothers, to their unease, noticed two 'mysterious' strangers wandering about the nearby fields suspiciously close to the hangar. They thought at first they were hunters, but there was little game to be had in the area and the men kept hanging around. Next morning they appeared again. One of them carried a camera. It became obvious their purpose was to spy on the aeroplane.

Realising they'd been spotted, the strangers eventually ceased all pretence and came over to the shed inside which Taylor was working on the *Flyer*. 'May we see it?' one of them asked. 'Sure,' said Wilbur, 'provided you don't take any pictures.' The men agreed and the one with the camera carefully put it down some distance away. He then asked if it was OK to look in the shed and was told to 'make himself right at home'. Was he a newspaperman? they asked. The stranger said he wasn't, though he sometimes contributed articles to publications. It was as far as he introduced himself. After the man and his companion had thanked them and gone, Taylor, who had been answering the questions, said, 'That fellow's no writer – at least no ordinary writer. When he looked at the different parts of the machine he called them all by their right names.'[14]

A few weeks later the Wrights were surprised to read in a New York newspaper a story that they had flown in secret experiments fifty times round their field. It was based on a lecture to the Aero Club of New York by Charles Manly of the Smithsonian Institution – Professor Langley's chief engineer and luckless pilot. Had Manly, they wondered, been one of the furtive visitors? Curious to know if they had innocently shown every detail of the *Flyer* to a rival designer, Wilbur immediately wrote to ask Chanute to describe Manly. 'Do you know any means of finding out whether he was wearing a moustache about the 1st of October?' he enquired. 'It is evident that the news was obtained by some underhand method.'

'Mr Manly,' Chanute replied, 'is about 5 ft 6 ins tall and with a brown moustache.' He had helped describe the visitor with the camera. Full confirmation later came from a newspaper picture of Manly.

So was Langley, whom they thought had abandoned his powered flying attempts, spying on them? The truth was that though the famous astronomer had turned his back on aviation and returned to astrophysics, he had agreed that Manly, using money offered by some loyal businessmen with undiminished faith in his experiments, should restore the failed *Great Aerodrome* to flying condition. This Manly had done. But he was to go much further. The doomed behemoth, structurally enhanced would, in extraordinary circumstances, one day return to haunt Orville. For the moment the Smithsonian engineer had gone away from Huffman Prairie with, if not the priceless data that had created it all, many of the *Flyer*'s control secrets in his astute head.

The brothers' rising sense of insecurity was daily made more acute by the spectators who came to watch their lumbering circuits. Having increased the size of the fuel tank they were tempted to take the *Flyer* on cross-country flights, but the rough and wooded surrounding terrain offered few places in which to put down intact in an emergency – and then there would be the complications of trying to recover it from the middle of a wood twenty miles away.

Their nervousness became alarm early in October when the newspapers began to take a serious interest in their antics. The incurious Luther Beard, the Dayton morning *Journal*'s managing editor, came to the field to see a flight the day Wilbur circled for the astonishing 40 minutes. But Beard dallied for too long. As he stood there concluding that even his city editor, Tunison, would regard this as worth a paragraph, he'd already been scooped. His evening rival, the Dayton *Daily News*, was at that moment on the city streets reporting the Wrights' sensational flights earlier in the week when Orville had flown 20 miles. A Cincinnati newspaper picked up the story fuelling public interest and bringing unwanted throngs now armed with cameras. It tipped the Wrights into a state of mild paranoia.

They halted the trials and shut the *Flyer* away in the shed. So fearful were they that news stories and pictures of these epochal flights would reveal their design to competitors that they embarked on drastic damage control. It was said – by one biographer – that 'with the help of a few influential friends the Wrights succeeded in keeping the news from going out over the wires – an achievement that gave rise abroad to a report that they had suppressed the news by buying up the entire edition of a Dayton newspaper'.[15] Unlikely as this was, they were now panicked into a complete cessation of flying.

Before shutting the programme down entirely they were keen that Chanute should see what the *Flyer* could do. They needed someone of his worldwide eminence to testify in support of their efforts to clinch a sale, imminently, they now hoped, with the British government. So they planned one final ambitious flight of the season in which they aimed to break the one-hour barrier. Wilbur wrote to tell Chanute. Their faithful admirer was only too keen to come:

> It is a perfect marvel to me that you have kept your performances out of the newspapers so long. With so curious a public as our own, and such appetite for sensation as obtains in the press, I felt convinced that some enterprising reporter would discover you sometime and make you famous. I think you must make up your mind to enforced publicity as to performance while preserving the secrets of your construction. From a military point of view it would be preferable to keep the whole thing secret, but I doubt whether it can be done. I shall be very glad to be present at your coming effort to fly for one hour.[16]

On 30 October, the Wrights summoned Chanute to Dayton. When he arrived, a violent storm was sweeping southern Ohio. It raged for so long the flight had to be abandoned. The storm killed not only the planned secret one-hour bid, but decided them to wrap up flying for the year.

Ironically, at the very point that they had finally perfected the world's first powered flying machine, eliminating almost every foible from its controls so that any dexterous person could be taught to fly it, it seemed, astoundingly, that no one was bursting to buy it. Foster, the British emissary, was still in Mexico, possibly ignorant of the instruction lying in his in-tray back in Washington; and the American War Department to whom, under Chanute's pressure, they had reoffered the invention had responded yet again with an obtuseness that beggared belief.

In a letter addressed to the Secretary of War himself, Wilbur wrote that, as the Board of Ordnance and Fortification appeared to have given their earlier offer 'scant consideration', they had decided to renew the offer. They could now supply a machine that would carry a pilot and observer and fly at least 25 miles at a minimum speed of 30 miles an hour. As had been proposed to the British, the price would be 'on a sliding scale' based on the distance flown in trials. However, they wanted a contract before demonstrating the aeroplane.

The reply from the president of the ordnance board reiterated that before it could even be considered, 'the device must have been brought to the stage of practical operation without expense to the United States'. The letter now demanded 'such drawings and descriptions thereof as are necessary to enable its construction to be understood and a definite conclusion as to its practicability to be arrived at'.[17]

Dumbfounded, Wilbur replied that the machine actually existed and was already flying. What specifications would the army seek? he asked. Would they want a global exclusive monopoly or would they permit it to be offered to other nations? Perhaps if Wilbur had sent a couple of photographs of the plane in flight, and a handful of affidavits from a few prominent citizens of Dayton, the board would surely have hesitated before sending them a letter recording what must rank as one of the biggest, most unfathomable blunders in military history:

> It is recommended that Messrs Wright be informed that the Board does not care to formulate any requirements for the performance of a flying machine or take any further action on the subject until a machine is produced which by actual operation is shown to be able to produce horizontal flight and to carry an operator.[18]

Exasperated, the brothers decided to give up on the US military. They would do business instead with the British, whose Colonel

Capper not only knew the war machine was tangible but understood its priceless value. Now puzzled why the nomadic Colonel Foster hadn't been in touch – but grateful for the opportunity it had given them to iron the remaining problems out of the machine – Wilbur wrote once more to the War Office in London. He said that acceptance of the aeroplane could now be dependent on a trial flight of a minimum of 50 miles rather than the 10 miles they'd previously proposed.

Meanwhile, more nervous than ever that their brainchild was at high risk of being pirated, they dismantled *Flyer III*. In the first week of November it was locked away in the Huffman Prairie shed. They wouldn't fly again for over two and a half years.

18

The French and British Connections

(1905–1906)

At the War Office in London, where Wilbur's letter guaranteeing a 50-mile range had arrived at the end of October 1905, there were already rumblings of concern at the silence from their Washington attaché. The strangely titled Inspector of Electric Lights, Major William Baker Brown, who was administratively responsible for the Balloon Factory and all British Army aeronautical operations, noticed from his files that after five months there had been no report from the attaché. When he prodded his superiors he was told that Colonel Foster had only just returned from his long absence in Mexico and would be addressing the matter as soon as he'd settled back into Washington. This was to take several more weeks, but at last, in the middle of November, the colonel got around to dictating a brief letter to the Wright Cycle Company. He said he'd been instructed to come to Dayton and see the aeroplane fly. He assumed it would be merely a matter of fixing a convenient date. He should have made no such presumption.

Wilbur's reply bewildered Foster. 'Of course we can not consent to show the machine to the representatives of the government which is considering the purchase of our knowledge and inventions until we are assured that the terms of sale will be satisfactory,' the attaché read to his surprise. 'It would,' the letter explained,

> be highly injudicious to place ourselves at the mercy of anyone by disclosing any part of our secrets with the expectation of arranging satisfactory terms afterwards . . . As a preliminary to the consummation of a definite contract, we will furnish incontestable evidence that we have done all that we claim to have done. By the terms of the contract not one cent need be paid out by the government until after the machine has fulfilled certain stipulated requirements in a trial trip in the presence of the government's representatives.

Wilbur said they would be pleased to welcome Colonel Foster to Dayton immediately. While there was no question of his even seeing the *Flyer* in its windowless hangar, they would be happy to introduce him to farmers and 'prominent citizens of Dayton' who had witnessed its flights of up to 24 miles. If an agreement were concluded with the British, the letter ended, they 'would set up the machine at some retired place and make a flight surpassing those to which we have already referred. We would have put the record much higher before quitting, but for the impossibility of securing privacy for further flights at that time and place.'[1]

Foster was baffled and annoyed by the response which one eminent aviation historian was to describe unkindly as 'Wilburian rigmarole'. 'The British government had not yet asked the brothers to disclose their secrets, and the attaché was not interested in the methods of construction or operation – he merely wanted to see the thing fly.'[2] He couldn't understand the Wrights' refusal to put it just once in the air for a genuinely keen and significant likely buyer – one of the world's most powerful nations – when, on their own admission, they had been openly flying for months in front of large numbers of people of every description. Brusquely he wrote back to clarify the instruction he was under which made it clear that a demonstration flight was an essential preliminary to the start of negotiations for British Army purchase:

> All I would therefore ask you is to say whether you will show me a flying trial, and if you will, to fix a near date. If you do not wish, I will so inform the War Office whose representative I am only for

> the purpose of seeing a trial. I am not their intermediary for negotiation with you and on that point I would ask you to communicate direct with the secretary for War, the War Office, London.[3]

The plain message seems still not to have registered in Dayton. Wilbur continued to argue with Foster as if he were a principal in the debate, now warning him that although they had offered the machine to the British, because of the delays in following it up the War Office was no longer the only interested purchaser in the running. It was 'possible that a crisis will be reached', Wilbur wrote, 'before the British War Office has all obtainable information before it and is ready to reach a decision . . .'

The other interest was very real. It came from France. Passionate scientific interest in human flight had existed there since the Montgolfier brothers had first floated aloft in the eighteenth century, but attempts to master fixed-wing flight had got nowhere until Chanute had startled the French aeronautical fraternity with his controversial address to the Aéro-Club de France early in 1903. His account and subsequently published article describing the success of the Wrights' gliders and their technical achievement in mastering three-dimensional control had sparked a major revival of French determination. When later the dramatic news that the Wrights had achieved brief powered flight had reached France, it had created a wave of chauvinistic fervour for the belief that French experimenters could still beat the Americans in the race for a truly practical aeroplane. Ferdinand Ferber, who had tried to buy their 1902 glider and was still unsuccessfully experimenting with his crude copy, declared, 'The aeroplane must not be allowed to be perfected in America.'

Leading the revival was a wealthy Paris lawyer and balloonist, Ernest Archdeacon, who declared: 'Will the homeland of the Montgolfiers have the shame of allowing that ultimate discovery of aerial science to be realised abroad?' Although no one in France properly understood how the Wrights' control system worked, or even why it was necessary, Archdeacon had set out to have built a vague replica of the Wrights' 1902 glider. He got Ferber and a young newcomer to aviation, a student architect called Gabriel Voisin, to fly it for him. The machine had no active roll control; it made a few short hops off a sand dune before being abandoned. An engineer, Robert Esnault-Pelterie, had also tried to clone the Wright glider. He couldn't make the wing warping work properly and replaced it ingeniously with aviation's first very crude ailerons – large moveable surfaces like horizontal rudders placed on struts projecting from the front of the lower wing. They were actually elevons in that they served as elevators as well. But this machine, too, was a failure.

Meanwhile, the determinedly persevering Ferber, who was now giving public lectures on aviation, had attempted free flight with a motorised glider. All he had managed was a short, uncontrolled powered glide. Nonetheless, he believed that with this precarious motorised hop he was at least beginning to emulate the triumph at Kill Devil. His satisfaction was shattered in October 1905 on receipt of a personal letter from Wilbur announcing that the Wrights had now flown for 20, 30 and nearly 40 minutes.

Ferber had already tried to buy a *Flyer* from the Wrights. Now they were offering one to his army. 'It is our present intention to first offer it to the governments for war purposes,' Wilbur wrote. 'If you think your government would be interested, we would be glad to communicate with it.'[4]

'Tell me the price which you want for your machine?' Ferber replied, adding untruthfully: 'I must tell you that considering the progress which I have made since June the government is no longer interested in paying as great a sum as it was . . .'[5]

Wilbur congratulated him on the success he privately doubted and offered the French Army their aeroplane for one million francs ($200,000 – around $4 million today) subject to a flight of 50 kilometres 'in not more than one hour of time'. Buoyed by the fantastic success of the finally modified *Flyer*, the Wrights were now very confident. If the fabulous invention wasn't wanted in their native land, then it would go to the highest foreign offer. In the hope of creating a bidding war they decided to spread news of its existence far and wide.

So, while waiting for Ferber's reply, they distributed three more reports of the still little-known Huffman Prairie flights. One went to Patrick Alexander in the hope he would spread the news within the British aeronautical establishment; another to the editor of the French aviation magazine *L'Aérophile* to tempt the French Army; a third to a German air magazine to excite its country's military. The letters listed the names of the now familiar Daytonian witnesses but asked that they not be identified in print 'as they would no doubt be flooded with enquiries'. And, just to make sure the French were left in no doubt that powered flight was available to them, another letter went off to the French ambassador in Washington inviting him to send his military attaché to Dayton at once. However, as with the deeply frustrated British attaché, the Wrights had no intention of giving his French counterpart even a peep of the *Flyer*. He would come to Dayton merely to hear from the sturdy citizens and farmers who had witnessed the flights.

Before this happened their overture to Ferber bore fruit. Ferber was the first man in Europe to learn the sensational details of the brothers' 1905 flights. What they didn't know was that his own gallant but unsuccessful flying experiments had not been meeting with the total admiration of his artillery superiors, who believed he was wasting his time and money; he was currently under something of a cloud. It didn't deter him from sending the Wrights' offer sideways to another quarter – to the officer in charge of French Army balloon and airship development, a Colonel Bertrand. But he, too, expressed disbelief and contempt.

The Wrights' letter to *L'Aérophile* excited much more interest. As the report arrived too late for the December issue, its editor, recognising its dramatic import, had passed it to a daily sporting paper, *L'Auto*, which carried it on 30 November complete with the stock assurance that the claims could be verified by 'a number of well-known citizens of Dayton'. Within hours the news of the lengthy flights by two American bicycle-makers was being read with scepticism within the Paris aviation community. Few could accept that such historically significant events could possibly have happened without being widely reported internationally. One prominent member of the Aéro-Club, though, was unwilling to reject the story.

Frank Lahm was a wealthy American businessman who had lived

in Paris for twenty-five years; his company had prospered selling Remington typewriters. Now in his late fifties, he'd become one of the Aéro-Club's most daring balloonists. His home town of Mansfield, Ohio, was only 120 miles from Dayton. It would not be difficult, he decided, to check the truth of the Wrights' assertions. 'VERIFY WHAT WRIGHT BROTHERS CLAIM. NECESSARY GO DAYTON TODAY. PROMPT ANSWER CABLE,' Lahm flashed to Henry Weaver, his brother-in-law, a Mansfield businessman. Weaver had never heard of the Wright Brothers. He sent a telegram blindly addressed 'Wright Brothers, Dayton, Ohio' seeking an explanation.

When the wire arrived at the cycle shop, Wilbur and Orville were equally mystified. They'd never met Lahm but had vaguely heard of him as a balloonist – a Frenchman, they had assumed – in France. After a further exchange of telegrams, Weaver began to recall that the Wrights had made some glider flights. Assuming his brother-in-law was trying to buy one of these machines, he hurried down to Dayton where he checked in to the Algonquin hotel. Here he was confused to learn that the Wright Brothers' business was bicycles.

Although it was a day of rest at Hawthorn Street, Orville volunteered to meet Weaver. He went to the hotel, where the mystery of Lahm's interest became clear to them both for the first time. Orville offered to take Weaver on a tour of the homes of witnesses of their remarkable powered flights. From house to house they went, finally travelling out to Huffman Prairie to listen to the farmers who had watched the *Flyer* droning overhead day after day. They went nowhere near the shed in which the dismantled aeroplane lay. No photographs of the airborne machine that might have confounded the world were produced.

Weaver was nevertheless deeply impressed by Orville. 'His very appearance could disarm any suspicion – with a face more of a poet than an inventor or promoter . . . very modest in alluding to the marvels they have accomplished.'[6] At the end of the tour Orville took his visitor home to Hawthorn Street to meet Wilbur, Katharine and Milton. Presided over by a retired bishop, it was a family, Weaver decided, he could trust. 'The older brother, Wilbur, I found even quieter and less demonstrative than the younger. He looked the scholar and recluse. Neither is married. As Mr Wright expressed it, they had not the means to support "a wife and a flying machine too."' Back in Mansfield Weaver cabled Lahm: 'CLAIMS COMPLETELY VERIFIED.'

A week later, on 12 December, a second investigator descended on Dayton. The French journalist Robert Coquelle, who worked for *L'Auto*, had been sent to New York to cover some cycle races when his editor had instructed him to go down to Dayton to check on the Wrights' claims. The brothers gave him the same treatment as Weaver. Coquelle was handed the witnesses' names and left to contact them. He met a few, but decided he could invent a more sensational story. 'WRIGHT BROTHERS REFUSED TO SHOW THEIR MACHINE,' he cabled his editor, 'BUT I HAVE SEEN SOME WITNESSES IT IS IMPOSSIBLE TO DOUBT.' His highly fanciful article, though clearly based on fact, appeared, complete with a remarkably accurate pirated sketch of the *Flyer*, in *L'Auto* shortly before Christmas 1905. 'Conquest of the Air by Two Bicycle Merchants' ignited a fierce debate within the Aéro-Club, which the previous year had boldly announced a trophy for the pilot of the first powered machine to cover a mere 25 metres.

Most regarded the story as total fabrication. The disbelievers were vociferously led by Ernest Archdeacon, who persuaded colleagues that the aeroplane was purely 'tentative' – that the Wrights needed the million francs they were demanding of the French 'to allow them to construct a better machine'.[7] But more disturbing evidence of the essential accuracy of Coquelle's heavily embroidered story was soon to follow.

At a meeting of the Aéro-Club's special committee for aeroplanes in late December, Frank Lahm read out a long letter he had just received from Henry Weaver summarising the evidence he'd collected from eyewitnesses of the flight which had made the unbelievable thirty full orbits of the field. The veracity of the report was hard to question. The journalist Coquelle stood up to say that he had personally met the patently truthful Wright family and was wholly satisfied that the flights had taken place – what had the dozens of witnesses, with no vested interest in the aeroplane, to gain by entering into a conspiracy of lies?

Archdeacon, who chaired the meeting, was an excitable man

with a falsetto voice. As the gathering erupted into shouting, gesticulation and argument between the factions, he was reduced, Brethren conference style, to banging on the table with a metal ruler to restore order. The room rang with one angry cynical question after another, most of the members apparently convinced that the Wrights had perpetrated a brazen bluff upon the world. They were known to be men of slender means. Who then had funded their work? They had done it entirely with their own private resources, said Lahm to loud laughter. Why, it was asked yet again, had the tenaciously prying American press not reported such historic events if they were really occurring so openly in public? Surely, if it were true, one of the greatest achievements in the history of the world would have been splashed across front pages everywhere. And why had not the American government, which had poured huge sums into Professor Langley's failed experiments, not snapped up the miracle machine? Lahm could not answer.

Sitting with uncharacteristic silence at the meeting was Captain Ferber. He had chosen not to reveal to his mocking colleagues an explosive piece of information: that, at that very moment, a French emissary with authority to negotiate a contract for the purchase of the *Flyer* was already in Dayton, gathered round a table in the room above the former cycle workshop, in earnest discussion with Wilbur and Orville.

When Colonel Bertrand treated the Wrights' offer with disdain, Ferber had taken it elsewhere. He'd gone to Paris to see the wealthy owner and publisher of the leading French daily *Le Journal*, Henri Letellier, who had made his money as a building contractor, and his son of the same name, a notorious Paris playboy and bon vivant. Ferber had persuaded the Letelliers to form a syndicate of rich business colleagues to purchase the *Flyer* as a gift to the nation and present it to the French Army. The syndicate, which Ferber had joined, appears to have had as its high-minded purpose – at least initially – no serious commercial motive other than providing *Le Journal* with a resounding scoop and some patriotic glory for its members, who saw the possibility of some Légion d'honneur awards – and, he hoped, for his initiative, promotion for Captain Ferber.

The younger Letellier, who was to play the most prominent part in dealings with the Wrights, despatched his secretary, Arnold Fordyce, to Dayton before Christmas to verify the truth of the Wrights' claims and conclude a swift deal. Fordyce, a clean-shaven chubby-faced Frenchman in his mid-thirties who radiated much Gallic charm and spoke excellent English, seemed an odd choice of envoy to investigate such a sophisticated invention in a technological field of which he understood practically nothing. He was an actor and playwright, with a string of plays already produced on the French stage plus a clutch of others he'd adapted from English. But on arrival in Dayton, he explained to the Wrights, who had been alerted by cable to his mission, that he didn't need to comprehend their flight secrets. Almost certainly he wouldn't have begun to understand them. His task, he made clear, was simply to confirm the truth that the contrivance could fly and sign a contract.

Fordyce failed to persuade the brothers either to show him the machine or to fly it for him. 'They were certainly the most impossible men I ever saw,' he later told a New York reporter exasperatedly. 'They wouldn't even allow me to approach their workshop and said that most of the reports I had read of their achievements were untrue.'[8]

The amiable Frenchman had begun to make his own investigations. Once more the obliging panel of patently honest witnesses, from bank managers to maize farmers, were wheeled out by the Wrights. Once more they recited the details of the astounding flights. Farmer Amos Stauffer, working almost under the flight path, had become a celebrity among the observers. He had just kept on cutting corn as 'the durned thing' had cruised by again and again on Wilbur's twenty-four-mile flight. 'I thought it would never stop,' he would tell people.

The Wrights were initially suspicious of Fordyce. Weeks earlier Ferber had written to ask if they'd be prepared to meet an official French government 'commission' if one were sent to Dayton. Assuming it would represent the French War Ministry, they had replied welcoming the idea, but instead of a commission there had arrived this engaging loose cannon. It had struck them as definitely suspicious. However, when Fordyce had explained that his civilian syndicate merely wanted to expedite French Army purchase to become the world's first military air power, the brothers finally agreed to enter into a contract. They would license the aeroplane's manufacture exclusively for 'government use'. It was not to be exploited commercially. And the deal would not – after three months – preclude them from selling the invention to the US or any other government.

The agreement they signed gave the syndicate a three-month option to buy for one million francs – a figure over which Fordyce had been instructed not to quibble. A trial flight of fifty kilometres had to be completed before 1 August 1906 and the deal required delivery of technical specifications to enable French manufacture. The syndicate agreed to deposit Fr25,000 ($5000) in escrow with the Paris branch of an American bank by 5 February 1906, leaving the French businessmen two months to raise the balance of the $200,000 purchase price. If the full one million francs was deposited by the first week of April, the brothers would sail to France and give the demonstration flights. If it wasn't, the agreement lapsed and they kept the $5000.

As Fordyce had begun to understand the brothers he had grown to like them – even asking them why two such exceedingly talented, eligible men in their mid to late thirties had never married? The neat response had been a variation on the standard theme. 'One of them said to me that women would be likely to object to their hazardous experiments, and that women who didn't object wouldn't be worth having – so they never married.'[9]

Before putting their signatures to the contract, Wilbur and Orville took the document to a lawyer who confirmed that it protected their interests. Thrilled that he had so easily given France the world's first true aeroplane, Fordyce immediately cabled the news to Letellier, who promptly hurried to the War Ministry. Having patriotically opened the door, the syndicate had no intention of putting their own money into the project. It was now over to the government.

The War Minister considered a million francs ridiculously high; yet he did not immediately reject the proposal. Just as the American government had been persuaded to fund Langley under the impetus of the Spanish–American war, so France faced a similar imperative – the real risk of conflict with Germany over the control of Morocco. Scouting aeroplanes could give the French Army a decisive advantage if it came to war. The ministry decided it would at least stump up the non-refundable $5000 deposit. The money was duly produced, but before committing itself fully, the War Ministry prudently decided to send a formal government commission secretly to Dayton.

Headed by Commandant Henri Bonel, the Army's Chief of Engineers, a confirmed sceptic of the Wrights' claims who had witnessed the futile take-off attempts of Clément Ader in his unflyable batwing machine nine years earlier, the five-man team comprised three military officers – one of them the already convinced Captain Ferber – and two civilians: the equally persuaded Fordyce, and an American lawyer, Walter Berry, legal adviser to the French embassy in Washington. Bonel and his team sailed from Cherbourg in the middle of March 1906. Anxious that no other country or the newspapers should learn of this hush-hush mission they booked into a modest hotel in Dayton, the army officers dressed inconspicuously as businessmen.

Day after day for nearly two weeks, sitting in the office at 1127 West Third Street, the five emissaries faced the Wrights in tense discussion, painfully protracted by the need to translate everything for Bonel who spoke hardly a word of English.

Assuming the commission had come to hear with their own ears confirmation of the accounts of the lengthy sustained flights, the brothers had quickly taken the five visitors from door to door on the now well-worn circuit of the patient witnesses; and as so much was at stake they daringly risked producing the irrefutable evidence of the photographs. They took Bonel and Fordyce and lawyer Berry back to their unpretentious wooden-planked home for dinner where, as unfailingly worked in their favour, the guests were duly impressed to enter the pious home of this upright retired bishop whose very presence breathed propriety upon the scene (Milton was even allowed to sit in on some of the meetings at the old cycle shop).

In no time the doubting Bonel had come to accept that the flights were most certainly real. However, as soon became clear, the commission's main object in coming to Dayton was actually to vary the contract they had signed with Fordyce. The War Ministry wasn't happy with an exclusivity option for as little as three months. They demanded world rights to the invention for at least fifteen months, during which the *Flyer* couldn't be offered to any other government. The brothers suggested five months. Bonel countered with one year. The Wrights said six months. The commission went back to their hotel from which a daily flurry of coded cables passed between the commandant and his masters at the War Ministry. What the brothers didn't know was that the Franco/German tensions over Morocco had now blown over. The ministry, already wincing at the demand for a million francs, could bide its time and drive a harder bargain.

Now that the boot was on the other foot, Bonel was instructed to raise the technical specifications as well. The French wanted the aeroplane's speed and payload lifted, plus an ability to fly at 1000 feet – above the reach of enemy gunfire, a great deal higher than it had ever climbed. Bonel, now genuinely keen for France to buy the aeroplane and ready to meet the Wrights halfway, faced ever hardening responses from Paris. He was also growing nervous that their presence in Dayton might not remain undiscovered for long. Returning to the hotel one evening, he and Fordyce had found a local reporter lying in wait for them in the lobby. The newspaperman had been tipped off by a telegraph operator, curiosity aroused by the unusual rash of mysteriously coded cables flowing in and out of such a modest place. What had brought them to Dayton, he wanted to know? Quick-wittedly Fordyce had drawn on his acting skills to explain convincingly that they'd come to study the city's water supply system. It seemed such a mundane mission the reporter decided there wasn't a story in it.

The option was due to expire in the first week of April, while the French were still in Dayton. As the negotiations, conducted hour after hour with great civility and courtesy, became bogged down and prospects for a lucrative sale receded by the day, Wilbur wired in desperation to Chanute to come and help them. Although particularly busy in Chicago at that moment with his timber preservation affairs, the old man immediately rearranged his diary and boarded the overnight train for Dayton.

The fellow Frenchmen Chanute was about to face in the small Dayton office were not fools. Furthermore they were convinced converts, and Bonel by now was actually urging his government to buy the invention before they lost it to another country. Chanute was torn between his preparedness to see the *Flyer* go to his native land and a sense that it really belonged to America. 'The best disposal of your machine would be,' he had earlier told Wilbur with amazing naivety, 'to have it go to the one single government who would keep it secret and thus promote peace.'[10]

Chanute's aura, his persuasive advocacy and his fluent French at the final meeting did not save the day. At the eleventh hour on the afternoon of 5 April, as the option expired, an ultimatum arrived from Paris. Decoded, Bonel showed it to them all. The War Ministry was still adamantly demanding twelve months exclusivity. It was their final offer. The brothers refused, and that night the commission, defeated, left Dayton to return to France.

Back at Hawthorn Street, Wilbur and Orville had second thoughts. They decided they'd been too inflexible. So Wilbur sat down to write a more conciliatory proposal to catch up with Bonel before he finally sailed home. They agreed to accept the twelve months and try to get the aeroplane up to 1000 feet – provided they could still offer it to the American government. 'Until we feel certain that there is no possible ground of agreement' they weren't disposed to demand the $5000 sitting in escrow. But it was too late. The French War Ministry eventually declined their belated offer. The option lapsed.

Walter Berry, the only non-Frenchman on the commission, later told the Wrights why the deal had collapsed. The French, he said, ultimately did not doubt that they had produced an aeroplane that had done everything they claimed; it was the million-franc demand that bothered them for the relatively brief one year of exclusivity. Berry offered to reopen negotiations if they would lower the price, but the Wrights, confident that other nations would soon be beating a path to their door, declined. Somebody, they knew, would have to buy the machine. Indeed the French commission had scarcely left Dayton when, to their surprise, the urbane Patrick Alexander arrived in town. Alexander was beginning to rival Octave Chanute for the vigour and span of his international aeronautical interest and the impressive currency of his knowledge. He had been in Italy making high-level balloon ascents, in France talking to Frank Lahm and in Germany helping Count von Zeppelin with his latest airship.

Almost the first thing he asked on arrival was: 'Is the French commission still here?' They were astounded. The covert mission had been surrounded by such intense secrecy that its members had even registered at the Dayton hotel under false names. Now quite convinced that their dangerously well-connected dilettante English friend was a member of the British Secret Service, they were concerned to learn that he had actually been talking in Paris to one of the French commissioners. They believed, in their ever-deepening suspicion of the world, that Alexander had been sent by the War Office in an attempt to catch Bonel's team actually in Dayton talking to the Wrights.

Their mistrust was further sharpened when they learnt that Alexander, who had come directly to Dayton from England, had hurried straight back – but they had no firm evidence and were too courteous to confront him with their fears. Instead they had again entertained him hospitably at Hawthorn Street.

Under pressure from Chanute, Wilbur and Orville now decided to make a fresh push into the market. Chanute had offered to have the US War Department's bureaucratic idiocy raised privately with Theodore Roosevelt, but Wilbur had immediately squashed the idea. 'We do not think there would be any advantage in bringing the matter to the attention of the President,' he had replied. It would serve no purpose, he said, unless Roosevelt was fully convinced in advance of the aeroplane's capability and value to the army.

Chanute, with his access to high places, had the ability, with a few persuasive letters, to have the existence of this incomparable new military weapon brought quickly to the notice of the most powerful figure in the land. Instead, the Wrights wrote offering it to the war ministers of Germany, Italy, Japan and Russia – the latter two, relevantly recently, at war with each other. They also decided, in the hope of shaming their own government, to revive the stalled negotiations with the British.

19

Fliers or Liars?

(1906)

Nearly a year after they had perfected a machine that could now almost unfailingly fly to the limits of its fuel capacity, the Wrights had failed to clinch a single sale of one of the most significant inventions of all time. They had created an impasse that was to continue for a long time yet, forestalling the age of powered flight.

As Adrian Kinnane said:

> I don't think that they at first understood that, after the Langley disaster, there was just no way the US government could even think of funding another flying machine without seeing it actually fly. But the Wrights had embarked on aeronautics from that background of solid Brethren righteousness with its twin corollaries of presumptive honesty and an equal readiness to mistrust. Who hadn't disappointed them? They could trust only each other. Yet they demanded that the world trust them – 'we are honest men, a bishop's sons: if it weren't true we wouldn't say it.'

The brothers' circular negotiations with the British had finally ground to a halt at the end of 1905. Pressed again by military attaché Foster to fly the machine for him, Wilbur had replied in his wordy style at the beginning of December with another infuriating letter:

> Even if there had been no other objection to showing our machine in flight it has now become hopeless to think of avoiding observation and publicity, for the newspapers have at last begun to realise the true situation and have been offering bribes to our friends for information on our extended movements. Under such circumstances only necessity could induce us to risk a flight to satisfy what may be only curiosity. You must admit yourself that up to the present your government has not shown in its communications such indications of a serious purpose to take the lead in this new art as would justify us in assuming a very serious risk. If circumstances should therefore lessen our objections to show the machine we will be pleased to inform you.[1]

Wilbur's reply prompted Colonel Foster to respond with a pithy summary. Curbing his exasperation, he wrote to say that he had sent Wilbur's letter to the War Office,

> to show the reason why you are not prepared to show me a flight. The fact seems to me that the War Office cannot commit itself to negotiations with a view to purchasing unless sure that your invention gives the flight it claims, while you do not wish to show its flight until the War Office have made some arrangement with you. There is thus a deadlock.[2]

Thus ended the fruitless exchange between the attaché and the Wrights. One historian questioned why Foster didn't make the 500-mile train journey from Washington down to Dayton at least to meet the brothers, who clearly had in their possession a machine – whether or not they would show it – that no military power, surely, could ignore. But the colonel was due to retire that month; he was busy clearing up his American affairs. In his last days in his Washington office he merely sent to London a memorandum addressed to the Directorate of Military Operations. His brief report said it all:

> They will not let me see the flight before the negotiations are made – as I am instructed to do. I therefore can do nothing by going to Dayton. They require an arrangement first. It seems most unreasonable, as so many people have seen the flight.[3]

If fear of newspaper interest in new flights was truly the Wrights' principal objection to a demonstration for a major customer, it has often been asked why they didn't do it at some other more remote location in the great expanses of the Midwest. They did consider it – but reasoned that sooner or later something as unusual as a flying machine would be discovered even in the wilderness. And had they moved to some secret place they would still have been reluctant to take military observers there for fear of revealing the *Flyer*'s mechanical detail.

Even when, at last, in May 1906, they were finally granted a US patent, they remained fearful the invention would be appropriated despite the legal protection it now enjoyed. Patent No. 821,393 was issued for 'an alleged new and useful improvement in flying machines'. It ran for seventeen years – until 1923 – and covered the principles of three-dimensional control embodied in the 1902 glider. In the three-year gestation of the final, excruciatingly legal-scientific wording of the patent document there had been months of argument between attorney Toulmin and the Patent Office officials over whether it should apply to a powered aeroplane as well as a glider. After endless redrafting they had eventually decided to settle for protection only of the sacred core of the invention of flight: its unique controls and aerodynamic principles. Patents for Britain, France and Belgium had already been granted. Austria, Germany and Italy would soon follow.

The Wrights believed that with something as revolutionary as their baby there would be no shortage of unscrupulous people out there happy to help themselves to its design and fight the legal battles later, so despite the patent documents now accumulating in their office they still denied anyone the merest glimpse of the machine that had not now been airborne for eight months. Redoubling their efforts to sell it, they decided to try and break the deadlock with the British.

On Colonel Foster's advice they resumed direct communication with the War Office. Extraordinarily, Wilbur's letter, addressed to the Secretary for War, stubbornly repeated that demonstrating the machine was not a necessary prelude to a purchase 'since the necessary safeguards can be included in the contract'. However, as soon as they had done a deal there would immediately 'follow a demonstration that the machine is all that has been claimed for it' – 'and before any money is paid to us'.

'We do not,' Wilbur concluded, 'ask for such advance payments as are customary in the building of battleships etc, nor for any assumption of risk whatever on your part . . . The invention is ready for sale to some one at once.'[4]

But, like the French, the British, too, were beginning to have second thoughts. 'How could the War Office face the nation after committing it to an invention which they had never seen and which was claimed by two bicyclemakers as far away as Dayton in the United States of America? It was, of course, permissible for the Envoy of his Britannic Majesty to interview local farmers, and even speak to such distinguished residents of Dayton as Mr E. W. Ellis, Mr Torrence Huffman and Mr C. S. Billman; but this was merely turning comedy into farce.'[5]

Before rejecting the Wrights' latest overture out of hand, the Director of Fortifications and Works decided to refer the matter once again to the top-level invention assessors at the Royal Engineer Committee. The committee, anxious to make the right decision, decided to consult Capper, now promoted to full colonel rank and to command of both the Balloon Factory and the Balloon School.

Capper didn't question the veracity of the brothers' claims. 'There appears to be little doubt that the machine has done all that the Wright Brothers claim for it, and that it is within their power to construct a similar machine capable of going much longer distances and of carrying one or more passengers,' he wrote. But he considered the £500 per demonstrated mile too high and the sliding scale unacceptably open-ended. He also suspected Wilbur would repeat his £25,000 demand for 50 miles and refuse to budge. Capper suggested that the British might have to go it alone, urging 'that we must do our utmost to build successful machines ourselves and learn their use'[6] – privately hoping that the honour of doing so would be allowed to fall to his own aeronautical unit.

The colonel's views were shared by the British Army's hierarchy, now exasperated by the unyielding secrecy with which the Wrights had enveloped their machine. In February 1906 a one-sentence letter had gone from the War Office to the Wright Cycle Company terminating the negotiations.

Privately, Capper had mixed feelings about the outcome. He had been so impressed by the Wright family that he was determined at least to maintain a personal friendship. Soon after the formal rejection letter had gone off on its two-week journey to Dayton he followed it up with a private and affectionate note to Wilbur, congratulating him on their spectacular flights at Huffman:

> However extended becomes the method of travel in the air by motor-driven aeroplanes, you will go down to perpetuity as the first to make it a practical success, and will be as such honoured and welcomed by the whole aeronautical world. May I be permitted most heartily to congratulate you on the immediate advance you have made over all your predecessors . . . I hope before long we may see you over in Europe. With kind regards from Mrs Capper and myself to your brother and Miss Wright.[7]

Encouraged by Capper's cordial letter and his obvious desire to keep the friendship alive, the brothers bravely decided it was worth making yet another approach to the British. Early in May 1906 Wilbur addressed a new proposal to the War Office – but it still stubbornly demanded a contract before demonstration of the machine. Wilbur now urged 'his Majesty's Government' to send a commission to Dayton to discuss a deal – as the French had done.

The British military mind in the bastion of Whitehall in 1906 still saw warfare in terms of vast numbers of foot soldiers, gun limbers drawn by teams of cantering horses, and great battleships with twelve-inch guns commanding the seas. No general or admiral could conceive of the destruction of armies and dreadnoughts from the air. Had they not read in *The Times* earlier that year 'that all attempts at artificial aviation . . . are not only dangerous to human life but foredoomed to failure.'[8] It was only a tiny minority of senior officers who believed that the Wrights had created a strategic weapon that would revolutionise the entire conduct of warfare. Two of these men were now to be involved in the War Office response to Wilbur's latest proposal.

The pro-aviation Fortifications and Works director, Brigadier-General Ruck, wasn't sure about the need for a commission but was unwilling to see the Wrights' latest overture spurned out of hand. It was decided to involve the new British military attaché in Washington.

Lieutenant Colonel Albert Gleichen was a career British Army officer who also, rather unusually, happened to be a German count. A phenomenon as remarkable as the Wrights in his own way, Gleichen was unusual not only for his acceptance as a foreigner into the senior ranks of the British Army but also, as a result of an epidemic of Anglo-German royal intermarriage, for his connections with the highest in the land. His father, Prince Victor Hohenlöhe-Langenburg, currently a serving admiral in the Royal Navy, was a nephew of Queen Victoria whose son, the reigning Edward VII, claimed Albert Gleichen as his cousin and godson.*

Educated in Germany and England, the noble attaché was a graduate of Sandhurst, a Grenadier Guards officer who had distinguished himself in action in the South African War, and served in British Military Intelligence at the War Office and as an equerry to his godfather Edward; he lived in private quarters at St James's Palace. He was said to move easily in the highest circles of international society. On his posting to Washington, the King, to smooth his way, had written a personal note to Roosevelt reminding the President of Gleichen's royal connections and 'to recommend him to your notice'. The colonel had become so patriotically anglicised that he had had to be removed from his last post as

*Albert Gleichen's father, the German Prince Victor, was the son of Princess Feodora, half-sister of Queen Victoria whose own husband was the German Prince Albert of Saxe-Coburg-Gotha. Colonel Gleichen was to serve bravely with the British Army in the First World War, eventually rising to the rank of Major-General. In 1917 he surrendered all his German titles and became, by Royal Warrant, Lord Edward Gleichen.

British military attaché in Berlin for outraging the Kaiser by his refusal 'to behave in the servile way the Kaiser required of those about him'. In Washington this singular aristocratic figure had immediately established himself as a sophisticated and hard-working diplomat of exquisite charm and polish. Less stiffly formal than his predecessor, he'd set out to mix his less than onerous military duties with extensive socialising and sightseeing travel. From a leisurely salmon-fishing expedition off the Californian coast in August 1906 he travelled back east direct to Dayton, to his first encounter with the Wright Brothers.

Instructed by the War Office, he had already been in correspondence with Wilbur about their latest offer. Unlike Foster he'd been given freedom to negotiate and had written to ask for a price for the *Flyer*; how soon it could be delivered; where the pilot training could be given; what its range would be. Unlike the former attaché, he had offered to come to Dayton to talk it over. Wilbur's reply offered one machine for $100,000 and their scientific knowledge, formulae and tables for a further $100,000. The aeroplane would now be guaranteed to fly an awesome one hundred miles, could be delivered by mid-1907, instruction given in England. Once more the British would get but fleeting exclusivity for their huge investment – just six months; and the US government was excluded even from that provision. Wilbur's letter ended with an anxious handwritten postscript: 'It would be well to avoid any mention of us at the hotels, in case you visit Dayton, as the hotel clerks notify the newspaper reporters.'[9]

The revamped proposal far from satisfied Gleichen. However, he decided to meet the secretive brothers face to face. As his train steamed into Dayton on 8 August, he was charmed to find them both waiting on the platform to greet him. He was immediately captivated. Within minutes the courteous, soft-spoken, bowler-hatted pair had cast their beguiling spell upon him. There radiated from them 'an indefinable aura of personality, apparently much stronger in Wilbur than in Orville'.[10]

Gleichen was whisked out to Hawthorn Street for a splendid meal at 'the paternal mansion', as he described it in his memoirs. The distinguished visitor was duly impressed by the atmosphere of utter goodness that emanated from this agreeable little family 'presided over by Mr Wright senior – a courteous old gentleman, bishop or dean of a local Christian church community'. Next day the count was taken on the ritual tour of Dayton's still obliging panel of witnesses. One, he recalled, was a chemist, another a bank manager. He was told the aeroplane couldn't be produced; it had been dismantled. But Gleichen was spellbound listening to the stories of their heroic struggle, 'telling me of their joy when it first rose into the air'.[11]

Back in Washington the convinced colonel decided, with astute diplomacy, to involve the British Foreign Office as well as the Army. He sent a long note to his ambassador, Sir Mortimer Durand, singing the praises of the Wrights, the bishop, and the flying machine that could bring Britain mastery of the air: 'The brothers Wright are two young men of about 30, intelligent looking, not "cranks", apparently honest – their venerable father being a bishop of some hazy denomination – and with little or none of the usual braggadocio of the Yankee inventor. Strange to say, they are modest in demeanour, and even shy.'

Gleichen had found Wilbur and Orville surprisingly forthcoming with details of the aeroplane and its dramatic capability, all of which he enthusiastically relayed to the ambassador. It would provide the army with an ideal scouting device:

> Flying at such a rate that it would be practically invulnerable . . . For transport it could be packed in a railway car or, if on the march, could either be carried on or in a wagon or, better still, keep up with the column by flying slowly . . . It would seem best to have a 2-man size as one could hardly expect that one man could attend both to the important duties of observation and to those of directing a novel mechanism. Messrs Wright assured me that after a few trials it came as natural and easy as riding a bicycle.[12]

What the Wrights had achieved was 'amost incredible', Gleichen told Sir Mortimer. In his professional opinion it was 'a device of almost incalculable military importance'. This compelling document reached the War Office via the Foreign Office almost simultaneously with Gleichen's separate report to the Military Operations Directorate with the less welcome news that the Wrights 'will not take a penny less than $100,000 for the flyer' and the right to manufacture. 'I gather,' the attaché wrote, 'that these rights are of little value unless accompanied by the "confidential scientific knowledge" for which they demand another $100,000. That is to say that though having bought the flyer you could manufacture as many more exactly like it as you please, you could not, without the "scientific knowledge" of formulae etc build any other of any other size or speed as the formulae vary according to size.'[13]

The British negotiations with the Wrights were going round in circles again. The correspondence was sent down to the Balloon Factory at Farnborough for the view of Colonel Capper, now regarded as the War Office's principal aviation adviser. He decided the time had come to deliver a lethal blow to the purchase:

> I have but little doubt that we shall be able, thanks partially to the scientific attainments and ability of Lieutenant Dunne, to turn out within a reasonable time a flying machine on much the same lines as that of the Wright Brothers – but we hope superior to it in several essentials, at an infinite fraction of the cost demanded by them.[14]

The prospect of a British rival aeroplane had made the Army Council hesitate. It was also pondering a recent widely publicised event in Paris. There the tiny rich Brazilian Alberto Santos-Dumont, who had begun to move from airships into fixed wing experiments, had just flown 60 metres in public. He'd done it in an ungainly box-like contraption, the *14-bis*, fitted with both undercarriage wheels and octagonal-shaped ailerons between the wings for roll control. He flew it standing up in a wicker open cockpit, operating the rudder and elevator with hand wheels and the ailerons by body harness. The French newspapers had hailed the short hop as the first true powered flight in Europe. The British press baron Lord Northcliffe had been in Paris at the time; it had added fuel to his obsession with the need for Britain to catch up. Back in London he had recently appointed to his *Daily Mail* the country's first air correspondent, launching a crusade 'to make the nation air-minded'. When, in early November 1906, Santos-Dumont had created a further sensation by flying more than 700 feet – almost as far as Wilbur's historic Kill Devil ride of 1903 – Northcliffe was outraged when the *Mail* dismissed the event with no more than a brief factual account:

> He immediately made one of those telephone calls which were a regular and continuing source of terror to his employees. He told his editor that the news was not that 'Santos-Dumont flies 722 feet,' but 'England is no longer an island . . . It means the aerial chariots of a foe descending on British soil if war comes.'[15]

The paper's chastened editor, fearful for his job, had responded with alacrity. Next morning the *Mail* declared more enthusiastically: 'M. Santos-Dumont has solved one of the great problems which have for more than a century baffled human intelligence . . . he has made of the aeroplane a practical machine.' And the following day, spurred by his lordship's anger, the newspaper hastened to make still further amends with a stirring editorial warning of the imminent threat to Britain of the powered aeroplane.

In America, where the Wrights' obsession with secrecy had limited recognition of their vastly superior feats to a mere handful of people, Santos-Dumont's achievement had ironically also been extravagantly praised by newspapers as a giant step for aviation. When Alexander Graham Bell publicly stated that Dumont had 'borrowed' the Wrights' ideas, the resentful Brazilian had told the *New York Herald* that there was no evidence that the brothers' secret machine had in fact ever flown.

Declared a hero by the French press and fêted at banquets, Dumont happily set out to seize from the Wrights the honour of being the first to fly. French aviation's wealthy patron Ernest Archdeacon rushed to laud his feat, proclaiming: 'He has achieved, not in secret or before hypothetical and obliging witnesses, but before a thousand people . . . a decisive step in the history of aviation.' France, Archdeacon told the Aéro-Club, 'will have been the first officially to have given birth to aviation, perhaps the greatest discovery made by Man since the beginning of the world.'[16]

Caught up in this wave of Gallic chauvinism, the Paris edition of the *New York Herald* had become a brutal doubter of the Wrights' claims, echoing the cynicism of the influential Archdeacon and the Aéro-Club. Under the headline FLIERS OR LIARS, it said: 'The Wrights have flown or they have not flown. They possess a machine or they do not possess one. They are in fact fliers or liars. It is difficult to fly. It is easy to say, "We have flown."'[17]

In Britain, the French 700-foot hop had jolted the War Office. Encouraged by Capper's hopes for their own aeroplane, the Army Council decided at last to expedite its own research. In the fond belief that the Balloon Factory would quickly, at modest cost, present them with something superior to the unsighted wraith of the undemonstrated *Flyer*, the council instructed Colonel Gleichen early in November 1906 to tell the Wrights that the British Army, 'especially in view of the great cost', had decided not to buy. In the first week of December the attaché, in a one-sentence, handwritten letter, did so.

But who then was going to solve the riddle for Britain? Who was Lieutenant Dunne?

John Dunne was a protégé of Capper's, a young, Irish-born serving lieutenant in the Royal Wiltshire Regiment. Chronic ill health had had him invalided home from the South African War where the fighting had convinced him of the value of aerial reconnaissance. Back in England he'd started experimenting privately, building model gliders. His work had somehow brought him to the notice of H.G. Wells, whom he'd begun to supply with technical information for use in his science fiction novels; he even used Wells' own garden for his experiments. Later he'd worked with Sir Hiram Maxim on another of the American inventor's fundamentally flawed aeroplanes.

Devouring information about the Wrights, Dunne had become envious and determined to cap their achievements. His work and his public school connections, combined with help from his father, a distinguished British Army general, had brought him to the notice of the War Office's Royal Engineer Committee, one of whose members had persuaded Capper to take him into the Balloon Factory. And so Dunne had been officially seconded there in the summer of 1906 with a brief to develop a flying machine for the army. His apparent grasp of the complex aerodynamics involved seems to have convinced Capper that his unit could actually soon overtake the Wrights. He didn't know that Dunne was deeply out of his depth – that he would not, in the foreseeable future, produce for Britain a machine that would rise successfully into the air.

When Gleichen's letter terminating the British interest arrived at the cycle shop, Wilbur and Orville were on the point of leaving for New York. They had been invited to a meeting with an investment banking firm, Charles R. Flint and Company. A lucrative part of its business was the sale of American weapons and military technology abroad. In the week before Christmas these international arms dealers – then one of the world's biggest, with offices in London, Berlin and St Petersburg – were to make a tentative offer for all foreign rights to the *Flyer* for the staggering sum of $500,000.

20

The Arms Dealer and the Dowager

(1906–1907)

'There is much in the papers about the Wright Brothers. They have fame, but not wealth yet. Both these things, aspired after by so many, are vain.'

Milton committed these pious moral observations to his diary on the last day of November 1906. The previous day an unexpected visitor had arrived at Hawthorn Street. Ulysses D. Eddy was a New York entrepreneur. He had read about the flying machine in the newspapers and, smelling an opportunity, had come to try and talk the inventors into a business deal.

Eddy knew virtually nothing about aeronautics. He was a deal-maker who had perfected his skills working with a celebrated investment banker and merchant, Charles R. Flint. Now long forgotten, Flint was, in international financial circles, a legend in his day. He enjoyed the friendship of men of power and wealth across the world, among them the President, Theodore Roosevelt, the British Rothschilds, Andrew Carnegie, J.P. Morgan.

He sailed ocean-going yachts, competing in the America's Cup, and at his large estate on New York's Long Island, where he hunted and fished, he would curry favour with his neighbour, President Theodore Roosevelt, sending him gifts of fat bass and woodcocks. No financial deal was too big or internationally sensitive and complex for Flint. He created giant corporations in the rubber and woollen industries, and, specialising in American armaments, had sold submarines to Russia, electric automobiles to France, torpedo boats to Peru, an entire naval fleet to Brazil. Wherever war flared between nations, Flint would speed there on the next ship with an eye to a sale to either belligerent of anything from battleships to machine guns. His sales tactics were high-pressure; he dealt with royalty, war ministers, admirals, ambassadors and grand dukes, sometimes imperturbably triggering diplomatic shock waves in his wake.

Flint thrived on international intrigue. He was also quick to seize the sales rights to American inventions of military potential. His former associate, Ulysses Eddy, was so convinced he would want to scoop up the Wrights' aeroplane before it fell into other hands that he had hurried to Dayton on his own initiative.

At Hawthorn Street Eddy was amazed to learn that the invention hadn't yet been sold to anyone. He had inevitably succumbed to the spell of the likeable, unpretentious family. His talk of large sums of money had so excited the brothers that Wilbur had immediately flashed the good news to Chanute: 'It seems that the favourable conditions we have been awaiting for six months have now arrived,' he wrote, describing the potential deal as 'the best from a financial standpoint that we have had'.[1] They hadn't committed themselves and were due to discuss the proposition further with Flint and Company in New York the following week.

Chanute was delighted. He had grown increasingly critical of the brothers' obsessive secrecy. He had also begun to question the huge sums of money they were demanding. He warned that the longer they delayed a public demonstration of the machine's patently remarkable capability for all to see, the greater the risk that someone else would overtake them – as Santos-Dumont, given time, might succeed in doing.

Wilbur responded defensively: 'We are not delaying an instant more than we consider necessary. We merely refuse to let our hand be forced.'[2] He also said, perhaps unkindly, 'Even you, Mr Chanute, have little idea how difficult the flying problem really is . . . When we see men labouring year after year on points we overcame in a few weeks . . . we know that their rivalry and competition are not to be feared for many years . . . We do not believe there is one chance in a hundred that anyone will have a machine of the least practical usefulness within five years. If our judgement is correct undue haste to force a sale would be a mistake.'[3]

To this Chanute, with disarming frankness, had responded: 'I cheerfully acknowledge that I have little idea how difficult the flying problem really is and that its solution is beyond my powers.' But, he added, 'Are you not too cocksure that yours is the only secret worth knowing and that others may not hit upon a solution' in less than five years? As there were many shapes of birds 'each flying after a system of his own, so there may be several forms of apparatus by which man may compass flight. Flapping wings for instance.'[4]

Wilbur told Chanute they were happy to let their rivals discover for themselves that cracking the scientific secrets of flight demanded time-consuming and complex research. The exploits of the unsecretive Santos-Dumont did not alarm them in the least. 'We estimate that it is possible to jump about 250 feet with a machine which has not made the first steps toward controllability and which is quite unable to maintain the motive force necessary for flight.'[5] Even when news reached America that Dumont had flown, apparently under control, for more than 700 feet and Chanute commented, 'I fancy he is now very nearly where you were in 1904', Wilbur refused to concede that they could be overtaken foreseeably. He doubted that Dumont had yet begun to attack 'the real problems of flight'. To which Chanute had cautioned: 'I still differ with you as to the possibility of your being caught up with if you rest on your oars.' On the contrary, Wilbur had reassured him, they had been developing a more powerful aeroplane that would carry two men 200 miles.

Ulysses Eddy was convinced the machine could bring riches to its inventors and promoters. He had wired his former associate urging him to snap it up – and persuaded Wilbur and Orville to meet senior executives of the Flint company in New York.

The brothers were going there anyway in the first week of December to attend an exhibition of the recently created Aero Club of America, formed by a group of wealthy men from the country's

Automobile Club. The brothers had joined the club and produced for it a detailed report of their historic, still largely unknown, long-distance Huffman Prairie flights of 1904 and 1905. Proudly the club had issued the report as a press release, which had forced the American newspapers to take their achievements seriously for the first time. Suddenly, at last, they were major celebrities in their own land. Even *Scientific American*, which until then had treated the flights with open doubt, was moved – after checking with some of the Dayton eyewitnesses – to eat humble pie and publicly acknowledge that they had become the first in the world to perfect a flying machine. Although there was no way the Wrights would agree to the *Flyer* appearing at the exhibition, they had sent one of their new engines – in which the four cylinders were now arranged vertically.

In New York Wilbur and Orville were Aero Club guests of honour and were pursued by reporters as famous men. Ulysses Eddy took them along to the sumptuous offices of Flint and Company. They thought they were going to meet the dynamic Charles Flint himself, but he was away in Europe. Instead they were told they would be summoned back to New York when the leader returned.

On the way back to Dayton the brothers, pumped with new hope that their invention was at last about to pay off, diverted to Coatesville in Pennsylvania to spend a couple of nostalgic days with George Spratt on his farm, 'spinning yarns as in the old days at Kitty Hawk'. The low-spirited Spratt's own obscure aeronautical experiments had got nowhere. He'd tried to patent a stall-proof aeroplane but the application had been rejected. Spratt received the Wrights hospitably. He kept to himself his resentment that he hadn't been credited for some significant contributions he was convinced he'd made to their conquest of the air. The hurt would silently simmer for nearly three more years.

Scarcely had the Wrights arrived back in Dayton when a telegram came from New York recalling them to meet Charles Flint. To avoid appearing too keen, they decided that only one of them should go. He could delay concluding any agreement until the other had been consulted. Orville went.

Charles Flint was a well-preserved, distinguished-looking man in his mid-fifties with silver wavy hair, a monocle, and an immense moustache that curled into sideburns. He exuded warmth and brimming confidence, and told Orville they had created something he could sell to the war ministers of the world. He was prepared, he said, to pay them $500,000 for all foreign rights to its manufacture outside the United States. The American market would remain theirs.

Staggered by the size of the offer, Orville said he would need to discuss it with his brother. Worth around $10 million today, it was a vast sum for two modest cycle-makers to contemplate. But there was something about the charmingly plausible Flint and the opulence of the palatial offices that slightly bothered Orville's cautious, frugal nature. It seemed somehow a bit too good to be true.

Back at Hawthorn Street where, that week before Christmas 1906, the first snow had fallen, Orville outlined the fabulous proposal. The money was actually to be paid in cash upon delivery of just one machine after a demonstration flight of 50 kilometres. But Wilbur shared his unease about this high-powered entrepreneur; he suggested they ask Chanute what he knew of these slick wheelers and dealers.

'What do you think of it?' Wilbur wrote, describing the unexpectedly generous proposition. 'Do you think them safe people to deal with under proper precautions? The price and terms are satisfactory and we would accept if we felt sure of their character.'[6]

To the brothers' astonishment Chanute replied to say that Flint had also been busy checking up on *them*. Even before Orville had arrived in New York the arms dealer had sent him two telegrams seeking a rundown on the substance and probity of the covert plane-makers. Chanute, finding himself sandwiched between the parties, had responded with customary helpfulness to both. He revealed to Wilbur that the telegrams had been followed by a 'friendly letter' from Flint asking if he would go to New York 'to talk about your machine'. 'I have known Mr Flint for 25 years,' Chanute said, 'but not closely, having had no business relations with him . . . I understand that he is a very rich merchant who has had extensive dealings with the South American republics and with European war departments. The terms and price ($500,000) which he offers you seem much better than I thought possible.'[7]

To Flint, Chanute wrote that there was abundant information on their long 1905 flights from eyewitnesses. From 'somewhat intimate acquaintance' with the pair, he told Flint, he could vouch for their absolute trustworthiness. 'They tell the exact truth and are conscientious, so that I credit fully any statement which they make.'[8]

Impressed by these warm endorsements from the aeronautical eminence, Flint moved quickly to seize the business. Not pausing for Christmas, which at Hawthorn Street was celebrated quietly that year without the usual invasion of relatives, he despatched one of his agents, George Nolte, to Dayton with instructions to get a contract buttoned up on the spot. After three days of fruitless negotiations, Nolte was forced to admit defeat. In January 1907 the talks resumed in New York. Here Wilbur and Orville learnt that some of Flint's European associates had objected to the generosity of the original deal, claiming that in France the Wrights had nothing exclusive to sell.

In the end the original proposals were dropped. Flint changed tack, suggesting instead that his company act as their sales representatives in all countries except the United States, on a commission basis. They agreed Flints would handle the foreign business while the Wrights would have control of the conditions of every sale and agree each customer. The company would pay their expenses; it would take 20 per cent commission on business up to $500,000 and a huge 40 per cent thereafter.

Flint was delighted with the new arrangement. In February he drew up an international campaign plan, exhorting his sales force to go out into the world and sell the *Flyer*. They were told to do it on a grand scale; Flint didn't believe in half measures:

> He planned to offer each of the governments an entire air force at one stroke. He proposed to offer fifty machines to each minister of war. If they hesitated to commit themselves to this number he would offer twenty machines at a time. If this proved too bold a proposition he was ready to sell ten machines to each of his clients. This daring attitude impressed the Wright Brothers. They approved of the new concept.[9]

Explaining it to Chanute, Wilbur said, 'The fact that we had the support of such influential people would make the governments less disposed to ignore us with the intention of stealing our invention later.'[10]

In Germany Flint briefed the Mauser gun company. The French, who believed they were close to inventing their own aeroplane, he left to his European operations staff. Russia and Britain he would deal with personally – beginning with Britain. His sales drive there launched an extraordinary phase in the tangled history of the marketing of the world's first aeroplane. It introduced a most unlikely sales agent: the elderly widow of a distinguished British general – an extraordinary lady of high aristocratic pedigree in her own right.

Seventy-six-year-old Lady Jane Taylour had been married to General Sir Richard Taylour, a veteran of the Crimean War, who had died two years earlier. The daughter of the Marquess of Tweeddale, she was a lively, highly intelligent Scotswoman, her vigour undiminished by age, who moved in the top circles of Edwardian English military and political society.

Originally Flint had planned to appoint as his English agents a large gun manufacturer, but it had occurred to him that Jane Taylour's connections with the establishment could bring 'quicker results and higher influence'. It was, on the surface of it, a shrewd move. Within days of concluding his deal with the Wrights, Flint wrote to her at her London home, inviting her to become his agent for the sale of a large batch of aeroplanes to the British government. His particular target was the Secretary of State for War, Richard (later Lord) Haldane. Flint hoped she might be able personally to persuade him to have reopened the doors that had so recently closed for the second time at the War Office.

Flint revelled in secrecy. He sent the doughty Lady Jane his company's commercial code book so they could communicate confidentially. He also told her that the prominent Aeronautical Society figure Major Baden Baden-Powell and the British Army's Colonel Capper could verify the existence of the amazing flying machine – almost certainly unaware that the balloon colonel had now persuaded the War Office to develop its own aeroplane and was busy trying to do so.

Jane Taylour, whom a photograph in her seventies reveals as a white-haired, formidable-looking dowager, was thrilled to accept the commission and entered zestfully into the spirit of the operation. Launching his code early in February, Flint got straight down to business: 'MAKE FIRM OFFER OF 50 AEROPLANES 2,000 POUNDS STERLING EACH', he cabled, confirming in a letter that the planes would be guaranteed to fly 30 miles in one hour.

From her home in fashionable Belgravia her ladyship immediately despatched by hand a personal and confidential letter to the War Minister – whom she did indeed happen to know personally. As Parliament was about to open, Haldane was excessively busy, yet he made time to see her.

The meeting that afternoon in February 1907 between the remarkable Jane Taylour and Richard Haldane – once described as one of the great twentieth-century servants of the State – has fascinated aviation historians ever since for the duel it began between these two singular individuals. A brilliant lawyer and tireless politician educated at universities in Edinburgh and Göttingen, Haldane had conceived an admiration for Germany and its thrusting, efficient way of doing things which would later enable him to create an effective British Army to enter the First World War. However, at the War Office at that moment, his reforms to modernise the army were being frustrated by his recently elected Liberal government's promises of strict economy in military expenditure. There was no way he could sell to his cabinet colleagues an investment of £100,000 on aeroplanes few people had been permitted to see actually fly.

Haldane, well briefed on the history of the Wrights' failed negotiations with his ministry, and confident that Lieutenant Dunne would soon give the army its own aeroplane, politely declined to reopen the matter. 'He was,' Jane Taylor later told Flint, 'most amiable but firmly refused to have anything to do with Wrights or anyone else's proposals until their superiority was established over all comers by public trial and competitions.'[11] Haldane suggested she urge them to come out in the open and enter a competition being organised by the *Daily Mail* at the behest of Lord Northcliffe, who was offering £10,000 to the pilot of the first powered aeroplane to fly from London to Manchester in one day.

Jane Taylour went back to Eaton Place, seized her code book and reported the disappointing outcome to Flint. She had problems mastering the elaborate code with its meaningless groups of letters. Her message reached New York in confusing form and she was forced to follow it up with a letter. Her coded messages began to exercise the British intelligence services; she was visited by an agent demanding to know precisely what she was communicating. Regarding this as utter impertinence, she refused to say.

All her reports were faithfully copied by the Flint company to the Wrights. When they read Haldane's demand for detailed specifications, they bridled. 'We positively will not furnish.' But Flint was far from ready to give up on the British. He asked Jane Taylour to get the details of the *Daily Mail* London–Manchester challenge. The Wrights' first response when they'd studied them was characteristic: 'We have no intention,' Wilbur told Flint, 'of going for the prize in the near future merely for the sake of the prize.'

On reflection the brothers decided they had been too negative about the Manchester flight. Wilbur wrote again to Flint to propose a deal: 'Haldane's willingness that we should show England how to fly by competing for the prize is very kind . . . If he would guarantee us an order for machines amounting to $500,000 [£100,000] conditional upon winning the prize, it might be worthwhile to sacrifice the chances of selling secrets on the Continent and go for it.'[12]

Flint pounced on this crack in the Wrights' intransigence, swiftly despatching a coded cable to his blue-blooded agent: 'WILL BUILD FOR HARMSWORTH* TRIAL TRIP BY JULY 1ST IF GREAT BRITAIN SECRETARY OF WAR AND GREAT BRITAIN SECRETARY OF NAVY . . . IS WILLING TO PURCHASE 50 AT 4000 EACH.' Flint had overnight doubled the aeroplane's sale price. The reason, he explained to the Wrights, was the 'far more rigorous' requirement of the 170-mile London–Manchester flight. 'An increased price for a machine of increased efficiency would cause them to take us more seriously.' He

*Lord Northcliffe was still known to many by his former name, Alfred Harmsworth.

directed Jane Taylour to approach the Royal Navy – even requesting she ask her brother, the retired Admiral Lord Hay, to privately lobby the Sea Lords. Again she went straight to the top, making an appointment to see the First Lord of the Admiralty himself.

Lord Tweedmouth was known for his determination to maintain Britain's naval superiority. Unfortunately he had few strong opinions of his own, little knowledge of naval warfare, and rarely interfered with his technical advisers, the Sea Lords. He greeted Flint's agent, she reported, with decidedly more interest than his colleague at the War Office – but betrayed a woeful lack of understanding of the value of air power, making the curious comment that 'a sea aeroplane would hardly have time to drop the shell on board before the ship had passed from under it'.

When Flint learnt the Royal Navy wasn't interested, he instructed his emissary to approach the War Minister again with a new sales ploy: the Wrights were now prepared to take the *Flyer* to Washington and actually demonstrate it secretly to the British ambassador. There was of course a condition: they would require a British government purchase contract first. Haldane's response was swift and to the point: 'The War Office is not disposed to enter into relations <u>at present</u> with any manufacturer of Aeroplanes.'[13]

Undeterred, Flint turned his sights on the fresh target of Lord Northcliffe. With the *Daily Mail*, *Evening News*, *Mirror* and *Observer*, the great newspaper proprietor owned a significant slice of the country's media. Flint wanted Lady Taylour to put the Wrights' Manchester flight proposition to him in the hope that she could persuade Northcliffe to force the War Minister to buy into the deal.

Obligingly, Jane Taylour, in the middle of April, confident she would quickly have the media mogul eating out of her hand, went to storm his headquarters at Carmelite House.

When she swept into Northcliffe's office that spring day in 1907, Lady Taylour found him in an ugly mood. He was suffering from a painful eye condition and was convinced he was going blind; it didn't help his unpredictable temper and slowly developing mental instability. The Scottish dowager was undeterred: well prepared, she proceeded to make a powerful case for British acquisition of the aeroplane. But Northcliffe was deeply sceptical of the Wrights' claims. 'They are never ready to talk business,' he said. 'They are always going to do, but do nothing that can be appreciated.'[14]

Northcliffe had been much impressed by the performances of Santos-Dumont, who always flew in public; he thought the Brazilian could well take the Manchester prize. But Jane Taylour said only the Wrights were capable of doing it. She spelt out their latest, startling offer – to supply a machine guaranteed to carry a pilot and observer a fantastic 200 miles non-stop. They would even pay the cost of a demonstration to prove it. At this Northcliffe pricked up his ears. It was, he said, the first practical proposal he'd ever heard the Wrights make. 'His ruffled feathers were entirely smoothed,' said Lady Taylour. But Northcliffe was unaware of the catch still attached to the proposition – a War Office contract first.

When Northcliffe failed to acknowledge her letter confirming the 200-mile flight offer, Jane Taylour made one final attempt to bully him. It was an even less happy encounter. Northcliffe's painful eye condition had worsened. He was 'in a terrible frame of mind'. Annoyed by her persistence, he issued a terse ultimatum: he demanded a typewritten statement, signed by the Wright Brothers, 'stating what they can do, will do, where they will do it, and what remuneration they demand and in what form'.[15] Only on receipt of such a document would he approach Haldane at the War Office. A letter of this description was never written.

Lady Jane retreated to Belgravia to report her latest disappointment to Flint. He was unfazed by her failure. He had already established many other beachheads. In Russia he'd offered the Czar's army a fleet of *Flyers*. In Belgium he was trying to negotiate directly with King Leopold, with whom he'd once been involved in a Congo rubber deal. In Germany he'd signed up an agent, Isidor Loewe of the Mauser company, to sell the German war ministry fifty planes. The ministry had countered with a not unreasonable proposal to buy just one for $10,000; if the plane did all that was claimed for it they wanted an option to take forty-nine more at the same price. Flint refused, telling the Wrights: 'You will note that the "walk into my parlour says the spider to the fly" proposition of Germany we respectfully decline.'

Jane Taylour, in desperation, tried to meet the Wrights' British Army friend, Colonel John Capper. With his known admiration of the Wrights' achievement he seemed an ideal person to persuade the War Office. Quite unaware that Capper was now frantically trying to help his protégé Lieutenant Dunne overtake the Wrights, she got his Farnborough address and wrote privately to him, beginning a correspondence of huge embarrassment to the colonel. There was no way he could help this pushy noblewoman and become involved in her commercial schemes. He referred her to the War Office, whose permission, he said, he would need before discussing military procurement matters with her. They never met.

Despite her awesome military connections, Lady Taylour achieved nothing for Flint. One of his biggest challenges remained the French. She offered to approach them through her friend, the French ambassador in London, but Flint, beginning to doubt her ladyship's effectiveness, decided to entrust France to his European sales chief, a remarkable figure, one Hart O. Berg.

21

Corruption in Paris

(1907)

Hart O. Berg was an enormously self-assured and ambitious American, based in Paris. He travelled throughout Europe selling military hardware for the Flint company. A legend in armament manufacturing circles who had worked at the Colt gun factory in America, he had managed an armament works in Belgium and established automobile plants in France and America, the latter turning out large cars that bore his name. France had made him a Chevalier de la Légion d'honneur. This rather cocky graduate engineer with huge nose and black moustache was a tenacious salesman. He moved confidently among Europe's royalty and top military leaders, dressed in the height of Edwardian elegance in bowler, huge cravat and striped trousers, frequently twirling a long cane.

Berg had no personal interest in aviation but joined the French Aéro-Club 'to widen his sphere of influence'. He had never even seen the machine he was expected to sell in large quantities for huge sums, and he had nagging concerns about it, doubting that something so spectacular could actually have been created by bicycle mechanics. And if it was real, he couldn't see how any government in peacetime would be willing, without getting exclusive rights, to pay the sort of money these obscure Americans were demanding.

Instead Berg proposed to Flint that, rather than continue to hawk whole fleets of aircraft to all and sundry, they should form a European Wright company and manufacture the machines themselves. The Wrights would be paid royalties on each sale. They and Flints would have a financial stake in the enterprise, which would seek European investment. The French millionaire oil magnate Henri Deutsch de la Meurthe, who owned three refineries and saw a new outlet for his petrol in aircraft engines, was, Berg decided, a likely source of capital. To sell the idea to him, however, he knew he would have to produce the inventors. It was their aeroplane. The time had come for them to convince dubious investors it was worth throwing money at. In the middle of May 1907 he cabled Charles Flint requesting that one of the brothers get the next ship to Europe.

When the summons arrived at the cycle company, Wilbur and Orville were in a state of renewed hope from another quarter. The US government, after two and a half years of bureaucratic lack of interest, had begun, for the first time, to take the invention seriously. What had brought about this change of heart?

It had begun with the wealthy Boston businessmen the Cabot brothers, who had sent congratulatory telegrams back in December 1903. Their subsequent offers of financial backing had been politely refused and the efforts of their celebrated relative, Senator Henry Cabot Lodge, to interest the War Department famously ignored. However, Samuel Cabot, with fresh concern that the aeroplane might be lost to America, had, through Chanute, renewed his offer of money. It wasn't funding they wanted but buyers, Chanute had explained. Subsequently, Samuel's brother, Godfrey Cabot, reading of the dramatic Huffman Prairie flights, had written to the Wrights in the spring of 1906 offering to help finance a company to exploit the *Flyer* commercially. Declining yet again, Wilbur had sent the rich Bostonian details of the bizarre correspondence that had passed between them and the War Department, describing the latter's letters as 'insulting'. Cabot was so astounded by what he read that he immediately decided that Senator Lodge should hear of the scandal. The senator leapt into the fray again, passing the tale of their cavalier treatment straight to Secretary of War Taft.

Taft sent the file to the obtuse Board of Ordnance and Fortification which had now acquired a new president, Brigadier General William Crozier. The general took the new approach seriously. He wrote to Senator Lodge telling him encouragingly that if the Wrights approached him direct 'any proposition they may have to make will be given consideration by the Board'. Cheered by this, Godfrey Cabot took the train to Washington and went to meet Crozier to show him detailed reports of the great 1905 flights. The general was much impressed. He said he would consider sending a War Department official to Dayton to meet the brothers. No official ever went.

When Cabot had communicated Crozier's interest to the Wrights, Orville, in one of his rare business letters, had written back haughtily:

> We are ready to negotiate whenever the Board is ready, but as the former correspondence closed with a strong intimation that the Board did not wish to be bothered with our offers we naturally have no intention of taking the initiative again.[1]

This wasn't entirely true. The previous month, Wilbur and Orville, in desperation, had decided on a bold move: they would go to see the President to warn him that the machine was in danger of going to a foreign power. Wilbur had written to Theodore Roosevelt's secretary, William Loeb, enclosing a statement of their achievements. Loeb had replied offering to make an appointment 'to pay their respects' to the President – 'if they would come to the White House any day at 12 o'clock, except Tuesdays and Fridays'. He warned, however, that he couldn't promise 'an extended interview'. Whether or not the prospect of such a brief meeting discouraged them, the Wrights abandoned the visit – they had come up with a much bolder idea to bring the invention to Roosevelt's notice: a sensational publicity stunt that Charles Flint would have applauded. It was to fly the aeroplane, uninvited, over a flotilla of US Navy battleships due to gather for a grand naval review late in April at Hampton Roads on the Virginia coast.

The event was part of the celebration of the three-hundredth anniversary of the founding of the first English colony at nearby Jamestown. The President would be there, flanked by his top generals and admirals, surrounded by reporters and thousands of ordinary people. Hampton Roads was within flying distance of Kill Devil. For safety in the event of engine failure over the sea, they would fit the *Flyer* with floats, take off from Albemarle Sound, and fly the seventy-five miles north to the review,

> circle the battleships and vanish southward, leaving the President and his party with mouths agape, aware that the air had been conquered but not quite sure by whom. When the truth came out, embarrassed War Department personnel would have trouble explaining to the President of the United States that the world's first practical flying machine had been offered to them three times and that three times they had let it slip through their fingers.[2]

It was a daring and, for the Wrights, unusually out-of-character stunt. But they had to abandon the idea when tests with propeller-driven floats in Dayton on the Miami River showed that to take off successfully from water demanded a lot more research.

Almost immediately there was a new development. On a visit to New York, Wilbur was introduced to a local congressman, Herbert Parsons, who offered to draw the President's attention to his government's obduracy. Parsons sent the President a magazine clipping about the *Flyer*. Roosevelt passed it to Taft recommending that some action be taken. For the first time the American President was asking his military heads to investigate the invention. Adding his own request that the aeroplane be regarded seriously, Taft passed the matter down yet again to the Board of Ordnance and Fortification. This time it had difficulty ignoring the invention that refused to go away. A request from the office of the President – commander-in-chief of the Army and Navy – endorsed by the War Secretary, compelled the reluctant body to do something.

Its secretary wrote to the Wright Cycle Company advising that it currently had before it 'several propositions for the construction and test of aeroplanes'. The unenthusiastic letter merely added: 'If you desire to take any action in the matter [the Board] will be glad to hear from you on the subject.'[3] Attached to the letter were copies of the endorsing notes from the President and Taft. The brothers reacted with deep cynicism. They had not the least doubt that the unwilling board had only written because forced to from on high. Yet they could hardly ignore it.

'We have some flyers in course of construction,' their reply said, 'and would be pleased to sell one or more of them to the War Department, if an agreement as to terms can be reached.' The letter said that the aeroplanes would carry two men and fuel for 200 kilometres – a great deal less, curiously, than the 200-mile range Flints were claiming for the aeroplane. Subject to the familiar caveat of a signed and sealed contract up front, they would demonstrate the machine's ability to fly at least 50 kilometres in one hour. They offered to come to Washington to talk it over or 'to submit a formal proposition'.[4]

At last the ice had been broken. But before the enforced dialogue could get properly under way Wilbur had gone. He had packed his small suitcase and sailed for Europe to help Hart Berg float a French company.

Wilbur had actually wanted Orville to go to Europe. In a letter to Milton he high-mindedly explained why. 'It was evident that the man who went to Europe would have to act largely on his own judgement . . . I felt that I was more willing to accept the consequences of any error of judgement on his part than to have him blaming me if I went.'[5] Another reason, he told his father, was that the brother who stayed behind would have to complete the latest *Flyer* they were building and later take it to France. Wilbur had wanted to oversee all that because 'I am more careful than he is – at least I think so.' But Orville had disagreed. Wilbur, who had become the public voice and correspondent of the partnership, would be more impressive in negotiation. And so it was Wilbur, having arrived at Liverpool and taken the train to London, whom Berg went to meet at Euston station.

Berg had never seen a picture of either of the brothers, or even read a description of them, but as the passengers streamed off the train that Saturday afternoon in mid-May he had no difficulty recognising his visitor. 'Either I am Sherlock Holmes or Wright has that peculiar glint of genius in his eye which left no doubt in my mind as to who he was . . . He arrived with nothing but a bag about the size of a music roll, but mildly suggested he thought it might be advisable for him to buy another suit of clothes. I fortunately found a shop open in the Strand and fixed him up at least for evening wear, as he came to the conclusion that he'd "guess he'd better have a swaller-tail coat."'[6]

They spent the afternoon together, shopping in the West End. The worldly arms dealer was enchanted by Wilbur's courtesy, his willingness to talk about the flying machine, and his daunting intellect. All his misgivings about the mysterious inventors melted away. He was soon a fully converted member of the Wright fan club. 'I am much pleased with Wright's personality,' he reported that weekend to Flint. 'He inspires great confidence and I am sure that he will be a capital Exhibit A.'[7] Behind the charm, however, he sensed a will of obstinate steel. He had difficulty penetrating Wilbur's protective shell:

> Mr Wright talked carefully, as if it was all mapped out in advance. It was obvious that he feared to be caught in a trap concerning his remarkable machine and what he wants to do with it. At the end of each question his clean-shaven face relapsed into a broad sphinx-like smile.[8]

Berg had difficulty winning Wilbur over to his company idea, 'which did not seem to please him very much'. Wilbur much preferred big contracts with governments who would do their own manufacturing. 'After a long talk,' Berg told Flint, 'I believe, please note that I say distinctly "I believe", that I made something of an impression as regards the impossibility of getting any sort of action in the near future from any government.' Berg thought the only exception might be Germany – 'and even there I assured him that we must look to the power greater than the government, that is, the Emperor himself.'[9]

By the end of the weekend Berg had convinced Wilbur that to make and sell the aeroplanes themselves was the best way into

Europe. Joined by Frank Cordley, Charles Flint's prudently cautious right-hand man from New York, they went to Paris to meet the powerful industrialist de la Meurthe, whom Wilbur was to describe as 'the Standard Oil King of Europe'. Things moved speedily. De la Meurthe expressed great interest in the *Flyer* and was keen to invest in it. But first, to ensure there would be a major French customer, he prudently went round to see the Minister of War, General Georges Picquart, who, after consulting Commandant Bonel (who had led the abortive mission to Dayton the previous year), said he was prepared to buy some – provided they could operate at 1000 feet and fly 50 kilometres.

With this encouraging news Wilbur, Berg and de la Meurthe set about creating a $700,000 company. The Wrights would have roughly a half-interest and receive considerable riches, $350,000 – $7 million today – for their efforts; they would control the European rights. Flint's company and de la Meurthe would each take a 20 per cent stake. There was talk of inviting investment from Britain, Germany and Italy as well.

But the international company was never born. The attempts to create it were to be bedevilled by intrigue, corruption, unpleasant battles for the sales rights and, saddest of all, by personal rows and recriminations between Wilbur and Orville.

It all started to go wrong when Bonel bumped into Arnold Fordyce, the French military commission member who was secretary to the Letelliers at *Le Journal*. Learning to his amazement that Wilbur Wright was in town negotiating with an entirely new group of Frenchmen, the cool Fordyce had been so shocked he had hurried to pass the news to young Letellier and his father – a bitter rival of de la Meurthe (whose own interests included a financial stake in the competitor newspaper, *Le Matin*). The Letelliers were incensed. Although the French Army's option on the *Flyer*, which had resulted from *Le Journal*'s initiative in funding the despatch of Fordyce to Dayton, had long ago lapsed, it seems that the younger Letellier still jealously regarded the French rights to the machine as his syndicate's property. He rushed to protest to Picquart, apparently demanding that any business the government did with the Wrights be done through him and his father's newspaper which had once held the rights to the story.

> Letellier became very angry. He insisted that he should be the sole French member of the new corporation to invest in it on a large scale. He demanded that Deutsch (de la Meurthe) should at once withdraw from the company.[10]

General Picquart who, earlier, had been caught up in the notorious Dreyfus case (in which a young Jewish army officer, falsely accused of passing state secrets to Germany, had been deported for life to Devil's Island), still carried mental scars from his own false imprisonment when wrongly accused of forgery. Anxious not to find himself at the centre of another major political scandal, he quickly took Letellier's side, telling de la Meurthe that any business the government did with the Wrights' aeroplane must be transacted through the Letelliers. Wilbur was dumbfounded. The brothers no longer had any contractual obligation to *Le Journal*, but before he could explain this to the furious de la Meurthe, the oil millionaire, whose money they so badly needed, had withdrawn in disgust. Suddenly Wilbur had no vehicle with which to launch the aeroplane into Europe.

He and Berg considered switching the offer to Germany, but, as the French War Minister had already responded positively to de la Meurthe's earlier feelers, they decided to give the negotiations one last chance. Wilbur and Berg, now unwillingly forced into bed with Letellier and Fordyce, reverted to their original demand for 1 million francs ($200,000). The ever-evolving package now offered six months exclusivity, 1000 feet and 50 kilometres with a passenger. After six months, what had become the Wright/Flint/Letellier syndicate would be free to sell to other nations. The negotiations quickly slid into murky waters. They found themselves directed to deal with a corrupt senator, Charles Humbert. Humbert was a friend and associate of the Letelliers and head of the Chamber of Deputies military budget committee. But Wilbur was not permitted to meet him. The War Ministry would deal only with Fordyce, who went to meet Senator Humbert.

Far from quibbling over the one million francs, Humbert coolly asked that the price be raised by 25 per cent to Fr1,250,000. He planned to pocket the quarter-million difference. If it wasn't agreed, he told Fordyce, the proposal's chance of success would be slim. When Fordyce conveyed the kickback demand to Wilbur he was appalled. 'I am very much surprised that such conditions obtain in this country, as Berg was of the impression that French officials were straight . . . I will not countenance any crookedness.'[11] Berg and Wilbur refused to pay the colossal sweetener – unless, at Wilbur's sharp insistence, Humbert's name was typed into the contract as the personal recipient of the money. If not they would pack their bags and take the offer to Berlin. Humbert declined but, unwilling to be responsible for France's loss of the aeroplane, agreed, unhappily, to push the bribeless million-franc proposal to the War Ministry. Here it was now to moulder amidst argument and confusion.

From over 3500 miles away, Milton's anxious warnings had continued to flow into Paris. 'It behoves you to be watchful of your interests and to be certain in any move you may make,' he had urged Wilbur. 'You may be sure that all dealing with you will try to reach into you as far as possible.'[12]

Milton's weren't the only misgivings being felt back home. While, in that Parisian summer of 1907, Wilbur was struggling to conclude an honest deal with people whose language he didn't speak and whose business morality seemed corrupted at every turn, Orville, waiting along with mechanic Charlie Taylor to bring over the latest version of the secret aeroplane, was becoming tetchy and restless. He was perplexed and unhappy with the precious little he could glean of the negotiations from Wilbur's cryptic cables and the infrequent letters that sometimes took twelve days to come. As co-inventor, he felt he wasn't being properly consulted. What's more, he had become exasperated with the Flint company, which had continued to ignore his pleading letters demanding the information he claimed Wilbur was withholding from him. The combination of slow mail and elliptically terse cables had begun to create such a nightmare of misunderstanding between the brothers that, for the first time in their long, harmonious partnership, personal tensions now burst into rare bitter words. To his brother on the other side of the Atlantic Orville began to appear obstructive. To the latest proposal he had simply cabled back bluntly: 'NOT APPROVE OFFER . . .

DO NOTHING WITHOUT I CONSENT.' He complained: 'I HAVE PRACTICALLY NO INFORMATION OF WHAT IS GOING ON.'

Almost immediately the harassed Wilbur, now impatient to abandon the impossible French, cabled 'EVERY TRADE IS OFF'. He asked the peeved and confused Orville to bring the *Flyer* urgently to Europe to show it to the Germans, but before he could book his passage yet another bald message arrived from Paris. Incredibly, it seemed, the French negotiations were on again. The War Minister's staff officer had agreed to all their terms. 'YOU AND CHARLIE COME HERE AS SOON AS POSSIBLE. EXPECT TO CLOSE,' Wilbur wired excitedly. But it was a false dawn. Within days the deal was off again.

By now, Wilbur had begun to suspect collusion between the Letelliers, Fordyce, the crooked Humbert and the War Minister's staff officer, Major Targe. The wine had flowed at lunches Fordyce would buy the senator and Targe. At one of these convivial gatherings, Fordyce later told Wilbur, Humbert had declared that 'he had no faith in the Wrights – that they were frauds'.

'The more we saw of the inside of French official life,' Wilbur told Chanute, 'the less we felt like taking any risks with such people . . . I am sure that our withdrawal was wise for many reasons, not the least of which was freeing ourselves from the odium of association with the disreputable Letellier crowd.'[13]

Nor was it only the French whose conduct unnerved him. Both he and Orville had by now independently developed serious doubts about the Flint company as well.

22

Fraternal Friction

(1907)

Orville's disenchantment with Flint's New York office had fused with his resentment at the sparsity of Wilbur's cables to reduce him to seething frustration. It communicated itself to Katharine and Milton – even to Lorin who came round daily for news – putting them all on edge as they waited anxiously for the perplexing cables and letters from France. Orville couldn't concentrate any longer on his aircraft assembly work. He kept going up to the post office to check for letters. They didn't always know where Wilbur was from day to day and some of their own letters, optimistically addressed simply 'c/o Hart O. Berg, Paris', had depressingly begun to arrive back in Dayton weeks later.

Misunderstandings between the two brothers had begun almost the moment Wilbur had arrived in Paris. When the French had insisted on the 300 metres/1000-feet altitude requirement, Wilbur had cabled Orville for his urgent agreement. They communicated in code. Orville's unhelpfully confusing reply 'THOUSAND IN AMERICA, HUNDRED FEET IN FRANCE', had annoyed Wilbur. It appeared to be a refusal, effectively, to do business with the French. Irritated, he had cabled back: 'IT IS QUESTION WHETHER REFUSE 1,000 FT IN EUROPE,' to which Orville had responded: 'WILL FULFILL TERMS WITH EXCEPTION OF HEIGHT WITHIN THE TIME. MAY REQUIRE AN ADDITION FOR 300

METRES.' Wilbur thought this to mean his brother needed extra time to develop a *Flyer* capable of rising to that flight level. He found this infuriating. Why hadn't Orville bothered to say how much more time?

Then Orville had refused to approve the one million franc offer. In that cable he had added a petulant clue to his unease: 'HAVE NOT YET RECEIVED ANY INFORMATION FROM FLINT & CO.' Wilbur was baffled. He had no idea what information Orville was demanding from Flints. He thought *he* was the only one dealing with the company. Wilbur, now angered by his brother's seemingly obstructive messages, sat down to write him a tough letter. 'I received your cable turning down the French Government deal this morning. At noon the Government also turned it down, so I am turned down on both sides, after both sides had, as I thought, indicated their approval quite definitely. 'I am,' wrote Wilbur peevishly, 'absolutely in the dark as to the reasons':

> I confess that I am a little hurt that you should refuse to take this job yourself and then turn down my recommendations after I supposed you had given your assent to every important point. I have had no letter from you since yours of June 11th, more than three weeks old and I have had not one word as to when you can come over with the machine, though I have asked for word both by letter and by cable.[1]

Stung by this litany of complaints Orville wrote back:

> I have had only one letter a week from you (these very short) in the last month or more. I have practically no information of what is going on. When you cable you never explain anything so that I can answer with any certainty that we are talking about the same thing . . . You have not answered a single question I have asked in my cables.[2]

Orville vented his exasperation with their sales agents. He was so unhappy with Flints that he'd cabled Wilbur a few days earlier suggesting he return to America urgently to get rid of them. Flints were disregarding his letters, ignoring his questions. 'I am so disgusted with them that I would like to sever our connection . . . I have had no information from Flint since you left. They surely have had advices of what was going on, but they have not sent me one word.' Nor had they responded to his questions demanding to know the exact level of commission they planned to take. 'They have been so tricky,' he declared. As to Wilbur's allegation that he had unreasonably vetoed the French deal, Orville said: 'I do not understand how you can say that when I did not know for a week after the proposition had been offered that you were thinking of making such a proposition!'[3]

Wilbur was also under attack from his father, equally baffled by events in Paris and cross that Wilbur was keeping them all in the dark. 'Your cablegrams have not been explicit,' he admonished, 'and have been therefore confusing to us and trying on Orville's nerves . . . I think it would be better if your business letters were more frequent and fuller of information and your cablegrams more explicit. Orville becomes nervous and Katharine still more excited and I have trouble to keep them in a practical frame of mind.'[4]

'We do not understand what your cables mean half the time.' Katharine's letters to Wilbur reveal how edgy and irritable the family had become as, day after day, they held their breath for word of the signing of a lucrative contract. 'News from Paris is becoming as scarce as hens' teeth,' she wrote at the end of June. 'Orv has just gone to the post office to see if there are any letters. It does seem as if you left off writing just as the exciting time came on. Orv can't work any. He is so uneasy and unsettled. The rest of us are in like condition. I do hope that some definite information will come soon.'[5]

Orville's resentment at what he perceived as the sheer greed of Flints at their expense had now infected them all. They had been staggered to learn that when the eventually stillborn European company had looked like getting off the ground, their agents had expected commission on the entire proposed $700,000 capitalisation rather than just the 50 per cent proportion of the Wrights' interest in the venture. To the family it ranked as usury. 'Orv was wroth,' Katharine told Wilbur, 'and said he was in favour of giving them notice to get out on the first of September when their time expires.'

Steeped in the common prejudices of the time, Katharine, having seen newspaper pictures of Wilbur with Hart Berg, had been quick to identify the reason for the vast commission that would have climbed into the region of 40 per cent. 'I can't stand Berg's looks. It has just dawned on me that the whole company is composed of Jews. Berg certainly looks it.'[6]

By early July the uncertainty of it all was beginning to affect everyone's temper at Hawthorn Street. 'We are all so nervous and worn out with the suspense that we can't any of us keep from being cross. Orv and I regularly fight every time we get together for five minutes. And poor Daddy does nothing but advise us to "be calm . . . be calm" while he is so excited that he can't hear anything we say. It would be funny if it weren't so desperate. But what has happened to the letters?'[7]

Charlie Taylor, whose working-class origins constantly offended Katharine,was also putting her on edge. Apprehensively awaiting the summons to take the aeroplane into the bewildering environment of a foreign country, he'd begun to leave the workshop and hang around the house demanding news. 'I can not endure his tiresome talk and he wants to come and sit for an hour twice a day. If his case isn't settled soon I shall be crazy . . . I want to cry if anybody looks at me.'[8] To Reuchlin, away from it all on his Kansas farm, Katharine wrote: 'This family is in such a fearful uproar the whole time it is a wonder that we keep our wits at all.'

Caught between shifty French officials and a family in a lather of agitation, Wilbur poured out his own frustrations in a bitter letter to Milton.

> The complaint that I have not written fully and promptly is incomprehensible to me as I have written every few days and kept back nothing . . . My telegrams were not intended to have any connections with my letters. Do you suppose I was so foolish as to mix letters and cables? . . . You people in Dayton seem to me to be very lacking in perspicacity . . .
>
> When Orville insisted that I should come I told him that I

> must be free to settle matters to the best of my judgement as they arose, as it would be impossible to wait for letters to pass back and forth or to explain things clearly by cable. Opportunities must be seized as they pass, or they are gone beyond recovery.

Wilbur said that he had urged Orville to get the aeroplane ready quickly and follow him to Europe. But,

> instead of attending to his work and letting me attend to mine, he seemed to have felt no responsibility as to his own work but the whole responsibility as to mine . . . I suppose he has been so worried that he has not been really himself. But it would have been much better if he had attended energetically to his department and avoided interference in mine.
>
> . . . it was an absolute impossibility in a negotiation which changed every few days like a kaleidoscope, to depend upon consultations with someone over two thousand miles away . . . I do not willingly assume the responsibility of deciding things alone, but when it is necessary I do not hesitate.[9]

Wilbur, having now learnt of Orville's complaint that their agents had taken him out of the loop, was amazed that his brother had even tried to put his spoke in the wheel. 'Flints were quite right in keeping silent. If they had attempted to communicate or negotiate directly with Orville there would have been a fuss here immediately.'[10] He castigated Orville who, after all, had pleaded to be left in Dayton to finish work on the new *Flyer* – 'he happened to be in one of his peculiar spells just then'. But, Wilbur added harshly to Milton, 'So far as his letters indicate he spent his time on things of no use . . . and left the necessary things undone.'[11] Had Orville come to Paris 'I would have given him a free hand till I could have followed to Europe myself – but I would have been ready to follow within one month instead of two'.

Wilbur had himself developed some deep reservations about their grasping sales agents, describing Flint and Berg as 'merely hustlers.'. He was disturbed by the large commissions demanded and by their brazen selling techniques. But, unlike Orville, he had refused to be intimidated. 'When I first came over,' he told Katharine,

> Berg and Cordley thought they were the business men and I was merely a sort of exhibit. But their eyes have gradually opened, and now they realize that I see into situations deeper than they do, that my judgement is often more sound, and that I intend to run them rather than have them run me . . . Now I control everything and they give advice and assistance.'[12]

'I am sorry,' Wilbur wrote to Katharine, 'that you are all so worn down by excitement . . . You people at home must stop worrying! There is no need of it. Orville and I can take care of ourselves all right and we will be found on top when the smoke has cleared away.'

Happily for the sake of their famously amicable relationship, the transatlantic discord was temporary. In the middle of July, Orville, who didn't believe in travelling as spartanly as his brother, packed his tuxedo and frock coat into a large trunk and left for Paris to join the sales team in the front line. In the weeks before he went there had been developments on the American front which had forced him to start writing the proposals to officialdom normally the exclusive preserve of Wilbur. The Board of Ordnance and Fortification, now aware of the President's interest, had unenthusiastically invited the cycle company to submit a proposition for the demonstration and sale of the flying machine which hadn't now flown for over eighteen months. 'For the sum of $100,000 we will furnish one flyer and teach an operator appointed by your Board to operate the same,' Orville had written. The aeroplane would carry two men 200 kilometres at 50 kilometres an hour. Additional machines would be supplied 'at a reasonable advance over the cost of manufacture'. He had added the familiar rider that 'since many of the features of our flyer are secrets, it would not be prudent to show the machine in advance of a contract'. The board had replied enquiring if the $100,000 sale would give the US Government exclusive rights to the invention. That was no longer possible, Orville had told them, whereupon the board, not convinced that a non-exclusive machine was worth so much money, had decided for the moment to pursue the matter no further.

In Paris, while waiting for Orville, Wilbur had begun to explore the city. He spent hours wandering through cathedrals and art galleries, several times drawn back to the Louvre where, he told Katharine, she would have been at home with the groups of other American schoolteachers he encountered 'prancing' about 'with red Baedeckers in hand'. He described the famous paintings in letters back home, critically appraising the work of his flying machine-designing predecessor. 'The Mona Lisa is no better than the prints in black and white. I must confess that the pictures by celebrated masters that impressed me most were not the ones that are best known. I like Leonardo da Vinci's "John the Baptist" much better than his "Mona Lisa".' He was unimpressed, too, by Notre Dame. 'It was rather disappointing as most sights are to me. My imagination pictures things more vividly than my eyes.'[13]

He took his first balloon ride, rising through the clouds to 3000 feet and drifting across the countryside for three and a half hours before landing in a wheat field near Orleans. The experience convinced him that it had no future as a sport. 'In ballooning a few glorious hours in the air are usually followed by a tiresome walk to some village, an uncomfortable night at a poor hotel, and a return home by slow local trains.'[14]

Getting to know some of France's own experimenters, he met Esnault-Pelteric, who had been trying out ailerons, the wealthy Archdeacon, still determined that America should not beat France into the air, and Gabriel Voisin, who had piloted Archdeacon's 1904 glider. Voisin, described as 'a dashing fellow and something of a ladies' man', was fond of regaling people with his lengthy catalogue of conquests – though he would not have been encouraged to share them with Wilbur – which, according to his memoirs, ranged from schoolgirls 'to seamstresses, dental assistants, postmistresses, landladies, prostitutes and errant wives'.[15] But he is better remembered for what he was to become – one of his country's leading aircraft manufacturers, who would survive into his nineties, into the 1970s.

Wilbur also met again the driven, frustrated Ferdinand Ferber. The army captain had feigned delight at the encounter – 'I grasped his hand and looked upon him with great emotion. Just to think that without this man I would be nothing . . . without him my experiments would not have taken place'[16] – though, as Wilbur had discovered, he was now busy behind the scenes doing everything he could to thwart a French purchase of the *Flyer*. Despite his earlier efforts to persuade his army to buy the aeroplane, Ferber had become 'infected with ambition and was largely responsible for the failure of the final negotiations in March 1906. Since then he has done all he could to prevent us from doing business here.' Ferber had joined the swelling ranks of the untrustworthy driven by cupidity: 'double-faced' and 'at bottom bitterly hostile'.

Orville arrived in Paris in the last week of July. Like Wilbur he didn't speak a word of useful French. Wilbur thought his brother appeared exhausted. Through the nervous suspense of it all he had lost weight and looked as lean as a stick. Even Chanute, back in Chicago, had commented on it. Seeing a picture of Orville in a French magazine he told Wilbur, 'I hardly recognised him.' Soon, however, Wilbur was reporting to his father that his brother was 'fattening up a little', adding bitingly, 'From what he says it seems he supposed I had come over here merely to talk, or for fun, rather than for business.'[17]

Orville was soon drawn into that business and was appalled by the web of aeronautical intrigue into which he had plunged. Bemused by the torrents of French, he left most of the talking to Wilbur whose English Berg would translate when necessary. In the interests of fraternal harmony, Wilbur had called a halt to the negotiations until Orville arrived. When the dialogue was resumed, the War Ministry, whose officials were divided between factions welcoming and opposing the foreign invention, almost immediately threw up a fresh obstacle. It announced that a technical committee would have to study the Wrights' proposals. It looked as if they would never do any business in France.

But, just as the prospects in France grew bleaker, back in America they began to brighten.

In Paris Wilbur had been befriended by Frank S. Lahm, the expatriate typewriter merchant and balloonist who had sent his brother-in-law to check on their flying exploits two years earlier.

Lahm had introduced the brothers to his son, Lieutenant Frank P. Lahm, a young West Point graduate who had that summer been assigned to the US Army's recently formed Aeronautical Division. It had become a unit of the army's Signal Corps which, since the Civil War, had been responsible for military balloon operations. The young Lahm, also a keen recreational balloonist who had the previous year flown from Paris 400 miles across the Channel and on into Yorkshire, was in France on temporary attachment to a cavalry school. His meeting with the Wright Brothers was to have historic consequences.

So excited was Lahm by their dramatic flying achievements and so amazed that the American Army hadn't seized the invention that he was moved to write and tell his new commanding officer, Brigadier General James Allen, about it. Head of the US Signal Corps, Allen was also a senior member of the four-man Board of Ordnance and Fortification that had shown such studied lack of interest in the aeroplane. When he read Lahm's plea he took serious notice. The upshot was that, for the first time, the army was stirred to initiative. It decided to break its detached silence and begin to pursue the Wrights.

A letter from the Ordnance Board actually inviting them to come to Washington caught up with them in Paris. There was, the board said, a problem: it was the price they were asking. The army was interested but $100,000 was more than it had at its disposal. To raise a sum like that would require a special appropriation from Congress – a slow process. The brothers replied that they were willing to negotiate on price. 'Fair treatment' and respect for their patents was more important than a high price. Privately they had agreed to sell a *Flyer* to their own government for as little as $25,000 – a quarter of their original asking figure. They had so little confidence now that a European sale was an even foreseeable likelihood that they were prepared to return to America on the next boat to discuss a final deal.

By the end of summer 1907 the French negotiations, bogged down between the Letelliers and pockets of corrupt bureaucracy, had got no further. Worse, French experimenters were starting to make public flights of ominous distance. Orville witnessed one. He'd gone out with Hart Berg to Issy-les-Moulineaux north of Paris and watched a man called Henri Farman fly a pusher biplane built by Gabriel Voisin. Farman, a bearded Englishman born and raised in France who spoke English with a heavy French accent, represented a new breed of aviator who were sportsmen rather than inventors. He cared much more for the thrill of it than the mathematics of the aerodynamics. One of France's leading racing cyclists, he had accumulated a considerable fortune selling motor cars in partnership with his brother Maurice. He had commissioned Voisin to build him an aeroplane.

The machine had undercarriage wheels but no roll control, yet Farman managed, in a wobbly circular flight, to remain in the air for a minute and a quarter and go just over a kilometre. The flight was immediately heralded in France, where the Wrights' claims were still not taken seriously, as 'a world record for mechanical flight'. Reporters who crowded round Orville at Issy pressed him for applause, but all he would say cautiously was that he and his brother 'never liked to pass criticisms on the work of others'. However, precariously controlled though it may have been, Farman's flight could not be ignored. As Chanute had warned, the others were starting to catch up – they were popping up everywhere, some now building monoplanes. One of them, Louis Blériot, was an engineer whose profitable business was the manufacture of automobile headlamps. He had progressed rapidly from gliders to single-wing machines with engine and propeller at the front, rear elevators and rudder and wingtip devices for roll control. In France it was believed that its aviators had already overtaken the Wrights – if indeed the American brothers had flown at all and were not merely *bluffeurs*.

'It seems that to the genius of France is reserved the glorious mission of initiating the world into the conquest of the air,' declared the President of the Aéro-Club. His colleague, the highly respected Archdeacon, told club members Farman's flight was 'an absolutely decisive stage in the history of aviation'. He dismissed the Wrights' 'phantom machine', saying they 'may today claim all they wish. If it is true – and I doubt it more and more – that they were the first to fly through the air, they will not have that glory before history . . .

The first authentic experiments in powered aviation have taken place in France.'[18]

Against such aggressive patriotic sentiment it was difficult for the French War Minister to rush into an expensive contract to buy a foreign machine that few French people had been allowed to believe existed. The safer course was to encourage Voisin, Farman, Santos-Dumont and others to overtake the Wrights – which they looked rapidly to be doing.

Meanwhile, wrote one biographer, 'the magic of Flint's name and organization proved of little avail . . . The dreary spectacle of the two brothers, sole possessors of a practical embodiment of man's oldest dream, cooling their heels in hotel rooms, patiently answering the imperious calls of petty officials, writing and rewriting lengthy contracts, calmly accepting the abuse of an unfriendly press . . . patiently defending their asking price – all this is enough to make anyone wish passionately that they had been able to throw caution to the winds and make just one electrifying flight.'[19]

In a final bid to find a European customer Wilbur and Berg took the train to Berlin early in August leaving Orville in Paris to handle the stalled French negotiations. While they were passing through Belgium, Wilbur astonished Berg with his unexpected knowledge of European history. He:

> noticed a sign indicating that they were in the little town of Jemappes. Then he recalled that a great battle took place there in 1792. He began to discuss the battle with an exact knowledge that astounded Berg . . . Over and over again Berg and others who dealt with Wilbur Wright were similarly impressed not only by the range of his reading but by the fact that no knowledge he had once acquired ever seemed to grow dim.[20]

Berg was also intrigued by Wilbur's choice of reading matter on their long train journeys together. He noticed that he carried in his pocket the same tiny book wherever they went and would be constantly immersed in it. It was a miniature volume of Shakespeare's *Romeo and Juliet*.

In the German capital they met Flints' agent, Isidor Loewe.

Things began promisingly. The Germans were much more businesslike than the French, and there appeared not to be a whiff of corruption anywhere. Loewe introduced them to all the right people in the aviation establishment – none, surprisingly, experimenting with heavier-than-air flight, all still preoccupied with balloons and the great new airships of Count von Zeppelin which would soon inaugurate the world's first passenger air services. At Loewe's suggestion, Wilbur had written a persuasive technical paper extolling the superiority of fixed-wing aeroplanes over airships, stressing their speed and manoeuvrability and the military vulnerability of bulky slow dirigibles to gunfire. Berg and Wilbur were invited to make a fresh proposal. The Germans were genuinely interested. But it soon became apparent that, not surprisingly, they weren't prepared to buy a single aeroplane until they had seen it fly.

Wilbur was now for the first time sorely tempted to break their rigid no-flight-before-contract rule, admitting to Katharine, 'We doubt whether an agreement will be reached before we have really made some demonstrations somewhere and stirred up some excitement.' It would have been simple to organise. Charlie Taylor had now arrived in France with the latest *Flyer*, which had upright seating for pilot and passenger and dual controls for tuition. The machine was in storage at Le Havre and could easily be railed to Berlin, but in the end Wilbur decided not to risk it. 'We did not like to disclose our machine at the tail end of the year and give imitators all winter to manufacture copies,' he explained to Chanute. 'We do not wish to get into lawsuits before we get the business properly organized and started. Our plan is to spend the winter building a half dozen new machines for the spring trade.'[21] Wilbur told Milton: 'We will probably put out a sign, "opening day, all goods below cost."'[22]

Back in Paris, where, in frustration, they had decided to terminate all negotiations with the French War Ministry, the brothers began to plan for that trade. They would break their holy vow, demonstrate the *Flyer* throughout Europe – and sell machines one at a time to any interested buyer. Orville began to talk to French engine manufacturers to find one who could build their motors locally; the airframes, five of which were partly completed back in their workshop, would be shipped over.

In Dayton their abortive negotiations with the French and Germans had been making headlines. Reporters had shadowed them around Paris and in Berlin, where Orville had gone briefly to join Wilbur. When Charlie Taylor had arrived in Paris to support the flying demonstrations that weren't now going to be needed, he tried to travel incognito, booking into a small hotel around the corner, at Orville's suggestion, under the name of 'C.E. Taylor, Lincoln, Nebraska', the town where he'd lived as a boy. They were worried that reporters might corner their unsophisticated mechanic when he'd had too much to drink and he'd disgorge a trove of secrets. But newsmen never found him and he hung dejectedly around Paris, a fish out of water, bored, lonely and homesick, badgering the brothers to send him back, and drowning his sorrows in the Parisian bars that Wilbur and Orville never entered.

The brothers were all too aware that Milton, fearful for their moral safety amid the fleshpots of Paris far from the reach of his steadying influence, was daily praying for their preservation from temptation. His letters monotonously expressed his concern at their exposure to peril 'among strangers'. His greatest anxiety was for the allurements of alcohol and women. Orville had been foolish enough to reassure him flippantly, 'We have been real good over here. We have been in a lot of churches and haven't got drunk yet!'[23] Wilbur, in more solemn vein, had reported, perhaps more reassuringly:

> As to drinking and dissipation of various kinds you may be entirely easy. All the wine I have tasted since leaving home would not fill a single wine glass. I am sure that Orville and myself will be careful to do nothing which would disgrace the training we received from you and from mother.[24]

Sternly Milton had written back: 'I did not anticipate that either of you would become intemperate or debauched, but I want you to show the foreigners that you are teetotallers and in every way maintain that high character that is most proper to have and which in the eyes of the best in America is the most approved.'[25] Milton began to lecture them on the evil of carnality. 'I am more and more convinced,' he said in a joint letter to them, 'that "the carnal mind is enmity against God." All observation attests this truth.' He went on to warn, 'true Christians under unfavourable circumstances do some strange things . . . Alas human depravity!'[26] In a later letter he set them sweeping goals: 'Be men – men of the highest type. Personally, mentally, morally and spiritually. Be clean, temperate, sober-minded, and great souled.'[27] Milton need not have worried. His parental training guaranteed there was no danger his sons would ever be tempted to stray from the straight and narrow.

'Though Wilbur was more inclined toward missionary seriousness about his behaviour than the genial Orville, neither ever deviated from strict adherence to the family's moral guidelines,' said Adrian Kinnane. 'Orville seems always to have worried his father and Wilbur a bit. They feared his accommodating sociability would somehow inadvertently compromise him. Milton and Wilbur had a solitary, zealous and righteous energy that reinforced their moral strength from the inside out. Orville, it was felt, needed reinforcing from the outside in. But he was really never in any great danger of corruption.'[28]

The bishop also had regular advice for their health. Orville became ill in Paris with a fever, diagnosed rightly or wrongly as malaria. 'You would better seek all practical exercise and rub your flesh to the bone every day, and take a daily bath. Rub on each side of the spine but not on the bone.'[29] He was also regularly xenophobically worried about their safety in the air should they be required to risk a demonstration among untrustworthy foreigners. 'Before making a flight you should inspect your machine carefully to see that no-one has tampered with it. Cultivate all worthy American friends and the American legation. A Frenchman is just as good as an American under like circumstances,' he explained, 'but human nature is curious . . . It is not a little thing to have been the first to cleave the air; but money will come in some safe way. Yours is already the credit; risk not too much in life and limb. Be not goaded into danger.'[30]

Almost every letter brought a report of the latest intrigues of the squabbling Brethren among whom Milton, despite retirement, had remained a formidable force. Still consumed by resentment at the continuing charmed survival within the breakaway White River district of his *bête noire*, the Reverend Millard Keiter, in one of his letters to Paris he reported that the crooked minister had begun stealing Brethren funds yet again. He had at last been forced to resign and had fled to Tennessee, spelling the end of the Keiter faction which, Milton wrote feelingly, 'will sink unwept, unhonoured and unsung'. With Keiter's departure his White River rebels had returned to the fold, and Milton had at last been acknowledged as a church hero for his unremitting efforts to dislodge the thieving parson. 'Who would have thought that I would live to be treated with respect and consideration by those that did their utmost to destroy me!' he told Orville.[31]

As the European autumn of 1907 faded into winter, Wilbur and Orville prepared to retreat. Before leaving Paris they decided to tackle Berg on the thorny matter of the sales commission that was beginning to sour the relationship. Orville appears to have lost some of his earlier determination to dump Flints altogether, but they still gave Berg a hard time when, in early November, they all sat down to try to resolve the unhappiness. The Wrights had quarrelled so often with Berg over their business relationship with his company that they determined this time to nail him down and hold him to what was agreed. A revealing, near verbatim note they later made of the discussion has survived.[32] It records the steely determination with which the brothers stressed once and for all that it was their invention and they intended to be the principal recipients of any profit from the still uncreated sales company.

'We want to make it perfectly clear,' Wilbur told Berg, 'that you are in no way entering into partnership . . . Your relation is simply that of agent.'

'I don't like that word "agent",' Berg had protested. 'Say "representative".'

But the brothers had stuck to 'agent' and set out to disabuse Berg of his hopes that Flints might become a major stakeholder in any sales company. The Wrights would be the sole owners and commission would remain at 20 per cent with no share in the company, but at 20 per cent of the *net* profit after deduction of the cost of building the machines and of demonstrating them. Berg had violently protested that Flints would be out of pocket – but the

Wrights knew the agency was potentially far too lucrative for Flint to abandon it.

While Wilbur was in Berlin, Orville had made a side trip to England. While there he'd gone down to Farnborough to spend a weekend with Colonel Capper and his wife at their country home. He and 'Jack' Capper were now warmly on first-name terms, and Orville's hope was to have a 'heart-to-heart' talk with the colonel about the prospect of rekindling British interest in the *Flyer*. After their disappointments in France and Germany they were considering knocking on the Whitehall doors yet again. He needed Capper's advice on tactics.

What did Orville learn in the peace of rural Hampshire that weekend? Did Capper reveal any of the closely guarded secrets of Lieutenant Dunne's rival machine? Or of a second British Army experimental aeroplane at that moment being built at the Farnborough establishment by one of the most unlikely of all history's inventors – an American cowboy, wild-horse tamer and music hall entertainer named Samuel Cody?

All that Orville ever recorded of his November 1907 visit is in a note to Katharine: 'I was out at the Cappers from Saturday noon to Sunday noon. Mrs Capper wants to send you a climbing rose. I told Will to get it if he goes out to see them on his way home.'[33]

There is no evidence that Wilbur, who went back to America with the disgruntled Charlie Taylor via England, ever collected the rose bush. When Orville followed them home early in December they still had not found a single customer anywhere in the world for their magnificent flying machine.

23

Supremacy Threatened

(1908)

In the last weeks of 1907, the US Army emerged at long last from its torpid lack of interest in military aviation. The intervention of Lieutenant Lahm had paid off. Through the doors his letter to the Chief Signal Officer had opened in Washington, Wilbur, on his way home from Europe, went to meet the cautious generals.

He was welcomed by the Chief Signal Officer himself, the man responsible for military aeronautics, Brigadier General James Allen, and came face to face for the first time with the reluctant members of the Board of Ordnance and Fortification who had so incomprehensibly turned their backs on the incredible new war machine. They were all much taken with the austere, messianic figure of Wilbur – impressed by his genuineness, articulate self-confidence and the obvious potential of the weapon he described.

As a result of the meeting, the board moved fast. Rather than snap up the *Flyer*, for which there wasn't a single rival anywhere in America, it decided, with bureaucratic correctness, to call for tenders for a military aeroplane. Lacking the smallest expertise in powered flight it sent the Wright Cycle Company, with quaint irony, some proposed specifications inviting their comments. One of the innocently listed requirements was automatic control. Wilbur leapt upon this, writing to Brigadier General Allen: 'If it is to be construed as a demand for something not possessed by any of the millions of flying creatures which have successfully navigated the air throughout the ages, we doubt the wisdom of retaining that sentence.' It was dropped in the advertisement that appeared two days before Christmas.

The notice invited bids for an aeroplane that could carry a pilot and passenger for one hour at an average speed of 40 miles an hour in a 10-mile flight. It had to hold fuel for 125 miles, be tested in the presence of army officers, be easily dismantled for road transport, and permit 'an intelligent man to become proficient in its use within a reasonable time'.

Newspapers greeted the advertisement with derision. The New York *Globe* said: 'One might be inclined to assume that the era of practical human flight had arrived . . . Nothing in any way approaching such a machine has ever been constructed (the Wright Brothers' claims still await public confirmation) . . . If there is any possibility that such an airship is within measurable distance of perfection any government could well afford to provide its inventor with unlimited resources and promise him a prize running into the millions.' The *American Magazine of Aeronautics* said: 'There is not a known flying machine in the world which could fulfil these specifications at the present moment . . . Why is not the experience of Professor Langley a good guide. We doubt very much if the government receives any bids.'

It received forty-one. Half were immediately discarded as preposterous – one came from a federal prisoner offering a flying machine in exchange for his release. Prices asked ranged from $850 to $1 million. Only two proposals could be taken seriously – the Wrights', seeking $25,000, and a rival one from an aviator with a significant record of well-documented experimentation, undercutting them at $20,000 – Augustus Herring.

Herring had come earlier to Dayton with another of his outrageous propositions. He said he planned to bid $5000 less than the Wrights in the hope that the army would be compelled to accept the lower price. The fact that he didn't have an aeroplane wouldn't be a problem: he would simply subcontract the work to the brothers. They had sent him away with a flea in his ear, regarding him as more pathetic than contemptible.

But Herring was still determined to compete with the Wrights for the army contract. He had set up an aeronautical workshop in downtown New York where he claimed to be building an aeroplane that would outperform the *Flyer*. The secret machine was extravagantly promoted by a friend, Carl Dienstbach, a musician who doubled as an aviation writer. Dienstbach described it in aviation magazines as a serious competitor, equal if not superior to the *Flyer*. They would meet in competition 'in the most remarkable rivalry America has ever witnessed'.[1]

Early in February 1908, the US Army Signal Corps accepted both bids and invited the rivals to bring their aeroplanes to Washington for demonstration before the end of August. To earn the full purchase price, the inventors had to fly at an average speed of 40 miles an hour throughout the test. For each mile per hour less than forty, $2500 would be deducted, but for each mile above the minimum there would be a $2500 bonus.

As the Wrights began to prepare a machine for railing to the capital, Herring's publicity agent coolly announced that his aeroplane, for which he was claiming the automatic stability the *Flyer* deliberately lacked, would have no need of shipping – Herring would fly it to the Washington army aerodrome from New York.

Scarcely had the Wrights begun to plan for the demonstration than there came the promise of more sales. In March 1908 their dispiriting French negotiations suddenly took a hopeful new turn. In Paris Hart Berg had found a fresh backer. Lazare Weiller, yet another wealthy Parisian, had a finger in many lucrative pies, including the city's electricity supply and its fast-growing motor taxi business; he agreed to head a new syndicate to be called La Compagnie Générale de Navigation Aérienne. He was immediately joined by the rich Deutsch de la Meurthe whom the angry Letelliers had cut out of the earlier venture. The latest French Wright company would purchase the brothers' French patents and the right to manufacture, sell and license their aircraft in France. It would be the country's sole supplier for both military and civil use.

What was in all this for Wilbur and Orville? After demonstrating the *Flyer* in France – required by the backers before the end of October – they would receive Fr500,000 ($100,000) on delivery of the first machine. Additionally they would get Fr20,000 ($4000) each for four more aeroplanes, as well as 50 per cent of the founders' shares in the company. Added to the $25,000 a successful US Army test would bring them, 1908 promised to bring the dawn of true reward.

Chanute was delighted by the two sales in quick succession. He had never stopped pressing them to reveal the aeroplane to the world and let it sell itself before someone else overtook them, but Wilbur had continued to insist they were still five years ahead of their French rivals who were now beginning to stay uncertainly in the air for minutes rather than seconds.

The competition, however, was advancing faster than they were prepared to recognise. Threats to their supremacy were rising on all sides. Early in 1908 one sprang from a new source, this time on their own doorstep in America. It came from a group of ambitious young inventors calling themselves the Aerial Experiment Association. The telephone inventor, Alexander Graham Bell, now a household name across the world, was the chairman. The group's initial $20,000 capital had been provided by his remarkable, profoundly deaf wife, Mabel, who took an active interest in his ceaseless scientific experimenting, playing a lively role at their meetings with her uncanny lip-reading ability. Rather as Chanute had done in the days of his Indiana dunes gliding trials twelve years before, Bell gathered around him a number of dedicated experimenters to try to solve the problems of powered flight independently of the Wrights. The association had begun its experiments at the Bells' remote summer estate, Beinn Breagh, on Cape Breton Island in Nova Scotia, where the inventor had built a huge rambling home resembling a French château.

It became the headquarters of this elite, well-funded group. They were paid salaries, worked in Bell's laboratory and held formal meetings at which everybody voted and minutes were taken. It was all a great deal more elegant than those other historic conclaves round the smoking stove at Kill Devil. In the evenings, Mabel would go to the piano and the hugely bearded Bell would burst into rousing song. 'It had been a band of comrades on a great adventure – for all they knew shaping man's future by their nightly discussion in

Bell's tobacco-fogged study. It had been a circle of good friends, happily relaxing with fencing and billiards, songs and stories, or tea with Mrs Bell before the great fireplace after a hard day's contest with wind and water.'[2]

Here, in this comfortable habitat, in late 1907, the group had begun to build a series of powered biplanes which the following winter they had taken south to Hammondsport on Lake Keuka in New York state. Among the sixty-year-old Bell's disciples was a young West Point artillery graduate, Lieutenant Thomas Selfridge, who had developed a passion for aeronautics and whom Bell had successfully persuaded his friend President Roosevelt to have the army second to him for the experiments. Selfridge had at first participated at Bell's insistence in flight trials of an enormous kite packed with thousands of tetrahedral cells and looking like a giant wedge of honeycomb. Towed behind a steamer, the artillery officer piloting this weird looking device had been lucky not to be drowned when it splashed into the sea.

Selfridge had been grateful to move on to more conventional flying machines and begin work at Hammondsport on an aeroplane he named *Red Wing*. It was a pusher biplane with, like the Wright *Flyer*, a canard elevator out front and a rear rudder. The pilot sat upright. In an attempt at lateral stability, Selfridge introduced spectacular dihedral, trussing the upper and lower wings so close together that they seemed nearly to touch. Unlike the *Flyer*, the *Red Wing* had no positive roll control, something that did not seem initially to have bothered Selfridge. However, while testing his ideas on a glider, he had written early in 1908 to the Wrights seeking advice on, among other things, the behaviour of the centre of lifting pressure on wing surfaces. Wilbur, not believing that any organisation headed by one as respected as Graham Bell would seek the information other than for research, and unaware that his group was resolutely embarked on a programme of designing powered aeroplanes to rival their own, generously answered the questions. He even – perhaps needlessly – referred Selfridge to their own sacred patent, which was now, unfortunately, a publicly accessible document.

Selfridge tracked down the Wrights' patent, which laid bare the sensitive secret of the means by which they turned so gracefully and safely, using wing warping in unison with the rudder. But he didn't attempt to copy the system, relying instead on the upward and downward swept wings for lateral stability and the rudder for skidding into unbanked turns. Early in March 1908, *Red Wing*, mounted on runners, was publicly flown off the frozen Lake Keuka by another of 'Bell's Boys', Casey Baldwin. The aeroplane made a successful take-off and flew for 100 yards before the tail buckled and it slammed back on to the ice. Five days later Baldwin tried again, but, lacking adequate roll control, it was tipped sideways by the wind and again crashed.

Bell had not witnessed the flights, but when he heard what had happened he wrote to Baldwin suggesting he solve the lateral control problem by fitting to the outer tips of the upper wing hinged flaps that could be moved in opposite directions to each other – in short: ailerons. Bell told him to try operating this roll device with a shoulder attachment. By moving his body from side to side he would raise or lower the opposing flaps to lift a dipping wing. Baldwin, who subsequently claimed to have hit upon the idea independently, incorporated it into his next aeroplane, *White Wing*. As well as ailerons, it was given a tricycle undercarriage.

Ailerons had made *White Wing* a controllable aeroplane. It was flown off the ground near Hammondsport by several members of the aerial association – most successfully by a young engineer called Glenn Curtiss whom Bell had appointed his 'director of experiments'. Curtiss flew the aeroplane nearly 340 yards. He and his colleagues, who always invited reporters to their demonstrations, had suddenly become serious American rivals to the secretive Wrights, whose machine was still so hush-hush that not even genuine buyers were allowed to set eyes on it.

Wilbur and Orville knew Glenn Curtiss. They shared a common background – Curtiss, too, had moved into aviation from cycling. A shy, reticent and rather dour man who found release in machinery and speed, he had opened a bicycle shop in Hammondsport which had expanded into a chain of stores. He had then started assembling and racing motorcycles, on one of which he had recently, at 130 miles an hour, created an American speed record. His motorbikes sold so well he'd set up a factory, soon numbering among his custmers the owners of airships looking for small power plants.

Keen to enlarge the trade, he had started approaching aeroplane builders, quickly singling out the Wrights for direct marketing. Back in May 1906 he had taken the liberty of writing to offer them a 'light and powerful motor' for the *Flyer*. He'd tried to come to Dayton to meet them – but they hadn't been interested. They were working on a new engine of their own and didn't want anyone else's. A persistent salesman, Curtiss had followed up the letter with a phone call, trying again to make an appointment. Again they had refused. However, several months later Curtiss had come to Dayton to work on one of his motors which was driving an airship on display at a local fairground. The brothers had gone out to look at the gasbag, operated by a travelling showman, 'Captain' Tom Baldwin, had met Curtiss and invited him and Baldwin back to their workshop.

In the light of subsequent unhappy events, it was an important meeting, much examined by historians for the crucial information the Wrights may or may not have disclosed to the engine-maker. They could not have known that his aviation ambitions would soon soar far beyond the production of motors.

It appears that Wilbur and Orville, who had helped Baldwin recover his airship when it drifted away, were exceedingly friendly to the visitors, showing, according to Baldwin, 'the frankness of schoolboys in it all and a rare confidence in us'. The confidence even extended to the unusual trust of showing Curtiss and Baldwin photographs of the *Flyer* confidently cruising above Huffman Prairie during its historic 1905 flights. The subject that apparently most interested the visitors had been propellers. Neither Curtiss nor Tom Baldwin had yet become involved with aeroplanes, but propeller efficiency was important in dirigible propulsion. The brothers apparently gave them some tips, for Curtiss later wrote to thank them for advice which had helped Baldwin remould his propeller blades into more effective shapes.

It had been over a year later, in the autumn of 1907, that Glenn Curtiss, now commissioned by Graham Bell to build a motor for his giant honeycomb wing contraption, had accepted an invitation to join the elderly patriarch and his team at their Nova Scotia base. For the first time he found himself working on fixed-wing aeroplanes, and in May 1908, to his delight, invited to fly the aileron-controlled *White Wing* across frozen Lake Keuka.

Wilbur and Orville were not immediately aware that a rival flying machine using the roll-controlling ailerons they believed to be their exclusive – and now patented – invention was making news up in New York state. They were busy preparing for the demonstrations to which they were now committed for the US Army in Washington and for their new company in France: a hopefully glorious simultaneous public debut of the *Flyer* on both sides of the Atlantic.

As neither brother had piloted the aeroplane now for two and a half years, they needed urgently to polish up their rusty flying skills – and master a radical new control system, flying no longer stretched out uncomfortably on their bellies, straining their necks to look ahead, but sitting upright.

Still obsessed with the need for concealment from prying competitors, they feared that flights at Huffman Prairie, now that people could arrive from near and far by motor car, would be too risky. Instead they decided to return to the isolation of the Outer Banks. In the first week of April 1908, Wilbur set off to recce their old camp at Kill Devil Hills. A depressing scene greeted him there. The two wooden buildings had been ravaged by gales, advancing sand and vandals. Only the roofless, half-collapsed original living quarters were still standing. The hangar was 'down and torn to pieces'. The water pump had disappeared. He stumbled on the skeleton of one of their 1902 glider wings protruding from a nearby sand hummock, its fabric stripped by local boys. In the hangar rubble lay the disintegrated remains of the two ill-starred Chanute machines. The melancholy of it all wasn't helped when Wilbur promptly developed acute diarrhoea.

The Bankers welcomed him back warmly. He was now a celebrated local hero, and the Kill Devil lifesavers found room for him at their station house while a big new 48- by 22-foot shed was erected by local carpenters. A second mechanic, Charles Furnas, whom they'd hired in Dayton, presently arrived, followed by Orville bringing the modified 1905 *Flyer*, which they landed at the Kill Devil jetty.

By the last week of April the three were installed, and, amid spring gales, rain and flying sand, had begun to assemble the aeroplane. With its skid undercarriage it looked almost identical to its 1905 incarnation – with the exception of the two safety-belt-less seats now clamped on to the lower wing to the left of the engine and two control levers. The pilot sat on the left with the passenger between him and the now more powerful 30 to 40 horsepower engine which gave the machine more than twice its original power. Ignition now came from spark plugs fired by a magneto controlled by a foot pedal. This, as there was still no throttle, was the only way of regulating the motor. The front elevator lever was at the pilot's left, the wing warping and vertical rear rudder controls, combined into a second single lever, between the seats. As they were back at sea level with brisk winds, they planned to launch, as in 1903, along the rail without the aid of the weight-dropping catapult.

On 6 May Wilbur made the first of twenty-two refamiliarisation flights. It was a short and rather ragged hop, as, sitting upright for the first time, he struggled to keep the aeroplane straight and level with the unfamiliar actions of the vertical steering levers, which at first were dangerously difficult to coordinate. The wings still extended horizontally without dihedral, the upward angling that would have given the machine more inherent stability. They were still convinced that successful flight must remain, no matter how exhausting, under the continuous control of the pilot.

In a series of swooping switchbacks, Wilbur managed to stay up for 22 seconds, flying just over 300 yards. Two days later they made eleven flights between them, on one of which Wilbur was airborne for nearly a minute. Once again the Kill Devil lifesavers helped them with the back-breaking work of lugging the heavy aeroplane to and fro across the soft sand – sometimes now taxiing it on a trolley with the propellers turning. Later in the week Orville did over three minutes in a complete circle. Then they each took Charles Furnas for a ride, Wilbur making him, for less than half a minute in the air, the first passenger in aeroplane history.

If they had thought that by retreating once more to the North Carolina coastal wilderness they would escape the attention of the newspapers, they were wrong. Their forthcoming US Army trials and the formation of their French company had been widely reported. Whether they liked it or not, they were now international news. There was no longer any hiding place. The moment they flew, the coastguard wires were buzzing.

On 2 May, even while they had still been assembling the machine, the Norfolk *Virginian-Pilot*, now edited by the promoted Keville Glennan, whose regard for the facts had, if anything, diminished with time, ran a startling front-page story declaring that they were back on the Outer Banks and had already made a ten-mile flight out over the Atlantic – 'the life-savers at Nags Head watched the peculiar shaped thing sail away in the distance until it resembled only a black speck on the horizon . . .'[3] The Wrights, who had yet to learn of the story, had been mystified to receive a cable from London from the globally pervasive Pat Alexander congratulating them on their remarkable ocean flight; it had made headlines in England.

When the unstoppable story reached the *New York Herald*, it was compelled to take notice. Like his colleague at the *Daily Mail* in London who was being bullied by Lord Northcliffe to treat aviation seriously, the *Herald*'s editor was also said to live in daily fear of his equally aeronautically enthusiastic proprietor, the legendary James Gordon Bennett. He therefore lost no time in despatching a reporter to investigate. A Norfolk freelance, D. Bruce Salley, was instructed to get the next boat to Manteo on Roanoke Island and sail across Albemarle Sound to the Outer Banks to see what was going on.

When Salley got there, he was disappointed to learn, after wading ashore and tramping for more than a mile through deep soft sand to their camp, that the story was false; the Wrights had not yet flown. Dismayed to see a reporter so soon, they greeted him coolly, making it clear they hoped he wouldn't be staying long. As the aeroplane appeared to be far from ready for flight, Salley, determining to be more secretive next time, had gone back to Manteo, deciding to give the Wrights a miss next day.

But that afternoon he'd been chastened to get a phone call at his hotel from a lifesaver telling him the *Flyer* had already been airborne. Dismayed that he'd failed the New York paper, he set out to try to save the situation. From information over the phone from the lifesavers, spiced with a bit of sensational fiction with which American newsmen routinely flavoured their stories at that time, he telegraphed a story to the *Herald*. The only fact he got right was the 1000 feet distance. He decided to put both the brothers on board together, reporting that they were about to make a fantastic flight of 150 miles along the coast.

When, two days later, Wilbur and Orville had made nine short flights, Salley was back at Kill Devil, this time observing from a hiding place in nearby woods. The first newspaperman to see the Wrights fly, he was so overcome by the spectacle that he finally broke cover and rushed across to their camp. His latest story to the *New York Herald* went to newspapers across America, deciding other editors to rush their own staff reporters to Kill Devil. Salley was soon joined at Manteo's Tranquil House hotel by a small contingent of the country's most able senior newsmen, including, to Salley's chagrin, the *Herald*'s own star reporter, the formidable Byron Newton. Fearful of Northcliffe's rage should they not have their own man on the spot, the London *Daily Mail* sent its chief American correspondent, P. H. McGowan. From *Colliers* magazine came both a writer and a photographer.

Led to his hide in the Kill Devil woods by Salley, the group set out daily at 4 o'clock in the predawn dark to make the uncomfortable journey across the sound in a small boat, and, as Newton was extravagantly to write, 'through noisome swamps and jungle, the thousands of moccasins, rattlers and blacksnakes, the blinding swarms of mosquitoes . . . determined to ambush the wily inventors and observe their performance from a hiding place'.[4] They got blisters on their feet and were soaked by heavy rain. As they approached the flying camp they would run, singly, crouching like advancing infantry, from one clump of trees to the next in the hope they wouldn't be spotted. Photographs of this historic little press corps, who were constantly bitten to distraction by ticks and mosquitoes, show them in collars and bow ties, sitting on the sand under the trees with their lunch basket.

The Wrights soon discovered they were there, but there was nothing they could do about it. With two crucial demonstrations looming they couldn't afford to cease operations. For the first time since they'd launched the *Flyer* nearly four and a half years earlier, they were forced to fly in full view of the media they had hitherto gone to such extraordinary lengths to avoid.

Byron Newton filed an awed account of the first flight he witnessed:

> On sped the great white craft straight toward one of the high sand dunes. Then to our bewildering amazement we saw the wings on one side warping slightly, saw the operator pulling at the levers and the craft heeled over slightly, turning in a graceful curve and came straight toward where we were hiding . . .
>
> No wonder we were paralyzed and dumb with the wonder of it all. It was something that few mortals had believed to be within the scope of possibility . . . There was something weird, almost uncanny, about the whole thing. Here on this lonely beach was being performed the greatest act of the ages, but there were no spectators and no applause save the booming of the surf and the startled cries of the sea birds.[5]

Although now overshadowed by the seasoned Byron Newton, Salley continued to file his own stories. As fast as he wired them, his reports were sensationalised by rewrite men across the country. Yet there were still newspapers that refused to believe the stories. The *Cleveland Leader* sent Salley a curt telegram telling him to 'cut out the wild stuff'; it refused to pay the collect charges. Even Byron Newton had difficulty with editors. When he tried to sell a longer version of his account to a magazine, it rejected it, saying, 'It does not seem to qualify either as fact or fiction.'

The *Colliers* photographer, Jimmy Hare, had less success than his reporter mates: his wide-angle lens had difficulty resolving the distant object circling the dunes. Nonetheless, his pictures remain historic – the first ever published of a Wright aeroplane actually flying.[6] They show the *Flyer* as a minute fuzzy shape cruising low over the sandy wastes.

The spate of dramatic flight reports from the Outer Banks was short-lived. On the afternoon of 14 May, Wilbur took off, making the longest journey so far, staying up for 7½ minutes and going 5 miles, 'sailing along serenely,' as one reporter romantically described it, 'like a thing endowed with life. Behind her floated a flock of gulls and crows that seemed at once amazed and jealous of this new thing of the air.'[7] The flight ended in disaster. In a moment of confusion with the new elevator control column, Wilbur moved it the wrong way, pushing it forward instead of back. With a tail wind boosting his speed to well over 50 miles an hour, he dived into the ground.

Through his binoculars Orville saw the plane appear to explode in a shower of sand as the tail rose vertically into the air. For an agonising thirty seconds until Wilbur appeared he feared his brother had been killed. But it was another miracle of survival. Unsecured, and with no head protection (something that today seems unthinkable given the whole project's utter dependence on their continued health and mobility), Wilbur had been flung forward into the crumpled top wing. Though badly shaken and probably concussed, he'd escaped again with only cuts and bruises.

The news team rushed out a flurry of lurid reports which next morning were spread across America's front pages. At Hawthorn Street, Milton and Katharine read to their consternation that the *Flyer* had been smashed into 'smithereens'. In the absence of a reassuring telegram they worried themselves into a stew for two days while the telephone rang incessantly and reporters hammered on their door for interviews. When at last a belated wire did come, Katharine was so relieved she sat down to write Wilbur a distressed letter reprimanding him for causing them so much worry. 'It wears me out for I am good-for-nothing this morning now that the suspense is over. And Daddy was so anxious waiting so impatiently for a telegram. You must think of that and spend a few dollars to keep us from this nerve-wracking uncertainty.'[8]

Down at Kill Devil the brothers had more than a wrecked flying machine on their minds. For several weeks a stream of agitated telegrams from Berg and Flint had been arriving. Even before it had been born, the new French syndicate was apparently in danger of self-destructing. To sort things out one of the brothers was needed in Paris urgently. What had gone wrong now?

The principal backers for the new French company, the taxi millionaire Lazare Weiller and the rich Deutsch de la Meurthe, were getting cold feet; they were talking of pulling out. The reason was painfully simple. The French experimenters, as Chanute had feared, were with quite alarming success starting to catch up. Henri Farman's much acclaimed leaps of around 1½ minutes and the faltering efforts of Santos-Dumont had now been appreciably eclipsed by the flights of a new aviator, Léon Delagrange, a prominent Parisian sculptor whose works were often exhibited at the Paris Salon. In a biplane built for him by Gabriel Voisin, he had the previous month flown 2½ miles. He had remained airborne under control for 6½ minutes – nearly as long as Wilbur's best most recent effort at Kill Devil. Delagrange's performance could hardly be dismissed by the Wrights as a mere hop. Their supremacy was under threat much sooner than they had thought possible.

Berg insisted that only one thing could now avert the collapse of the syndicate: an urgent public demonstration in France of the mythical *Flyer*. There was no time to lose. The brothers agreed that Wilbur should go. To catch the next ship, leaving from New York in a few days, he would have to rush straight from Kill Devil to Paris and fly the machine that was still sitting in its crate at Le Havre. The panicking Flints convinced them that, if they wanted to save their company, there wasn't even time to go home first to Dayton. Wilbur wired Katharine to pack his bags and send them to New York before his ship sailed on 21 May.

24

Triumph at Le Mans

(1908)

With the bishop fussing over her, Katharine rushed about the house gathering up the clothes she thought Wilbur would want for his new French mission. 'I hope I sent everything you needed,' she wrote to New York to tell him. 'It will be a great scrape if I put in the wrong dress coat . . . I could not find the key for your hat box but I am enclosing in this letter your trunk key. Besides your suits I sent shirts, socks, including your silk ones, your patent leather shoes, collars and cuffs, a very few handkerchiefs, mostly Orv's, some underwear and your beloved bath-robe. I did my best to get everything that old Jullam would want.'[1]

She even packed some pieces of equipment, including sprocket wheels and tyre cement, which Charlie Taylor had insisted he might need. Taylor was irritating her again. He 'says he has no work', she told Wilbur. 'Please give me some idea what to tell him to do. My opinion is that he has plenty but is shirking. Write something pretty sharp and I will read it to him.'[2]

Alas, the lovingly packed things did not include Wilbur's bowler and straw hats. 'I wish,' he wrote from New York, 'that you had raised the lid of my hatbox, which was not locked, and put some of my hats in it before sending it on. However, a man can buy hats almost anywhere.' Wilbur went on to confide elder-brotherly concern for Orville, whom they had agreed would go from Kill Devil to Washington to inspect the field at the Fort Myer military base from which they would have to operate the *Flyer*; he would then come on to France to get some more flying practice for the army demonstration. 'If at any time Orville is not well, or is dissatisfied with the situation at Washington, especially the grounds, I wish you would tell me. He may not tell me such things always.' The letter ended: 'Good-bye to Sterchens for a few months. PS: See other side for postscripts #1, #2, #3 &,&.'[3] The other side was blank.

Wilbur hadn't yet received a letter from Katherine in which she explained that they couldn't find his sacred bowler and she 'didn't know where to put your straw hat. I tried to get it in . . . I took it out of the hat box at the last minute because the lid wouldn't go down.'[4] Hoping the letter would reach him before he sailed, Katharine quoted a newspaper report of an interview in Paris with the now famous Delagrange, who was planning a much longer flight than his last. The French aviator had some discouraging things to say about the Wrights' latest syndicate, whose backers were faltering. 'Delagrange is very patronising – so is Farman,' Katharine said. 'Show 'em a few things, Jullam.'[5]

When Wilbur arrived in Paris in the last week of May, he was dismayed to learn from Hart Berg that the resurgence of French aviation success that was gripping France had all but killed their new syndicate, which Berg had led them to believe would be financed by wealthy men. The venture was distinctly '"looking upward,"' he reported to Orville, 'in other words, flat on its back.' Their backers, Weiller and Deutsch de la Meurthe, aware of the recent substantial flights of Farman and Delagrange, had got cold feet. Furthermore, disbelief in the existence of the Wrights' aeroplane was still widespread. Soon after his arrival, the big-circulation weekly *L'Illustration* published one of the fuzzy photographs of the *Flyer* airborne at Kill Devil. The image had been heavily retouched to help it resemble an aeroplane at all. 'Its appearance is quite dubious,' said the magazine; it was an obvious 'fabrication'.

Wilbur found France in such a public fervour of patriotic pride in the triumphs of its own emerging aviation heroes that he wondered how a foreign aeroplane could now get a foot in the door.

Farman and Delagrange, he told Orville, 'will probably make fifty kilometres before I am ready for the demonstrations . . .'[6]

If he had ever truly believed that their discoveries were so complex it would take rivals five years to catch up, Wilbur certainly didn't any longer; but he was never prepared to concede that their obsessional fears had lost them years of commercial advantage, sacrificed great wealth, and retarded the evolution of the flying machine. Despite the fact that challengers on both sides of the Atlantic were now treading on their heels, he remained convinced that their own machine's unique superiority of control, and their exclusive aerodynamic research data on ideal wing shapes, would still win the day. Philosophically he told Orville: 'The first thing is to get some practice and make some demonstrations. Let the future be what it may.' It did not look immediately bright.

Three weeks after he wrote that, Delagrange, in Milan in the last week of June, flew for 18½ minutes, going 9 miles. To the Paris newspapers it was a world record. How could the Wrights hope to compete with this on French soil?

As others, despite their less perfect machines, began to catch up, Wilbur grew more and more concerned that rivals' aileron devices were breaching their patents. In New York he had seen a report of the flights of the Aerial Experiment Association's *White Wing* which, he had promptly written to Orville, 'intimates that Selfridge is infringing our patent on wing twisting'. Wilbur had suggested they now urgently put their mark publicly on their invention as a warning to infringers that they intended to defend it:

> It is important to get the main features originated by us identified in the public mind with our machines before they are described in connection with some other machine. A statement of our original features ought to be published and not left covered up in the patent office. I strongly advise that you get a stenographer and dictate an article and have Kate assist in getting it in shape if you are too busy.[7]

In New York Wilbur had gone to meet the editors of the widely read *Century* magazine. He'd promised them a world exclusive article about the entire process of the evolution of their aeroplane, but as he was about to sail he had casually lumbered Orville with the assignment. Orville didn't enjoy writing – though he always did so effectively, often with wit and humour – but he wrote the article which stands to this day as one of the best subjective records of their failures and triumphs since they'd first dabbled in aeronautics. It was published under their joint names.[8] He also took the precaution of sending a full account of the latest Kill Devil flights to several aviation magazines. The publicity drive had not the least effect on what they saw as outright piracy by their European and American competitors, who were increasingly being compelled to use wing devices to make their machines roll. Aeroplanes had to bank and there weren't really a lot of ways of doing it. The Wrights had twisted the wing tips; others had more effectively begun to use hinged flaps – various forms of the ailerons that were to be universally adopted.

It was, of course, an inevitable development – but it didn't deter the brothers from now pursuing every aviator anywhere in the world whom they perceived to be stealing their system. When Orville had read to his shock that the Experimental Association was offering its machines for public sale at $5000 each, he wrote to Wilbur: 'They have got good cheek!' It was just the beginning. When later that summer Glenn Curtiss had flown yet another of his group's aileron-equipped aeroplanes, the *June Bug*, it had won at Hammondsport a *Scientific American* trophy for a flight of 1 kilometre. To Orville's consternation it had then gone on, amid much publicity, to make flights of more than 2 miles and to demonstrate complete figures of eight in the air. This, Orville decided, demanded some action. He wrote to Curtiss: 'I learn that your *June Bug* has movable surfaces at the tips of the wings, adjustable to different angles on the right and left sides for maintaining the lateral balance.' When, he said, they had referred Curtiss's colleague, Lieutenant Selfridge, to their American patent, they had not intended 'to give permission to use the patented features of our machine for exhibitions in a commercial way'. Those features, the very core of their brainchild, were the combination of rudder and wing warping that was central to their aeroplane's success.

'We believe,' Orville told Curtiss, 'it will be very difficult to develop a successful machine without the use of some of the features covered in this patent.' He invited Curtiss to 'take up the matter of a license to operate under our patents'.[9] It was the first shot the Wrights were to fire in patent battles that would continue, heartbreakingly, for nearly ten years.

As reports of fresh successful flights by rivals began to make news almost by the month, they knew they were now in a race against time: Orville in Dayton rushing to get a machine ready for the crucial US Army acceptance trial at Fort Myer; Wilbur in Paris trying to salvage the collapsing syndicate by showing the French at long long last what the *Flyer* could do. By July it was clear that Orville would have no time before the Washington trial to go to France to share the flying there with Wilbur. For these critical events, upon which the whole commercial future of their invention now depended, each for the first time was on his own without the power of brotherhood.

Separation, as each began to acquire fame in his own right, spawned a brisk correspondence between them that tried to keep the threads of their interdependence intact. Had the fax machine or email existed they would have been sharing their news, thoughts and problems daily, but in the summer of 1908, impatient waits for replies to each other's sea-mail letters quickly put new strains upon their celebrated rapport. The previous year Orville had been frantic with despair at his brother's seemingly wilful refusal to keep him informed of the French government negotiations. Now the boot was on the other foot.

'I am a little surprised that I have no letter from you yet,' Wilbur wrote to Orville with unusual tartness in the first week of June. 'The fact that the newspapers say nothing of a visit to Washington leads me to fear you did not stop there in returning home. It is a great mistake to leave a personal inspection of the grounds go till the last minute.'[10] Wilbur had added a catalogue of peremptory demands for things he wanted Orville to send him at once, from the precise records of their recent Kill Devil flights and data on the performance of their latest engine to patent information and copies of a host of letters in their files.

In fact Orville had been to Washington and cast a critical eye over the Fort Myer flying field. Although intended for airships and balloons and not as big as Huffman Prairie, it was smoother and just big enough for the *Flyer*. He was at that very moment writing a long letter about it. But while his report was creeping across the ocean, Wilbur's impatience snapped. 'I have no word from Orville since leaving Kitty Hawk,' he wrote bitingly to Katharine. 'Does he not intend to be partners any more? It is ridiculous to leave me without information of his doings and intentions.'[11]

The truth was that Orville had simply been too busy to write with the speed Wilbur expected. Back in Dayton, where a heatwave had prostrated everybody, he had been swamped with work created by their rising celebrity. He couldn't keep up with their mail which had increased 'tenfold', or with a plague of demands from companies trying to sell them equipment and new gadgets. He had been at it day and night preparing all the articles Wilbur had demanded – and about which there kept arriving from France streams of instructions: 'I hope you bring out the fundamental difference between our methods and those of Chanute'; 'call attention to the fact we have obtained very broad patents'. Every day, it seemed, a fresh directive would arrive. Orville was so pressurised he was having difficulty finding the time even to visit the workshop to oversee Taylor's work preparing the *Flyer* for Washington, on top of which a ceaseless flow of reporters and well-wishers kept coming to the door. The family was also in distress for quite separate reasons: Lorin had just been run over on his bicycle and painfully injured by a drunken motorist, and his fifteen-year-old son, Milton, had gone down with typhoid; he lay in a high fever.

Overwrought by these events, and wilting in 34°C of heat, Katharine, incensed by Wilbur's never-ending strictures, had leapt to Orville's defence. 'It isn't much fun to get Jullam's letters when they are all complaints from one end to the other,' she responded.

> Sister takes a look and if it doesn't look encouraging – back goes the letter into the envelope. I'm too tired to be worried with such stuff. It may be hard for you over there but you must remember

> that Orv has a terrible load on him and you both ought to be more considerate.
>
> Right in the midst of everything, he had to stop to get the Century article off and the weather was blazing too. Now he has the Washington machine to get ready for packing . . . Orv looks perfectly terrible – so pale and tired all the time. I wouldn't fuss at him all the time. You have your troubles too but I can't see any sense in so much complaining at him.[12]

Trying to calm the troubled waters, Milton wrote an affectionate letter to Wilbur reminding him of the current load on Orville and repeating again his concern that Wilbur was so distant from his reach to bring a Christian influence to bear upon his grievances. 'I do not like to have you so far from us all, with your cares and experiments.'[13] Earlier he had been moved to pledge his special affection for him: 'I do not forget the valiant and victorious struggle you had with embezzlement and its apologists. Nor do I forget your care of your Mother.'[14]

If Wilbur was placated, all changed when he opened the crates that had been stored at Le Havre. He was shocked to find the *Flyer* in a damaged mess. Automatically blaming his brother and Taylor, he sent Orville one of the most scathing letters he was ever to write him:

> I opened the boxes yesterday and have been puzzled ever since to know how you could have wasted two whole days packing them. I am sure that with a scoop shovel I could have put things in within two or three minutes and made fully as good a job of it. I never saw such evidences of idiocy in my life. Did you tell Charley not to separate anything lest it should get lonesome? Ten or a dozen ribs were broken and as they are scattered here and there through the surfaces it takes almost as much time to tear down and rebuild as if we could have begun at the beginning . . . Never again pack anything else in the surface [wings] box.[15]

Wilbur proceeded to itemise the damage in fine detail:

> The cloth is torn in almost numberless places . . . The radiators are smashed; the seat is broken up; the magneto has the oil cap broken off, the coils badly torn up . . . The only thing I ever saw resembling the interior of the boxes is the rattler at a foundry. Please bear in mind hereafter that everything must be packed in such a way that the box can be dropped from a height of five feet ten times, once on each side and the other times on the corners.

The letter left Orville in no doubt that he had set back the public displays of the aeroplane by weeks. Yet it hadn't been his fault. He and Taylor had packed the aeroplane with their usual meticulous care; every component had been firmly secured before shipping. The blame lay with the French customs officials at Le Havre. In their zealous inspection of the first flying machine ever to come their way they had unpacked everything but failed to resecure it all.

Wilbur had more setbacks. Bariquand and Marre, the company they had commissioned to build some duplicate engines for use in France, were slow to deliver. When he went along to their Paris works to check on progress, he was appalled. 'Nothing was ready,' he complained in his diary. 'I fear they will have the old American motor ruined before I can get it out of their hands. They are such idiots! and fool with things that should be left alone. I get very angry every time I go down there.'[16]

The horrifying discovery of the damaged *Flyer* was made at a car factory at Le Mans, 125 miles south-west of Paris, where Wilbur had acquired facilities to assemble the machine. It wasn't far from the Hunaudières race course from which he planned to fly as soon as he'd repaired and assembled the mutilated aeroplane. In Paris, where Berg had wanted to dump Weiller from the whole venture, Wilbur had firmly taken control of the business. He had vetoed dropping the taxi magnate, so convinced was he that he would be only too quick to join the venture once he'd seen the *Flyer* in the air. Gingering up the now defeatist Berg, he had briskly set about searching for a flying field, meeting many French aviators in the process. He lunched with Henri Farman, whom he warmed to, and was offered by Louis Blériot the use of his shed at Issy-les-Moulineaux; but he felt that Issy, which had seen some recent spectacular French flights, was too close to the city, too public for his liking. When Berg had taken him down to Le Mans to meet the car factory's owner, Léon Bollée, he knew at once he'd found the right place.

Bollée, 'a jolly rotund man with a saucy little beard', who had as little English as Wilbur had French, was an enthusiastic aeronaut. He was president of the local aéro-club and flew his own spherical balloon. Wilbur took to him instantly; he and the Bollée family became fast friends. The car manufacturer generously offered him, not only a wing of his plant in which to assemble the *Flyer*, but also the help of his staff. What's more, the place was a long way from the prying eyes of Paris and the crowds now drawn to the flying fields. Le Mans was 'an old-fashioned town,' Wilbur wrote with delight, 'almost as much out of the world as Kitty Hawk.'

It took him seven weeks to repair and assemble the aeroplane. Still simmering over the damage, his mood was not helped by his almost total lack of French. The few simple words he attempted were invariably misunderstood. For some reason he resisted the smallest effort to acquire even the rudiments of the language in an environment where little English was spoken. Léon Bollée effectively had none. Nor did anyone at the Le Mans hotel where he initially stayed. Between Wilbur and the mechanic, Bertrand, who had been assigned to him and who had a useless smattering, there was constant impasse and misunderstanding. 'I have to do practically all the work myself as it is almost impossible to explain what I want in words to men who only one-fourth understand English,' he grumbled to Orville.

Notwithstanding the language barrier, Wilbur, labouring day after day at the car plant, was the subject of wide admiration. He was known as 'Veelbure Reet'. In pronunciation it sounded like *vieille burette* – old oilcan. It became his nickname. His routine endeared him to the French workers, who had expected the inventor of a flying machine to be more aloof and self-important. They were amazed when this man donned workman's clothes and mucked in with them:

> He worked away at his apparatus from 6 a.m. till nightfall. He would come in with the staff, and when the factory whistle

> sounded he would immediately drop whatever he had in his hand, take off his overalls, and go out to dinner with the men.[17]

In the first week of July Wilbur turned his attention to the motor. It was the original, which the French company had been trying to copy. Running the engine up to test its revolutions, he was standing directly in front of it with shirt sleeves rolled up when a radiator hose flew off, spurting a jet of boiling water on to his body and severely scalding him. Bollée, who happened to be there, caught him as he staggered backward and lowered him gently to the floor before rushing off to get some picric acid with which to treat the burns, which raised enormous blisters on his arm and body. He is said stoically to have insisted on walking the mile back to his hotel where a doctor came to dress the burns with oil-soaked cotton. Unable to bend his left arm, which had a blister a foot long, he couldn't work properly for a week – during which, in a highly strung-up state, he vented his pain and disappointment once more on Orville (from whom he had not yet heard the explanation for the packing fiasco):

> I would really save time by getting into bed and staying there till entirely well, as nothing is done down at the shop except irritate my arm and nerves. If you had permitted me to have any anticipation of the state in which you had shipped things over, it would have saved three weeks' time probably. I would have made preparations to build a machine instead of trying to get along with no assistance and no tools. If you had any conscience it ought to be pretty sore . . .[18]

Long before he received this unpleasantly sarcastic note, Orville had read of the accident. The story had gone round the world and got dramatic headlines in Dayton. 'We just had about sixteen different kinds of fits,' Katharine wrote. Milton, also anxious for his welfare, sent an affectionately blunt lecture on his worth to mankind:

> Aside from the value of your life to yourself and to ourselves, you owe it to the world that you should avoid all unnecessary personal

> risks. Your death, or even becoming a cripple . . . would seriously affect the progress of aeronautical science, and a record of its advancement . . . You have much that no-one else can do so well. And alone, Orville would be crippled and burdened. Soon others can do the flying, but you have a field for truth and science that no-one can fill.[19]

Katharine thrived on crisis. There was not only the injured Lorin to fuss over but his desperately ill son's temperature began to soar. As it hit 104°F and they rightly feared for his life, she swept into the house and took over his medical care. She had no faith in Lorin's family doctor, who wrongly diagnosed malaria, nor in Netta's treatment of her ailing son. She had a row with her sister-in-law and called in the bishop's long-serving GP, Dr Spitler, to whose treatment her nephew slowly began to respond.

Katharine now alternated the latest in the never-ending stream of her acute anxieties with worry about her brothers. Not only did she want Orville to be in France as Wilbur's support system, she wished Wilbur could help keep Orville safe in Washington. 'I do hate to have Orv to have to make these government demonstrations alone. May be you are coming,' she enquired somewhat pointlessly of Wilbur. 'We all miss Jullam so much . . . Grandpa is anxious about you all the time. You are the "apple of his eye" all right. Everybody wants Jullam home again.'[20]

It would be a long time before he went. Overburdened with his lonely responsibility, and disheartened by the setback of his accident, Wilbur seems at this point to have carefully cast around for every apparent failure of Orville's he could now seize upon for rebuke. He had asked him urgently to ship across a part. The request had gone through Flints, from whom Orville had gathered there was 'no rush'.

'I cannot conceive how you get such an idea,' Wilbur pounced, 'when I have been writing time and again to forward goods as fast as they are finished.' Then he proceeded to admonish Orville for a yet further failure: 'You have never sent me a copy of your letters to British War Dept. I ought to see them . . . you seem never to notice requests or instructions.'

They had earlier agreed that Orville would make yet another overture to the War Office – a perhaps surprising move given that they were both already overstretched trying to fulfil their French and US Army commitments. Nonetheless, as Wilbur had set off for Kill Devil, Orville had written to make their third approach to the British. He had renewed their offer of a scouting machine, now much improved in design, payload and power since their last offer. The War Office had been invited to buy it – or to build it themselves under licence.

Orville's letter had passed into the ponderous systems of the British Army whose own flying machines were now nearing completion. To buy some time, it had sent the Wrights, at Colonel Capper's suggestion, lengthy finicky specifications the colonel had now painstakingly drawn up for a military aeroplane. Orville had been aghast to read them. The machine must now operate at an impossible 5000 feet, stay up for two hours and, something the *Flyer* didn't routinely do, 'rise from the ground under its own power without special starting devices'. These were impossibly unreasonable stipulations, calculated to keep the Wrights at arm's length indefinitely. What Orville may not have known was that a cold wind of change had begun to chill the War Office's attitude to aeroplanes. A new Chief of the General Staff, an undistinguished soldier but brilliant administrator, General Sir William Nicholson, had arrived. Nicholson was a powerful, querulous and pedantic figure who had spent much of his army career in India; known to his enemies as 'Old Nick', he was fundamentally opposed to aviation in any form: he didn't want flying machines, airships or even balloons anywhere near the British Army. He believed 'that an observer in an aeroplane or airship would be either too high, or moving at too great a speed, to observe accurately, or to perform any other valid military function. No argument could change his mind . . . He did not readily tolerate opposition to his ideas, theories or opinions.'[21]

While Orville was packing his aeroplane for Washington, he probably hadn't yet seen a statement – issued by the British War Office under Nicholson's influence – to reassure the public that aeroplanes foreseeably posed no threat to Britain. If the country were to be attacked from the air, high-angle gunfire 'with high explosive shells' would quickly knock any invaders out of the sky.

The harsh new British specifications may have reflected Nicholson's lack of interest in air power, or Capper's unremitting determination to thwart the *Flyer*'s sale to the British Army to protect his own unpromising machines. Whatever it was, Orville was now too busy to be drawn into futile correspondence over conditions neither they, nor anyone else anywhere in the world, could yet meet. Wilbur, despite his curt demands to see the letters, appears not to have pursued the matter. By the end of July his burns were nearly healed and he had become too involved with more urgent things to hound his brother any further.

In the first week of August, the French *Flyer*, assembled at last, was ready to fly. It was towed by one of Bollée's cars, under cover of darkness to avoid newsmen, on a carriage five miles to the Hunaudières racecourse where a wooden hangar had been erected. Into this basic Kill Devil-type shed – this one didn't even have a floor – Wilbur now moved. He didn't want the machine out of his sight and had decided to sleep beside it. The hut soon became a replica of its Outer Banks predecessors, its shelves neatly stacked with an array of food supplied with the compliments of a local cannery. Unlike the Kill Devil headquarters, the new one even had 'an outdoor privy erected a discreet distance away'. There was a small restaurant down the road for his evening meal, and to supply water and milk a nearby farmhouse where 'a little boy about five or six years old talks English and German. At least he replies very politely "Oui Monsieur" when I say "Parlez vous Anglais" . . . and he looks like a truthful little chap.'[22]

Not far from the flying shed there now gathered every day an intimidating posse of reporters and photographers. The French newspapers had continued to treat the Wrights' claims with scepticism, and intense interest surrounded Wilbur's preparations for the flight that would put the *Flyer* through its paces before a cynical public for the first time. Had they come to witness the launch of a manned moon ship there could not have been greater excitement as, day after day, people gathered in the racecourse's small grandstand to await the event. A photograph, looking like a scene in an Impressionist's painting, shows a group of elegantly dressed people, the women in huge decorated hats anchored with flowing silk scarves, the men in their Sunday best and panamas with downturned brims, waiting expectantly on the tiered benches. Some had come down from Paris by train, bringing lunch baskets and bottles of wine. However, rain forced the flight's postponement for several days.

Wilbur refused to be rushed. 'For four long days he kept us all on the tiptoe of expectation, going about everything in a deliberate and indolent manner that was maddening to men who had left their beds at four o'clock in the morning lest he should take it into his head to make the first flight at dawn,' wrote the London *Daily Mail* reporter Joseph Brandreth.[23] Brandreth was lucky to have been accepted into the press corps. A predecessor from his newspaper had so displeased Wilbur he had been replaced: 'The *Daily Mail* had a little scamp here, but we saw the manager and had him called off.'[24]

Brandreth was to write some piercingly critical things about Wilbur:

> We voted him 'mule-headed', 'eccentric', 'unnecessarily surly' in his manner towards us, for it was impossible to discover from such a Sphinx what he intended to do or when he intended to do it.
>
> 'I did not ask you to come here,' he said. 'I shall go out when I'm ready. No, I shall not try and mislead you newspaper men, but if you are not here I shall not wait for you.'
>
> When, however, exasperation became acute, the genial Mr Hart O. Berg, who is responsible for Mr Wright's visit to Europe, would come out of the shed and tell us some amusing story about his principal that would put us in a good humour again.[25]

Berg was in fact on tenterhooks, concealing with his abiding charm the tension that gripped him as the public promoter of this unproven machine. He knew the Wrights had recently flown again at Kill Devil, but he had never seen it with his own eyes. He had suffered months of ridicule and abuse in France for his inability to produce proof of their claims, and the pressure had only grown as more and more Frenchmen began to make impressive flights for all to see. If Wilbur, who hadn't flown for weeks, were accidentally to mishandle the controls again and crash before this doubting crowd of journalists and aviators, he knew it would be hard to recover his reputation.

Léon Bollée had much less to lose. He had become Wilbur's local press officer and sang his praises, describing him as 'a marvel of inventive genius' and his machine as 'the most perfect instrument of flight known up to the present time'. Bollée happily discoursed on Wilbur's austere existence and his neurotic distrust of anyone else to lay a finger on his aeroplane. 'He will not allow anybody to touch his machine or handle so much as a piece of wire. He even refuses to allow mechanics to pour oil into his reservoir. In his opinion they don't do it the correct way.'[26]

Brandreth saw for himself this strange American's spartan living arrangements.

> In a corner of the shed was his 'room.' This consisted of a low packing case from which the top has been removed. Resting on the edges of the case was a narrow trundle bed. Nailed to the side of the shed was a piece of looking-glass and close by a camp washstand. This together with a cabin trunk, a small petrol cooking stove – he cooks his own breakfast – and a camp stool, comprised the whole furniture. He takes his baths from a hose-pipe attached to a wall sixty feet away. He sleeps practically under the wings of his aeroplane. And early in the day he starts to work, whistling the while . . .'[27]

When Brandreth finally managed to persuade Berg to arrange an interview, Wilbur reluctantly stopped what he was doing on the *Flyer* and emerged.

> There was something strange about the tall, gaunt figure. The face was remarkable, the head suggested that of a bird, and the features, dominated by a long prominent nose that heightened the bird-like effect, were long and bony. A weird half-smile played about the clean-shaven chin and puckered lips, and the skin was deeply tanned with wind and sun. Behind the greyish blue depths of his eyes there seemed to shine something of the light of the

> sun . . . From the first few moments of my conversation with him I judged Wilbur Wright to be a fanatic – a fanatic of flight, and I had no longer any doubt that he had accomplished all he claimed to have done. He seemed born to fly.[28]

It was not until Saturday 8 August, when the skies cleared, that Wilbur at last announced he would fly. All through that day the crowd and newsmen waited patiently while Wilbur unhurriedly worked on the aeroplane inside the shed. All that was to be seen was the launching rail and its four-legged wooden pylon. Some famous aviation figures had come down from Paris, among them the Wright brothers' most outspoken critics, the cynical patron of French aviation, Ernest Archdeacon, and a number of other prominent experimenters, including Louis Blériot, who had flown in a monoplane for 8½ minutes just a few weeks before.

Early in the afternoon the crowd of less than a hundred people stirred as the shed doors were opened and the *Flyer* was drawn out into the sunshine. Hart Berg, immaculate in his bowler and formal striped trousers, appeared before the grandstand with a loudspeaker. He harangued the restless spectators, warning them that taking photographs of the aeroplane would not be allowed – 'except from a distance' (Wilbur had sold exclusive rights to *Century* magazine). The machine was moved out to the starting rail and connected to the launching weights already hoisted to the top of the tower.

Wilbur still refused to be hurried. Seemingly oblivious of the crowd, he wandered between shed and machine, fussing over it and making small adjustments. It was not until half past six that evening, when the wind had died to calm, that he prepared at last to fly. Dressed in his standard grey suit and high starched collar, he turned his peaked cap backwards and climbed on to the left-hand seat. As he did so, Archdeacon, up in the stand, was loudly pointing out to anyone who would listen the design features of the *Flyer* that would prevent it from performing as well as its French rivals. He was still discoursing when the propellers were swung and Wilbur tripped the heavy metal weights.

Its wings steadied by Berg's chauffeur, Fleury, the aeroplane leapt forward; within seconds it was climbing into the sky. With only fifteen minutes' piloting experience with the new controls, Wilbur was still far from proficient – the inherently unstable machine threatened to dive into the ground with the slightest misjudgement. Never before had so much been at stake as Wilbur fought successfully to keep it under control, desperate to avoid moving one of the levers the wrong way.

As he cruised away, heading straight for some tall poplars, it seemed to those on the ground that he could not possibly avoid them, but at the last moment they were astonished to see him execute a magnificent steeply banked turn. The watching aviators had never seen a machine do this before. Murmurs of applause rippled through the stand as the aeroplane made two perfectly banked circuits of the small racecourse before gliding down on its skids to a safe landing just fifty feet from the starting rail. 'In the excited babel of voices one or two phrases could be heard again and again. "*Cet homme a conquis l'air.*" "*Il n'est pas bluffeur!*"' The flight had lasted less than two minutes; but it had changed the face of European aviation.

The French pilots in the crowd had never witnessed such impeccable flight control. They were stunned. Their own wobbling excursions, crabbing clumsily through wide flat turns, were crude by comparison. Here was astounding superiority. The crowd burst into generous applause as they poured out of the stand on to the ground to surround Wilbur. To his embarrassment, people seized him, kissing him on both cheeks. A new aviator, Paul Zens, whose biplane had flown into a haystack the previous week, exclaimed: 'Mr Wright has us all in his hands.' Another, René Gasnier, told reporters, 'It is a revelation . . . we are as children compared with the Wrights.'[29]

Archdeacon wasn't quite able to bring himself to eat his words, commenting stubbornly to the *New York Herald* man: 'We can do as well with our machines in France.' They were superior because they had wheels and didn't need the help of rails. But Louis Blériot, more competent to recognise the technical achievement, couldn't contain himself. 'It is marvellous,' he said. 'A new era in mechanical flight has commenced.'

The French press agreed. Next morning Wilbur's flight was lauded across the country. The bicycle-maker was not a charlatan. He had become a national hero. Life for the Wright Brothers would never be the same again.

25

The Trumpet Blasts of Fame (1908)

Wilbur's Hunaudières flight on 8 August 1908 lasted only 1 minute and 45 seconds, yet it marked a triumphant turning of the tide. On that memorable day, European aviation had been revolutionised in one dramatic leap. The sheer, undeniable perfection of the flight was enough to convince the entire doubting world at last that the small-town American brothers had truly conquered the air. Their French critics were astounded. They had never before seen a machine with the seemingly effortless manoeuvrability of a bird.

Ecstatically Berg had pleaded with Wilbur to fly again next day, but it was the sabbath. The aeroplane would not leave the shed until Monday. Then a much bigger crowd was waiting. Only a few score had come on Saturday; thousands now flocked to the racecourse as Wilbur, nervously gaining skill with the new controls, went on that week to make longer and longer flights. He flew at Hunaudières eight more times, building his graceful circuits, now with perfect figures of eight, to flights of more than 8 minutes in which he circled seven times to roars of cheering. Even when he once fumbled the controls and bounced into the ground, people just cheered when he climbed out.

It was dazzling success – yet, absurdly, it did not soften his relentless objection to photographs of the aeroplane. After his second flight, watched by 2000 people who overflowed the grandstand and spilled along the racetrack, his eagle eye spotted a French Army captain pointing a camera at the *Flyer* as it was being towed past the stand. In an instant Wilbur leapt over the fence and confronted the man. He demanded the plates be handed over or the images exposed in front of him. The captain, shocked by this unexpected aggression, refused. It looked as though an ugly scene was developing as people quickly gathered round, awestruck and astonished by the flying hero's unseemly loss of control. As Wilbur folded his arms and waited threateningly, they wondered if they were about to witness a fight, but finally the embarrassed officer yielded. Reluctantly he opened the camera, removed the offending plate and handed it to Wilbur.

The incident seems in no way to have tarnished his golden image as word of his flights swept from France across the world. In the space of a few days he had become an international hero of towering fame. In Fleet Street editors quickly realised that something of tremendous significance was occurring in France, and weren't slow to respond. THE MOST WONDERFUL FLYING MACHINE THAT HAS EVER BEEN MADE the *Daily Mirror* proclaimed. *The Times* said the Hunaudières flights proved that the Wrights 'have long mastered the art of artificial flight' and awarded them 'the first place in the history of the flying machine'.[1] 'Mr Wilbur Wright is the hero of the hour', the *Daily Telegraph* said. 'Anyone who has seen M. Delagrange, Mr Farman, M. Santos-Dumont, M. Blériot, and others practise with their machines will at once see the immense superiority of the Wright method.'[2]

At the *Daily Mail,* Lord Northcliffe, who had spurned Lady Taylour's attempts to promote the invention, swiftly made amends. His paper was instructed to reflect his enthusiasm. 'The scoffer and the sceptic are confounded,' it said. 'A bird could not have shown a more complete mastery of flight.' So thrilled was Northcliffe, and so anxious now to jump on the bandwagon, that he wrote to Wilbur with a pressing invitation to enter his London to Manchester challenge flight. He even offered him, at his home in Kent, 'an absolutely private practice ground in my own park'. Their aeroplane had elevated itself to world status. It already had the Aeronautical

Society's prominent Major Baden-Powell pronouncing grandly 'that Wilbur Wright is in possession of a power which controls the fate of nations is beyond dispute'.

Octave Chanute's congratulations were more muted. He was still smouldering with disapproval at the way the Wrights had needlessly withheld the machine from the world. Only a few weeks earlier, in a German aviation magazine, he had accused them of wasting two fruitless years, refusing demonstration, and demanding 'an absurdly high price'.[3] When at last Chanute wrote to Wilbur at Le Mans, all he could bring himself to say was: 'I have been much gratified in reading from day to day of your successes and triumphs in France, and it is pleasant to learn that frank admiration has succeeded distrust.'[4]

Overnight the French newspapers had abandoned their scepticism, their taunts that the American bicycle makers were hoaxers and bluffers, and joined the tidal wave of euphoric praise. *Le Figaro*'s reporter exclaimed: 'I've seen him; I've seen them! Yes I have today seen Wilbur Wright and his great white bird, the beautiful mechanical bird . . . there is no doubt! Wilbur and Orville Wright have well and truly flown.'[5]

The French aviation community generously joined in the acclamation. *L'Aérophile*, the powerful voice of the aeronautical establishment, was moved to utter: 'Not one of the former detractors of the Wrights dare question today the previous experiments of the men who were truly the first to fly.'[6] The outspoken, chauvinistic chairman of the Aéro-Club, Ernest Archdeacon, who had sat in the stand at Hunaudières rubbishing the *Flyer* and had for so long used his wealth to foster France's own aviation development, made an almost embarrassing turnaround: 'For a long time, for too long a time, the Wright Brothers have been accused in Europe of bluff . . . They are today hallowed in France and I feel an intense pleasure in counting myself among the first to make amends for that flagrant injustice.'[7] Even France's own hero of the hour, Léon Delagrange, who had flown for nearly 20 minutes, joined the chorus of admiration. He had gone to Le Mans to see the *Flyer* in the air. 'It is marvellous,' he said as he watched with incredulity one of Wilbur's perfect figures of eight, adding, famously: 'We are beaten.'

'The newspapers and the French aviators nearly went wild with excitement,' Wilbur wrote elatedly to Orville. 'Blériot and Delagrange were so excited they could scarcely speak . . . You would have almost died of laughter if you could have seen them.'[8] He explained that he had still not fully mastered the new control system. He urged Orville in Washington: 'Be awfully careful in beginning practice and go slowly.'

The control problems were hardly surprising. Today's pilots, accustomed to operating the rudder with a foot bar pressed in the direction of the turn required, would be aghast at the very thought of the unnatural action of doing this by moving a lever backwards and forwards to roll into a bank. Again and again Wilbur found that whenever he moved his left hand (controlling the elevator) forward to dive gently to increase speed, some instinctive reflex made him do the same with the other hand. This put the machine into a dangerously sharp turn 'which consumes power awfully fast' and before he could rectify things he would stall and start sliding into the ground. 'I am about,' he told Orville, 'to discard all fore-and-aft movement of the right hand as dangerous.'

In America, Wilbur's Le Mans flights had hit the front pages everywhere. In Dayton he was a local celebrity. Katharine, sending him news that young Milton was at last out of danger, said she hoped the fame wouldn't go to her brother's head. 'The Dayton papers are proposing a "welcome home". But that can be headed off – there is no surer way to make oneself odious!'[9]

Wilbur's bald head and long, unhappy-looking face were now familiar to all Americans, thanks to the news pictures from Le Mans. They led Katharine to pounce on his sloppy appearance:

> We just laughed and laughed over the bouquets and things which the ladies are sending Jullam . . . I think myself that you look pretty tough, going around with that vest on and no coat. Couldn't you wear a decent looking shirtwaist? It makes me kind of sick to see so horribly many pictures in that outfit. I always did despise that way of dressing anyway. Other people either wear coats or have regular shirt-waists and wear nothing over them. I can't half enjoy the pictures on account of that.'[10]

Katharine Wright, her skirt decorously hobbled with a cord, prepares for a flight with Wilbur at Pau in southern France in February 1909 – watched by Orville at left. *Special Collections and Archives, Wright State University*

A joking Mrs Hart O. Berg brings a rare smile to Wilbur's lips in this 1909 picture taken at Pau. Katharine (*at right*), who disliked Mrs Berg, looks on disapprovingly. The others, from left: Louis Blériot, pupil pilots Paul Tissandier and Captain Paul Lucas-Girardville. Count Charles de Lambert stands between Katharine and Mrs Berg. *Special Collections and Archives, Wright State University*

Katharine Wright, at the age of twenty-four, on her graduation from Oberlin College. *Special Collections and Archives, Wright State University*

Wilbur in characteristic pose in Hart O. Berg's apartment at Le Mans, 1909. *Special Collections and Archives, Wright State University*

The crash at Fort Myer in September 1908. The *Flyer*'s wings are being raised to release the badly injured Orville from the wreck. His passenger, Lieutenant Selfridge, lies dying among the spectators on the right. *Special Collections and Archives, Wright State University*

Wilbur and Orville on the rear porch at 7 Hawthorn Street, at the peak of their fame, in June 1909. *Special Collections and Archives, Wright State University*

Orville with walking stick, still recovering from his crash injuries, with the Wrights' European sales agent, Hart O. Berg, in Paris in January 1909. *Special Collections and Archives, Wright State University*

Enthusiastic Germans spontaneously wave their hats as Orville flies overhead, demonstrating the miracle of flight to Berliners in the summer of 1909. *Special Collections and Archives, Wright State University*

Brothers in step. Orville (*left*) and Wilbur in a picture that symbolised their unique togetherness. They were at a 1910 air-race event at Belmont Park, New York. *Special Collections and Archives, Wright State University*

Orville chats in Berlin to German Crown Prince Friedrich Wilhelm, whom he later took for a flight. Hart O. Berg is on the right. *Special Collections and Archives, Wright State University*

Concealed in the woods near the Wrights' Kill Devil Hills camp in the spring of 1908, newsmen, devoured by ticks and mosquitoes, secretly watch and photograph the *Flyer*. The brothers were brushing up their flying skills, not having flown for two and a half years. *Special Collections and Archives, Wright State University*

Augustus Herring, the rival experimenter and confidence trickster, who tried to steal the Wrights' invention. *Special Collections and Archives, Wright State University*

Glenn Curtiss, a commercially more successful aircraft manufacturer than the Wrights who relentlessly pursued him through the courts, alleging illegal use of their patented flying control system. *Special Collections and Archives, Wright State University*

Griffith Brewer (*left*), the first Englishman to be given a flight by the Wrights, about to take off with Wilbur at Auvours in France in October 1908. *Royal Aeronautical Society*

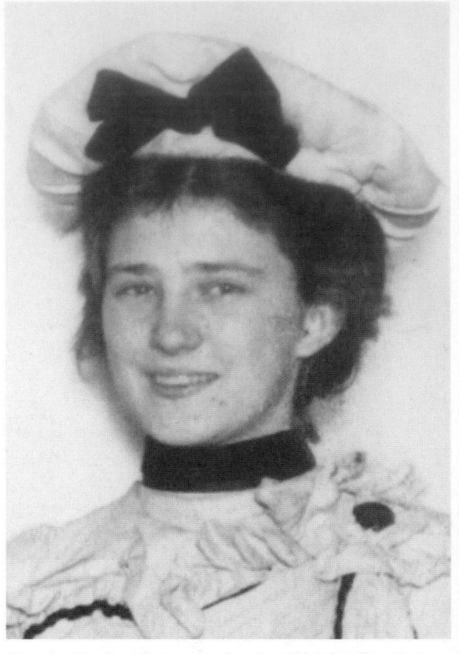

Carrie Kayler Grumbach, the Wright family's devoted housekeeper. Hired by Bishop Wright when she was fourteen, she remained for nearly fifty years. *Special Collections and Archives, Wright State University*

Hawthorn Hill, the stately Dayton mansion into which Orville, Katharine and Milton Wright moved in 1914, two years after Wilbur's death. *Special Collections and Archives, Wright State University*

The dishonestly strengthened and modified Langley aeroplane that had originally failed to take off, flies off Lake Keuka, New York State, in 1914, sparking a long and bitter feud between Orville and the Smithsonian Institution. *NASM, Smithsonian Institution (SI 2003-20560)*

Below: Mabel Beck, Orville's intimidating, long-serving secretary and gatekeeper, inherited from Wilbur. *Kettering-Moraine Museum, Ohio*

Bishop Wright in his eighty-seventh year with Orville and Katharine in 1915. *Library of Congress*

Katharine Wright in her early fifties, around 1925, when she became secretly engaged but was afraid to tell Orville. *Special Collections and Archives, Wright State University*

Henry J. Haskell, the Kansas City newspaperman with whom Katharine was to enjoy only two years of married life. *Haskell family collection*

Orville, at seventy-six, with the wind-tunnel device he and Wilbur used to measure the lifting power of miniature wings – in this case the eliptical-shaped one clipped to the top bar. *Library of Congress*

She had also read, to her concern, that he 'had been treating the French ladies scandalously and would not even put on your coat when they talked to you. Of course, we know that it is all rank nonsense but it reminded me to tell you to be sure to be extra nice to everyone you can and not to give them any excuse for offence.'[11]

Wilbur replied with customary glee. An artist had just done a portrait of him, 'trying to catch that enigmatic smile which the papers talk so much about – but I feel you will raise an awful fuss when you see it. It is worse than shirt sleeves! . . . It was rather cold and to shut out the wind during the flight I slipped on a blue jumper and overhaul jacket. It left about two inches of my coat sticking out at the bottom.' He had also been photographed yet again in garb that he knew would upset Katharine.

Accompanied by their wives, Lazare Weiller and Deutsch de la Meurthe, both of whom had predictably leapt to back the floundering syndicate – de la Meurthe had telegraphed Wilbur within hours seeking 100,000 francs' worth of stock – had come down to Hunaudières. A news photographer had 'slipped up and snapped us. Mrs Weiller laughed heartily when I told her how you objected to shirt-sleeve pictures and how pleased you would be to see that I had on two coats. She is a jolly woman and very intelligent.'[12]

As more and more good-looking French women began to appear in the photographs of Wilbur seen with the rich and famous, Katharine's curiosity was aroused. She wondered if, unaccompanied by Orville and far from their father's influence, her brother, in his forty-second year, might, in the heady atmosphere of fame, be tempted for the first time to take some interest in womankind. She demanded fewer reports about the minutiae of his flying operations and more about his social life in France – 'all about the fun. Suppose you tell me about a few things when you write! What do I care about the position of the trees on the practice ground? Hey! Hey! Sterchens wants to hear all about the beautiful young ladies and the flowers and champagne!'[13]

But Wilbur refused the invitation; there was nothing to tell. His letters spoke only of chaste admiration for some of the elegant wives who had entered his world. 'Mrs Berg is raking Berg over the coals in great shape and demanding whether he prefers Wright to herself.

Mrs Berg is a very smart woman and has an excellent command of language. There are times when Berg reminds me a little of our patent medicine faker who used to come sometimes. However Mrs Berg has many redeeming qualities and is really a charming woman, like yourself (I put my head under the table when I wrote this – instinct I suppose).'[14]

A few of the French pioneers fought a rearguard action, continuing to insist that their machines were the equal of the Wrights', conceding them only 'momentary' superiority. Gabriel Voisin said in *Le Matin* that if French aviators had derived a little helpful information from the *Flyer*, the Wrights had 'also profited from French genius in large measure'.[15] Archdeacon reminded people that the French aeroplanes took off on wheels without the need for crude catapulting devices, and Blériot was quoted as hopefully doubting, on reflection, that the *Flyer* could make the 50-kilometre flights required by their French syndicate contract. 'But such criticism,' said Wright Brothers historian Tom Crouch, 'was scarcely noticed outside limited aeronautical circles. After years of relative obscurity the Wrights were swept along on a wave of popular acclaim that drowned out any dissent.'[16]

For Wilbur the adulation had just begun. The Hunaudières racecourse had been surrounded by trees and buildings. In the middle of August he was invited by the French Army to move to a much larger, unobstructed field at a nearby artillery testing ground called Camp d'Auvours. Moving the *Flyer* and its shed, again by road to avoid risking the seven-mile flight over open country, he was soon startling France again. By the middle of September his flights were confounding the most doubting of his critics as he began to approach 50 kilometres and 40 minutes. People came from England and from as far away as Russia to see the miracle of perfect flight.

'All question as to who originated the flying machine has disappeared,' he told Katharine. 'The furore has been so great as to be troublesome. I cannot even take a bath without having a hundred or two people peeking at me . . . we have even been set to music and everyone is singing a song "Il Vol" (he flies) of which I will send you a copy . . . You really can have no comprehension of the enthusiasm with which the flights have been greeted.'[17]

To Orville he said: 'The French have simply become wild. Instead of doubting that we could do anything they are ready to believe that we can do everything . . . People have flocked here from all over Europe.' Again he reminded Orville of the perils of flying the wickedly unstable aeroplane – warning, too, of the distractions of fame:

> I advise you most earnestly to stick to calms till you are sure of yourself. Don't go out even for all the officers of the government unless you would go equally if they were absent. Do not let yourself be forced into doing anything before you are ready . . . Do not let people talk to you all day and all night. It will wear you out before you are ready for real business. If necessary appoint some hour in the day time and refuse absolutely to receive visitors even for a minute at other times. Do not receive any one after 8 o'clock at night.[18]

Orville had arrived in Washington in the third week of August to join the two Charlies, Taylor and Furnas, who'd gone on ahead with the other aeroplane, and was preparing to fly it for the US Army. He hadn't been prepared for his own elevation to eminence: he was treated like royalty. Swooped upon by Chanute's old friend, the flight experimenter Albert Zahm, now a maths and physics professor and a prominent member of the Aero Club of America, he was plucked out of a comfortable, modest hotel and installed at the city's exclusive Cosmos Club, where the great Samuel Langley had once resided in splendour among judges and senators. Suddenly the painfully shy Orville, who couldn't utter even a one-sentence speech, found himself daily fêted and dined by the upper strata of the city's scientific and academic community. All too soon he was to appreciate the wisdom of Wilbur's advice. He wrote to Katharine:

> I haven't done a lick of work since I have been here. I have to give my time to answering the ten thousand fool questions people ask about the machine. There are a number of people standing about the whole day long . . . I find it more pleasant here at the club

> than I expected. The trouble here is that you can't find a minute to be alone . . . I have trouble in getting enough sleep.[19]

The Washington reporters followed Orville everywhere. They began to write about the 'society belles' who 'flock' around him. 'I don't know whether you have seen the Washington papers or not,' he wrote to Katharine, anxious she shouldn't get the wrong impression. 'I am meeting some very handsome young ladies!' But, he quickly added, 'I will have an awful time trying to think of their names if I meet them again.'[20]

Reading of his brother's popularity, Wilbur wrote to say, 'I see by the papers that the women & men are kissing you in genuine French fashion.' But, as with Wilbur, even the aphrodisiac of fame could not overpower Orville's incurable discomfort in the presence of unmarried women, with whom he would happily engage in jokey conversation – so long as they kept their distance.

The army base at Fort Myer, next to the Arlington National Cemetery on the west side of the Potomac, has long since been engulfed by the spreading metropolis of Washington, but in 1908 it was mostly surrounded by open country. The flying field was a small army parade ground. When Orville and his mechanics arrived, it was being used by the Signal Corps – hedging its bets – for the acceptance trials of another aerial vehicle, an airship for which Tom Baldwin was seeking a contract. In the air it was being steered by Baldwin and its engine nursed by its manufacturer, Glenn Curtiss, someone Orville now regarded with suspicion as a purloiner of their sacred patents. The distrust deepened when Baldwin confided in Orville a warning about Curtiss and his experimental colleagues. 'I hear them talking,' he said. The rival work they were doing at Hammondsport openly infringed the Wright patents; Curtiss had no qualms about helping himself to all their secrets.

Nor was Curtiss the only predator lying in wait at Fort Myer. To Orville's dismay, Lieutenant Selfridge, to whom the brothers now regretted so freely giving technical advice to help build a rival machine, was also there. The army had recalled Selfridge from Bell's experimental group to join the Fort Myer acceptance board that would decide the fate of the *Flyer*. With good reason, Orville regarded him as totally compromised by his own aviation ambitions. However, he was partly reassured when he heard the names of the other four members of the board. One, to his delight, was their old ally Lieutenant Frank Lahm, who had helped force the army to take the invention seriously. Another, Lieutenant Benjamin Foulois, as determined as Lahm to see the army create an air corps, he quickly warmed to. The three lieutenants had been selected to receive the contractual pilot training on both the airship and the *Flyer* – if it made the grade. The other two members of the board, not destined to fly, were a major and a captain.

With these five men lay the military fate of the Wright brothers' baby. But at these historic trials there was surely someone missing? Where, Orville enquired, was Augustus Herring, who had told America he would fly his rival offering to Fort Myer? There was not a sign of him or his much vaunted aeroplane – it was still in Herring's workshop in New York. The motor had been shaken to pieces during a test, injuring – or so he claimed – one of its inventor's fingers. The Signal Corps had granted him an extension to the middle of September. Army officers told Orville they would be surprised if the Herring machine ever turned up.

Orville had also been having problems with his engine. It was overheating, running rough and kept stopping. But the snags were ironed out and the *Flyer* began its formal trials. After some quick partial dismantling it was loaded on to a combat wagon and deemed adequately portable for army use – and ready for the proving flights. They were due to begin on 3 September.

It was a much more low-key event than Wilbur's debut at Hunaudières. The Washington newspapers took the view that it was unlikely to prove any more special than the 3-minute, 2-mile demonstration, at Hammondsport the previous week, of the experimental association's *June Bug*. Certainly no more amazing than the increasingly longer flights now regularly being made in Europe. Only a handful of reporters went out to Fort Myer to join a few hundred curious people who, like Orville, travelled there by streetcar from the city. Tediously, they were all kept hanging around most of the day before he decided it was calm enough to fly.

At around half past four in the afternoon the machine was taken from its temporary tent and placed on the launching rail:

> The motor refused to start; but after a second try it sputtered to life and the weights under the derrick thumped to the ground. With a popping of valves and clattering of propeller chains the *Flyer* left the starting rail, brushing the tops of the weeds on the parade ground before beginning its sharp rise.
>
> A collective gasp of astonishment was supplanted by a hearty burst of handclapping. When Orville reached the end of the field he turned east toward Arlington cemetery at an altitude of thirty-five feet . . . As he banked and passed over the road where most of the spectators were congregated, a few of them ducked. Most roared their approval.[21]

The cheering was short-lived. Starting a second circuit, Orville, struggling to master the disconcerting levers, moved one the wrong way. Suddenly he found himself heading, at a low level, straight for the aeroplane's tent. He was forced to make an abrupt landing. As the *Flyer* hit the ground in a swirl of dust, it damaged its skids and front elevator. He had been in the air, unamazingly, for just over a minute.

An unspectacular flight ending in anticlimax, it was not calculated to excite the newspapers. The Washington *Evening Star* buried its report – desperately headlined STAYS UP OVER A MINUTE – on page three. Curtiss had done much better than this at Hammondsport. In France, Delagrange, three days later, was to fly for half an hour. However, Orville soon began to master the tricky levers and get into his stride. He started making momentous flights. The crowds grew. Soon he was exceeding all of Wilbur's flight times, creating world records.

As word 'spread through the corridors of government buildings across the river . . . desktops were slammed down. Offices were shut up. Government officials, reporters, embassy personnel, and the merely curious, poured across the river by the thousands.'[22] The Secretary of War and the Navy Secretary were among those who rearranged their diaries and rushed over to watch. Charles Flint, filled with excitement, travelled down from New York. Chanute came from Chicago. Orbiting the parade ground, often, astoundingly, more than fifty times, successively breaking his own records, Orville was staying up for more than the magic hour. His exploits moved to the front pages; they joined Wilbur's as startling world news. Nearly five years after its first flight, Americans were seeing for the first time one of their country's greatest ever inventions.

'You ought to seen it! You ought to seen it! Great big sing!' Wilbur wrote rapturously to Katharine:

> I refer to the excitement roused by Orville's dandy flights . . . When I made my first over here the sudden change from unbelief to belief roused a furore of excitement I had not expected to see renewed, but the news from America seems to have been sufficient to repeat the stir. I have had almost as many congratulations on Orville's success as I had a month ago. I suppose Orville must be overwhelmed with them. Well, it was fine news all right and lifted a load off my mind.[23]

At Fort Myer people were losing count of Orville's incredible circuits. The secretary of the Aero Club of America, Augustus Post, who had dashed down from New York, made a mark on the back of an envelope every time the *Flyer* rumbled overhead. Charlie Taylor climbed on top of a shed with a pot of white paint. 'When fifty minutes had passed he painted a big 50 on the roof for Orville to see. Then a large 55. When Orville had been in the air for one hour Charlie raised both hands.'[24]

To satisfy the acceptance requirements, he began had to begin to fly army observers. He was hoping it wouldn't be Lieutenant Selfridge. Selfridge was due to go with Baldwin's airship to another base, and Orville prayed he would be gone before the passenger tests. 'I will be glad to have Selfridge out of the way,' he said to Wilbur. 'I don't trust him an inch. He is intensely interested in the subject and plans to meet me often at dinners etc where he can try to pump me . . . I understand that he does a good deal of knocking behind my back.'[25]

Wilbur was now at his new airfield at Auvours. He'd re-created his shed habitat; his bed, to the fascination of the French reporters, a heavy piece of canvas nailed to strips of wood, was now hauled up and stored under the roof during the day. His early flights at Auvours were not immediately as awesome or record-breaking as Orville's; Orville was now breaking records by the day. On 10 September he flew for 1 hour and 6 minutes, reaching the then staggering altitude for a flying machine of 200 feet. Wilbur didn't believe this when he read of it. He told Orville the report must surely be exaggerated. Two days later Orville rose to over 300 feet. And he repaid their debt to Frank Lahm by taking the jubilant lieutenant up for six circuits; then flew the acceptance board chief, Major Squier, for 9 minutes – a new record for two-man flight.

As Wilbur began to get his second wind at Auvours, his times also started to soar. On 16 September he flew for 39 minutes, travelling 48 kilometres, breaking all French records. Across the width of Europe he was the biggest show in town. The crowds at the airfield began to grow by the week as trains brought people down from Paris in thousands, and the Le Mans taxis did roaring business shuttling them to and from the airfield. Some enthusiasts came by bicycle from as far as sixty miles away. Top French Army officials arrived to watch, rubbing shoulders with military attachés from almost every part of Europe – commanded by their governments to report on the phenomenon that could change the whole balance of international power. So big had the throngs become that Berg had been forced to institute an entry ticket system.

The brothers had not expected anything quite like this. They had difficulty coming to terms with it as the price of fame. Its terrifying pressures began to create unimaginable strain; flying the potentially lethal aeroplane was demanding enough. The maelstrom of interest and adulation threatened to overwhelm them as each struggled to survive without the once vital complementary support of the other. But they only admitted their fears very privately, often in letters to Katharine. Wilbur had written:

> I have not done much for several weeks partly because of windy weather, partly because of accidents which have necessitated

> repairs, and partly because I have been so nervous and worried that I have not felt like doing much hustling. You can scarcely imagine what a strain it is on one to have no one you can depend on to understand what you say . . . It compels me to do almost everything myself and keeps me worried.[26]

To Milton Wilbur poured out his growing detestation of the clamour from which there was no escape, and the fatigue and stress threatening his health to the point where he actually wanted to run away from it all:

> The excitement and the worry, and above all the fatigue of an endless crowd of visitors from daylight till dark had brought me to such a point of nervous exhaustion that I did not feel myself really fit to get on the machine . . . I sometimes get so angry at the continual annoyance of having the crowd about that I feel like quitting the whole thing and going home. But when I think of the sacrifices some of them have made in the hope of seeing a flight I cannot help feeling sorry for them when I do not go out. If I can get through this season in such a way as to make a reasonable competence secure I am done with exhibitions & demonstrations forever. I can't stand it to have people continually watching me. It gets on my nerves.[27]

At Hawthorn Street, Milton, who was sending Wilbur an almost daily tally of Orville's stupendous flight times, sat at the small desk in his upstairs bedroom, torn between immense pride and nagging concern both for his sons' safety and for the risk of their moral corruption. 'They treat you in France,' he said to Wilbur, 'as if you were a resurrected Columbus; and the people gaze as if you had fallen down from Jupiter. Enjoy fame ere its decadence, for I have realized the emptiness of its trumpet blasts.' His letter concluded with the familiar mantra: 'I wish it were so you could be in the home circle . . . You are so alone, if not lonely.'[28]

But it was Orville's flights that were really stunning the world, Wilbur told his father. They are 'making more of a sensation than my first flight over here and I thought then people would go crazy they were so excited. Well, it will be a relief to me to have some of the responsibility removed from my mind. While I was operating alone there was the constant fear that if I attempted too much and met with a serious accident we would be almost utterly discredited before I could get the machine repaired with no materials and no workmen.'[29]

Wilbur's worst nightmare was about to happen. Early on the morning of 18 September a big crowd had gathered at Auvours to watch him make a bid for a rich French aviation prize – the Coupe Michelin. Funded by the great tyre manufacturer, it was to be awarded for the longest flight of 1908 and was worth a useful 20,000 francs ($4,000) – around ten years' salary for an American schoolteacher like Katharine.

Wilbur was out at the starting rail making his usual fastidious inspection of the *Flyer* when he was called back to the shed by Berg, who handed him a telegram just arrived from America. Wilbur read it with deep shock. Orville had crashed at Fort Myer; he was seriously injured. His passenger, Lieutenant Selfridge, was dead.

26

Disaster in Washington (1908)

The accident had happened with terrible speed. Tom Selfridge's airship assignment had been delayed; Orville was asked to take him up. The thought of having a determined competitor spying on him at close quarters in the air had not thrilled him, but he knew that Selfridge, as a member of the appraisal board, was entitled to a flight.

Their take-off, late on the afternoon of 17 September, had been sluggish, for Selfridge was a big man. Struggling under its unaccustomed load, the *Flyer*, instead of its usual clipping of the grass, dragged along the ground on its skids for more than thirty yards before lumbering away to the now standard round of cheering from the spectators. They went up to 100 feet and Orville flew three smooth circuits of the parade ground. He was beginning a fourth when there was a slight tapping behind him. A glance over his shoulder showed nothing was obviously wrong, but within seconds two loud thumps announced a structural failure.

The aircraft began to shake violently and slewed to the right. People on the ground saw a propeller blade come tumbling down. Thinking that one of the driving chains had snapped, Orville shut off the power and prepared to glide back, but immediately ahead was a gully filled with trees. Warping the wings, he had just managed to bank towards the parade ground when the levers ceased to control the machine and it pitched down into a near vertical dive. The petrified Selfridge turned to him and uttered a barely audible 'Oh! Oh!'

'The first fifty feet of that plunge,' Orville later recalled, 'seemed like half a minute . . . I can hardly believe it was over one second at most.' Around twenty-five feet from the ground something hopeful happened – the machine began to respond to the elevator; it started to come out of the dive. 'A few feet more and we would have landed safely.' It was too late. At high speed they slammed into the ground. The wings folded up, the motor tore loose and the skids collapsed. The appalled spectators saw the *Flyer* disappear with a loud thump into a boiling cloud of dust:

> A tense silence pervaded the parade ground. Nobody moved. Then everybody seemed to move at once and there was a wild dash onto the field. Three mounted cavalrymen galloped ahead, followed by half a dozen reporters and more soldiers on foot and on horseback. As the crowd closed in, a cavalry officer could be heard shouting, 'If they won't stand back, ride them down' . . . Gradually the clouds of dust stirred up by the crowd of men and horses settled, and the extent of the damage became visible . . . Orville and Selfridge were pinned beneath the upper wing, their faces buried in the dust.[1]

Both men were lifted from the wreckage and laid on the grass. Selfridge, a large bleeding gash on his head, was unconscious. Orville, with a cut above one eye and bloodied face, was conscious, moaning quietly. Charles Flint, who'd come down again from New York and witnessed the crash, rushed to the scene. A colleague with him (he wrote in his memoirs) 'noted for his powers of observation' had looked carefully at the hands of the two victims. '"Lieutenant Selfridge", he said, "will probably die – he does not move his fingers – but Orville does, and will probably survive."'[2]

Charlie Taylor had been among the first to reach the aeroplane. He had stooped over Orville, loosened his stiff collar and tie, and undone his shirt. As Orville was carried away on a stretcher Taylor is said to have leant against one of the upturned wings, 'buried his face in his arms and sobbed'. He said he was to have been the passenger that afternoon – that Orville had promised him the ride but Selfridge had pulled rank and claimed the seat.

Army doctors worked hard to save both men. Outside the base hospital a group of officers, foreign military attachés and reporters waited for news. Among them was George Spratt, who'd come from his Pennsylvania farm to watch the trials. The Signal Corps' Major Squier paced up and down, heard again and again to mutter distractedly, 'It's frightful! It's frightful!' Chanute was there, having come back to Washington to watch another flight. Shocked to see the *Flyer* career to earth, he was the first to attempt an explanation – a broken propeller. He was right. One blade in the nine-foot long right propeller – they were now six inches longer than the original ones – had split, causing it to vibrate and lose thrust; it had slipped out of line to clip one of the wire stays that braced the rear rudders. The rudders had twisted, rendering the machine uncontrollable. The rudders had been tilted so far out of the vertical that they'd begun to function as elevators, ceasing to turn the *Flyer* and sending it instead into a dive.

Around half past eight that evening an army doctor emerged with a bulletin. Lieutenant Selfridge's skull had been badly fractured; he had died without regaining consciousness – the world's first powered aircraft fatality. Orville had a broken left thigh, several fractured ribs, scalp wounds and an injured back. Although in deep shock, he was expected to survive. The small crowd listened to the news in stunned silence, presently broken only by the quiet weeping of one of Selfridge's fellow officers. Spratt slipped quietly away. He went off to send a perhaps too cheerful telegram to Bishop Wright to reassure him that Orville was 'NOT SERIOUSLY HURT NOW FULLY CONSCIOUS'.

At Auvours that morning Wilbur did not cry. For a long time after reading the cable he remained in the shed, speaking to no one, pacing around the *Flyer*, twisting a piece of wire in his hands. When at last he appeared, it was to announce he was cancelling all flights until further notice. He said he was going into Le Mans where further cables from Washington would reach him more promptly.

He climbed on to his bicycle and, said one of his biographers, 'set off alone, bent over the handlebars . . . along the country lanes under the pines and horse chestnuts, where any tears he had to shed could be shed in private'.[3]

News of the accident reached Milton in Indiana. He'd gone to a Brethren conference where he'd just had a report phoned to him of Wilbur's flight of nearly 40 minutes. Within twenty-four hours had come the news of Orville's crash. The message had been delayed until the doctors knew for certain he would live. Milton seems to have taken it extraordinarily philosophically, noting in his diary that night an almost casual reference at the end of a lot of conference minutiae. All he was moved to write was: 'Orville injured. Orville's disaster at 5.00; Selfridge death.' But he cancelled the rest of his church business in Indiana and set off home to Dayton.

Katharine had just got back from school when the telegram arrived. She phoned her principal, demanded immediate indefinite leave and began to pack her suitcase, determined to hurry to Orville's bedside on the night train. She would supervise her brother's nursing care.

On arrival in Washington next day, Katharine, met by Charles Flint and Lieutenant Lahm, was driven straight to the army hospital. With scarred face and left leg suspended from the ceiling in a cradle, Orville was in a delirium of pain. He'd had a bad day and she was only allowed a short stay. The two Charlies had earlier brought him some fragments of the broken propeller; he had feverishly tried to work out the fateful sequences of the disaster – but had been too ill to make sense of it.

He was to remain in hospital for nearly seven weeks. And Katharine, boarding nearby, stayed there throughout, keeping constant vigil at his bedside. Now thirty-four, she would never return to teaching.

'When I went in his chin quivered and the tears came to his eyes, but he soon braced up again,' she wrote to Lorin.

> The shock has weakened him very much, of course. The only other time that he showed any sign of breaking down was when he asked me if I knew that Lieut Selfridge was dead . . . I bathed

that part of his face that was exposed, and his chest and shoulders. That quieted him some.[4]

What neither of them knew, as Orville lay there in much pain, was that the army doctors had actually missed some of his injuries. Twelve years later, X-rays were to reveal a dislocated hip and three hip bone fractures.

Katharine told Lorin that Orville was enormously popular at Fort Myer. 'Both doctor and nurse are devoted to him. I found the room well filled with flowers and a great basket of lovely fruit sent by some newspaper man. They like Uncle Orv tremendously. Uncle Orv immediately asked about Whacks [Milton junior] and I told him that Whacko was doing fine.'[5]

People also made a fuss of Katharine. Chanute came to see her, dispensing his famous charm to ask if there was anything he could do, but Flint and his wife had already assumed responsibility for her comfort and welfare. She liked the Flints, despite finding their pretensions mildly preposterous. 'They are very kind hearted people, but make me laugh with their immense amount of blowing and affectation.'[6]

With her unique flair for criticism, Katharine soon found fault with the army nursing staff. 'The night nurse has never been satisfactory. He goes away and leaves brother by the hour. I do not understand such neglect but fortunately I am here and brother likes to have me take care of him anyway. I shall not leave him until he is out of this place . . . school can go and my salary too . . . little bubbo shall not be neglected as long as I am able to crawl around.'[7]

Not only did she physically nurse Orville through those dark days, reading to him, regularly sponging him and initially sitting there sleepless, a guardian angel through the entire night, she also became his secretary. Piles of telegrams, flowers, fruit and letters of sympathy had poured in from around the world. Week after week she sat at a desk in his room dutifully acknowledging every gesture – in between wiring progress bulletins to Wilbur, Lorin and Milton and dodging newsmen determined to photograph and interview the hero's devoted sister.

The rival contender for the army aeroplane contract had finally pitched up at Fort Myer. Augustus Herring arrived in a taxi with an assistant who was carrying two suitcases containing parts of a twin-engined flying machine. In the army's balloon shed he had assembled only the centre-section of what appeared to be a very small biplane. The mysterious aeroplane had been the subject of outright derision by the newspapers. When reporters had asked to be shown what was inside the cases, Herring had brusquely refused. 'I don't like publicity,' he said. His machine travelled 'at express train speed' and needed a bigger airfield than Fort Myer. 'I prefer to hold its preliminary flights in secret.'

'The Herring airship is packed in a suitcase,' reported the *New York Herald* next day. 'This is the safe way to use it.' *Harper's Weekly*, which took it more seriously, quoted its inventor's claim that it could carry from six to twelve men, needed no catapult to launch and 'was as safe and easy to use as a motor car'. Because the Wrights, following Orville's accident, had been given an extension, the Signal Corps decided, in fairness, to allow Herring one as well. The embryonic aeroplane, that was to have been flown to Washington from New York, left as it had arrived – in a taxi in a couple of suitcases. If Herring went to visit his injured rival in his hospital bed at Fort Myer there is no record.

Orville's crash sparked an outpouring of family correspondence. Now back in Dayton, still vigorous at seventy-nine, Milton sent Orville a lengthy homily, comforting him with the assurance that out of disaster would emerge triumph:

> I am afflicted with the pain you feel and sympathise with the disappointment which has postponed your final success in aeronautics. But we are all thankful that your life has been spared . . . We learn much by tribulation, and by adversity our hearts are made better.[8]

Milton had such faith in Orville's full recovery that, in a letter that week to Wilbur in France, he didn't mention his damaged son until the last page. The letter was much more concerned with his recent Brethren conference and the satisfying news that his *bête noire*, the Reverend Millard Keiter, who had fled to Tennessee, had been indicted there for a land deal fraud. When he got around to mentioning Orville, it was merely to say he was 'sad' that he'd been hurt. His greater concern was with Wilbur in his isolation from the family at this tragic time. 'The brighter day will come to you,' he said. 'We all sympathise with you in your isolation, trials and perplexities.'[9]

Wilbur, still refusing to fly at Auvours, brooded over the mechanical failure at Fort Myer, blaming himself for leaving his younger brother alone with the stressful responsibility of proving the *Flyer*'s perfection to its most important customer. He told Katharine:

> I cannot help thinking over and over again 'If I had been there it would not have happened'. The worry over leaving Orville alone to undertake those trials was one of the chief things in almost breaking me down a few weeks ago – and as soon as I heard reassuring news from America I was well again. A half dozen times I was on the point of telling Berg that I was going to America in spite of everything. It was not right to leave Orville to undertake such a task alone.[10]

It was not, Wilbur said, that he thought Orville was incompetent, but that he would be dangerously distracted when surrounded by thousands of people keeping him from proper rest:

> Here Berg helps to act as buffer and gives me some chance to be alone when I work. People think that I am foolish because I do not like the men to do the least important work on the machine. They say I crawl under the machine and over the machine when the men could do the thing well enough . . . Hired men pay no attention to anything but the particular thing they are told to do and are blind to everything else.[11]

Wilbur sent Katharine sympathy for all the distress their invention – and their nephew's illness – had brought her:

> I am awfully sorry that you have had to pass through so much trouble of a nerve-wracking character this summer. However I am

> sure that as soon as Orville is well on his way to recovery you will enjoy yourself immensely at Washington. Orville has a way of stepping right into the affections of nice people whom he meets, and they will be nice to you at first for him and then for yourself, for you have some little knack in that line yourself.
>
> I am glad you are there to keep your eagle eye on pretty young ladies. I would fear the worst if he were left unguarded. Be careful yourself also.[12]

All Wilbur's letters to the family at this time reflect the wholly unjustified guilt that gnawed at him for months. 'It is the only time that anything has broken on any of our machines while in flight in nine years experience,' he agonised to Milton, again wrongly attributing the accident to the distractions that had surrounded Orville. 'He is too courteous to refuse to see people . . . I will never leave him alone in such a position again.'[13] To Orville he wrote that he had been 'refusing all invitations, and all but a few visitors for six weeks nearly. I found it necessary to take the bull by the horns or break down.'[14]

Wilbur's near Trappist asceticism kept him going. After grounding the *Flyer* for three days, he decided to go back into the air. On 21 September he created a sensational new world record of 1 hour 31 minutes when he flew over 40 miles. 'Little Bubbo smiled and smiled' when he heard, said Katharine. 'We both wish you were here to help take care of him.'[15] The seemingly never-ending flight, watched in awed amazement by a crowd of 10,000, won for Wilbur a French Aéro-Club prize worth $1000. They needed this sort of money rather badly now; Flints had had to advance them $500 to keep the wolf from the door. 'I will try to send some home,' Wilbur told Orville. Staggering as the *Flyer*'s success had been, it had yet to find a single customer or produce a cent of sales income.

As Orville lay in hospital at Fort Myer slowly mending, his brother's flights, more fabulous by the week, had become the talk of Europe. Wilbur became aviation's first popular idol. His flying headgear, a nondescript green workman's cap picked up cheaply in Paris, was seized upon by the fashion industry. Copies were soon being displayed in shop windows everywhere as 'Vreecht caps'.

Souvenir postcards went on sale across the country on which Wilbur was caricatured, depicted cruelly gaunt with hawklike nose and protruding Adam's apple. He'd sent one to Chanute, who had written back: 'Dear me! How thin you have grown! Your sister said that you were emaciated and nervous but I had no idea it was to this extent.'[16]

Despite the crowds that milled around the shed, he continued to cook and sleep there. He now had a dog for companionship, a mongrel which acquired the unimaginative name 'Flyer'. When the fans, come to observe the miracle of flight, tried to force their way inside, soldiers from the Auvours base were called to drive them away. To work on the aeroplane and catch up with his correspondence he was forced to lock the door, whereupon people queued to climb on a box to peer at him through a window. A woman even bored a hole with a gimlet through the back of the shed to spy on him. All his letters home spoke of his misery as a public exhibit. 'For three months,' he told Chanute, 'I have had scarcely a moment to myself except when I take my bicycle and ride off into the woods for a little rest. How I long for Kitty Hawk! Yet I have been received in France with a friendliness scarcely to be realized. I never hoped for such treatment. In the reaction from former abuse they seem [to be] trying to make up for lost time.'[17]

Milton urged him to be tolerant of the crowds. 'The friendship of the people is a beautiful thing towards a stranger. I hope you will ever maintain and cherish it . . . What compassion Jesus showed toward the multitude drawn out by curiosity!'[18]

Gifts of fruit and flowers arrived along with the flood of letters which, despite help from Berg's secretary, went mostly unanswered. A German crown prince cabled congratulations, and the dowager Queen Margherita of Italy came to Auvours to meet him. 'Princes and millionaires are as thick as fleas,' he told Orville.[19]

Almost every week he set new records. He rose to 90 metres, then to 115 metres (380 feet), earning two more money prizes. At receptions and banquets he was presented with medals, some, he told Katharine, 'the size of a small can'. The French Senate summoned him to Paris to hear speeches of praise. The same day he was the guest of honour at the Academy of Paris, to which some of the country's most distinguished statesmen, scientists and writers flocked to meet him. Again and again, with eulogies ringing in his ears, he was expected to stand up and speak. His aversion to this was only a little short of Orville's. He developed a standard response which has been borrowed by tongue-tied aviators ever since: 'I know of only one bird, the parrot, that talks – and he can't fly very high.' After which he would immediately sit down. People applauded. It always seemed to work.

He began to take up passengers. Bollée, who had almost abandoned his work at the car factory to function as his aide at Le Mans, was first. Getting the seventeen-stone (109 kilogram) Bollée off the ground severely taxed the *Flyer*: the skids perilously brushed the grass for yards before staggering into a climb. Hart Berg went up with him, and Mrs Berg, her long skirt discreetly hobbled around the ankles with a cord, became the world's first woman aeroplane passenger. He flew their French financiers, Weiller and de la Meurthe. By early October the machine had fulfilled all the passenger and distance requirements of the syndicate, and the Compagnie Générale de Navigation Aérienne was formally launched, thus triggering the agreed payment of $100,000 (worth around $2 million today), the first chunk of serious wealth to come their way.

To their great delight, Wilbur agreed to take reporters up; he'd already begun to put them to work helping to hoist the starting weights. 'They considered it a privilege to be allowed to haul the *Flyer* out of its shed, to fetch and carry tools for the great Wilbur.'[20] He flew Bollée's eleven-year-old nephew, the Italian tyre magnate Giovanni Pirelli, and an equerry of the King of Spain. He flew Russians and Germans.

In England, the Aeronautical Society and the Aero Club rushed to award gold medals to both brothers. Inspired by the Auvours and Fort Myer flights, Lord Northcliffe, whose London–Manchester prize had yet to be won, announced a yet more spectacular prize: £1000 (around £60,000 today) for the first man to fly the Channel. Everyone assumed that Wilbur would attempt it. After all, he had now, many times, flown distances much greater than the width of the Dover Straits. He knew he could probably do it, and was sorely tempted when Northcliffe (who had recently visited Orville in hospital) offered a tempting inducement that would have raised the prize to $2500 as well as a slice of the receipts of a London exhibition of the machine.

Behind Northcliffe's Channel challenge was much more than desire for an historic aviation event. In Britain, fear of German invasion, spearheaded by giant Zeppelin airships, to destroy the navy's battle fleets as they lay in port, was mounting. Northcliffe's primary agenda was to awaken the War Office by showing that the nation was no longer a safe island fortress.

But with one *Flyer* a heap of wreckage back in America, Wilbur decided not to risk another of their precious machines just when demonstration flying had become so vital. A plea from Orville may finally have dissuaded him. 'I do not like the idea of you attempting a Channel flight when I am not present,' he wrote with concern. 'I haven't much faith in your motor running. You seem to have more trouble with the engine than I do.'[21] It was left to Blériot in a monoplane with wing warping copied from the Wrights to achieve immortality with the first crossing the following year.

Meanwhile, a steady flow of balloonists from England were making the pilgrimage to the shrine of flight. One of them, Griffith Brewer, was the first Englishman to be given a ride. A well-to-do London patent agent in his early forties, Brewer had been swept up in the flying fervour that was gripping many of his contemporaries among Edwardian England's leisured wealthy. He was a passionate balloonist and had helped to found the Aero Club of the United Kingdom. At the Aeronautical Society he mixed with the cream of the country's aviation intelligentsia, rubbing shoulders with Baden-Powell, Sir Hiram Maxim, Pat Alexander and the Honourable Charles Rolls, another balloonist, who had recently co-founded the Rolls-Royce motor company. Brewer described how news of Wilbur's flights had lured him to France:

> My old associate in balloon races, Charles Rolls, when he heard that I was going to Paris by the night train invited me to dine with him and enquired in a whisper: 'Brewer, why are you going to Paris?' to which I replied: 'Don't tell anyone, but I am going to see

> Wilbur Wright fly.' He laughed and said: 'Well, don't tell anyone, but I have just returned from seeing him fly.'
>
> This is how flying came to us in Europe. We at once recognised the miracle that had taken place. From that moment we kept our balloons for pleasure races and accepted the arrival of mechanical flight.[22]

Arriving at Auvours, Brewer approached the *Flyer*'s shed with trepidation. A crowd surrounded Wilbur as he worked on the machine out in the open, so he decided not to join the throng but to sit down discreetly by the shed and smoke his pipe. Presently, when a mechanic came over to fetch a spanner, Brewer gave him his card for Mr Wright. He saw Wilbur glance at it and nod briefly in his direction:

> Time went on and there was no flight. Ultimately the machine was wheeled back to the shed. The crowd dispersed; they all went back to Le Mans and I began to think that I was forgotten . . . The machine had gone back inside and Wilbur Wright had gone inside. I wondered whether I should sit out there indefinitely. Then out came Wilbur Wright and said: 'Now Mr Brewer, let's go and have some dinner.' We went across to Madame Pollet's inn and had a very nice simple dinner. We talked of all things American and I did not bother him with aviation. That was probably his first rest from the subject of flying since he left his home in Ohio many weeks before . . . When we strolled back to the shed where Wilbur turned in for the night I said goodbye and felt that I had known him for a very long time.[23]

It was the first of several visits Brewer made to Auvours that summer. On one of them he was accompanied by Rolls and Baden-Powell. 'In some unaccountable way we had hopes that Wilbur would carry his English friends as passengers, but we knew if he did so the invitation would come from him and it would be useless to ask for this greatest of privileges.' But Wilbur did offer, and all the English aviators were given a flight.

Griffith Brewer, whose patent expertise was later to help the brothers protect their invention in Britain, became a lifelong friend of the Wrights. Charles Rolls, the son of Lord Llangattock, had become a dashing motor racing figure, demonstrating the perfection of his company's then little-known cars. For two years he had pestered the brothers, demanding to buy a *Flyer* and to be allowed to market it for them in Britain, where he wanted to be the first to own and pilot one. When he heard that Wilbur had arrived in France in the summer of 1908, Rolls had immediately gone to Paris to plead with him yet again for a machine and the sales agency. Rolls had a reputation for parting with his own money reluctantly. His plan actually was for a wealthy friend to buy it for him to fly and demonstrate. His first customer, he had already decided, though he didn't disclose this to Wilbur, was to be the British Army. Wilbur had been tempted, writing to Orville. 'If we can get an order it might be well to take it.' They had agreed to do a deal with the persistent Rolls and had begun to discuss with him an arrangement by which the aircraft could be made by a British manufacturer on a royalty basis under licence.

Now that Rolls had at last powered into the air aboard the *Flyer* he was more than ever determined to possess one and be fruitfully involved in its financial success. Aware of Colonel Capper's rival clandestine experiments which were getting nowhere, he was convinced that if he could dazzle the doubting hierarchy of the War Office with a Wright machine, they would have no option but to snap it up. He naturally didn't want a word of his secret design to reach Capper's ears. 'I did not half thank you for giving me that ride,' he wrote to Wilbur when he got back to his Mayfair office. 'It was the realisation of several dreams and I could think of nothing else for a long while . . . You will of course keep private the fact of my negotiating for a machine etc as such things are so quickly apt to get into the Press which can do no good, at any rate at present.'[24]

To build the aeroplane in England, Rolls intended to offer the work to two London balloon makers – Eustace and Oswald Short. In their small workshop under an arch of Battersea railway bridge – chosen for its proximity to the gasworks – they had made sporting balloons for both Rolls and Brewer. After reading of Wilbur's startling flights under perfect control at Auvours, Oswald is said to have exclaimed to Eustace: 'This means the end of ballooning.' The Short brothers had decided to move into fixed-wing aircraft. They persuaded a third brother, Horace, a steam turbine design engineer with some understanding of aerodynamics, to join them. The three each put up £200 to form a company which would become one of the great British aircraft manufacturers. But in the autumn of 1908 they didn't yet have an airfield and had still to acquire from Charles Rolls the *Flyer* construction business he'd promised them.

The Short brothers were not alone in their dream to introduce the aeroplane to Britain. Nor was Rolls the only contender for the sales agency. A young marine engineer from Manchester, Edwin Alliott Verdon Roe, another in the long line of those inspired by the flight of albatrosses – he had been moved to launch gliders off some of the ships he had sailed in – had also written to the Wrights pleading to handle their British business. Roe, who would launch a production dynasty that would give birth to the Lancaster bomber, had, in a shed beside the Brooklands motor racing track, already built an aeroplane. It owed much to the *Flyer* – though it refused to make more than an unhistoric hop of around 50 yards.

All the while, over at the army's Balloon Factory at Farnborough, Colonel Capper was still manfully trying to overtake the Wrights. The machine upon which all his original hopes had centred, that of his much vaunted protégé, Lieutenant Dunne, was proving depressingly unsuccessful. Dunne's brainchild was a tailless swept-back V-shaped biplane. Its inspiration was a winged seed which Dunne had noticed glided with perfect trim and stablity. Under a blanket of military secrecy the prototype had been tested at a remote grouse moor of the Marquess of Tullibardine in the Scottish highlands, the site closely guarded by soldiers, ordered to dress as civilians. The Secretary of State for War, Richard Haldane, had himself made the long journey to Scotland to watch British aviation history in the making. He was to be gravely disappointed. In test after test over many weeks, both with and without engines, Dunne's aeroplane proved unflyable.

Capper had slightly more luck, however, with his second experimental machine, by now being secretly tested at Farnborough. It was the invention of an extraordinary man called Samuel Cody.

Though Dunne is today largely forgotten, Cody has remained one of aviation's legendary curiosities, remembered more for his unconventional, larger-than-life character and dauntless courage than for any valuable contribution to the development of the aeroplane.

A flamboyant and very likeable expatriate American, Cody, whose real name was Cowdery, was a Texas cowboy and horse whisperer who came to live in England and made a living in the music halls as a Wild West showman. His hobby was kite flying. His enormous man-lifting, winged box kites – made to roll like the *Flyer* with wing twisting – attracted the interest of both the Admiralty and the War Office. After some impressive demonstrations at the Balloon Factory, during one of which Capper was lifted 1000 feet into the sky, Cody was engaged as the British Army's 'Chief Kite Instructor'. Lacking any technical training, with little education and no theoretical aerodynamic knowledge, Cody, appointing himself 'Colonel', branched into aeroplane design and, by the autumn of 1908, produced a primitive powered biplane made of bamboo, fabric and piano wire, heavily derived from the Wrights'. It was designated British Army Aeroplane No.1. Airborne on this machine on Farnborough Common in October 1908 for 27 seconds, Cody made what is recognised as the first sustained powered flight in Britain. Considering what was happening in France, it was not a particularly historic event, yet for this insignificant flight he had been hailed by Britain's newspapers next morning as a national hero.

There is no record of the Wrights' reaction to this underwhelming development in British aviation. They could only have been bewildered that such acclaim had greeted a flight so timorous when the British Army could, years earlier, have acquired the *Flyer* and created whole squadrons of aeroplanes capable of flying reliably to the limits of their fuel. At Auvours only a few days earlier, Wilbur had travelled 50 miles in a flight of 1 hour and 10 minutes. People continued to pour into Le Mans to watch him, now giving flying instruction – as required by the Weiller syndicate deal – to three trainee pilots. He flew on, despite freezing weather, into the winter. The week before Christmas he set a new world record, staying up, in bitter wind and stinging snow showers, for nearly 2 hours.

Concerned that one of his French rivals might wrest from him the $4000 Michelin prize with a longer flight in 1908, Wilbur determined to make a flight of two hours before the year's end. It was more important, he decided, than going home to Dayton for the family Christmas. On the afternoon of 31 December, in coat, cap and gloves, above a landscape now mantled with snow, he pounded on through a freezing drizzle of sleet and rain for nearly 90 miles. When, at last, in the twilight, he landed, he had been up for just over 2 hours and 20 minutes. That evening he learnt that the French government had bestowed on him and Orville the Légion d'honneur.

Orville received the news at Hawthorn Street. After more than six weeks in hospital he had arrived back in Dayton in a wheelchair. 'His mind,' Milton had noted, 'is as good as ever and his body promises to be in due time.' But full recovery was to be slow. The family doctor disapproved of the army's traction treatment of the fractured femur and encased the leg in plaster. Orville hobbled about on crutches while Charlie Taylor began to wheel him down to the workshop to supervise repairs to the smashed *Flyer.*

It would be months before he could fly it again for the army – and there was now a new priority: Wilbur urgently needed help in France. Potential business all over Europe was crying for their attention; he couldn't cope with all the negotiations and continue to fly the demonstrations. 'I very strongly suggest,' Wilbur had written to Orville, 'that you and Kate, and Pop too if he will, should come over to Europe immediately. It is important to get machines ready for the spring business . . . You could superintend and design when you could not actually work. There is more to be done than I can do.'[25]

There was also, quite suddenly, ample funding – Wilbur had just sent Lorin and Reuchlin each a generous $1000 gift – to bring the family contingent to France. In a persuasive letter to Katharine he pressed her to take a year's leave from Steele High School and come over for 'a good rest':

> I know that you love 'Old Steele' but think you would love it still better if the briny deep separated it from you for a while. We will

> be needing a social manager and can pay enough salary to make the proposition attractive, so do not worry about the six [dollars] per day the school board gives you for peripateting about Old Steel's classic halls.[26]

Milton, now eighty, though still in robust health, felt he was too old to go. Katharine had needed no second bidding. She'd taken leave and fixed for Carrie – now in her early twenties and married to an odd-job man, Charlie Grumbach – to move with her husband into the house to care for the bishop. In the first week of 1909 Katherine and Orville, now managing with a pair of canes, sailed for France.

As their ship steamed towards Cherbourg, people back in America were stunned on the morning of 8 January to read some deeply shocking news – an allegation that was apparently being made in France against the nation's man of the hour. WILBUR WRIGHT IS NAMED IN DIVORCE SUIT BY FRENCHMAN, declared one appalling headline. TONGUE OF SCANDAL, said another, HAS REACHED WILBUR WRIGHT.

27

Tongue of Scandal

(1909)

The allegation against Wilbur – that he had indulged in a brief, sordid affair with the wife of a French Army officer, a Lieutenant Goujarde – was the unthinkable. The lieutenant, based at a camp near Auvours, the Dayton *Herald* reported, had named 'the famous aeroplanist' as co-respondent in a divorce suit:

> Mme Goujarde, the lieutenant's wife, is said to be an enthusiast on the subject of aeronautics and she has been seen many times among the interested spectators of Wright's flights. Goujarde, who is well-known in French military circles, accuses his wife of having made love to Wright as the result of a wager with a friend that she could captivate the heart of the American. She was led to make this wager by the many stories concerning Wright's alleged indifference to women.
>
> Goujarde declares his wife was absent from her home in Champagny overnight in Wright's company. When she returned home the husband refused to admit her. Mme Goujarde immediately returned to Wright . . . and the two spent an entire week together at a hotel in Le Mans. The plaintiff says he has convincing proofs of every one of his charges.[1]

The Dayton newspapers handled the story cautiously. The *Herald* took the precaution of phoning Lorin, who was thunderstruck. 'My brother isn't that kind,' he was quoted as saying in a footnote to the United Press report from its Paris bureau. The story was 'absolutely false', probably circulated by rival aviators whose feats had been put in the shade by Wilbur. It was, Lorin suggested, 'a malicious blackmailing scheme'.

Lorin's disbelief was echoed by one of Wilbur's oldest Dayton friends, Ed Ellis, now the assistant city auditor. 'In the first place he is too clean a man, he is too moral to do a thing like that,' Ellis said. 'In the second place he has too much good sound sense to associate with another man's wife.' Despite these expressions of incredulity the stories had nonetheless run, but next day the home town newspapers were forced to admit they had been hoodwinked. The story was a complete fabrication. Enquiries in France had established that Lieutenant Goujarde did not exist. The French Army had no record of him. Nor was there at Le Mans a cavalry unit to which he was said to belong. There was no divorce court record of any proceedings involving the famous American. Wilbur was quoted as saying it must be a practical joke. One lame explanation offered by the Dayton *Herald* was that 'one of Mr Wright's mechanics has been showing much attention to the wife of a sergeant in the local garrison, and this man was confused by the people of Le Mans with Mr Wright himself'. The damaging fiction, it turned out, had been concocted by a United Press reporter and the Paris bureau had cavalierly put it on the wire to its subscribers across America. The journalist had been fired and UP had sent a hasty letter of apology to Wilbur.

Wilbur's first instinct was to sue United Press, but in the end he didn't bother. Refusing to let the allegation die quietly, he went on the warpath. He threatened the Dayton papers with retribution, composing a stinging letter in the vein of those he had often crafted so fiercely for his father when the target had been a shifty Brethren minister. 'The people who had a hand in the concoction and publication of this outrageous lie will be punished,' he warned the editor of the *Daily News*, describing the report as 'a libellous fake' and an 'infamous outrage'. Even the excuse that he had been confused with a philandering mechanic was a lie.

> No-one has complained of me in court or out of it. I have never given anyone cause for complaint. I have never been under suspicion. My bill of health is absolutely clean . . .
>
> The French people seem to be amused that I do not smoke or drink wine and their caricaturists for a joke accordingly represent me with a pipe in my mouth . . . There was no excuse whatever for smirching my good name. It will be a scandal if the local paper, which published such a lie about a man who has tried to bring honour rather than dishonour to Dayton, goes unpunished by public opinion.[2]

Although United Press had never publicly apologised, the Dayton newspapers corrected the original story and it quickly died. Wilbur's indignant letter, arriving a month later, merely revived it, reigniting the scandal. The story appears never to have been published in France, where the revelation of human frailty would likely have been approved of as a refutation of his monkish image; his rival French pilots, themselves accustomed to the temptations of aeronautical fame, would have understood a dalliance. But Delagrange would still have doubted it. 'Even if this man sometimes deigns to smile, one can say with certainty that he has never known the *douceur* of tears. Has he a heart? Has he loved? Has he suffered? An enigma, a mystery.'[3] Wilbur's elusive sexuality never ceased to preoccupy the French newspapers, who delighted in running cartoons of him, in one of which he was shown, with angel's wings, sourly resisting the advances of a beautiful woman.

Orville and Katharine arrived in Paris in the second week of January 1909. Wilbur, still uncomfortably attired from an evening function, met them off the train with Berg and his wife at the Paris terminal at one o'clock in the morning. 'I spied old Jullam,' Katharine told Milton, 'in a silk hat and evening clothes!' Arnold Fordyce was there and stepped forward to present her with a bouquet of roses into which he had stuck an American flag. At their hotel the three Wrights sat up until half past three in the morning, catching up with the events of the last six months.

They weren't to stay long in Paris. To escape the bad flying weather of the Le Mans winter Wilbur had decided to move his base to southern France. At the suggestion of one of his pupil pilots, a balloonist, Paul Tissandier, the *Flyer* had been shipped to the winter resort town of Pau on the edge of the Pyrenees. Wilbur went down to inspect the field selected for him at Pont-Long, a few miles away, and Orville and Katharine followed two days later.

At Pau they were welcomed by the mayor and treated like royalty. They were made guests of the town, honoured at a municipal reception, put up at one of the best hotels and showered with invitations to lunches and dinners. Wilbur refused to stay at the hotel. He insisted on living at the airfield, again eating and sleeping in the *Flyer*'s shed. When the mayor heard of this he was shocked; he insisted on providing him with a chef – as well as having a special telephone installed. The chef's cooking didn't satisfy Wilbur: he soon fired him – and his successor; cook no. 3, briefed on her brother's eating habits by Katharine, survived.

The two months in the late winter of 1909 that the trio spent at Pau saw them thrust on to a pinnacle of international fame that they could not in their wildest imaginations have bargained for:

> The great and the near-great of Europe were fascinated and impressed by the Wrights. There was a straightforward honesty about them, coupled with rare poise, common sense and wit. Men of wealth and power would never turn the heads of these three American heroes. 'Kings,' Katharine remarked to a reporter, 'are just like other nice well-bred people.'[4]

To Milton, of an eight in the morning royal visit, she wrote more candidly: 'The Kings are a nuisance all right. They always come at such unearthly hours.'[5]

The world knew about the brothers; it had been far less aware of the existence of their uncommonly self-possessed and outspoken sister. Almost overnight Katharine became a celebrity too. The French newspapers were quick to credit her with a gloriously romanticised role as a pivotal force within the brotherly invention team:

> There was no shortage of stories about her. It was stated seriously that her knowledge of mathematics was behind her brothers'

> success, and that her life's savings had kept the family from starving while the *Flyer* was being perfected. Her experience as a trained nurse, it was said, had hastened Orville's recovery after the accident at Fort Myer.[6]

Now in her mid-thirties, Katharine did not always photograph well. While a few of the many newspaper and magazine pictures reveal her looking almost sensually elegant, most of the press photos at the flying field show her as a bespectacled, slightly old-maidish, almost masculine figure. The impression is not helped by the rimless pince-nez permanently clamped to her nose under a great hat like a nesting bird secured with voluminous scarves underhung with diffusing veils.

Journalists, however, hastened to reveal a quite different image. Glamorous sketches depicted her as ridiculously young and beautiful, piloting herself alone in the air with hair flying. 'Miss Wright is petite, dark and good-looking. She looks the sister of her brothers. Her manner is most attractive. Like most American girls the aviators' sister has very decided views of her own.'[7]

The myth that somehow her brothers owed much of their success to her began to grow and feed upon itself. 'Without meaning to detract in any way from the greatness of Wilbur and Orville Wright, it can be claimed that, but for a woman, they would probably be repairing bicycles or automobiles for a living, unknown and unsung.'[8] One story went as far as to claim that Katharine had not only joined the inventors in a study of aeronautics, she had also 'made the calculations and her brothers made the experiments . . . Before her brothers had tested the machine they were building Miss Wright knew that it was possible for man to fly . . . She was willing to stake what little money she had saved from her salary as a school teacher . . . upon the outcome of the device to be made according to her instructions.'[9]

When at Pau Wilbur rewarded her love and care with the excitement of a seven-minute flight, the news was immediately cabled to America. THE AMERICAN GIRL WHOM ALL EUROPE IS WATCHING, one headline said. 'The Silent Partner of Orville and Wilbur Wright . . . in the Aerial Triumphs of the Intrepid Brothers'.

Not only was it now being said that she had immediately mastered the controls and was 'in charge of the machine throughout the latter part of the trip', but that she had 'made one of the most successful landings on record'. Neither brother was churlish enough to attempt to redress these extraordinary stories. However, nearly forty years later, when pressed for the truth towards the end of his life, Orville was at last to set the matter straight. In a guardedly brief statement, issued through his secretary, he said that 'his sister was his and his brother's closest confidant and comrade, but it was without foundation that she contributed to their success scientifically or financially'.[10]

There was no doubt, however, about Katharine's value as a social asset in France. Everywhere she went she compensated with her naturally bubbling extrovert charm for the dourness of Wilbur and the sometimes debilitating shyness of Orville. She reached out to people to put a warm and human face upon the famous family. With no one was she not at total ease – one moment being photographed with a broom showing Wilbur's uniformed cook how to sweep out the shed properly, the next chatting away with one of the kings who'd come to the small grass aerodrome. Singularly devoid of airs and graces, unaffected by the stupendous fame of her brothers, she charmed them all, radiating the middle-class modesty of the plain folks of the Midwest. Spain's King Alfonso, who came with his entourage, was captivated, much quotedly describing her as 'his ideal of American womanhood'. Alfonso had wanted to go up with Wilbur, but the queen had made him promise not to; he had to be satisfied with sitting in the passenger seat on the ground while Wilbur explained how the controls worked.

England's 68-year-old Edward VII was driven across from his winter quarters at Biarritz in the royal Daimler. Katharine was presented to the portly monarch, who is said to have made a flattering comment about her. But Edward wasn't as interested in the flying machine as the younger Alfonso; he asked no questions and 'was observed to be engaged in conversation with a member of his suite while the *Flyer* was being launched'.[11] One historian claimed that the King's famed mistress, the beautiful, luminous Alice Keppel, who used to accompany him on his winter sojourns in Biarritz, was given a flight by Wilbur.[12] None of the Wrights' records appear to confirm this, but the logs of their passengers were not always complete. On the other hand, notwithstanding the respectable face the King's adulterous affair had acquired, they may have been so scandalised by the sinful relationship that they simply decided not to document it.

The kings were but two of the royal personages who flocked to Pau that February and March 1909. As the pictures and stories went out to the world, the southern French town became a Mecca for the famed and affluent. If man had suddenly begun lifting off regularly on missions to another planet the phenomenon couldn't have created a bigger stir. Once again a procession of prominent political figures, dukes and princesses, lords and ladies jostled at Pont-Long for a sight of the *Flyer* and its heroic pilot.

Some of the most picturesque images ever recorded of the aeroplane in the air were captured at Pau. One photograph caught the *Flyer* lumbering low over an ox wagon piled high with hay, on top of which a man, pitchfork in hand, has stopped work to look up in wonder. In another, Wilbur and a passenger are passing over a group of horses and carriages. One of the top-hatted, liveried coachmen is restraining a shying horse. Other photographs show lines of parked motor cars from whose open tops chic and stylish women in plumed hats gaze up at the aeroplane.

Some revealing human interest studies have survived. One chanced to catch a magic moment in which a laughing Mrs Hart Berg appears to be flirting with Wilbur, for she has actually brought to his lips the rarity of an almost full smile. Wilbur, in leather jacket, baggy trousers and cap, often tieless, contrasts sartorially with the always distinguished-looking Orville; in every picture, with his smart overcoat, gloves, polished shoes, bowler hat and cane, he could be mistaken for a visiting diplomat. Still not yet fit enough to fly, Orville, who masked his crippling shyness with, outwardly, a disarming affability, was for the moment on the edge of the limelight.

In the flow of important visitors there was no let-up. Their names read like the pages of a pan-European Debrett: Lord and Lady Galway; the Duke and Duchess of Manchester; the Duke of

Leuchtenberg; Marquis Edgard de Kergariou; Lieutenant General Sir Henry and Lady Settle; Count Castillon de Saint-Victor. Day after day they arrived in box-shaped motor cars and horse-drawn carriages with retinues of servants. In the second week of February, Britain's former prime minister, the leader of the Conservative Party, the aloof and aristocratic Lord Balfour, made the journey; he'd been invited by Lord Northcliffe to join him there. Northcliffe, now obsessed with the belief that to defend its shores the country needed urgently to equip with Wright machines, had planned a fresh tactic. He wanted the Tory leader to join with his newspapers – now calling Britain's lack of a functional military aeroplane a national humiliation – to press the negligent War Minister Haldane into doing business with the brothers. Balfour accepted the invitation. Deciding to rough it, he wrote back to the press lord: 'I am greatly looking forward to my visit to Pau. I shall bring a servant but no secretary.'

The ex-prime minister was predictably bewitched by the Wrights and ecstatic about their aeroplane. Insisting to Wilbur that he be allowed to involve himself with 'the miracle', he volunteered to join the line of helpers hauling on the rope to raise the starting weights, which had grown to two-thirds of a ton. He was photographed as he strained on the line next to Northcliffe, the latter sheathed conspicuously like a grizzly bear in a voluminous ankle-length fur coat. Not satisfied with this excitement, Balfour pressed Wilbur for a flight. However, the weather had worsened and they couldn't go.

A single aeroplane, Wilbur told Balfour, would be of greater value to the British Army than an entire regiment of cavalry. From Pau, Northcliffe had written personal letters to Haldane and Lord Esher, a close friend of Edward VII and an influential and highly respected figure in the British establishment, pleading with them to seize the Wrights' aeroplane. To the War Secretary he had described what a laughing stock British Army Aeroplane No. 1 was in France. The French aviators, he said, were calling it 'the steamroller'. He questioned why the War Office hadn't bothered to send someone down to Pau 'to find out why it is this aeroplane gets off the ground and can fly for ten minutes or ten hours if it chooses and your Aldershot [he meant Farnborough] aeroplane which is a very bad copy of the bad French aeroplanes, is unable to leave the ground.'[13]

To Lord Esher he was even more scathing about Britain's pilot folk hero, Samuel Cody. 'The English aeroplane arrangements have been put in the hands of an American who, on his own statements, knows nothing about aviation. He got the appointment because he knew something about kites . . . I might as well attempt to produce my newspapers by the aid of a man who confessedly knows nothing of printing.'[14]

Northcliffe's ploys to enlist the eminence of Balfour and the patronage of the King of England had no effect. The anti-aeronautical lobby, driven by the closed-minded and dominant General Sir William Nicholson, was impervious to pressure. Northcliffe's appeal to Lord Esher made not a shred of difference.

Esher had begun chairing a high-level defence committee charged by Prime Minister Asquith with investigating the country's military aviation needs against the threat of invasion. A galaxy of powerful figures had been asked to involve themselves in this historic review. They included two future prime ministers, David Lloyd George and Winston Churchill, as well as War Minister Haldane and a cavalcade of generals and admirals, most rooted in the land warfare philosophies of the nineteenth century. The committee had summoned before it some seeming experts – Major Baden Baden-Powell, the Honourable Charles Rolls, Colonel Capper, and the eccentric inventor Sir Hiram Maxim.

As the country's aeronautical experts filed before the committee, General Nicholson treated the fixed-wing aviators with contempt. Not only did he doubt that pilots would be able to breathe at cruising level, but he had argued with Rolls that no observer in an aeroplane travelling at 30 miles an hour could possibly see what an enemy was doing. He knew this, he said, from travelling at 30 miles an hour in his motor car. No one on the committee felt able to point out to him that even in a train moving at 60 miles an hour, while the telegraph poles were whizzing by, the cows in the nearby fields were plainly visible. In any case, Nicholson declared: 'As soon as we have made a very good aeroplane, other nations will make aeroplanes in the same way and we shall be no better off.' Maxim had arrived to claim he was 'the first man in the world' to make a powered machine lift off; he dismissed the Wrights as a pair of amateurs merely treading in his footsteps. 'They are,' he told the committee, 'a couple of clever young men, without any trade, who learnt to make bicycles.'

As Balfour and Northcliffe were being astounded by the effortless performance of the *Flyer* day after day at Pau that February of 1909, the report of Lord Esher's committee with the weighty responsibility of setting an air defence policy for Britain was circulating under secret cover in Whitehall and Downing Street. General Nicholson won the day. The report concluded that while more experimental work deserved to be done on airships, the aeroplane had yet to prove itself as a military vehicle for the army or the navy. It was recommended that all aeroplane development should cease forthwith.

Before it disbanded, the august committee discussed a proposal it had received from Charles Rolls inviting the government to participate in trials he planned to make with the *Flyer* he was trying to buy from the Wrights. Haldane had supported the offer and the use of army facilities for evaluation flying, but Churchill, then President of the Board of Trade and a member of the parent committee of Imperial Defence, had disagreed. A champion of air power, he was soon to take flying lessons himself. He thought the proposal smacked of amateurism; he had a much better idea. 'We should,' he urged, 'place ourselves in communication with Mr Wright himself and avail ourselves of his knowledge.'

But the committee was not in the business of dealing directly with any flying machine inventor. The recommendations turning Britain away from military powered flight went, via the Imperial Defence Committee, to Downing Street where Prime Minister Asquith endorsed them.

The decision to spurn the aeroplane brought the death of any further hope of War Office negotiations with the Wrights. It also spelt the end of Colonel Capper's brave attempts to compete with the technological brilliance of the *Flyer*. Capper was replaced as superintendent of the Balloon Factory and eventually posted back to the Royal Engineers whence he had come. Dunne and Cody were dismissed. The era of the amateur plane-makers at Farnborough was over – though it wouldn't be the last the aviation world would hear of either Dunne or Cody.

While Britain's military leaders were deciding in the early months of 1909 to have nothing to do with the aeroplane, the *Flyer* was continuing, at Pau, to rush the world headlong into the age of the flying machine. Other nations were less reluctant to welcome it as a necessity of future warfare. Invitations had already arrived to demonstrate the aeroplane in Germany and Italy; both countries had despatched military observers to see it fly. And a French Army officer, Captain Paul Lucas-Girardville, had become one of Wilbur's three pupil pilots. He was already doing circuits and bumps at what, against the backdrop of the snow-covered Pyrenees, had become the world's first powered flying school.

The pupil sat on the lower wing, precariously unharnessed on the right-hand seat, with Wilbur on his left – both with feet resting out in space on a rail. There were three levers: dual elevator controls on the outside of the two men, and a third stick between them, which they shared, for wing warping and rudder operation. Although the *Flyer* had gained a reputation as an unstable aeroplane needing acrobatic skill to fly it, the first pupils quickly got the hang of it. Paul Tissandier wrote:

> It was at Pau that I was first initiated into the secrets of this artificial bird . . . I steered the aeroplane for the first time – Wilbur Wright remaining with his hands on his knees – after seven lessons. When I was sufficiently advanced with the elevation rudder [the front elevator] Wilbur Wright allowed me to take the second rudder [the rear steering rudders] the operation of which is more delicate, but with which I was soon familiar. After this my education was practically finished, for on February 18 and 19 I was in full charge with my professor at my side closely watching all my movements and ready to interfere if I made a mistake. But there was no need to interfere, for I made no mistake and after this test I was allowed to take the mechanical bird aloft with my companion and friend, the Comte de Lambert as passenger.[15]

While Captain Lucas-Girardville had, owing to short-sightedness, some difficulty mastering the controls of the frisky *Flyer*, Tissandier and de Lambert proved apt pupils. They learnt to fly it in just a few hours and in the last week of March both went off solo, each to make a 25-kilometre flight qualifying them for French Aéro-Club licences.

Count de Lambert was a Russian aristocrat of French ancestry whose wealth enabled him to indulge his speed machine passions by amusing himself with cars and powerboats. He and his wife became firm friends of Katharine, who found herself in demand by the cream of European society. Her letters to Milton regaled him with blow-by-blow details of the endless social activity that had exploded around the trio in this small town. She took some of the heat off her brothers, for Orville, oppressed by his role as an exhibit, had fled to Wilbur's shed at Pont-Long, re-creating there the cosy fraternal atmosphere they had enjoyed over the years at Kill Devil. Back in Pau, Katharine became a much sought-after celebrity in her own right.

'Every time we make a move,' Katharine told Milton, 'the people in the street stop and stare at us. We have our pictures taken every two minutes.'[16] Unintimidated by the lofty status of many of those converging on Pau, Katharine treated them all with her customary unabashed, egalitarian warmth. Her private opinions she confided only to the family. The gushing, glamorous Mrs Berg was definitely not on her list of favourites; she did not share Wilbur's liking for her. 'Pretty as a picture and about the best dressed woman I ever saw,' she told Milton. 'But she is a regular tyrant and as selfish as anyone can be. We will be glad when she goes . . . She has been very busy cultivating the people whom she thinks influential. She makes us all very weary.'[17]

With the blunt-speaking Lord Northcliffe she got on famously. 'He is good company,' she wrote, adding that Lord and Lady Northcliffe were surprisingly 'very simple in their manners'. The Northcliffes issued the three Wrights a firm invitation to stay with them at their Kent estate on their way back to America.

Back in Dayton, the bishop was basking in the international fame of his children. As their venerable father he was being respectfully greeted wherever he went. Happy and well, he was still actively engaged in Brethren business; he was regularly commuting to his Indiana farm and had written the first 50,000 words of his autobiography. He poured out letters almost daily to Wilbur, Orville and Katharine exhorting them to set a Christian example by their conduct. 'You had better,' he warned Katharine 'look to yourselves that you behave well and live straight.' 'Dear Sons, I am glad to notice that they credit Wilbur for Sunday observance and freedom from tobacco. It will do more good to Europe than all the worth of the money you will ever get out of your invention. European countries need reformation and our own country needs to beware.'[18]

Katharine was by now less concerned about her example than the preservation of her phenomenal stamina. 'I have had too much excitement seeing people,' she finally reported. She retreated to her hotel room, refusing to emerge for two days.

Yet the exhausting, triumphant progress through Europe had only just begun. The reports and pictures of the *Flyer* that had gone to every corner of the world had made the self-effacing brothers huge celebrities. Their names and images were on cinema screens everywhere. The Wrights became more internationally familiar than any other inventor in history. The money was now rolling in too. In just one consignment Orville sent home a cool Fr110,000 for Lorin to place on deposit 'at 4 per cent'. The $22,000 would today be worth nearly half a million dollars. The days of counting the pennies were over.

By the end of March the French pilots had completed their training and the Wrights went back to Paris to prepare for the next mission – to Italy. In Paris they were fêted with renewed fervour. The newspapers were perpetually fascinated by the trio's unmarried state. When a journalist asked Wilbur about his little-known older brothers, he 'gestured vaguely, "The others?" he said. "They're married."' The media reserved their greatest curiosity for Wilbur, delighting in running cartoons of him in which he would be depicted in dissipatedly louche poses with cigarette, and attractive women gazing into his eyes. What few French were to divine was that with the brothers it wasn't bachelorhood at all – it was celibacy.

They took the train to Rome early in April. The Italian tyre mogul Pirelli had now given them a $10,000 contract to make demonstrations to an aviation club subsidised by the Italian government. The deal required them to train two military pilots. The *Flyer* Wilbur had used in France was given to Lazare Weiller and the Wrights' French syndicate, while another machine, its parts shipped from Dayton, was railed to Rome. For the first time machines were being manufactured for sale: six more came from Dayton to France to be fitted with Wright-designed engines produced by Bariquand and Marre.

In Rome the adulation began all over again. Wilbur, Orville, Katharine and Berg were entertained by the mayor, presented to King Victor Emmanuel and lionised at banquets. The machine was shipped across the city on a wagon drawn by grey horses to a flying field at Centocelle. Again Wilbur did all the flying. A bevy of Italian cabinet ministers, dukes and princes queued for rides. The king and the dowager Queen Margherita came to watch. A picture shows Orville looking like an ambassador, resplendent in morning coat and top hat, mixing with the royals. Some days Wilbur made more than ten flights. The aeroplane never faltered. A naval officer and an army lieutenant, Umberto Savoia, later to become one of his country's leading aircraft manufacturers, were taught to fly, and cinematic history was made when Wilbur took up a newsreel cameraman to record the first-ever sequence shot from an aeroplane. He also made several successful launchings without the rail and weights, taking off on the grass on the *Flyer*'s skids unaided.

At the end of April they returned to Paris to be presented with more medals before crossing to London. Fleet Street hailed them as heroes and there ensued another fevered round of banqueting and medal-giving. At the glittering Aero Club dinner at the Ritz, Wilbur rose to tell his hosts how ironical it was that flight had at last been achieved at a time when the tide of aviation in Britain, which boasted in George Cayley a man who more than a hundred years earlier had advanced the science of flying to heights it had never reached before, had sunk to such a low ebb.

When War Minister Haldane invited Wilbur and Orville to come to see him, the London newspapers rushed to speculate that the government was about to invest in the *Flyer* and create an 'aerial navy' at last. Nothing could have been further from the truth. The War Office had no intention of acquiring the Wrights' machine; most of its generals were still happy with balloons and horses. Yet the Asquith government was at that very moment being attacked in both houses of parliament for its neglect of any form of air defence against the threat of Germany's Zeppelins. A powerful lobby group, the Aerial League of the British Empire, supported by some of the country's most prominent peers, military leaders and political figures, had taken over the Mansion House in London to hold a public meeting to warn that the city could be devastated from the air. The presence in the capital amid this foment of the Wright Brothers, 'the most eminent living symbols,' as one historian put it, 'of the new age of the air', only served to heighten the bumbling irony of it all.

Instead of a major sale to the British government, they had to settle for the deal with the Short Brothers that Rolls had pressed them to conclude. It was agreed that the Shorts would build *Flyers* under licence, for each of which the Wrights would be paid £1000 – a very modest sum even by today's values; after paying Shorts to build the machines and supplying the French-built engines, their net profit was barely £600 on each aeroplane. The deal had been negotiated by Griffith Brewer, who had persuaded the Wrights to appoint him their British patent agent.

To build the six English *Flyers* the Short brothers had found a field at Eastchurch on the Isle of Sheppey in the Thames Estuary. Here, on the understanding that the farmer would move his sheep whenever they needed to fly, they set up one of the world's first aircraft factories. Wilbur and Orville went down to see the place and visited the Shorts' shed under Battersea Bridge where the first machines were taking shape.

Machine No. 1 was earmarked for Charles Rolls. Quietly awaiting its first flight and demonstration to his own aeronautical staff was none other than the Secretary of War. Richard Haldane didn't want it for its uniqueness; he wanted it for the secrets he hoped it would reveal to the team of engineers and designers he had appointed to succeed the aeronautically inexpert Colonel Capper.

Yet to learn of the War Office's ulterior motive, Wilbur, Orville and Katharine sailed home to America early in May. As their ship entered New York harbour an exuberant welcome was awaiting them.

28

The Lawsuits

(1909)

As the *Kronprinzessin Cecile* crept through the Narrows into New York in May 1909, it was surrounded by an armada of small boats. The decks of every ship in the harbour were packed with cheering, waving people; the band playing on the German liner's afterdeck was drowned out by a bedlam of whooping whistles and sirens. The Wrights were whisked through the customs shed, Wilbur now nearly a stone heavier and Orville walking at last without his cane. New York had planned a tickertape welcome with a ceremonial drive through Manhattan, but the brothers had nipped it in the bud with a cable from mid-Atlantic.

However, a full-scale welcome in their home town they couldn't avoid. When their train steamed into Dayton, 10,000 people were waiting to greet them. As factory whistles hooted and a thirty-gun salute boomed out, they were driven home in a cavalcade of carriages led to Hawthorn Street by a band. The house had been decorated with banners and balloons. The speeches went on for hours. It was only the beginning.

To their great dismay, the mayor and a bevy of officials arrived next morning to reveal details of a mammoth carnival the proud city had arranged for them a month hence in the middle of June. 'The Dayton presentation,' Wilbur complained to Chanute, 'has been made the excuse for an elaborate carnival and advertisement of the city under the guise of being an honour to us.'[1] Chanute had replied soothingly:

> I know that the reception of such honours becomes oppressive to modest men and they would avoid them if they could, but in this case you have brought the trouble upon yourselves by your completing the solution of a world-old problem, accomplished with great ingenuity and patience at much risk of personal injury to yourselves.[2]

They were summoned to the White House to be presented with gold medals by the President. The Dayton carnival they dreaded went ahead. The entire city, shops and schools virtually completely shut for two days to be given over to a continuous rhapsody of parades, receptions, band concerts and fireworks. Congressional, state and city medals were successively presented to Wilbur and Orville as they stood stiff and unsmiling on a dais, uncomfortable in morning coats and top hats, privately hating every moment of it.

At the point in the programme designated 'Responses by the Wrights', reporters seized their notebooks. Rising to speak for them both, Wilbur uttered just three words, 'Thank you, gentlemen', and promptly sat down. Given the trouble their home town had gone to and the pride it felt in their famous sons – and Wilbur's great ability, when he wished, to find appropriately courteous words – it appeared needlessly churlish.

'They frankly,' said Adrian Kinnane, 'mistrusted and disliked any form of public attention. They never learnt to use it or adapt to it. So they went down in history with an image largely as famously described by the Philadelphia newspaper which said they looked like "a pair of clerks in a village hardware store", whose pleasure it was to attend the Wednesday night prayer meeting – nothing "devilish or daring" about them. This near cult of the virtuous ordinary man – the bicycle makers from Dayton – became the dominant motif for them both, helpfully enabling them to shun publicity, dodge personal probes and get on with their work building aeroplanes.'

Even before the tumult of bands and fireworks had subsided they were back in workshop aprons, preparing for Fort Myer. Orville was at last fit enough to fly again – though this time Wilbur demanded to be there. In Washington he insisted they stay out of sight at a modest hotel. They kept themselves to themselves, declining to be interviewed and refusing to be pressurised into flying before they were confident to do so. On the day scheduled for the first flight, the Signal Corps, seeking funds for military aeronautics, had rashly invited every member of Congress to Fort Myer. Both houses had adjourned and hundreds of senators and representatives had streamed out to the airfield; but instead of being allowed to meet the great flyers, on Wilbur's instructions they were kept away, standing restively in fierce heat and humidity while he and Orville fussed with the machine in the distance. Congressmen began to complain they might as well have gone to the ball game. Their frustration spilled into anger when a wind came up and the promised flight was abandoned altogether. The incident produced some damaging headlines in the *New York Times* next morning: WRIGHTS FAIL TO FLY – SNUB CONGRESSMEN – BROTHERS NO DIPLOMATS.

It was another three days before they were ready to put the machine in the air. Now the Signal Corps appraisal officers grew impatient. 'They tinkered and fussed and muttered to themselves from dawn to dusk,' wrote Lieutenant Foulois. 'It seemed as if they would never say they were ready to go.'

> When you spoke to the two of them it would be Orville who would answer, and Wilbur would either nod assent or add an incomplete sentence as his way of corroborating what his younger brother had said. At no time did I ever hear either of them render a hasty or ill-considered answer to any question I asked, and sometimes they took so long to reply that I wondered if they had heard me.[3]

When flying finally did get under way, things didn't immediately go well. Orville had to relearn the controls yet again, familiarising himself with a spark-retarding pedal for throttling the engine and with a split-handled lever he'd designed: the hinged top now twisted to add, if needed, extra movement to the rudder and the whole lever pushed backwards and forwards for banking. On the second day, fumbling with all this, he smashed a skid on landing. Then the engine stopped in midair and, gliding in to land, he hit a tree, crumpling a wing.

As Orville emerged, dazed, from the damaged aeroplane, spectators rushed across to help themselves to souvenirs from the broken bits. At the sight of this brazen looting, Wilbur once again lost his cool. Spotting a photographer taking pictures, he seized a piece of splintered wood and hurled it at the man, then proceeded to grapple with him, demanding the exposed plate. Taken aback, the shocked photographer stammered that he was a War Department official just doing his job. The story, reporting Wilbur's embarrassment and eventual apology, merely added to his reputation as a brilliant oddball.

Back in the air, Orville's confidence grew. He began to make long flights, setting new records. One of 1 hour and 20 minutes with a Signal Corps observer met the army's duration requirement. Milton travelled to Washington to watch and was joined by the family black sheep, Reuchlin, who had come all the way from his farm in Kansas to see his brothers fly for the first time.

The final demonstration was the speed trial which would decide the price the army paid for the *Flyer*. Orville did it with Lieutenant Foulois – the latter armed with map, compass, aneroid barometer and two stopwatches – on a ten-mile round-trip cross-country flight south over forested hills and ravines to Shooter's Hill near Alexandria.

It went off faultlessly. When, watched by the President waving his hat from an open limousine, Orville swept over the finishing line, the 15-minute journey was finely calculated to have been flown at an average speed of 42.583 miles an hour. The Wrights were credited with two extra miles at $2500 each as a bonus on top of the contractual $25,000. Thus the US Army paid $30,000 (around $600,000 today) for its first aeroplane. In the first week of August 1909 (since Cody's machine in Britain was never regarded as such) it became the world's first military flying machine, acquiring the designation Signal Corps Airplane No. 1. Disappointingly for the Wrights, the army did not immediately buy more.

What had happened, people were asking, to Augustus Herring's revolutionary rival machine? Herring was to claim that he had later assembled it and made a test flight somewhere on Long Island, remaining airborne for 100 yards before crashing. He was never able to produce a witness, and a few weeks before Orville's successful demonstrations the Signal Corps had declared his contract void, the deposit forfeited.

Although the Wrights remained American heroes, their greatness was suddenly in danger of eclipse. On 25 July, two days before Orville's Fort Myer cross-country feat, Louis Blériot successfully flew the Channel from France to England, shattering for ever Britain's sense of security as an island nation. Wilbur and Orville had made much longer flights, but they had prudently never strayed far from their airfields. Never had they dared risk going out over the sea. Blériot's 23½ mile, 37-minute flight in his frail monoplane captured the imagination of the world far more electrifyingly than had their own inaccurately reported first flights at Kill Devil five and a half years earlier. By proving that man, equipped with a pair of wings, could successfully fly over the ocean, Blériot had reclaimed the legend of Icarus. At a banquet at the Savoy hotel in London, Lord Northcliffe, whose newspapers were trumpeting again that expensive dreadnoughts would no longer save Britain, had presented to the French aviator the £1000 prize his lordship had so badly wanted Wilbur to win.

Arriving back in Paris, Blériot, who had nearly bankrupted his car headlamp business building a succession of eleven flying machines, in which he had broken more bones than any other aviator of the era, had been mobbed at the Gare du Nord by 100,000 people. Unlike the Wrights, his flight would eventually bring him magnificent reward in the shape of orders for around 800 of his aeroplanes, some to France's first military air corps.

Blériot's Channel crossing has remained an heroic legend. Wilbur could have taken it in his stride – perhaps years before had they not, distrustful of a wicked world, locked their incomparable device away for over two and a half years. Now, suddenly, other aviators were competing for the headlines. An array of inventors all over the world had sprung up to improve and perfect the aeroplane. The genie had burst from the bottle.

By the middle of 1909, controllable, more or less reliable flying machines were being built everywhere. The aeroplane was rapidly becoming big business – far too significant to remain the exclusive property of two cycle-makers from the American Midwest. Although the aura that surrounded them would survive for ever, their magic machine, with its unique technology, was about to lose its dominance. Aeroplanes were taking to the air in Russia, Austria, Sweden, Romania, Spain, Portugal, Canada. Almost every month someone flew further, higher, stayed up for longer. The world's first big international aviation race meeting was held at Reims in August 1909, organised and funded by the champagne industry. It marked a turning point in the acceptance of the aeroplane as an established mode of transport that had arrived to change life on the planet. Thirty-eight machines, most of them French, all capable of banking, turning and circling safely in the air, entered for big prizes.

A crowd of more than 200,000 came by specially built railway to the Reims flying ground where, in four grandstands, bars and restaurants dispensed champagne and bands played. At times the multitude was treated to the spectacle of six aeroplanes circling in the air at once. As they flew past his box, the French president kept shouting, 'Bravo! Bravo!' Lord Northcliffe was there along with the British Chancellor of the Exchequer, Lloyd George, who declared, 'Flying machines are no longer toys and dreams. They are an established fact. I feel as a Britisher rather ashamed that we are so completely out of it.'[4] Wilbur's portrait on the cover of the programme led people to believe that the master of flying would be taking part.

They were to be disappointed; the Wrights had deliberately stayed away. 'I do not compete for trophies,' Wilbur had loftily told a journalist, 'unless I can win them occasionally through those flights I am obliged to make by my contracts.'

As the inventors of the aeroplane the Wrights saw no reason to compete with newcomers to the field – particularly when they regarded most of the newcomers as patent infringers. As Wilbur had once told Chanute, they refused to play the mountebank game with mountebanks.[5]

It was being suggested that it was not only the mountebanks that kept the Wrights away from the great aviation festival. A much more compelling reason was the high risk that they might no longer be certain of winning anything. In this, perhaps, they were wise, for the event saw one after the other of their famous records tumbling. Henri Farman, now seen as Wilbur's equal as a pilot, took the distance grand prix of $10,000 with a flight of over 112 miles, breaking both the 100-mile barrier and the 3-hour endurance one as well. A French Antoinette machine clawed its way up to a hitherto unattainable 500 feet, and Blériot recorded a speed over 10 kilometres of 48 miles an hour. The Wrights' absence was made all the more stark not just by the appearance of three French-built *Flyers* flown by pilots Wilbur had trained, but by the arrival of Glenn Curtiss, their now deadly serious American competitor, who had risen to threaten their entire business.

Curtiss became the hero of Reims when he took the American newspaper publisher James Gordon Bennett's trophy for the quickest time round the pylons over 20 kilometres. Beating Blériot by a few seconds, he was proclaimed the fastest aviator in the world. In Paris the equally taciturn and publicity shy Curtiss was hailed as a successor to Wilbur Wright, but the sweet taste of success was soured by news from America that the Wrights had just filed suit against him: they accused him of infringement of their control system patents.

A new V-8 engined biplane, looking today, with its uncovered fuselage, like a piece of scaffolding, Curtiss's 'Reims Racer' had been fitted for banking with ailerons. Unlike those of today, the hinged flaps – which Curtiss operated with a shoulder yoke – were fitted as separate surfaces between the wings. He had been careful not to copy the *Flyer*'s warping controls, in which the rear part of the outer wings were made to twist. His wings were rigid: they could not be flexed to induce rolling. But this did not satisfy the Wrights.

Learning of the device, Wilbur had heard that Curtiss was about to seek glory with it in France. Worse, he had built for the newly formed Aeronautic Society of New York another machine, the *Golden Flier*, that would incorporate the same inter-wing ailerons. It was, Wilbur had decided, time to declare war. He went to New York to launch a preliminary volley of actions to force the copyists to desist – or pay up.

For the Wrights' image, the timing could not have been worse. When news of the lawsuits reached Reims, the aviation community responded angrily. The legal actions were seen not only as an attack on Glenn Curtiss but as the start of a campaign to establish an international monopoly on the manufacture and operation of all aircraft using any means of roll control. The Americans at Reims were furious that the Wrights had targeted their own country's sole representative at races the brothers had not seen fit to enter themselves.

What the astounded Curtiss didn't know was that the timing of the legal thunderbolts had actually been exquisitely arranged. The Wrights wanted to ensure that the shock would ricochet among the world's leading aviators while they were all conveniently gathered together in camaraderie. From New York Orville had written to Wilbur urging: 'If suit is brought before the races at Reims the effect will be better than after.'[6] The injunctions were not confined to the new American superpilot. To try and halt its use of the *Golden Flier*, they fired them also at the Aeronautic Society of New York – of which, awkwardly, the Wrights had been made honorary members; and, with the most devastating consequences of all, upon a brand new company Curtiss had just formed in partnership, quite incredibly it would seem, with, of all people, the notorious Augustus Herring.

Having failed to gain for himself a slice of the Wrights' modest riches, Herring, who had himself still not produced even the promise of a practical flying machine, had seen, in the success of Curtiss's aeroplanes emerging from Graham Bell's experimental group, a new opportunity. Surviving with boundless plausibility and upper-class polish and charm, he had continued to mix in aviation's highest circles, promoting his claims to hold the innermost secrets of flight. He had built around himself a reputation as an 'aeronautical wizard', impressing, it seems, many people. One was the president of the Aero Club of America. A wealthy New York banker, Cortlandt Field Bishop was a shy and studious man who collected books and paintings and spent half the year abroad in France, where he enjoyed ballooning. Bishop had been persuaded by Herring that the time to make money out of aeroplanes was now – before the Wrights tried to monopolise the business by tediously hounding all other plane-makers through the courts. Keen to seize the moment, the prominent banker had agreed to invest $20,000 in the company; his brother stumped up another $16,000. According to Curtiss's biographer, 'the best final estimate on Herring's cash outlay was $650.'

Extraordinarily, Herring had managed to convince Curtiss that he held aeronautical patents that predated those of 1906 granted to the Wrights. What he hadn't told Curtiss was that he'd made a similar but unsuccessful approach to the Wrights after their first flights in 1903. Glenn Curtiss was not as astute as the brothers. Blinded by Herring's hints of a glittering array of patents, he had agreed to join forces.

What were these purported rival inventions of the aeroplane? Herring was later vaguely to describe them as 'automatic devices to produce stability' and 'surfaces that were of a high degree of efficiency'.[7] Whatever they were, Curtiss had innocently accepted that these crucial patents existed. He was further deceived into believing that Herring had access to a large amount of investment finance.

To Graham Bell's horror, Curtiss had gone ahead with the deal to form the Herring-Curtiss Company as America's first aircraft manufacturer. In a moment he was to regret all his life, Curtiss turned over to the company all his property, including his profitable factory and personal real estate – even his shares in patents applied for by Bell's experimental group. Herring's biggest contribution, indeed the company's greatest presumed asset, were the patents he claimed to hold, now assigned to the business, and which nobody, including the Herring-Curtiss president, a retired county court judge, Monroe Wheeler, had ever bothered to verify; nor had anybody verified the blueprints of the secret aeroplane for the US

Army that Herring was continuing to keep under wraps, reassuring the Signal Corps that 'a force of mechanics' was busy working on it. Curtiss became general manager of the new company and Herring a vice-president, both on the then mammoth salaries of $5000 a year.

To announce the historic launch of America's aircraft industry, Bishop had proudly called a press conference in New York at the Aero Club. 'We have lost the Wrights,' he told reporters, because the brothers were setting up their factory in France. The new company would retain 'Herring's genius for the USA'.

Bishop's excitement was to be distressingly short-lived. In France a few weeks later, in the spring of 1909, he met the brothers on their way home from Wilbur's epic flying demonstrations. Bishop was shocked to hear that they planned to move against the company he had helped to create. The Wrights carefully detailed for him the history of what they regarded as the seizure of their revolutionary three-axis control system: Herring's 1902 visit to their gliding camp at Kill Devil where, under their trusting eyes, he had familiarised himself with every detail; the visit in 1906 to the cycle shop by Curtiss and the airship operator Tom Baldwin when the brothers had shown them, in confidence, photographs of the *Flyer*; the expertise they had shared with the now dead Selfridge on the understanding that it was for scientific research, not commercial purposes; Orville's warning to Curtiss that the *June Bug*'s controls infringed their patents when he invited him to pay for a licence. Most fundamental of all – and on their weakest ground – they succeeded in convincing Bishop that Curtiss's mid-wing ailerons blatantly copied the sacred wing-warping technique that lay at the very heart of their success.

Bishop was in an embarrassing bind. He was president of the Aero Club from which had split off the New York society that had bought the allegedly infringing *Golden Flier*. He was also on the board of the Herring-Curtiss company, and its biggest investor. Alarmed at what he had been told, he shot off a letter to the company president, the upright Monroe Wheeler. The Wrights, he informed the judge:

told me certain things which, if true, put matters in a very bad light, both on moral and legal grounds. If the facts are as they state them I shall regret having anything to do with the aeroplane part of the business . . . There are certain phases of the subject which I hope will be kept out of the papers for the sake of us all. I have great respect and esteem for the Wrights and for Curtiss and I hope we will all be discreet and not talk to reporters.[8]

Bishop told Wheeler that defending the Wrights' suits would be enormously expensive. 'I certainly will not put up more money, nor will my brother. The Wrights have ample funds and unlimited backing; we would have no chance.'[9] But into the courts and into the newspapers the actions were nonetheless to go. 'The brothers,' Wright historian Tom Crouch said, 'had spent their earlier years watching their father settle his church-related problems in one courtroom after another. Wilbur had helped Milton prepare legal briefs. Neither doubted that the courts existed to defend the virtuous.'[10]

The injunction Wilbur filed in the New York court sought to restrain the aeronautical society from exhibition of the *Golden Flier*, asked for damages, and drastically demanded the surrender of the machine for destruction. The bill of complaint claimed that Curtiss had broken his written undertaking to Orville that his aileron-controlled aeroplanes were not intended for exhibition flying. What the New York society was planning to do would 'practically destroy' a large source of revenue that was the entitlement of the Wrights. At Hammondsport further papers were served on the secretary of the Herring-Curtiss company.

Glenn Curtiss couldn't believe it was happening. When he'd first heard about it, as the plaudits were being showered upon him as the man of the hour at Reims, he had been unable to take it seriously. 'Everyone here,' he wrote home, 'thinks the Wrights' suit is only a bluff. No-one thinks there is any infringement.'[11] All the other aviators at Reims had expressed disgust that the Wrights were trying to establish what they saw as an outrageously grasping monopoly on the institution of flight.

An amiable, rather private man, popular with his colleagues,

Curtiss had tried to remain friends with Wilbur and Orville. He had gone to Fort Myer to watch Orville flying the latest army tests. He'd wanted to say hello to the brothers, but wasn't allowed to get near them. He had witnessed the flight on which the *Flyer*'s motor had stopped and Orville had hit the tree on landing. Later he had written a friendly letter to them both with a helpful suggestion to make their engine more reliable with a different type of magneto. The real point of the letter, however, had to do with the lawsuits he feared were coming his way. Convinced that the patent difficulty could be solved in civilised fashion between friends, without recourse to the courts, he wrote: 'I want to suggest that, if you contemplate any action, the matter be taken up privately between us to save if possible annoyance and publicity of lawsuits and trial.'[12]

But the Wrights no longer trusted Curtiss. And now that he was in bed with the disreputable Herring, the last shred of belief in his integrity had gone. The courts would decide the matter.

Up at Hammondsport the president of the troubled company, Judge Wheeler, was appalled at the furore. He put out a statement saying the suits would be strenuously defended. The records of the patent office, he was foolish enough to say, would show that 'many of the infringements alleged were fully covered by patents taken out by Mr Herring and his associates before the Wrights applied for patents'. It was true that a patent application for Curtiss's aileron-controlled *June Bug* had been filed. At the time, in the days of the by now defunct experimental association, Graham Bell, supporting the application, had gone to meticulous lengths to distinguish between the ailerons and the Wrights' wing-warping for roll control. Bell, who had faced something like 600 lawsuits challenging the supremacy of his own telephone invention, was particularly sensitive to the fine print of patent protection. 'We do not twist our aeroplanes or any portion of them for any purpose whatsoever,' he had declared in a memorandum to the patent attorney. Whereas the Wrights' wing-twisting had to be supplemented for banking by the rear rudder, the association's ailerons would roll the aeroplane unaided by rudder forces. The patent application, however, had yet to be granted. It made more urgent the need to know if the closely guarded Herring patents, purportedly predating the *Flyer*'s, provided a separate practical alternative to the control of an aeroplane in three dimensions.

For several months Curtiss had been pressing Herring for a sight of the patents upon which the new company's survival now rested. He had tried again, also, to view the design drawings of the secret army machine. Herring had failed to produce either. Relations between the two had begun to bristle with tension and suspicion.

While the Wrights' Damoclean threat hung over America's first aircraft production business – and, by inference, over Europe's new aileron-using aeroplane builders as well – the brothers were busy, through the late summer and autumn of 1909, clinging to the supremacy they were so briefly to enjoy. As Curtiss reeled at Reims from the news of their first salvo, Orville, Katharine and Hart Berg had arrived in Berlin. Sponsored by a newspaper, Orville was to demonstrate the *Flyer* to the Germans for a large fee. He had also gone to finalise with a group of businessmen arrangements for the production of machines locally under licence.

Orville responded with delight to the news in the German newspapers of their lawsuits. 'I think it would be a good plan,' he wrote immediately to Wilbur, 'to give out an interview in which announcement is made of suing all who have any connection with infringing machines.'[13] All, increasingly, was going to apply to almost every other rival aeroplane on earth. Already their ruthless policy was beginning to lose them the sympathy of valuable old friends and admirers – prominent among them the most constantly and devotedly supportive of them all. Octave Chanute, who had dedicated so much of his later life to sharing aeronautical know-how with the world, was thoroughly shocked. 'I think,' he wrote to the editor of *Aeronautics*, 'the Wrights have made a blunder by bringing suit at this time. Not only will this antagonise very many persons but it may disclose some prior patents which will invalidate their more important claims.'[14]

Chanute's criticism was seized upon by newspapers: they demanded elaboration of his strictures, and he obliged them. While Wilbur and Orville were entitled to be rewarded for their great achievement, he told the Chicago *Daily News*, their wing-warping claim was not absolutely original: 'Many inventors have worked on it,' he said, 'from the time of Leonardo da Vinci.' Chanute had struck at the aerodynamic Holy Grail – one of the Wrights' crucial discoveries that had finally cracked the problem of safe manned flight. His hurtful remarks spelt the beginning of an acrimonious end to a once very special relationship.

29

A Precious Friendship Sours (1910)

The ten-year-long friendship between the Wrights and Octave Chanute had been dying for a long time. The affectionate correspondence that provided for posterity the single most important record of the invention of the aeroplane had virtually dried up. Strangely, for someone who figured so eminently at the centre of the world's aeronautical information web, and who had been immersed for so long in the theory of aerodynamics and the evolution of manned flight, Chanute had still not fully grasped the groundbreaking significance of the control system the brothers were now aggressively determined to monopolise. Unshakeably he clung to the belief that they hadn't actually discovered the means safely to turn and bank – they had simply devised their own mechanism to do something that had been known long before they came on the scene.

The rift had boiled to the surface in the middle of 1908 when Chanute had begun publicly to criticise their approach to the sale of the *Flyer*. Milton had been peeved to read one such attack in the *Independent*. Chanute had criticised the brothers for demanding contracts 'for a secret machine', wasting years 'in fruitless negotiations' while the French aviators were catching up. Sending the critical clipping to Wilbur in France, Milton had urged his son's forbearance of the elderly outpourings. 'Age and premiership are to be considered . . . Better no rupture with a former friend.'[1]

Chanute's crusade to minimise the Wrights' technical achievements had spread to Europe. In German and French scientific magazines he had set out to play down the uniqueness of the *Flyer*'s controls, claiming that its warping system had been not only invented but patented years earlier by the French artist and glider experimenter Louis-Pierre Mouillard. Mouillard's dabbling in North Africa with flight control devices had been encouraged by Chanute, who had helped him financially and in 1887 obtained an American patent in their joint names. It had been for a primitive steering device in which outer wing flaps could be lowered to allow their resistance to turn the machine like the paddles of a canoe. These left and right drag brakes were not differentially connected like ailerons, and they could, if needed, be simultaneously lowered to reduce the glider's speed. In no way did they resemble the Wrights' physically interconnected wing-twisting surfaces which controlled the aircraft with great precision when used in conjunction with the rudder – a feature that Mouillard's glider totally lacked.

Chanute was now busy reminding the aviation world that he had sent a copy of the Mouillard patent to the Wrights well before their celebrated first flights in 1903. In interviews he'd begun to enlarge, too, on his own contribution to the creation of the *Flyer*. When the Wrights wanted to start flying, he told the Chicago *Daily News*, 'they wrote to me that they had read my book on gliding and asked if I would permit them to use the plans of my biplane.' The brothers had done no such thing. They had rejected at the outset Chanute's crude body-swinging methods of control inherited from Lilienthal.

Wilbur was conscious that advancing years were playing havoc with Chanute's memory and refrained from entering into a fight. His restraint, however, was exhausted by the appearance in a New York newspaper in December 1909 of a provocative article condemning the Wrights for 'their persistent failure to acknowledge their monumental indebtedness to the man who gave them priceless assistance'. It was, said the writer, Arnold Kruckman, 'one of the most puzzling mysteries in their careers'.[2]

It was too much for Wilbur. Incensed, he wrote to the author using the letterhead of the Wright Cycle Company to link Orville into the complaint: 'We wish to say to you, Mr Kruckman, that your accusation is most unjust and undeserved.' All they had borrowed from Chanute's gliders had been their construction; they had used the same strong wing-trussing system. But wing warping was entirely their original concept. Acknowledging Chanute's consistent encouragement of their experiments, Wilbur said it was:

> one of the chief stimulants which kept us at work till we attained success. We therefore owe him a great debt of gratitude which we have not the least thought to repudiate. Without it we might have quit and thus failed. But the impression which has grown up in some quarters that we began our work with a copy of one of his machines as a continuation of his experiments, and that we worked under his teachings and instruction, and even at his expense, is quite false. Except in the matter of sympathetic interest we are less indebted to him than to Lilienthal.

The stories alleging that their invention owed its ideas to a stream of knowledge from the Chanute fountain had embarrassingly begun, Wilbur said, 'to build up a legend which takes the place of truth'. Attempts to correct it gave the appearance of

> ungratefully attempting to hurt the fame of Mr Chanute. Rather than subject ourselves to criticism on that score we have preferred to remain silent . . .
>
> Mr Chanute is one of the truest gentlemen we have ever known and a sympathetic friend of all who have the cause of human flight at heart. For many years we entrusted to him many of our most important secrets, and only discontinued it when we began to notice that his advancing years made it difficult for him to exercise the necessary discretion.[3]

Chanute would not have seen this letter when, two days later, on 23 December, he sent Wilbur a warm note begging 'to tender to yourself, to Miss Katharine, to Orville and to your father my best wishes for a merry Christmas and a happy New Year. May all your desires be achieved and your anticipations fulfilled'.[4] Alas, the seasonal spirit was to endure only fleetingly.

In the weeks before Christmas 1909, Wilbur and Orville had been amassing their legal artillery. At long last they had formed a company. Wealthy presidents and stockholders of giant corporations from the US Steel Corporation to the Packard Automobile Company rushed to take shares. Leading the prominent names was the multimillionaire Cornelius Vanderbilt. The famous J.P. Morgan had wanted shares but withdrew when told the other investors feared his domination of the company. Formed with a capital stock of $1 million (around $20 million today), the Wright Company paid the brothers $100,000 in cash and shares for their patent rights and expertise. They were given a one third share of the stock and were to be paid a 10 per cent royalty on each machine sold. Wilbur had become president, Orville a vice-president. An aircraft production plant was being built in Dayton and the company's headquarters established in smart offices on Fifth Avenue, New York. To the Wrights' huge relief, the company, now owning their patents, had assumed responsibility for the licensing of rights, the hunting down of infringers, and the rising cost of prosecution. The company lawyers had quickly found themselves immersed in the first of the patent battles.

The case, *Wright Company v Herring-Curtiss Company and Glenn H. Curtiss*, had been heard by federal judge John Hazel in the circuit court in Buffalo, New York, in whose jurisdiction the Herring-Curtiss business came. At the trial, the defendants' attorney had swiftly moved to cut the Wrights down to size. Their fame, he said disparagingly, was based merely on their skill as 'airplane chauffeurs'. But Judge Hazel had decided otherwise. In the first week of January 1910 he handed down his judgement. It declared, surprisingly, that ailerons were the equivalent of wing warping. 'Dissimilarities in structure had no bearing on the case, since both mechanisms achieved an identical result.'[5] Pending a full hearing of the complex technical issues, the judge granted an injunction preventing the Curtiss company from manufacturing, selling or exhibiting aeroplanes.

Curtiss was flabbergasted. He immediately filed an appeal. On payment of a $10,000 bond he was allowed, while awaiting the hearing, to continue production. His appeal against the injunction later succeeded and the bond was returned. The trial of the substantive infringement suit was to be an appallingly protracted business. It would be four long years before the US Circuit Court of Appeals finally delivered a decision. Meanwhile the Herring-Curtiss company was free to go on building, demonstrating and selling its aileron-controlled aeroplanes across the country.

The decision, at least temporarily in Curtiss's favour, was a blow to Wilbur and Orville, but it didn't deter them from tracking down others they believed to be flouting their patents. Convinced of their rightfulness, they set out to pick them off one by one.

Within twenty-four hours the Wright Company launched its second strike: it filed an injunction against a French pilot called Louis Paulhan. A newcomer to aviation, Paulhan, who had taught himself to fly and had become one of the star performers at the Reims meet, had come to America to give flying exhibitions. Innocently he had brought four machines – two Farmans and two Blériots. On arrival in New York a shock awaited him. As he walked down the gangway he was served with injunction papers. All his aeroplanes, he was informed, breached the Wright patents – the Farmans with ailerons, the Blériots with wing warping. It was a month before the case was heard; Paulhan quickly used the breathing space to great profit. Demonstrations, including long cross-country flights, brought him, within weeks, a magnificent $20,000 – before he found himself in a New York court. The now inevitable injunction ordered him to post a huge $25,000 bond – half a million dollars today – or cease flying. Paulhan ignored the order and went on flying – until US marshals caught up with him in Oklahoma. As they served papers upon him 'Paulhan raised his clenched fists and emitted a stream of French invectives'. He decided to cut his losses. Abandoning the tour, he shipped his aeroplanes back to France.

Even in their homeland French aviators and aircraft builders were not safe from the long arm of the Wrights. Later that year their French company, Compagnie Générale de Navigation Aérienne, sued no fewer than six rival manufacturers. Many of the leading plane-makers – Blériot, Farman, Esnault-Pelterie, Antionette and Santos-Dumont – were among them. The suits were vigorously defended. The honour of French aviation, which had hoisted the first men into the air in balloons, was at stake. When the case came to trial, the defendants were united in protestation that the Wrights' patent application was invalidated by 'prior disclosure' of the brothers' technology. The French lawyers had been busy. They had combed through the records of every description ever given of the *Flyer*'s mode of control. To their delight they struck gold. Had not the eminent authority, Octave Chanute no less, helpfully divulged the vital essence of it all in his unfortunately revealing 1903 lecture that had created such a stir at the French Aéro-Club – followed by his article with scale drawings, moreover, in *L'Aérophile*? So, too, they insisted, had Wilbur himself in his acclaimed 1901 address to Chanute's fellow engineers in Chicago in which he had referred to their use of torsion of the wings to control 'lateral equilibrium'.

Increasingly Chanute's 1903 lecture and article were to return to haunt the Wrights. Aviation historians over the years have searched the records of his enthusiastic utterances during that Paris visit. No verbatim note was apparently made of his Aéro-Club lecture, but the excited chairman, Ernest Archdeacon, recalling much of the illuminating detail, had immediately written a full account for *La Locomotion*. In this he quoted Chanute's fatal words – not only that Wilbur was one of his 'intelligent and daring pupils' but his description of the Wrights' lateral control 'by means of warping upon the right and left sides of the wing and, simultaneously, by the movement of the vertical rear rudder'.[6] In his *L'Aérophile* article a few months later Chanute had revealed the heart of the matter again: their glider was steered 'to the right or left by the torsion of the wings which are framed loosely and by the vertical rudder behind'.[7]

As their latest litigation began to grind with numbing complexity through the French courts, Chanute's injudicious disclosures of seven years earlier appeared to be making a gift of their unique device to the world. Beneath the conventional civilities of seasonal greetings, the air between them by early 1910 was brimming with mistrust.

In 1909 Chanute had tried to block the award to them of a prestigious honour. The Smithsonian Institution had established a Langley medal in memory of its former chief. It was to be awarded annually for 'specially meritorious investigations in aeronautical science'. The brothers were an overwhelmingly obvious choice for the inaugural honour. Unfortunately, the awards committee chairman was Octave Chanute. He held that, against the spirit of the award, they had gone to unusual lengths to keep their invention secret. The board of regents had brushed his objection aside; but when Wilbur and Orville went to Washington to receive the award Chanute was absent.

The final showdown was triggered by a further New York *World* interview with Chanute in which he repeated his mantra that the principle of wing warping had been known for half a century. When Wilbur saw the story he was livid. He cut it out and sent it to Chanute, demanding that he identify the previous users of wing warping. As Mouillard, so frequently quoted by Chanute, did not, who, then, were the others?

Chanute sent a list of nineteenth-century aviation thinkers and experimenters who, he claimed, had alighted on the wing-warping idea, written about it and thus put this roll control method permanently into the public domain. Two of those he retrieved from the past were enterprising French pioneers – a sea captain, Jean-Marie Le Bris, celebrated in the 1850s for raising himself with galloping horses 300 feet into the air in a large albatross-winged glider; and a French count, Ferdinand d'Esterno, who'd described in an 1864 book a glider he'd designed but never flown. Wilbur's research established that neither machine had any provision for roll control and he wrote and told Chanute so. If the courts decided, Chanute replied, that the Wrights were 'the first to conceive the twisting of the wings so much the better for you, but my judgement is that you will be restricted to the particular method by which you do it.' With the harshest words he had ever used in a letter to Wilbur, he repeated his condemnation of their witch-hunt. 'I am afraid, my friend,' he said, 'that your usually sound judgement has been warped by the desire for great wealth.'[8]

Chanute had another bone to pick with Wilbur. The brothers had attended a dinner in Boston organised in Chanute's honour; Wilbur had been asked to speak. No precise record of what he said that evening appears to have survived, but whatever it was it deeply wounded Chanute, striking at the very root of their friendship:

> In your speech at the Boston dinner, January 12th, you began by saying that I 'turned up' at your shop in Dayton in 1901 and that you then invited me to your camp. This conveyed the impression that I thrust myself upon you at that time and it omitted to state that you were the first to write to me, in 1900, asking for information which was gladly furnished, that many letters passed between us, and that both in 1900 and 1901 you had written to me to invite me to visit you, before I 'turned up' in 1901. This, coming subsequently to some somewhat disparaging remarks concerning the helpfulness I may have been to you, attributed to you by a number of French papers, which I, of course, disregarded as newspaper talk, has grated upon me ever since that dinner, and I hope that, in future, you will not give out the impression that I was the first to seek your acquaintance, or pay me left-handed compliments, such as saying that 'sometimes an experienced person's advice was of great value to younger men.'[9]

In Dayton, where construction had started that January of 1910 on the Wright Company's aeroplane factory, Wilbur and Orville read Chanute's hostile words with incredulity. They had no idea that the friend they had for so long valued as their patron, soulmate and confidant even at times their adviser had been smoulderingly nursing such an embittered sense of grievance behind his flow of courteous and supportive letters. Wilbur waited five days before bracing himself to reply. When he did it was the most biting, emotionally charged letter he had ever sent to the old man.

He and Orville, he said, found the things Chanute was saying quite incredible.

> We had never had the slightest ground for suspecting that when you repeatedly spoke to us in 1901 of the originality of our methods, you referred only to our methods of driving tacks,

> fastening wires etc, and not to the novelty of our general systems. Neither in 1901, nor in the five years following, did you in any way intimate to us that our general system of lateral control had long been a part of the art and, strangely enough, neither your books, addresses or articles, nor the writings of Lilienthal, Langley, Maxim, Hargrave etc made any mention whatever of such a system. Therefore it came to us with somewhat of a shock when you calmly announced that this system was already a feature of the art well-known, and that you meant only the mechanical details when you referred to its novelty.
>
> If the idea was really old in the art, it is somewhat remarkable that a system so important that individual ownership of it is considered to threaten strangulation of the art was not considered worth mentioning then, nor embodied in any machine built prior to ours.[10]

As to greed, surely, Wilbur said, 'the world owes us something as inventors, regardless of whether we personally make Roman holidays for accident-loving crowds.' The gloves off at last, Wilbur went on to pour out some of the resentments they had been quietly harbouring against Chanute for eight years. Chief among them was their hurt that he had continually described them in France as his pupils who had merely

> put into material form a knowledge furnished by you; that you provided the funds; in short that you furnished the science and money while we contributed a little mechanical skill, and that when success had been achieved you magnanimously stepped aside and permitted us to enjoy the rewards . . .
>
> The difficulty of correcting the errors without seeming to disparage you and hurting your feelings kept me silent, though I sometimes restrained myself with difficulty.

Wilbur reminded Chanute of their true and exclusive achievements: the historic breakthrough of their brilliant wind tunnel experiments that had produced the data that led to the creation of efficient wings; their groundbreaking scientific work that solved the propeller problem. He reminded him that they alone had designed, built and flown 'all of our machines from first to last' at their own expense. They had not made a single flight in any of Chanute's own machines.

As to the Boston dinner remarks that had precipitated it all, Wilbur said that he had had 'no thought of intimating either that you had or had not been the first to seek an acquaintance between us'. But when it came to the sensitive heart of Chanute's grievances – their consistent failure to acknowledge the smallest indebtedness to his own aeronautical expertise – Wilbur was merciless. 'I confess,' he said hurtfully, 'that I have found it most difficult to formulate a precise statement of what you contributed to our success.' The air would perhaps be cleared 'if such a statement could be prepared', relieving 'a situation very painful to you and to us . . . There is no pleasure to us in the situation . . . We have no wish to quarrel with a man toward whom we ought to preserve a feeling of gratitude.'[11]

In one of the most penetrating letters he had ever written, Wilbur, in putting their friendship under the microscope, had not a word for the incalculable number of unpublicised things the other man had actually contributed: his kindness and generosity of spirit, his unstinting encouragement, his rallying words when, depressed by failure in 1901, Wilbur had declared that 'not in a thousand years would man ever fly'.

Chanute, now in failing health, was shocked beyond comprehension by this brutal broadside. The cruel candidness of Wilbur's words and his righteous fury hastened the end of one of aviation's most remarkable fellowships. The ageing engineer was too stunned to reply immediately. A few days later he wrote to George Spratt, who was still futilely struggling on his Pennsylvania farm to find his own solution to the conundrum of flight. Chanute told Spratt that he had received a 'violent letter' from Wilbur 'in which he disputes my opinion, brings up various grievances, and quite loses his temper. I will answer him in a few days, but the prospects are that we will have a row.'[12]

Chanute did not reply. His silence began to bother Wilbur: Chanute usually responded within the week. When three months had passed, Wilbur became worried. In the last week of April, anxious to keep the relationship alive, he sat down to write a kinder note to the man who, beyond his own family, had once been his most valuable friend and confidant, and with whom he had shared in such precious trust so many of the agonies of invention:

> I have no answer to my last letter and fear that the frankness with which delicate subjects were treated may have blinded you to the real spirit and purpose of the letter . . . My brother and I do not form many intimate friendships, and do not lightly give them up. I believed that unless we could understand exactly how you felt, and you could understand how we felt, our friendship would tend to grow weaker instead of stronger. Through ignorance or thoughtlessness, each would be touching the other's sore spots and causing unnecessary pain. We prize too highly the friendship which meant so much to us in the years of our early struggles to willingly see it worn away by uncorrected misunderstandings which might be corrected by a frank discussion. My object was not to give offence but to remove it. If you will read my letter carefully I think you will see that the spirit is that of true friendship.[13]

Wilbur suggested, once again unfeelingly, that the wounds could be healed and the air cleared by publication of 'a joint statement' that would 'do justice to both and injustice to neither'.

What would such a statement have contained? Would it have succeeded in correcting some of the claims the internationally revered old gentleman had so unwisely made thousands of miles from America in a foreign language so many years before? Would it have soothed the grievances that had for so long been festering between them? We will never know.

Wilbur was unaware that Chanute was ill; he was away resting and recuperating in New Orleans. When he returned to Chicago he responded at last, but his letter conceded nothing. 'I am in bad health and threatened with nervous exhaustion,' he wrote,

> and am now to sail for Europe on the 17th of this month.

> Your letter of April 28 was gratifying, for I own that I felt very much hurt by your letter of January 29th which I thought both unduly angry and unfair as well as unjust.
>
> I have never given out the impression, either in writing or speech, that you had taken up aeronautics at my insistence or were, as you put it, pupils of mine. I have always written and spoken of you as original investigators and worthy of the highest praise. How much I may have been of help I do not know. I have never made any claims in that respect, but I may confess that I have sometimes thought that you did not give me as much credit as I deserved.14

On wing warping Chanute still firmly refused to yield an inch; he would not acknowledge that they were the true originators. Adamant to the bitter end, he would go no further than accepting that 'you are entitled to immense credit for devising apparatus by which it has been reduced to successful practice'. The letter ended on a conciliatory note: 'I hope, upon my return from Europe, that we will be able to resume our former relations.'

On his visit to Europe that summer of 1910, Chanute contracted pneumonia. From France he had been due to go to England to receive the great honour of the Aeronautical Society's gold medal. He had to cancel the visit. Barely well enough to withstand the voyage back to America in October, he died in Chicago, aged seventy-eight, the following month.

30

'Keep Out of My Air' (1910–1911)

Wilbur, when he got the telegram, dropped everything and took the train to Chicago. He had had no idea that Chanute was so ill, for the two had long ceased to share news of these more personal things. Milton duly recorded the death in his diary that evening, according it second place to news of the execution of the American wife poisoner Hawley Crippen: 'Crippen was hung for killing his wife in England. Chanute, Octave, died in Chicago aged 79 years nearly . . . I do not believe that Crippen killed his wife.'

The funeral was a private occasion, family and close friends. Though he was never to concede that the celebrated French-American had brought anything of aeronautical significance to their invention, Wilbur was generous in his praise for the impetus his international agency had given the birth of the aeroplane. 'The world has lost one whose labours had to an unusual degree influenced the course of human progress,' he wrote. 'If he had not lived the entire history of progress in flying would have been other than it has been.' In an appraisal of his aviation work for *Aeronautics,* Wilbur factually recalled Chanute's own experiments and his dogged, unsuccessful attempts to create a machine with automatic stability. The railroad engineer who became obsessed with human flight had been defeated by the success 'of the Wrights', Wilbur said, with their philosophy of control by 'human intelligence'. Nonetheless, Chanute's labours 'had vast influence in bringing about the era of human flight'. His lucid writings had helped the world to an intelligent understanding of the technical problems of flight. He had 'inspired and encouraged all who were devoted to the work. No-one was too humble to receive a share of his time. In patience and goodness of heart he has rarely been surpassed. Few men were more universally respected and loved.'[1]

In another tribute Wilbur credited Chanute with having, along with Lilienthal, the greatest influence of their generation on the development of human flight. Chanute had been 'a missionary of the cause'. His books and correspondence had 'inspired and encouraged others to action'.[2]

No one can doubt the genuine respect and love Wilbur had felt for Chanute; but he was greatly concerned about the technical secrets they had so willingly shared with him over the years. The huge correspondence, more than 400 letters, would be a trove of incalculable aeronautical value to the rivals now determined to fight their infringement lawsuits. Within the letters there lay invaluable aerodynamic information about almost everything they had struggled to understand and perfect – from the data involved in the creation of efficient wings and propellers to the triumphs of three-dimensional control. On all of this they had trustingly bared their inventive souls to Chanute, initially sharing their exciting discoveries almost as if he'd been another brother. If the letters got into the public domain they could spell the end of all hope of successful prosecutions, the death of future revenue.

Within weeks of Chanute's death he wrote anxiously to Charles Chanute, Octave's son, to enquire about the fate of the letters. 'I do not know whether you have any intention of turning his papers over to a biographer soon, but I am writing to request that you do not permit any person <u>interested in flying as a business</u> to have access to these papers and talks at this time.' Wilbur said they had communicated freely with his father on the understanding that all their disclosures were treated as confidential. He told the son, with some justification, that the correspondence would one day have 'historic value'. Charles Chanute replied that as his father's estate now owned the correspondence he could give no assurances about its disposition.

In fact, earlier in 1910 Octave had already moved to protect the priceless correspondence. He had had typewritten copies made of all his letters to Wilbur. Charles Chanute agreed similarly to protect all of Wilbur's to his father. The Chanute–Wright correspondence, today renowned among aviation historians for what it reveals about the frankness, scientific intelligence, philosophic spirit and simple charm out of which flight was born, was not to become publicly accessible – in the Library of Congress – until the early 1950s. But long before then Wilbur's concern for their confidentiality was proved to be well founded.

Professor Albert Zahm, who had persuaded Chanute to go ahead with his 1893 Chicago international aviation conference and had made such a fuss of Orville on his 1908 army demonstration visit to Washington, cultivating both brothers the following year, had joined the patent litigation saga as a new threatening force. By 1910, now secretary of the Aero Club of Washington and established as a widely recognised academic and aeronautical scientist – he had done his own wind tunnel experiments at Catholic University and published learned aerodynamic works – he had seen a chance to capitalise on the action against the Herring-Curtiss company. Having earlier provided Wilbur with a helpful technical affidavit that was harmful to Curtiss, he decided to offer his services as a scientific witness to the brothers again, writing to Wilbur: 'You will probably regard me as a renegade friend if the defence in the approaching litigation succeed in securing my professional service against you, but I hope you will remember that I have never declined, or hesitated, to serve you when the opportunity arose.' When the Wrights rejected the offer a tense exchange ensued. Wilbur wrote: 'Naturally we regret that you will be lined up against us . . . in the legal struggles, but we do not think that such a service carried out in a spirit of friendliness need interrupt the friendship which has always existed between us.'[3]

Zahm replied angrily: 'Apparently you are not very much concerned about my position in the patent litigation, seeing that you made no effort to secure my professional services.'

From that moment Zahm became calculatedly hostile towards the Wrights. He executed an affidavit for Curtiss that contradicted the technical statement he had earlier sworn for Wilbur. Overnight he became a star witness for Curtiss. And, getting wind of the treasure chest of the all-revealing aeronautical dialogue that lay sleeping in the custody of the Chanute estate, Zahm persuaded the executors to let him see the documents. He went to Chicago and began to devour the revelatory letters.[4] Sinister as this may have appeared, it seems that his limited perusal may not have reached as far as disclosures of the crucial flight control system. When Curtiss's appeal against the drastic injunction was allowed and the substantive hearing embarked on its tortuous processes to decide the issue, the defence lawyers would, for the moment, continue passionately to argue in court that ailerons were quite different control surfaces which the Wrights had not invented.

Many agreed with them. The technical argument divided an aviation world at the dawn of its bursting into a vast global industry. Most people were bewildered by the abstruse technical issue and the Wrights' sweeping demand that anyone using, it seemed, any protruding device on their wings to bank their aeroplanes must pay them royalties for the privilege. If the Wrights had invented the wheel, it was asked, would they have been entitled to patent their invention? Or, more precisely: if they had invented the wheel but patented the axle, without which the wheel couldn't operate, would they have been entitled to a fee from every man who used the wheel?[5]

The tenacious British aviation historian Charles Gibbs-Smith, a stickler for historical truth, made, in the 1970s, a careful study of the fine print in the Wrights' 1906 patent that they believed supported their lawsuits. He concluded that, while they had clearly established an exclusive right to the wing-warping device, they had no legal grounds at all for the prosecution of those, like Curtiss and Cody, who had fitted ailerons 'as separate surfaces' between the wings – or indeed separate moveable banking devices anywhere that were not, like the warping system, a part of the wing itself. Gibbs-Smith felt so strongly about this that, in 1974, he dictated a memorandum to be filed with his aeronautical papers at the National Museum of

Science and Industry in South Kensington. It said that careful examination of the patent text revealed:

> no statement which clearly covers separate winglets or separate ailerons; all references are to portions of the main wings . . . Orville himself seemed in no doubt about his own patent at the time he accused the AEA [Graham Bell's Aerial Experiment Association] of infringing it. For we have him writing to Wilbur in Europe on August 16 1908: 'If you have a copy of our American patent I wish you would look it over and give me your opinion of the claims that cover the Curtiss machine ie one using separate pieces on the ends of the wings that can be adjusted.'[6]

The Aerial Association's early machines had attached ailerons to the wingtips – but Curtiss's successful *Golden Flier* had deliberately relocated them as separate devices between the upper and lower wings. The aeroplane and its *Reims Racer* sister did not, Gibbs-Smith claimed, infringe the Wrights' patent.

'There never would be any legally satisfying answer to the question,' wrote Wright biographer Fred Howard (who helped edit the brothers' technical papers at the Library of Congress), 'but the battle in the courts would go on for seven long years, gathering size and momentum like a large snowball,' leaving in its wake 'a sordid trail of hatred, invective and lies that muddy the pages of aeronautical history to this day'.

Some of this hatred and invective, sparked off by the Wrights' lawsuit against it, burst spectacularly within the precarious Herring-Curtiss company, quickly tearing it apart. The Herring patents and inventions which he had assigned to the business and which underpinned the partnership were suddenly of critical importance to its very survival. Curtiss, apparently quite sincerely believing that in joining forces with Herring he was allying himself with an aeronautical genius, now urgently needed the proof. His lawyers demanded to inspect the unseen documents; the company's directors ordered Herring to hand them over. When he failed to do so, he and his lawyer were summoned to a special meeting at the Hammondsport headquarters. There the directors moved to file an injunction requiring Herring to produce the material.

While these injunction formalities were being attended to there was a pause in the proceedings. Herring excused himself and left the room. A few minutes later his lawyer also left the room. When neither man reappeared, a search by car was made through the streets of Hammondsport. Herring and his lawyer had disappeared. They lay low for the night and next day fled by train to New York. For three weeks Herring remained in hiding there to avoid being served the papers. There was no workable invention; the patents did not exist; all that he possessed were rejected applications dating back to 1896 – all refused by the Patent Office for lack of proof that any of them were practical. By the time Herring emerged from hiding, the Herring-Curtiss company had begun to sink into debt, and Curtiss was forced into paying the staff out of his own pocket. He now only wanted to get rid of Herring. Unfortunately the latter, through some financial chicanery, had acquired the major stake in the company. When Curtiss tried to buy him out, Herring refused. Curtiss responded by putting the company into bankruptcy. Injunctions flew between them. Herring, trying to patch it all up, offered to drop his suit, urging they 'get together and put the Wright Brothers out of business'.[7]

It was, however, the Herring-Curtiss company that met that fate. It was formally declared bankrupt in December 1910. Curtiss promptly started up a new business. Within four years it was to become the Curtiss Aeroplane Company, the biggest and most successful aircraft manufacturer in the United States. Herring, left with a parcel of worthless shares, went off to lick his wounds, protesting that the bankruptcy had merely been a desperate device to dump him. Curtiss had still not heard the last from him.

During all this tumult the Wrights had been making more headlines. In September 1909, when the tensions between them and Curtiss were just beginning, Wilbur had astounded millions in New York with a lucrative twenty-mile flight from Governor's Island up the Hudson River to Grant's Tomb and back. He had been paid $15,000 – around a third of a million dollars today – to do it. Watched by crowds waving to the box-kite contraption from the tops of Manhattan's skyscrapers and serenaded once more by ferry whistles and foghorns, he had, with an emergency flotation device fitted between the skids, made an orbit of the Statue of Liberty followed by a 33-minute journey up the river that had been the talk of the city.

Meanwhile, in Germany, Orville and Katharine, in that early autumn of 1909, had once more been enjoying the fruits of fame. Accommodated in a luxurious hotel, they were being treated like a visiting king and queen. Orville had set a new unofficial world altitude record of over 1600 feet and a new passenger-carrying record of over an hour and a half. He trained pilots for the newly formed German Wright company, Flugmaschine Wright Gesellschaft, and gave exhibition flights for the newspaper *Lokal-Anzieger*. Two hundred thousand people, including Kaiser Wilhelm, had gone out to Berlin's army parade ground at Templehof to watch the *Flyer* making its immaculate orbits. On the ground, escorted again by Hart Berg, who was now joined by his boss Charles Flint, Orville was mobbed.

Everywhere brother and sister were treated with awe. So frightening was the crush that they had to be escorted by a posse of bodyguards. A troop of soldiers in spiked helmets permanently guarded the *Flyer*'s shed. And every time they tried to enter their hotel, a squad of police on horseback had to force a passage for them. 'Dear Pop,' Katharine wrote home, 'the crowds have been enormous . . . The likes of this social whirl in Berlin we have never seen before. We refuse every invitation we decently can but nevertheless we are out every evening for dinner.'[8]

Unlike France, Germany had been slow to develop the flying machine; its military had long favoured airships. The Kaiser introduced Katherine and Orville to von Zeppelin and the count took Orville for a 50-mile flight in his giant dirigible. In Berlin they constantly hobnobbed with members of the royal family, top generals and wealthy industrialists. The Kaiser and the Empress had them to dinner and the Crown Prince, Friedrich Wilhelm, pleaded to be taken for a flight. 'I have now had a half dozen or more conversations with the Crown Prince on the telephone. We are getting quite chummy!' Orville told Wilbur. 'He says he doesn't want to miss getting a ride. Everyone tells me that I had better get the consent of the Emperor before taking him, as there might otherwise be trouble.'[9] The Kaiser had agreed – news of the Berlin flights had been pouring back to America. 'I see you in front of the crowds with the empress and princesses etc and not writing any letters, but all right for you,' Wilbur complained to Katharine. 'Just wait till the winter comes and then you get the bad of it like any other grasshopper after the festive season is over. I have had <u>one</u> letter since you left home more than six weeks ago.'[10]

If not letters, certainly money was flowing back to Dayton from Berlin. 'I am sending a draft for $40,000,' Orville wrote to Lorin, who had become their investment manager, telling him what to do with the tidy sum that would today be approaching a million. 'If Will is not at home please place it in different building associations.'[11]

In Berlin Orville found himself competing with French aircraft builders also chasing German buyers for their machines; but the French pilots couldn't compete with the *Flyer*. 'The French aviators are pretty sore because the Royal Family all paid so much attention to Orv but found no time to see them,' Katharine proudly told Milton. 'They knew all right to whom the credit belongs and they were not slow about showing it.'[12]

Increasingly, however, the credit was being disputed and the Wrights' relentless pursuit of almost every competitor through the courts bitterly criticised. The avalanche of litigation they launched changed not only attitudes towards them but the entire pattern of Wilbur's and Orville's lives. It forced them for the first time to work on different fronts. From 1910 to 1912, while Orville was busily training pilots, Wilbur virtually ceased to fly, his energies now consumed by the demands of the patent suits sizzling on both sides of the Atlantic. He was constantly away from home, wrestling with technical affidavits, moving from court to court, standing for days giving evidence and being exhaustingly cross-examined by aggressive lawyers. If he wasn't on the stand in New York or Buffalo he would be at a patent hearing in Paris or Berlin. For Wilbur it was like a rerun of the Brethren wars. Inspired by the biblical associations, he leapt to defend their unyielding position:

> When a couple of flying machine inventors fish, metaphorically speaking, in waters where hundreds had previously fished for thousands of years in vain, and after risking their lives hundreds of times, and spending years of time and thousands of dollars, finally succeed in making a catch, there are people who think it a pity that the courts should give orders that the rights of the inventors shall be respected and that those who wish to enjoy the feast shall contribute something to pay the fishers.[13]

The Wrights' deadly pursuit of Louis Paulhan had caused particular uproar. American newspapers ran cartoons of the brothers brandishing their fists at an aeroplane as they shout: 'Keep out of my Air!' The *New York Herald* had headlined the story FLY NO MORE IF YOU DO NOT HIRE WRIGHTS' WINGS. The French aviation fraternity saw them as grasping monopolists. The Fédération Aéronautique Internationale complained to the Aero Club of America: unless the Wrights would guarantee not to 'molest' foreign fliers, no European pilots would attend the next races, due to be held this time in America, for the prestigious Gordon Bennett trophy. The hero-figure Louis Blériot joined the expressions of disgust. 'It was regrettable,' he declared, 'to see at the dawn of a science (to encourage which all should have united in their efforts), inventors make the unjustifiable claim of monopolising an idea and, instead of bringing their help to the collaborators, prevent them, for no reason, from profiting by some ideas which they should have been happy to see generalised.'[14] The Wrights refused to make the least concession. Moral right was on their side. They suggested that the French create a fund to compensate them for those of its country's aviators who used 'infringing' machines.

In France the court battle, launched by the Wrights' French company against six leading aircraft manufacturers, was to go on for more than five years. A technical adviser engaged by the judges decided that the patent had been invalidated by the prior disclosure revealed by Wilbur himself to the Chicago engineers, and by Chanute so candidly spilling the secret beans right there in Paris. Chanute's 1903 address was also seized upon. Their German patent was declared invalid and the Imperial Supreme Court upheld that ruling.

In America, where many of the recipients of injunctions decided it was cheaper to pay up, they had better luck. While the Herring-Curtiss case was still grinding its way through the legal system, with Curtiss trying to prove he could safely bank his machines without use of the rudder, the Wright Company eventually succeeded in getting an agreement with the Aero Club of America by which all flying exhibitions would be sanctioned by the company and royalties paid as a percentage of prize or gate money. 'There was grumbling,' said biographer Fred Howard, 'that the Wrights were arrogating to themselves complete control of aviation in America.' The brothers' response was to enter the highly profitable exhibition flying business themselves. They formed a team and Orville trained an elite pilot group at a flying school they set up on their old airfield at Huffman Prairie, now called Simms Station. The barnstorming pilots travelled the country, introducing the aeroplanes to Americans from coast to coast, breaking new records and, at a fee that would now amount to $100,000 per appearance, creating a healthy income stream – a cash flow that would have been even larger had Wilbur and Orville allowed them to fly on the sabbath.

Competing for the crowds 'crazy to see flights' and the revenue was Glenn Curtiss. For the moment the court still allowed him to fly, and he'd formed a rival team of exhibition pilots. Still anxious to come to terms privately with the Wrights, Curtiss asked his marketing manager and publicist, Jerome Fanciulli, a former newsman, to go to Dayton. According to Curtiss's biographer, C.R. Roseberry, Fanciulli had got to know Wilbur and Orville as a reporter covering their flights. Curtiss wanted Fanciulli to go and meet them 'to see whether the Wrights would be friendly to him' – whether they would consider forming 'a combination' or make an arrangement to end the patent litigation.

Fanciulli didn't go to Dayton. It seems that he used his connections to test the water and discovered that the Wrights 'were very bitter'; a visit would be pointless. Later in 1910 the brothers had made their own approach: an offer to settle by which Curtiss would pay $1000 royalty on every machine he built plus $100 for each day one of his aeroplanes flew on exhibition business. The proposal, however, had a tough condition – that it retrospectively cover all past flights by Curtiss machines as well. Curtiss refused.

In the autumn of 1910 the Wright and Curtiss flying teams met in competition at a big international air tournament at Belmont Park on Long Island. The major event was the second running of the James Gordon Bennett speed race for which entrants included pilots from England and France who, under the Wrights' deal with the Aero Club, all paid hefty participation fees for the privilege of using their wing warps or ailerons. Ironically, neither a Wright nor a Curtiss machine won the big race. Curtiss withdrew his aeroplane, deciding it wasn't powerful enough. The Wright entry, to be flown by one of the exhibition pilots, was the favourite: a new high-speed machine with an eight-cylinder 50 to 60 horsepower engine, called the *Baby Grand*. Orville had already clocked a sensational 70 miles an hour in it. But the company pilot due to race it suffered an engine failure on a test run and crashed.

The Gordon Bennett trophy went to a British pilot, Claude Grahame-White, flying a Blériot, its wing warping licensed just for the event. Earlier in 1910 Grahame-White, the wealthy son of an English woollen mill family who had bought one of Blériot's machines and taught himself to pilot it, had become a flying celebrity in England. He'd taken up Lord Northcliffe's challenge and set out to fly from London to Manchester in twenty-four hours. It had become a tense race between him and his only other rival, the Frenchman Louis Paulhan whom the Wrights had driven out of America. Paulhan had taken the £10,000 *Daily Mail* prize, despite Grahame-White's desperate efforts to catch him up – flying by night, perilously trying to follow northbound trains through the dark along the London–Manchester railway. Subsequently Grahame-White had also come to make some big money barnstorming in America. He had the following year, in 1911, captured headlines with his daring flights, been personally welcomed by President Taft and once taken off dramatically before an excited crowd in one of his Farmans from the street beside the White House. But he, too, was to fall prey to the rigour of Wilbur's witch-hunt from which, it seemed, there was simply no hiding place. Grahame-White was believed to have amassed a small fortune – a huge $100,000 (two million today) – with his exhibitions across the country. In December 1911 the Wright Company sued him for half that. Unlike the European courts, the American judge found in their favour – but awarded them, and not until twelve months later, only a token $1700.

While the American decisions upheld the claim that all the practical means of laterally controlling an aeroplane were the exclusive property of the Wrights, it was a hollow victory. The message to the growing ranks of the violators was that, effectively, on payment of their costs and a small fee, they could fly their Blériots and Farmans in America with impunity. Moreover, not all the Wrights' swoops upon American air-show organisers were successful. As Wilbur set out methodically to pick them off – 'showing our teeth a little' as he put it to Orville – he began to meet increasing resistance. The Aero Club of Illinois refused to pay. The Wrights had problems, too, extracting the income due to them from the organisers of the big Belmont Park meet. 'The Belmont swindlers,' Wilbur described them angrily to Orville.

More and more of their old relationships began to fall apart. Albert Zahm, now actively helping Curtiss prove the Wrights weren't the first to think of wing warping, had become a formidable enemy. It wasn't helped by the former mathematics and physics professor's status now as one of the country's few academics who fully understood the esoteric aerodynamics of the flying machine. While the case was still being heard, Zahm published a book tracing the history of aviation.[15] In it he said that Chanute's 1896 biplane glider could have been easily converted to a successful powered machine. 'Any intelligent artisan could power a Chanute glider and soar aloft,' he'd gaily written, adding: 'The aeroplane would thus appear to be the sudden outgrowth of fertile and mature conditions, rather than the product of uncommon originality.' Zahm went even further. He asserted that, back in 1893, he himself had delivered a paper to the historic Chicago aviation conference proposing the three-axis control system the Wrights had subsequently patented. The brothers never forgave Zahm for this misrepresentation, and when they tripped up the aerodynamics professor in court on a technical point, publicly humiliating him, the enmity between them became a permanent, hostile rift.

'It is rather amusing,' Wilbur wrote to the dreaded Edward Huffaker (whom they had considered – but in the end didn't – asking to give evidence of their 1901 Kill Devil control success), that 'after having been called fools and fakers for six or eight years, to find now that people knew exactly how to fly all the time.'

Another old friend to go was George Spratt. In the autumn of 1909 he'd written to them claiming that their success owed something to his suggestion in the smoke-filled hut at Kill Devil that they measure the lift/drag relationship of their wings as a ratio of one another. They had not, he said, ever given him public credit for his contribution, nor anything in return. Wilbur had replied, freely acknowledging that they'd used his idea. 'We have not wished to deprive you of the credit,' he'd said, 'and when we give to the world that part of our work, we shall certainly give you proper credit.' He had been 'surprised and a trifle hurt', he told Spratt, that he was complaining they hadn't repaid his contribution. In fact, he'd reminded him, they had trustingly sent him all their groundbreaking wind tunnel data. 'My ideas of values may be wrong but I cannot help feeling that in so doing we returned the loan with interest.'[16] Spratt had disagreed and the friendship had ended.

Old, once valuable friends may have been fading away, but the brothers' financial fortunes were not. Wealth undreamed of in the frugal days of the cycle shop began to accumulate in their prudent investment accounts. Towards the end of 1910 Wilbur confided the scale of it in a letter to Hart Berg: 'As for the American Wright company it has made a net profit of more than a hundred thousand dollars this year. Orville and I will take out more than fifty thousand clear for our share . . . in the past 16 months we have received about two hundred thousand dollars in cash in America.'[17] The money had come from the US Army's initial purchase, the sponsored New York flights, from royalties, and from the $100,000 paid to them for the sale of their patents to the Wright Company. They had also, of course, received a further $100,000 on the formation of their French company. Three hundred thousand dollars is not, for many people, a vast fortune any more – but in 1910 it had the purchasing power of $6 million today.

It enabled the Wright family to consider moving upmarket. Fame had greatly increased the spread of their worldly possessions; the modest house in Hawthorn Street, which they had occupied for nearly forty years, could scarcely contain it all any longer. And the middle-class character of the street was receding with an influx of artisan families. Early in 1910 they began to look around for somewhere to build a bigger home. Wilbur and Orville chose a small lot in West Dayton about a mile away to the north. However, Katharine opposed it as being too near the city centre. She wanted the tranquillity of a more secluded site on the wooded Oakwood hill to the south of downtown Dayton. Her brothers demurred, reluctant to move into this conspicuously affluent suburb, but eventually agreed. They bought a seventeen-acre spread and commissioned an architect to design what was to become a colonial mansion. Not in memory of the street where they'd lived, but because of the trees that cloaked the site, it was to be called Hawthorn Hill.

31

'A Short Life Full of Consequences'

(1912)

Hawthorn Hill was to take longer than the aeroplane to create. Katharine persuaded her brothers they needed something elegant and spacious – a fitting place in which to entertain aeronautical dignitaries. Orville was to have a much bigger hand in its nativity than his spartan brother. Inspired by stately plantation homes he'd seen in Virginia, he produced the basic floor plans from which architects came up with a design for a huge, fifteen-room, Georgian-style mansion on three levels. Reposing majestically at the end of a long sweeping drive, its front would be dominated by tall white fluted columns, the first floor on two sides giving out on to great balconies supported by smaller columns. The roof of this grand pile was to be topped by an eyrie, a large open balustraded viewing platform. It would be a home fit for aviation kings and it would take four years to complete.

Wilbur was too busy, too often away hunting down patent infringers, to take much interest in the time-consuming venture. He rarely involved himself in the detail apart from once writing cynically to Orville from Paris: 'I see that most of the rooms are smaller than in the original plans, and only the price has been enlarged. You are wasting entirely too much space on halls etc . . . I see plainly that I am going to be put into one of the south rooms so I propose a new plan for them. In any event I am going to have a bathroom of my own, so please make me one.'[1]

Orville, supervising the factory and the flying school at Simms Station, had made Hawthorn Hill, as it began to rise out of the woods, a personal project that verged on an obsession. 'Everything about the house had to be perfect,' said Tom Crouch. 'Painters unable to match the precise shade of red stain for the doors and woodwork were taken off the job. He did the work himself . . . the house was Orville's machine for living. He designed the basic plumbing, heating and electrical systems himself.' To feed pure water to the house he piped rainwater from the roof through a system of pumps, filters and cisterns to remove sediment and odour. In his vast second-floor bathroom it was dispensed through a series of circular shower pipes surrounding the bather from shoulder to knee. 'It was the same with the heating system,' said Tom Crouch who, seeking atmosphere for his biography of the brothers in the 1980s, spent a night in Orville's bedroom. 'Standard controls were not acceptable. Orville regulated the temperature with a wire running from the furnace in the basement through the living room and on up to his bedroom. He was especially proud of an industrial vacuum system built into the walls so that Carrie had simply to plug her hose into an outlet in a room and throw the switch.'[2] She rarely used it.

But all this was still in the future and the family still quartered in Hawthorn Street in November 1910 when the Wright aircraft factory opened in Home Road, Dayton and began turning out aeroplanes at the rate of two a month. Determined to escape at last from the rising mountain of paperwork, they'd appointed a manager, Frank Russell. Neither of the brothers was a natural businessman. Once the production line was running smoothly and the patent litigation concluded, all they wanted now was to devote their time to further aeronautical research and experiment. To distance themselves from the day-to-day administration of the factory they continued to use their old office above the former cycle shop. A few days after Russell's arrival, Wilbur called on him carrying a basket filled with an accumulation of letters addressed to the new company. 'I don't know what you'll want to do about these,' he is much quotedly reported to have said. 'Maybe they should be opened. But of course if you open a letter there's always the danger that you may decide to answer it and then you're apt to find yourself involved in a long correspondence.'[3]

The Wrights kept a close eye on the construction process: they paid meticulous attention to the finest details. An assistant who later worked for Orville in the factory recalled that he 'directed all of the design work in the shop, even the small metal fittings. Many a time I had designed some detail and made a fine drawing of it, only to find that meanwhile Orville had gone into the shop and with one of his trusted mechanics such as Charlie Taylor . . . he would not only have designed the part, but had made it right there.'[4]

Manufacturing their own aeroplanes was one thing – finding buyers quite another. They had sold just one machine to the US Army; five years later it had bought barely a further dozen. Most of the buyers were wealthy private individuals keen to take up flying. The first had been Robert Collier, publisher of the famous *Collier's* weekly. Figures for the volume of sales remain elusive to this day, but the production plant was never, under the brothers, to become very large. Photographs convey a sense of cottage industry. One shows just three men at work on an assembly line of aeroplanes under construction. In another a lone woman sits at a table with a sewing machine stitching a section of wing fabric.

The Wright factory would only ever produce a hundred aeroplanes, for though they had bequeathed the flying machine to the world, their own aircraft was slow to evolve technically beyond the design of the revolutionary *Flyer* that had started it all. While their competitors were fitting wheels, the Wrights continued to launch off a rail with teams of people straining on a rope to hoist clumsy iron weights inside their quaint wooden tower. Their controls threatened to defeat all but the most apt pupils. One of these, Henry 'Hap' Arnold, an army trainee, who soloed after twenty-eight flights in 3 hours 48 minutes, and who was to become the US Air Force's first five-star general, recalled: 'No two types of controls were the same in those days and from the student's point of view the Wright system was the most difficult.'

As the *Flyer* evolved, its controls became steadily more

unfriendly. By 1910, to make a simple turn the pilot had to move one lever to the front or rear to begin to bank, while remembering simultaneously to bend his wrist one way or the other if he needed to give the rudder extra movement – all the while not forgetting to operate with fine delicacy the sensitive elevator controlled by his other hand. Pilots preferred the relative simplicity of Curtiss's machines in which the controls worked in the natural sense in that they had to be moved in the direction the pilot wanted the plane to go. 'A new pilot had to *think* about flying a Wright machine, and that was a dangerous thing.'[5]

Before risking their necks in the air, Orville introduced his pupils to the world's first flight simulator – an engineless *Flyer* that had been retired from service and mounted at the back of the factory on a wooden trestle. It was a bit like trying to ride a bucking bronco:

> The lateral controls were connected with small clutches at the wingtips and grabbed a moving belt running over a pulley. A forward motion, and the clutch would snatch the belt and down would go the left wing. A backward pull and the reverse would happen. The jolts and teetering were so violent that the student was kept busy just moving the lever back and forth to keep on an even keel. That was primary training and it lasted for a few days.[6]

The trainees' first solos out at Simms Station must have been scary experiences, for the machines they had volunteered to fly were potentially lethal. In pictures the pupils are seen with Orville in their caps, waistcoats and ties in a smiling group around a *Flyer* looking like office workers. As members of the Wright flying team they had been lectured on the strict rules they must observe: no drinking, no gambling, no Sunday flying. Some of them were not to live very long.

As they went out across America on modest salaries to earn huge performance fees for the brothers, thrilling crowds with their (by today's standards) unspectacular demonstrations – no one yet dared attempt a loop, roll or spin; they simply made dives and steep turns dangerously close to the ground – the fatalities began to mount. It was still not considered necessary to secure pilots with harnesses and some, during violent crowd-pleasing manoeuvres, were simply flung out of their seats to gasps of horror from their audiences. Others, struggling to handle the unnatural actions of the control levers, made fatal errors and plunged to the ground – at which point crowds would rush to claw through the wreckage for souvenirs.

The flights, heavily promoted by local newspapers, drew crowds of 30,000 and more; but the Wrights became alarmed by the human sacrifice that had become the price of their new prosperity. Every few months, it seemed, they were at another pilot's funeral or comforting a distraught widow. Wilbur issued an urgent instruction to one pilot, Arch Hoxsey:

> I am very much in earnest when I say that I want no stunts and spectacular frills put on the flights. If each of you can make a plain flight of ten to fifteen minutes each day keeping always within the inner fence well away from the grandstand and never more than three hundred feet high it will be just what we want . . . Anything beyond plain flying will be chalked up as a fault and not a credit.[7]

Plain flight, however, was not what the crowds were paying to see. The stunt flying went on. Three months later Hoxsey was killed in a crash at Los Angeles. Of the nine men who joined the initial Wright exhibition team, six were dead within a few months.

Not only in America had pilots begun to kill themselves; they were dying in crashes all over Europe. As the infant industry burgeoned in a meteoric boom which saw flights of over 300 miles and heights reached of over 10,000 feet, the casualty list began to soar. The world's first mid-air collision occurred at Milan. A Peruvian pilot, Georges Chavez, was killed in a crash in a Blériot monoplane in Italy at the end of a dramatic first flight over the Alps. The French pioneer Léon Delagrange perished before a big crowd at Bordeaux when his Blériot's wing collapsed in a sharp turn. Ferdinand Ferber, a revered figure in France to this day for his pioneer enterprise, but whose early friendship with the Wrights had turned to antagonism, died at an air show at Boulogne, also stalling off a steep turn only twenty-five feet above the ground. In England the Honourable Charles Rolls who, in June 1910, had flown the Channel both ways in his Wright *Flyer*, was killed the following month. A friend and admirer of the brothers, who had tried so hard to infiltrate the *Flyer* into the uninterested portals of the War Office, Rolls had been flying at a Bournemouth air show. He had made his own modifications to the machine, adding wheels and an auxiliary elevator in the tail; the second elevator had collapsed in a dive with disastrous consequences.

Nor were people safe on the ground. One of the aircraft leaving Paris at the start of an air race to Madrid had veered out of control, killing the French War Minister and severely injuring the great patron of French aviation Deutsch de la Meurthe. Around a quarter of the thirty-five men who had died in crashes by the end of 1910 were killed in Wright-type machines. Flying had become a lethal sport. Grim drawings started to appear in France depicting aviators with angels of death as their grinning passengers.

But the death toll did nothing to arrest the rise and rise of powered flight into one of the greatest industries of the twentieth century. Aircraft types proliferated and were being offered to private buyers at trade fairs. At an aeronautical show at Olympia in London in 1910, no fewer than eighteen aircraft constructors exhibited their machines and aero engines. There was not a Wright *Flyer* to be seen. Its British licensed manufacturers, Short Brothers, were already exhibiting their own new machine.

New designers, soon to become household names, had begun to join those already on the scene: Hugo Junkers in Germany, Louis Breguet in France, Anthony Fokker in Holland, Igor Sikorsky in Russia, Glenn Martin in America, Geoffrey de Havilland, Tom Sopwith, Harry Hawker, Frederick Handley Page, John Moore-Brabazon and the Bristol Company's Sir George White in Britain. By 1910 the Wright *Flyer*, despite design improvements, had been resoundingly surpassed by its European rivals.

The French had rocketed ahead in the technological race. What they brought to aviation was something Wilbur and Orville had persistently rejected: inherently stable machines that didn't, like theirs, require the pilot to wrestle with the controls every instant he was in the air. In France – and England – designers had quickly developed machines that were, as today, both stable and controllable. They were safer and easier to fly, and had much less frightening controls. From 1910 there now occurred almost every week some startling new aviation milestone.

The first woman – the French Baroness de Laroche – qualified as a pilot; another woman, the beautiful Harriet Quimby, whose face to this day continues to appear on postage stamps, would fly the English Channel. The first air passenger services – admittedly still by airships – began in Germany. Night-flying arrived. Aerodromes were created everywhere. In London one had sprung up on Hounslow Heath. From another at Hendon a French pilot had flown a Blériot non-stop to Paris in under four hours. Airmail flights began. Cabin planes, amphibians and flying boats took to the air and the first all-metal aircraft appeared along with retractable undercarriages. In America the first coast-to-coast flight was made in a Wright machine; the pilot, who suffered five crashes en route, took eighty-four days. A Curtiss plane was flown 90 miles over water from Florida to Cuba. The aeroplane was also used for the first time in warfare. An Italian military pilot dropped four grenades from a Blériot on enemy troops during hostilities with Turkey in Libya in 1910. And the US Army the same year conducted live bombing tests from a Wright *Flyer*.

In Britain, where the blinkered army chief General Nicholson had helped the War Office and his Prime Minister and cabinet to bury their heads in the sand, the tide had begun to turn. Orchestrated by aviation pressure groups, by Northcliffe's newspapers, which began to attack Nicholson personally, and by angry MPs at Westminster, criticism of the country's continued defencelessness against air raids and its unshakeable reliance on great battleships had risen to fever pitch. Public concern had started to threaten support for Asquith's Liberal government. Though the dominant, seemingly mesmerising figure of General Nicholson – soon to become a field marshal and be elevated to the peerage – was still Chief of the Imperial General Staff, his Luddite views had ceased to be tenable. As aeroplanes began to fly the Channel, and Germany, developing airship bombers, was seen as a threatening menace, things at last began to change. Lord Esher, who had chaired the fateful Imperial Defence Committee which, in 1909, had been instrumental in having the aeroplane banished and Colonel Capper and his experimenters Cody and Dunne swept away, had made a complete about-turn. Convinced that world war was approaching, he had, in October 1910, urged the government to equip the army and navy immediately with squadrons of fighting aeroplanes.

The running down of the Farnborough aeroplane development establishment was reversed. To re-energise it the War Minister, Haldane – now Lord Haldane of Cloan – appointed a new superintendent, a brilliant scientist, an Irishman, Mervyn O'Gorman, to produce some effective warplanes. O'Gorman, creating at Farnborough the scientific spirit of what was to become Britain's celebrated Royal Aircraft Establishment, proceeded to draw freely on development expertise anywhere he could find it. He engaged the already proven designer Geoffrey de Havilland and acquired a batch of the latest French aeroplanes. Charles Rolls, before his death, had delivered for the War Minister's inspection one of his two Wright *Flyers*. But Haldane's earlier plan to acquire its control secrets through the back door from Rolls had now been overtaken by events: O'Gorman soon had in his possession more advanced and safer Farmans and Blériots. The *Flyer* was no longer the aeronautical prize it could once have been.

As Britain rushed to catch up, an 'air battalion' was first hastily established within the Royal Engineers, then superseded, at last, in April 1912, by a dedicated aeronautical service – the Royal Flying Corps, destined to become the Royal Air Force. Ironically its aeroplanes were all of French origin – Farmans and Blériots or English versions of them; there was not a Wright machine in sight. And none would ever join the Royal Flying Corps: the handful that Short Brothers produced under licence went to private buyers. Had Wilbur and Orville been prepared to astound Colonel Capper with even a five-minute demonstration of their fantastic machine back in 1904 it might have been a different story. Now the world from which they had been so obsessed to conceal the invention had taken it from them.

Back in Dayton the Wright Company was turning out more aviators than aeroplanes. At their flying school at Simms Station, around 120 pilots, three of them women, would learn to fly, many taught by Orville. Bishop Wright was given a seven-minute flight. The 81-year-old Milton, overwhelmed with excitement, apocryphally shouted as they orbited the field: 'Higher, Orville! Higher!' It ranked almost as an afterthought in his diary that night: 'Orville took me up 350 feet and 6.55 minutes.' On the same day, in May 1910, Wilbur flew as Orville's passenger. It was the only time they ever broke their pledge never to fly together.

At the small West Dayton factory, the brothers were slow to introduce the design features that were now taking other people's aeroplanes more and more reliably and safely into the future – propellers and engines in front, wheels, ailerons, rear elevators, cockpits, control columns and foot-operated rudder bars that did the things the pilot wanted in a logical way. A development of the faithful *Flyer*, which they labelled the Model B, embodied a few concessions to progress when it began to come off the production line in the summer of 1910, incorporating the first major design changes since 1903. Immediately different from its predecessors, it dispensed at last with the palaver of catapult launching, having acquired wheels mounted on the skids. No longer a canard, the front elevator was removed to the rear and now sat behind the vertical rudders. The Model B was instantly recognisable by a pair of triangular blinkers fitted for stability to the front of the skids.

True stability with positive control as pilots know it today still eluded the Wrights. Much earlier, back in 1908, they had applied for a patent on an automatic stabiliser. It had a pendulum to detect roll and yaw and a vane to monitor pitch. When these devices sensed changes in the aircraft's attitude, they activated the wing warping and elevator controls through compressed air cylinders. While Wilbur was in Europe testifying against infringers in the autumn of 1911, Orville took the system down to the Outer Banks with Lorin to try it out on a glider he'd especially built for the purpose. Joining them was an English pilot, Alec Ogilvie, whom Orville had taught to fly in Dayton along with their British patent agent Griffith Brewer. But no sooner had they restored the gale-wrecked huts and installed themselves in the sand wilderness than a group of newsmen trooped in across the dunes, curious to see what the famous aviator was up to. Orville was so convinced the reporters would describe the still unpatented invention to the world that he refused to test it. While the secret device remained hidden from prying eyes in the hut, he and Ogilvie filled in the time gliding off the big sandhills. All that the expedition achieved was a world soaring record when Orville stayed up for nearly 10 minutes – a time that was to stand for ten years.

The auto-stabiliser remained untested for two more years. Still using a primitive pendulum and vane, but with the controls now operated by servomotors powered by a wind-driven generator, Orville would eventually prove (at the end of 1913) that it worked, flying again and again past admiring observers with his hands in the air, and winning a trophy for his efforts. But a vastly more sophisticated and precise gyroscopic auto-pilot system, invented by a young man called Lawrence Sperry, almost immediately gave aviation a better solution; it would be relieving pilots of the physical tedium right up to the twenty-first century.

By 1911, while the Dayton factory was gently turning out, still mainly for private fliers, its increasingly old-fashioned-looking aeroplanes, Wilbur and Orville found themselves more and more occupied in their unremitting war against violators on both sides of the Atlantic. The new Curtiss company, free for the moment both from the clutches of the appalling Herring and from restraint to build and sell aeroplanes and train pilots, was going from one commercial triumph to another. Curtiss had begun to enjoy much more dramatic success with the US military than the Wrights. He had concentrated on the navy, staging the first take-off and landing on a vessel at sea; soon he would be building practical flying boats for which big orders would come not only from the US Navy but from European navies as well.

The Wrights saw Curtiss as the Millard Keiter of aviation. Planning a visit to Dayton with his wife, Curtiss had sent ahead a friendly telegram to Orville trying to tempt him and Katharine to a meal. It was almost as if the Devil himself were about to arrive in town. Writing to Wilbur in Europe, Katharine said scornfully: 'He had the nerve to telegraph Orv and invite us to lunch with him and Mrs Curtiss! Needless to say we declined.'[8]

The sense of injustice that the invention copiers created within the brothers consumed large amounts of their income as the Wright Company poured money into travel and legal expenses to pursue the hopeless witch-hunt. They now took it in turns to rattle the cages in Europe. When Orville had gone to France at the end of 1910 he'd been dismayed to discover that their French company, Compagnie Générale de Navigation Aérienne, had collapsed in a sea of intrigue and incompetence. The French management had acquired such a bad reputation that the French government had refused to do business with it. CGNA had subcontracted the building of *Flyers* to another company, an airship manufacturer called Astra. In a welter of legal complications, Astra had swallowed the Wright aeroplane business – yet appeared not to have sold any machines. Royalties had dried up in France.

In Germany the news was equally depressing. Flugmaschine Wright Gesellschaft was turning out aeroplanes from its Berlin factory efficiently enough, but the zealous engineers had been busy modifying the design, adding so many 'improvements' that the flying performance was seriously undermined. There had been two fatal control-handling accidents, and when Orville examined the company's books he found that more machines had been built than royalties paid. The plant manager, he decided, was incompetent; and the company wasn't even bothering to prosecute infringers. The whole business had become entangled with other companies, including the huge General Electric, whose president Walther Rathenau also sat on the Wright company board. 'I have little hope,' Orville wrote gloomily to Wilbur, 'of its ever being successful . . . I have about made up my mind to let the European business go. I don't propose to be bothered with it all my life . . .'[9]

In 1911 it was Wilbur's turn to make the European pilgrimage. In Paris in March he went straight to the Wright company and demanded to see the books. He set out to examine them with the same ruthless thoroughness he'd once brought to bear on the defalcations of the Reverend Keiter, but here he didn't stumble on evidence of fraud. The commercial failure of their French operations was 'partly incompetence, partly a poor system of bookkeeping . . . and principally bum motors.'[10]

Although unreliable, locally built engines had lost them several precious French Army contracts, the hard truth was that they couldn't now hope to compete with the rapidly expanding colony of French aircraft manufacturers, many subsidised by their government. The War Ministry, busy rearming in the face of the threat of German invasion, had already bought 250 French-designed planes. How many of these might have been the once amazing Wright machine, had its creators not refused to give even a glimpse of it to Commandant Bonel's eager mission to Dayton, or to Arnold Fordyce, who'd come to see them with a virtually open chequebook?

In Paris Wilbur had tried unsuccessfully to salvage something from a scene in which the technology of flight had overtaken them. Wearily he testified against a string of twelve French infringers, listening to desperate defence arguments that Santos-Dumont, Ader and – Chanute's favourite – Mouillard had all produced wing warping systems that predated theirs. Santos-Dumont hadn't flown an aeroplane until 1906, Ader's hadn't left the ground and Mouillard's creation had never been built.

In Germany – where Wilbur made his last-ever flight and visited the holy aviation shrine of Otto Lilienthal's fatal gliding hill, meeting his financially distressed widow, Agnes – things were exactly as Orville had described, except that here his corruption-sensing antenna soon locked on to some identifiable villains. With manifest pleasure he set out to expose the suspects, tempted to wrap up, in the process, their whole German operation. He wrote to Orville:

> If I could get free from business with the money we already have in hand I would rather do it than continue in business at a considerable profit. Only two things lead me to put up with responsibilities and annoyances for the moment. First the obligations to the people who put money into our business and, second, the reluctance a man naturally feels to allow a lot of scoundrels and thieves to steal his patents, subject him to all kinds of trouble or even try to cheat him out of the patents entirely . . . For the good of the public and the protection of others we ought to do our share to discourage such people a little.[11]

With undisguised zest, Wilbur prepared for the fray, disclosing to Katharine, that Berlin summer of 1911, his battle plan. It was to have translated into German a letter distributed to all the company's stockholders, threatening dire consequences if the board did not clean up its act:

> I have not had so much fun since I wrote those Keiter papers . . . If the first does not effect a cure I am intending to carry the fight into the courts and into the newspapers and if possible bring it to the attention of the Emperor as a national scandal.[12]

The Keiter figure in Berlin was Dr Rathenau. He was a prominent German industrialist who mixed in royal circles and put money into an aviation development company that was the Kaiser's special baby. Rathenau, Wilbur suspected, had been syphoning off their royalties into his own electrical company. This forceful company director, well connected in German high society, had obtained for his electrical giant a licence to manufacture *Flyers*. Wilbur wanted to know what had happened to the royalties that should have streamed from the deal. He suspected the German magnate was the latest robber baron to prey on their success. All the anti-Semitic feeling endemic in the bishop's household, but rarely expressed beyond its walls, burst to the surface. In a letter to Orville, he wrote:

> Our friend Dr Rathenau is a good substitute for Keiter. But I think he has wandered into his own net and that when he discovers where he is, and whom he has to deal with, he will have a sad awakening. I feel certain that, like all Jews, he lacks courage for an open fight, however much he may bluster with these poor idiots here who are afraid of him.[13]

Telling Orville in a certain reference to their agent, Hart Berg, that 'our people have not the nerve to negotiate in the way I could negotiate,' Wilbur had written the scorching letter to their German shareholders, 'explaining what Rathenau is doing and calling them to kick him and his "dummies" out of the board . . . I expect the temperature of Berlin will rise a few degrees when the doctor reads the letter.'[14]

Wilbur knew the aeroplane they'd invented was now virtually everybody's property. Even the German courts had refused to acknowledge the genius of its premiership. The rushing from one hole in the bursting dyke wall to another had become futile. Wilbur's plaintive legal protestations were but a minor irritant on the fringes of the aircraft production boom that was driven more and more by fear of war. Even in England, where the *Flyer* was admired as the symbol of creation, it was not going anywhere. The Short-produced machines went only to a wealthy elite.

The six frustrating months Wilbur spent in Europe in the spring and summer of 1911 were made more miserable by a severe cold he caught in France and couldn't shake off. Count de Lambert and his wife had befriended him in Paris, and the countess made a big fuss of him, dosing him with patent medicines. Wilbur had been so unwell that he'd stopped writing to Hawthorn Street. Katharine, who had long ago given up teaching to run the home and be a good aunt to Lorin's children and hostess to the stream of aviation visitors Orville brought home from the flying school, became alarmed. When no letter came for nearly a month, she declared a state of emergency. She cabled Berg's Paris office to ask if her brother was all right. 'Dear Ullam,' she later reprimanded her brother, 'I was getting very uneasy and was dreaming about you every night.'[15] She urged him to come home quickly, they were all missing him so badly.

Dayton was being seared by a heatwave, the worst for fifty years, when Wilbur finally arrived back in August 1911, tired out of his mind and physically run-down by travel, illness and the stress of fighting his corner in lands where he didn't speak the language. Almost immediately he was sucked into further rounds of patent litigation. The psychological traumas of the still unresolved case against Curtiss were compounded by nuisance suits now being brought against them. One had come from the Californian jeweller Charles Lamson who had built man-lifting kites and the oscillating wing glider that Chanute had forced upon them at Kill Devil in 1902. Lamson was now claiming that they owed their success to his kite design. The absurd case dragged on wearily for months. But Wilbur, who had left all the flying now to Orville, refused to abandon a single fight.

From long days in witness boxes and lawyers' offices he would return, Orville began to notice, looking drawn and unusually white-faced. Milton, too, had started to worry about him. For over two weeks on end in February 1912 Wilbur occupied the stand in Dayton testifying against Curtiss. Day after day, for the benefit of judge and lawyers, he reduced to simple terms the functioning of the control system. Milton, an elderly, alert, white-bearded figure in clerical garb, sat in at some of the hearings and wrote in his diary: 'Wilbur began his examination . . . The amount of his intellectuality in describing their invention was marvellous. It must have greatly wearied him.'[16]

Righteous litigation seemed somehow as necessary to Wilbur as it had been to his father in the tempestuous years of the Brethren wars. With equally aggressive passion, Wilbur thrived on conflict, the hounding of transgressors and argument in which no quarter was given. Yet in his heart he regretted the need for it. 'It is much more pleasant to go to Kitty Hawk for experiments than to worry over lawsuits,' he confided to a friend in France:

> We had hoped in 1906 to sell our invention to governments for enough money to satisfy our needs and then devote our time to science, but the jealousy of certain persons blocked this plan and compelled us to rely on our patents and commercial exploitation. We wished to be free from business cares so that we could give all our own time to advancing the science and art of aviation . . . When we think what we might have accomplished if we had been able to devote this time to experiments we feel very sad – but it is always easier to deal with things than with men.[17]

At the end of April 1912 Wilbur made the long train journey to Boston. It is not clear what the purpose of the trip was – probably to meet a lawyer. At his hotel he was taken ill after a fish meal. When he arrived back in Dayton he was feeling a little better, but was still unwell. He managed to join Orville, Katharine and Milton on a picnic in the woods up on Hawthorn Hill at the site of their new mansion, but when they got home he had a temperature. Milton called in a doctor, who diagnosed malaria. Next morning the temperature had risen, but Wilbur refused to go to bed. He continued to work, making trips out to Simms field to inspect a new model *Flyer* ordered by the US Army, and going to the office above the cycle shop to write for the Aero Club of America's bulletin an appraisal of the groundbreaking gliding experiments of Lilienthal, to whose near destitute widow, Agnes, he and Orville had sent a cheque for $1000 – worth $20,000 today.

He also wrote an irate letter to the Wright Company attorney, Frederick Fish, who had dared to suggest they postpone hearings of the seemingly endless Curtiss case for six months until the autumn. This was not good enough for Wilbur:

> Unnecessary delays by stipulation of counsel have already destroyed fully three-fourths of the value of our patent. The opportunities of the last two years will never return again. At the present moment almost innumerable competitors are entering the field, and for the first time are producing machines which will really fly. These machines are being put on the market at one half less than the price which we have been selling our machines for.[18]

The real money-making flying season, Wilbur told Fish, was from September to November. If the case was postponed until autumn they could effectively lose a whole year's revenue if Curtiss was finally ordered to pay the fees he was evading.

It was the last letter Wilbur was ever to write. The next day he was forced to take to his bed. Again the doctor was called. This time he was not so sure the fever was malaria; he began to suspect typhoid. A chill of apprehension went through the family. Typhoid had nearly taken Orville from them in 1896. When their elderly GP, Dr Spitler, confirmed the suspicion, Wilbur sent for his secretary, Mabel Beck, and a Dayton lawyer, Ezra Kuhns, to come to his bedside and dictated his final will.

A hush settled on Hawthorn Street. When neighbours learnt how seriously ill Wilbur was, children were sent to play in other streets;

'grown-ups tip-toed gravely past the house'. There was nothing doctors could do but hope the deadly infection would run its feverish four- or five-week course. As a deep shadow descended upon the house, Lorin came every day to sit beside him and Reuchlin was summoned from Kansas.

By the middle of May, when a specialist was called in from nearby Cincinnati, the doctors believed there was still hope. Reassured, Orville had gone off to Washington to deliver a new *Flyer* to the Signal Corps. When Wilbur heard that he'd gone he became so agitated he had to be calmed with a sedative injection. Entering the critical third week of fever, his condition began to deteriorate again. Two nurses were engaged to care for him in shifts. When Orville, urgently recalled from Washington, arrived on Monday 20 May, he found his brother had lapsed into unconsciousness.

Milton's diary had begun to log his condition:

> *Saturday 18 May:* Wilbur is no better. He has an attack mentally, for the worse. It was a bad spell. He is put under opiates. He is unconscious mostly.
>
> *Sunday 19 May:* Wilbur ceases to take opiates, but is mostly quiet and unconscious. His sickness is very serious.

Milton was so worried that he couldn't sleep properly. He started getting up in the middle of the night and walking anxiously about the house. He went to bed with his clothes on. News of the illness was going out to the world; cards and telegrams started to pour in. A concerned cable arrived from Lord Northcliffe. Doctors came twice a day as Wilbur's kidneys began to fail.

> *Monday 27 May:* They think the case very bad. His fever was higher and he has difficulty with his bladder and his digestion is inadequate . . . We thought him near death. He lived through till morning.

> *Tuesday 28 May:* I slept some in the night. I awoke at 4.00. Wilbur is sinking. The doctors have no hope of his recovery . . . At 6.30 eve. the doctor thought him dying.

> *Wednesday 30 May:* Wilbur seemed no worse, though he had a chill. The fever was down, but rose high. He remained the same till 3.15 in the morning when, eating his allowance, he expired without a struggle. His life was one of toil. His brain ceased not its activity till two weeks of his last sickness had expired. Then it ceased.

The sense of shock in the house was profound. That evening, with customary precision, Milton wrote in his diary a touching, elegiac lament for his favourite son:

> This morning at 3:15 Wilbur passed away, aged 45 years, 1 month and 14 days. A short life, full of consequences. An unfailing intellect, imperturbable temper, great self-reliance, and as great modesty, seeing the right clearly, pursuing it steadily, he lived and died.[19]

32

Feud with the Smithsonian (1913–1917)

Wilbur's death in May 1912 plucked from the family's heart an exceptional brother and son. It ended one of the greatest, most fruitful partnerships in the annals of invention. They never quite recovered from the unexpectedly cruel loss of his powerful immanence at the peak of his fame and remarkable powers.

CONQUEROR OF THE AIR, FATHER OF FLIGHT, INVENTOR OF THE AEROPLANE, THE MAN WHO MADE FLYING POSSIBLE. Around the world Wilbur made his last headlines. By the end of the day he died around a thousand telegrams and a mountain of flowers had arrived in the family's stunned midst. A wire came from the President, another from Lord Northcliffe. Glenn Curtiss sent one. So did some of Europe's crowned heads. The family wanted a quiet funeral, but Wilbur's celebrity made it impossible. Milton wrote in his diary on the day of the funeral:

> I awakened before midnight and got up nearly two hours. I slept then till nearly 5:00. Arose and washed off and dressed till near seven. The undertakers put Wilbur in the burial casket. Took him to the church at nearly ten. Many relatives come; many friends. Wilbur's body lay in state at First Presbyterian Church from 10 till 1:00 . . .[1]

Twenty-five thousand people filed past the coffin before the brief service, conducted without music. Although Wilbur had been alienated from the Brethren – 'he had chosen to practice his Christianity in a private manner' – the church, at Milton's pleading, sent a minister who read the words of Martin Luther's hymn 'A Mighty Fortress Is Our God'. As Wilbur was taken from the horse-drawn hearse and laid to rest next to his mother, Susan, on a tree-lined slope in the city's Woodland cemetery at half-past three that afternoon, the whole of Dayton fell silent. While church bells tolled, all traffic came to a standstill for three minutes. The streetcars stopped, the manual phone service was halted and people stood in the streets with heads bowed.

> *Monday 3 June:* Wilbur is dead and buried! We are all stricken. It does not seem possible that he is gone. Probably Orville and Katharine felt his loss most. They say little.

For weeks the Wright family went about in a daze. Orville thumbed through the great pile of letters and telegrams, quite unable to absorb or answer any of them. Katharine stopped sleeping properly, became unwell and the doctor had to be called. Milton and Orville began to escape from the house – quickly fumigated by health officials – going on long drives into the countryside in the family's first car, which Orville had only just bought. They appear to have cruised numbly and rather aimlessly about in the small open tourer, staying away from Hawthorn Street for hours at a time, sometimes visiting the site of the new house that Wilbur would never see. The passing days did nothing to soften their sorrow. 'I felt Wilbur's absence as never before,' Milton wrote a week after the funeral.

The family grief was tinged by bitterness. They blamed the patent infringers, who had forced Wilbur to pursue them through the courts, for wearing him down and undermining his resistance. At Hawthorn Street his death was transformed into a kind of martyrdom. 'The death of my brother Wilbur,' Orville was to say publicly, 'is a thing we must definitely charge to our long struggle . . . The delays were what worried him to his death – first into a state of chronic nervousness and then into a physical fatigue . . . We were fighting foes whose strategy was played in the dark.'[2]

The blame was particularly directed at one quarter. 'Orville and his sister Katharine,' said the Wright factory's production chief, Grover Loening, 'had preying on their minds and characters the one great hate and obsession – the patent fight with Curtiss. It was a constant subject of conversation.' Another visitor to Hawthorn Street, a young naval officer called Holden Richardson, was a friend of Curtiss. Because of this he claimed he was treated with only the barest civility. 'Katharine especially was terribly bitter toward Curtiss,' he recalled. At the funeral it was said that Katharine had turned to someone and uttered: 'I suppose the Curtiss crowd will be glad now Wilbur is gone.'[3]

'When Wilbur died,' said Adrian Kinnane,

> the entire quality of life in the Wright household changed. Gone was that sense of mission that had coloured the marketing of the invention with the bright hues of moral purpose. Gone also was some of the aggressiveness that had pushed with it the fortunes of the whole family. From the date of his death the Wright home would be marked as much by his absence as by the presence of those who remained. His brilliance, though, had isolated him in many ways into a technological cloister. The self-discipline created a uniquely single-minded life of work and self-denial. It had also bred the righteousness, the reclusiveness, the intolerant zealot – the ultimately rather lonely figure.[4]

For nearly a hundred years, historians and psychologists have tried to identify the respective contributions of the brothers to the triumph of human flight. It is an impossible task for, notwithstanding their quite different characters, there existed a unique symbiosis between them in which they seemed to function as a single, remarkable, inventive entity. It was the potent product of the union – whether or not Wilbur, as the elder, led and dominated, whether his interest in the challenge of flight was aroused first, whether he was the more visible, addressing learned societies and handling most of the ongoing stream of technical correspondence with Chanute that accompanied the process, whether his was the inspiration for the breakthrough of wing warping and the connection of the warp and rudder controls; whether his strengths were the broader picture and Orville's the mechanical solutions; whether the turning point lay in Orville's flair behind the wind tunnel that produced the crucial wing design or his sleepless ruminations on the critical need to swing the rudder, or his original drawings for the engine. Either of them alone, without the stimulus, the shared values and explosively fierce arguments with the other, would probably not have launched an aeroplane into sustained powered flight. Nor would it likely have happened but for the indissoluble force of brotherhood nurtured in the morally charged environment of the bishop's domain.

There are other theories. One, the subject of a study by two doctors at Dayton's Wright State University School of Medicine in the early 1980s, believes that the magic mix of ability that solved the problem of flight lay in the complementarity of the brother's respective left- and right-brain hemispheres. One of the researchers was Dr Stanley R. Mohler, the university's Director of Aerospace Medicine. He said:

> The best-known function of the left hemisphere is speech and verbal communication. It is characterised by well-organised, unemotional, rational and logical thought processes. Wilbur was one such person – scientific, analytical with strong verbal memory, a good orator with a well-structured style. Orville was almost certainly right-brained. Right-brain dominant people tend to be creative, perceptual, nimble-fingered and skilled in complex spatial tasks – such as piloting an airplane. Orville was markedly different from his brother: he was inventive and more adept with complex mechanical devices. He was, as Wilbur conceded, the better aviator of the two. Although Orville originated new ideas and would launch a number of new projects of his own he tended to lack his brother's analytic ability to shape them into practical form. Together they produced a formidable team in which the whole was greater than the sum of the parts.[5]

It was said that for years Wilbur's spirit lingered so powerfully at Hawthorn Street that they had difficulty accepting that at any moment he wouldn't enter the room and join the conversation with some dry and droll remark. Everywhere they seemed to hear his voice.

Wilbur left an estate valued at around $280,000 – of the order, today, of $5.5 million. Fifty thousand dollars each went to Katharine, Lorin and Reuchlin, making them all relatively rich and independent. Aware that the others would care for their father to the end of his days, he left Milton only a token $1000 with 'my earnest thanks for his example of a courageous upright life, and for his earnest sympathy with everything tending to my true welfare'. The money was 'to use for little unusual expenditures as might add to his comfort and pleasures'. The remainder of the estate, including all the patents and shares in Wright companies, went to Orville. His brother 'who has been associated with me in all the hopes and labours both of childhood and manhood', he was sure, 'will use the property in very much the same manner as we would use it together in case we would both survive to old age.'[6]

The close-knit force that the brothers had presented to the world had gone. Orville had not the least desire to step into Wilbur's shoes and become an aviation industrial tycoon. He wanted none of the stresses he'd seen destroying his brother as president of the Wright Company. 'Orville,' said Tom Crouch, 'had almost none of his brother's restless ambition, nor the energy and drive to succeed that came with it.'

> Alone with his friends he was a delightful conversationalist; among strangers he grew silent and withdrawn. He had few illusions about his capacity for leadership. The thought of attending a board meeting, let alone presiding at one, was abhorrent to him. Moreover, with the single exception of Robert Collier, he felt little other than contempt for the rich New Yorkers whom Wilbur had regarded as friends and associates.[7]

Orville did become president of the company, but he detested his management role and in Dayton insisted on working out of the old cycle shop office. He tried to avoid confrontation by working through intermediaries and was protected by the sharp-tongued secretary he had inherited from Wilbur, Mabel Beck.

Orville became more reclusive as the years passed. He saw the *Flyer* in its reluctant evolution at the small Dayton factory left far behind in the technological revolution it had fathered. Unwilling to embrace the advances that had rendered the difficult-to-fly machine so swiftly obsolete, Orville went on flying until 1918, testing new models as they all too slowly evolved for markets that didn't now want them. He never piloted the ultimate descendant of the *Flyer* – the Wright Model L, a biplane that looked at last like the sort we all know: a single-seat military scout plane with engine and propeller in the nose and, inevitably, the dreaded ailerons and modern controls that he and Wilbur had been so determined to keep at bay – for it would surely have been tantamount to selling their souls to the Devil.

He continued to fight patent battles – though never with Wilbur's deadly messianic verve. Against the infringers he saw some moral victories, but not a lot of money flowed from them. In Berlin with Katharine in 1913, he heard their claim finally rejected on the grounds of prior disclosure. In Paris, the French high court favoured the Wrights, but its decision to allow another panel of experts to study the history of alleged earlier invention meant that the defendants could keep the arguments boiling now until the French patent expired in 1917. Mainland Europe had become a lost cause.

In England he fared better. Griffith Brewer and Alec Ogilvie had helped him form a British Wright Company to license the use of the local patents. It issued few licences, but Brewer later persuaded the British government to make a lump sum payment effectively buying out the right to use the contentious control system on all its military aeroplanes. The deal added a helpful $75,000 – $1 million today – to Orville's estate. In England he learnt that not only was Mervyn O'Gorman's Farnborough establishment preparing for war, busy turning out British-designed machines at last for the Royal Flying Corps, but so were a growing host of private manufacturers. Samuel Cody, whom the War Office had hoped would quietly disappear, had gone on with his own resources, astonishingly, to perfect a succession of machines, on one of which he'd flown more than 1000 miles round Britain. He'd become the country's aviation idol – but was to crash to his death in August 1913 when his aircraft broke up in mid-air over Hampshire. Even Colonel Capper's protégé, John Dunne, likewise dismissed by the establishment, had gone from strength to strength and in his tailless biplane triumphantly flew non-stop from Eastchurch in Kent to Paris.

Back in Dayton in March 1913, the Wright family had to flee Hawthorn Street when the Miami River burst its banks to flood large areas of the city. A tide of brown water surged into the downstairs rooms, and the manuscript of the bishop's precious autobiography was lost. He was evacuated by canoe, Orville and Katharine on a horse wagon. Into the garden shed, where they'd stored all the precious glass-plate negatives that had recorded the birth of flight, the water poured, peeling off delicate emulsions. Yet by some miracle the priceless image of Orville rising into the air off the rail at Kill Devil in 1903 survived with damage to only one corner of the plate. At the inundated cycle shop on West Third Street the water rose to twelve feet, just failing to reach the first-floor office where all the treasured aeronautical data were filed. The world's first flying machine in the rear shed was buried under several feet of mud, but when the waters receded it was found to be intact, preserved by the yellow ooze.

For a time Orville resumed battle with Glenn Curtiss, whose company was defiantly going from strength to strength; its successful flying boats now dominated the US Navy market. The patent war became a personal feud between Orville and Curtiss. It came to a climax early in 1913 when, after four years of courtroom argument that had examined almost the entire history of man's attempts to fly, Federal Judge Hazel handed down his final decision, finding for the Wrights. Hazel had decided that the brothers' solution of the combination of rudder and banking controls had achieved 'a new and novel result'. They had attained success where others had failed and 'may rightly be considered pioneer inventors in the aeroplane art'. In other words, ailerons were the equivalent of warping and infringed the patent. It was a terrible blow for Curtiss. To him, and to many other aviators, ailerons were a radically different means of banking from warping, and his alma mater, the Graham Bell experimental group, had actually patented the superior system. The judge's view, which swept up every practical means of rolling an aeroplane into one blanket innovation, seemed irrational and absurd. It threatened once more to put Curtiss out of business, yet still he refused to give up; again he filed an appeal. But early in 1914 the appeal judges upheld Hazel's decision. Curtiss was in Europe when the news reached him. Bitterly he sent a two-word cable to Orville: 'CONGRATULATIONS CURTISS'.

Orville issued a rare press statement that attacked Curtiss personally – many outside the Wright camp thought unjustly. Orville now demanded a 20 per cent royalty on every Curtiss aeroplane built 'plus retroactive settlements'. No Curtiss plane would be allowed to fly without a licence from the Wright Company. Defending his ruthless policy, Orville said, 'This is not an act of harshness. It is an act of great benefit to aerial navigation . . . what incentive was there to do hard thinking when anyone could loot the thinking?'

Curtiss refrained from responding. Orville's demand would have crippled his business. He couldn't afford to pay him $1000 from every $5000 aeroplane he built. Quite extraordinarily, it seems, he still hoped that he and Orville could reach some happy accommodation helpful to both their companies. Again he tried to meet Orville. He sent telegrams. He wrote letters suggesting they meet to discuss a beneficial merger. Orville ignored the overtures. When he replied to none of the friendly messages, Curtiss issued his own press statement. It was mild compared with Orville's, denying that he had ever consciously drawn on any of the *Flyer*'s features in designing his own machines. There was much public sympathy for Curtiss. A Boston newspaper complained that 'America has become a closed book to all makers of aeroplanes based on the Wright principle'. A 20 per cent royalty was outrageous. 'It is difficult to believe that Mr Wright is actuated by other than personal animosity . . . The effect of the Wright decree will beyond question numb what little life remains in aviation in America.'[8]

Appalled by Orville's unbending determination to maintain an aviation monopoly, the great car manufacturer Henry Ford had, early in 1914, come to Curtiss's aid, offering the services of his company's attorney, who had become skilled fending off a major patent challenge to his mass-produced, low-priced automobiles. The Ford lawyer suggested a redesign of the control system, so Curtiss disconnected the interlocked right and left ailerons to let them operate independently. Immediately Orville sought a fresh injunction.

While this was dragging through the courts, Curtiss turned to an even more desperate tactic.

The Smithsonian Institution had begun to talk of restoring the Langley aeroplane, the *Aerodrome*, that had twice so disastrously plunged into the Potomac ten years earlier. The conspirators, as they were quickly to be perceived by Orville, wanted to demonstrate whether the *Aerodrome* – had it been successfully launched back in 1903, just nine days before the Wrights flew – might not have been actually capable of sustained free flight. Langley's successor as the Smithsonian's chief, Charles Walcott, was keen to make the experiment. So was Orville's arch enemy, Professor Albert Zahm, who had joined the institution as director of its aerodynamics laboratory, inheriting the battered remains of the ill-fated Langley aeroplane. When Henry Ford's lawyer, W. Benton Crisp, heard of the scheme, he seized upon the potential it offered to undermine the legal primacy of the Wrights. Curtiss, desperate to escape Orville's clutches, needed no persuading that the experiment, if successful, might lead the courts to reverse their view of the Wrights' entitlement. It would 'go a long way toward showing that the Wrights did not invent the flying machine as a whole but only a balancing device and we could get a better decision next time,' Curtiss had written to one of his exhibition pilots.[9]

The Langley machine had been pulled out of storage and rebuilt by Curtiss at Smithsonian expense at his Hammondsport factory. 'Curtiss, the Smithsonian, and Zahm all stood to benefit,' said Tom Crouch:

> Curtiss could return to court arguing that the pioneer status granted the Wright patent was unwarranted. Walcott would demonstrate to the world that his old friend Langley had not

> really failed after all. And Zahm would gain revenge on Orville for the supposed slights offered him at the outset of the patent suit in 1910.[10]

Curtiss and Zahm announced that the *Aerodrome* would be faithfully restored to its original 1903 condition. Instead they made a number of improvements. They made the shape of the wings more efficient, they made propeller enhancements, and they also strengthened the structure in the very places that had catastrophically failed. Like the original machine it had no banking control, so why it was hoped it could compete with the *Flyer*'s three-axis control system is not clear. Rejecting Langley's dangerous catapult launch method, Curtiss fitted the tarted-up *Aerodrome* with pontoons and invited a horde of newsmen to watch him fly off Lake Keuka in May 1914. The *Aerodrome* became airborne briefly and skimmed the water for 50 yards.

Concerned by this dubious activity, Orville decided to send a spy to Hammondsport. His English friend Griffith Brewer agreed to go. To avoid suspicion, Brewer masqueraded as a London reporter and brought back photographs confirming that the original aeroplane had been considerably modified. Brewer wrote an indignant letter to the *New York Times* telling Americans that the Langley machine had not been honestly restored to its 1903 state. Curtiss was quite unfazed. He made even more improvements and fitted a more powerful engine. A year later, in mid-1915, another pilot started flying the *Aerodrome* off the lake; the dishonestly modernised plane now began to achieve distances of over 300 yards. This time Orville sent Lorin, armed with camera and binoculars, to Hammondsport. Lorin, registering at a hotel in a nearby town under the name of 'W.L. Oren', proved less skilful than Brewer. Watching a take-off attempt through glasses he'd been the startled witness of disaster. Under his very eyes the rear set of wings had broken off and folded up. As the wrecked machine was hauled back up the slipway Lorin had started dutifully taking photographs. Caught in the act, but not recognised as a member of the Wright family, a Curtiss company executive demanded he hand over the film. However, Orville believed that Brewer's pictures had given him all the evidence he needed.

There is another version of what Brewer actually saw at Lake Keuka. It came from Curtiss, who told the *New York Times* that he had already flown the Langley machine in its original unmodified condition. 'I do not know why Brewer brings all this up,' he protested. An angry chorus of Curtiss and Smithsonian supporters had risen to the defence. An aeronautical engineer who had witnessed the first test asserted that the *Aerodrome*, despite making only short hops, had been proved to be a 'practical flying machine'.

The Curtiss lawyers now wanted to argue that Langley's aeroplane had, after all, been capable of flight before the Wrights'. They were never to get the opportunity. In 1917 the whole wretched, destructive row was ended by the US government. When the country entered the war in Europe it suddenly needed hundreds of warplanes in a hurry: it was forced to end the patent stranglehold, which by then included many from Curtiss himself. His company and the Wright interests both surrendered their rights for $2 million each. The patent war, which had stultified the development of aviation in America, was effectively over. Sadly it was to be just the beginning of a new, equally bitter and highly publicised one, now between Orville and the Smithsonian. This one would last for nearly thirty years.

By the time the patent unpleasantness had finally ended, Orville had long since vacated the battlefield. Uncomfortably aware of his temperamental unfitness to manage the affairs of a big organisation, he'd decided the time had come to turn his back on it all. Now (since April 1914) ensconced in his luxurious mansion, Hawthorn Hill, he had sold the Wright company in 1915 and retired, a wealthy man, to gentler pursuits.

Retirement did not, however, bring the peaceful existence out of the limelight that he craved. The Smithsonian had felt that it and its revered former chief were vindicated by the Hammondsport flights of the souped-up *Aerodrome*, and was emboldened to make the highly contentious public claim that Langley, not the Wrights, had invented the aeroplane. Brave enough to put his name to the astounding assertion was Albert Zahm. In the Smithsonian's 1914 annual report he declared that the rebuilt *Aerodrome* had proved that 'with its original structure and power, it is capable of flying with a pilot and several hundred pounds of useful load. It is the first airplane in history of which this can truthfully be said.' The machine, Zahm claimed, had been flown 'without modification'; it had proved that, shed of its floats, it could make 'a voyage lasting practically the whole day'.[11]

Orville read these words in his library (where he'd installed a special chair with leg-rest to ease his back pain) with shocked disbelief; yet he did nothing at that point to refute the inaccurate claim. The institution's 1915 annual report gratuitously repeated the statement, this time going as far as to say that the tests had 'shown that former Secretary Langley had succeeded in building the first aeroplane capable of sustained free flight with a man'.[12] The Langley aeroplane, returned to the Smithsonian in Washington after the 1915 flights, had been restored to its true 1903 condition which modern experts believe was certainly incapable of sustained controlled flight. It was then put on display with a provocative label: 'The first man-carrying aeroplane in the history of the world capable of sustained free flight.' This would have had Wilbur drafting an immediate injunction, but it still didn't move Orville into action. To have publicly denied the outrageous claims being made on Langley's behalf, he was later to tell the chairman of the Smithsonian Board of Regents, 'might have been looked upon by the public as a jealous attack upon the word of a man who was dead'.[13] Although resentful at what he called 'the subtle campaign to take from us much of the credit then universally accorded us',[14] Orville was to let the matter rest for ten years.

Not until 1925, when he was in his mid-fifties, did Orville finally decide to do battle. The Smithsonian claims had never been withdrawn, and the institution's scientific reputation had helped their public acceptance. The belief was slowly infiltrating the record of aviation history. For the first time, Orville decided to challenge the Smithsonian's regents, seeking a retraction. They refused, so at last he made a gesture of which his brother would have been proud. The Smithsonian had long prevaricated on the sensitive matter of how it should exhibit a Wright *Flyer* alongside the rival Langley machine. Orville now announced he would solve the difficulty for them. Declaring that the Smithsonian had 'perverted' the history of flying, he said that unless the national museum publicly recognised it as the world's first successful aeroplane, the hallowed 1903 machine would be shipped to England – to the Science Museum in London. Nobody took his threat seriously.

Meanwhile, Orville's sale of the Wright Company in 1915 had freed him to live the life he preferred. In West Dayton he'd built a small laboratory in which he set up a wind tunnel and a lot of machine tools. In the outer office he had installed a watchdog, his intimidating secretary, Mabel Beck, who grew increasingly possessive of him, ruthlessly keeping the unwanted at bay and generally terrifying people with her aggressive demeanour. Orville used this retreat largely to tinker, often pointlessly, or to create domestic appliances that were simply mechanical curiosities – a record changer that smashed more records than it changed; a gauge to ensure that bread was cut to a uniform thickness; a toaster that compressed the slices to stop them curling and burning. If he wasn't devising new gadgets he was dismantling others to discover how they worked. He took Mabel Beck's typewriter to pieces and no one could reassemble it. He punched holes in the carburettor of his car to improve its performance; when it didn't he filled in the holes with wooden pegs. He made toys for Lorin's children and continued at every opportunity to play elaborate schoolboy practical jokes on people. A certain unwarranted mystique hung over the laboratory – there was an understandable belief that one of the inventors of the aeroplane was perhaps incubating some startling new flying technology. But apart from a device, never fully developed, to increase the lift of aircraft wings and a practical stall-warning indicator to try and stem the alarming death toll of *Flyer* pilots, nothing of further aeronautical brilliance was ever born there.

Orville suffered to the end of his days from bouts of severe pain from his Fort Myer crash injuries. Dr Stanley Mohler, the aero-medical specialist who arrived at the brain hemisphere theory to identify the brothers' individual strengths, had also, in his research into their lives, been shown a copy of an old X-ray of Orville's fractures. One of the pictures, taken ten years after the accident, was especially revealing to a modern doctor. 'It showed the hip fracture,' he said. 'The broken femur had not fully united. It had never healed properly – the bones had joined up crookedly and become arthritic, trapping the sciatic nerve. His whole hip was unstable. No wonder it affected his mobility and often caused so much pain when he walked.'[15]

Not everyone knew the extent of the constant excruciating sciatic pain that remained with Orville to the end of his days. In 1915 it had put him to bed for two weeks, where he was cared for by Katharine and two nurses. Later a team of specialists had rediagnosed the problem bequeathed by the Fort Myer doctors and given him a wide supportive belt to wear tightly round his hips. Today surgeons would have quickly ended his pain and suffering: he would have been given a hip replacement – an artifical joint would have replaced the floating broken neck of his femur.

To reduce the discomfort of travel, Orville had heavy duty shock absorbers fitted to his car. He tended to drive erratically and sometimes dangerously. Once he took the car all the way up into Canada to a summer house he had acquired on Lambert Island in Lake Huron's Georgian Bay. He had bought the whole island, rebuilt the main house and its cluster of cottages, replumbed the water supply and constructed a cable railway to haul supplies from the jetty.

At Lambert Island there was blissful retreat for six summer weeks from the demands of fame and controversy. Back in Dayton he could never entirely dodge the duties that celebrity never ceased to bring. Famous people, presidents and other aviation heroes would come specially to the Midwest city to meet him. People tried to persuade him to write his memoirs and record fully the brothers' story of the birth of flight, but Orville could never bring himself to do it. Though he wrote entertainingly and his letters were models of clarity, he found writing of any description a burden – people sometimes had to wait months for a reply. His reluctance to put pen to paper was only equalled by the paralysis that seized him at the merest suggestion that he stand up and utter a few words in public. Year after year he continued to be presented with medals, honorary degrees and doctorates. Amid pomp and ceremony he would receive them all in silence – not able, most times, even to bring a bare thank you to his lips. Many times he was approached for radio interviews;

he declined them all. No recording of his voice – or indeed of Wilbur's – is known to exist.

Preferring to work unobtrusively out of public view, Orville joined the US National Advisory Committee for Aeronautics created in 1915 to help the country's aircraft industry with research and development. It was a far from onerous role: the committee met infrequently. Orville is said to have taken part in discussions – his interest being principally for the encouragement of small inventors – but never to have emerged as a force within the agency.

From time to time ghosts would arise unhappily from the brothers' past. The most persistent of all was that of the Californian 1880s gliding experimenter John Montgomery, so excessively commemorated in his home state. Montgomery, who never contributed anything of value to aeronautical science except foolhardy enthusiasm, had around 1903 built some tandem-wing gliders which brave pilots had flown in circus stunts, descending from balloons. One of them had been killed in front of the crowd, and in 1911 Montgomery himself had died crashing one of his machines. Fuelled by his publicist, an extensive myth had sprung up that the deceased aviator was an unsung aerodynamic genius whose contribution had been ignored by mankind. In this heady atmosphere Montgomery's widow, his ageing mother and other members of his family had, in 1917, filed suit alleging that the Wrights' wing design had infringed a 1906 Montgomery patent. Although Orville had left the organisation, he was inevitably involved as a key witness. The case dragged on for four years, forcing him to get the 1903 *Flyer* out of storage and reassemble it as evidence of the futility of the claim.

Curtiss and Herring had ceased to be a source of angst – except to each other. Curtiss had become immensely wealthy, accumulating a personal fortune, vastly greater than the Wrights', of hundreds of millions of dollars from his large wartime contracts supplying the British and American governments. One of his machines alone, the famous JN-4D 'Jenny', got orders from the US Signal Corps for 6,000. By the early 1920s his company was producing aeroplanes that could fly at over 200 miles an hour and climb to 35,000 feet. He had moved on to a more peaceful existence in property development in Florida – where, sadly, his tranquillity was soon rudely shattered.

Herring, having quietly bided his time for seven years, suddenly leapt from obscurity to remind Curtiss that he still held stock in the Herring-Curtiss company. No one, unfortunately, had ever bothered to have the defunct company legally dissolved. Herring called a meeting of surviving stockholders and had himself elected president of the resurrected company. One of his first actions was to revive the earlier lawsuit against Curtiss, renewing the allegation that their joint company had been bankrupted simply as a means of getting rid of him. The case rumbled on until 1923. The suit was dismissed. Herring appealed and succeeded. A panel of arbitrators was set up to fix compensation. But neither Herring nor Curtiss was to live to hear its verdict.*

In the final year of Curtiss's life came the greatest irony of all – merger of his aircraft business with that of the descendant company of the former persecuting Wrights. When, in 1915, Orville had sold out for a reputed $1.5 million, the new management had failed with the rudimentary *Flyer* to keep pace with the meteoric surge in aviation technology. The Dayton factory had finished up producing the British DH4 fighter-bomber designed by Geoffrey de Havilland for wartime service. A host of complicated mergers had followed Orville's departure, culminating in a marriage that created the arrangement Glenn Curtiss, with his olive branch, had tried but failed to interest Orville in: the giant Curtiss-Wright Company. Orville was reported to have 'waxed indignant' on hearing that Curtiss's name would precede that of Wright.[16] There was no longer anything he could do about it.

When, in 1917, America entered the war in Europe, Orville was commissioned as major in the US Army's air reserve. He was asked to do very little and never wore a uniform; his base of operations remained his office in West Dayton. The war did not much affect

*Augustus Herring died of a stroke in 1926 – but the claim for $1 million did not. His son and daughter kept the case alive and Curtiss, himself now ill, was hauled back into court for days' more testimony. He died in 1930, aged only fifty-two, before it was over. His widow, desperate to get Herring's family out of her life, settled out of court at a figure believed to have been around half a million.

the even tenor of his pottering existence and his pampered life at Hawthorn Hill, where he was still fussed over by Katharine and fed and waited upon by their devoted housekeeper Carrie Grumbach, whose husband Charlie had become the estate's odd-job man.

Milton, with his own large bedroom and bathroom, saw out his twilight years in the great house, moving serenely from his mid- to late-eighties with growing pride in his longevity. 'My age is greater than that of any of my ancestors for several generations,' he wrote in his diary on his eighty-eighth birthday in November 1916. The diary, which he religiously kept up until his last evening, maintained its daily record of the comings and goings at Hawthorn Hill, the weather and the visits of the grandchildren, the eldest now in their twenties. He read his Bible, researched his ancestors, and began to take naps during the day. He remained spry and intellectually alert to the end, and in his eighty-ninth year was still taking mile-long walks, proudly boasting that he was as well preserved as men twelve years younger. In one of the last photographs of him he is sitting in his favourite rocking chair on one of the house's big balustraded porches, where he would watch the grey squirrels and the bluejays as he mused over his tempestuous sixty-seven years' ministry in the disunited Brethren Church. To the end he still spoke with pride of the forces of darkness he had vanquished: his diary had recorded with quiet satisfaction the news of Keiter's subsequent shady dealings and his death in Tennessee in 1913.

On the evening of 2 April 1917, four days before the United States entered the First World War, Milton retired early as usual to his room. According to his biographer Darryl Elliott, 'he read the newspaper as usual, as well as the poets Byron, Pope and Poe. Later the bishop wrote several letters to friends and made an entry in his diary. Throughout the evening he visited Katharine's room several times, remarking that his shoulder ached before he finally went to bed.'[17]

Next morning Milton failed to appear at breakfast. When Orville went up to his room he found that his father had died peacefully in his sleep.

33

Spinster in Love

(1918–1925)

Katharine Wright had been her father's devoted carer and housekeeper for twenty-eight years. As a schoolgirl of fifteen she had compliantly bent to his wishes; she had seamlessly assumed the role, and many of the burdens, of his departed wife, becoming, as well, her brothers' replacement mother. Now that Milton was gone, all the devotion she had lavished upon him went to Orville as the two adjusted to life cosily together in the great house. Still attended by Carrie and Charlie Grumbach – now virtually family themselves, with their own apartment – they had acquired an enormous pet, a St Bernard dog they named Scipio. People said they treated Scipio as if he was their child, lavishing affection on him and addressing him with baby names. Orville was so devoted to the great dog that he kept photographing him and carried his picture about in his wallet.

For more than nine years after Milton's death, Orville and Katharine lived together in the spacious comfort of their home on the hill. People who didn't know them invariably assumed they were married. Pictures show them together, sitting side by side like Derby and Joan in rocking chairs on one of the mansion's stone porches. Companionably they sat at the dining table, waited upon by Carrie who would summon them each evening with a sonorous

Chinese gong. They co-hosted the flow of important visitors who came to Dayton especially to meet the legendary Wright brother. They went on holiday together, to the summer house on the Canadian lake. They appeared regularly in public as VIP guests of honour. They looked like an ageing couple wholly comfortable in each other's space, moving gently into their last years together. Not only did Katherine sometimes wear two rings Orville had given her, but there was said to have been an unspoken assumption by both that in sickness and health neither would ever leave the other.

In 1926 Katharine shocked Orville with the news that she had fallen in love and wanted to marry.

At the centre of this cataclysm was a long-standing friend of them both. Henry J. Haskell was a prominent newspaperman, the chief editorial writer on the Kansas City *Star*. He had spent his early life in Bulgaria where his American parents, and later his brother and sister, were Congregationalist missionaries. He and Katharine had been fellow students at Oberlin College in the 1890s, where he had tutored her for a while. In 1901 he had married another graduate, Isabel Cummings. The couple had remained lifelong friends of Katharine's, later becoming good friends of Wilbur's and Orville's too. Haskell had begun to take an interest in aviation and had earned Orville's admiration by publishing articles highly sympathetic to the Wrights during the Smithsonian's controversial attempts to usurp their sovereignty over the birth of flight. The Haskells sometimes visited Katharine and Orville, and the Wrights had been guests of the journalist and his wife in Kansas City.

What Orville didn't know was that back in her Oberlin days, Henry Haskell had secretly fancied Katharine – and she, very privately, him. Although she'd found him a trifle aloof and uninterested in girls, she had been much drawn by his good looks, his intellect and the sane and balanced view of the world he had later taken so successfully into journalism.

But Katharine had become engaged to another student, Arthur Cunningham. Little is known about their relationship, which Katharine may not have revealed to her family – certainly Bishop Wright, who studiously recorded such important things, never dropped a whisper of it into his diaries; yet the secret engagement had lasted for nearly two years. 'Then by a miracle, not my own wisdom,' she much later confided to Haskell, 'I saw that he really didn't care much about me – not the way I have to be cared about if I am going to care so much.' She had broken it off. Cunningham later became a doctor, married and went to practise in Washington State.

In advanced middle age the once glamorous aura of the aviation heroine had faded. White-haired – in photographs she would now pass for sixty – Katharine came across as a formidable, schoolmarmish, confirmed spinster whom everyone thought would go to her grave caring for her reclusive, sciatic, crippled brother.

In September 1923 Isabel Haskell died and the course of Katharine's life changed. Her regular, innocently chatty, fellow-alumni letters to Henry became expressions of sympathy and comfort. Quite quickly they turned to something warmer. Her letters cheered Haskell when he returned to the empty house in Kansas City from a long holiday in Europe to assuage his grief. Katharine, flatteringly praising his journalistic abilities and personal qualities, and reminding him of the future he still had, had encouraged him out of his black despondency.

They corresponded first weekly, then daily, then frenetically three or four times each day. They discussed everything from the iniquities of the Smithsonian and Henry's growing job insecurity at the *Star*, to politics, the fallibility of the Pope, the meaning of life, and her favourite theme – the inequality of women in a man's world. They chatted about mutual friends and shared their memories of Oberlin, of which Katharine, still actively organising reunions of the class of 1898, had recently become the first woman on the board of trustees. They discussed life's disappointments, Orville's 'old enemy', his hip pain, and the Kansas City widows already in pursuit. They began to write so frequently and at such length – her daily output sometimes ran to twenty-four pages – that one wonders how either found time to do anything else.

By Christmas 1924 they were exchanging gifts, and she was daringly sending him a fragment of a new dress she was having made and asking him to imagine her in it. Her letters exuded affection and concern. 'Tell me, are you sleeping now? Are you over the nervous attacks?' How Harry replied we will never know; his letters during this period, despite many searches by biographers, have never surfaced. Indeed the hundreds Katharine wrote of what by early 1925 had become passionately uninhibited love letters did not become public until 1991. They unveiled a woman very different from the one widely portrayed for seventy years – the Wright Brothers' prim and correct sister – revealing someone hungry for affection, companionship and physical love. They also revealed how her decision to keep the merest whisper of her developing relationship from Orville led her ever deeper into a cauldron of stress and guilt that threatened to shatter her life.

In the twelve months following Isabel's death, the correspondence was correctly formal – 'Dear Katharine', 'Dear Harry', and very properly signed 'Sincerely, Katharine Wright'. But early in 1925 Harry threw caution to the winds. He openly declared his love for her and suggested they might get together. With great speed she reciprocated, confessing her long-standing love for Haskell – but torn between joy at the prospect of a new life and concern for the trauma it would precipitate for Orville. As she and the newspaperman began to discuss the home they would create in Kansas City and the life they would share, her loyalties to the two men became hopelessly divided. 'When I don't think of what being with you means for Orv, I am so happy and full of plans,' she wrote.

More and more her life was consumed with secret letter-writing and the precautions to keep her brother unaware of the increasingly torrid correspondence. The volume of letters grew by the week. Some days she would post one in the morning, another in the afternoon and would rush down in her car to the station to despatch a third to catch the westbound night train. She would sit at the desk in her bedroom, pouring out her heart to Haskell, his picture in front of her, often until three o'clock in the morning. At the start of every day she hopefully looked down the long drive to see if the white flag on the mailbox heralded a new clutch of letters from Kansas City. Seldom was she disappointed. She confided it all to Carrie so the maid could help keep incriminating letters from Mr Orville's sight.

Meanwhile, Katharine and Harry pretended to Orville that

nothing had changed – that Harry was still no more than a good family friend. Indeed he continued to come and stay on working visits to the east when Orville would hospitably make him welcome. But when Orville was safely in bed she would creep into 'the blue room' where Harry was staying. In keeping with the premarital seemliness of the 1920s Midwest, nothing improper ever occurred. Nonetheless, the blue room, she wrote, 'was such a sweet place to love you, with the lovely moonlight for our only light. You were so sweet to me dear. I love to have you so close to me.'[1] Just how close was revealed by another letter whose frankness, when it surfaced in the 1990s, astonished those accustomed to describing the bishop's daughter in terms of her maidenly spinsterishness. Fantasising about the day when they might be married, she wrote:

> You have come home and I have run down to meet you and you kissed me and put your arms around me and we went upstairs, arm in arm, and you kissed me a lot of times on the way up and we are all prepared to be very very silly. Then I'll put my face up to be kissed before we sit in the big chair and you'll hold me very close and maybe slip your hand down where I like it so much to have it and maybe I won't have any stiff clothes on and will stay that way a little while. Then we'll sit in your big chair and have such a dear time together. It will be such a blessed happy time together, dearest.[2]

Had he stumbled on one of these letters Orville would have reeled in shock, but so secure was he in the comfortable partnership that he was quite unaware that his sister had fallen in love. And to help keep it that way, Katharine would cheerfully read to him newsy extracts from the Kansas City letters that did not approach the intimacy that lay on other pages. Indeed she instructed Harry to write from time to time the sort of letter that could safely be shown to Orville in its entirety.

Katharine and Harry were acutely aware of the appalling impending emotional cataclysm for Orville: they discussed it in almost every letter. By the middle of 1925, they were impatient to be together; Orville, like a towering obstacle, was all that stood in their path. It sometimes made Katharine ill to contemplate it as, daily, she studied her brother's face for the smallest sign of suspicion. What troubled her to distraction was Orville's utter dependence upon her. She was his housekeeper, escort, nurse in his constant suffering, confidante, counsellor in his business affairs. Even their birthdays were on the same day. Had the position been reversed:

> It would have almost killed me if he had, in these latter years, wanted someone else more than me. I can't desert him now . . . I have taken care of him so much. I have lived in his life so long . . . I love him so, Harry, and we are so happy together. Since Will and Father have been gone we have been everything to each other. And he is so good to me.
>
> I don't see how Orv could get along without me. And it would break my heart not to stay by him after all he has been to me. It would. No-one else knows all there is between us.[3]

She began to doubt that she would make a good and worthy enough wife – 'I'm not much good – you would be really disappointed and disillusioned if you saw too much of me', beset, too, with guilt that she'd improperly encouraged him to turn to her with her flow of sympathetic letters after Isabel's death – 'I wonder if I should not have been more restrained'.[4]

But restraint proved difficult. In the middle of June, Katharine began rashly to propose a daring assignation, seizing advantage of Orville's absence on a forthcoming brief business trip to Philadelphia and Washington. Harry, on some pretext, would come to Dayton and stay at Hawthorn Hill as soon as Orville had gone. 'If you could come Tuesday evening and stay until Wednesday evening that would be absolutely sure,' she briefed Harry. 'It isn't like me to keep things from Orv but I'll have to this time. I wouldn't for anything worry him so just now. Please don't let Orv or anyone guess anything of this . . . I haven't had any sleep worth speaking of for two nights . . . I do wonder who is walking around here in my shoes . . . I would sit down and cry for a day if it would do any good.'[5]

Katharine had a few days earlier been up at Oberlin attending a trustees' meeting. While she was there there had been a burst of express letters and telegrams between them. Harry was tantalisingly suggesting they meet in the middle, rendezvousing at a hotel in Chicago. One of his letters urging this was in her hand, unopened, when, in a café, to her alarm, she bumped into one of Haskell's closest friends, the university's psychology professor, Raymond Stetson. By further coincidence Stetson happened to be with Harry's sister, Mary, another Haskell Congregational missionary, who was visiting Oberlin from her station in Bulgaria. 'Paralysed', she had hastily stuffed the letter into her pocketbook 'so they wouldn't see the handwriting . . . Oh Harry such a time. I thought of you waiting for a telegram and there I sat rooted to the spot.'

What she may not have known was that the psychology professor, once described 'as an eccentric in his own right', who had maintained a close friendship with Harry, was in fact exceedingly well informed about the secret affair. Urging him to marry Katharine and leave Orville to his own devices, he had been dispensing a stream of professional wisdom to Haskell in a flow of letters passing between them. Stetson typed his using a form of speed-writing in which many of his words were inconsistently compressed to cardinal consonants:

> As for leavg th inventor-bro, I've no notn how she's feel about tt . . . He has means and cd always tke care of himslf – marry his housekpr aft few years, or smthng of th sort . . . She's already done a lot for inventor-bro and mebbe it's time for new venture in life. As for riskg her happiness – well, tt's true to form; I s'pose tt you shd ve solicitous about tt. But hang it, th risk wd be worth it. The only way to live is to risk being unhappy; and I'd rath be unhappy w person I loved than cat-by-the-fire . . . No, go to Dayton before there's another attack and find out the land and get it settled.[6]

From Oberlin Katharine had not gone to meet Harry in Chicago – she wasn't prepared to risk it. The idea of a covert meeting there scared her. If Orville ever heard she'd gone solely to meet Haskell – and at a hotel – their secret would have burst shockingly into the open, and she was not yet ready for a trauma like that. 'NEVER COULD EXPLAIN TO ORV', she wired Harry. Instead she'd suggested the Dayton alternative when Orville was out of the way. His stay at Hawthorn Hill could later be represented to her brother in some perfectly innocuous way. In fact she urged him to stay over until the end of the week actually to meet Orville on his return, thus proving the innocence of the visit.

In Dayton the carefully planned tryst had gone badly wrong. The day before Harry was due to come, her hand was forced. While she and Orville were having breakfast, Carrie came in: Western Union was on the line with a telegram for Miss Katharine. She rushed guiltily to the phone alcove in the entrance hall to take the latest message from Kansas City. It was from Harry confirming his arrival. Obliged to explain, she came back and announced casually:

> 'Harry's coming tomorrow night.' Orv said, 'He is? How does that happen?' So I said, 'Going East.' That struck him as opening a chance that he might see you in Washington, so he says, 'Going to Washington?'
>
> 'No,' says I, 'New York.'
>
> Stupid lie. Of course I might as well have said I didn't know but I was playing a new role of 'creative artist.' So that passed with Orv expressing regret he could not stay home to see you.[7]

As soon as Orville was out of the way she wired Harry: 'PLEASE COME'. That afternoon she drove her brother to the train for Philadelphia. On her return she went up to her bed to rest. She fell asleep – but was presently awakened by the sound of a car coming up the drive. Rushing out on to her bedroom balcony she saw it was their close friends and neighbours, Frank and Anne McCormick. As they got out of the car she called down to them. To her horror Frank shouted up, 'Orville hasn't gone. He's been trying to get you.' Her heart nearly stopped. 'I was so scared,' she later told Harry, 'I couldn't say anything but "Hasn't gone? Hasn't gone?" I was sure he had met with some accident.'

Orville had unexpectedly returned and was back at his Dayton office, carless and trying to get Katharine to drive down and collect him. He'd been frantically phoning while she was asleep. 'Well,' she told Harry, 'I nearly had a fit.'

Hurriedly dressing, she rushed downstairs where Anne told her that Frank had already gone to collect Orville. The whole situation degenerated into French farce. She had only minutes to telephone Western Union and wire Haskell before he boarded the night train for the eighteen-hour journey to Dayton. When she dialled the number no one answered. In mounting panic she dialled again. Still no response. In desperation she phoned a rival cable company. 'I got hold of a blockhead (man, of course!) who couldn't understand anything' – she was so overwrought. When she calmed down, she dictated the warning message – but decided she wanted to see Harry so badly he should still come and she would give Orville some credible explanation: 'ORVILLE MISSED TRAIN. COME ANYWAY IF YOU WILL. WE CAN MANAGE'. 'By this time I was expecting Orv and Frank might walk right into the telephone booth.'

When, a few minutes later, Orville arrived home, he explained what had gone wrong. Soon after he'd boarded the train 'little Bubbie discovered he didn't have any ticket, any sleeping reservations, any money, any of his correspondence . . .' He had left it all in another suit and, less than twenty miles from Dayton, had left the train and caught another back. Katharine, Orville and the McCormicks went out to dinner. When they arrived back at Hawthorn Hill the phone was shrilling. In fresh panic Katharine hurried to seize it, dreading further embarrassment. Another telegram from Harry: he'd prudently decided to abandon the visit. In case Orville received the message all he said, blandly, as if to them both, was: 'OHIO TRIP HAS BEEN POSTPONED'.

'So, as casually as I could, I told Orv you weren't coming after all. I felt as if he could see I had been deceiving him all day.' Terrible guilt now assailed her. At breakfast next morning she sat at the table looking at him, convinced more than ever that he must surely suspect something. When Carrie brought in yet another express envelope from Kansas City and she saw Orville glancing enquiringly, the fresh love letter seemed to burn a hole in the table. 'Unless Orv is a great deal stupider than I think, he saw that something was wrong . . . Lies are always a mess . . . please don't send any special delivery letters or telegrams unless you have to . . . I want them but I can't manage it.'[8]

'I can't bear to begin doing what I have never done – doing things in a way that isn't frank – when we have always been so frank with each other about where we are and what we are doing,' she wrote in one of many letters on the subject. She dwelt on the failed assignation for months, later saying of it: 'It was God's judgement on us that Orv missed the train that day.'

The toll the still grinding feud with the Smithsonian was taking on Orville's health had begun to alarm her. Although he had yet to play his trump card and send the *Flyer* to England, the Smithsonian chief, Dr Walcott, encouraged by the Wrights' enemy, Albert Zahm, had been stepping up their public relations campaign to revise the history of the aeroplane. Langley was now openly being proclaimed 'Discoverer of the Air'; the media in some quarters had even begun to question the Wrights' claim to fame. The Smithsonian regents had ignored Orville's stream of protests. In April 1925, as Katharine and Harry Haskell had begun to pledge their love, Orville had made public his long-delayed shock announcement: as his own country was unprepared to recognise the *Flyer*'s primacy, it would now definitely be going to London's Science Museum. The museum's management could not believe their good fortune in acquiring such a prize.

'This Smithsonian business gets on his nerves,' Katharine told Haskell. 'I am seriously concerned about Orv – as I have been much of the time since Will died . . . he looks thin and worn and tired and <u>old</u> now . . . I'd never forgive myself or be able to live in peace, if I failed Orv now – after all we have been through together and after all he has been to me.'[9]

But the new life that Haskell held out for her was too tempting. She went on living dangerously. She manufactured excuses to Orville to explain her several-times-a-day journeys merely to post letters. When her own mail to Harry at the Kansas City newsroom began to attract attention there, she started typing the envelopes and putting Orville's name as the sender – risking the calamity of the postal system returning them to him. To prevent the office tongues wagging, Harry took a private mailbox.

Through the summer of 1925 the need to choose between Harry and her brother tormented her. It was a choice between two equally beloved men. She had never really needed to marry until now because 'I had Orv who was more like a lover (someone else said that of him) than a brother (in some ways!).' Besides 'men were not inclined to have "feelings" about me.' They 'were not the least interested in me, except as a friend'.[10]

As Harry's letters piled up in her bedroom drawers, her sense of shame weighed on her. She and Orville had shared everything:

> enjoyed everything together, endured everything together. I am sure almost no-one on earth would understand our relation . . . Orv never goes anywhere without me . . . He never considers anything without asking what I think about it – just as any good husband would do . . .[11]

Wilbur and Orville had 'made' her life, she said. She had been a part of their exclusive team, always considered as much as they did each other. 'There was a reason why none of us married.' The three had shared 'all the joys and sorrows and wild delights and bitter griefs'. She pleaded with Harry to be patient, wondering desperately if there might not be some happy compromise – Orville perhaps coming to live with them. But in her heart she knew it wouldn't work. 'What can I do, dear?' she kept pleading in letter after letter. Whatever Haskell said, he was prepared to wait.

Fresh opportunities to be together presented themselves. Orville had to go again to Washington. Harry came and stayed the night. They kissed and cuddled again in the 'blue room'. 'I'm glad you came,' she wrote afterwards. 'You almost frightened me, dear, when you showed so much feeling.'[12]

With Orville's warm agreement she invited Harry to join them on their 1925 summer holiday at their Lambert Island retreat on Lake Huron. 'We will tell him up there where all is peace and quiet and Orv will be in a happy mood.' But Orville was under fresh strain: he was now having publicly to defend his decision to send the *Flyer* to Britain. The news had created outrage in some quarters; at least one senator was trying to have the plan reversed. But the Smithsonian was unmoved. It refused to retract its claims, which were now embedding themselves in history, that Langley's aeroplane had solved the problem of flight first. The *Flyer*, Orville repeated, would definitely go to London.

Harry's visit to Lambert Island passed without the revelation being made. Katharine and Harry went out of their way to conceal their true feelings from Orville, waiting for him to go off fishing in his boat before seizing each other in the privacy of her bedroom or at the rear of the island, where they would go like much younger lovers, buckets in hand, blueberrying. They never found the courage to tell him, and Orville pressed Harry to come again the following summer.

From Lambert Island Orville and Katharine went up into the wilds of northern Ontario as guests of some old Dayton friends – Colonel Edward Deeds, a prominent Dayton industrialist, and his wife. Orville hurt his back at the remote log cabin and collapsed. For days he was crippled with pain, unable even to dress himself. They eventually had to carry him on to the train on which he travelled back to Georgian Bay on an inflatable mattress. At the island, as Katharine nursed him, helping him to dress and to walk, she had flashbacks of him lying in pain in hospital at Fort Myer where she'd rarely left his bedside. As she sat writing to Harry, Orville now lay incapacitated again, stretched out on the floor beside her. How could she even contemplate abandoning someone now more than ever so utterly dependent upon her. 'Who,' she asked, 'will take care of little brother if I don't? . . . He looks at me so appealingly it breaks my heart.'[13]

When Orville began to walk again and they went home to Dayton at the end of September, her desire to be permanently with Harry returned overwhelmingly. Her letters began to address him 'My darling, darling Harry', and to end 'Your little Katie Wright'. As she and Orville sat by the fire at Hawthorn Hill reading to each other, he had not the least idea that his sister was struggling to engineer a way to leave him decently.

When Katharine asked Harry if they were actually engaged, he immediately proposed, and as autumn arrived she made several attempts to tell Orville. Always she faltered. When she composed the words and saw his unsuspecting face, always 'my heart fails'. Meanwhile she began to refurnish Harry's Kansas City home. On her travels with Orville to New York or Washington he would have been stunned had he known his sister was busily shopping around the big stores looking for furniture, rugs, linen, china and wallpaper for another man's house.

She began to fear that her indecision might lead Harry to give up in frustration and turn to someone else, to one of the wealthy 'aggressive' widows – 'widders', she called them – some of whom had their eye on the now available newspaperman. She need not have worried. Harry's patience was seemingly inexhaustible. He was, it appeared, prepared to wait for ever.

As Christmas 1925 approached and their separation grew unendurable, it looked as if the impasse might finally end. They hatched a new devious plan – for Harry to be invited to Hawthorn Hill for part of the holiday. He arrived on Christmas Day. It was a happy occasion. Orville, without a flicker of suspicion, welcomed him warmly, playing the affable host. Katharine and Harry, fearful of betraying themselves with a glance or inadvertent word of endearment, acted out their former role of old college friends. Again Orville wasn't told. Though Harry was ready to do so, wretchedly as he must have contemplated the shock it would deliver under his old friend's roof at Christmas, of all times, Katharine beseeched him to delay for a little longer. She was beginning to have qualms about the rightness and selfishness of it, wondering if the lust Harry had awoken in her was not just an ephemeral thing that should not be allowed to dictate her destiny:

> I can't think passionate love will last, dear. The other will. I really didn't realize how strong my attachment to Orv was. That is the kind of love that lasts, it seems to me.[14]

Adrift in a sea of doubt, and convinced she was letting both men down, she veered back to the hope that she could have them both, that they could all live happily in some sort of *ménage à trois*, perhaps even at Hawthorn Hill. It would be essential, whatever happened, that she could always be with Orville 'if ever he needs me in sickness'. With sublime optimism, she wrote, 'If Orv knows how generous you are, dear, it seems to me he will be generous, too, to you.'

Through the early months of 1926, the burden of the awful secret and the serial deceits it spawned, grew daily heavier upon Katharine. Every time she tried to compose herself, rehearsing the words with which to make the shattering confession, she saw Orville's face receiving the news of betrayal and shrank from delivering it. It began to affect her health. 'I am so on edge,' she told Harry, 'I suppose what will finally drive me to tell Orv will be a strain I can't stand any longer . . . I know the look that will come on his face.'[15] She tried yet again to explain the pivotal role she'd held for so long as the family linchpin and carer. She'd been only seven when she'd been expected to help nurse her sick mother, Susan. By the time she'd gone away to university she had already been 'old in my ways and old looking'.

'I lay awake thinking what a good-for-nothing I'd become.' Weary of life, she had given everything to her Father, Will and Orv and had now 'come to the end of it all . . . How have I made us both so unhappy?' she wailed. 'You are really so young – much younger than I am dear.* All your friends will wonder why you wanted to marry someone so much older than you are and will come to the conclusion that you got "roped in" and couldn't escape!'[16]

Again and again she crafted her confessional. 'Last night I thought I would tell Orv but I couldn't.' It would have been a heartless moment, for Orville had become depressed and irritable, nagged by a fresh bout of acute sciatic pain.

Still Haskell didn't give up. His ardour was uncooled by the seeming hopelessness of it all. There exists just one glimpse of his stoicism: only one undated page of one of his letters from this period has survived. It is in the brisk, emphatic, hard-to-read handwriting of a busy newspaperman, but reflects his enormous, philosophical patience:

> I understand perfectly and you mustn't blame yourself. You have done your best. If there is any blame it is on me. But K you have been under great strain . . . When I went to D [Dayton] last June,

*They were actually born in the same year.

> do you remember I told you I wanted to help you find out what was in your heart. I haven't changed since and I couldn't possibly ask you to do what you thought you shouldn't. You know that you don't have to decide right away. There is plenty of time to think it over. I know your feeling for Orv, dear. If you finally decide you can't leave him – even for the part of the time I have talked about, it will be all right dear. I'll do my best. I love you, K whatever happens.[17]

Harry had proposed that she share her married life between the two, living in Kansas City but regularly commuting to Dayton to spend time with her brother. Whatever the time-sharing suggestion was, it was never to be raised as a sop with Orville as he went on living with the greatest deception of his life. But the risk that Orville would get wind of the secret romance was growing by the week. Stetson was pressing Harry to bring matters to a head speedily; he thought Miss W was 'exaggerating her indispensability' to her brother. The professor warned Haskell of the risk that Orville would learn of it from another source with consequences none of them could bear.

In the middle of February Katharine tried to tell Orville, but she was so overcome she couldn't go on. She lost courage. Whatever Orville was told, it appears not to have alarmed him. Perhaps she only got as far as reminding him of her fondness for their old friend – which wouldn't have surprised him. Life at Hawthorn Hill went on smoothly.

Meanwhile, at the Kansas City *Star* a management upheaval began to threaten Harry's own security. The *Star*'s owner had suddenly died and the paper was about to be sold; a string of telegrams reported the worrying news to Hawthorn Hill. Suddenly it wasn't clear if he would have a job to support her. Harry and five other employees were trying to buy the paper; Katharine offered to send him $10,000, but he refused to accept it. Job or no job, she insisted, she would still marry him.

In the middle of May 1926, the management buy-out of the newspaper was happily concluded. Harry Haskell's future – now as a director – was resecured. He found a business excuse to come once more as an overnight guest to Hawthorn Hill. This time, it had been agreed, he would arrange to see Orville on his own.

Katharine's every worst fear of the devastation it would wreak upon little Bubbo's psyche was shatteringly realised. Orville was felled by Harry's announcement. He reeled in shock and scandalised disbelief. Had he just learnt that his sister had been killed in an accident he could not have been more deeply stunned. The gentle hint Katharine had given him months earlier had just not registered. Scarcely able to believe his ears, Orville told Haskell that the proposed marriage broke an immutable arrangement that he and Katharine had entered into to remain single for each other. It was all too tragically clear that he believed quite absolutely that they had bonded for life.

34

'Little Brother' Alone (1926–1929)

The atmosphere in the stately house changed for ever. Orville was inconsolable:

> I am so sick with heartache. I ought to have foreseen how it would be. I didn't quite; and I blame myself. I couldn't go through many more days like today dear . . . How it hurts me to hurt him so. He didn't show it much last night but today – oh, Harry, dear. I feel just as if someone in the family had died . . . This is the first time there has been any trouble to amount to anything between Orv and me. He looks so pitiful, so dark under the eyes – just as he used to look when he was terribly worried and sick besides. I don't know what to do dear.[1]

In the days that followed, Katharine walked about in a daze, crying much of the time. She tried to talk to Orville but he began to avoid her – 'he won't stay in the house a minute'. He'd started getting up at the crack of dawn and leaving home, not to reappear all day. From her bedroom she would hear his car, its motor somehow expressing his deep hurt, roaring off down the drive at the unheard-of hour of half-past six in the morning. Where he went we do not know – probably to his office where he just may have shared his grief with the other woman in his life, the formidable Mabel Beck.

Orville lived in a black mist, lying awake through two nights, doping himself with aspirin, waiting for the first crack of dawn so he could rush out of the house away from the sight of his sister. It was several days before she could pin him down. His pathetic state so melted her heart that it threatened her wavering resolve. She learnt that so deep had been his trust in the form of 'marriage' that had bound them that he had been blind to every clue that should have aroused suspicion. He could not find words to express his despair and unhappiness. His state of mind so alarmed her that she was forced to restore some grains of hope. 'I didn't know what to do so I told Orv not to worry so. I wasn't going to leave him now.' The idyllic life she'd yearned for with Harry would, for her own sanity, have to be postponed. 'We must let Orv get used to the idea before we press it again,' Harry would have read, surely with dismay.

Consideration of the devastated Orville was to prolong everyone's unhappiness through the entire summer and autumn of 1926. The letters continued to go back and forth, but hers were now much briefer and no longer daily. Among those that have survived there are suddenly unexplained gaps of several weeks in the continuing pledges of her love and expressions of remorse.

At Hawthorn Hill a leaden gloom settled over Katharine's once very special relationship with her brother. Their extraordinary kinship had been ruptured beyond repair. Orville, now fifty-five, his moustache and remaining hair going grey, his hip giving him constant pain, had retreated into a pit of long silences and self-pity. The poisoned atmosphere had brought an awkwardness between them neither had ever known. His withdrawal into wounded martydom made it almost impossible for Katharine to discuss their futures as she braced herself for the final act of departure:

> I have been trying all day to talk to Orv but I couldn't do it . . . I have started four times but I can't get anywhere when I see that look on his face. It is what I always call his 'little boy look' – it nearly breaks my heart.[2]

She'd always known it would end this way. They would still get married, but there could be no question of a formal wedding. Haskell continued to show the patience of Job. His letters went on pouring balm upon her suffering. He was, it would appear, prepared to wait until the end of time.

And now, as the fateful year dragged on, Orville suddenly began to cling to the hope that when it came to the crunch, Katharine would not, after all, abandon him. It kept him cheerful through their annual summer holiday on Lambert Island where, with the new awkwardness between them, the marriage wasn't even mentioned.

By October Katharine was nearing the end of her tether. 'I am at my nerves' end,' she wrote. 'I am worn out, dear . . . I am sorry to fall down so – and so ashamed.' She hadn't really been free to leave Orville in the first place. Now she was paying for her selfishness. 'I see for the first time what a relief from responsibilities death could be,' she said bleakly. 'No-one can help me.'[3] Her expressions of shame and remorse are almost embarrassing to read. Every time she looked at Orville she knew she couldn't go. 'I feel as if I were in chains and I'm not sure I can break out.'[4] She began to go out less and less. Her normally busy social life and her involvement in a raft of worthy causes began to wind down. She started looking at all the possessions spread about the big house, realising how few she dared take without upsetting Orville. As it grew more and more impossible to discuss their future, she thought of just walking out with a few things of her own without the heartbreak of saying goodbye. That final moment she could not face.

She wanted to confide in Lorin but feared he would never forgive her 'for tearing up everything' the staunchly united family had ever stood for. When, late in October, she managed at last to broach it, she was surprised how sympathetic the now 64-year-old Lorin and Netta were. Next to Wilbur and Orville she had been closest to Lorin who, as a young man, used to braid her hair before she went off to school. Lorin already knew of the crisis – Orville had told him. He and Netta were, to her surprise, full of compassionate understanding. She had, after all, been a marvellously caring and generous aunt to their children, rushing to help nurse them whenever they were ill. They had all adored her. They believed the wedding should now quickly go ahead; they promised to look after Orville.

Her other sister-in-law, Lulu, was equally supportive. 'Lou' was now sixty-one and widowed: Reuchlin had died at fifty-nine in Kansas City six years earlier. Lou, in recent years, had become rootless; now a regular visitor to Hawthorn Hill, she was currently staying there in full sight of the domestic drama simmering around her, adding womanly support to the encouragement Carrie was also giving Katharine.

To the last, Orville still clung to the hope she wouldn't go. To her relief he had cheered up. After all, she told Harry, her brother owed her something too. 'I have always stuck by him – against everyone else – even against Will . . . Maybe he has got used to the idea a little.'[5] But Orville had not. He brought matters to a head, one version of these searing events claiming that he finally pointed the pistol. Said to have been 'alternately furious and inconsolable', declaring that he was not prepared ever to be shared, he had delivered an ultimatum: 'choose between me and him'. In October 1926 Katharine chose Haskell. She agreed that they should marry as soon as possible.

Harry sent her a ring and they fixed the date for Saturday 20 November. When Orville was told, he announced he would boycott the wedding. He went further, telling Lorin that he was forbidding his famous name to be used in any announcement of the event. However, the two Wright family figures in this melodrama were internationally celebrated in their own right. The newspapers seized the story of the wedding a few days before, when Haskell came to Dayton to obtain the licence. Katharine's picture went on the front pages. The sister of Orville and Wilbur Wright, inventors of the aeroplane, was about to be wed 'in the deepest secrecy'.

Orville had forced the covert ceremony upon them. Determined that he shouldn't be humiliated and the story of the rift burst into full public view, Katharine went to unusual lengths to have the ceremony conducted in private away from media eyes. They decided to do it at Oberlin College, whose president, Dr Henry King, agreed to marry them at the home of one of the couple's old university classmates, another professor, Dr Louis Lord. Lorin and Netta didn't go in the end; Katharine decided it would split the family down the middle and risk souring their own relationships with Orville. She had wanted Lorin's daughter Ivonette, now thirty and married to Harold Miller, who operated a finance company, to sing at the wedding and Lou to play the piano. Ivonette didn't go, and it's not clear whether Lou did either. However, Harry's son, 24-year-old Henry Jr., himself now a fully fledged newspaperman, and Harry's missionary sister Mary were there. So, fittingly, was the psychology professor Raymond Stetson, who had helped to steer Haskell safely to this destination. The only member of Katharine's family to turn up was Lorin's daughter Leontine, with her husband; now living in Cleveland they could attend without embarrassing the Dayton clan.

Orville remained conspicuously absent. No card of congratulations, no wedding present could he bring himself to send. There is no record of how he spent possibly the blackest day of his life, grieving in anger and self-pity over his sister's elopement, nor of the moment of their parting. Katharine, it is said, went with very little – just her own things. She even left behind a photograph of Wilbur and Orville in France that had hung for years in her bedroom. Perhaps she thought its rightful home was Hawthorn Hill. As he had to come to Dayton for the licence, Harry may have collected her in his car; but another version has them travelling separately to Oberlin, for propriety's sake.

However Katharine left Dayton she did so almost invisibly. From this city in which she ranked as one of its most prominent women, with a large circle of friends, she felt obliged, to avoid embarrassment to Orville, to leave like a thief in the night. She denied herself the flood of congratulations and wedding gifts that would have showered upon her; but she protected Orville from the appalling public revelation of how badly he was behaving. She confided her precipitate exit to only two people – her old friend Agnes Beck, and Colonel Deeds' wife. 'It was all so undignified, going away as I did,' she told Griffith Brewer. 'I shall never forget that. I hated it so.'[6]

From that day Orville excised Katharine from his life. The severance was total. But in Kansas City in her marriage to Harry Haskell Katharine found the full happiness she had dreamed of.

'If she'd had even a whim of a doubt that her life with Harry would not have been completely wonderful, I don't think she would have chosen that path – for she did like firm ground,' said historian Lois Walker at the USAF's Tyndall airbase in Florida where, in 2002, she was working on a biography of Katharine Wright. 'But she loved and trusted Harry and felt completely secure in her future with him. So she left the old and comfortable behind. I think Orv never thought she would actually go through with it. Fooled him, she did. That's what you get for sending a woman to college and letting her develop a sense of her own self-esteem.'[7]

'It's a wonder she pulled it off really,' said Adrian Kinnane when he read Katharine's letters to Haskell for the first time. 'I think it underscores her courage and her good sense and, not least, the underlying sense of fairness and doing what's right that all the Wrights possessed. Orville was, as was his father, outwardly a champion of women's rights who'd even once joined her on a suffragette march through the city – until, it seems, it interfered with his own needs.'[8]

In Kansas City in late 1926 Katharine was welcomed into Harry's wide circle of friends. Invitations poured in, and at their house in Charlotte Street they regularly entertained prominent personages, from the Missouri state governor down. Harry, who became editor of the *Star*, moved, she discovered, in the highest strata of city society. And their reward for the protracted torment of the preceding two years was a marriage, people said, that could have been made in heaven.

Orville's punitive hostility hung over the blissful union as a permanent sombre cloud. It was uncompromising, without a grain of mercy. He could not bring himself to open the door he slammed on his relationship with his sister by even the tiniest compassionate crack. Katharine hoped his petulance would fade with time; she had truly wanted to keep a large corner of her life free for him. Indeed she had wanted to spend whole weeks, even months, of her year back at Hawthorn Hill, an arrangement that the unusually generous Harry had happily supported. She also badly wanted to keep in touch, through Orville, with the aviation world and his continuing feud with the Smithsonian, from all of which she was cut off in Kansas City. But Orville remained implacable. He didn't want to share his aviation interest with her any more. He never wrote, never phoned, never mentioned her in his letters to common friends. He did not speak of her in conversation.

Katharine remained a trustee of Oberlin College and regularly travelled to meetings there from Kansas City. She had hoped these journeys back to Ohio would enable her to go down to Dayton to spend time with her unhappy brother. But when, several times, she wrote to him to suggest this, he did not reply; pointedly he returned the letters unopened.

'I couldn't regret doing what I did, but Orv is a great shadow over my happiness all the time,' Katharine told the Wrights' old family friend, the polar explorer Vilhjalmur Stefansson:

> If he would only let me come and stay with him all I can. I could be there often and stay for weeks – as I intended to do. I never thought of anything but that. Sometimes I wonder if I won't wake up from a bad dream and find him as he always was.[9]

'I think,' Stefansson commented, 'Orv is punishing himself worse than you. But it is bad for everybody, including people like Griff and me.'[10]

Griffith Brewer maintained his close friendship with both Katharine and Orville. He still travelled regularly to America and would stay with Orville at Hawthorn Hill and up at his Canadian summer retreat, where Stefansson was also a welcome visitor. Occasionally Brewer would make the long train journey west to Kansas City where he would be the guest of Katharine and Harry. Brewer and Stefansson had found themselves in the middle of this tragic rift. Katharine and Harry regularly confided their sorrow to both men.

In letters to Brewer, Haskell wrote of the sadness Orville's unrelenting sulk had cast upon the happiness of the marriage:

> His attitude is a calamity to Katharine; a calamity all round. But I see no way to change it. He assumes that Katharine prevented his marrying when a younger man, and that an implied agreement resulted that she should never marry. So far as I can learn he is

> mistaken. He was so absorbed in his work he had no inclination to marry. Through her companionship and her part in making a home, he felt no need of marrying. If he, with his determination and will, had met somebody whom he had wanted to marry I believe he would have married. It would have been Katharine's duty to accept the situation and make the best of it. Just as it is his duty to make the best of her marrying.
>
> But Orville is not a man who can be argued with. He made his great success thro his independence of character, his refusal to listen to others. The same qualities now get in the way of his being influenced . . . She has been a devoted sister to him. She gave up her career as a teacher – work that she enjoyed more than anything else she has ever done – to devote herself to looking after him and Wilbur. He waves all that aside as negligible. But I have no real hope of any change.[11]

Harry Haskell saw Griffith Brewer as the one person who might have enough influence with Orville to persuade him to relent. 'It is barely possible he might open up the subject with you and that you might be able to work a miracle. I know you would if you could!'

While on holiday at a mountain hotel in the Rockies a few weeks later in the summer of 1927, Katharine poured her heart out to Brewer:

> No-one can ever realise how heartbroken I was to do what I did – but it came finally to the place where I thought it was the only right thing to do. I do not expect everyone to agree with me. As far as you are concerned, I only want you to be the good friend to Orv that you have always been . . . I expected to devote a great deal of my time to him. Harry was willing and expected nothing else.[12]

What explained Orville's heartless obstinacy? Biographers over the years have touched only lightly on the brutal rejection from his life of the sister who had mothered and sustained him in sickness and health for so long. Katharine's account of the secret courtship and anxiety about Orville's reaction, which only surfaced in the

1990s, told only half the story. Orville, as far as is known, studiously committed not a molecule of his feelings, his burning sense of betrayal, in letters to anyone. History was left to guess at the reasons for his apparent callousness, his determination to make his sister pay for her 'infidelity'.

'Orville was a difficult character to fathom,' said Tom Crouch. 'His niece, Ivonette, told me, "You know, he was the kind of man who hid behind women – who always had to have a woman to do the hard things, and that's what Mabel Beck did for him. She was useful in that way and he was willing to pay a very high price for that." Orville was someone who wanted to live life on his own terms. He wanted it to be as easy and comfortable as he could make it. By making use of women like Mabel and Katharine, they fulfilled those needs for him. When Katharine left him it was as if she'd walked out of a marriage. I can understand his reaction, but still it was not a pretty picture.'[13]

Those of Orville's descendants old enough to remember Uncle Orv tried to find a sympathetic explanation when the full harshness of his response finally became public more than forty years after his death. 'Could it have been,' said Orville's great-niece Marianne Hudec, in Boston, 'that building Hawthorn Hill for her constituted an unspoken contract? Or was there some understanding flowing from the brothers successfully persuading her to quit her job as a teacher to be supported for the rest of her life? If there was no pact between her and Orville never to marry I can't imagine why he felt so injured. Orville was not a vindictive man looking for injury where none existed. He was a rational sensitive man. I don't think Katharine handled the situation very well at all. Had she been up-front with Orville and not kept her relationship with Harry a secret things might well have turned out very differently.'[14]

Mrs Hudec, a granddaughter of Lorin, had, by the new millennium, become the Wright family spokesperson. Orville, whom she remembered as a child in the 1930s and 1940s, with much affection, as a kindly, elderly great-uncle has, she said, too often been cast as the villain in these sad events:

> It must have been very hurtful to learn that the person he felt

> closest to in the world did not share her feelings about Harry with him before presenting him with a *fait accompli*. Katharine, he felt, was his adored and adoring sister and Harry his valued friend. His confidence in her loyalty to him was destroyed. His Victorian sensibilities would have been jarred to say the least. I don't think he would have understood the strong pull of being in love – he had never had that experience. But certainly when he decided that a wrong had been committed he would never flinch from making a painful decision.[15]

In the mid-1920s the Wright family had been quite unaware, Mrs Hudec said, of the secret engagement. Her mother, Lorin's daughter Ivonette, had not learnt of it until nearly seventy years later when, in her late nineties, some of the love letters were read to her. 'She had supported Katharine's decision to marry and had known that it had upset Orville. What she hadn't known until she heard the letters was how long the romance had gone on before he was told. That really stunned her.'

But Katharine's letters were not to be the only source of enlightenment on the matter. Early in 2003, research for this biography uncovered in London some long-lost correspondence between Harry Haskell and Griffith Brewer; the cache also included some unseen letters of Katharine's. One of Haskell's letters reported to Brewer, in January 1928, the only explanation on record for his actions by Orville himself.

Few people who had been witness to the tragic events had been bold enough to challenge him. One who did was Anne O'Hare McCormick. A prominent *New York Times* foreign affairs writer, the first woman to win a Pulitzer Prize in journalism and later a confidante of President Franklin D. Roosevelt, she and her husband lived in Dayton. As neighbours and close friends of Orville and Katharine at Hawthorn Hill, the domestic drama had erupted before their astonished eyes. A probing journalist 'unintimidated by men' and especially fond of Katharine, Anne decided to seek an explanation. In January 1928 she'd gone to put some hard questions to Orville. A few days later, on a visit to Kansas City, she had reported his grievances to Katharine and Harry – who later relayed them to Griffith Brewer:

> Mrs McCormick was determined to talk to him about Katharine and thought she knew him well enough to do so.
>
> The reason he gave her was that Katharine hadn't treated him fairly in that she was the cause of his not marrying thirty years ago. As I understand he said about the same thing to her that he did to me. There was nothing definite, but the fact that he felt that Katharine wanted to keep house for her brothers and did not want them to marry, deterred him from 'going out with the girls' and so prevented his forming any attachment that might have led to marriage.
>
> Mrs McCormick says she laughed at him and told him that was about as flimsy an excuse as she had heard. The fact was, I suppose, that his concentration on his work prevented any social activities on his part, and Katharine was making them so comfortable at home that he was not driven out to find somebody to make him a home. Mrs McCormick told him he was simply making himself unhappy and hurting Katharine without any real reason. I don't know that she made any progress with him . . .[16]

'What an emotional child was the father of flight,' said Adrian Kinnane. 'It really does smack of the bitterness of divorce.'[17]

In Kansas City Katharine never managed to free herself of guilt. Thoughts of Orville haunted her, stirred by regular news of him from Carrie who continued to care for Orville at Hawthorn Hill, where Lorin's family were constant visitors. Carrie told Katharine that she had kept trying to ease Mr Orville's loneliness, suggesting he invite friends to dinner. But, 'he just smiles, she says,' Katharine told Agnes Beck. She'd heard a wild rumour that Orville had become engaged to a widow named Mrs Barnes. 'I shouldn't imagine that there was much likelihood of that,' she commented with much truth to Agnes.

Katharine declined an invitation in March 1927 to go and stay with Agnes in Dayton:

> I can't go home . . . I can't go to Dayton yet. Lorin thinks I ought to come and see them but I can't do it yet. I don't see how I ever can . . . In my imagination I walk through that house, looking for

> Little Brother and at all the dear familiar things that made my home – but I never find Little Brother and I have lost my old home forever, I fear. Harry is so unbelievably good to me and is so happy about my being here that I can't spoil his happiness.[18]

Katharine became firm friends with Henry Jr., now working on newspapers in the east. 'They were supremely happy,' the younger Henry Haskell recalled in 1977. 'She and I had a wonderful relationship. She was an angel.' Henry spoke of his stepmother's alienation from her famous brother. He told a writer, Dr John Crane, planning a biography of the Wrights:

> My impression – amounting almost to a certainty – is that Orville never wrote to his sister after her marriage. It was both a painful and an extraordinary situation. My father and Orville had been friends for many years . . . I believe Orville more than once made it clear that his objection to the marriage had nothing to do with my father. Apparently it was the thought that Katharine could leave him which he found intolerable. I heard, at second-hand, Orville's alleged explanation that <u>he</u> had not married on her account. Frankly, such an excuse seems wholly unpersuasive . . . Katharine foresaw the opposition, tried hard to win her brother over, but failed, and only then, on my father's gentle insistence, with great reluctance, agreed to brave his wrath . . . I have difficulty in forgiving Orville, who was a fine man otherwise. But I hope that if you must deal with this sad episode you will do so with the discretion – and compassion – it deserves.[19]

Henry Jr. said that his father's relationship with Orville ground, at least temporarily, to a halt. 'In the circumstances to try and maintain it would have been impossible.'

Life in Kansas City for Katharine wasn't, on a newspaperman's income, quite as financially comfortable as it had been with Orville. 'About once a day Harry and I take pencil and paper in hand to figure when we will be out of debt. The latest figure showed that, barring untoward events, we ought to be pretty nearly out of the pit in the spring of 1930.'[20]

Their finances improved sooner than that. By the end of 1928 she and Harry were able to plan a holiday together to Europe. Then suddenly things started to go wrong. At the end of January 1929 Haskell had to undergo what was then major surgery for the removal of a kidney stone. As she had done over twenty years earlier for Orville, Katharine remained constantly at his bedside for two weeks at the Mayo clinic in Rochester, Minnesota. Back in Kansas City she went on nursing him as his wound continued to drain. They decided nonetheless to go ahead with their holiday, now booked, to Greece, Italy and England.

They were never to go. The day they returned from the clinic Katharine became ill. It began as a severe cold contracted in the sub-zero weather of Minnesota; it developed into pneumonia. In the absence of antibiotics it was immediately life-threatening. Harry wrote to warn Lorin.

The attack had been a recurrence of a severe bout of flu earlier in December which had so alarmed Harry and his sister Mary that the latter had taken the bold step of addressing to Orville a diffident letter. Writing from Oberlin College, she said:

> You will be as surprised to receive this letter as I am to be writing it, but something has happened that impels me to write . . . One day last week came a letter from Harry saying that Katharine was in bed with the flu and 103 temperature. I could not sleep. I may be all wrong, but I kept on wondering – you see when I have written to ask Harry whether he was forgiven for taking away Katharine, he did not answer and I did not repeat the question, only wondered.
>
> When Harry called me to K City in '26 to tell me of this prospect I thought I had never seen him so happy – the only sorrow being that his gain was your loss. But he said, "Katharine will just have to commute between Dayton and K City." He also remarked, "Of course Katharine's being sorry for me has much to do with her marrying me."
>
> Before our Mother died we spoke together of the possibility of that marriage and Mother said, "She will never leave her brother!" . . . Perhaps dear Katharine reasoned it out that if she

> married Harry she could spend lots of time in Dayton and so make you both happy . . . I felt dreadfully about the dilemma myself but then I concluded that Harry too is a human being and if God had pity on him in giving Katharine this love to him, would not the great Father in some way make up the loss to her brother . . .[21]

The alarm bell from Harry's missionary sister ended, 'This letter isn't one that has to be answered.' It appears that Orville did not. Nor a few weeks later, in the last week of February 1929, when Katharine's pneumonia had worsened and her life was suddenly hanging in the balance, was he immediately willing to make the 600-mile journey to Kansas City.

When Harry phoned Lorin he asked him to tell Orville that Katharine was dying. Lorin did – but Orville was moved neither to phone Kansas City nor to send the briefest telegram of concern. Three days later Katharine, her lungs filling with fluid, was in a delirious fever; as she lapsed in and out of consciousness she asked for Lorin. When Harry called him, Lorin booked himself on the next train to Kansas City. He phoned Orville, but Orville was not willing to join him on the overnight train. Lorin told him that if he didn't go to Katharine, none of the family would ever speak to him again. With enormous reluctance Orville capitulated. Still in no hurry, he booked himself on a later train and coldly wired Harry that he was coming.

When Lorin got to Katharine's bedside in the Haskell home she was unconscious. They managed to arouse her briefly. 'She smiled and said, "Why, it's Phiz [Lorin's nickname]" and then drifted off,' Harry later recalled. 'When Orville arrived she was still weaker. I asked her if she knew him, and finally she aroused and said, "Of course I do."'[22]

They were the last words Katharine ever spoke. She did not regain consciousness. The following evening, on Sunday 2 March, 1929, she died in front of Harry, Lorin, Henry Jr. and Orville.

35

The Twilight Years

(1930–1948)

Katharine's death produced not a perceptible quiver of emotion or sorrow in Orville. He shocked Harry Haskell, telling him 'that Katharine had died for him three years ago and that he had gone to Kansas City entirely on my account, not hers,' Harry wrote to Griffith Brewer. 'I had hoped her death would change his attitude.'[1] It had changed nothing. He had written his sister out of his life and no corner of his heart remained for her. He was never to speak of her again, and the family protected him by discreetly avoiding mention of her name. It was almost as if she had never existed. His true emotions as he looked upon her coffin in the Kansas City house we shall never know.

Harry felt that Katharine should be buried in her home town, in the family plot back in Ohio. After a funeral service in Kansas City, her body was shipped by train to Dayton. Harry, Orville and Lorin travelled with her, despite their strained relations, drawn together by bitter poignancy. Orville was stiffly cordial to Harry, who was still in much pain from his kidney operation and numbed with grief and heartbreak.

Katharine lay in the big, flower-heaped living room at Hawthorn Hill, that had once rung with her emphatic voice as she charmed her brother's important guests, during the simple service she had wanted. Whether or not at Orville's request, the Episcopalian minister, oddly it seems, made, according to a local newspaper report, 'no personal reference to the deceased'. But her old friend Agnes Beck told reporters, 'She enriched every life she touched.' At Woodland cemetery, Katharine, in her fifty-fifth year, was buried next to Wilbur as aircraft from Wright Field, the air base that had sprung up next to Huffman Prairie, flew over, dropping flowers.

She left an estate of around $54,000. It would be worth more than half a million dollars today. The lion's share went to Harry, but she made bequests to her nieces and nephews and to Lorin, Reuchlin's widow Lulu ('Lou'), Carrie Grumbach and even her laundress, Lottie Jones, who'd bought the Hawthorn Street house. Lorin, who had struggled financially most of his life, got a generous $10,000. To Orville 'who has abundant means of his own, in loving remembrance', she left $1000.

Her death sparked a renewal of the spurious claims that she had been a true partner of her brothers, a third member of the inventing team, guiding them with her superior academic qualifications to the complex aerodynamic truths as well as pouring her own money into the project. At that awful moment Orville made no attempt to correct them; but a Cincinnati newspaper dug out of the files an earlier interview in which he'd said it was 'just another newspaper fairy story. Indeed my brother and I had even more money saved perhaps than my sister.'[2]

Orville and Haskell were to resume their interrupted friendship, and Harry was to be accepted with great warmth by all the other Wrights as a much liked and respected member of the family; they found him stimulating company. He was never to leave Kansas City, but, being a man who didn't enjoy living on his own, two years later he remarried; his third wife, Agnes Hadley, was the widow of a former governor of Missouri.

In a column he wrote for the Kansas City *Star*, Haskell never lost an opportunity to champion the Wright brothers, deriding the scandalous efforts of the Smithsonian to belittle their monumental achievement. In his seventies he began an autobiography. As far as it got before his death in 1952, it made little reference to the Wright family; but had he accepted an invitation in 1948 by Lorin's daughter Ivonette to write the full story of the invention, he would have had to confront the emotions aroused in addressing the lives of both the brothers and their unique sister, with whom he'd become bewitched. Deteriorating health induced him to decline the daunting project. 'It would be a fascinating job,' he told Ivonette. 'Unhappily . . . I haven't the time – and am afraid, the energy because of an imperfect heart – and the eyesight – to go into the work . . . I have a feeling that Katharine would have liked me to do it if I could, she was so proud of Wilbur and Orville and of their great achievements.'[3]

Haskell memorialised the family in another way: he paid for a monument to Katharine to be built at Oberlin College. A memorial fountain, it was a replica of a sculpture in Florence of a boy and a dolphin by the fifteenth-century artist Verrocchio, one of whose pupils, Leonardo da Vinci, had explored the mysteries of flight.

The atmosphere within the grand house in Oakwood had never been the same again for Orville after Katharine's departure two years earlier. It must have seemed, at first, a bitterly lonely place without even the great St Bernard to keep him company, for Scipio had died. The only women in his life now were Carrie, who continued to cook and care for him, even tying his shoelaces when his sciatica prevented him bending, and Mabel Beck, whom Katharine had always disliked for the aggressive way she barred his office against all comers – including his own family. Mabel, whose not unattractive appearance in photographs belies her intimidating reputation, had begun to form an important part of his public life.

There were rumours that Mabel Beck may have become rather more in Orville's life than his secretary. In the 1990s one of the Wrights' biographers, Rosamond Young, in her column in a Dayton newspaper, ran a startling item in which she claimed an elderly local man had described to her how, as a boy, over sixty years earlier, he had one day peeped through the window of Orville's office and seen him with Mabel on his lap. 'I've wondered if the man had become senile,' commented Marianne Hudec. 'My own view is that the story is so out of character for Uncle Orv as to be laughable. If he were going to romance someone, it would not be in his office.'[4]

Occasionally Mabel would accompany Orville to the sorts of

events to which he would once have automatically taken Katharine. She went with him in 1932 to the dedication of the Wright Brothers memorial, the great granite obelisk built at the site of the first flight among the Kill Devil sand dunes – linked at last to the mainland by a long bridge across Albemarle Sound. And it was claimed by one author that he had had a posh house built for her in affluent Oakwood, its architecture suspiciously modelled, at her request, on nearby Hawthorn Hill. Indeed Orville had been seen laying out for her a driveway she had wanted modelled on his.

He may have laid out her driveway, said Marianne Hudec, 'but he never paid for nor built her mini-Hawthorn Hill. There was never a possibility that he would marry her – nor was there ever a romantic relationship between them. He always called her Miss Beck and I can hear his professional tone of voice when he said it. I'm sure she tried every trick in her arsenal to promote a romance – but he never was interested.'[5]

Orville went through life propped up by the women around him. Katharine, effectively a wife, had been hostess to his visitors and his public consort, Carrie had run his household and cooked his meals in the fussy way he demanded, Mabel, who acquired from his files an astonishing grasp of the history of the Wright contribution to aviation and had sewn for him the new muslin covering on the *Flyer*'s wings before it went to England, had taken possession of his business affairs with ferocious competence. He was never, despite speculation, ever to even contemplate marriage – to anyone.

Orville survived Katharine by nearly two decades. Although the frail flying machine he had helped to invent had by now become a quaint museum piece, they were years in which his personal status as a reluctant national treasure soared to greater heights in his own country than had ever been accorded him and Wilbur when they'd tried to offer the aeroplane to a cynical world. Medals and awards were heaped upon him in an unceasing cascade. In 1928 he was declared one of the four greatest living Americans, his genius linked to that of Homer. Harvard and Yale and even universities in Europe presented him with honorary doctorates. He was in constant demand for his prestigious name and his aeronautical wisdom to serve on an array of aeronautical boards and commissions. President

Franklin Roosevelt, Charles Lindbergh and Henry Ford made special pilgrimages to Hawthorn Hill to see him. Obligingly, despite his permanent hip pain, he would turn up around the country at huge formal receptions determined to honour him, load him with gold medals and trophies, but at which, in his self-effacing way, he was only ever heard to say a subdued 'thank you'. Although the aeroplane and the science of aerodynamics had long since leapt into realms of sophistication far beyond the Wrights' discoveries, he was still seen as the fountainhead of it all.

'A grey man now, dressed in grey clothes,' is how a disappointed *New Yorker* reporter, expecting to find some manifestation of genius, described him after a 1930 visit to the Dayton laboratory as Orville approached sixty. 'Not only have his hair and moustache taken on that tone, but his curiously flat face . . . a timid man whose misery at meeting you is obviously so keen that, in common decency, you leave as soon as you can.'[6]

Orville's family, with whom he could be himself, saw a quite different man; especially so his nieces and nephews, who worshipped him. They all spoke with great affection of the interest he took in them, his patience and ability to communicate, the trouble he would take to entertain them for hours at a time; of the mystique that surrounded his fudge, its temperature monitored during cooking with a regularly inserted thermometer; of the dinner plates that suddenly, mysteriously, began to migrate across the table, pulled by a concealed cotton thread; of the Christmas Day turkey that had been grafted on to a duck: they enjoyed the adolescent jokes and the teasing. They found it awesome to go flying with him out at Simms field or fishing on the lake at Lambert Island. It was only the outside world to which he presented an image of such shyness and disappointing ordinariness.

Little of the glory that attached to him did Orville ever enjoy. He would try to escape from the limelight to his laboratory with its big roll-top desk, draughting table and photograph of Wilbur on the wall, where he went on happily tinkering and dismantling things for sheer curiosity. Pictures show him, a little elderly, bald, impeccably dressed man, screwdriver in hand, earnestly taking a clock to pieces. The story is told of two schoolboys who secretly watched him, in awe, through the window one day. 'What's he doing?' one asked. His friend replied scornfully, 'He's inventing, of course!' This was true, but no more aeronautical innovation from Orville Wright would astound the world. His inventive flow was now confined to domestic devices like the special tool he designed to hang or take down the luxurious damask that covered some of Hawthorn Hill's walls and which had to be washed and rehung every year.

He became fanatically finicky. William Lewis, a popular black servant who worked from time to time for various members of the Wright family, recalled Orville inspecting the symmetry of the dining-room table before a dinner party. He would say, 'William, the table cloth is one inch longer on this side than the other. Please reset the table and change the cloth.' William was instructed to use a ruler to measure the distances between the plates and the gaps between the laid-out cutlery. 'During dinner whenever Orville tapped his water goblet, William knew that a guest had taken a drink. The tapping was the signal for him to refill the glass because Orville insisted that the water level in each must remain the same.'[7]

The bishop's family shrank further in 1939 when Lorin died at the age of seventy-seven. He had never known prosperity until Wilbur's $50,000 legacy had arrived to bring him a measure of security in his fifties. The brother who had spent his life unspectacularly in modest jobs as a clerk and bookkeeper, or sprinkling streets with his horse-drawn water tanker on municipal contracts, had been a devoted part of the inventing team, helping launch the gliders on the Outer Banks and keeping their business affairs straight during their constant absences from Dayton as famous men. The legacy had helped him in the mid-1920s – when he had become a Dayton city commissioner – to buy into a small local company manufacturing novelty items. The company flourished and he became its president. One of its most successful products was a children's toy created and patented by Orville – a contraption on which a clown was sprung on to a revolving trapeze.

Occasionally the past would come back to unsettle Orville's life in the shadows. In 1928, Carlotta, the widow of Léon Bollée, the French car manufacturer who had befriended and entertained Wilbur at Le Mans twenty years before, suddenly arrived in Dayton with her daughter, now the Countess Elizabeth Jean de Vautibault. When they came to stay at Hawthorn Hill, Orville's niece Ivonette was brought in for propriety's sake. It soon became clear why Carlotta, now fifty, had come to this dull, unscenic Midwest town. She was in financial distress and it wasn't long before she was dropping in Orville's direction less than subtle hints at marriage. She even tried to invite herself on a cosy holiday with him at his island fastness where he was soon due to go. In a panic he told her he could not possibly make her and the countess comfortable at his summer camp and swiftly diverted them to Niagara Falls. It wasn't the last he would hear from the penurious widow. For years thereafter he was plagued with letters from France beseeching him for money. There is no record that he ever sent any.

Other ghosts were to arise. At his Pennsylvania farm, George Spratt had continued to smoulder with unresolved resentment. In 1922, Orville, briefly toying with the idea of writing the book he would never in fact get around to, wrote to him asking if he would be kind enough to send copies of the letters he and Wilbur had written – but failed to copy – in happier days two decades earlier. Orville had been shocked by the rancorous response. Spratt had refused, repeating his bitter complaint that they had still not given him public credit for his 1901 lift/drag measurement suggestion. He went on to unleash all his festering animosity, accusing them of secretiveness and obstructing the development of the aeroplane by others. 'Aviation,' his letter said, 'deserved a leadership of greater vision and generosity than the Wrights seemed capable of.'[8] Spratt, who remained among aviation's visionary dreamers, had never ceased his attempts to find his own solution to heavier-than-air flight. A month before his unhappy life ended in 1934, he lurched briefly into the air in a frail, purportedly stall-proof biplane he had at last built.

Another of those who had shared the discomfort and excitements of the Kill Devil camp had also refused to abandon attempts to create a perfect flying machine. Edward Huffaker, back in Tennessee, was still, in his eightieth year, pleading with the Smithsonian for money to experiment with a revolutionary flying wing that dispensed with fuselage and tail. He had been refused and died two years later in 1937 having never flown in an aeroplane.

The enigmatic Patrick Alexander had lost interest in the Wrights once their success had been universally proclaimed. The eccentric, once wealthy Englishman they had suspected of being a British government spy had moved into the realms of fantasy, trying to develop aeroplanes powered by electricity extracted from the air in which they flew. He had eventually spent or given away all his money, and died destitute in 1943.

As the surviving inventor of the aeroplane, the biggest cross Orville had to bear was his continuing public feud with his own country's leading scientific establishment. In spite of his dramatic reprisal in 1928 when he shipped the *Flyer* to London's Science Museum, where it had been welcomed unreservedly as the world's No. 1 aeroplane and ceremonially unveiled by King George V no less, the Smithsonian maintained its obtuse refusal to back down. The stalemate, which caused irreparable damage to the famous institution, continued unresolved for decades, during which the impostor Langley machine remained in its place of honour in the national museum in Washington. Viewed from the twenty-first century, the conduct of the august body is hard to understand; through the 1920s and 1930s it left many Americans wondering who, after all, had invented the aeroplane. 'In my 9th grade science textbook,' said Marianne Hudec, 'as late as 1948 it was stated that the Wright plane was not the first to be capable of flight. That credit was actually given to Langley. No wonder people were bewildered.'

The controversy continued to be stirred by the Wrights' avowed enemy Dr Albert Zahm, now regarded as one of the country's pre-eminent aeronautical scientists. As he moved from the Smithsonian to a succession of prestigious posts, amassing awards for his pioneer aviation work, he went to untold lengths in his personal crusade to belittle the Wrights' 1903 triumph. When the Hammondsport trials with the dishonestly repowered, strengthened and partly redesigned Langley *Aerodrome* began to look increasingly disreputable, he unearthed another contender for the invention honour – an obscure German-American called Gustav Weisskopf (Whitehead) who claimed to have made a seven-mile flight in a powered machine over Long Island Sound in 1902. The flight proved to be a myth, but the story was seized by the media, throwing even further doubt on the Wrights' supremacy. In London, Griffith Brewer and Lord Northcliffe joined the fray. The press lord condemned the Smithsonian for its attempts, he said, 'to rob the Wright Brothers of the credit of their invention'; the Wrights had taken 'a beggarly sum for one of the greatest inventions of the world'. But in America it did not prove easy to overturn the orthodoxy of a body, however perfidious, that was regarded in the scientific community, almost by definition, as the ultimate authority.

In Congress there were calls for an investigation. BRING BACK OUR WINGED EXILE newspapers demanded, and the pilot hero of the hour, Charles Lindbergh, was invited to mediate. He decided the fault lay largely with the Smithsonian, but found Orville 'not an easy man to deal with'. He failed to resolve the dispute and it was still unsettled when the Second World War arrived to bring higher priorities than this academic squabble.

In 1942 the Smithsonian finally capitulated. Its annual report declared that the decision to try and prove that Langley's steam-powered machine would have been 'capable' of sustained, controlled flight 'was ill considered'. The 1914 tests did not warrant the claim that had remained so damagingly attached to the aeroplane in the famous museum for nearly a third of a century.

Orville accepted the apology graciously, opening the way, at last, for the *Flyer* to come home. But in 1942 this was no longer possible. In England it had been removed from the Science Museum and stored in an underground shelter to protect the international treasure from German bombs.

The unpleasant feud finally settled, Orville returned to the routines of his life in Dayton, driving each day to his laboratory where he was pursuing a private bit of war work, developing a code machine for the military that would never be adopted. As the Second World War in the air began to spread destruction across the world, and awesomely powerful devices wrought never-before-seen havoc upon two Japanese cities, newspapers sent reporters to ask how one of the architects of it all felt about his invention of the delivery vehicle. Orville had been forced to modify his and Wilbur's rosy view of the flying machine as an agency for permanent world peace: 'Now I wonder if the aeroplane and the atomic bomb can do it,' he said. But in his last years, during which he remained spry and active, he witnessed a succession of fantastic developments destined to revolutionise the service aviation brought to mankind.

Orville saw the military air power that General Sir William Nicholson had dismissed as useless decide the fate of nations. He saw airlines spread networks like spiderwebs across America and around the world, and even flew over Dayton himself in a four-engined Lockheed Constellation airliner in 1944. Invited on to the flight deck with its bewildering array of instruments, he sat in one of the pilot's seats and handled the hydraulically powered controls of the 300-mile-an-hour machine.

He did not see man go into space, but did witness the arrival of the jet engine that before long would power 400 people in one aeroplane across the world in comfort above the weather in giant twelve-hour strides. He lived into the era of supersonic flight that would take champagne-sipping Concorde passengers across the Atlantic in three and a half hours at 25 miles a minute. He saw the beginnings of pressurisation that would cruise passengers safely at the very edge of space. He saw radio beacons, radar and landing beams start to bring flying machines with great precision to their destination runways through cloud and darkness in appalling weather. Although he wouldn't live to see it, by the turn of the twenty-first century the world's airliners would be carrying 1.8 billion people a year in the great-great-grandchildren of the *Flyer* he helped to create.

One day, in October 1947, Orville, a conscientiously punctual man, was bounding up the front steps of an office in Dayton, late for a meeting. Halfway up he had a heart attack. He was rushed to hospital, where he spent four days recovering in an oxygen tent. It was said that he delighted in teasing the nurses and suggesting ways of improving the design of the tent. He was discharged with warnings to slow down his life, and bounced back to work.

In the last week of January 1948, as Dayton lay under snow, a problem developed with the front door bell at Hawthorn Hill. Orville spent much of one freezing morning trying to fix it, darting in and out of the house and up and down the basement steps. When late that morning he arrived at his office, he collapsed in front of Mabel Beck. It was another heart attack.

When he arrived in hospital he greeted the nurse who had looked after him last time, 'This is the only way I could get to see you again.' But this time his condition was more serious: congestion began to develop in one of his lungs. Carrie Grumbach, now grey-haired and 'grandmotherly', his faithful servant now for nearly half a century, came to visit him. While she was there a nurse came in to ask if he would like something to eat or drink. Yes, he said, he would have a bit of scraped apple and a few sips of ginger ale. 'After the nurse had begun to prepare the food, Orville Wright, full of solicitude for Carrie who had cared for him and for Wilbur and Katharine and his father for so long, said gently: "You had best let Carrie do that, Miss – she knows all my cranky little ways."'[9] A few days later, on 30 January 1948, Orville died. He was seventy-six.

As he lay in state on a flower-decked bier at the mortuary, 1500 people queued back into the street to file past the open coffin to view the dead inventor. Although his passing was reported round the world, most in the international aviation community were, strangely, surprised to know that he had still been alive. So low was his profile that many thought he had been dead for years.

Despite the pervasively religious environment that had nourished the bishop's children, it had been nearly fifty years since Orville had been regularly to church or shown the least interest in spiritual matters. There were, he had often told people, few clergymen he actually admired. He had chosen a Baptist pastor, who conducted the service and officiated at the snow-covered grave site. Here in Woodland cemetery, where Lorin had been buried separately beside a lake, Orville joined Milton, Susan, Wilbur and Katharine. Katharine lay between her famous brothers. As Orville was lowered beside her, four jet fighters swooped over Dayton and roared low over the grave.

Orville Wright left an estate of just over $1 million – worth more than $7 million today. Not a lot of money, at the end of the day, for a creation so epoch-making for humankind. He had forgotten few of the people who had touched his life. There were modest bequests to Reuchlin's widow Lou, Carrie, his boyhood playmate Ed Sines, mechanic Charlie Taylor, Mabel Beck and, as Katharine in her will had done to the family's long-serving laundress, Lottie Jones. While most of the fortune was divided among his tribe of nephews, nieces and their children, he left the generous sum of $300,000 to Oberlin College, the Alma Mater of the sister who had broken his heart.

He did not live to see the return of the *Flyer* he'd fought for so long to have accorded the honour due to it in his homeland. The controversial machine did not come back to America until late in 1948. On 17 December, the forty-fifth anniversary of the first flights, it ceremoniously joined the Smithsonian's aeronautical collection in Washington. The label read, unequivocally, that it was the world's first 'power-driven, heavier-than-air machine in which man made free, controlled and sustained flight'. It went further: 'By original scientific research the Wright Brothers discovered the principles of human flight. As inventors, builders and flyers they further developed the aeroplane, taught men to fly and opened the era of aviation.'

In Dayton, Ohio, No. 7 Hawthorn Street is now an empty lot. In 1936 Henry Ford had swooped upon the house and the cycle shop at 1127 West Third Street. With Orville's agreement, both buildings were removed in their entirety to a 'pioneer America' museum village that Ford had established near his great automobile plant in Detroit. Today the Hawthorn Street area presents a depressing vista. Although ambitious attempts are being made to revive its former vibrancy, it remains visibly depopulated and in sad decay. Houses and shops are abandoned. The paint peels from weatherboards, windows are boarded up or glassless, collapsed gutters dangle from roofs. Many of the white families who once lived in this, the cradle of aviation, fled in the late 1960s when threatened by the violence of racial riots.

Where the bishop's house stood is a patch of rock-strewn grass. At the beginning of aviation's centennial year, 2003, the only reminder of its special status was a small sign on a steel pole declaring bleakly, 'Aviation Trail: Wright Family Home Site'. It was as if the family had been expunged from the world. Elsewhere in Dayton one of their celebrated aeroplanes is on display at a museum; one of their six cycle shops has been preserved with much of its original atmosphere. But here in this urban wasteland in which were played out so many of the ecstasies and agonies of the birth of flight, no sense of their presence lingered.

However, the physical dimension of their great achievement does live on, preserved in the yellowy golden sands of the Kill Devil hills on North Carolina's Outer Banks. The once isolated sand island, now traversed by two busy parallel highways, is connected to the mainland by two great bridges. Manteo, on Roanoke Island, from where reporters came in boats to spy on the lonely flying camp, is today but a few minutes' drive from the banks, which have become a sprawling coastal city of holiday homes, motels and restaurants, visited every summer by hordes of people. Some come to emulate the Wrights, hang-gliding off the huge dunes that brought the brothers there.

The big hill off which they flew their remarkable wings and proved their singular control system was subsequently to migrate under the force of the ceaseless wind. At the rate of twenty feet a year, it travelled for 200 yards across the sand waste. Engineers finally arrested the runaway dune, planting grasses on its restless slopes. On the stabilised summit the great memorial has been erected. At its base sit replicas of the weatherboard huts. Up in the rafters of one are re-creations of the sagging sack beds in which they had tried to escape from the all-devouring mosquitoes. Cans of food of the sort they ate line the shelves.

Nearby are four rough-hewn stone markers. They stand, grey sentinels, in a row. When they were first conceived, back in 1928, nobody was any longer sure of the exact spot from which the *Flyer* had been famously launched off its rail that morning in December 1903. The whole shifting sandscape had radically changed. The problem was solved when some of the surviving lifesaver witnesses of the flights were taken there to try and work it out. Between them they eventually fixed upon a location where, they were agreed, the rail had been. In the cause of aviation history they solemnly swore affidavits to record the fact.

The first of the markers says: *End of 1st Flight – time 12 seconds – distance: 120 ft – Dec 17, 1903 – Pilot: Orville.* The last, a significant two-minute walk away, says: *Time 59 seconds – distance 852 ft – pilot: Wilbur.* In those moments, that day, man had, for the first time, truly flown.

Notes

Abbreviations

MW Milton Wright
WW Wilbur Wright
OW Orville Wright
WB Wright Brothers
KW Katharine Wright
LW Lorin Wright
RW Reuchlin Wright
SW Susan Wright
HJH Henry J. Haskell
OC Octave Chanute
WSU Wright State University, Dayton, Ohio
LOC Library of Congress
WHMC Western Historical Manuscript Collection, University of Missouri, Kansas City (Katharine Wright Haskell papers)

1 The Bishop's Sons

1 Wilbur Wright, deposition of 3 April 1912 in *The Papers of Wilbur and Orville Wright*, ed. Marvin W. McFarland.

2 Milton Wright, 'Ancestors', undated note, *c.*1912, box 8, file 8, Wright Collection, WSU.

3 Curtis Wright, Carthage, Missouri, 1915, *Genealogical and Biographical Notices of Descendants of Sir John Wright of Kelvedon Hall, Essex, England; in America Thomas Wright of Wethersfield, Conn 1610–1670 and Dea Samuel Wright of Northampton, Mass.* (Higginson Book Company, Salem, Massachusetts).

4 William G. Hunt, Windsor Herald of Arms, College of Arms, London, in letters to author, 27 December 2000 and 4 August 2001.

5 Letter from Bishop Wright to unknown addressee, Dayton, Ohio, 7 January 1916, Wright Collection, WSU.

6 Milton Wright, 'My Grandparents and my Parents', 12 February, 1912, Wright Collection, WSU.

7 Milton Wright, 'Ancestors', 6 April 1913, box 8, file 8, Wright Collection, WSU.

8 Ibid.

9 Ibid.

10 Kinnane, *The Crucible of Flight*.

11 Crouch, *The Bishop's Boys*.

12 Milton Wright, 'The Wright Ancestry', undated note, Wright Collection, WSU.

13 Milton Wright, *Diaries*.

14 Elliott, *Bishop Milton Wright, Quest*.

15 MW to WW, 4 July 1908, box 6, Wright Papers, LOC.

2 A House of Piety

1 Milton Wright, 'National Convention Opposed to Secret Societies', *Religious Telescope*, 22 June 1870.

2 McMahon, *Fathers of Flight*.

3 'The Telescope and Bishop Weaver', *United Brethren Tribune*, 15 September 1874.

4 Crouch, *The Bishop's Boys*.

5 McMahon, *Fathers of Flight*.

6 Ibid.

7 Kinnane, *The Crucible of Flight*.

8 Crouch, *The Bishop's Boys*.

3 Trials of the Righteous

1 McMahon, *Fathers of Flight*.

2 Milton Wright, 'Notes for Who's Who', 26 October 1907, in Miller, *Wright Reminiscences*.

3 'Wilbur Wright Born in Henry County', interview with Milton Wright, undated newspaper article in 'Wright Scrapbooks', 1909, Wright Papers, LOC.

4 LW to KW, 12 November 1888, box 5, Wright Papers, LOC.

5 WW to Revd. W.J. McGee, 13 April 1888, box 41, Wright Papers, LOC.

6 SW to MW, 1 June 1888, file 10, box 8, Wright Collection, WSU.

7 WW, 'Scenes in the Church Commission During the Last Day of its

Session' (Wright Brothers, Job Printers, Dayton, Ohio, 1888)

8 SW to MW, 19 June 1888, Wright Collection, WSU.

9 WW to MW, 23 August 1888, box 6, Wright Papers, LOC.

10 MW to KW and OW, 11 August 1888, Wright Collection, WSU.

11 SW to MW, 20 September 1888, ibid.

12 MW, 6 October 1888, *Diaries.*

13 Elliott, *Bishop Milton Wright, Quest.*

14 Bishop William Dillon, 'General Conference', *Christian Conservator*, 23 May 1889.

4 The Bird-watching Bicycle-makers

1 MW, 4 July 1889, *Diaries.*

2 MW, 4 July 1894, *Diaries.*

3 Brunsman, *Wright & Wright, Printers.*

4 MW to KW, 15 October 1887, box 5, Wright Collection, WSU.

5 MW to KW, 30 May 1888, ibid.

6 MW to KW 30 May 1888, ibid.

7 MW to KW, 9 August 1889, ibid.

8 MW to KW, 12 September 1892, box 5, Wright Papers, LOC.

9 MW to KW, 12 September 1892, Wright Papers, LOC.

10 MW to KW, 12 September 1892, ibid.

11 MW to WW, 15 September 1894, ibid.

12 McFarland, *Papers.*

13 Elliott, *Bishop Milton Wright, Quest.*

14 MW, 25 December 1891, *Diaries.*

15 WW to KW, 18 September 1892, box 5, Wright Papers, LOC.

16 McMahon, *Fathers of Flight.*

17 Miller, *Wright Reminiscences.*

18 Kelly (ed.) *Miracle at Kitty Hawk.*

19 McMahon, *Fathers of Flight.*

20 WW to MW, 12 September 1894, box 6, Wright Papers, LOC.

21 Orville Wright, *How We Invented the Airplane.* Orville's comments were contained in a deposition of 13 January 1920 he prepared for a court case that year. The action had been brought against the US government by members of the family of the 1880s glider experimentalist John Montgomery, claiming that aircraft it had purchased from the Wrights had infringed the former's patent.

22 Probably James Bell Pettigrew, *Animal Location, or Walking, Swimming and Flying, with a Dissertation on Aeronautics*, Appleton, 1874.

23 'Brief and Digest of the Evidence for Complainant on Final Hearing, Wilbur Wright (Wright Company) vs Herring-Curtiss Co and Glen H. Curtiss in Equity No. 400 (copy in Wright State University archives)

24 WW to the Smithsonian Institution, Washington, DC, 30 May 1899, McFarland, *Papers.*

5 Some Aeronautical Theories

1 WW to the Smithsonian Institution, Washington, DC, 30 May 1899, McFarland, *Papers.*

2 Otto Lilienthal, 'Practical Experiments in Soaring'; Louis-Pierre Mouillard, 'Empire of the Air'; Samuel P. Langley, 'Story of Experiments in Mechanical Flight'; E. C. Huffaker, 'On Soaring Flight'.

3 *The Aeronautical Annual*, Boston, 1896.

4 Ibid.

5 'On Aerial Navigation', triple paper by Sir George Cayley, *Nicholson's Journal of Natural Philosophy, Chemistry and the Arts*, 1809–1810.

6 Coachman's quote from flight witness, Cayley's then ten-year-old granddaughter, Mrs Dora Thompson, in 1933.

7 *The Times*, 18 December 1857.

8 *Der Vogelflug als Grundlage der Fliegekunst*, Berlin, 1889. (English translation from second edition of 1910: *Birdflight as the Basis of Aviation*, Longmans Green, London, 1911.)

9 Orville Wright, *How We Invented the Airplane.*

10 Ibid.

11 Wilbur Wright, *Brief & Digest of the Evidence*, 'Brief and Digest of the Evidence for Complainant on Final Hearing', The Wright Co vs Herring-Curtiss Co and Glen H. Curtiss in Equity No. 400 pp.4–25 (copy in WSU).

12 'Some Aeronautical Experiments', lecture by WW to the Western Society of Engineers, Chicago, 18 September 1901 (Journal of WSE, December 1901; text reproduced in McFarland, *Papers*).

13 Wilbur Wright, *Brief & Digest of the Evidence*, 'Brief and Digest of the

Evidence for Complainant on Final Hearing', The Wright Co vs Herring-Curtiss Co and Glen H. Curtiss in Equity No. 400 pp.4–25 (copy in WSU).

14 Orville Wright, *How We Invented the Airplane.*

6 To Ride a Flying Machine

1 'Some Aeronautical Experiments', lecture by WW to the Western Society of Engineers, Chicago, 18 September 1901 (*Journal of WSE*, December 1901; text reproduced in McFarland, *Papers*).

2 Wilbur & Orville Wright, 'The Wright Brothers' Aeroplane', *Century Magazine*, New York, September 1908. (Article in fact written entirely by Orville.)

3 Crouch, *The Bishop's Boys.*

4 *Buffalo Courier*, 26 August 1886.

5 Eugene Husting, 'Augustus M. Herring', *WWI Aero*, No 130, November 1990.

6 Letter from Augustus Herring to OC, 25 May 1895, Box 1, Chanute Collection, LOC.

7 Complexities of the Invisible Forces

1 'Some Aeronautical Experiments', lecture by WW to the Western Society of Engineers, Chicago, 18 Sept 1901 (*Journal of WSE*, Dec 1901; text reproduced in McFarland, *Papers*).

2 Kelly, *Miracle at Kitty Hawk.*

3 Ibid.

4 Ibid.

5 Ibid.

6 Ibid.

7 Elliott, *Bishop Milton Wright, Quest.* (Fowlerton was originally Leach township when Milton Wright developed it.)

8 WW to OC, 13 May 1900, in McFarland, *Papers.*

9 Ibid.

10 Ibid.

11 OC to WW, 17 May 1900, in McFarland, *Papers.*

12 WW to OC, 1 June 1900, ibid.

13 Ibid.

14 Joseph J. Dosher, weather station, Kitty Hawk, to WW, 16 August 1900, in Kelly, *Miracle at Kitty Hawk.*

15 William J. Tate, Kitty Hawk, to WW, 18 August 1900, ibid.

16 Wilbur & Orville Wright, 'The Wright Brothers' Aeroplane', *Century Magazine*, New York, September 1908 (article written by Orville).

17 OW to Alexander Klemin, 11 April 1924, in McFarland, *Papers* (p.44, note 1).

18 WW to MW, 3 September 1900, in Kelly, *Miracle at Kitty Hawk.*

19 KW to MW, 5 September 1900, ibid.

8 A Place Called Kitty Hawk

1 In McFarland, *Papers*, p.27 n.3.

2 WW to MW, Elizabeth City, 9 September 1900, in Kelly, *Miracle at Kitty Hawk.*

3 WW, 'Memorandum', *c.* 13 September 1900, in Macfarlane, *Papers.*

4 Parramore, *Triumph at Kitty Hawk.*

5 Kirk, *First in Flight.*

6 Parramore, *Triumph at Kitty Hawk.*

7 Ibid.

8 Kirk, *First in Flight.*

9 WW to MW, Kitty Hawk, 23 September 1900, in Kelly, *Miracle at Kitty Hawk.*

10 Crouch, *The Bishop's Boys.* Tom Crouch created this highly probable reconstruction of Wilbur's first venture into the air from his own experience flying a replica 1902 Wright glider built by a celebrated Wright aircraft builder and restaurateur, Rick Young, of Petersburg, Virginia, in the 1990s.

11 OW to KW, 18 October 1900, in McFarland, *Papers.*

12 OW to KW, 14 October 1900, ibid.

13 Parramore, *Triumph at Kitty Hawk.*

14 Parramore, *Triumph at Kitty Hawk.*

15 OW to KW, 14 October 1900, in McFarland, *Papers.*

16 Kelly, *The Wright Brothers.*

17 Parramore, *Triumph at Kitty Hawk.*

18 'Some Aeronautical Experiments', lecture by WW to the Western Society of Engineers, Chicago, 18 September 1901 (*Journal of WSE*, December 1901; text reproduced in McFarland, *Papers*).

9 The Maestro's Disciples

1 WW to OC, 16 November 1900, in McFarland, *Papers.*

2 OC to WW, 1 December 1900, in McFarland, *Papers.*

3 WW to MW, 2 June 1897, box 6, Wright Papers, LOC.

4 WW to OC, 26 November 1900, in McFarland, *Papers.*

5 WW to OC, 3 December 1900, ibid.

6 McFarland, *Papers*, p.57 n.8.

7 William F. Trimble, 'The Amateur in Aviation: George A. Spratt and the American Aeronautical Community', *Pennsylvania Magazine of History and Biography*, July 1981.

8 Ibid.

9 Ibid.

10 OC to WW, Chuckey City, Tennessee, 29 June 1901, in McFarland, *Papers.*

11 WW to OC, 1 July 1901, ibid.

12 OC to WW, 3 July 1901, ibid.

13 WW to OC, 4 July 1901, ibid.

14 OW to KW, Kill Devil Hills, 28 July 1901, ibid.

15 Ibid.

16 Ibid.

17 'Some Aeronautical Experiments', lecture by WW to the Western Society of Engineers, Chicago, 18 Sept 1901 (*Journal of WSE*, December 1901; text reproduced in McFarland, *Papers*).

18 Parramore, *Triumph at Kitty Hawk.*

19 Ibid.

20 Wilbur Wright, *Brief & Digest of the Evidence for Complainant on Final Hearing*, The Wright Co vs Herring-Curtiss Co and Glen H. Curtiss in Equity No. 400 pp 4–25 (copy in WSU).

21 Kelly, *The Wright Brothers.*

10 A Wing of Perfect Shape

1 KW to MW, 26 August 1901, box 4, Wright Papers, LOC.

2 WW to OC, 29 August 1901, in McFarland, *Papers.*

3 KW to MW, 3 September 1901, ibid.

4 WW to OC, 6 September 1901, in McFarland, *Papers.*

5 KW to MW, 25 September 1901, box 4, Wright Papers, LOC.

6 KW to MW, 11 September 1901, ibid.

7 WW to MW, 24 October 1901, in Kelly, *Miracle at Kitty Hawk.*

8 Jakab, *Visions of a Flying Machine.*

9 OC to WW, 18 November 1901, in McFarland, *Papers.*

10 OC to WW, 19 December 1901, in Kelly, *Miracle at Kitty Hawk.*

11 OC to WW, 19 December 1901, in McFarland, *Papers.*

12 WW to OC, 23 December 1901, in McFarland, *Papers.*

13 Orville Wright deposition of 2 February 1921, quoted in McFarland, *Papers*, p.551.

14 WW to OC, 19 January 1902, in McFarland, *Papers.*

15 WW to OC, 23 January 1902, ibid.

16 RW to MW, 17 September 1901, box 6, Wright Papers, LOC.

17 WW to RW, 20 May 1902, box 7, ibid.

18 WW to MW, 15 February 1902, ibid.

11 Tumult in the Church

1 WW to OC, 16 May 1902, in McFarland, *Papers.*

2 KW to MW, 7 September 1902, box 4, Wright Papers, LOC.

3 KW to MW, 25 September 1901, ibid.

4 KW to MW, 7 December 1901, ibid.

5 KW to MW, 20 August 1902, ibid.

6 Ibid.

7 Howard, *Wilbur and Orville.*

8 OW Diary B, 1902, 24 September 1902, in McFarland, *Papers.*

9 Jakab, *Visions of a Flying Machine.*

10 WW to OC, 29 May 1902, in McFarland, *Papers.*

11 WW to George Spratt, 23 January 1902, ibid.

12 Fetters, *Trials and Triumphs.*

13 KW to MW, 3 September 1902, box 4, Wright Papers, LOC.

14 KW to WW and OW, 4 September 1902, ibid.

15 KW to MW, 9 September 1902, ibid.

16 WW to MW, 12 September 1902, box 7, Wright Papers, LOC.

17 Ibid.

12 An Unscrupulous Guest at Kill Devil Hills

1 OW Diary B, 23 September 1902, in McFarland, *Papers.*

2 Ibid.

3 Ibid.
4 KW to WW and OW, 5 October 1902, box 4, Wright Papers, LOC.
5 Crouch, *The Bishop's Boys*.
6 OW Diary B, 14 October 1902, in McFarland, *Papers*.
7 Howard, *Wilbur and Orville*.
8 Kelly, *The Wright Brothers*.
9 WW to MW, 2 October 1902, in Kelly, *Miracle at Kitty Hawk*.
10 OW to KW, 23 October 1902, in McFarland, *Papers*.
11 KW to WW and OW, 4 September 1902, box 4, Wright Papers, LOC.
12 Professor Samuel P. Langley to OC, 7 December 1902, in Kelly, *Miracle at Kitty Hawk*.
13 WW to OC, 3 November 1902, in McFarland, *Papers*.
14 Parramore, *Triumph at Kitty Hawk*.
15 Gibbs-Smith, *The Rebirth of European Aviation*.
16 Howard, *Wilbur and Orville*.

13 'Our Turn to Throw'

1 Gertrude Bacon, *Memories of Land and Sky* (publisher unknown, London, 1928).
2 OC to WW, 30 June 1903, in McFarland, *Papers*.
3 WW to OC, 2 July 1903, ibid.
4 WW to OC, 24 July 1903, ibid.
5 OC to WW, 27 July 1903, ibid.
6 WW to OC, 22 July 1903, ibid.
7 Charles E. Taylor, 'My Story of the Wright Brothers', *Collier's*, 25 December 1948.
8 Ibid.
9 Wilbur and Orville Wright, 'The Wright Brothers' Aeroplane', *Century Magazine*, New York, September 1908 (article written by Orville).
10 Anderson, *A History of Aerodynamics*.
11 OW to George Spratt, 7 June 1903, in McFarland, *Papers*.
12 WW to George Spratt, 20 April 1903, ibid.
13 WW to George Spratt, 27 April 1903, ibid.
14 Parramore, *Triumph at Kitty Hawk*.
15 Vaeth, *Langley*.
16 WW to OC, 16 October 1903, in McFarland, *Papers*.

14 Twelve Famous Seconds

1 WW to OC, 14 November 1901, in McFarland, *Papers*.
2 OW to KW, 1 November 1903, in Kelly, *Miracle at Kitty Hawk*.
3 Ibid
4 OC to WW, 24 October 1903, ibid.
5 OW to MW and KW, 15 November 1903, ibid.
6 WW to his family, 23 November 1903, in Kelly, *Miracle at Kitty Hawk*.
7 WW to MW and KW, 23 November 1903, in McFarland, *Papers*.
8 KW to MW, 7 October 1903, box 4, Wright Papers, LOC.
9 KW to MW, 4 October 1903, ibid.
10 KW to MW, 25 October 1903, ibid.
11 OW to Charles Taylor, 20 October 1903, in McFarland, *Papers*.
12 Ibid.
13 Ibid.
14 Ibid.
15 Ibid.
16 Ibid.
17 OW to MW and KW, 19 November 1903, ibid.
18 Vaeth, *Langley*.
19 *Congressional Record*, 27 January 1904.
20 WW to OC, 8 November 1906, in McFarland, *Papers*.
21 Orville Wright, 'How We Made the First Flight', *Flying*, December 1913.
22 Ibid.
23 William O. Saunders, 'Then We Quit Laughing', *Collier's*, 17 September 1927.
24 Ibid.

15 'Damn'd if They Ain't Flew' . . .

1 James Ferber, interview with Orville Wright, *New York Times*, 17 December 1933.
2 'Orville Wright Foresees Great Progress in Next Decade', *St Louis Post-Dispatch*, 7 November 1943.
3 Interview with John T. Daniels, 1943, unidentified N.Carolina newspaper.
4 OW Diary D, 17 December 1903, Wright Papers, LOC.
5 William Tate, 'With the Wrights at Kitty Hawk', *The Aeronautical Review*, December 1928.
6 Orville Wright, 'How We Made the First Flight,' *Flying*, December 1913.

7 Robert Mason, 'When Flying Was News', *Virginian-Pilot*, 17 December 1950.

8 Kelly, *Miracle at Kitty Hawk*.

9 Norfolk *Virginian-Pilot* and *Washington Post*, 16 December 1928.

10 *Virginian-Pilot*, 18 December 1903.

11 MW to Carl Dienstbach, 22 December 1903, in McFarland, *Papers*.

12 Hunt, *Cooking the Wright Way*.

13 MW, 31 December 1903, *Diaries*

14 WW to OC, 28 December 1903, in McFarland, *Papers*.

15 Statement by Wright Brothers issued to Associated Press, 5 January 1904.

16 'The Machine that Flies', *New York Herald*, 17 January 1904.

17 OC to WW, 14 January 1904, in McFarland, *Papers*.

18 WW to OC, 18 January 1904, ibid.

19 OC to Patrick Alexander, 18 January 1904, Chanute Papers, LOC.

16 Shattering the Five-Minute Barrier

1 WW to OC, 8 January 1904, in McFarland, *Papers*.

2 *Illustrierte Aeronautische Mitteilungen*.

3 OC to WW, 9 April 1904, in McFarland, *Papers*.

4 WW to D.A. Willey, 1 March 1904, ibid.

5 WW to Willard A. Smith, Advisory Committee, St Louis air race, 28 March 1904, in McFarland, *Papers*.

6 Bishop Halleck Floyd, 'The Ego', *Christian Conservator*, 25 May 1904.

7 WW to OC, 5 May 1904, in McFarland, *Papers*.

8 WW to OC, 5 June 1904, ibid.

9 WW to Arnold Fordyce, 8 January 1906, in Kelly, *Miracle at Kitty Hawk*

10 Kelly, *The Wright Brothers: A Biography Authorized by Orville Wright*.

11 Charles E. Taylor, 'My Story of the Wright Brothers', as told to Robert S. Ball, *Collier's*, 25 December 1948.

12 Amos Ives Root, 'What God Hath Wrought', *Gleanings in Bee Culture*, 1 January 1905.

13 WW to OC, 5 October 1904, in McFarland, *Papers*.

14 Godfrey Lowell Cabot to Senator Henry Cabot Lodge, 31 December 1903, in Kelly, *Miracle at Kitty Hawk*.

15 Walker, *Early Aviation at Farnborough*.

16 Ibid.

17 Air 1/1608/204/85/36 'Aeronautics': Visit to USA in Sept to Nov 1904 by Brevet Lieut Colonel J.E. Capper CB, Commanding Balloon Sections, Royal Engineers, Aldershot, 15.12.1904.

18 Kelly, *The Wright Brothers*.

17 Unwanted Baby for Sale

1 WW to OC, 1 June 1905, in Kelly, *Miracle at Kitty Hawk*.

2 WW and OW to Congressman Robert M. Nevin, 18 January 1905, in Kelly, *Miracle at Kitty Hawk*.

3 Major-General G.L. Gillespie, Board of Ordnance and Fortification, to Congressman Nevin, in Kelly, *Miracle at Kitty Hawk*.

4 WW to OC, 1 June 1905, in McFarland, *Papers*

5 Dr Adrian Kinnane, in interviews with author, Washington, DC, November 1999.

6 Gibbs-Smith, *The Rebirth of European Aviation*.

7 WW and OW to Lt. Col. J.E. Capper, 10 January 1905, in Walker, *Early Aviation at Farnborough*.

8 Lt. Col. J.E. Capper, Officer Commanding Balloon Sections, to GOC Royal Engineers, Aldershot Command, 30 January 1905, in Walker, *Early Aviation at Farnborough*.

9 Elliott, *Bishop Milton Wright, Quest*,

10 Fetters, *Trials and Triumphs*.

11 WW to OC, 28 May 1905, in McFarland, *Papers*.

12 Dr Adrian Kinnane, in interviews with author, Washington, DC, November 1999.

13 KW to OW, WW and MW, 10 July to 1 August 1905, box 4, Wright Papers, LOC.

14 Kelly, *The Wright Brothers*.

15 Howard, *Wilbur and Orville*.

16 OC to WW, 22 October 1905, in McFarland, *Papers*.

17 Major-General J.C. Bates, president, Board of Ordnance and Fortification, to Wright Cycle Company, 16 October 1905, in Kelly, *Miracle at Kitty Hawk*.

18 Captain T.C. Dickson, Recorder of Board of Ordnance and Fortification, to Wright Cycle Company, October 1905, ibid.

18 The French and British Connections

1 WW to Colonel H. Foster, British Military Attaché, Washington, 20 November 1905, in Walker, *Early Aviation at Farnborough*.
2 Walker, *Early Aviation at Farnborough*.
3 Colonel H. Foster, British Military Attaché, Washington, DC, to Wright Cycle Company, 23 November 1905, in Walker, *Early Aviation at Farnborough*.
4 WW to Captain Ferdinand Ferber, French Army, 9 October 1905, in McFarland, *Papers*.
5 Captain Ferdinand Ferber, French Army, to WW, 21 October, 1905, ibid.
6 Kelly, *The Wright Brothers*.
7 Gibbs-Smith, *The Rebirth of European Aviation*.
8 'France to Own First Real Airship in the World', *New York Herald*, 7 January 1906.
9 Ibid.
10 OC to WW, 21 December 1905, in McFarland, *Papers*.

19 Fliers or Liars?

1 Wright Cycle Company to Colonel H. Foster, British Military Attaché, Washington, 5 December 1905, in Walker, *Early Aviation at Farnborough*.
2 Colonel H. Foster, British Military Attaché, Washington, DC, to Wright Cycle Company, *c.* 8 December 1905, in Walker, *Early Aviation at Farnbough*.
3 Colonel H. Foster, British Military Attaché, Washington, DC, to Directorate of Military Operations, War Office, London, 28 November 1905, quoted in Walker, *Early Aviation at Farnborough*.
4 Wright Cycle Company (WW) to the Secretary, War Office, London, 28 November 1905, in Walker, *Early Aviation at Farnborough*.
5 Walker, *Early Aviation at Farnborough*.
6 Ibid.
7 Colonel J.E. Capper to WW, 19 February 1906, Wright Papers, LOC.
8 *The Times*, 24 January 1906.
9 Wright Cycle Company to British Military Attaché, Washington, 31 July 1906, in McFarland, *Papers*.
10 Walker, *Early Aviation at Farnborough*.
11 Major-General Lord Edward Gleichen, *A Guardsman's Memories – A Book of Recollections*, William Blackwood, London, 1932.
12 Lt. Col. Gleichen to Sir Mortimer Durand, 17 August 1906 (War Office 32/8595) in Gollin, *No Longer an Island*.
13 Lt. Col. Gleichen to Director of Military Operations, War Office, London, 11 August 1906 (Air 1/728/176/3/33), in Walker, *Early Aviation at Farnborough*.
14 Colonel Capper to Director of Fortifications and Works, War Office, 6 September 1906, in Walker, *Early Aviation at Farnborough*.
15 Graham Wallas, *Flying Witness: Harry Harper and the Golden Age of Aviation* (publisher unknown, London, 1958).
16 Gibbs-Smith, *The Rebirth of European Aviation*.
17 *New York Herald (Paris Edition)*, 2 February 1906.

20 The Arms Dealer and the Dowager

1 WW to OC, 1 December 1906, in McFarland, *Papers*.
2 WW to OC, 10 October 1906, ibid.
3 Ibid.
4 OC to WW, 15 October 1906, ibid.
5 WW to OC, 2 November 1906, ibid.
6 WW to OC, 20 December 1906, ibid.
7 OC to WW, 22 December 1906, ibid.
8 OC to Charles R. Flint, 26 December 1906, Octave Chanute Papers, LOC.
9 Gollin, *No Longer an Island*.
10 WW to OC, 28 January 1907, in Kelly, *Miracle at Kitty Hawk*.
11 Lady Jane Taylour to Charles R. Flint, 15 February 1907, Wright Papers, LOC.
12 WW to Charles R. Flint, 16 February 1907, ibid.
13 Richard Haldane, Secretary of State for War, to Lady Jane Taylour, 12 April 1907, ibid.
14 Lady Jane Taylour to Charles R. Flint, 17 April 1907, ibid.

15 Gollin, *No Longer an Island.*

21 Corruption in Paris

1 Kelly, *The Wright Brothers.*
2 Howard, *Wilbur and Orville.*
3 Board of Ordnance and Fortification, US War Department, to Wright Cycle Company, 11 May 1907, Wright Papers, LOC, as quoted in Kelly, *The Wright Brothers.*
4 Wright Brothers to Board of Ordnance and Fortification, War Department, 17 May 1907, in McFarland, *Papers.*
5 WW to MW, Paris, 20 July 1907, ibid.
6 Hart O. Berg to Flint and Company, New York, 26 May 1907, in Kelly, *Miracle at Kitty Hawk.*
7 Ibid.
8 Miller, *Wright Reminiscences.*
9 Hart O. Berg to Flint and Company, New York, 26 May 1907, in Kelly, *Miracle at Kitty Hawk.*
10 Gollin, *No Longer an Island.*
11 WW Diary, 31 July 1907, in McFarland, *Papers.*
12 MW to WW, 22 June 1907, box 5, Wright Papers, LOC.
13 WW to OC, 9 December 1907, in McFarland, *Papers.*

22 Fraternal Friction

1 WW to OW, Paris, 2 July 1907, in McFarland, *Papers.*
2 OW to WW, 11 July 1907, ibid.
3 Ibid.
4 MW to WW, 9 July 1907, box 5, Wright Papers, LOC.
5 KW to WW, 30 June 1907, box 4, Wright Papers, LOC.
6 Ibid.
7 KW to WW, 5 July 1907, ibid.
8 KW to WW, 5,24 & 28 July 1907, ibid.
9 WW to MW, Paris, 20 July 1907, in McFarland, *Papers.*
10 Ibid.
11 Ibid.
12 WW to KW, 17 July 1907, in Kelly, *Miracle at Kitty Hawk.*
13 WW to KW, 8 June 1907, ibid.
14 Wilbur Wright, 'Flying as a Sport – Its Possibilities', *Scientific American*, 29 February 1908.
15 Gabriel Voisin, *Men, Women and 10,000 Kites* (Putnam, London, 1963).
16 Captain Ferdinand Ferber to Georges Besançon, *L'Aérophile*, June 1907.
17 WW to MW, Paris, 2 August 1907, in Kelly, *Miracle at Kitty Hawk.*
18 Gibbs-Smith, *The Rebirth of European Aviation.*
19 Walsh, *One Day at Kitty Hawk.*
20 Kelly, *The Wright Brothers.*
21 WW to OC, 9 December 1907, in McFarland, *Papers.*
22 WW to MW, 22 November 1907, in McFarland, *Miracle at Kitty Hawk.*
23 OW to MW, Paris 23 August 1907, ibid.
24 WW to MW, Paris 27 August 1907, ibid.
25 MW to OW, 5 September 1907, box 5, Wright Papers, LOC.
26 MW to WB, 15 October 1907, ibid.
27 MW to WB, 30 October 1907, ibid.
28 Kinnane, *The Crucible of Flight.*
29 MW to OW, 1 September 1907, box 5, Wright Papers, LOC.
30 MW to WB, 4 August 1907, ibid.
31 MW to OW, 10 October 1907, ibid.
32 Notes of conversation between Wilbur and Orville Wright and Hart O. Berg, Paris, 6 November 1907, in McFarland, *Papers.*
33 OW to KW, Paris, 12 November 1907, ibid.

23 Supremacy Threatened

1 'Herring's Work', *American Aeronaut*, May 1908.
2 Bruce, *Bell: Alexander Graham Bell.*
3 'Wright Brothers Sail Over Land and Sea with Aeroplane', *Virginian-Pilot*, Norfolk, Va, 2 May 1908.
4 Byron Newton, 'Watching the Wright Brothers Fly', *Aeronautics*, June 1908.
5 Gollin, *No Longer an Island.*
6 *Collier's*, 30 May 1908.
7 Bill Hoster in *New York American*, quoted in Kirk, *First in Flight.*
8 KW to WW, 17 May 1908, box 4, Wright Papers, LOC.

24 Triumph at Le Mans

1 KW to WW, 17 May 1908, box 4, Wright Papers, LOC.

2 Ibid.
3 WW to KW, 19 May 1908, in McFarland, *Papers*.
4 KW to WW, 18 May 1908, box 4, Wright Papers, LOC.
5 Ibid.
6 WW to OW, Paris, 1 June 1908, in McFarland, *Papers*.
7 WW to OW, New York, 20 May 1908, ibid.
8 Wilbur and Orville Wright, 'The Wright Brothers' Aeroplane', *Century* magazine, September 1908 (article written by Orville).
9 OW to Glenn H. Curtiss, 20 July 1908, in McFarland, *Papers*.
10 WW to OW, Paris, 3 June 1908, ibid.
11 WW to KW, Paris, 9 June 1908, ibid.
12 KW to WW, 2 July 1908, box 4, Wright Papers, LOC.
13 MW to WW, 25 June 1908, box 5, Wright Papers, LOC.
14 MW to WW, 5 June 1908, ibid.
15 WW to OW, Le Mans, France, 17 June 1908, in McFarland, *Papers*.
16 WW Diary T, 8 June 1908, in McFarland, *Papers*.
17 Joseph Brandreth, interview with Léon Bollée in 'Mr Wilbur Wright: The Fanatic of Flight', *Daily Mail*, 17 August 1908.
18 WW to OW, Le Mans, France, 9 July 1908, in Kelly, *Miracle at Kitty Hawk*.
19 MW to WW, 2 August 1908, box 5, Wright Papers, LOC.
20 KW to WW, 26 July 1908, box 4, Wright Papers, LOC.
21 Gollin, *No Longer an Island*.
22 WW to KW, Le Mans, 2 August 1908, in Kelly, *Miracle at Kitty Hawk*.
23 'Mr Wilbur Wright: The Fanatic of Flight', *Daily Mail*, 17 August 1908.
24 Ibid.
25 Ibid.
26 Ibid.
27 Ibid.
28 Ibid.
29 *New York Herald*, probably 9 August 1908.

25 The Trumpet Blasts of Fame

1 *Daily Mirror*, 13 August 1908; *The Times*,14 August 1908.
2 *Daily Telegraph*, 10 August 1908.
3 *Illustrierte Aeronautische Mitteilungen*, 1 July 1908.
4 OC to WW, 25 August 1908, in McFarland, *Papers*.
5 *Le Figaro*, 11 August 1908.
6 *L'Aérophile*, 11 August 1908.
7 *L'Auto*, 9 August 1908.
8 WW to OW, 15 August 1908, in McFarland, *Papers*.
9 KW to WW, 18 August 1908, box 4, Wright Papers, LOC.
10 KW to WW, 30 August 1908, ibid.
11 KW to WW, 18 August 1908, ibid.
12 WW to KW, Le Mans, 13 September 1908, in McFarland, *Papers*.
13 KW to WW, 27 August 1908, box 4, Wright Papers, LOC.
14 WW to KW, Le Mans, 13 September 1908, in McFarland, *Papers*.
15 *Le Matin*, 5 September 1908.
16 Crouch, *The Bishop's Boys*.
17 WW to KW, Le Mans, 22 August 1908, in Kelly, *Miracle at Kitty Hawk*.
18 WW to OW, Le Mans, 25 August 1908, ibid.
19 OW to KW, Washington, DC, 27 August 1908, ibid.
20 OW to KW, Washington, DC, 31 August 1908, ibid.
21 Howard, *Wilbur and Orville*.
22 Ibid.
23 WW to KW, Le Mans, 13 September 1908, in McFarland, *Papers*.
24 Howard, *Wilbur and Orville*.
25 OW to WW, Washington, DC, 6 September 1908, in Kelly, *Miracle at Kitty Hawk*.
26 WW to KW, Le Mans, 10 September 1908, ibid.
27 WW to MW, Le Mans, 13 September 1908, ibid.
28 MW to WW, 9 September 1908, ibid.
29 WW to MW, Le Mans, 13 September 1908, ibid.

26 Disaster in Washington

1 Howard, *Wilbur and Orville*.
2 Flint, *Memories*.
3 Howard, *Wilbur and Orville*.
4 KW to Lorin Wright, Fort Myer, 19 September 1908, box 4, Wright Papers, LOC.
5 Ibid.
6 Ibid.
7 KW to WW, 24 September 1908, box 4, Wright Papers, LOC.
8 MW to OW, 20 September 1908, box 5, Wright Papers, LOC.

9 MW to WW, 19 September 1908, ibid.
10 WW to KW, Le Mans, 20 September 1908, in McFarland, *Papers*.
11 Ibid.
12 Ibid.
13 WW to MW, Le Mans, 22 September 1908, ibid.
14 WW to OW, Le Mans, 23 September 1908, ibid.
15 KW to WW, Fort Myer, 24 September 1908, box 4, Wright Papers, LOC.
16 OC to WW, 7 October 1908, in McFarland, *Papers*.
17 WW to OC, Le Mans, 10 November 1908, ibid.
18 MW to WW, 24 September 1908, in Kelly, *Miracle at Kitty Hawk*.
19 WW to OW, Le Mans, 9 October 1908, ibid.
20 Howard, *Wilbur and Orville*.
21 OW to WW, 14 November 1908, in McFarland, *Papers*.
22 Brewer, *Fifty Years of Flying*.
23 Ibid.
24 Hon. Charles S. Rolls to WW, 14 October 1908, Wright Papers, LOC.
25 WW to OW, Le Mans, *c.* 14 November 1908, in McFarland, *Papers*.
26 WW to KW, Le Mans, 7 December 1908, in Kelly, *Miracle at Kitty Hawk*.

27 Tongue of Scandal

1 Dayton *Herald*, 8 January 1909.
2 WW to editor of the Dayton *Daily News*, Pau, France, 24 January 1909.
3 *L'Illustration*, 5 August 1908.
4 Crouch, *The Bishop's Boys*.
5 KW to MW, Rome, 20 April 1909, box 4, Wright Papers, LOC.
6 Howard, *Wilbur and Orville*.
7 *The World Magazine*, 11 April 1909.
8 *Elmira Star*, 16 July 1909.
9 Ibid.
10 Grace Goulder, *Ohio Scenes and Citizens* (World Publishing Co., Cleveland, Ohio, 1964).
11 Howard, *Wilbur and Orville*.
12 Penrose, *British Aviation*.
13 Lord Northcliffe to R.B. Haldane, Secretary of State for War, Pau, 19 February 1909, in Gollin, *No Longer an Island*.
14 Lord Northcliffe to Lord Esher, Pau, 26 February 1909, Esher Papers, in Gollin, *No Longer an Island*.
15 Paul Tissandier, quoted from *Le Figaro* in *Automobilia and Flight*, June 1909.
16 KW to MW, Pau, 24 January 1909, box 4, Wright Papers, LOC.
17 KW to MW, Pau, 1 February 1909, ibid.
18 MW to WB, 21 March 1909, box 5, Wright Papers, LOC.

28 The Lawsuits

1 WW to OC, 6 June 1909, in McFarland, *Papers*.
2 OC to WW, 16 June 1909, ibid.
3 Benjamin D. Foulois, *From the Wright Brothers to the Astronauts*, (McGraw-Hill, New York, 1968).
4 Gibbs-Smith, *Aviation*.
5 Crouch, *The Bishop's Boys*.
6 OW to WW, New York, 10 August 1909, in McFarland, *Papers*.
7 Roseberry, *Glenn Curtiss*.
8 Ibid.
9 Ibid.
10 Crouch, *The Bishop's Boys*.
11 Roseberry, *Glenn Curtiss.*.
12 Ibid.
13 OW to WW, Berlin, 24 August 1909, in Kelly, *Miracle at Kitty Hawk*.
14 OC to Ernest L. Jones, editor, *Aeronautics*, 26 August 1909, in McFarland, *Papers*.

29 A Precious Friendship Sours

1 MW to WW, 13 June 1908, box 6, Wright Papers, LOC.
2 New York *World*, 12 December 1909.
3 WW to Arnold Kruckman, 21 December 1909, in McFarland, *Papers*.
4 OC to WW, 23 December 1909, ibid.
5 Howard, *Wilbur and Orville*.
6 Ernest Archdeacon, Report of Octave Chanute address to Aéro-Club de France, *La Locomotion*, 11 April 1903.
7 Octave Chanute, 'Aerial Navigation in the United States', *L'Aérophile*, August 1903.
8 OC to WW, 23 January 1910, in McFarland, *Papers*.
9 Ibid.
10 WW to OC, 29 January 1910, ibid.
11 Ibid.
12 Howard, *Wilbur and Orville*.
13 WW to OC, 28 April 1910, in McFarland, *Papers*.

14 OC to WW, 14 May 1910, ibid.

30 'Keep Out of My Air'

1 Wilbur Wright on the death of Octave Chanute, *Aeronautics*, January 1911.
2 WW to Colonel William A. Glassford, 30 November 1910, in McFarland, *Papers*.
3 WW to Dr Albert Zahm, 29 January 1910, ibid.
4 Source of Zahm's perusal of Octave Chanute correspondence on 14 August 1911: in McFarland, *Papers*, 1008n.
5 Howard, *Wilbur and Orville*.
6 Charles Gibbs-Smith memorandum of 11 October 1974 in his aviation papers at the National Museum of Science and Industry, London.
7 Roseberry, *Glenn Curtiss*.
8 KW to MW, Berlin, 27 August 1909, box 5, Wright Papers, LOC.
9 OW to WW, Berlin, 23 September 1909, in Kelly, *Miracle at Kitty Hawk*.
10 WW to KW, 26 September 1909, ibid.
11 OW to Lorin Wright, Berlin, 9 September 1909, ibid.
12 KW to MW, Berlin, 11 October 1909, box 5, Wright Papers, LOC.
13 'Are the Wrights Justified?', *Aeronautics*, April 1910.
14 Blériot, quoted by C.B. Hayward in *Practical Aeronautics* (American Technical Society, Chicago, 1917).
15 Albert F. Zahm, *Aerial Navigation: A Popular Treatise on the Growth of Aircraft and on Aerial Meteorology* (Appleton, New York, 1911).
16 WW to George Spratt, 16 October 1909, in McFarland, *Papers*.
17 WW to Hart O. Berg, 16 November 1910, in Kelly, *Miracle at Kitty Hawk*.

31 'A Short Life Full of Consequences'

1 WW to OW, Paris, 26 May 1911, in Kelly, *Miracle at Kitty Hawk*.
2 Crouch, *The Bishop's Boys*.
3 Kelly, *The Wright Brothers*.
4 Grover Loening, *Our Wings Grow Faster* (Doubleday, Doran, New York, 1935).
5 Crouch, *The Bishop's Boys*.
6 Henry H. Arnold, *Global Mission* (Harper, New York, 1949).
7 WW to Arch Hoxsey, 19 September 1910, in McFarland, *Papers*.
8 KW to WW, 23 April 1911, box 5, Wright Papers, LOC.
9 OW to WW, Berlin, 27 November 1910, in McFarland, *Papers*.
10 WW to OW, Le Mans, 31 March 1911, ibid.
11 WW to OW, Berlin, 30 June 1911, ibid.
12 WW to KW, Berlin, 6 July 1911, box 7, Wright Papers, LOC.
13 WW to OW, Berlin, 6 May 1911, ibid.
14 WW to OW, Berlin, 8 July 1911, ibid.
15 KW to WW, 9 July 1911, box 5, Wright Papers, LOC.
16 MW, 14 February 1912, *Diaries*.
17 WW to M. Hévésy, 25 January 1912, in McFarland, *Papers*.
18 WW to Frederick P. Fish, 4 May 1912, in McFarland, *Papers*.
19 MW, 30 May 1912, *Diaries*.

32 Feud with the Smithsonian

1 MW, 1 June 1912, *Diaries*.
2 Roseberry, *Glenn Curtiss*.
3 Culick and Dunmore, *On Great White Wings*.
4 Kinnane, *The Crucible of Flight*.
5 Dr Stanley R. Mohler in an interview with the author, Dayton, Ohio, December 1999, and Stanley Mohler and Dr. David A. Tipton, 'The Wright Brothers: A Personality Profile', *Aviation, Space and Environmental Medicine*, June 1983.
6 The will of Wilbur Wright, 10 May 1912, in McFarland, *Papers*.
7 Crouch, *The Bishop's Boys*.
8 Boston *Transcript* newspaper, March 1914, quoted in Roseberry, *Glenn Curtiss*.
9 Howard, *Wilbur and Orville*.
10 Crouch, *The Bishop's Boys*.
11 A.F. Zahm, 'The First Man-Carrying Aeroplane,' in the Smithsonian Institution *Annual Report*, Washington, DC, 1914.
12 Smithsonian Institution *Annual Report*, 1915.
13 OW to William Howard Taft, 14 May 1925, 'Smithsonian Controversy', Wright Papers, LOC.
14 OW, 'Why the 1903 Wright Machine is sent to a British Museum', March 1928, in McFarland, *Papers*.
15 Dr Stanley R. Mohler in an

interview with the author, Dayton, Ohio, December 1999.

16 Howard, *Wilbur and Orville.*

17 Elliott, *Bishop Milton Wright, Quest.*

33 Spinster in Love

1 KW to HJH, 4 April 1925, WHMC.

2 KW to HJH, 6 May 1926, ibid.

3 KW to HJH, 13 June 1925, ibid.

4 Ibid.

5 Ibid.

6 Professor R.H. Stetson to HJH, 9 June 1925, WHMC.

7 KW to HJH, 16 June 1925, WHMC.

8 Ibid.

9 Ibid.

10 Ibid.

11 KW to HJH, 22 June 1925, WHMC.

12 KW to HJH, 29 June 1925, ibid.

13 KW to HJH, 12 September 1925, ibid.

14 KW to HJH, 12 January 1926, ibid.

15 Ibid.

16 Ibid.

17 HJH to KW, undated page of letter, WHMC.

34 'Little Brother' Alone

1 KW to HJH, 14 May 1926, WHMC.

2 KW to HJH, 19 September 1926, ibid.

3 KW to HJH, undated – probably October 1926, ibid.

4 KW to HJH, undated letter No. 46: Oct/Nov 1926, ibid.

5 KW to HJH, undated letter No. 20 *c.* Oct 1926, ibid.

6 KW to Griffith Brewer, Kansas City, 23 November 1927. Brewer Papers, Royal Aeronautical Society, London.

7 Lois Walker, letter to author, 22 August 2002.

8 Dr Adrian Kinnane, letter to author, 24 August 2002.

9 KW to Vilhjalmur Stefansson, Kansas City, 1 January 1928, Stefansson Papers, Rauner Special Collections Library, Dartmouth College, New Hampshire.

10 Vilhjalmur Stefansson to KW, 8 August 1927, ibid.

11 HJH to Griffith Brewer, 31 July 1927, Brewer Papers, Royal Aeronautical Society, London.

12 KW to Griffith Brewer, Longs Peak, Colorado, 27 August 1927, ibid.

13 Tom Crouch in interview with author, Washington, DC, November 1999.

14 Marianne Miller Hudec in letters to author, 27 May 2003.

15 Marianne Miller Hudec in letter to author, 28 August 2002.

16 HJH to Griffith Brewer, 20 January 1928, Brewer Papers, Royal Aeronautical Society, London.

17 Dr Adrian Kinnane, letter to author, 28 January 2003.

18 KW to Agnes Beck, Kansas City, 12 January 1928, WHMC.

19 Henry C. Haskell to Dr John B. Crane, 17 November 1977, ibid.

20 KW to Agnes Beck, 12 January 1928, ibid.

21 Mary Haskell to OW, Oberlin, 9 December 1928, Box 32, Wright Papers, LOC.

22 HJH to Griffith Brewer, 14 March 1929, Brewer Papers, Royal Aeronautical Society, London.

35 The Twilight Years

1 HJH to Griffith Brewer, 14 March 1929, Brewer Papers, Royal Aeronautical Society, London.

2 *Cincinnati Enquirer*, 4 March 1929.

3 HJH to Ivonette Wright Miller, 16 April 1948 (letter in possession of Henry J. Haskell's grandson, Harry Haskell).

4 Marianne Hudec, letter to author, 24 August 2002.

5 Marianne Hudec, letter to author, 23 August, 2002.

6 Eric Hodgins, 'Heavier than Air', *New Yorker*, 13 December 1930.

7 Young and Fitzgerald, *Twelve Seconds to the Moon.*

8 George Spratt to OW, 27 November 1922, in McFarland, *Papers.*

9 McFarland, *Papers*, p.1179, n.1.

Date	Location	Aircraft & Pilot
Dec 17, 1903	Kill Devil Hills	Wright Flyer (Wilbur)
Nov 9, 1904	Dayton	Wright Flyer (Wilbur)
Sept 29, 1905	Dayton	Wright Flyer (Orville)
Oct 4, 1905	Dayton	Wright Flyer (Orville)
Oct 5, 1905	Dayton	Wright Flyer (Wilbur)
1906 & 1907	Wright Flyer locked away from public view	
Nov 9, 1907	Issy-les-Moulineaux, France	Voisin-Farman (Henri Farman)
Jan 11, 1908	Issy-les-Moulineaux, France	Voisin-Farman (Henri Farman)
April 11, 1908	Issy-les-Moulineaux, France	Voisin-Delagrange (Delagrange)
May 14, 1908	Kill Devil Hills	Wright Flyer (Wilbur)
June 23, 1908	Milan	Voisin-Delagrange (Delagrange)
July 4, 1908	Hammondsport, USA	Aerial Experiment Association's 'June Bug' (Glenn Curtiss)
July 6, 1908	Issy-les-Moulineaux, France	Blériot VIII (Blériot)
July 6, 1908	Issy-les-Moulineaux, France	Voisin-Farman (Henri Farman)
Aug 29, 1908	Hammondsport, USA	AEA 'June Bug' (John McCurdy)
Sept 12, 1908	Fort Myer, USA	Wright Flyer (Orville)
Sept 16, 1908	Auvours, France	Wright Flyer (Wilbur)
Sept 17, 1908	Issy-les-Moulineaux, France	Voisin-Delagrange (Delagrange)
Sept 21, 1908	Auvours, France	Wright Flyer (Wilbur)
Oct 2, 1908	Bouy, France	Voisin-Farman (Henri Farman)
Oct 3, 1908	Auvours, France	Wright Flyer (Wilbur)
Oct 10, 1908	Auvours, France	Wright Flyer (Wilbur)
Oct 30, 1908	Bouy to Reims, France	Voisin-Farman triplane (Henri Farman)
Oct 31, 1908	Toury to Artenay, France	Blériot VIII (Blériot)
Nov 17, 1908	Bouy, France	Voisin-Farman triplane (Henri Farman)
Dec 17, 1908	Hammondsport, USA	AEA 'Siver Dart' (John McCurdy)
Dec 18, 1908	Auvours, France	Wright Flyer (Wilbur)
Dec 31, 1908	Auvours, France	Wright Flyer (Wilbur)

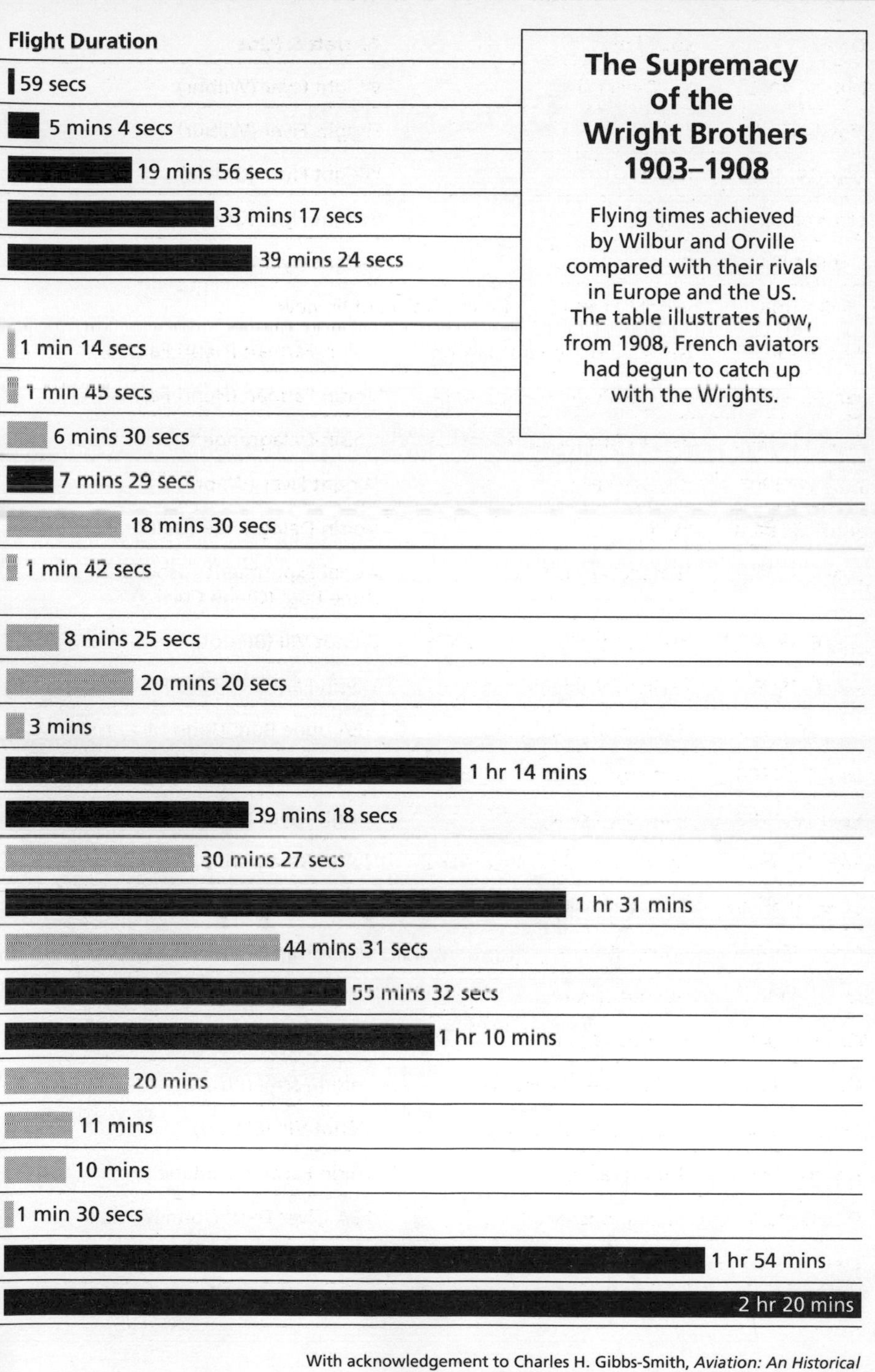

With acknowledgement to Charles H. Gibbs-Smith, *Aviation: An Historical Survey from its Origins to the End of World War II* (HMSO, London, 1970)

Select Bibliography

Anderson, John D. Jr. *Introduction to Flight*, McGraw-Hill, New York, 1979
A History of Aerodynamics, Cambridge University Press, 1997

Barfield, Rodney. *Seasoned by Salt: A Historical Album of the Outer Banks*, University of North Carolina Press, 1995

Bernstein, Mark. *Grand Eccentrics: Turning the Century: Dayton and the Inventing of America*, Orange Frazer Press, Wilmington, Ohio, 1996

Boyer, Chip. *The Door: A Narrative and Commentary Concerning the Funerals of the Wright Brothers and of Other Wright Family Members, 1912–1948*, published by the author, Dayton, Ohio, 2002

Brewer, Griffith. *Fifty Years of Flying*, Air League of the British Empire, London, 1946

Bruce, Robert V. *Bell: Alexander Graham Bell and the Conquest of Solitude*, Cornell University Press, New York, 1973

Brunsman, Charlotte K., and E. August. *Wright & Wright, Printers: The Other Career of Wilbur and Orville*, Trailside Press, Kettering, Ohio, 1989

Burton, Robert. *Bird Flight*, Facts on File, New York, 1990

Chanute, Octave. *Progress in Flying Machines*, M.N. Forney, New York, 1894

Chapman, William R., and Jill K. Hanson. *Wright Brothers National Memorial Historic Resource Study*, National Park Service, Atlanta, 1997

Combs, Harry, with Martin Caidin. *Kill Devil Hill: Discovering the Secret of the Wright Brothers*, Houghton Mifflin, Boston, 1979

Crouch, Tom D. *A Dream of Wings: Americans and the Airplane, 1875–1905*, W.W. Norton, New York, 1981
The Bishop's Boys: A Life of Wilbur and Orville Wright, W.W. Norton, New York, 1989

Culick, Fred E.C., and Spencer Dunmore, *On Great White Wings*, Hyperion, New York, 2001

Cullingham, Gordon. *Patrick Young Alexander: Patron and Pioneer of Aeronautics*, Cross Manufacturing Co., Bath, England, 1984

DuFour, Howard R., with Peter J. Unitt. *Charles E. Taylor: The Wright Brothers' Mechanician*, Prime Printing, Dayton, Ohio, 1997

Dyson, James. *A History of Great Inventions*, Carroll & Graf, New York, 2001

Elliott, Brian A. *Blériot: Herald of an Age*, Tempus Publishing, Stroud, England, 2000

Elliott, Daryl. *Bishop Milton Wright and the Quest for a Christian America*, Drew University, Madison, New Jersey, 1992

Fairlie, Gerard, and Elizabeth Cayley. *The Life of a Genius: Sir George Cayley: Pioneer of Modern Aviation*, Hodder & Stoughton, London, 1965

Fetters, Paul R. (ed.). *Trials and Triumphs: History of the Church of the United Brethren in Christ*, Church of the United Brethren in Christ, Huntington, Indiana, 1984

Fisk, Fred C., and Martin W. Todd. *The Wright Brothers from Bicycle to Biplane*, published by the authors, West Milton, Ohio, 1995

Flint, Charles R. *Memories of an Active Life*, Putnam, New York, 1923

Freudenthal, Elsbeth E. *Flight into History: The Wright Brothers and the Air Age*, University of Oklahoma Press, 1949

Gibbs-Smith, Charles H. *A Brief History of Flying: From Myth to Space Travel*, HMSO, London, 1967
Clément Ader: His Flight Claims and his Place in History, HMSO, London, 1968
Leonardo da Vinci's Aeronautics, HMSO, London, 1967

Sir George Cayley's Aeronautics, 1796–1855, HMSO, London, 1962
The Aeroplane: An Historical Survey, HMSO, London, 1960
The Rebirth of European Aviation, 1902–1908: A Study of the Wright Brothers' Influence, HMSO, London, 1974
The World's First Aeroplane Flights, HMSO, London, 1965
A Directory and Nomenclature of the First Aeroplanes 1809–1909, HMSO, London, 1966
Aviation: An Historical Survey from its Origins to the End of World War II, HMSO, London, 1970

Gollin, Alfred. *No Longer an Island: Britain and the Wright Brothers 1902–1909*, Stanford University Press, California, 1984
The Impact of Air Power on the British People and their Government, 1904–1914, Stanford University Press, California, 1989

Greenwall, Harry J. *Northcliffe: Napoleon of Fleet Street*, Allan Wingate, London, 1957

Harper, Harry. *My Fifty Years in Flying*, Associated Newspapers, London, 1956

Howard, Fred. *Wilbur and Orville: A Biography of the Wright Brothers*, Alfred A. Knopf, New York, 1987

Hunt, Melba. *Cooking the Wright Way: A Unique Profile of the Wrights from the Aspect of Food*, Kettering-Moraine Museum, Kettering, Ohio, 1998

Jakab, Peter L. *Visions of a Flying Machine: The Wright Brothers and the Process of Invention*, Smithsonian Institution Press, Washington, DC, 1990

Jakab, Peter L., and Rick Young (ed.). *The Published Writings of Wilbur and Orville Wright*, Smithsonian Institution Press, Washington, DC, 2000

Jenkins, Garry. *'Colonel' Cody and the Flying Cathedral: The Adventures of the Cowboy who Conquered Britain's Skies*, Simon & Schuster, London, 1999

Johnson, Mary Ann. *A Field Guide to Flight: On the Aviation Trail in Dayton, Ohio*, Landfall Press, Dayton, Ohio, 1996

Kelly, Fred C. *The Wright Brothers: A Biography Authorised by Orville Wright*, Harcourt, Brace, New York, 1943

Kelly, Fred C. (ed.). *Miracle at Kitty Hawk: The Letters of Wilbur and Orville Wright*, Farrar, Straus and Young, New York, 1951

Kinnane, Adrian. *The Crucible of Flight*, an unpublished psychological study of the Wright family, Washington, DC, 1982

Kirk, Stephen. *First in Flight: The Wright Brothers in North Carolina*, John F. Blair, Winston-Salem, North Carolina, 1995

Lilienthal, Otto. *Birdflight as the Basis of Aviation*, original German edition pub. 1889; first English language edition pub. Longmans Green, London, 1911

Lissarrague, Pierre. *Au Temps de Clément Ader*, Teknea, Toulouse, 1994

Longyard, William H. *Who's Who in Aviation History*, Airlife Publishing, Shrewsbury, England, 1994

McFarland, Marvin W. (ed.). *The Papers of Wilbur and Orville Wright: Including the Chanute Wright Letters and Other Papers of Octave Chanute* (2 volumes), McGraw-Hill, New York, 1953

McMahon, John R. *The Wright Brothers: Fathers of Flight*, Little, Brown, Boston, 1930

Miller, Ivonette Wright. *Wright Reminiscences*, The Air Force Museum Foundation, Wright-Patterson Air Force Bureau, Ohio, 1978

Ogilvie, Gordon. *The Riddle of Richard Pearse*, A.H. & A.W. Reed, Wellington, 1973

Owen, Louise. *The Real Lord Northcliffe: Some Personal Recollections of a Private Secretary*, Cassell, London, 1922

Parramore, Thomas C. *Triumph at Kitty Hawk: The Wright Brothers and Powered Flight*, North Carolina Department of Cultural Resources, Raleigh, NC, 1999

Pelham, David. *The Penguin Book of Kites*, Penguin, London, 1976

Penrose, Harald. *British Aviation: The Pioneer Years 1903–1914*, Putnam, London, 1967

Pritchard, J. Laurence. *Sir George Cayley: The Inventor of the Aeroplane*, Max Parrish, London, 1961

Renstrom, Arthur G. *Wilbur and Orville Wright: A Bibliography*, Library of Congress, Washington, DC, 1968
Wilbur and Orville Wright: A Chronology Commemorating the Hundredth Anniversary of the Birth of Orville Wright, August 19, 1871, Library of Congress, Washington, DC, 1975

Rodliffe, C. Geoffrey. *Wings over Waitohi:*

The Story of Richard Pearse, Avon Press, Auckland, NZ, 1997

Rolt, L.T.C. *The Aeronauts: A History of Ballooning 1783–1903*, Walker & Co, New York, 1966

Roseberry, C.R. *Glenn Curtiss: Pioneer of Flight*, Doubleday, New York, 1972

Ryan, A.P. *Lord Northcliffe*, Collins, London, 1953

Scott, Phil. *The Pioneers of Flight: A Documentary History*, Princeton University Press, 1999

Shaw, W. Hudson, and Olaf Ruhen. *Lawrence Hargrave: Explorer, Inventor and Aviation Experimenter*, Cassell Australia, Sydney, 1977

Shea, George. *First Flight: The Story of Tom Tate and the Wright Brothers*, HarperCollins, New York, 1997

Shulman, Seth. *Unlocking the Sky: Glenn Hammond Curtiss and the Race to Invent the Aeroplane*, HarperCollins, New York, 2002

Stein, Ralph. *The Great Inventions*, Playboy Press, Chicago, 1976

Thompson, D.D. *Our Bishops: A Sketch of the Origin and Growth of the Church of the United Brethren in Christ*, United Brethren Publishing House, Dayton, Ohio, 1904

Vaeth, J. Gordon. *Langley: Man of Science and Flight*, Ronald Press, New York, 1966

Walker, Percy B. *Early Aviation at Farnborough Vol II: The First Aeroplanes*, Macdonald, London, 1974

Walsh, John Evangelist. *One Day at Kitty Hawk: The Untold Story of the Wright Brothers and the Airplane*, Crowell, New York, 1975

Whedbee, Charles Harry. *Legends of the Outer Banks*, John F. Blair, Winston-Salem, North Carolina,1966

Wohl, Robert. *A Passion for Wings: Aviation and the Western Imagination, 1908–1918*, Yale University Press, 1994

Wright, Orville (ed. Fred C. Kelly). *How We Invented the Airplane*, McKay, New York, 1953

Wright, Bishop Milton. *Diaries 1857–1917*, Wright State University, Dayton, Ohio, 1999

Wykeham, Peter. *Santos-Dumont: A Study in Obsession*, Putnam, London, 1962

Young, Rosamond, and Catherine Fitzgerald. *Twelve Seconds to the Moon*, Journal Herald, Dayton, Ohio, 1978

Sources and Acknowledgements

Most of the original source material for this biography was in the public domain. Two libraries supplied much of it: the Manuscript Division of the Library of Congress provided most of the aeronautical papers relating to the birth and development of the aeroplane; the Paul Laurence Dunbar Library at Wright State University in Dayton, Ohio, provided the prolific Wright family private correspondence, including the diaries of Bishop Milton Wright. The papers of Octave Chanute were also in the public domain at the Library of Congress.

Katharine Wright's letters to Henry J. Haskell and to Agnes Beck, likewise publicly available, were at the Western Historical Manuscript Collection, University of Missouri, Kansas City. Katharine's correspondence with Vilhjalmur Stefansson was in the Rauner Special Collections Library at Dartmouth College, New Hampshire.

I wish to express my gratitude to the following people who helped me with information about the Wright Brothers and their family:

Hazen Allen (librarian, Rauner Special Collections Library, Dartmouth College, New Hampshire); John D. Anderson (Professor of Aerospace Engineering, University of Maryland); Costaguta

Attilio (International Civil Aviation Organisation, Montreal); Fred Bartenstein (historian and author, Dayton, Ohio); Roland Baumann (archivist, Oberlin College, Ohio); David Boutros (Western Historical Manuscript Collection, University of Missouri, Kansas City); Chip Boyer (Dayton, Ohio); Tom Bredenharn (Public Affairs Department, City of Dayton, Ohio); Ruth Brookshire (Wilbur Wright Memorial Museum, Millville, Indiana); Nancy Villa Bryk (curator, Henry Ford Museum and Greenfield Village, Dearborn, Michigan); Clive Bunyan (assistant curator, aeronautics, National Museum of Science and Industry, London); Sarah Spink Downing (assistant curator, Outer Banks History Center, Manteo, North Carolina); Denis Parks (curator, Museum of Flight, Seattle); Powers Museum (Carthage, Missouri); Scott Price (historian, US Coast Guard, Washington, DC); Paula Sadler (Maud Preston Palenske Memorial Library, St Joseph, Michigan); Simine Short (aviation historian, National Soaring Museum, Elmira, New York); William F. Trimble (Department of History, Auburn University, Auburn, Alabama); John Wallach, Elli Bambakadis and Nancy Horlacher (Dayton and Montgomery County Public Library, Ohio); Don Weckhorst (historian, Octave Chanute Aerospace Museum, Rantoul, Illinois); Jane Wildermuth, John Sanford and John Reynolds (archivists, University Libraries, Wright State University, Dayton, Ohio).

I am also indebted to the Royal Aeronautical Society for permission to quote from Henry and Katharine Haskell's correspondence with Griffith Brewer in the society's collection of the latter's papers; to the National Museum of Science and Industry, London, for allowing me access to the Charles Gibbs-Smith papers; and to Becky Rehling of Dayton, Ohio (daughter of Katharine Wright's friend, Agnes Beck) for a copy of her unpublished manuscript, *Swesterchen* (*sic*) about Katharine's life.

The richest sources of photographs of the Wright Brothers' aeronautical activities, and of their family, are the picture libraries of the Library of Congress and the Paul Laurence Dunbar Library at Wright State University. The LOC holds the original glass plate negatives taken by the Wrights to record the process of invention.

For permission to use extracts from their books, I am grateful to:

Tom D. Crouch, author of *The Bishop's Boys: A Life of Wilbur and Orville Wright*; Fred Howard, author of *Wilbur and Orville: A Biography of the Wright Brothers*; Adrian Kinnane, author of the unpublished *The Crucible of Flight*; Peter L. Jakab, author of *Visions of a Flying Machine: The Wright Brothers and the Process of Invention*; The Air League of London, publisher of Griffith Brewer's *Fifty Years of Flying*; Historical Publications Section of the North Carolina Department of Cultural Resources, publisher of *Triumph at Kitty Hawk* by Tomas C. Parramore.

I also wish to thank: Henry J. Haskell, of Guildford, Connecticut, and his sisters, Judith Zernich, Tamme Haskell, Ingrid Vrooman and Elizabeth Park, for permission to quote from the unpublished letters of Katharine Wright Haskell held in the Western Historical Manuscript Collection, University of Missouri, Kansas City. And to the Rauner Special Collections, Dartmouth College Library, Hanover, New Hampshire, for permission to quote from correspondence between Katharine Wright and Vilhjalmur Stefansson contained in the Stefansson papers.

Index

WB denotes Wright Brothers

12 Pages
In Two Parts

VOL. XIX. NO. 68. NORFOLK, VA., FRIDAY DECE

LYING MACHINE SOARS 3 MILES IN SAND HILLS AND WAVES

LLY SHEETS WILL DECIDE CONTEST

irman Dey Forced to rn From Richmond to Ge Sheets For Committee

HY FACTION HAS ADVANTAGE THUS FAR

Proxies Ruled Out of Meeting by Decisive Vote Before Fight Began

TH SIDES TO ABIDE BY FINAL DECISION

(Special to Virginian-Pilot.)

RICHMOND, VA., Dec. 17. th all indications pointing to victory for the Treby faction, the state ocratic committee, after spending the hearing the Norfolk election con- adjourned just before midnight 10 o'clock tomorrow morning, after icy session, in which some radical n was taken. Meanwhile Captain W. Dey, under instructions from the mittee, left for Norfolk, accompa- by his two deputies and by Police missioner Reid. They are expected turn here in the morning and pro- the books and tally sheets of the ion of October 13, which Dey has ed in his safe in the seaside city. rt from this, the important feature e day was the passage of a resolu- doing away with proxies for good all. The committee will probably h a decision by tomorrow night. e committee met at Murphy's hotel oon. Chairman Ellyson, who pre- , re the call for the meeting, and etary Button called the roll of mem- showing the following present at time or later during the meeting, ies a number of persons holding ies of absentees: rst District—Lloyd T. Smith, Clag- B. Jones, J. Boyd Sears, R. L. All- h and H. H. Wallace.

U. S. LANDING PARTY FINDS STRONG CAMP OF COLOMBIAN TROOPS

Natives Order American Flag Hauled D... Cutter But it S...

(By Cable ...

ties he ... cision of ... mit to ... spirit he ... that he and ... who ever ... of the duly ...

Mr. Lawle... ers, referred ... tion asking ... production o... the election.

DISCREPANC...

Chairman E... written two le... to Mr. Dey, re... of the tally she...

Mr. Cabell the... ther of the two ... received, and th... notice of contest had ever been served on the contestees. He had never heard the petition read until it was read by the

TO D...

... Spinners to Meet in Manchester to Discuss Curtailing the Production—Inter-

visit, state... matter up ... vened and ... the next ... sion for ... and deepen...

SCAR...

Form No. 168.

THE WESTERN UNION TEL...

INCORPORATE... CABLE

23,000 OFFICES IN AMERICA.

This Company TRANSMITS and DELIVERS messages only on conditions limiting its l... Errors can be guarded against only by repeating a message back to the sending station fo... in transmission or delivery of Unrepeated Messages, beyond the amount of tolls paid there... after the message is filed with the Company for transmission. This is an UNREPEATED MESSAGE, and is delivered by request of the sender, un...

ROBERT C. CLOWRY, Presiden...

RECEIVED at

Via Norfolk

176 C KA CS 33 Paid.

Kitty Hawk N C Dec 17

Bishop M Wright

7 Hawthorne St

Success four flights thursday morn... wind started from Level with engin... through air thirty one miles long... home ~~####~~ Christmas .